CRIME AND CRIMINAL JUSTICE

Crime and Criminal Justice provides students with a comprehensive and engaging introduction to the study of criminology by taking an interdisciplinary approach to explaining criminal behaviour and criminal justice.

The book is divided into two parts, which address the two essential bases that form the discipline of criminology. Part One describes, discusses and evaluates a range of theoretical approaches that have offered explanations for crime, drawing upon contributions from the disciplines of sociology, psychology, and biology. It then goes on to apply these theories to specific forms of criminality. Part Two offers an accessible but detailed review of the major philosophical aims and sociological theories of punishment, and examines the main areas of the contemporary criminal justice system – including the police, the courts and judiciary, prisons, and more recent approaches to punishment.

Presenting a clear and thorough review of theoretical thinking on crime, and of the context and current workings of the criminal justice system, this book provides students with an excellent grounding in the study of Criminology.

Ian Marsh is Principal Lecturer in Criminology at Liverpool Hope University and is a widely published textbook author. His recent publications include *Theories of Crime* (Routledge 2006 – with Gaynor Melville, Keith Morgan, Gareth Norris and Zoe Walkington), *Criminal Justice: An Introduction to Philosophies, Theories and Practice* (Routledge 2004 – with Gaynor Melville and John Cochrane), *Sociology: Making Sense of Society* (4th edn, Pearson, 2009), and *Crime, Justice and the Media* (Routledge 2009 – with Gaynor Melville).

Gaynor Melville is Lecturer in Criminology at Liverpool Hope University. She has co-written and contributed to a number of books including *Crime, Justice and the Media* (Routledge 2009), *Theories of Crime* (Routledge 2006) and *Criminal Justice* (Routledge 2004).

Keith Morgan is Senior Lecturer in Criminology and Psychology at Liverpool Hope University and contributed to *Theories of Crime* (Routledge 2006).

Gareth Norris is Lecturer in Criminology at Aberystwyth University and contributed to *Theories of Crime* (Routledge 2006).

John Cochrane is Lecturer in History and Criminology at Liverpool John Moores University and contributed to *Criminal Justice* (Routledge 2004).

CRIME AND CRIMINAL JUSTICE

Ian Marsh,

with Gaynor Melville, Keith Morgan, Gareth Norris and John Cochrane

 Routledge
Taylor & Francis Group

LONDON AND NEW YORK

First published 2011
by Routledge
2 Park Square, Milton Park, Abingdon, Oxon, OX14 4RN

Simultaneously published in the USA and Canada
by Routledge
711 Third Avenue, New York, NY 10017

Routledge is an imprint of the Taylor & Francis Group, an informa business

British Library Cataloguing in Publication Data
A catalogue record for this book is available from the British Library

Library of Congress Cataloging in Publication Data
Library of Congress Cataloging-in-Publication Data
　　Crime and criminal justice / by Ian Marsh . . . [et al.].
　　　　p. cm.
　　1. Criminology. 2. Criminal behavior. 3. Criminal justice, Administration of.
　　I. Marsh, Ian, 1952–
　　HV6025.C678 2011
　　364—dc22   2010039195

ISBN: 978–0–415–58151–6 (hbk)
ISBN: 978–0–415–58152–3 (pbk)
ISBN: 978–0–203–83378–0 (ebk)

Typeset in Garamond and Frutiger
by Keystroke, Station Road, Codsall, Wolverhampton

Printed and bound in Great Britain by the MPG Books Group

CONTENTS

LIST OF FIGURES

LIST OF TABLES

LIST OF NUMBERED BOXES

LIST OF CASE STUDY BOXES

PREFACE

The intention of this book is to provide students (and tutors) with an interdisciplinary approach to explaining criminal behaviour and criminal justice. Its aim is to encourage students to develop a deeper understanding of classic and contemporary theorizing about crime and of the context and current working of the criminal justice system.

CONTENT

The book consists of two main parts – the first focused on explaining criminal behaviour and the second on criminal justice. Essentially, these two areas form the basis of the discipline of Criminology, so the book will provide a thorough grounding in that subject area that is suitable for a wide range of Criminology and related courses.

The first part describes and reflects on a range of theoretical approaches that have offered explanations for crime and applies them to specific forms of criminality.

Chapter 1 provides a brief overview of the history of criminal behaviour, considering the relative nature of crime and how changing definitions and perceptions impact on studying the history of crime. Chapters 2, 3 and 4 examine the ways in which the different disciplines of biology, psychology and sociology have tried to explain criminal behaviour. In Chapter 2 the focus is on biological explanations. Written by Keith Morgan, with help from Sue Aitken, this chapter considers the controversy over attempting to explain criminal behaviour in biological terms. It starts by debating the value of biology in this context and after looking at the history of biological theorizing it considers in some depth the importance of evolution, genes, physical characteristics of offenders and brain structures in affecting behaviour and, particularly, criminal behaviour. Chapter 3, written by Gareth Norris, with help from Zoe Walkington, looks at the range of different explanations for crime that psychologists have offered. It considers these theories in terms of criminality as being an element of personality, and then examines the precursors, or reasons, why a person may become involved in criminal behaviour. It also highlights how psychological and social factors interact and need to be considered together in offering a full explanation for crime. Chapter 4 turns to explanations offered from sociological perspectives. Although the differences between the different disciplines of biology, psychology and sociology are not absolute or rigid, the emphasis in sociological theorizing is on the social context in which crime takes place – crime and criminal behaviour can only be fully understood in relation to the social structure, to specific social conditions and processes. The chapter starts by looking at classical criminology that emerged in the late eighteenth century, then considers the major early founding writers in sociology (including Durkheim and Marx) and how the theoretical approaches they developed have helped to explain crime. It looks at examples of theorizing within the sociology of crime and deviance that have developed from these major theoretical positions, including interactionism and labelling theory, feminist criminology, the postmodern influence and, more recently, cultural and environmental criminology. The final two chapters apply the different theoretical approaches and perspectives to explaining the patterns of criminal behaviour of women and of ethnic minority groups. Chapter 5, written by Gaynor Melville, looks at how theorizing from the major disciplines has helped provide an understanding of the criminal behaviour of women. After looking at the history of women and crime and the changing patterns and trends in female criminality it discusses a range of theoretical explanations, including naturalistic, biological, psychological, sociological and feminist explanations. Chapter 6, by Ian Marsh and Gaynor Melville, offers a similar approach to considering the criminal behaviour of ethnic minority groups. After reviewing the patterns and trends in ethnic minority criminality, it looks at explanations under two main categories: first, ethnic minority, and especially black, crime is a social reality and the reasons for the greater criminality amongst such groups needs to be examined; second, that the criminal justice system is biased against certain ethnic minority groups and this can explain the higher rate of crime amongst such groups.

The second part provides an examination of the historical, philosophical and theoretical context of criminal justice followed by a systematic overview of the major criminal justice agencies. Chapter 7 considers the basic question 'Why should offenders be punished?' It does this by looking at the justifications for punishment and the philosophies that lie behind them. There are various plausible justifications for punishment and there are different ways of categorizing them. Here these justifications are examined under three main headings: deterrence, retribution and rehabilitation. The contradictions and tensions between the different philosophies of punishment are highlighted through examples of different forms of punishment at different periods of history. Chapter 8 focuses on explanations for punishment and, in particular, addresses the question 'What have social theorists said about the role of punishment in society?' The main theoretical approaches that are examined are Durkheim's argument that punishment produces social solidarity; the Marxist tradition that punishment is part of a class-based process of economic and social regulation; and the more recent theorizing of Foucault emphasizing the interrelationship between punishment, power and regulation. Chapter 9, written by John Cochrane, relates and applies these and other theoretical approaches to the history of the policies and practices of crime and justice. Essentially it tries to understand this history in terms of the nature of the particular governments and societies responsible for introducing these policies and practices. Chapter 10, written by Gaynor Melville, shifts the focus to an examination of the role of the victim within the criminal justice system. It charts the emergence of the discipline of victimology and considers the main theoretical positions within it. In doing this, it distinguishes between victims of different forms of criminal behaviour, with a particular focus on victims of domestic violence (private crime) and of corporate crime (public crime).

The final three chapters in Part II examine the major different elements and agencies of the contemporary criminal justice system. Chapter 11 looks at police and policing, setting the context for an examination of police culture through a consideration of how historical changes, and especially those of the post-1960 period, have shaped the current form and style of policing. Chapter 12 turns to the courtroom and examines issues around the trial and sentencing of offenders, in particular issues of impartiality, focusing on gender, ethnicity and class bias. After this, it looks at those who sentence offenders – the magistrates and the judges – considering their backgrounds, appointment and ideologies. Chapter 13 looks at prison, the most severe penalty available in our criminal justice system; it provides data that enable a consideration to be made of the extent to which the current prison system is in 'crisis', and looks at some of the issues facing the prison service, including overcrowding, security and the different needs of long-term and other prisoners. The chapter concludes by examining the background to and success of community sentences. Issues of inequality – in particular in terms of gender, ethnicity and class – are raised and discussed in relation to each of the main agencies of the criminal justice system that are examined in Chapters 11, 12 and 13.

FEATURES

Crime and Criminal Justice adopts an interactive approach that actively encourages the reader to engage with and respond to the text and think for herself or himself. There are question breaks throughout the book that provide opportunities for reflection. Some of these breaks include stimulus material from original studies or media accounts and ask questions based on that material; others are just short stop-and-think questions based on the material in the text. Throughout the book there are extracts from academic sources, official reports and contemporary press reporting which will encourage students to read a range of original sources. At the end of each chapter there are suggestions for further reading and research, including key texts and, where appropriate, relevant websites.

This book, along with previous publications including *Criminal Justice* (2004), *Theories of Crime* (2006) and *Crime, Justice and the Media* (2009), has been a collaborative venture, and the authors would like to thank Gerhard Boomgarden, Jennifer Dodd and the rest of the production team at Routledge for their help and support with the development of this book.

PART 1

EXPLORING AND EXPLAINING CRIME

CHAPTER 1

Crime – The Historical Context

INTRODUCTION

Crime, criminals and how they are dealt with by society are topics of endless fascination. Look at any newspaper or glance at what's on television or at the cinema and it is immediately clear that there is a vast and seemingly insatiable interest in crime and criminals. We are interested both in 'real life' crime and criminals and in fictional accounts. We could ask why there is so much interest in this area; even if many people break the law from time to time, most people are not involved in spectacular criminality, yet we seem to love to watch and read about it. Maybe such an interest demonstrates a sense of moral outrage and the enjoyment of seeing the wrongdoer punished and justice being done – given that in most fictional crime stories the criminals tend to come off worse eventually. Or perhaps it reflects a sympathy with the underdog and a degree of admiration for those who try to beat the system, with yesterday's public enemies and villains having a habit of becoming present-day cult figures. Or maybe this interest just demonstrates the excitement and enjoyment gained from reading about and watching that which we ourselves would not engage in – a sort of substituted excitement or vicarious pleasure. Whatever the reasons, murder, robbery, fraud, drug smuggling, gang warfare, rape, football hooliganism and so on make good subjects of conversation and exciting and profitable films. Indeed a visitor from another culture might assume crime was a basic and ever present feature of everyone's everyday lives. Yet apart from minor law breaking, very few people go on to become professional criminals.

QUESTION BREAK: CRIMINALS AS CELEBRITIES

'Mad Frankie Fraser' a notorious (ex)gangster is now a popular speaker at social functions. The following extracts are taken from his own website:

Frank has been a contract strong-arm, club owner, club minder, company director, Broadmoor inmate, firebomber, prison rioter but – first and last – a thief. 26 convictions. 42 years inside. In the 60s Ron and Reggie Kray sought his services but Frank chose to pitch in with Charlie and Eddie Richardson and their South London alleged 'Torture Gang'.

GUEST APPEARANCES

Frank is available for guest appearances at weddings, birthdays and all special occasions.

Make it a night to remember!

For more info please telephone:

Also available for After Dinner Speeches, Functions and Boxing Tournaments

---

- List other criminals that have become celebrities.
- Why do you think people admire such criminals?

This interest in criminality has been present throughout history. The briefest scan of the history of literature reveals the central role played by crime and criminals – from the Greek tragedies, to Shakespeare's *Hamlet*, to Bill Sykes in Charles Dickens' *Oliver Twist*, to George Orwell's *1984*. Dostoevsky's *Crime and Punishment* is a classic work of criminal psychology, while the New Testament story of Jesus tells of wrongful accusation, arrest, trial, conviction and execution.

However crime is not a clear cut or static phenomenon. What was viewed as criminal in the past was often quite different to current notions; just as many contemporary criminal acts would not have been viewed so in earlier times. Indeed in studying crime and punishment over time one of the most obvious 'findings' is the relative nature of crime. What is seen as and defined as criminal varies according to the particular social context in which it occurs, as the extracts and questions below illustrate.

QUESTION BREAK: THE CULTURAL AND HISTORICAL RELATIVITY OF CRIME

It is easy to think of examples of behaviour which one society sees as criminal and another as quite acceptable and normal; and there are behaviours which are seen as criminal now but which were perfectly acceptable in previous times. Consider the extracts below and the questions that follow them.

> It is easily observable that different groups judge different things to be deviant. This should alert us to the possibility that the person making the judgement of deviance, the process by which the judgement is arrived at, and the situation in which it is made will all be intimately involved in the phenomenon of deviance . . .
>
> Deviance is the product of a transaction that takes place between a social group and one who is viewed by that group as a rule breaker. Whether an act is deviant, then, depends on how people react to it . . . The degree to which other people will respond to a given act as deviant varies greatly. Several kinds of variations are worth noting. First of all, there is variation over time. A person believed to have committed a given 'deviant' act may at one time be responded to much more leniently than he would at some other time. The occurrence of 'drives' against various kinds of deviance illustrates this clearly.
>
> (From H. S. Becker, *Outsiders: Studies in the Sociology of Deviance*, 1963, pp. 4–12)

Burning and hanging women as witches was commonplace in Europe in the 16th and 17th centuries. Witches were believed to have made pacts with the Devil which gave them supernatural powers. They were blamed for all sorts of personal and social misfortunes – illnesses, bad weather, loss of and damage to property.

Although many people associate burning at the stake with witchcraft it was used much less in England than other parts of Europe – particularly France, Switzerland and the Nordic countries. Only a few witches were burnt in England, the majority were hanged, possibly as a cost saving exercise and possibly because the public would not tolerate such a barbaric punishment. Scotland did burn witches and there are at least 38 recorded instances, the last being in 1722.

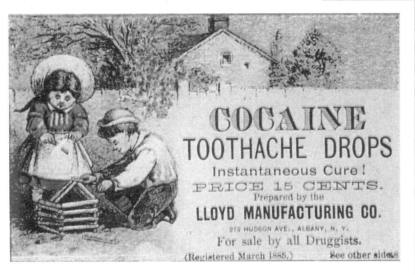

In the late 19th century cocaine was widely used as a pain killer in the USA – much as aspirin is today – and advertised with pictures of children at play. (From A. G. Johnson, *Human Arrangements*, 1989, p. 249)

1 Alcohol drinking and bigamy illustrate the relative nature of crime and deviance.

   (a) List other types of behaviour that have been categorized as criminal or deviance in one society but not another.
   (b) Give examples of behaviour that has been criminal or deviant at certain periods of time but not at others.

2 In looking at responses to crime and deviance Becker refers to 'drives' against certain types of behaviour. What types of crime or deviance have been subject to such drives in recent years in the UK?

The fact that crimes, and the ways in which they have been punished, vary from place to place and time to time highlights the importance of social reaction in determining what behaviour is categorized as criminal. There is no particular action that is criminal in itself – an action only becomes criminal if society defines it as such. So even an action such as killing another person, which, in the form of murder, can be the most serious of crimes in modern society, in many contexts can be quite acceptable. Indeed in some situations killing other people can be seen as heroic and people can be punished for not wanting to engage in killing – conscientious objectors were imprisoned in Britain in the First World War as were those who tried to 'dodge the draft' to fight for the US army in Vietnam in the 1960s.

Bearing in mind the relativity of crime and how it is dealt with, it would be useful to consider the history of crime before examining theoretical explanations for it in later chapters. In considering the history of crime we will examine the historical myths and traditions that surround the way in which crime has been and is viewed. Although there is a general awareness that there was horrendous violence and crime in the past, it is a widely held notion that modern, Western societies have become more and more criminal and dangerous places to live in. Given this tendency to think that things are much worse nowadays, we will start our historical overview by considering if there ever was a 'golden age', when 'things were so much better', when violence and criminality were only a marginal part of everyday life.

THE HISTORY OF JUVENILE CRIME

We will start our account by referring Geoffrey Pearson's study of the history of juvenile crime (1983). Pearson used literary and journalistic accounts of crime to argue that it was important not to view criminality in modern society as a new or unique problem and to make the point that, when examining the history of crime, an appropriate sub-title would be 'there's nothing new under the sun'. Pearson takes issue with the notion of moral degeneracy (of young people in particular), not in an attempt to underplay the problem of violent crime in modern society but to demonstrate that, if anything, it is a continuation of traditions rather than a new phenomenon. He shows that for generations Britain has been plagued by very similar problems and fears that the myth that Britain has historically been a stable, peaceful, law-abiding nation and that violence is somehow foreign to our national character shows little sign of waning.

The most striking aspect of the history of delinquency is the consistency with which each generation characterises the youth of the day and the way of life of twenty years previously. In 1829 Edward Irving is quoted as inquiring, 'Is not every juvenile delinquent the evidence of a family in which the family bond is weakened and loosened?'. He talks about the 'infinite numbers of unruly and criminal people who now swarm on the surface of this great kingdom' (see Pearson 1983). Thus, while hooliganism and delinquency still make news as alarming and unusual, such behaviour is clearly not new.

QUESTION BREAK: JUVENILE CRIME – THERE'S NOTHING NEW UNDER THE SUN

The following quotes are taken from press, political and literary sources; many are taken from Pearson (1983) although some more recent ones have been added. Place these quotes in historical order and suggest when they might have been said. (The answers are at the end of the chapter – but see how many you can locate correctly before turning to them.)

(a) One of the most marked characteristics of the age is a growing spirit of independence in the children and a corresponding slackening of control in the parents.

(b) We have to recognize where crime begins . . . we must do more to teach children the difference between right and wrong. It must start at home. And it must also be taught in our schools.

(c)   Looked at in his worse light the adolescent can take on an alarming aspect:
he has learned no definite moral standards from his parents, is contemp-
tuous of the law, easily bored.

(d)   The morals of the children are tenfold worse than formerly.

(e)   (On the increase in juvenile crime).In many cases they [juveniles] find
themselves in a large city without friends, without family ties, and belonging to no social circle in which their conduct is either scrutinized or
observed.

(f)   Parents failed to instil respect in their children . . . neighbourliness had
broken down in villages, towns and cities. Decades of poor parenting and
increasing selfishness have made life a misery for the police.

(g)   People are bound to ask what is happening to our country . . . having been
one of the most law-abiding countries in the world – a byword for stability,
order and decency – are we changing into somewhere else?

(h)   The most characteristic part of their uniform is the substantial leather belt
heavily mounted with metal. It is not ornamental, but then it is not
intended for ornament.

(i)   There seems to be a general corruption throughout the kingdom . . . the
spirit of luxury and extravagance that seems to have seized on the minds of
almost all ranks of men.

(j)   These people are simply savages, angry, blind and brutal. They are in this
condition because of what they have been drinking. They are all so ill-
educated or made crude by inadequate civilizing influences in their homes
that they seem unable to drink in an acceptable 'continental' fashion.

(k)   Any candid judge will acknowledge that manifest superiority of the past
century; and in an investigation of the causes which have conspired to
produce such an increase of juvenile crime, which is a blot upon the age
. . . Is it not [the case that] the working classes have generally deteriorated
in moral condition?

Pearson starts his study by looking at contemporary society – and, as the book
was published in 1983, at the late 1970s and early 1980s. In introducing his historical
account he makes the point that if each generation has a tendency to look back fondly
to the recent past, it is sensible to start with present-day society and compare it with
the situation twenty or so years previously, and then to compare that generation with
its predecessor. Of course, there are bound to be difficulties in comparing different
ages and periods – there will be differing definitions of crime and different measuring techniques and, in particular, a lack of adequate records in previous times.
Nonetheless, an impression of the style and extent of crime, and of the popular
concerns about it, can be gained by looking at contemporary accounts from
newspapers and books of the particular period.

As mentioned, Pearson's study starts with present-day attacks on our 'permissive
age' by contemporary public figures and 'guardians of morality'. In March 1982 the
Daily Telegraph suggested that 'we need to consider why the peaceful people of

England are changing . . . over the 200 years up to 1945, Britain become so settled in internal peace'. There were warnings of a massive degeneration among the British people which is destroying the nation. Kenneth Oxford, the Chief Constable of Merseyside, prophesies that the 'freedom and way of life we have been accustomed to for so long will vanish'. There are numerous instances of such statements from prominent politicians and public figures alleging that contemporary society is witnessing an unprecedented increase in violence and decline in moral standards. Indeed there is a great consistency in the view of Britain's history was based on stability and decency, and that the moderate 'British way of life' is being undermined by the upsurge in delinquency.

QUESTION BREAK: IMAGES OF CONTEMPORARY YOUTH

- How are youth viewed today?
- What words are commonly associated with contemporary youth? (Consider how many of these words are negative and how many positive.)
- Looking back a generation, how would you characterize British society in the 1960s?
- What words would you associate with British youth of the 1960s?

Twenty years previously, however, we can find remarkably similar comments. At the Conservative Party conference in 1958 there was discussion of 'this sudden increase in crime and brutality which is so foreign to our nation and our country'. The Teddy Boys were arousing similar apocalyptic warnings of the end of British society. The Teds' style of dress was derived from men's fashion of the reign of Edward VII, which explains the name of Teddy Boys. Rock and roll was the musical focus of this youth subculture, and the reaction which the Teddy Boys engendered was one of outrage and panic. The press, in particular, printed sensational reports of the happenings at cinemas and concerts featuring rock and roll films and music. A letter in the *Daily Sketch* (a popular newspaper of the period) in 1956 announced that 'the effect of rock'n'roll on young people is to turn them into devil worshippers; to stimulate self-expression through sex; to provoke carelessness, and destroy the sanctity of marriage', while an article in the *Evening News* of 1954 suggested that, 'Teddy Boys . . . are all of unsound mind in the sense that they are all suffering from a form of psychosis. Apart from the birch or the rope, depending on the gravity of their crimes, what they need is rehabilitation in a psychopathic institution [*sic*].' This reaction was widespread; off-duty soldiers were banned from wearing Teddy Boy suits and Teddy Boys were viewed by the rest of society as 'folk devils'.

Nowadays when we look back at old photographs and films of the 1950s rock and roll craze and the Teddy Boys we might wonder what all the fuss was about. In comparison to groups who have come since then, they look quite straight. If anything, Teds are remembered with a degree of nostalgia and viewed as something quaint. Quite a contrast with the reaction in the mid 1950s illustrated above.

Pearson asks whether it was pre-war Britain that was characterized by a law-abiding youth and a stable society. In fact the Second World War has been seen as a kind of watershed with the post-war period being morally inferior to the 'full rich back street life and culture of pre-war England'. However, when looking more closely at this period familiar declarations and allegations appear. In the 1930s there was a similar bemoaning of the 'passing of parental authority' and the 'absence of restraint'. The targets of criticism have a common ring, football rowdyism and the increasing crime and disorder. In the 1920s there were fierce street battles in North London between Spurs and Arsenal fans, some of whom were armed with iron bars and knives; while a part of Bradford football ground was closed in 1921 after the referee had been pelted with rubbish. It is sometimes implied that such incidents, and delinquencies in general, have become 'more serious' or 'more violent' over time, and since the war. The evidence would not seem to back up such suggestions. Crime in the interwar years was characterized by razor gangs, feuds between armed gangsters, vice rackets, and so on.

Moving back to the turn of the century and pre-First World War period Pearson suggests that we seem little nearer to finding the traditional way of life based on a 'healthy respect for law and order'. A wide range of popular culture came under severe criticism in the early twentieth century. The music halls, professional football and the noisy presence of working-class people at seaside resorts on Bank Holidays were all attacked. There was even a good deal of excitement and panic over the 'bicycle craze' of the late 1890s. There are newspaper accounts of youths whizzing about madly on their bikes, dashing along quiet country roads and through peaceful villages with loud shouts, causing pandemonium among the traffic and knocking over pedestrians, with headlines such as 'The Dangers of City Cycling' (*Daily Mail*, 1898) and 'Cyclomania' (*News of the World*, 1898). As ever, youth of the period were compared unfavourably with previous generations. Baden-Powell in his *Scouting for Boys* published in 1908, suggests that professional football is betraying the British traditions of 'fair play' and sportsmanship:

> Thousands of boys and young men, pale, narrow-chested, hunched up, miserable specimens, smoking endless cigarettes, numbers of them betting, all of them learning to be hysterical as they groan and cheer in panic unison with their neighbours – the worst sound of all being the hysterical scream of laughter that greets any little trip or fall of a player. One wonders whether this can be the same nation which had gained for itself the reputation of being a stolid, pipe-sucking manhood, unmoved by panic or excitement, and reliable in the tightest of places.

Neither does nineteenth-century, Victorian Britain provide any comparative baseline of a tranquil, law-abiding society. The first officially named 'Hooligans' of the 1890s and the 'Garrotters' of the 1860s do little to kindle nostalgia for Victorian city life and culture. It was in the late 1890s that the words 'Hooligan' and 'Hooliganism' were used, to describe delinquent youth. There were regular news reports of Hooligan gangs smashing up coffee-stalls and public houses, robbing and assaulting old ladies, attacking foreigners and setting upon policemen in the streets. In line with later youth subcultures and gangs, Hooligans had a distinct style of dress, a recognizable look.

As with so many of the later youth subcultures, there was no doubt an over-reaction to Hooligans. Nevertheless, whether correct or not, there was a widely held feeling that hooliganism was a major problem.

Earlier in the Victorian period in the winter of 1862, panic swept through respectable London over a new variety of crime called 'garrotting', a type of violent robbery that involved choking the victim. A Victorian parallel with present day 'mugging' perhaps. The press reacted in familiar manner, with *The Times* observing that it was 'becoming unsafe for a man to traverse certain parts of London at night'. *Punch* magazine launched an 'anti-garrotte' movement, which invented a variety of somewhat bizarre anti-robbery devices, metal collars with long steel pikes being favoured forms of protection against throttling.

The possibility that it was industrialization that destroyed the stable and peaceful life of pre-industrial Britain does not appear to hold up either. Certainly in the mid nineteenth century it was widely felt that life in the previous century was greatly superior and that the increase in juvenile crime was a blot on this age. However, writing in 1751 Henry Fielding (London magistrate and well-known author) paints a very similar picture with his prediction of an imminent slide into anarchy when the streets of our cities 'will shortly be impassable without the utmost hazard'.

It is difficult to find evidence that there has been a massive deterioration in the morality and behaviour of the common people, in comparison to the pre-industrial world. From the late seventeenth century there have been complaints of increasing wickedness, crime and disorder, while the streets of pre-industrial London were extremely dangerous, with no effective system of street-lighting nor a police force.

It is not just societal reaction and fears that echo one another through the ages, and Pearson also examines the recurrent nature of different explanations of the criminal question. Time and again a permissive present is contrasted with the not too distant past. If such accusations are accepted, we would be forced to conclude that with each generation crime and disorder has increased dramatically. The over-representation of youth in the criminal statistics is rediscovered in each wave of concern over crime and delinquency. Looking back over Pearson's historical review, it is hard to believe that Britain's cities are any more perilous today than those of pre-industrial Britain, or when they were frequented by gangs of Garrotters and Hooligans.

STUDYING THE HISTORY OF CRIME

While contemporary sources are important indicators, it is necessary to consider how these sources relate to the findings of historians on crime levels in the past. However, in measuring the history of crime, a statistical approach, while essential, is fraught with difficulties. Sharpe (1995), in examining the different approaches to studying the history of crime, argues that the counting of crimes has to go hand in hand with interpreting the meaning of crime to different communities at different times and with considering the changing definitions of crime. The term 'crime' encompasses a massive variety of activities, from petty theft to fraud to rape and murder and it has always been the case that it is the more serious crimes that get reported and recorded and the more minor ones which are less likely to figure in the statistics. Emsley (2005) suggests that although small-scale and opportunist theft was statistically the most common crime during the eighteenth and nineteenth centuries, the appetite for reading about violent crime fed by the media and literature of the day obscured the petty nature of most criminality. As he puts it, 'violent crime was what worried people; it was central to the moral panics and crime waves; it provided good copy' (Emsley 2005).

The statistics of crime

Although crime statistics are usually quoted as 'hard facts', and as such are used by governments and public bodies for making policy decisions with regard to crime and its treatment, they are far from being perfect indicators of the extent or character of crime. There are two major and important deficiencies with them – first, the problem of omissions in that only a proportion of crimes and offenders are included in official figures; and second the problem of bias in that those crimes and offenders that are included might not provide a representative picture of all crime and of all offenders. The amount of crime that is not officially known about is termed the 'dark figure' of crime and there are many factors which lead to the non-reporting and recording of crime.

QUESTION BREAK: THE DARK FIGURE OF CRIME

There are many reasons why crime statistics might underestimate the amount of criminal activity, including:

- victims being unaware that they are victims of specific crimes
- victims not wanting to waste time or money in reporting a crime
- victims feeling that there is no point in informing the police
- victims dealing with matters informally, outside of the legal system
- victims' embarrassment
- victims (or witnesses of a crime) not trusting or liking the police
- victimless crime – crimes where all parties involved do not wish the police to know about it

Consider each of those reasons and suggest how much more (or less) relevant they would be in relation to measuring crimes at different periods of history.

- What other factors might have stopped people from reporting crime in the past?

Sharpe (1999) makes the point that the importance of the dark figure would be reduced if there were a constant relationship between recorded and unrecorded crime.

If, for instance, the same proportion of crime, however large or small that proportion, was invariably reported, the changes in the crime statistics could be said to indicate changes in the actual level of criminal behaviour. However, there do appear to be substantial variations in the willingness of people to report criminal behaviour – during periods of 'moral panic' the public seem much more ready to report crimes. And the practices and efficiency of the police and other criminal justice agencies will also have an effect on the crime statistics. Even if the phrase itself was not used, contemporary commentators were aware of the 'dark figure' from at least the end of the eighteenth century. Emsley (2005) cites Patrick Colquhoun reflecting in his *Treatise on the Police in the Metropolis* (1796) that 'under the present system there is not above one offence in one hundred that is discovered or prosecuted'.

Of course, it is highly likely that these problems and deficiencies would be more marked when looking at criminal statistics from hundreds of years ago; and that the 'dark figure' of unrecorded crime would be 'darker' the further back in history we go. Indeed there are no official statistics for crime in England before 1805, and historians examining previous periods have to search court records for their data. The further back we go, the fewer official records and sources have survived. Court records, for instance, are rarely complete and, even where they are, they only show how particular systems operate at particular periods in history (Newburn 2007).

However, there have been attempts to assess and quantify the extent of crime. For instance, the beginning of the eighteenth century was a low crime period compared to the previous century, but with increasing urbanization the later 1700s in England were characterized by a significant rise in crime. The growth of an industrialized nation, along with the demobilization of soldiers and sailors after eighteenth-century wars and the defeat of the French in 1815, led to large numbers of the labouring classes living in the growing urbanized areas without adequate incomes; a situation that led, in turn, almost inevitably to a massive rise in property crimes. The relationship between property crime and the growth of an industrial capitalist society was an area of explanation considered by historians of crime. Emsley (2005) points out that the increase in crime in the eighteenth century could be partly accounted for by the increase in population along with the increasing possessions, urbanization and the spread of capitalism generally. So, the first half of the 1800s was a period when there were real concerns about rising crime combined with fears of social disintegration; however, by the end of the nineteenth century such fears were diminishing, along with the rise of a more prosperous, 'respectable' Victorian working class and a society that was better policed than ever before. Indeed explanations for the emergence of the modern police in the early to mid nineteenth century highlight this fear of the 'dangerous classes' – the new urban, industrial proletariat.

This notion of the 'dangerous classes' is conflated with that of the 'criminal classes'. Sharpe (1999) indicates that by the 1850s, the idea of a criminal class was generally accepted. It was seen by Victorian scholars as a product of industrialization and urbanization which concentrated the 'lower orders' in poor, dangerous groups who lived mainly on the proceeds of crime and who were separated from both the bourgeoisie but also from the 'respectable poor'. The Victorians saw this new 'criminal class' as essentially the product of rapid and vast economic and social change. However, Emsley (2005) suggests that while there may have been groups of habitual criminals such groups did not necessarily form what might be called a 'class', which implies a large and homogenous group of people. The overwhelming majority of offences in the eighteenth and nineteenth centuries were not organized and large-scale crimes but rather petty thefts and disorderly behaviour. Emsley points to the convenience for 'respectable' society of the idea of a criminal class who act as a sort of alien group committing crime on law-abiding citizens. And it is important to emphasize that even if the existence of such a class is dubious, the idea that there was one was certainly widely believed in by the Victorian population.

Indeed the notion of a 'criminal class' persisted throughout the nineteenth century and beyond. However, even though it was the case that small, professional gangs may have committed some crimes, the majority of crimes were almost certainly committed by those who felt they needed to steal for economic reasons.

It is also worth noting that changes in the law also had a major impact on crime rates and statistics; and the eighteenth century saw a wide range of new legislation – for instance, the creation of income tax led to the new crime of tax evasion, while the extension of compulsory education introduced by the Elementary Education Act of 1870 led to thousands of parents being prosecuted for not ensuring their children attended school (Emsley 2005).

COMMUNITIES AND THE CONTROL OF CRIME

Studying how the law was enforced in different communities also helps to fill out the picture of the history of crime and criminals. Certainly informal sanctions played an important role before the emergence of the modern police and will have played a part in the under-recording of criminal activity. Community action against nuisance offenders was commonplace and the widespread opposition from working-class communities to the new police ensured that informal controls existed long after the emergence of a professional police force (and they still do of course – criminals and gangsters throughout history have rarely been willing to involve formal bodies in sorting out their affairs).

In providing an overview of the 'early modern criminal' of the sixteenth and seventeenth centuries, Sharpe (1999) argues that there was little organized or professional crime at this time, 'the pathetic, small-time whore and the opportunistic pilferer were more typical, if more elusive, figures than the high-class madame or the criminal entrepreneur' (p. 171). While there were some people regularly on the wrong side of the law, criminal associations were casual and ad hoc in manner; gangs of highwaymen and horse thieves may well have existed but, outside of London, organized crime was 'rarely very sophisticated or permanent'. Sharpe suggest there was little evidence of anything approaching a criminal subculture or class; and he makes the point that if there was a 'dangerous class' then those in it were far more of a danger to one another than anybody else – as always, the poor stole from the poor, and assaulted and killed each other rather than those from different backgrounds.

CHANGING DEFINITIONS OF CRIME

As we suggested above, while there are some actions which virtually all societies will define as criminal and sanction accordingly, there are many more activities which are seen as criminal or not depending on the time or place in which they occur. In broad terms, Sharpe (1995) suggests that historians of crime have pointed to a transition from notions of crime based on sin to notions of crime based on concern over ownership of property. In the period up to the mid seventeenth century there was little attempt to separate out the different categories of sin and crime (male homosexuality, for instance, was made a capital offence in 1563). This is not to say that the link between religion and crime disappeared in the 1700s; the connection between law enforcement and Christian morality remained strong through the next two centuries, and arguably still plays a role in our criminal justice processes. However, secular concerns, and in particular concerns over the need to protect property, gradually came to replace the notion that crime and sin were intimately related. Also, and certainly by the early twentieth century, early criminologists were expounding the idea that crime was often the result of inbuilt hereditary deficiencies or of the degrading urban environments in which many people lived (Godfrey and Lawrence 2005).

So while it is clear that crime is a problem in contemporary society, and that we are experiencing serious law and order problems, our predecessors have from time to time felt similar concerns. Sharpe (1995) points to the periods from around 1580–1650 and 1800–60 as ones of severe economic dislocation but also as times when the fears about crime eventually proved groundless; and these periods were soon followed by periods of relative stability and harmony. The history of crime shows us how little attitudes have shifted between different 'thens' and now. The panics about Victorian garrotters and Elizabethan vagrants can be seen as examples of the criminal stereotyping that is still prevalent in modern society. The garotters were commented on earlier (p. 10), while Sharpe (1999) refers to the increase in vagrancy in the later sixteenth century being seen as a threat to the social order of the day. Vagrants were not solely criminals and included, as Sharpe puts it, 'the pathetic and the bizarre'. The crimes that were committed by vagrants tended to be opportunistic and small-scale thefts.

Although property crime has always been the most common form of offence, it has always been violent crime that has frightened people and made the most news-worthy stories. In concluding his study of crime between 1750 and 1900, Emsley (2005) suggests that while periods of economic slump and hardship might have increased the temptation towards property crime, the 'steepest overall increase in the criminal statistics during the period 1750 to 1900 coincided with fear for the social order, fear of "the mob", fear of revolution and . . . anxiety about "the dangerous classes".

SUMMARY

This chapter has looked briefly at the history of criminal behaviour. The rest of the first part of the book considers the major theoretical explanations for such behaviour. In particular the next three chapters look (respectively) at biological, psychological and sociological approaches to examining crime – they review early examples of these different theoretical approaches through to current theorizing about crime in each discipline. Chapters 5 and 6 then apply these varied theoretical approaches to explaining the criminal behaviour of women and of ethnic minorities.

FURTHER READING

Emsley, C. (2005) *Crime and Society in England 1750–1900* (4th edn), Harlow: Longman. An analysis of the period that highlights the scale of crime in the first part and then explores changes in the courts, police and systems of punishment in the second part.

Godfrey, B. and Lawrence, P. (2005) *Crime and Justice 1750–1950*, Cullompton: Willan. The focus of this book is more on the history of the criminal justice system; however, it does include interesting discussions on the changing perceptions of crime and criminals and on changing patterns of female and juvenile criminality.

Pearson, G. (1983) *Hooligan: A History of Respectable Fears*, London: Macmillan. This is a journey back through the history of youthful delinquency and responses to it. Making use of contemporary accounts, including newspapers and pamphlets, it shows that for generations Britain has been plagued by the same problems and fears that today we see as unique to our own society.

Sharpe, J. A. (1999) *Crime in Early Modern England 1550–1750* (2nd edn), Harlow: Longman. A wide-ranging analysis of crime, criminality and punishment in the early modern period. The book explores the extent, the causes and the control of crime and its impact on society.

WEBSITES

Two easy-to-navigate websites that provide contemporary accounts to illustrate different periods and enable users to look for coverage of criminal behaviour during those times are www.eyewitnesstohistory.com and www.bbc.co.uk/history/society

Answers to questions on pp. 7–8

(a) M. Barrett, *Young Delinquents,*1913
(b) M. Howard, Home Secretary, 1993

(c) British Medical Association, *The Adolescent*, 1961

(d) Lord Ashley, House of Commons, 1843

(e) W. Morrison, *Juvenile Offenders*, 1896

(f) D. Blunkett, Home Secretary, 2004

(g) *Daily Express*, 1981

(h) *Daily Graphic*, 1900

(i) Daniel Defoe, *The Complete English Tradesman*, 1738

(j) Judge Charles Harris, QC, *The Times*, 2005

(k) H. Worsley, *Juvenile Depravity*, 1849

CHAPTER 2

Biological Explanations for Criminal Behaviour

INTRODUCTION

In this chapter we examine the controversy over attempting to explain criminal behaviour in biological terms. We consider the main types of biological explanation for human behaviour that are used within the subject of criminology and the evidence that underpins them. Typical biological theories are that some people are more likely to commit violent crimes because of the genes they have inherited; or that there is more chance of acting in an impulsive way that breaks the law if you have attention deficit hyperactivity disorder (ADHD), because it involves a reduction in activity in a part of the brain that helps us both to control our own actions and to see their consequences.

It will be clearer if, before we engage with the criticisms of a biological perspective on criminal behaviour, we set out a very brief outline of why biology must be relevant.

- Human beings are surely just one species out of the millions of living creatures on the earth.
- Criminal behaviour is still behaviour even if what is regarded as 'criminal' changes over time and place.
- All our behaviour, thoughts, feelings, etc. are rooted in our biology.

Given these points, it must be possible to learn about criminal behaviour by taking a biological perspective.

THE DEBATE OVER THE VALUE OF BIOLOGY

When the contents of this textbook were first proposed, several criminologists considered the outline. Some thought that a chapter on biology was valuable, but others said that a chapter about biological explanations of criminal behaviour did not belong in a criminology book. This reflects a lively controversy within criminology (Wright and Miller 1998).

We have sympathy for those who oppose the use of biology within criminology because of two interrelated strands of the history of the social sciences.

First, for the majority of the twentieth century social scientists rejected biological explanations for human behaviours (Tooby and Cosmides 1992), especially social behaviours, of which criminal behaviour is an example (Walsh 2002).

Second, biological explanations of human behaviour were used by politicians to legitimize inhumane and invalid policies. This was seen in major countries with diametrically opposed political systems from the first to the last decade of the twentieth century. For example, 'Social Darwinism' refers to a group of theories that claim that Darwinism could be applied to social institutions as well as to organisms. It is best known in the version proposed by the philosopher Herbert Spencer (1820–1903), who wrote on psychology, sociology, evolution and philosophy and influenced Charles Darwin (1809–1882). Darwin published *The Origin of the Species* in 1859, in which he first set out his theory of evolution by natural selection.

Spencer and Darwin were both heavily influenced by Thomas Malthus (1766–1834). In 1798 Malthus published his 'demographic theory' proposing that famine and conflict were inevitable because population grows exponentially (i.e. 2, 4, 8, 16, 32) while resources increase only arithmetically (i.e. 1, 2, 3, 4). He argued that the poor, but not the wealthier members of society, should show moral restraint by having fewer children. His arguments were used to justify laws that made life harder for the most vulnerable.

This type of Social Darwinism was popular from late Victorian times until the Second World War. The results were used to justify the inequalities of wealth found in capitalist society as the natural consequence of the survival of the fittest – a term coined by Spencer – as well as the exclusion of would-be immigrants from Eastern Europe to the USA. They were rejected on the grounds that they were poor because they lacked the biological potential to succeed. Therefore, if they were allowed to enter the USA they would interbreed with, or outbreed, the established American population from largely Western European backgrounds and bring down the country by degrading its biological, genetic, quality.

This position, which now seems clearly to reflect the prejudice of those who supported such policies rather than being an objective consequence of biological theory, was taken up by other governments, including the UK, and was a factor in trapping so many Jews in Nazi Europe where they were the target of genocide (Rose 1997).

Another consequence of this crude application of biological principles to political and social issues was the widespread acceptance of eugenics by both left-wing and right-wing political thinkers. Eugenics is selective breeding, whereby people with 'good biological stock' were encouraged to reproduce and those with 'poor biological stock' were discouraged, in the extreme by sterilization and abortion. The Nazis appealed to 'science' to justify their campaign to exterminate the Jews, Slavs, Gypsies, gays and the mentally handicapped – all of whom were said to have inferior biological make-ups. This was used to demand their destruction for the good of humanity. Because the Nazis so enthusiastically embraced eugenics it was publicly rejected by most societies after the Second World War, though even then it was used covertly in several Western countries.

Two American controversies since the 1950s show how biological explanations are still being used to justify discriminatory policy.

First, the claim that black children do badly at school (and, indeed, in life – including their higher rates of criminal conviction) because they are inherently less intelligent than other racial groups for biological reasons (see the discussion of Murray and Herrenstein's book *The Bell Curve* in Chapter 5, p. 170).

Second, and directly concerning criminal behaviour, were two American projects to apply biology to criminal behaviour in the inner cities. In 1966 three Harvard professors, Frank Ervin, Vernon Mark and William Sweet, were involved in a federally sponsored, low-profile research programme set up in response to serious inner-city riots. They proposed using brain surgery for the ringleaders and other treatments for those who took part. The argument was that the causes could not be poverty, racial discrimination and social breakdown, because then all the people in the area who were subject to the same factors would have rioted. Fortunately the public became aware of what was going on and the government abruptly changed its policy and removed all funding for research into brain surgery; unfortunately some individuals had already been experimented on and left permanently damaged (Breggin 1995).

Things then went quiet until President George Bush announced the Federal Violence Initiative in 1992 with the goal of identifying biological factors in, and interventions for, criminal behaviour. Once again, as soon as people began to talk about what was going to be done in detail it looked as if it was based on the idea that Black American young males were obviously biologically different. This difference explained their higher levels of violent crime, rather than social, economic and political factors. The respected researcher, Frederick Goodwin, chosen to head the programme, compared unusually aggressive and sexually active monkeys seen in natural populations to inner-city youths (Breggin 1995). After a period of media and political debate Goodwin resigned; later the funding for the overall programme was withdrawn but several of the individual projects are still going on.

The problem here is the implicit assumption that the reason that some groups are poorer, more anti-social, have shorter life-spans, and so on is a result of their different biological make-up. The solution is to 'fix' their biology with surgery, electrodes or drugs rather than considering the environmental disadvantages that are much more likely to be relevant.

QUESTION BREAK

- Can you think of any other examples of how biological explanations could be used to justify social policies?
- As some policies based on biology have had terrible consequences, do you think biological explanations should be ignored? Give reasons for your answers.

The historical factors (as shown in these examples) of the political misuse of biological explanations to justify extreme discrimination and of the dominance of non-biological theories within the social sciences make the distrust of biological explanations by criminologists very understandable. However, there is growing support for the recognition of the key role of biology in understanding human behaviour. This chapter argues for the Biosocial Interaction (BSI) model (e.g. Raine 2002b) which recognizes the critical contribution of other factors such as family environment, the peer group and the opportunities to behave in particular ways. BSI is consistent with the vertical integration approach to understanding.

Vertical integration recognizes that we can validly examine something like anti-social or criminal behaviour at many distinct levels of explanation, and that these are arranged in a ladder going from the lowest levels, like physics, through increasingly higher levels such as chemistry to biology to psychology to sociology (Rose 2003a).

Mayr (1982) sets out how explanations of the way that something is caused (for example, rape) need to match both the level of the perspective being used and the question being asked. Explaining rape in terms of physics seems pointless; using a biological perspective may treat rape as being just heterosexual sex against the female's wishes (see the section below on evolution, p. 29); while a sociological approach can include factors such as political change, shifting gender roles and sexual politics. However, a sociological approach is blind to biological factors such as brain systems. One crucial element of this model of understanding is that the rules, relationships and laws at a particular level cannot be predicted simply by knowing all about the lower rungs of the ladder. Even if one could understand all the biology of human development through adolescence it would be difficult to see patterns crucial to the psychology of adolescent development (Steinberg and Morris 2001) such as the experience of first love, or relationships like that between skin colour and the chance of being imprisoned. The world as seen from a higher rung is said to 'emerge' from the world as seen from those rungs below it. Consciousness, a key psychological phenomenon, is often held to be an emergent property that is based on biology and yet cannot completely be explained from a biological perspective.

This example may help: everything that a computer does is based on physics, because a computer is a physical, material thing. If you sit down at your keyboard and compose a love poem it would be possible to give an explanation of this at the level of physics (e.g. how the 'L' of 'Love' was created on the screen by directing electrons using structures and processes within the computer, and even in terms of quantum mechanical interactions within some of the essential components). This could be accurate and correct; however, it can never be complete because the world of physics does not have concepts like 'love' – something essential for a full understanding and totally unpredictable from a knowledge of physics alone.

No level is absolutely best: the levels that you use need to reflect the question you want to answer and provide information suitable for the task at hand.

Today's biological researchers largely accept three propositions:

- The brain is the cause of the mind (whatever goes on in your mind is the result of physical processes in your brain).
- The mind is modular (made of many specialized parts, each largely independent of the rest but taking their input from other modules and sending their output to yet others).
- The brain is also made of largely separate, interacting systems.

This suggests certain research questions: for example, which systems are involved in aggression? Are they different in those convicted of violent crimes? How are they different, and can we change this or compensate for it? Are particular brain systems important in impulsive aggression?

Most current biological researchers also accept that the way to understand subjects as complex as human beings is to reduce the complexity by breaking them down into simpler parts: this is termed reductionism. Reductionism suggests that the way to understand, say, road rage attacks is to look for the parts of the brain involved; the organization and activity of neurons that make up those critical parts; the functioning of the chemical messengers that mediate communication between those neurons; the involvement of genes in that functioning and communication; and the effect of all of these on road rage behaviour.

The reductionist approach has been incredibly successful across science and seems rational, but it has limits. For example, suicide bombings are an extreme behaviour so one might expect to find evidence that suicide bombers are different in some biological way. Or if not, that there are clear differences between their experiences and those of other people.

It is important to realize that biologists have no problem with the idea that our biology may predispose us to behave in particular ways in response to outside forces. In this case things like having seen your family maltreated, or how extreme your religious or political education has been, appear plausible suggestions.

However, researchers have looked hard for signs of differences between suicide bombers and others without much success. This is true at the level of personality (an aspect of ourselves clearly connected to our biology (Davidson 2001)) and of experience. Some researchers think they have found slight differences in both areas but they are not enough to suggest that suicide bombers are basically different from the rest of the world. Instead it seems to be largely social pressures that lead to their actions (Bond 2004).

Stanley Milgram's studies, inspired by the savage behaviours of concentration camp guards and other staff during the Second World War, had a very similar outcome. To the amazement of experts and lay people it turned out that almost all normal people can be made to give an innocent stranger apparently lethal electric shocks simply by being told to (Milgram 1983; Blass 2000).

From these two examples of the most extreme anti-social behaviour we can see that biological differences are not necessarily present just because the perpetrators do what most people agree is wrong. In this chapter the emphasis on the interaction of biology with other factors at higher levels is an admission that reductionism cannot explain criminal behaviour.

Biological researchers are also predominantly materialists. This means that they see the real world as being made of physical 'stuff' – matter and energy. If you believe this then you are likely to ask questions about material things such as genes, chemicals and brain structures.

Finally, the majority of modern biologists are determinists. This means that they believe that everything that happens is caused by something else. For example, if someone sexually abuses a child we can assume that the behaviour followed some facilitating thoughts and was motivated by some strong feelings. These in turn will have been caused by other factors such as genetic predispositions or low activity in brain systems involved in self-control.

Our approach is to argue for a 'weak' determinism which suggests that criminal behaviour is determined not solely by the person's biology but rather by the inter-action of various factors including biological ones. The complexity of the interplay between different elements cannot be resolved. This is why we cannot say that one cause is more important than others for criminal behaviour; instead we must look at what seems to increase a person's chance of displaying criminal behaviour and in which environments this is the case.

As they tend to be reductionists, materialists and determinists, biological researchers give more importance to the simpler, biological processes. This easily slips into treating biological factors as causing the psychological, behavioural and sociological phenomena that are relevant to criminal behaviour. BSI explicitly takes biological and non-biological factors as equally important, which reduces the risk of invalidly assuming that our 'biological essence' is the real cause of criminal behaviour.

Critics attack the very assumptions upon which most biological criminology rests (Poole 1994), but the biological perspective on humans is becoming more dominant. Politically and economically the biological paradigm fits with the spirit of the age (American Psychiatric Association 1997; Herbert 1997), and the simple stories it tells are convincing even when the evidence and argument are not really sound (Rose 1997). Indeed the history of biological approaches to human nature demonstrates how easily popular prejudices can be transformed into apparently 'scientific' truths (Sennett 1977).

However, non-biological researchers are just as likely to make these errors: the last century saw the blaming of mothers for every sort of social problem from 'refrigerator mothers' producing schizophrenia in their children to poor mothering creating criminals (Ladd-Taylor and Umansky 1998). It is important to remember that whichever approach we use carries the risk of ignoring factors from other levels of explanation. The BSI model supported here is an example of a non-additive inter-action model because the effect of two different factors cannot be predicted reliably by simply adding the effect that the first would have by itself to the effect the second factor would have by itself. Think of a recipe: a cake does not taste like raw flour plus raw eggs and the other ingredients.

When researching rape, what questions do you think that biological criminologists might ask?

- What might they hypothesize leads to rape?
- What questions and hypotheses do you think psychological or sociological criminologists might use instead?
- Do you think that a biological approach to understanding rape is likely to be a good thing? Why?

Before we briefly consider the history of biological theories of criminal behaviour, there is one simple biological factor that is associated with a big increase in risk of criminal behaviour. Stop here and try to think what this might be before reading the next paragraph.

The factor can be seen from several biological perspectives:

- possession of a Y chromosome
- having a penis and testes rather than a vagina and ovaries
- having higher levels of testosterone
- behaving more aggressively
- being a male.

Why should this be so unless the biological differences between males and females are also connected to the very different levels of crime they commit?

Unfortunately it is plausible that such differences could arise from social and cultural factors, together with incidental consequences of the differences in strength and in time spent looking after children, for example. In summary, then, we believe that the differences in criminal activity are due both to biological and to other factors.

THE HISTORY OF BIOLOGICAL THEORIES OF CRIMINAL BEHAVIOUR

Now that you have thought about some of the wider issues concerning the value of biological explanations of criminal behaviours we will consider the history of this type of theory.

Since the time of the earliest surviving records, ugliness, disability and deformity have been taken as reflections of evil and criminality. Egyptian papyri, the Bible and Homer's *Iliad* all take the link as valid and this belief has survived to the present day. Physiognomy (assessing personality from facial features) traces its roots to ancient

Greece where the concept that mind, morality and body were intimately interrelated was widely accepted, even by Aristotle (perhaps the most scientific of the ancient Greeks). Socrates was condemned to death partly on the evidence of a physiognomist that his face showed him to be a cruel drunk.

In medieval Europe physical imperfections, such as warts, moles and third nipples, were taken as proof of demonic possession (Einstadter and Henry 1995) and in ordinary, secular, law if two people were under equal suspicion then the uglier was to be found guilty (Wilson and Herrnstein 1985).

The pre-existing belief that appearance reflected inner worth was first woven into a more scientific version of physiognomy by Della Porte (1535–1615). Della Porte studied dead bodies and claimed he had found a connection between facial features such as small ears and large lips with criminal behaviour. Later physiognomists such as Beccaria ('On Crimes and Punishments', 1764) and Lavater ('Physiognomical Fragments', 1775) extended Della Porte's theory.

Many of their claims are still heard in everyday conversation, for example 'weak chins' and 'shifty eyes' are still remarked upon as if they were true indicators of moral weaknesses.

The increasing status of scientific methods encouraged the search for physical signs of moral degeneracy. Phrenology was a theory adopted and publicized by Gall (1758–1828). It proposed that the surface of the skull was raised where it lay over parts of the brain that were more active than average. In many ways it prefigured our present view of the brain as made of many largely independent modules each with a specific task. Indeed, Gall correctly predicted the location of a part of the brain concerned with producing spoken language.

Some of the 'bumps' that phrenologists linked with criminal behaviour actually have some empirical support. The 'destructiveness centre' behind and above the left ear really is prominent in about 17 per cent of criminals, and there are others at the back of the skull that seem to reflect abnormalities of two parts of the brain, the hippocampus and amygdala. You will see that these are thought to be important in violent anti-social or criminal behaviour (see the section below on brain structures, p. 49). It may be that things that distort the development of our brains can also disturb the growth of the neighbouring bone, or vice versa. Injuries later in life certainly can damage the skull and the underlying brain tissue.

The methods, and philosophical understanding, to test Gall's theory did not exist in his lifetime and his attempts to get around these problems ended by invalidating the project. Indeed, the popular success of phrenology (it became quite fashionable to 'have one's bumps felt') led to a counter-movement that focused not only on the problems of testing its claims but also on the idea that our brain was built of largely independent systems.

Phrenology is a well-known enough fashion for it to have appeared in *The Simpsons*. When Homer's mother comes back and Mr Burns spots her resemblance to an ancient 'Wanted' poster the Springfield officers interview him. Officer Friday asks 'Are you sure this is the woman you saw in the post office?' Burns replies 'Absolutely! Who could forget such a monstrous visage? She has the sloping brow and cranial bumpage of the career criminal.' When Smithers objects to Mr Burns's use of phrenology by saying 'Uh, Sir, phrenology was dismissed as quackery 160 years ago', he is met with the unanswerable riposte 'Of course you'd say that: you have the brainpan of a stagecoach tilter' (Appel 1995).

- Have these old ways of thinking about humans disappeared?
- If not, where can you see their influence?

The next major step on the road to current biological theories comes with Lombroso, one of the people who founded modern criminology. As Garland (1997) points out, the founders of criminology as we now understand it were very open to the idea of biological factors leading to criminal behaviour. Lombroso (1876) used Darwin's theory of evolution by natural selection to argue that criminals were biological throwbacks (i.e. their looks, morality and behaviour were atavistic – or like their primitive ancestors). Criminals were physically and morally degenerate.

Biological positivism is the term for theories that claim that criminal behaviour is caused by biological factors: most current criminologists regard it as either false or simplistic. When the claims of physiognomy, phrenology and other similar 'sciences' were disproved by empirical data, biological theorizing in general was brought into disrepute.

However, even if the specific claims were wrong there could still be other biological bases for criminal behaviour. If you are not convinced by Lombroso's claim that prostitutes' feet showed the same prehensile (or gripping) form as our primate relatives (e.g. apes and monkeys), the link between looks and criminal behaviour could still be true. After all, why would an idea have such a long history if it had no basis in reality or was completely invalid? Indeed these ideas are so attractive that they appear in the wider popular culture. For example, in his novel *Crime and Punishment* Dostoyevsky makes a point of the central character's good looks. He does not want readers to assume that his evil acts are a consequence of an innate weakness that would show itself as both a physical and a moral deficiency. Dostoyevsky knew that at that time, 1866, people believed that the two went together in most criminals. Charles Dickens often makes the connection between physical appearance and morality in his novels. Think of *Oliver Twist*, where Oliver, even though he does not know it, is from a 'good family' and thus carries 'good genes' (although that term did not exist then). Oliver turns out to be good because of his biological inheritance while the Artful

Dodger, from a classic deprived background, is destined to go to the bad because of his (Dickens 1897).

Lombroso himself studied 383 criminals looking for a set of signs (stigmata) that he argued showed atavism. These included such things as excess digits and an asymmetrical face. He found that over two in five had at least five signs. On this evidence he argued that five or more stigmata indicated that someone was born biologically destined to be a criminal.

In a later study he found that about one in three anarchists (people who believed that violence was justified to gain their political aims) showed the stigmata compared to about one in eight members of other extreme political factions. He did compare his criminals to a control group of soldiers and used simple statistics but he did not control for variables such as mental illness and ethnic origin. The criminal groups showed more mental illness and had more Sicilian people: both of these would accentuate any differences between criminals and controls. As the methods were not adequate for the task his data cannot be relied upon and should be treated as of historical interest.

The problems with Lombroso's work illustrate the importance of methodology and statistics. Lombroso and Gall both struggled to get around the relatively primitive methodology of their times.

An English scientist responded to Lombroso's claims with one of the earliest convincing tests of the atavism hypothesis. Goring (1913) compared over three thousand habitual criminals with large, varied control groups over a decade: he used objective measures for 37 possible signs of atavism and found no differences other than that the criminals were, on average, two inches shorter and about five pounds lighter. Goring took this as support for his own theory that criminals had inherited a poorer set of genes but it is also consistent with the hypothesis that if people grow up in impoverished environments then they are likely to be physically less developed and more likely to turn to crime.

Interestingly, 26 years after Goring's book, Hooten (1939) published the results of a study of nearly 14,000 prisoners compared to 3,200 controls using 33 measures, many of which could have come from Lombroso, including malformed ears and sloping foreheads. Hooten found the criminals to be 'inferior' on all the body-part measures. Unfortunately Hooten's study had serious flaws, such as unsuitable controls and the same plausibility of environmental explanations for the physical differences as for Goring's results. He also claimed differences between types of criminal although many had been previously convicted for different offences. However as mentioned earlier, one would expect people to engage in behaviours for which they are physically suited, so big people are more likely to be able to use force effectively. In addition Hooten's theory and style of writing embody racist assumptions of the time. Indeed, Hooten's work was dismissed with contempt (e.g. Merton 1938) particularly for the circular reasoning that criminals were biologically inferior and therefore whatever physical differences they showed must indicate biological inferiority that must explain their criminality . . . and so on.

- Do you think it is reasonable to think that there may be a link between looks and criminality?
- What biological explanation(s) might explain any connection?
- What non-biological explanations can you think of?
- How could you test whether looks themselves caused criminal behaviour?

The idea that looks and crime are somehow connected via biology continued to develop, and after the Second World War Sheldon (1949) published a book that proposed a theory that body type was linked to personality. There have been ideas like this for hundreds of years – think of Shakespeare having Caesar say that he did not want lean men like Cassius around him as they were dangerous: 'Yond Cassius has a lean and hungry look, He thinks too much; such men are dangerous' (*Julius Caesar*, I.ii.194), but Sheldon used scientific methods to support his hypotheses. There were three extremes: the round, chubby endomorph who is tolerant, extrovert and likes food and people; the ectomorph who is slender and artistic, sensitive and introverted; and the mesomorph who is muscular, shaped like a triangle pointing down, and aggressive, competitive, fearless and risk-taking. If you imagine a triangle with each extreme at one point we all fall somewhere within it – few people are 'pure' meso-morphs, endomorphs or ectomorphs – but the more a person approached the mesomorphic point then the more likely Sheldon thought they were to be criminal. He produced data to show that convicted offenders are more mesomorphic on average than the rest of the population.

Other researchers have confirmed this: in one study by Eleanor and Sheldon Glueck 60 per cent of delinquents compared to only 30 per cent of non-delinquents had mesomorphic body characteristics (Glueck and Glueck 1950). But the Gluecks' theory is vulnerable to the criticism that of course muscular people are more likely to commit crimes involving aggression and violence. However, you will see later in this chapter that there is some biological support linking testosterone levels with both mesomorphic bodies and aggressive criminal acts.

Whatever the reason there does seem to be a connection between looks and the risk of conviction: Cavior and Howard (1973) took 159 photographs of male juvenile delinquents and 134 of male high-school seniors. University psychology students rated them for attractiveness: the high-school seniors were significantly more likely to be judged attractive.

Even more convincingly Kurtzberg *et al.* (1978) took one hundred 'ugly' convicts from one of the USA's toughest prisons, Rikers Island, New York, at their release and gave them plastic surgery. They were compared against a control group of equally ugly convicts who did not receive surgery. After 12 months those who had had plastic surgery were significantly less likely to have been rearrested. Finally, Saladin, Saper and Breen (1988) showed that there is a bias to believe that uglier people are more likely to be criminal by showing two psychology classes a set of photographs. The first class rated them for attractiveness and the other rated them on the chance they would commit murder or robbery: those rated less attractive tended to be judged more likely to commit serious crime. All of these studies of attractiveness should remind you of the claims of the physiognomists and the historical beliefs that physical beauty reflects goodness.

This takes us into the 'modern' period of biological thought on which the rest of this chapter concentrates. As you will see, studies of the possible genetic basis of factors related to criminality had already been going on for decades. A set of studies by Bohman (1996) are a milestone in the development of methods which highlighted the interaction between biological and social factors: the biosocial interaction model that is the most promising in this area. Also Wilson's revolutionary book (1975) argued that human social behaviour had biological roots and was evolved.

The rest of the discussion is divided into five sections:

- Evolutionary perspectives, to give you a framework within which to interpret the other viewpoints.
- Genes, as the bridge between evolution and our working bodies and brains – this subsection also covers the transmitters that carry signals within the brain.
- Physical characteristics, as some are related to your risk of criminal behaviour.
- Brain structures, as the organ with which we sense, process and respond to the world.
- Development of the brain, as this process ties together the other biological perspectives.

EVOLUTION

The most useful way to begin looking at particular approaches within biology is to consider criminal behaviour from an evolutionary perspective. As the geneticist Dobzhansky (1973) wrote: 'Nothing in biology makes sense except in the light of evolution.' To give you an idea of how this may help in understanding criminal behaviour, after introducing the concept of evolution below, we will look at three applications: first, one of the most convincing, which explains the age–crime curve for males (Kanazawa 2003); second, one of the most interesting but contested claims – that step-parents are much more of a danger to children than biological parents (Daly and Wilson 1988, 2002); third, one highly controversial hypothesis – that rape is a behaviour that has evolved as it has increased men's chance of leaving the greatest number of offspring (Thornhill and Palmer 2000).

Introducing evolution

Evolution applies to populations of animals (including humans) not to individual animals. You *are* the product of many generations of evolution, but the pattern of change that evolution produces can be seen only by looking at the whole population that you are a member of.

Individuals differ in their genes and so in their characteristics. Different characteristics give you differing chances of surviving and leaving successful offspring.

Those offspring will carry their parents' genes into the next generation. The more successful descendants a person leaves, the more successful they are in evolutionary terms. (See Dawkins (1976) for an explanation of how it is really genes that are 'successful' or not. You should also expect our understanding of genetics to change rapidly due to new methods.)

Thus, if you look at the population as a whole over time you will see evolution: an increase in the proportion of the population carrying versions of genes that fit them well to the environment.

The production of different combinations of genes is ruled by chance. The success of the combinations is tested by the particular environment. Evolution is shooting at a moving target: the best combinations of genes now in Latvia is not likely to be the same as the best in a thousand years' time in Surinam. The environment 'selects' those genes that lead to more offspring. However, evolution does not produce 'progress'; we are no 'better' than our ancestors; what is good now was not, and will not be, good in other environments.

Humans are as highly evolved as every other living organism, no more, no less. Owing to our shared evolution we share genes with other living things: the more closely related we are (i.e. the more recently that we shared a common ancestor with another species) the more of our genes are shared with them. We share about half of our genes with the banana (Begley 2002), even though that is obviously only distantly related to humans, but chimpanzees and humans have over 96 per cent of their genes in common (Holmes 2005).

Recently researchers have found clear evidence that we are still evolving quickly. Two genes that control development of the brain have versions, or alleles, that are being selected by the environment – this means that people who have the preferred versions are leaving more successful offspring. This seems to be an extension of the differences between humans and chimps and has led to the selected alleles becoming much more common over the last 6,000–30,000 years, broadly speaking up to the period that city life first appeared (Inman 2005). Evidence showing substantial human evolution over the last fifteen thousand years across at least seven hundred of our 25,000 genes has been published with the expectation that many more will be recognized (Douglas 2006).

Evolution will tend to make a really useful adaptation spread throughout the population, for example the impulsivity, competitiveness and high sex-drive of 15–30-year-old males are typical of males in general (just as antlers are typical of sexually mature male red deer). This is thought to be due in part to sexual selection where members of one sex prefer mates with certain traits, as when female deer prefer bucks with larger antlers. Then, even if those traits have other disadvantages, the genes that underlie them will become more common. This will go on until the disadvantages (of say huge antlers or extreme competitiveness) outweigh the advantages, always in terms of how many successful offspring you leave. As a general rule, in humans, females prefer high-status males while males prefer young, sexually mature females (Miller 2001).

There is more than one successful strategy possible. For example one view of psychopaths is that they are a relatively small group within the population who carry genes selected by evolution that suit them for a life of preying on the rest of us (Mealey

1995). Humans are highly adapted for co-operation (Ridley 1996) and are a social animal that relies on working with the group. This often means that we assist someone now and trust them to help us if we need it in the future (reciprocal altruism); however, this creates a niche for cheats who take the help now but never repay it (Katz 2000). Thus psychopaths are seen not to feel guilt or remorse, to be impulsive and egocentric, and not to be deterred by negative consequences. They understand how others' emotions work but do not care if they hurt someone else; this combination helps them to manipulate others in crime, business life and so on (Babiak, Neumann and Hare, 2010).

While psychopaths make up about 1 per cent of the general population, because of their persistent and varied offending from an early age, about 20 per cent of prisoners are psychopaths. They commit an even larger fraction of the most extreme offences: in 1992 the FBI found that over ten years about half the law enforcement officers killed at work were victims of psychopaths (Hare 1996).

Ellis (2005) uses this style of explanation to cover criminal behaviour in general. Testosterone and related male hormones lead to more competitive or victimizing behaviour while higher intelligence results in this behaviour being less violent and less criminal.

Animals have evolved flexibility and will change their behaviour as the social and physical environment changes. Humans do the same. The Hadza society (a hunter-gatherer people from Tanzania) was regarded as the hardest-hearted he had ever come across by an anthropologist who just happened to have studied them during a severe famine. Evolution produces a range of possible strategies: we are evolved to use unconsciously the one that is most appropriate for the circumstances.

The idea that we do not think out what is best to do, but our behaviour is unconscious, wired into our brains, is crucial. For example, women appear to present themselves in a more sexual way when they are at their most fertile point in the menstrual cycle, but women are not consciously aware of when this is (Miller 2001). In 2010, Lovatt claimed that 'dad dancing' had evolved to show they were not sexually available, not a very convincing claim, even though we know that humans do use dancing to assess various attributes of possible partners.

Modern humans and evolution

Presumably something that we would recognize as criminal behaviour must have existed as long as humans have lived in cities. At the moment the oldest city that we have good evidence for is Tell Brak, from about 6,000 years ago, although it is thought that in Iraq cities may have been established from 8,000 years ago (Lawton 2004). Some of our earliest written records, for example Hindu texts, the Old Testament, ancient Greek philosophy, discuss issues concerning anti-social behaviour and practical moral issues. Over this time the social and physical environment must have changed drastically, many times, yet – as far as we can make out – crime has always been there and at roughly comparable levels.

Evolution can produce rapid change in biologically determined characters: for example the specialized beaks of the finches that Darwin collected in the Galapagos

Islands change in response to the sharp changes in the type of food available (Weiner 1995). However, most biologists believe that humans now are biologically very similar to those from 10,000 years ago.

Biology not only affects physical things such as hair colour, height and risk of heart disease, it also underlies how we behave. There is good evidence that biology underpins our emotions (Damasio 2003) and thoughts (McGinn 2000) – two factors that motivate and guide our behaviour. Later you will see evidence that the behaviour patterns of attention deficit with hyperactivity disorder (ADHD), a condition that gives an increased risk of criminal convictions and delinquent acts, are due to biological factors. These seem to be often inherited from the person's parents and these behaviours may have been an advantage to their carriers in the past.

When E. O. Wilson published *Sociobiology: A New Synthesis*, in 1975, he argued that, just as in other animals, human social behaviours such as altruism and courtship were based on biology. Although most biologists agreed that there were some human behaviours largely under genetic control there was a powerful negative response to extending this to what were felt to be behaviours shaped by our education, society and moral beliefs, and for which we held people responsible. Wilson's view was attacked from one side for being a right-wing attack on the liberal-left consensus, and from the other as excusing bad behaviour and undermining responsibility (Segerstråle 2000). It is still difficult to get a productive debate going with researchers adopting a feminist perspective, but nonetheless there are a number of feminists who believe an understanding of the role of evolution can help produce a more effective feminism (Vandermassen 2005).

Since 1975 Wilson's ideas have been a crucial influence on human evolutionary psychology. Most evolutionary biologists believe that the genes we carry now evolved to suit our modern human ancestors' way of life. This is typically argued to be on the African grasslands about 60,000 years ago (Dunbar and Barrett 2010).

For our purposes evolutionary researchers who work in the areas of evolutionary psychology, sociobiology and human behavioural ecology are the most important. They argue that criminal and delinquent behaviour has been shaped by evolution because it has an impact on reproductive success. These approaches will be referred to collectively as human evolutionary psychology (HEP), as Daly and Wilson (1999) suggest.

Three examples of evolutionary explanations of criminal behaviour

The male age–crime curve

The male age–crime curve (MACC) shows how the number of male offenders per thousand males changes as their age increases. There are very few offenders up until about 11 years of age (in the UK the age of criminal responsibility is 10 years), the curve increases steeply until the proportion who are convicted offenders reaches a peak at about 18 years. From there it drops – steeply at first, but reducing more gently after about 25 years of age. The MACC has been called 'the best accepted fact in criminology' (Gottfredson and Hirschi 1990), although there is disagreement over how universal it actually is, and there have been many attempts to explain it in sociological terms. However, the evolutionary explanation is both interesting and useful.

Kanazawa (2003) presents a readable account of his hypothesis that the bulk of offenders are just young men displaying behaviour that evolved as it increased their chances of finding a mate and having children. Remember that producing successful children is what drives evolution: we might suspect that the MACC relates to this. We might also guess that the ways in which young males differ from young females are more likely to be linked to reproduction (think of the different mature sexual organs such as the vagina versus the penis, ovaries versus testes, breasts versus chests). We know that young men are more aggressive, impulsive, novelty-seeking and sexually driven than young women and also less empathic. We also know that there are biological changes through puberty and beyond that underlie these differences. One example is the male surge in testosterone levels that begins at about 11 years of age and does not decline until about 30 years of age. In many situations, women find men who show the physical changes associated with higher levels of testosterone more sexually attractive (Miller 2001).

QUESTION BREAK

- What is happening to males from about 11 years until about 18 years old?
- What might tend to be happening in men's lives between about 18 and 27 years of age?
- Why do you think young men show off so much to their peers?

Puberty in males begins at about 11 to 13 years of age and usually continues into the late teens. The biological purpose of puberty is to create a sexually mature person who can find a good mate and have children; males are interested in sex and capable of fertilizing a woman from early puberty.

Kanazawa argues that the initial rise in the MACC is triggered by puberty; he thinks that the increase in criminal behaviour reflects young males' increased drive to behave aggressively and/or impulsively. Therefore he proposes that these changes are concerned with finding a good mate. Recently it has been claimed that although young women do not prefer risk-taking men, men get higher status among their male peers by taking risks and women prefer men with higher status. Similarly you could argue that aggression and competition between young males are to do with establishing their status in their peer group. In the last 15 years or so there has been much research into the changes in the brain during adolescence (examples of this work include Oriz, 2004 and Steinberg, 2010 – both providing clear and accessible summaries).

If this is so then one might expect criminal behaviour to be only one type of behaviour that young men will adopt to compete with their fellow males. Kanazawa says that this is exactly what you find with sport, art, music and scientific achievement, and he shows that the curves for each of these for different ages have very similar shapes and characteristics to the MACC.

QUESTION BREAK

- Why do you think that evolutionary psychologists expect young women to have evolved different behaviour patterns than young men?
- What differences do you think there are in what a woman compared to a man looks for in a sexual partner?

The differences between male and female behaviour we see are expected by human evolutionary psychologists. We will use Miller's (2001) account as the basis for our discussion.

Sex has different costs and benefits for males and females. When men have sex they produce millions of sperm each time: sperm are tiny and cheap to produce. Women, once a month, release one (sometimes two) of the eggs that they have stored in their ovaries from birth. Eggs are much more substantial than sperm and women have only a limited number. This is called anisogamy; it fits women investing more in reproduction than men. It is important to remember that men do produce lots of sperm, so the overall difference in investment is much smaller than it may appear; however, women seem to invest a lot more after birth. This matters as it alters the best strategies for each sex.

If one of the man's sperm fertilizes a woman's egg then he can leave her to bring up his child while he fertilizes more women, leading to lots of potential offspring for him – think of the harem system where powerful men had sexual access to many women who bore them many children. The highest recorded number of children to one man – 1,042 – are attributed to Moulay Ismail the Bloodthirsty (who was also reputed to have killed over 30,000 people!); while genes from Genghis Khan have passed down to about 16 million Asian men. If a woman is pregnant then she is stuck with nine months of pregnancy, using large quantities of energy and exposing her to health risks and making her less able to look after and defend herself. Human birth is a dangerous event: in rich countries we forget that women used to face, and still do in poorer states, a serious chance of dying around the time of giving birth. And for a child the most serious problem is to lose their mother.

Because of this difference women are less keen on promiscuity than men (although contraception has changed behaviour, remember that these tendencies evolved over long periods and act below the level of consciousness) and more selective in whom they choose to have sex with. In particular women want someone who is healthy and carries successful genes *and* who has significant resources and is reliable. Most males do not combine both types of qualities.

HEP (Human Evolutionary Psychology) can explain the differences in criminal behaviour between males and females naturally. In many species males compete amongst themselves, with the winners having the best chance of being chosen as a mate by the females. Attributes increasing a male's chance of impressing potential mates are then selected by evolution. Females also compete, usually using social and verbal aggression, and there is evidence that the number of young female criminals is increasing, especially for violent crimes (see Chapter 5 for data on female criminals).

The HEP hypothesis that criminal behaviour is often just a way of impressing possible mates by out-competing your peers suggests that schemes that offer alternative ways for young males to compete in public should reduce both crime and anti-social acts. For example, there are projects for young men convicted of joyriding that teach them to repair old cars and then to race them. It also implies that there needs to be an element of genuine danger and that competition itself is necessary for adolescents. Another lesson is that we should expect youths from more disadvantaged homes to be more likely to show anti-social or criminal behaviour because they tend to have poorer educations and fewer opportunities to engage in other competition that satisfies their evolved drives. We should not think that males from less supportive environments are more 'naturally criminal' even if they are more likely to display behaviour for which they could be convicted.

QUESTION BREAK

- Has this view helped you to understand young male anti-social or criminal behaviour?
- Can you see any practical lessons or implications for policy from it?

'The Cinderella hypothesis'

The hypothesis being proposed here is that step-parents are much more dangerous to children than biological parents, and that this is because the step-parents do not share genes with the children. Therefore they have less interest in the children's survival and may even benefit from their death. (This section is based on Daly and Wilson 1998 and 2002.)

This is what we see in numerous animal species, the best known example being the African lion. Lions live in groups of closely related females called prides. Each pride has one or two sexually mature males who are closely related, often brothers, and who fight off others to keep their right to have sole access to mate with the females. Eventually another pair of males will come along and defeat them. When the new lions take over one of their first acts is to search out any young cubs and kill them. There are two reproductive benefits: they do not want to waste any of the resources they could use to bring up cubs of their own on unrelated cubs that will compete with their offspring; and the lionesses will not come back to peak fertility until they stop producing milk.

QUESTION BREAK

- Suggest some reasons why step-parents might look after their stepchildren less carefully than their biological offspring.
- What evidence can you think of that suggests that step-parents might be unhappy to support their stepchildren?
- What sorts of conflict might exist?

In human culture we have worldwide stereotypes of stepmothers (e.g. in 'Cinderella', 'Snow White' or 'Hansel and Gretel') and stepfathers (e.g. King Claudius in *Hamlet*) as being cruel to the children from previous relationships. Although there are many more wicked stepmothers in fiction, in real life it is often stepfathers who are more dangerous. Sociologists looking at how people actually behave find high levels of conflict in Western stepfamilies. Anthropologists have described the accepted practice in the Pacific island of Tikopia by which new stepfathers publicly state that they are not willing to bring up unrelated children and insist that they are either fostered or killed.

Daly and Wilson analysed evidence on crimes against children within the family. For abuse the US data showed that in 1976 under-three-year-olds were almost seven times as likely to be recorded as abused if they lived with a stepfather rather than two biological parents. To check that this was not due to cultural bias against stepfathers they looked at more serious cases, ending up with 279 fatalities from nearly 88,000 cases. These records are likely to be accurate because of the seriousness of the crime. When they did this they found that stepchildren were at one hundred times more risk than children living with both biological parents.

There have been criticisms of this work, but most of them do not convincingly undermine the hypothesis.

A sociological perspective would suggest that stepfamilies are under greater stress than first families: there are the effects of whatever led to the break-up of the previous relationship, tensions between step-parent and children due to loyalty to the missing parent, psychological issues such as anger and jealousy, the strain of managing on less income (thinking of the average stepfamily) with the consequential impact on education, housing, diet or recreational opportunity. And all these factors can increase the risk of criminal behaviour via mediating variables like substance misuse and bad peer group, while reducing the protective elements of a happy family life.

The factors in the previous paragraph are clearly relevant and there is great variety of quality within both different stepfamilies and different biological families. After all humans adopt unrelated children (although there is a preference for relatives in adoptions) and invest heavily in them. This may reflect the fact that many adopting parents cannot have children of their own.

A natural history of rape?

The final hypothesis examined is based on a book by Thornhill and Palmer (2000) with the same title as this section. The point they are trying to establish is that human rape is sexually, or reproductively, driven rather than being an act of violence reflecting unbalanced power relations between men and women as Brownmiller (1975) proposed. Brownmiller's position has been dominant for the last 30 years and she does not accept a sexual, reproductive explanation for rape.

Mealey (1999) shows that rape has several causes; she takes a 'life history' approach to identify several distinct routes ending in rape. This insight follows from sociological, psychological and biological evidence; it also means that one approach will not explain all cases and that a range of strategies to reduce rape are required.

Thornhill and Palmer use evidence from animals, including the scorpion fly – an insect whose mating behaviour Thornhill has studied. The normal way for a male scorpion fly to get sexual access to a female is for him to bring her a piece of food. Similarly human females prefer mates with resources, and men who give their partners gifts and treat them affectionately are much less likely to be domestically violent. Some male scorpion flies cannot manage this but they have an alternative strategy – the males have a notch in their wing with which they can hold an unwilling female in the correct position for sex. They propose that this is a model of human rape.

To make this argument work, Thornhill and Palmer have to define rape very tightly: it must involve vaginal sex as this is the only way that rape could produce a child. This seems to miss out a sizeable proportion of human rape, for example rape with objects, anal rape, rape followed by murder – especially in conflicts where rape is widely practised, sometimes as a deliberate weapon of terror – or rape of women past reproductive age or of pre-pubertal girls. This is necessary because they want to argue that men show adaptations that help them rape women that are encoded in the genes and so can be selected by the environment, but this can happen only if more copies of their genes are passed down the generations because they rape women. They do not suggest that men have physical adaptations like the scorpion fly but Thornhill thinks that men show psychological adaptations inclining them to rape. Mealey would see them as developing a theory that fits many rapes well, but that is not relevant to all.

It is certainly true that rape is common, especially when you include date rape and coercion that falls short of legal rape. Rape is found in all cultures and has been so throughout recorded history. It also seems that males try to push for sex more often than women do. Together this is consistent with some biological factor being important. Palmer's position is also plausible: he argues that rape is a side-effect of male traits that do tend to result in more offspring, such as aggression and high sex-drive.

Virtually every aspect of their project has been attacked, from their definition of rape to their interpretation of the statistics, to their suggested advice based on their work, for example that young women should not wear provocative clothing. While their hypothesis may be flawed, the idea that there is a biological side to rape is reasonable, even though it does not yet seem to have produced any useful applications. We would not argue that human rape is the same as forced sex in other species because rape has other dimensions and meanings that do not exist in other animals.

Human culture and intelligence are likely to be relevant to this, but evolutionary factors such as men's vulnerability in bringing up another man's child and the importance to a woman of choosing her own mate may help us understand the horror that rape arouses.

Summarizing evolution

We have considered the evolutionary perspective at some length to encourage you to see this as the view that unifies and makes sense of the other biological approaches. It has the advantage that it reunites us with the rest of the living world and evolution is being applied many new areas with impressive results. You will see that the later biological approaches to understanding crime make more sense if you have an evolutionary framework in which to interpret them. The sociological and psychological theories looked at in the next two chapters can also be integrated with this perspective. The evolutionary perspective sees the way that we behave as depending partly on our genes but also on the environment: this is an example of biosocial interaction. (The application of evolutionary theory to crime is relatively new, and useful sources of study include Duntley and Shackleford 2008 and Salmon and Shackleford 2007.)

GENES

We have seen how evolution can provide a framework for understanding human behaviour: now we will take a brief look at how genes provide the link between evolution and the biological factors that more directly underlie criminal behaviour. The evidence supports the biosocial interaction model.

The debate over the importance of genes in behaviour has always been intense, from the eugenics movement at the start of the twentieth century right through to the present (for example, Joseph 2003). Critics, some from within biology, have attacked the implication that genes largely determine our behaviour as well as the interpretation of the data from some of the methods that form the cornerstone of the genetic approach. For most of the twentieth century the 'nature versus nurture' debate, in which one side argued that biology, especially genes, determined our behaviour and the other that the environment determined how we behaved, was how disagreements were presented. More recently it has become clear that the evidence makes sense only if the biosocial interaction model is used (e.g. Raine 2002b).

No serious biologists think that there is 'a criminal gene': they are looking for genes that make criminal behaviour more probable. If genes can influence our impulsivity, and we know impulsivity makes you more likely to become an offender (Morgan and Norris 2010), then those genes increase the probability that you will perform criminal acts.

We now have compelling evidence that genes are important in establishing the likelihood that we will display particular anti-social and criminal behaviour. For example Brunner *et al.* (1991) showed that one defective version of a gene that makes an enzyme crucial in how some of our neurons work leads to a massively increased risk of very violent behaviour.

The combination of sustained criticism and improved understanding has resulted in the recognition that the impact of genes depends on the social and physical environment that the person lives in. Investigating the contribution genes make to a behaviour also reveals the importance of the environment. Parens (2004) gives a clear account of our present understanding of the role of each and of the difficulties in interpreting the results from such studies.

As with evolution there are several distinct approaches within genetic research. We will consider two: behavioural genetics and molecular biology.

Behavioural genetics

Behavioural genetics tries to identify how important genes are, in particular behaviours using methods that rely on comparing how similar different relatives are on that behaviour. Different relatives share different, predictable proportions of their genes. Humans share about 99 per cent of their genes because most are for crucial biological systems such as your heart and liver. Humans all need genes to do the same tasks, so we may all seem to have the same set of genes. However, remember that there will be a variety of versions of the same gene so we will end up with different genotypes. Almost all the genes we have do not appear to be relevant to how likely we are to be anti-social or criminal; that leaves a much smaller number where variations in the versions, or alleles, that we inherit may alter our predisposition to criminality. If you share half of your alleles in general with a relative then you will also be likely to share half of those alleles relevant to criminal behaviour.

Identical twins share all their genes; non-identical twins and other brothers and sisters share half their genes; parents share half their genes with each child; an aunt or uncle shares 25 per cent of their nieces' or nephews' genes, and so on. This means that by studying families we can compare how similar they are on, say, having a criminal record and see whether those who share more genes are also more alike on criminality.

QUESTION BREAK

- If a study finds that children with criminal parents are more likely to be criminals than those parents' nephews, does this show that being a criminal has genetic roots?
- Why do you think researchers often use twins to study the role of genes in criminal behaviour?
- Studies of twins separated at birth are regarded as especially powerful. Why do you think this is?
- Studies comparing adopted children's behaviour with their biological versus adoptive parents' behaviour are also useful. Why?

Twin studies have shown that genes are relevant to anti-social and criminal behaviour. If we ignore those with small sample sizes (as a rule the larger the sample the more valid the results) there are two early projects that stand out: Dalgaard and Kringlen (1976) and Christiansen (1977). They both compared identical twins with nonidentical twins on how alike each type of twin was on adult criminal behaviour (not adolescence-limited anti-social and criminal behaviour). This similarity is called concordance, and can range from 0 per cent (meaning no similarity) up to 100 per cent (meaning if one twin was a criminal the other always was too).

If we combine their results, the concordance for identical twins was 31 per cent and for non-identical 12.9 per cent. As both types of twins share much of their environment this is interpreted as showing that genes are important because sharing all your genes makes you much more alike in adult criminal behaviour than if you share half your genes.

Cloninger and Gottesman (1987) added more subjects to Christiansen's set and reanalysed the data. Now the concordance for identical twins was 74 per cent against 47 per cent for non-identical. This was then used to calculate the importance of genes in adult crime, also called its heritability. They found that 54 per cent of the differences between adults in criminal behaviour were due to genetic differences.

Genes were more important in males than females. Perhaps this is because some of the genes are on the Y sex chromosome that only the male inherits (e.g. the MAO, Mono-Amine Oxidase, genes). Or maybe there is less reproductive advantage to females in carrying these genes and therefore female adult criminals are more likely to behave like that either because of biological damage or because of their past or present environment.

More recently Taylor, Iacono and McGue (2000) tested about 140 male twins and found evidence that genes are involved in early-onset delinquency. This is known to be a good predictor of a persistent criminal lifestyle lasting through adulthood.

At this point you need to be aware of some of the criticisms of twin studies. For example, identical twins may be treated more similarly than non-identical twins because of their appearance (identical twins are often dressed identically by their parents): this would make them more alike for non-genetic reasons (see Allen 1976). Also, there is evidence that we seek out environments that suit our genes (Beaver et al. 2008) so identical twins tend to choose similar friends and activities – including anti-social and criminal ones. Beaver, Wright and DeLisi (2008) found one gene allele that only biased children from 'high-risk' families to seek out delinquent peers – a major risk factor in anti-social and criminal behaviour. This is an example of the complexity of environment–gene interactions: similar genes lead people to choose similar environments that amplify the effect of those genes, and increase their risk of delinquency, although that is also contingent on exposure to other factors.

Adoption studies are another way of looking for genetic effects. These look at people adopted at an early age and see whether, in later life, they are more like their biological parents (which would suggest that genes are important) or their adoptive parents (which would suggest that the environment dominates).

Mednick, Gabrielli and Hutchings (1984) looked at all adoptions in Denmark from 1924 to 1947, an unbiased set of over 14,000 cases. They found strong evidence of genetic influence, with about half of the sons convicted of crimes having criminal biological parents compared to about a third of the sons without criminal convictions. Genes were more important in persistent offending, as in the twin studies. These results are consistent with other studies, including Bohman *et al.* (1982) who looked at over 1,750 Swedish cases from their central register.

As with twin studies there are criticisms of adoption studies. Some studies have included children adopted by relatives, or adopted by an aunt living in the same street as the biological parents with whom they spent a lot of time (Lewontin *et al.* 1984). Also adoption agencies tend to place children with families similar to their biological one, which will make it more difficult to separate out environmental from biological effects (Jones 2006).

The different methods do seem to find compatible results even though there are differences in the precise figures they produce. Rhee and Waldman (2002) combined the data from 51 twin and adoption studies in a meta-analysis: their conclusion was that genes and environment are both important factors in explaining anti-social behaviour for both males and females. Similarly, Raine (1993) combined results from twin studies and, separately, from adoption studies and made a convincing case for the importance of genes in criminal behaviour across cultures. There is also evidence that this genetic influence is relevant to non-violent property crime but not to violent crime. In the sections on the brain and development we will see how biologists explain violent criminal behaviour.

There are many studies showing evidence that factors we know to be strong predictors of persistent criminal behaviour, such as early bullying, certain personality traits and conduct disorder have genetic components. For example Slutske *et al.* (1997) used over 2,500 pairs of twins to show that genes are a strong risk factor for conduct disorder, while Eley *et al.* (1999) tested over 1,500 twins and found a genetic factor underlying early onset aggressive bullying. Krueger *et al.* (1994) directly measured the link between the personality traits of rejection of conventional values, sensation seeking and recklessness and anti-social behaviour in over 800 participants and found evidence of a significant genetic influence.

We know that being abused as a child can have dramatic effects in later life, including anti-social behaviour and Caspi *et al.* (2002) showed that this negative impact only hit children with one version of a gene for MAO A function. Caspi and colleagues also showed a parallel effect for physical abuse and later psychiatric problems mediated by this allele, both from their own research and from an analysis of other similar research findings. Interestingly, in 2008 Binder and colleagues discovered a similar pattern of vulnerability to Post-Traumatic Stress Disorder following abuse, but that it depended on which allele of a completely different gene a person has. Other studies have shown such interactions involving more than one gene; for example a teenager's chance of showing conduct disorder and other anti-social behaviour, where the version of each of two genes was only important in conjunction with the version of others (Beaver *et al.* 2008). Genes underlie between 40 and 45 per cent of the differences as to whether people get victimized; and when only repeat victims are considered about 64 per cent of the differences are due to genetic variations.

In summary, the genes you inherit do put you at more or less risk of anti-social and criminal behaviour but their impact depends on the environment you grow up in. One early study illustrates the dominance of this non-additive interaction. Cloninger *et al.* (1982) carried out an adoption study and found that the risk of becoming a criminal if the adoptee had criminal biological parents was 12 per cent, if they had criminal adoptive parents their risk was 7 per cent, but if they had both then the risk shot up to 40 per cent. This shows that we must consider both biology and other factors together if we want to understand crime.

Molecular genetics

Molecular genetics involves the use of sophisticated laboratory-based methods to identify precisely which genes, and which alleles, are linked to particular traits and behaviours. This connects the findings of behavioural genetics to the functioning of brain systems and structures. We will give a flavour of this work because it will suggest how the transmitters and related structures and processes that carry signals within the brain relate to anti-social and criminal behaviour.

Most of this work has focused on the molecules involved in communications between the brain cells (or neurons). To be even more precise, the clearest evidence implicates elements of the communication systems concerned with the neurotransmitters serotonin and dopamine.

Genes connecting criminal behaviour to serotonin systems

Low serotonin activity has repeatedly been associated with criminality, for example conduct disorder (Coccaro *et al.* 1997), anti-social personality disorder (Dolan *et al.* 2002) and young adult offending (Moffitt *et al.* 1998). Other analyses have shown a clear link between low serotonin and high levels of impulsive violence, with changing serotonin activity altering human aggression (Berman *et al.* 2008). Therefore it is not surprising to find that genes involved in different aspects of serotonin function have been linked with various types of anti-social and criminal behaviour.

Brunner *et al.* (1991) reported a Dutch family with at least six generations of males showing extreme violence and learning disability. One was convicted of raping his sister at 23 years old. In the institution he was sent to he repeatedly got into fights with the other criminally insane inmates; at 35 he drove a pitchfork into the chest of a prison officer. Another relative made his sisters strip at knifepoint; another drove at his sheltered workshop manager when he was criticized. No females showed these behaviours, which made Brunner's team suspect the genetic flaw was on the female sex chromosome (the X). This is because the X is larger than the male Y chromosome and holds more genes. If one of the 'extra' genes is faulty males do not have a matching gene to cover the flaw: this is why genetic developmental disorders are so much more common in males.

The 'Brunner version' cannot be common in violent criminals because it produces learning disabilities and extreme behaviour that are rarely seen in offenders. Offenders like the Dutch family members above are held in special hospitals as they are both very dangerous and felt to be not legally responsible for their violence. MAO A and

B (monoamine oxidases) destroy surplus molecules of some neurotransmitters (e.g. serotonin and dopamine), and it seems clear that differences in this set of systems alter the chances of criminal behaviour. McDermott *et al.* (2009) found that those with low activity MAO systems punish opponents in a 'game'; more severely than those with high MAO activity, which suggests MAO activity may be important in personal violence, crime and even politics. Beaver and colleagues (2010) found that low activity MAO in adolescent males predicted twice the risk of joining a gang and over four times the chance of using a weapon – so we can see connections between sociological, psychological and biological levels of explanation.

Considering the process by which signals are received by serotonin-using neurons, Quist *et al.* (2000) found that one version of a gene (the HTR2A gene) that builds one of the serotonin receptors makes a child significantly more likely to have ADHD. ADHD is a substantial risk factor for later criminal behaviour. Fletcher and Wolfe (2009) found all three types of ADHD are substantial risk factors for later criminal behaviour.

QUESTION BREAK

- From what you have read, if serotonin activity and the genes that influence it are likely to be relevant to a person's chance of committing criminal offences, what offences are they more likely to carry out?
- What sort of biological interventions to deal with such behaviour do you guess people might suggest?

There are always problems in carrying out and interpreting these types of studies – for example serotonin activity is almost always measured indirectly because of problems in accessing the brain safely and comfortably. The overall picture suggests that genes that influence serotonin function will affect their holder's tendency to be involved in impulsive and aggressive behaviour.

Because of these links, researchers have tried using drugs that increase serotonin activity in offenders. The SSRIs (Selective Serotonin Reuptake Inhibitors) increase the activity of serotonin-using neurons by preventing neurons re-absorbing serotonin so that it is able to continue stimulating receptors. Prozac and Seroxat are two common brand names in Britain. A small number of male paedophiles who, despite hating their behaviour so much that some had considered suicide, were almost totally unable to resist their urges have been treated with SSRIs with some apparent success (see Rowe 2002, chapter 7). Similarly other researchers have suggested using the same drugs to reduce crime levels in the inner cities (Breggin 1995). Although some are sceptical of the benefits of using such measures widely there is a case for testing them on offenders who seem to be desperate to stop impulsive violent or sexual behaviour and who show signs of low serotonin activity. MDMA (better known by the street name Ecstasy) is known for its enhancement of empathy and positive feelings towards others and it acts primarily by boosting serotonin activity for several hours.

Lawyers have already tried to use molecular genetics research into serotonin systems to excuse or mitigate their clients' criminal acts. For example, Stephen Mobley ('the Domino's Pizza Killer') robbed a pizzeria at gunpoint in Georgia, USA, in 1991 and then for no apparent reason chose to shoot the manager in the back of the neck. At his murder trial his defence tried to have his death sentence commuted to life imprisonment on the basis of a family tree (like that Brunner constructed) showing several relatives with violent and criminal records. The court ruled that this was not relevant, and did not allow him to undergo biological tests of levels of the enzyme (MAO) that was malfunctioning in the Dutch family Brunner studied, or of the relevant transmitter, serotonin (Deno 1996). Mobley was executed on 1 March 2005. You may be interested to know that one of Mobley's brothers, sharing half his genes, became a self-made millionaire. This should make you distrust simplistic genetic determinism as an explanation of anti-social or criminal behaviour.

Genes affecting dopamine function

The other transmitter system that has been researched with encouraging results is the dopamine system. One part of the brain's dopamine system is known to be involved in experiencing reward, or in the motivation to get a reward. Cocaine and amphetamine act directly on these neurons and other drugs act on it indirectly (Julien 2007).

One type of transmitter will be used in several systems in the brain, each carrying out a distinct function. There are also several different receptor types for each transmitter, and we assume that these create different results in the neurons that carry them. The Dopamine 4 receptor (D4) has been implicated in characteristics relevant to criminal behaviour, with different versions creating different tendencies to act in particular ways. This type of research is relatively recent. Ebstein *et al.* (1996) found that Israeli students showed greater novelty-seeking if they carried the '7 repeat' version of the D4 gene. Although this has been retested by several groups with mixed results, it did trigger a burst of research into the gene itself.

The '7 repeat' version of the D4 gene has often been associated with ADHD, a risk factor for anti-social or criminal behaviour. Faraone *et al.* (2001) reviewed all the studies that could be found (including unpublished data) and concluded that there is clear evidence for a significant link between the '7 repeat' version and ADHD. Interestingly Rowe *et al.* (2001) found that adults who said that they had been more involved in teenage delinquency were also more likely to have the '7 repeat' allele, but only in males.

There is an evolutionary perspective that regards the characteristics of ADHD as useful in some situations, leading to more offspring. Now we make children sit in busy classrooms and judge their progress by how well they can ignore distractions, sit still, be quiet and concentrate on often dull material (Jensen *et al.* 1997). Indeed many famous people showed traits that we now interpret as elements of ADHD, for example Edison, Mozart, Churchill, Einstein, John Lennon and many sportspeople.

Practical implications

How then might we use the information from genetics? There is already a genuine debate about using genetic information to show that an offender has a predisposition towards anti-social or criminal behaviour, and on that basis altering the sentence they receive (Evansburg 2001). In at least one case in the USA a death sentence has been reduced to life in prison on grounds including genetic vulnerability (see the case study of John Eastlack at the end of the chapter, p. 57).

We could intervene biologically by altering the diets of children with low levels of a transmitter and increasing the amount of the 'building blocks' of that transmitter, or the chemicals involved in making it. For example tryptophan is part of a normal diet and is essential for constructing dopamine; it is easy to eat more foods that contain it. Vitamins, minerals, omega-3 and related essential fatty acids (found in oily fish, cod-liver oil and some plants, such as flax seeds) are essential for the effective functioning of our brains. Well-designed studies have clearly and repeatedly shown that simple, cheap supplements in tablets decrease the amount of criminal behaviour. In a series of studies over more than 14 years involving all the relevant children in Mauritius, there was much less anti-social and criminal behaviour in the teenage years if supplements were given in childhood. Poor diets at three years old were linked to criminal behaviour in adulthood. Kirby *et al.* (2010) found that omega 3 essential fatty acid levels in children were lower in those who had greater behavioural problems, and lower levels have been claimed to be found in ADHD.

In England Gesch *et al.* (2002) studied males detained in a young offenders' institution and randomly assigned to two groups. One was given a simple supplement, the other was given identical-looking tablets without the supplements. At the end of the trial the records of the supplemented group showed 25 per cent fewer disciplinary offences than those of the unsupplemented group, with the greatest difference for the most serious offences such as hostage-taking and assault (Lawson 2003). These findings raise the question as to why such cheap, effective measures are not applied in prisons, in schools and in schemes for the under-fives – perhaps because there are no great profits to be made? Moore, Carter and van Goozen (2009) also showed the negative impact of childhood diet; using adults followed since their birth in 1970 as part of large study they found that, at the age of 34 years, the adults who had eaten sweets ('candy') daily when younger had a 69 per cent chance of being convicted for violence compared to 42 per cent of those who had not eaten sweets so frequently. While this may be a reflection of the standard of care they were given in general, it is also consistent with popular worries about additives and sugar in children's diets.

Genetics is not destiny: to use a metaphor, it is more like playing a long session of poker where each card is a version of one of the genes we inherited from our parents. We need to play until we have been dealt about 25,000 cards (one per gene) so luck is unlikely to be a major factor. Also your hand can be judged only in the context of the other players' cards, and your success depends partly on who you are playing with. So a child with genes associated with a higher risk of anti-social or criminal behaviour who is brought up in a supportive environment is much more likely to have a happy and successful life than one who has high-risk genes and a poor social and physical environment.

Biosocial interaction is once more the best model. Evolution works because some combinations and versions of genes, in a particular environment, result on average in the person that inherited them leaving more offspring. Those offspring then carry those genes into the next generation.

We have seen how the next step of the process (when the genes produce different characteristics in their holders) works with respect to communication between the neurons that we think are the key brain cells underlying emotions, thoughts, our physical responses and motivations, etc. Note that most of the findings we discussed apply to the sort of traits – for example impulsivity, novelty-seeking, aggression – that we saw evolution has selected in young men in general. However, we also saw that 'faults' can also help to explain some criminal behaviour, as in Brunner's team's work with the Dutch family.

Systems using serotonin and dopamine, both controlled by MAO, are important in the prefrontal cortex and temporal lobe of the brain. In the brain structures section (pp. 49–53) you will find that these parts of the brain are implicated in criminal behaviour, and this helps to tie together the different biological perspectives. First, we will look at how those who seem predisposed to criminal behaviour differ from the majority of the population in various physical factors.

PHYSICAL CHARACTERISTICS OF OFFENDERS

In this section we will consider ways in which offenders differ physically from non-offenders. Bear in mind the proposed differences in attractiveness and physical characteristics that you read about in the introduction to this chapter.

QUESTION BREAK

- In what ways do you think offenders differ physically from non-offenders?
- Which ideas mentioned in the introduction to this chapter does this remind you of?
- If we could find differences between offenders and non-offenders what actions or policies do you think would be suggested?

Mesomorphy and testosterone

We looked earlier at Sheldon's theory that males fell into three general body types. Of these the mesomorph, having a muscular body, little body fat and adventurous, fearless, competitive, low-empathy, risk-taking personality, is the most likely to become a criminal. It makes sense that physically strong and aggressive people are better equipped for crimes involving force and intimidation. Mike Tyson and Bernard Hopkins are both world champion professional boxers who have committed serious crimes of violence. More recently, 'cage fighters' have been appearing in crime stories – for instance Lee Murray was convicted in June 2010 for organizing a £53-million armed robbery in the UK, and in the USA, David Tyner was arrested in 2009 for alleged involvement in a gang-related murder case.

Sheldon's work is now seen as simplistic and also as perhaps confusing cause and effect (for example skinny, anxious people are unlikely to be successful armed robbers even if they really want to be); however that is not to say that he was totally mistaken. Even if you cannot tell that someone is a criminal just because they are mesomorphic there is evidence that the physique and personality do often go together, and that they are more common in offenders. Eight studies have tested this relationship and all have found that mesomorphs are more often offenders than the other body types; one study has also found this for males with anti-social personality disorder (Ellis 2005).

In considering why this might be, Ellis convincingly argues that the underlying biological factor that leads to the personality and physical characteristics of the mesomorph that in turn make them more likely to become criminals is the hormone testosterone. Testosterone shapes the brain before we are even born and sets it up to respond in a particular way when puberty sets off the massive increase in testosterone levels many years later. This time delay explains why we do not see large correlations between adult testosterone levels and criminal behaviour, although there are consistent associations between them. There is also evidence that testosterone is especially important in violent offences including domestic violence and other aggressive crimes. Eysenck's criminal personality theory (pp. 91–94) explains psychoticism, which fits closely to the concept of psychopathy as reflecting testosterone levels and an increased risk of ADHD.

This theory might help to explain why females are so much less likely to be involved in such crimes. Baby girls are not set up in the womb to respond to testosterone in the same way as baby boys, and later levels of testosterone are much lower in females.

Fight or flight

Our response to danger depends on a web of systems that predispose us either to flee from the threat or to fight. There are significant and well-established links between criminal behaviour and different aspects of these systems.

Fearlessness is a trait with biological underpinnings that is linked to offending and anti-social acts. Gao et al. (2009), using a large sample of about 1,800 children, found that 3-year-olds who show a less than normal intensity fear response to a noise had an increased chance of being convicted by the age of 23 years. The notion of fearlessness is associated with the heart rate – which Raine (2002a) has called 'the best-replicated biological correlate of antisocial and aggressive behavior in children'. Low resting heart rate has been linked to conduct disorder but not to other psychiatric conditions (i.e. it is specific to a condition diagnosed by extreme anti-social and criminal acts). Five studies that measured resting heart rate at a young age – one at three years old, all before any criminal behaviour – have found that low rates predict aggressive and delinquent behaviour later in life. Moreover, low resting heart rate, by itself, is a predictor of later violence; more so than having a criminal parent!

Males as a group have lower heart rates than females, but among females those with low rates are at greater risk of criminal behaviour. This indicator is particularly good at predicting the small group of anti-social young people who go on to become life-long offenders. In addition to these reasons to take it seriously, heart rate is also known to be heritable (it is genetically determined to a substantial extent). A high rate protects against other risk factors and it interacts with other, non-biological risk factors (see Raine 2002a).

It could be argued that this factor is so important because of a link with fear-lessness; indeed decorated bomb disposal operatives have very low resting heart rates and low reactivity to threat (Cox *et al.* 1983), as do decorated British paratroopers (McMillan and Rachman 1987). A more general explanation is that it is part of a general low level of arousal in the several systems underlying fight or flight responses. This is supported by recent research by several groups showing that other measures of arousal are associated with anti-social and delinquent behaviour in children. It also fits with the higher levels of sensation-seeking seen in anti-social, delinquent and criminal populations. The connection is thought to exist because we all have a level of arousal that we find preferable. If we are biologically highly aroused then we do not want to be more stimulated because that takes us past the optimal level; if we are biologically under-aroused then we will seek out stimulation to bring us up to that preferred arousal level (Eysenck 1987).

Joy riding, burglary, street fighting and many other criminal acts are clearly very exciting and arousing and so would be expected to be seen more often in those with low biological arousal than in other people. As there are many other ways to be excited we can also see how this fits with sociological theories linking criminal behaviour with lack of opportunity and with exclusion as this in turn limits access to legal ways of experiencing risk and excitement.

There are other factors that are thought to reflect low arousal and reactivity such as low pulse rate, low levels of sweating when emotionally challenged (galvanic skin response or GSR) and low levels of hormones released in response to stress, especially cortisol (see Raine 2002a and Ellis 2005).

Overall the evidence for lower than normal activity in the body's arousal systems of anti-social, delinquent and criminal persons seems convincing and plausible; it also relates to psychological and sociological theories. It makes sense in the evolutionary framework within which we are considering biological factors. However, it should be obvious that having a low arousal level cannot, by itself, cause crime any more than any other biological factor can. After all besides bomb disposal officers, it is likely that risk-taking sportsmen and women, such as racing drivers or mountaineers, and entrepreneurs would also have low resting arousal levels and responsivity to stress; indeed it is another example of the critical role of interaction between biology and other types of factors.

The final biological factor we will consider concerns those brain structures and functions that seem to be particularly relevant to understanding criminal behaviour.

BRAIN STRUCTURES

This section focuses on research into the frontal lobes of the brain (especially the prefrontal cortex) and the temporal lobes (especially the amygdala and hippocampus). It also considers differences between the two halves of the brain. The reason for looking in some detail at the brain is that a significant proportion of the most extreme, life-course-persistent offenders show clear signs of significant brain damage in exactly the parts of the brain where we would predict would lead to immoral, impulsive, violent, anti-social and unpredictable behaviour.

The prefrontal cortex

In 1848 Phineas Gage, a respected, diligent railway worker, survived a one-metre-long, 6-kilogram, iron rod being blasted through the frontal lobe of his brain, landing about 10 metres behind him. The destruction was mostly on the left, mainly impacting the prefrontal area, and showed us that traumatic damage to the prefrontal cortex can change a person's character and behaviour dramatically for the worse (Macmillan 1999/2005). Phineas was not allowed to return to his job because his employers said that he had changed from their most capable, reliable, efficient and businesslike foreman into an unreliable, disrespectful, offensive man who could not deal with his fellow workers and showed impulsivity, obstinacy and an inability to decide on and follow any plan. He was said to 'no longer be Phineas Gage', abandoned his family, showed no respect to his fellows, swore, gambled, drank and ended up as a freak exhibit for the Barnum museum in New York and working in stables in Chile (Macmillan 2000). Although we must be careful in our interpretation (as a lot of the evidence is only anecdotal), notice that the way Phineas was after damaging his prefrontal cortex is similar to the collection of characteristics that are seen in many of those who have been convicted of crimes.

Less sudden damage to the frontal and/or temporal cortex can also produce anti-social behaviour in people with frontotemporal dementia (FTD). Miller *et al.* (1997) compared 22 patients with FTD against 22 with Alzheimer's dementia (which damages structures further back in the brain). Their families said that the FTD group had been responsible, competent, reliable citizens before their dementia began; therefore it is unlikely that the FTD 'unmasked' pre-existing anti-social characteristics. The diagnoses were made before the dementia was severe enough to explain their anti-social actions as due to cognitive difficulties.

There was a large difference between the groups: ten out of the 22 with FTD had records of socially disruptive behaviours including theft, assault, inappropriate sexual behaviour, unethical behaviour at work and even one hit-and-run. Three had been arrested and two others had avoided arrest only because their families persuaded the police that they were ill. The Alzheimer's group had only one patient with a socially disruptive record. Once again we can see the same types of behaviours that are seen in criminals, especially those with anti-social personality disorder and those who belong in the life-course-persistent subgroup of offenders.

Many children thought to have conditions predisposing them to criminal behaviour (especially the disruptive behaviour disorders that include conduct disorder, oppositional-defiant disorder (ODD) and the attention deficit disorders (ADHD)) show differences in brain function (and even structure) when compared to children who do not have these conditions.

There are also cases of brain injury in children. It is generally agreed that conduct disorder and other behaviour problems commonly appear after such damage (Raine 2002a). The frontal lobes and the tip of the temporal lobe (where the amygdala and hippocampus lie) are particularly vulnerable to head injury. More specifically, children can have damage limited to the prefrontal cortex. For example, Anderson *et al.* (1999) studied two young adults whose prefrontal cortex had been damaged before 16 months. One was a 20-year-old woman who was intelligent but stole, abused others verbally and physically, lied, was sexually promiscuous, never expressed guilt and had no empathy for her illegitimate child. The other was a 23-year-old man who was apathetic, slovenly, financially reckless, lied, physically assaulted others, stole in ways that were easily detected, never showed guilt and also had no empathy for his illegitimate child. Both had good environments but had shown such behaviours consistently since the damage with no apparent effect of punishment; also neither had been able even to learn social and moral conventions, let alone act upon them.

Vargha-Khadem *et al.* (2000) report on two British teenagers with childhood frontal damage who then developed delinquent behaviour that got worse until they were found guilty of criminal offences. Pennington and Bennetto (1993) discuss nine other children with frontal damage under the age of ten years. All showed behavioural disorders after their injuries, seven of them having conduct disorder, while one showed impulsive, unpredictable behaviour and another uncontrollable behaviour.

This evidence shows that childhood damage to the prefrontal cortex can cause later criminal behaviour, and is consistent with childhood abnormalities of structure or function being strong predictors of adult anti-social or criminal behaviour.

It is important to understand that, although you may be born with this type of brain, it is also easy to produce this pattern of damage by direct physical abuse.

Shaking a baby or infant, falls and other blows can produce damage to the prefrontal cortex. McKinlay *et al.* (2009) found that children with even mild brain trauma before they were five years old had a greater chance of ADHD, behavioural disorders and substance abuse at the ages 14 to 16 years. Perron and Howard (2008) adopted an opposite approach by studying juvenile offenders and asking if they had been knocked out for at least 20 minutes – they found one in five offenders had been, compared to about one in 250 in the general population. Even more worryingly it is now established that simply growing up in a family where it witnesses domestic abuse is associated with brain changes that make the child more likely to respond violently in future (Margolin and Gordis 2000).

In adults there is much more direct evidence of abnormal function and structure in the prefrontal cortex being linked with criminal behaviour. There have been several reviews of functional brain-imaging studies. These look at studies using diverse methods and testing different types of anti-social or criminal individuals; also the number of subjects tested is often low. Bearing these issues in mind it is impressive to what extent there is agreement that violent offenders show abnormal patterns of activity in their prefrontal cortex (Raine 2002a). Probably the best studies are a series by Raine's team which ended up by comparing 41 murderers to 41 non-offenders matched for age, sex and schizophrenia. They found an underactive prefrontal cortex in the murderers, with the reduction being greater in impulsive, emotion-driven murderers than in predatory murderers who killed to achieve a goal. Craig *et al.* (2009) had a slightly different view; after examining nine chronically violent psychopaths, they argued that poor connections between the amygdala and orbitofrontal cortex tended to encourage psychopathic behaviour.

Paedophilia has also been associated with prefrontal damage. Langevin reported that paedophiles' brains were structurally different in a series of papers from 1985, but the methods did not allow very fine resolution (Freund 1994). In 2003 Burns and Swerdlow described a 40-year-old married male teacher with conventional sexual behaviour who had begun visiting child pornography websites, using prostitutes and propositioning young children. His wife left him and he was soon convicted of child molestation; then he was expelled from his treatment programme for soliciting sex from the women on the course. Fortunately he went to hospital complaining of headaches and a fear that he would rape his landlady. The doctors spotted other signs of brain dysfunction and scanned his brain, finding a large tumour in his right prefrontal cortex. An operation removed the growth and he returned to his old self. Some time later his sexual deviance returned and they found that the tumour had regrown. On its removal he once again became his original, sexually conventional self. This is strong evidence that his behaviour was caused by the tumour impairing prefrontal functions.

More recently, Tost *et al.* (2004) used tasks based in the prefrontal cortex to show that four paedophiles were very impaired, while their performance on tasks associated with other brain structures was normal. Schiffer *et al.* (2007) found various differences between paedophile, heterosexual and homosexual males' brains, especially in serotonin- and dopamine-using systems related to impulsivity, addiction and compulsion. In 2008 a study found that paedophiles' brains tended to have weaker connections between sexual areas in the brain (Cantor *et al.* 2008), consistent with the poor performance on prefrontal task found by Tost. Together they suggest some brain abnormality in paedophiles, not specific to sexual behaviour, in the prefrontal cortex and related systems.

There are also many cases where previously law-abiding adults who have had their prefrontal cortex damaged have then developed anti-social, psychopathic characteristics, including low arousal, thus supporting the research we have discussed.

The temporal lobe

The temporal lobes have a covering of cortex like a tablecloth on a table. Under this is a sizeable space where the amygdala sits: this is known to be critical in strong negative emotions like anger and fear. Along its lower side the sheet of cortex is rolled up like a Swiss roll: the edge that ends up in the centre of the roll is hemmed with the hippocampus, a structure critical in anxiety, memory and controlling anger. Damage to the hippocampus, amygdala and the front half of the temporal cortex on the left side of the brain has been shown to often produce violent behaviour, and the amygdala is part of a system including the prefrontal cortex that controls aggressive behaviour. Damage to the amygdala can result also in an inability to empathize with others, the loss of emotional memory and emotional under-arousal, all factors which we have seen to be linked to criminal behaviour (Martens 2002).

Mendez and colleagues (2000) found that two patients with homosexual paedophilia starting after brain damage showed substantial underactivity in the front half of their right temporal lobe. One was a case of frontotemporal dementia, the other had damage to the hippocampus on both sides of the brain. This is consistent with other evidence that damage to the right temporal lobe can produce an increase in sexual behaviour, especially inappropriate sexual acts.

So how can we make sense of all this? Bufkin and Luttrell (2005) reviewed 17 brain-imaging studies on aggressive, violent offenders. They argue that the prefrontal cortex and the temporal lobe in the amygdala and hippocampus region work together in a system to regulate negative emotions. Kiehl *et al.* (2001) found that criminal psychopaths showed significantly less emotionally related activity in the temporal cortex and in part of the prefrontal cortex as well as in a connected part of the brain important in producing behaviour (the striatum). At the same time the rest of their prefrontal and temporal cortex was over-active.

This seems to tie together the studies that implicate the frontal cortex with those highlighting the temporal lobe: both are part of a system critically important in emotional processing and controlling impulsive, aggressive and sexual behaviour.

The two sides of the brain

There is evidence that lower than normal right-hemisphere functioning might be important in the lower heart rate clearly linked to higher risk of criminal behaviour. Damage to the right side of the brain in adulthood has been shown to reduce the patient's response to negative emotional stimuli. This supports the idea that the fearlessness and impaired ability to learn from negative consequences known to be risk factors for criminal behaviour might be due to right-hemisphere underactivity (Raine 2002a).

Dysfunction of the left hemisphere has been convincingly associated with violence and criminal behaviour in psychopaths, sex offenders, people with conduct disorder, children showing anti-social behaviour, male violent offenders and others, using several methods (Raine 1993). More recently, Raine *et al.* (2003b) have measured the size of the corpus callosum (the great band of fibres connecting the two halves of the cortex) in 15 men with anti-social personality disorder and high psychopathy scores and in 25 controls. They found several differences that imply greater connectivity between the two halves in the anti-social group. The greater the volume of the corpus callosum the lower the men's response to stress was and the more they showed the signs of psychopathy.

The type of evidence outlined here, although quite detailed and technical, suggests that the balance of activity between the hemispheres might be abnormal in those predisposed to criminal behaviour, although it is not yet clear how best to interpret it.

- Do you think that frontal damage, or frontal malfunction from birth, should be taken into account when deciding guilt?
- What about when deciding sentence?
- What should we do with such people after they have served their sentence?

In summary, there is evidence that the brains of some offenders are different in function and structure from those of non-offenders. This is particularly striking for life-course-persistent, impulsive, violent offenders.

DEVELOPMENT OF THE BRAIN

This section brings together many of the ideas from this chapter and will help you to understand how the different biological perspectives interlock. It also emphasizes the biosocial interaction at the heart of human life.

Anti-social behaviour is not unusual, so it is unlikely that much of it is caused by dramatic problems such as tumours, maladaptive genes or injuries. Over the last 50 years researchers have begun to understand the normal processes by which our brain develops in response to our environment (Schore 1997). This development certainly continues into our early twenties (Andersen 2003) and in all likelihood will be found to go on past the age of 30. In this section on early development we look at what happens up to puberty.

Even in the womb the baby is sensitive to the mother's environment. At the end of the Second World War there was a famine in the Netherlands where the population was reduced to eating such things as tulip bulbs, grass and rats (Hart 1993). Women who were in the third trimester of pregnancy at the time gave birth to underweight babies. However, those in the first trimester had overweight babies on average and when the females grew up and went on to have their own children they too were heavier than average (Motluk 2004). This was unexpected and shows the power of the environment to change biology: it is argued that this is a response to adapt the baby to the environment it is going to be living in (Vines 1998) and it may be working by a mechanism called imprinting where genes can be turned off for long periods before being passed on to the next generation or even beyond.

Even more dramatic effects can be seen in many mammals if a pregnant female is stressed during pregnancy: for example rabbits will reabsorb growing embryos and, after birth, stressed guinea pigs will eat their own babies. Both of these behaviours save resources for when they can be better used to bring up offspring successfully. In humans it is suspected that maternal stress can predispose a child to be anxious and in one study to double the chance of hyperactivity in boys (Glover and O'Connor 2002).

In humans, babies exposed to alcohol in the womb can have their development impaired. If the mother drinks heavily the babies may show foetal alcohol syndrome

(FAS) which is seen in about one in 500 births worldwide. FAS is due to brain damage, especially to the prefrontal cortex, which leads to impulsivity, hyperactivity, attention difficulties, learning disabilities and problems with thinking things out – all of which, as we have seen, are risk factors for criminal behaviour. Unsurprisingly when they grow into their teens and beyond such children are at significantly greater risk of being imprisoned (Boland *et al.* 1998). Recently there has been evidence that even low levels of drinking during pregnancy can lead to less severe forms of these problems (Hall 2005). Greenbaum *et al.* (2009) found FAS to have significantly more severe effects than ADHD, including a substantially greater risk of anti-social or criminal behaviour; only about 8 per cent of FAS (even defined loosely) ever live truly independently, and about 60 per cent are locked up in custodial institutions.

Using drugs such as cocaine (powder or crack), heroin or methamphetamine can have severe consequences for the baby's brain, behaviour and likelihood of later criminal behaviour (MedlinePlus 2005). People are often surprised that smoking tobacco during pregnancy has been shown to increase the child's chance of criminal behaviour: in eight studies since 1992, six showed clear evidence and two limited support. These are not small effects: one study found twice the risk of a criminal record at 22 years.

Besides drugs, exposure to toxins such as lead, mercury, pesticides, industrial chemicals that mimic hormones (such as pthalates which are used to keep some plastics soft) and many other environmentally widespread poisons can distort brain development and lead to increased chances of criminal behaviour (Galen 2000). If there are medical problems during pregnancy, for example bleeding or infections, there is an increased chance of the baby having minor physical anomalies (MPAs) such as lower ears than average or a furrowed tongue. These are an indicator of disturbed development and mean that is likely that the brain has also been slightly affected. MPAs are associated with aggression, impulsivity and behavioural problems at school in children from the age of three years. They have also been shown to indicate a higher risk of teenage conduct disorder and adult violent offending (Raine 2002a). Note the link to earlier beliefs that to be physically ugly indicated moral weakness.

The next danger is at birth itself where complications such as lack of oxygen, forceps delivery and pre-eclampsia have been linked to conduct disorder, delinquency, impulsive crimes and violence as an adult in a range of studies (Raine 2002a).

In case you are now terrified of having a child, or feeling guilty for having given birth to the next serial killer, here is the good news: there is very strong and convincing evidence that all of these factors can be counteracted by a stable, supportive upbringing (Raine 2002b). As we have repeatedly seen, it is when there are both a biological predisposition and then a bad environment that the most serious problems arise. This is an example of biological research showing the importance of the non-biological environment and gives a very encouraging message to parents as well as suggesting how governments might reduce biologically influenced anti-social or criminal behaviour without doping our children up on the latest pharmaceutical product.

QUESTION BREAK

- What type of environment do you think will lead to successful biological development?
- How might a child's upbringing change the impact of early biological disruption?
- How might growing up as a witness to domestic violence or as a subject of abuse disturb normal biological development?

As regards the complex interactions between mother and baby, and identifying some of the key factors leading to successful early maturation, it is now believed that the first two to three years of life are crucial in the development of emotion (or affect). In the aftermath of the Second World War there were a great many orphans and the World Health Organization funded research into their needs. In a famous report Bowlby (1951) showed the dire effects of being brought up with enough food, clothes and other physical staples but without real emotional contact with a carer. Such children grew up to be emotionally damaged. These findings have been replicated many times in group settings (e.g. Groza *et al.* 2003) and in individual cases of extreme neglect (e.g. Rymer 1993).

The more recent studies do show the possibility of counteracting the damage by providing a supportive, patient family environment through later childhood but also emphasize the long-term consequences in behaviour, emotional sensitivity and expression and mental health if early neglect is not dealt with effectively. These studies emphasize the interplay between biology and the social and physical environment. A person's earliest experiences shape the development of their brain and so change the way they will respond in future. We know that children with the types of behavioural patterns that make them more likely to become criminals are also more likely to have had neglectful or abusive childhoods.

The evidence that genes are important in conduct disorder (AACAP 1997) and that systems using the transmitter serotonin are disturbed (Lahey *et al.* 1993) highlights the biological-environmental interaction at the heart of human development. This seems to be a common way in which biological systems have evolved: our genes describe a generally useful set-up but the set-up then adapts to the environment we happen to have been born into. This is a powerful way of dealing with the fact that evolution is 'blind' and cannot tell what the world will be like in the future.

One of the psychological constructs most clearly linked to development is that of attachment. Bowlby (1951) and Harlow (1962) set the stage for later work, especially by Ainsworth and her colleagues (Ainsworth *et al.* 1978). Cicchetti and Barnett (1991) found that a massive 80 per cent of abused or maltreated infants showed signs of attachment disorders. Evolutionary psychologists have hypothesized that the 'poor' attachment styles are actually ways of adapting to life in a world where people are less supportive or more dangerous than is usual in the UK; although the actual style developed affects the person's whole life (Brune 2008).

In addition to attachment researchers have shown that the style of discipline in a family has important long-term consequences (Wade and Kendler 2001). Discipline styles may be summarized as warm-consistent (clear rules, talking not hitting), warm-inconsistent (rules not clear, but talking not hitting), cold-consistent (clear rules, physically enforced) and cold-inconsistent (rules not clear with hitting not talking): these styles interact with attachment styles and together lead to long-term consequences (Kerr *et al.* 2004; Johnson and Smailes 2004).

It is clear that these psychological differences reflect biological differences and will also make it more or less likely that a person will engage in anti-social and criminal activity – for example an impulsive, uncontrolled person who has grown up without clear rules in an atmosphere of arbitrary violence is more likely to behave anti-socially as an adult (Hirschi 1995; George and West 1999).

Extreme or chronic stressful experiences, such as abuse or witnessing domestic violence, lead to high levels of stress-related hormones that damage the brain, including the hippocampus which is critical in memory, dealing with stress and controlling aggression (McEwen 1999).

Case studies of serial killers often find that their childhood attachments and family discipline seem to be one of the building blocks that lead to their extreme criminal acts. Harvey Carignan, convicted of multiple rape and homicide, was the illegitimate son of a 20-year-old who could not cope. She passed him round numerous temporary carers, thus undermining any proper attachment and exposing him to inconsistent but physical discipline. He grew up to be a very hostile man who hated all women (Berry-Dee 2003).

We are now in a position to see how all the biological threads can be drawn together to suggest a consistent model of the biology underlying criminal behaviour. The evidence also shows how preposterous it is to suggest that biology alone, or even more ridiculously just one biological factor, can explain criminal behaviour – only a biosocial interaction model is consistent with the evidence.

QUESTION BREAK

- Which aspects of early family life might be important in how an infant develops as a person?
- Thinking about yourself, your children or people you know, can you identify behaviours that we have seen are linked to offending?
- Did they always show them or was it more obvious at one period of their lives?
- Do you think people can be anti-social and delinquent in their teens and early twenties but good citizens later in life?

CONCLUSION

In concluding this chapter we will use two case studies to try to draw the various threads and issues together. Read through them and then consider the questions at the end.

John Eastlack

John Eastlack was sentenced to death for brutally beating an elderly Tucson couple, Kathryn and Leicester Sherrill, to death in their home in 1989. At appeal his sentence was reduced to life imprisonment. In her decision the judge said that the biological vulnerabilities caused by his previously undiagnosed foetal alcohol syndrome, together with his genetic vulnerability – deduced from his biological family's history of generations of substantial mental illness and criminality – made him less able to understand what was right and wrong, not able to feel guilt and less able to control his behaviour.

Eastlack was taken from his mother at birth, then went through various foster homes (one of which had handed him back so the foster parents could more easily go on holiday). His father was shot to death soon after John's birth when caught stealing cash from a pinball machine.

By the time he was adopted by a loving, supportive family he was already a habitual liar and thief with learning difficulties. Bringing up a child who was so demanding, and who soon began to get into trouble at school and ended up in an institution for juvenile criminals for theft, was a reason behind the divorce of his adoptive parents.

Eventually he was sentenced to nine years' imprisonment for credit card fraud but he escaped from the Arizona State prison, and was on the run when he broke into the Sherrills' home. At the trial he said that the wife had attacked him with a poker and he had then beaten them both to death and fled in their car. He said that he had felt as if he was watching events unfold rather than as if he was actually committing them himself (Revere 1999).

This is a typical case of biological damage and illustrates the interaction between the biological and environmental factors that make it almost impossible to decide what was the ultimate cause of his actions that night.

Charles Whitman

This case also illustrates the danger that taking the 'obvious' biological view may lead you to miss the environmental factors that are at least as important in understanding an offence.

Whitman was one of the first 'spree' killers to be widely covered in the media. In 1966 he shot his wife and mother before climbing the University of Texas Tower and spent 96 minutes shooting randomly chosen victims before killing himself. At autopsy he was found to have a tumour on the amygdala, an area known to be critical in intense negative emotions. Stimulation of the amygdala in animals, or damage to it in humans, is known to be capable of causing extreme violence. Therefore that may well have been a critical factor behind the murders he committed that day.

However, a more detailed examination of his story reveals evidence of other possible biological factors. Whitman's father had an extreme temper, leading to his beating his wife and son. This is consistent with a genetic vulnerability in his son, but of course also illustrates a family environment that taught the use of violence. As with John Eastlack, the domestic violence he witnessed and experienced is likely to have led to biological changes that increased the likelihood of him offending as well.

If his, relatively small, tumour was important we might expect his violence to be something that began near the time of the murders. Several years previously he had said to a number of people that the tower would be a perfect place from which to shoot passers-by, suggesting that the thought patterns shown in his crime were already present, in part.

He was sponsored by the Marines to attend university, but without clear rules he began to display criminal and violent behaviours. He was arrested for poaching deer, did not pay gambling debts and got poor grades, ending his sponsorship. Back at a Marine camp at the end of 1963 he was court-martialled for gambling, unauthorized possession of firearms and threatening a fellow soldier over a debt of $30. In addition, he had beaten his wife on several occasions: although he made efforts to stop this behaviour with some success, he also had fits of temper; she filed for divorce in 1966.

In early 1966 his wife did report that he had been getting depressed and anxious, which is consistent both with a tumour and with the growing pressures in his life. He went to a doctor, and told him that he had fantasized about shooting people from the tower.

Whitman then began using amphetamines to help him work. Amphetamine use increases the chance of violent behaviour. Drug or alcohol abuse is perhaps the most important risk factor for violent crime in general: it increases a person's risk to others by about 14 times (in comparison severe schizophrenia increases a person's danger to others by only about four times) (Eisenberg 2005).

In his suicide note he did state that his violent fantasies had been increasing and that his treatment had not helped. He also wrote that he was going to kill his wife and mother because the world was such an awful place that he did not want to leave them to suffer. This is not an unusual theme in cases where depression drives a parent to commit suicide and also kill their own children: depression is influenced by both biological and environmental factors.

He then killed his mother, followed by his wife, and completed his thorough preparations to enact his fantasy. During his killing spree he murdered 14 passers-by and wounded dozens more.

The case studies above illustrate some of the difficulties in determining causes of criminal behaviour – and the difficulty of settling on either biology or the environment as *the* cause.

Do you agree with the appeal court judge's comments concerning John Eastlack? Suggest reasons for and against her decision that Eastlack was not as culpable as someone without the same biological vulnerabilities that had been thrust upon him.

On consideration of the second case, do you think the genes Whitman inherited made him more likely to act violently, or that his environment was a more convincing cause? Why might people feel that he was less culpable if his biology had been an obvious cause than if the dominant cause was his family and later environment?

SUMMARY

As we have stressed, modern biologists do not look for 'the crime gene', they look for genes that increase a person's probability of committing particular types of offence in certain environments. The large majority of them do not think that black young men in the USA and Britain are more likely to be imprisoned because of their biology. Even if there were to be biological differences there are clear factors such as poverty that are much more plausible causal factors (Jones 2005).

Evolutionary psychologists do not think that biological explanations will destroy the utility of concepts such as responsibility and morality. If a child shoots a friend dead while playing a game of soldiers with the father's loaded handgun we accept that they are not morally, or legally, responsible owing to their age and consequent immaturity. Surely we can find a way to deal with cases of people who, for other biological reasons, may have reduced culpability? At the moment, biology is not even fully integrated into clinical psychology, a discipline relevant to understanding anti-social and criminal behaviour.

Violent and other crimes seem to be universally found in human societies: indeed the evidence suggests that levels of violence and murder are considerably higher in pre-state, hunter-gatherer groups than in the type of state we find in Europe and many other parts of the world (Pinker 2005); when the state structure breaks down, as in the former Yugoslavia, crime rates soar. Surely we do have evolved tendencies to behave in certain anti-social and criminal ways in certain circumstances, and part of normal male development is to compete in ways that include criminal behaviour. Although this does not mean that we have to accept behaviours that harm other members of society, 'natural' does not mean 'moral' or 'right'.

As to the role of biological perspectives on anti-social and criminal behaviour in helping to understand and deal with such behaviour, maybe the effective response is not to try to ignore biology but to learn enough so that you can understand it and make an informed contribution to the debate (Stangroom 2005). The greatest dangers have arisen when people without scientific knowledge (including politicians like Stalin or Hitler) have taken up scientific hypotheses with no real understanding and based policies upon their own ignorance.

FURTHER READING

Daly, M. and Wilson, M. (1998) *The Truth About Cinderella*, London: Weidenfeld & Nicolson. A very short and easy read. Clearly sets out their argument that stepfathers are much more dangerous to children than biological fathers. Puts it in an evolutionary psychology framework.

Duntley, J. and Shackleford, T. (2008) *Evolutionary Forensic Psychology*, Oxford: Oxford University Press. The application of evolutionary theory to criminal behaviour is relatively new and this book does this in relation to a variety of crimes.

Raine, A. (1994) *The Psychopathology of Crime: Criminal Behavior as a Clinical Disorder*, New York: Academic Press. The most important text in this area. Sets out to address the most common criticisms made of the biological approach to explaining crime. Clearly written but does assume some knowledge.

Rowe, D. (2002) *Biology and Crime*, Los Angeles: Roxbury. A short textbook that is especially good on the genetic and evolutionary explanations. If you are new to this area read it with a 'Dummy's Guide' to genetics and evolution by your side and you should be able to understand it all.

WEBSITES

www.crime-times.org/ A website devoted to spreading the word about biological explanations of crime. Very clear and covers the latest research and has archives going back at least ten years.

www.crime-library.org/ contains a range of information, including the links between injuries, brain damage and crime.

CHAPTER 3

Psychological Explanations for Criminal Behaviour

INTRODUCTION

Psychology and its theories have been used to expand our understanding of criminal behaviour for over a century, despite there being no real agreed consensus on whether there exists an overall 'criminal personality' type. Indeed, at many points throughout its short history, psychological theories of criminality have been rejected outright as viable explanations of lawbreaking and deviance. Despite the advances in the field, policy makers and politicians often favour sociological and related justifications for criminality depending upon the nature of the crime problem and the dominant research paradigm at that moment in time. Additionally, psychology as a discipline itself has a number of competing and often contradictory schools of thought, which dominate discourse and research within the field. Throughout its short history, psychology has swayed towards more prevailing and/or emerging theories that attempt to explain behaviour, including that of a criminal nature. This chapter will provide a brief account of these major fields within psychology and detail research that has emerged from within the criminological domain over time.

In our quest to make sense of criminal behaviour, we often attach 'labels' to criminals and attempt to explain their behaviour through describing them as possessing a certain character trait(s). For example, a *psychopath* is identified as someone who has little regard for moral codes, is often manipulative and appears to have little conscience or show much remorse for their crimes (Hare 1980). Labels or classifications such as these have been developed by psychologists and criminologists to help us understand the different types of personality category that people fit into. Not all of these are necessarily criminal – many successful politicians and businessmen are thought to exhibit psychopathic tendencies, for example – but it is assumed that many criminals possess similar personality characteristics. Clearly there are some important factors to criminality that can be explained by situational and social factors, but there is also the psychological element to criminal activity that can be relatively unique to that individual. One possible explanation for our interest in uncovering the psychological traits of offenders is that it can provide a quantifiable difference between 'us' and 'them' and to some extent further defines law-breakers as being almost another 'type' of person.

QUESTION BREAK

- Consider your own personality and list the key characteristics of it.
- Where do you think these characteristics come from?
- Describe what you think a criminal personality might consist of.

You might find it interesting to refer back to your 'answers' when you have finished the chapter.

However, before we become too engrossed in attempting to explain criminal behaviour through an all-encompassing classification system, we should keep in mind that the vast majority of criminal activity is a behaviour like any other and that many of us will break the law at some point in our lifetime, no matter how slightly. Statistics show that approximately a third of men under the age of 35 have a criminal record of some description. Although serious criminality, involving violence or sexual behaviour, and those people who are persistent offenders throughout the life course, are potentially different to more everyday crimes (e.g. burglary, deception, drug taking, etc.), they constitute only a very small percentage of recorded crime in most societies. The majority of criminal behaviour is often unsolved and even unnoticed and is committed by a range of people, many of whom appear otherwise law abiding and respectable. In order to understand criminal behaviour, we will begin by examining the psychological antecedents to these behaviour patterns and conclude by identifying some of the most basic individual differences between criminals and non-criminals, including a 'grand theory' that attempts to integrate social and psychological factors in explaining crime.

EARLY BEGINNINGS – FREUD AND PSYCHODYNAMIC THEORY: 1900s ONWARDS

A major early theory which was applied to explain criminal behaviour is known as *psychodynamic theory*. The psychodynamic approach is based closely around the ideas of perhaps one of the most well known psychologists, Sigmund Freud (1856–1939).

Freud's ideas have been developed and modified by other psychologists over the years; however, the work of Freud and his followers is still generically referred to under the general banner of psychodynamic theory.

Psychodynamic ideas are extremely complex but a key notion is that of the 'unconscious mind'. Freud believed that much of our *conscious* behaviour is in fact determined by *unconscious* influences of which we are largely unaware. The mind has a complicated structure which is built up through various stages of development. Freud believed there were three key elements to the mind: first, there is the *id*, which Freud saw as the basic instincts that drive our behaviour; second, the *ego* controls these basic urges by operating according to the reality principle; third and finally, the *superego* is a form of internalization of the standards of society. At each stage of development the instincts of the *id* (within the unconscious mind) are expressed. You may have heard of, for example, the 'oral stage' where babies have an instinct to explore objects with their mouths. During this stage, if you give an infant a new toy, it is very likely that the infant will put the toy in its mouth. Freud thought that later psychological problems arose when there were problems in the expression of these basic instincts at different stages of development.

Freud himself had little to say on the subject of criminality, and believed that often people engaged in such behaviours in order to be punished for other indiscretions or morally reprehensible activities they have committed at earlier periods in their lives (Freud 1953). These were often unconscious processes that were unearthed during psychotherapy and such interventions have been practised with offenders in an attempt to get to the root cause of their offending, often with mixed success. However, many of Freud's contemporaries applied his ideas directly to crime and offenders. One such psychologist, who was strongly influenced by these ideas of Freud, was John Bowlby (1907–90). Bowlby took particular interest in the close relationship formed between a parent and a child or more formally known as the concept of *attachment*. Attachment refers to the strong social and emotional bond between an infant and its carer. He argued that the bond works both ways; carer and child provide comfort and warm feelings for one another and this attachment process is critical in shaping the future behaviour of the infant. Bowlby (1946) examined a sample of '44 juvenile thieves' who had all been convicted of theft and were referred to a child guidance clinic. He found that compared to a non-delinquent control group (who also attended the guidance clinic), a much higher proportion of the delinquents (almost 40 per cent compared to 5 per cent in the control group) had been separated from the mothers for more than 6 months during the first five years of their lives. This evidence is consistent with the idea that early relationships with the mother are important for a child's psychological development. Despite this finding, other researchers such as Rutter (1971) have pointed out that the research of Bowlby in this area has not been substantially replicated. Rutter argued that separation from the mother in itself is not the problem, but found that failure to form a bond with a caregiver (not necessarily the mother) was critical in future delinquency.

CASE STUDY BOX 3.1 FREUD AND RESEARCH

Freud carried out his research not by conducting experiments but by in-depth observations of individual patients. The image of a patient on the psychologist's 'couch' stems from Freud's work in understanding behaviour. Freud drew inferences about the human mind from the detailed cases which he observed. He was deeply impressed by work on the phenomenon of hysteria. His psychodynamic theory is complex and capable of almost infinite variation, meaning it can be adapted to explain almost any occurrence. However, this is all on the basis of inference (i.e. Freud inventing his own possible explanation predicated on his own hypotheses) and not experimentation.

The main problem with psychodynamic theories is that because they rely on unconscious processes they are hard to test empirically and this has been one of the major criticisms of this approach more generally, not just in regard to crime. Because they focus on internal conflicts and unconscious processes (which are things we cannot see or measure), it is largely impossible ever to prove or disprove them. It is worth noting that in the present day many theorists (although not all) feel the role of explaining criminality using psychodynamic theory is limited.

QUESTION BREAK: THE KRAY TWINS

Ronald and Reginald Kray were two highly feared notorious London gangsters. They were both sentenced to life imprisonment for murder, and both twins have since died in prison. Yet both of the twins were famously very close to their mother, Violet, and valued their family identity very highly. Read the following extract from Pearson's account of their lives and consider the questions below.

The Krays were an old-fashioned East End family – tight, self-sufficient and devoted to each other . . . The centre of their world was to remain the tiny terrace house at 178 Vallance Road where they grew up and where their Aunt May and their maternal grandparents still lived . . . The area . . . was one of the poorest parts of the entire East End and a breeding ground for criminals . . . For Violet none of this mattered. Her parents where just around the corner: so was her sister, Rose. Her other sister, May, was next door but one, and her brother, John Lee, kept the café across the street. And old grandfather Lee . . . would sit with the twins for hours in his special chair by the fire . . . And sometimes the old man would talk about the other heroes of the old East End, its criminals.

(Adapted from Pearson 1972: 12–27)

- What does this say about maternal deprivation as an influence on criminal behaviour?
- More generally, do you think the behaviour of children can be blamed on their parents? (List the arguments for and against.)

BEHAVIOURISM AND SOCIAL LEARNING THEORY: 1920s ONWARDS

Whilst Freud proposed that our behaviour is the result of tension and conflict between psychodynamic forces that cannot be seen, other theorists have proposed an alternative approach which focuses much more on observable behaviour.

Behaviourism relies on the fact that any behaviour can be learned. The behaviourists would posit that there is no such distinction as 'us' (non-criminals) and 'them' (criminals). Rather, they would argue that as we develop and interact with other people we learn, through trial and error, how to behave in different ways. Depending on how and what we learn, we either may or may not learn to behave in criminal or non-criminal ways.

These underpinnings of behaviourism began at the turn of the century with the work of Ivan Pavlov (1849–1936) whose ideas of 'classical conditioning' or 'learning by association' had a huge impact on the development of psychology and criminology in the twentieth century. Pavlov's first significant discovery came about by chance when he was studying the digestive systems of dogs. Whilst it is quite normal for dogs to start to salivate at the sight of food, he noted that the dogs would start to salivate at cues associated with the presence of food, such as the sound of food being prepared. He explained this behaviour by noting that stimuli (i.e. environmental events such as the sound of the dog bowl scraping as the food is prepared) can be associated with a natural reflex response (i.e. salivation). This response can become conditional on the stimuli. So by ringing a bell before the dogs were fed, he noted that they would begin to salivate even if he didn't actually feed them. For this reason, learning by association is called 'classical conditioning'. The main tenet of this approach was that people's behaviour could be explained not by forces inside a person (as in psychodynamic theory) but by the interaction between the person and their environment. Behaviour could be learned through interacting with the world.

This newly developing approach to psychology was termed *behaviourism* and many researchers have expanded upon it since Pavlov. For example John B. Watson (1878–1958) argued that humans are born with various innate stimulus–response reflexes, in the same way that some animals are. He argued that through 'learning by association' humans could develop increasingly complex chains of behaviour. Pavlov and Watson, like Freud, had started a new way of thinking about the world and upon these behaviourist ideas were based some important criminological theories.

▎ CASE STUDY BOX 3.2 GIRL GANGS

Rates of girls joining gang culture have increased rapidly over the years. Gangs first emerged in the 1930s, and were predominantly male gangs. However, even in such gangs women could often be seen on the periphery of gang activity. Women would often hide weapons for the men and get involved at the fringes of fights. In the present day female gang membership has risen sharply, particularly in the USA. Read the following extract and consider the questions below it.

> Two teenage girls who led a violent gang in Surrey were jailed for life at the Old Bailey yesterday for kicking and beating a man to death at a drunken party. The court heard how the teenagers from Walton-on-Thames, Surrey, spent their time with a 'violent peer group' drinking heavily and taking drugs. The group aged between 14 and 19 were notorious in the area according to police. Detective Chief Inspector Graham Hill, who led the murder inquiry, said the girls were part of a group of teenagers who hung around the local area causing criminal damage and generally making a nuisance of themselves. 'They existed in a culture in which there was a hierarchy within the group and these two were in it' he said. 'They spent their time engaged in anti-social behaviour and causing chaos. They felt they could get away with anything.'
>
> (From Sandra Laville, the *Guardian,* 9 February 2005)

- What are the social conditions which you could identify which may account for such a rise?
- How could you explain why women may join gangs by using learning-based theories?

From 1930–35 a researcher at Harvard developed the ideas of Pavlov further to provide a more comprehensive account of behaviour acquisition. His name was Burrhus Skinner (1904–90) and the new approach he championed was *behaviour analysis.* Skinner formulated, through experimental research, the principles by which we can understand the relationships between behaviour, the consequences of behaviour and the learning of new patterns of behaviour. Skinner's early work was conducted with animals (much like the researchers who had gone before him) but rather than focus on classical conditioning he looked at what is known as *operant behaviour.* Operant behaviour is the sort of behaviour which operates on the environment to produce *consequences*: for example if a rat in a cage pushes a lever to receive a food treat as a reward, the rat operates on the lever, which produces a consequence (the food). The relationship between behaviour and its consequences he termed a contingency, and he identified two types of contingency: reinforcement and punishment.

In the USA, at around the same time as Watson was developing the behaviourist approach, a group of researchers were dissatisfied with the biological and Lombrosian approach of 'the criminal man' (as outlined in Chapter 2, pp. 22–27). During the 1920s and 1930s this Chicago University-based research group developed the idea that crime was not the result of biological or psychological factors associated with individuals, but was instead the product of social forces. They noted that people who lived in areas of community disorganization with poorer social conditions had an increased risk of being delinquent. They hypothesized that once a delinquent culture became established in a particular neighbourhood, other youths would be drawn into this subculture by associating with the delinquent group.

Edwin Sutherland (1883–1950) was a member of the 'Chicago School' and had an interest in both the social creation of crime but also the role of the individual in that process. He was interested in establishing how criminal behaviour was transmitted through the generations and why some people would be drawn into crime when others would not. He was particularly interested in how criminal behaviour can be learned. Sutherland argued that crime is defined socially and that those with power within society decide what is and what is not considered a criminal act. Therefore crime as a concept has both a social and a political dimension. So why, asked Sutherland, do some people obey these socially and politically created laws when others do not? Sutherland argued that this depended on the person's 'definitions', i.e. their attitudes towards breaking the law. A definition, according to Sutherland, is the way a person views crime, depending on the social forces in their life. Some individuals will hold definitions that are favourable to crime and others will not. Therefore to understand a person's criminal behaviour we need to understand their history of individual learning experiences. Sutherland argued that learning took place through association with other people, and that the learning might be about specific criminal techniques as well as about attitudes towards committing crimes. The important point is that each person's learning experience is different, depending on whom they are exposed to, and so the theory was termed *differential association* (Sutherland 1947). Sutherland believed that learning criminal behaviour was no different to any other sort of learning. Sutherland's theory was highly influential, but it left many questions unanswered. For example what social conditions are likely to lead to learning criminal attitudes? How does the learning actually happen?

Crimes can be rewarding in many ways. They can be materially rewarding in terms of financial gain; however, they can also be rewarding in terms of peer status. Yet, on the other hand, they can also have aversive effects such as imprisonment and the subsequent disruption of family relationships. Each individual will have a unique learning history so that their individual history of reinforcement and punishment will determine their risk of criminal behaviour when the opportunity arises. Therefore the precise circumstances that lead an individual to commit crime will be unique to that person, depending on the context they find themselves within.

BOX 3.1 BEHAVIOURISM AND RESEARCH

The behaviourist school discovered their 'facts' by using rigorous experimentation in a laboratory. Their participants were usually animals, rather than humans, but this allowed their researchers a great deal of control over their experiments. For example, because of being able to totally control an animal's environment the researchers are able to isolate the one variable of interest, and make sure that apart from that variable, absolutely everything else was the same about the groups of animals being tested. This is at the heart of experimental psychology. Unless we can be sure that there is only one variable that is different we cannot be sure that our results are due to that variable. This is very hard to achieve outside a laboratory setting and for ethical reasons it is particularly hard to control when we are working with humans.

One obvious problem of this approach is that real life does not work like a laboratory. In real life several forces may operate at once, rather than there being tight control. Additionally some theorists have been critical of the concept of studies which have at their basis animals as participants – they argue that because humans are so much more complex than animals it is hard to draw conclusions from observing animal behaviour. Another drawback is that behaviourists are only interested in observable behaviour, they are not interested in a person's innermost thoughts, yet a lot of people believe that our inner thoughts are what set us apart from animals, and are at the heart of what being human is about. When trying to use such theories to explain criminal activity it is obviously very hard to find out about a person's unique learning history, due to the complexity of human life. This therefore makes some of the theories based in behaviourism hard to apply.

QUESTION BREAK: LEARNING HISTORIES

Think about your own life to date. Think about the situation you are now in. For example, you may be working full time and studying at night school, or you may have just enrolled in an undergraduate degree.

- What do you think are the most significant learning experiences have contributed to you being in your current situation?
- How do you think these experiences reinforced your behaviour along the way? For example, did you have particularly encouraging parents or did a particular teacher put you off education?
- Do you think it is possible to try and view your current situation as a result of many individual learning experiences?
- How might 'learning history' relate to involvement (or not) in criminal behaviour?

An alternative theory that has been suggested is the idea that although criminal behaviour may be learned, this isn't necessarily from a person with whom the individual physically interacts. This is the central tenet of *Media Aggression Hypothesis*. There have been concerns for several years that exposure to violence, via television or video games, may cause an increase in aggression. Much of the research has looked at short-term increases in small acts of aggression in children, which may only have limited application to criminologists. The 'bobo doll' experiments conducted by Albert Bandura are an example of this (see Bandura 1977). However, some research has also looked at longer-term effects on criminal violence. From those who believe that media can cause aggression the current view is that filmed violence has a small significant effect on viewers (e.g. Passer and Smith 2001). It has been shown that various factors can interact with the effect of the media on aggression. For example, research suggests that if the violence is depicted as being justified it has a greater effect, and there are individual differences in the extent to which people are affected by media violence. In addition, certain individual factors such as unpopularity and low educational attainment are also involved in the interaction (Blackburn 1999).

Despite this research many criminologists and psychologists adopt a critical stance on the studies conducted in this area (e.g. Fowles 1999). This is largely due to the problem of how media aggression has been studied. Much of the research has looked at short-term influences on minor acts of aggression, and has been based in laboratories. However, it is hard to extrapolate from such lab-based research whether or not viewing violent material would be likely to make someone be physically violent in the real world. Other research has attempted to take real violent criminals and find out about the level of violence in the television programmes they used to watch, but this can be very difficult – for example, how do you rate and compare violence in a cartoon, to violence in an 18-rated film? And how likely is it that a 'true figure' can be established on how much violence someone has actually been exposed to? These are just a few of the reasons that the research in this area remains controversial.

QUESTION BREAK: MEDIA AGGRESSION RESEARCH

Imagine you are a media aggression researcher wanting to establish whether or not violent video games cause violence in adulthood.

- How would you design such a study?
- What problems might you encounter with a design such as this?

There are various problems with the research into media and aggression. First, the relationship is likely to be bi-directional, i.e. the aggressive person is more likely to *seek out* violent television/play violent videogames. This then can influence the level of aggression further. Most of the research in this area comes from laboratory-based studies – is this appropriate when we are trying to use media aggression hypotheses as an explanation for serious crimes such as murder? Second, when using field based retrospective studies (i.e. taking a sample of violent adults and asking them if they were exposed to media violence as they grew up) there will be huge problems with remembering what was watched many years ago.

QUESTION BREAK

Above are just a few of the reasons why researchers are often sceptical about the research conducted into media aggression.

- Can you think of any other arguments against the view that violence in the media leads to violent and aggressive behaviour?
- Are there any convincing arguments or incidents that lend some support to the notion of a link between media violence and aggressive behaviour?

DEVELOPMENTAL ISSUES: 1950s ONWARDS

Following the Second World War, many large-scale social policies were implemented in an attempt to address poverty and improve conditions for many families and children in particular. Juvenile delinquency was seen as a reaction to poor upbringing and it was thought that various interventions could help prevent later adult criminality. Despite some successes, researchers and policy makers are still only just uncovering some of the more salient features of the developmental processes that could be reliable predictors of later criminal tendencies. For example, there is a common belief that offenders are more likely to have been raised in homes where one or more parents are not present due to separation, divorce or death. Indeed early research seemed to find evidence to support this view.

Wells and Rankin (1991) conducted a 'meta-analysis' of 50 studies published between 1926 and 1988 that investigated the relationship between delinquency and broken homes. A meta-analysis is a type of research project where instead of gathering data at first hand the researchers re-analyse the data collected by previous researchers that includes the information from lots of different studies on the same topic. This allows people to draw some broad-based findings on a specific topic. In their meta-analysis, Wells and Rankin found that the prevalence of delinquency in broken homes was between 10 and 15 per cent greater than from 'intact' homes.

The relationship was stronger for less serious *status* offences (a status offence is only an offence due to the age of the offender, e.g. drinking under the age of 18) than for more serious *index* offences (e.g. burglary and assault). Interestingly, it would seem that simply having one parent absent does not lead to such high levels of delinquency. For example, in families where one parent had died compared to families where there had been a divorce, the children were less likely to become delinquent (Wadsworth 1979). So the common belief that offenders more often come from homes where only one parent is present seems to be a little misleading.

As a possible explanation for such a finding, McCord (1982) looked at the prevalence of offending behaviour among groups of boys who were raised in 'intact' and 'broken' homes, but also took into consideration the presence of a 'caring' mother and overall parental conflict. McCord found that the prevalence of offending was:

- Broken home, without a caring mother – 62 per cent
- Intact home, with parental conflict – 52 per cent
- Intact home, no parental conflict – 26 per cent
- Broken home with a caring mother – 22 per cent

Offending appeared to be highest in the broken home without a caring mother. However, with a caring mother present, even in a broken home, the prevalence of offending was lower than in intact homes with no parental conflict at all.

QUESTION BREAK: CARING MOTHERS – DIFFERENT EXPLANATIONS

As we have discussed previously it is common for psychologists to come up with alternative theories to explain essentially the same phenomenon. How do you think the different theories we have covered would explain this finding?

- What would a psychodynamic theorist argue?
- What would media aggression theory provide as an explanation?
- Can we apply differential association theory to this research, and if so, how?
- Can you think of any other explanations for McCord's findings?

There is little doubt that the family is a highly influential social institution. Most of us look to our family upbringing to explain our own behaviour as an adult. References to this in popular culture are common; for example, the anti-hero in many movies was only 'turned bad' by some tragic or traumatic experience as a child. This idea is at least in some way supported by research which shows that family functioning plays a large role in how children adjust and develop (Rankin and Kern 1994). Early work on the relationship between how a family functions and delinquency led to the formulation of 'typologies' of parenting style (e.g. Baumrind 1978). A typology attempts to put different types of behaviour into categories of some kind. For example, Baumrind evaluated parental behaviour through interviews with parents, teachers and through direct observation of parents with their children. From this she devised four different types of parenting style:

- *Authoritarian* – parents place value on obedience and favour punitive punishment in order to exert control over children.
- *Permissive* – parents nurture their children, but prefer to allow them freedom of expression.
- *Indulgent and neglectful* – parents neglect their children.

- *Authoritative* – parents fall between the extremes of the authoritarian and permissive styles, and use an inductive style of discipline.

(adapted from Baumrind 1978)

Baumrind found that of these types of parenting style, the authoritative style was found to be least associated with producing delinquent children and also considered the most effective parenting style overall. It is perhaps unsurprising (having covered behavioural theory earlier on in this chapter) that psychologists agree that for discipline to work effectively it needs to be applied consistently, and needs to depend on the child's behaviour. However, further research by Hoffman (1977) identified that there are differing styles of delivering discipline, which have different associations with the development of delinquency.

Hoffman (1977) identified three types of disciplinary practices:

- *Power Assertion* – includes the use of physical punishment, criticism of the child and threats of maternal deprivation (e.g. saying to the child 'You are a bad little boy. Mummy won't love you any more if you do that')
- *Love Withdrawal* – involves expressing disapproval, but not in a physical way and the witholding of affection (e.g. saying to the child 'that's a bad thing to do' and not cuddling the child)
- *Induction* – involves reasoning with the child, and talking through the consequences of the child's behaviour to others (e.g. saying to the child 'it makes Jimmy upset if you steal his toy rabbit and it hurts his feelings. If someone did that to you you would be upset too, wouldn't you?')

Of these three types of discipline *Power Assertion* was the technique most used by the parents of delinquent offspring.

QUESTION BREAK: DISCIPLINING CHILDREN

Power assertion was the technique most used by the parents of delinquent offspring. How do you think these different theories would explain this finding?

- Psychodynamic theory
- Behaviourist theory
- Developmental theory

Take a sheet of paper and write the three theories as headings. Try to think about how each theory might explain this finding (you may need to refer back to each theory in order to help you do this).

Finally under each explanation which you have created, try to think of some possible criticism showing why that theory may not fully explain the finding – when you do this you will be critically analysing that theory.

What must be kept in mind when considering parenting skills is that even parenting that closely meets the ideal may be disrupted by stressful experiences, which in turn may have an effect (temporarily or longer term) on the approach being utilized. External stressors such as unemployment, poverty, illness and parental conflict could all disrupt the most effective parenting techniques. The coping strategy of the parents in dealing with such stressful life events will play an important mediating role in how these factors may affect the children they raise.

One such area is that of parental criminality. Many common phrases refer to the fact that our personality type often seems to be passed down from generation to generation. Phrases such as 'like father, like son' and 'he's a chip off the old block' reflect this. Once again some research seems to support this. McCord (1979) noted that criminal fathers tend to have criminal sons. In support of this finding, West and Farrington (1977) found that having a convicted parent predicted later offending in both adolescence and adulthood in their longitudinal study. Twin and adoption studies (see Box 3.2, p. 79) have been instrumental in showing the impact of parental criminality, with children from non-criminal families who are adopted into those with at least one criminal parent being significantly more likely to engage in criminal behaviour themselves. This phenomenon also works in reverse, with children from 'criminal families' showing a reduction in the risk of offending when adopted into a non-criminal environment. Whilst genetics arguably plays a larger part and there are a number of other factors to consider (e.g. socio-economic status), there nevertheless exists an identifiable influence resulting from whether parents have a criminal record or not (Farrington, Barnes and Lambert 1996).

QUESTION BREAK: LIKE FATHER LIKE SON?

There are a number of possible explanations for the finding that criminal fathers tend to have criminal sons.

This time try to consider not only the theories covered in this chapter, but also the explanations offered in other parts of this book. How do you think the finding can best be explained? Choose any two theoretical positions (e.g. biological explanations versus learning theory for example – or from the sociological theories looked at in Chapter 4).

- First try to work out how each theory you selected might explain the findings.
- Second, try to work out how each theory would criticize the assumptions of the other.

Whilst parental criminality can have an impact upon their offspring's chances of also becoming a criminal, many non-criminal families have children who will go on to offend. Hence, we must often look outside of the family to evaluate other potential influences upon the developing youngster. Children have strong **peer attachments** and friendships are critical to their development; for example, with regard to delinquency it is a common saying that a child 'fell in with the wrong crowd'. Research has found that friends can play a role in encouraging or inhibiting delinquent behaviour. There are two consistent findings in the literature:

- Delinquents are more likely than non-delinquents to have delinquent friends;
- Adolescents with close friends who are delinquent are more likely to behave delinquently (West and Farrington 1973).

Both of these findings hold true both for self-reported crime and crime as recorded in official statistics. This is an important point, as not all people who commit crime get caught and so do not show up in the official crime statistics.

Moffit (1993) came up with an intriguing theory to explain why many adolescents become involved in offending when they are teenagers, but then desist from offending when they become adults. He argued that the peak in offending rates which happens in adolescence conceals two different types of offender. The first type is the *adolescent limited offender*. They will be likely to have a short period of time (during their teenage years) in which they offend, before they 'grow out' of the behaviour. The second type is the *life-course-persistent offender* who is likely to progress from offending in adolescence to further and more prolific offending in adulthood. Moffit argued that life-course-persistent offending is very different in its etiology to the adolescent limited offender. Indeed it is likely that there may be some element of neuropsychological risk in the life course of persistent offending which can be worsened by problem interactions, and by the individual becoming ensnared as a result of their offending lifestyle. What is most interesting is why the adolescent limited offenders ever become involved in criminal activity in the first place. Moffit argued that in modern society children in their teenage years are held in a sort of 'maturity gap'. They are not considered adult enough to have jobs, and yet they are no longer children. As a result they can become frustrated and seek ways to break away from their parents' control. Other adolescent offenders – these more 'exciting' peers – can effectively become role models, and the adolescent limited offenders become involved in deviant and/or criminal behaviour in an attempt to emulate the life-course-persistent offenders.

This goes some way to explain the sharp rise in offending around 17 years old. The adolescent limited offenders are able to stop offending – by adapting to changing contingencies; i.e. when it becomes more beneficial to them to stop offending they can do. When they realize they will gain more benefit from getting a job, or continuing with education, they desist from offending. However, the life-course-persistent offenders do not adapt (or cannot) to these changing contingencies and continue to offend into adulthood.

QUESTION BREAK: THE PEAK IN CRIMINAL BEHAVIOUR

Moffit's theory is of particular interest because it combines elements of several of the theories we have discussed in this chapter. Try to work through Moffit's theory and identify the different elements which may come from the theories we have studied.

There are a myriad of factors which can be useful in exploring why certain individuals are more likely to engage in criminal behaviour, and developmental psychologists are routinely engaged in research into uncovering 'tomorrow's criminals'. For many, identifying and dealing with these factors early will hopefully prevent many young people from developing a life of crime. Here are some other areas that have been identified in the research literature:

Unemployment: Recently a lot of attention has been paid to the idea that if someone is employed then they are subsequently less likely to be involved in criminal activity. Research indicates that the most important issue is someone's ability to hold down a job to which they are committed (Jeffery 1977). It has been reported that offenders have higher rates of unemployment than non-offenders (Freeman 1983). However, there is a complex relationship at play because it can be harder for someone, once they have a criminal record, to obtain employment. Once released from prison if the person is able to find employment they are less likely to re-offend (Rossi, Berk and Lenihan 1980).

QUESTION BREAK: EMPLOYING OFFENDERS

We know that if offenders can be released into the community with a job which they are committed to it will reduce their risk of re-offending. Imagine you are working with ex-offenders and trying to secure jobs for them.

- What challenges do you think you will face in convincing employers to give ex-offenders jobs?
- How might you go about overcoming these challenges?

Child abuse: Research has shown that children who have been victims of severe physical abuse in the home are around three times more likely to use alchohol and drugs, to deliberately damage property and to get into fights. Additionally they are about four times more likely to be arrested than other children (Gelles 1997). Wisdom (1989) carried out a 20-year follow-up study of children who had been abused or neglected and found they were more likely than the control group to have been arrested as juveniles, as adults, and for violent crimes. One thing that must be borne in mind though when considering research into people who have suffered abuse, is that, first, it is hard to know exactly who has been abused as many people never report the abuse; second, the findings can be problematic as sample sizes are often small, so that it is harder to make generalizations from the research.

Academic Acheivement and Schooling: A consistent correlation between academic ability and delinquency has been found. However, more important than ability, it has been found that performance is the key measure in predicting delinquency (i.e. how the child actually performs at school regardless of how *capable* they may be academically). The relationship between performance and delinquency is robust and remains when other factors associated with delinquency have been controlled for (Patterson and Dishion 1985). Those who fail academically at school are at increased risk of delinquency regardless of whether the outcome measure of success is self-report or using official criteria (Elliot and Voss 1974). Interestingly, despite individual variation between pupils the prevalence of delinquency is not evenly distributed between schools (Farrington 1972). Due to this finding, some theorists have attempted to explain delinquency in terms of the school itself. For example, Power, Alderson, Phillipson and Morris (1967) looked at the delinquency rate of 20 inner London schools. They calculated the delinquency rate of each school for six years, using the measure of the number of court appearances of children. They found that rates of delinquency did not relate to the catchment area, and concluded it must be something within the school itself that caused the difference in rates. On the other hand some researchers argue that the individual characteristics of pupils lead to so called delinquent schools. Farrington (1972) studied boys from six primary schools with similar delinquency rates and found that when the boys moved on at age eleven there were differences in delinquency rates between the schools. Farrington therefore argued that the 'delinquency proneness' of the schools' intake has an effect on its delinquency rates. In summary the relationship between school factors and delinquency is a complex one, with the nature of the association between the school and delinquency being quite unclear. It seems unlikely that the school itself can cause delinquency, although it could act as a catalyst for later conduct problems.

This section has covered just a few of the social factors which have been shown to have some link with criminality. However, there are many others we have not had the opportunity to explore in more detail, for example family size and poverty. It must be kept in mind that no one social factor can really be taken out of context and seen as an explanation in isolation. In reality, several social as well as individual factors will interrelate and all play a role in the risk of someone potentially engaging in criminal behaviour.

COGNITIVE THEORIES: 1970s ONWARDS

One area of psychology that has a lesser acknowledged link with criminal behaviour is known as cognitive psychology. The majority of research conducted by cognitive psychologists concerns internal mental processes, such as attention and memory, and for this reason is generally studied in a laboratory setting. Although it is perhaps easier to understand how people can acquire criminal tendencies by learning them from other criminals, identifying how 'thinking' in a criminal way leads to offending is often more difficult. Vast and identifiable differences between people are readily observable in everyday life (e.g. in education and employment) and researchers have expended considerable effort in trying to identify those individual differences that could characterize offending behaviour.

One prominent idea surrounding the nature of criminal behaviour concerns the notion of intelligence. When we talk about 'intelligence' we are generally referring to a person's intellectual ability or IQ. Your IQ relates largely to your ability to learn and adapt to various environments and, subsequently, often how successful you can expect to be; this is particularly relevant in relation to education and employment. Whilst many offenders are of above 'average' intelligence (consider, for example, white-collar and computer-related crime), a large proportion of offenders have been identified as recording below-average IQ scores. It is suggested by some that it is this limited capacity which results in the majority of criminal behaviour. One of the first to propose this was Goddard (1914) in his book called *Feeble-Mindedness: Its Causes and Consequences*. Here it was proposed that low intelligence made criminals unable to learn socially acceptable conduct and resist offending behaviour. A later study by Zeleny (1933) postulated that criminals were nearly twice as likely to be low scorers on IQ tests as non-criminals. These studies and many similar ones have suggested that people who have low intelligence are for many reasons (mostly the inability to learn and adhere to the complex rules of society) more likely to become criminals. Due to its simplicity, this theory has endured for many years and still does has a significant research interest in more recent times.

Longitudinal studies – those which follow groups of people over an extended time period (see p. 90) – have consistently shown that intelligence scores in children are a relatively reliable predictor of later adolescent and adult offending. One such examination, the Cambridge Longitudinal Study (see Farrington 1992), followed a group of males from birth into adulthood. Farrington reported that over a third of the 8–10-year-old boys who scored less than 90 (significantly below average) on a test of intelligence (non-verbal), were later convicted of a criminal offence. This was twice as likely as the remainder of the sample. It was also discovered that this low level of (non-verbal) intelligence was particularly characteristic of recidivism in juveniles and of those who were to be convicted of offences when aged 10–13 years. There is support, however, for the differences between offenders and non-offenders on measures of intelligence reflecting only *verbal* intelligence. Psychologists largely disagree on what actually constitutes IQ and many believe that it can (and should) be broken down into a number of different components rather than relying on one overall index (i.e. IQ) (see Anastasi and Urbina 1997 for a review of intelligence testing). The difference between verbal and non-verbal intelligence relates generally to the ability to use language in the former, and the capacity for problem solving in the latter. Hirschi and Hindelang (1977) found limited support for any real discrepancies between the two groups in *non-verbal* intelligence. Hence, it might be that offenders demonstrate limited capabilities with regard to activities that require verbal skills (including reading and writing). Research has shown that up to 70 per cent of offenders in prison are illiterate (Rice, Howes and Connell 1998) and amongst people with learning difficulties, criminality is three times more likely than in the general population. Low intelligence can also lead to poor school performance and later job success.

There could be a number of other explanations as to why intelligence (both verbal and non-verbal) may be related to criminal behaviour in this way. First, there is a possibility that those with low intelligence could be more likely to be caught when committing crime (West and Farrington 1977); in the evaluation and selection of crimes they may not be as successful as those who are more astute. However, West and Farrington also found that this link remained even when the measurement of offending was not arrest data, but individual self-report measures (see p. 94). The second possibility is that the less intelligent could simply be more ready to admit to committing crime. This could be in an interrogation by the police or in self-report evaluations. Quay (1987) believes this could be also a result of those with lower intelligence not fully understanding the charges being presented to them and the consequences of their co-operation with the police. More recent criminal justice policy has recognized the need to protect those who are intellectually 'subnormal' (i.e. have an IQ below 70) or else have recognized learning difficulties, e.g. autism spectrum disorder. Responsible adults and specially trained interviewers are often employed in these situations (Bull 2010). In severe cases, these individuals may not be deemed fit to stand trial and in jurisdictions where there is capital punishment, they may be saved from the death penalty even if convicted.

However, alongside these early assumptions regarding intelligence and criminal behaviour there are a number of problems in simply accepting this apparent link. First, defining exactly what we mean by 'crime' and similarly 'intelligence' is not as simple as it may appear. Although the development and use of IQ tests has improved considerably since the days of Goddard and Zelany, there is still debate as to what intelligence actually is (Anastasi and Urbina 1997). For example, some people may be highly competent mathematicians, but have poor social skills; others could be excellent artists but relatively poor at organizing themselves. Additional propositions, for example, the concept of emotional intelligence (Goleman 1996), complicate our discussion on the nature of intelligence. Second, what makes somebody a 'criminal' is also open to some debate along many different legal, moral and philosophical lines. It cannot be assumed that what makes a person a 'criminal' is the fact that they have been convicted of breaking a law (for example, what about people who purposely break the law to expose apparent injustices, such as unfair taxes or business practices that damage the environmental?). The majority of people have also most probably committed a crime of some description – even if it was as seemingly minor as breaking the speed limit whilst driving – so it is inappropriate that just because someone was caught, they should then be seen as different from those who eluded apprehension and/or conviction. In addition, there are significant differences between the personalities and behaviours of someone convicted of financial fraud compared with a violent murderer, in which intelligence probably plays a small part. For the latter, it is therefore difficult to both define and measure intelligence and crime so easily.

Despite the limitations in allowing us to understand and explain criminal behaviour in relation to intelligence alone, there are many studies that include intelligence as a variable when assessing offenders. There is now, though, the recognition that low intelligence might not be a personality feature of the individual *per se*, but in fact a result of poverty or other social factors (Herrnstein and Murray 1994). Instead of low intelligence causing crime, it could equally be possible that coming from a poor neighbourhood influences the educational skills available to a person. There is extensive research to support the idea that people with low incomes and limited access to employment are more likely to be involved in criminal activities (Sampson, Raudenbush and Earls 1997). On the other hand, controversial theories of intelligence suggest that racial differences in IQ could account for some of the large discrepancies in incarceration rates for different ethnic groups (Herrnstein and Murray 1994). Additionally, Hirschi and Hindelang (1977) reviewed many studies reporting the link between crime and intelligence, and discovered, overall, that when socio-economic factors are statistically controlled for, the pattern remains. However, there are many other factors that may also vary in their influence on the propensity for unlawful behaviour. It is almost impossible to separate the link between intelligence and criminal behaviour from environmental and even possible hereditary factors (see Chapter 2). Nevertheless, there is a vast amount of research into intelligence and crime which highlights the difficulties in researching criminal behaviour in general and finding one simple answer to explain this type of activity. It should be remembered that although there is often a relationship between intelligence and crime, it is seldom proposed that low intelligence actually *causes* crime.

QUESTION BREAK

- How would a researcher go about testing whether criminal behaviour was a result of a poor upbringing or a result of poor intelligence?
- Suggest the advantages and disadvantages of different research methods.
- What other areas of social research have used similar methods?

BOX 3.2 TWIN STUDIES

When researchers are interested in finding out whether behaviour is a result of genetics or the environment which an individual grows up in, they often try to isolate one variable by using twins as their subjects. Mono-zygotic (MZ) or identical twins have exactly the same DNA, meaning they should have exactly the same physical and mental attributes. Research into intelligence has made significant use of such methods. If intelligence is genetically based, then two identical people (i.e. MZ twins) should have the same IQ score even if they were raised in different environments. Similarly, if crime were genetically based, then two MZ twins would have the same predisposition for crime. However, Blackburn (1999) reports that most MZ twins reared apart show comparable levels of intelligence, and similarities on personality and attitude measures. Twin studies are popular in the social sciences as they allow

continued

any genetic influence to be controlled and the behaviours that are observed be accounted for by other factors. Such research is expensive and although many twins volunteer to be included in studies, access to samples is difficult and drop-out rates are high.

Aside from intelligence, there are other individual differences that have been implicated in the acquisition and maintenance of criminal tendencies. One such area is *impulsivity*. From a clinical perspective, being impulsive describes behaviours where people are likely to act almost on instinct and seldom weigh up the consequences of their actions. This process of 'acting without thinking' has found a receptive audience amongst criminologists and psychologists in providing another way of explaining why some people commit crime and others largely don't. Glueck and Glueck (1950) were early pioneers of such thought, and believed that poor self-control mechanisms led to impulsive and often criminal behaviour. Early sociologists debated the idea that there were differences in the social classes' ability to *delay gratification* – people from higher social classes were assumed to be able to plan for the future and set a path to reap greater rewards in return for sacrificing earlier gains. From a more individual perspective, criminals have been assumed to act in a way that seeks to maximize their immediate desires without considering the likely future consequences that these actions may have, such as imprisonment. Criminals are therefore assumed to have poor control mechanisms that cause them to seek immediate satisfaction of their needs (see Gottfredson and Hirschi 1990 and Chapter 4, pp. 115–118). Longitudinal studies that follow individuals over a period of time or even their whole lifetime have shown this to be a relatively enduring and stable trait amongst offenders (e.g. Farrington 1992). However, as with intelligence, the link between impulsivity and crime is not so simple. Indeed much criminal behaviour is meticulously planned. Many financial frauds and robberies require a complete lack of any impulsive behaviour.

Support for the link between impulsivity and crime has been mixed; apparently reckless and spontaneous activity of a criminal nature is often observed in conjunction with many other personality and situational variables, e.g. offenders who are under the influence of drugs and alcohol. Other researchers have elaborated on the nature of impulsivity and seldom describe it as an umbrella term to encompass any behaviour that has shown irresponsible and uncontrolled factors. For example, Dickman (1990) hypothesized that impulsivity was composed of two separate entities: functional and dysfunctional. Impulsive behaviour does not necessarily lead to offending behaviour, and indeed some spontaneity is often applauded in certain situations. Increased activity, adventurousness, and enthusiasm were characteristic of the functional type of impulsivity. Hence, dysfunctional impulsivity is more closely linked with offending in that the behaviours generally have negative consequences for the individual. Disorderliness, poor appraisal of facts, and lack of concern for the consequences of actions, were symptomatic of people exhibiting the more dysfunctional style of impulsivity. Impulsive criminals have also been seen to behave in a generally reckless – not necessarily criminal – way and to seek excitement in many situations (Raine 2002).

QUESTION BREAK

Draw a line and write impulsivity at one end of it and careful planning at the other.

Place the following crimes at where you feel to be the appropriate place on this line:

- Shoplifting
- Drug dealing
- Fraud
- Burglary
- Assault

Think of some other crimes and add them to the line. Is there really such a thing as an impulsive crime or is there an element of planning and deliberation involved – no matter how small – in all offending?

Part of the problem with assessing impulsivity as a correlate of criminal behaviour is the differing theoretical perspectives that underpin the explanation of this personality trait. For example, as with psychodynamic theory (see pp. 62–65) impulsivity is suggested to be a result of poor ego-control. The drive impulses of the id are not adequately suppressed and the individual seeks to satisfy them in a manner that may infringe on current laws. Conversely, social learning theorists see the suggestion of impulsivity as a lack of self-control as being determined by situational forces as well as the individual's own inner narrative. Regardless of the theoretical paradigm where impulsivity is believed to originate from, there is also a practical problem in its measurement and intensity. Blackburn (1999) reports numerous measures of impulsivity that have originated from more general personality inventories, such as the MMPI and 16-PF. One problem with using these scales is that they have usually not been validated on offender populations. When personality measures are created, they are tested and re-tested on very large samples to ensure that they are valid and reliable. If it is valid and it measures what the researchers hoped it would (i.e. a personality feature) then they must make sure that it could do this over and over again for reliability in identifying this trait. This means that a 'normal' score is based upon certain factors and generally applies to the population that they tested while developing these scales. Hence, offenders might score differently only because they interpret the questions differently, not because they are actually unalike. Nevertheless, they do show some marked differences between the control 'non-offender' samples. There is also the question of whether impulsivity merely predicts the prevalence of offending behaviour rather than its simple occurrence.

BOX 3.3 ADHD

Attention Deficit and Hyperactivity Disorder (or ADHD as it is commonly abbreviated), is a personality disorder that was proposed in the American Psychological Society's *Diagnostic and Statistical Manual* (DSM). The DSM lists a number of symptoms that psychologists and psychiatrists have identified as defining a particular abnormal pattern of behaviour. Those for ADHD are:

- Symptoms of inattention: missing important work details, not listening, forgetting instructions, forgetful, always losing things;
- Symptoms of hyperactivity: frequent fidgeting, excessive talking, inability to remain seated;
- Symptoms of impulsivity: blurts out answers to questions, can't wait their turn, constant interruption of others.

Researchers have only recently explored the link between ADHD and crime. There is also some debate about the diagnosis of ADHD and that it is being used to explain any children who have even minor behavioural problems (Morgan and Norris 2010). But the link with impulsivity and crime is a compelling one and the role of the frontal lobes of the brain is implicated in explaining both ADHD and impulsivity (see Chapter 2 for a detailed discussion on the brain and behaviour). Research in this area is relatively new and no firm conclusions can be drawn as yet. What is apparent though, is that many of the symptoms of ADHD have been found in longitudinal studies of juveniles and their likelihood of committing crime (see Farrington 1992). Moffitt (1990) and many other researchers also believe that ADHD sufferers are at increased risk of becoming chronic alcohol and drug users. Coupled with the interpersonal effects of impulsivity, there are then the added dangers that the well-documented links with drugs and crime pose.

Another psychological factor also related to criminal behaviour is the concept of *locus of control* (Rotter 1975). Whereas impulsivity was concerned with the way in which offenders might not adequately anticipate the consequences of their actions, the idea of having a 'locus of control' describes the way in which people accept 'explanations' for things that happen. For example, people with an *internal* locus of control commonly perceive events as being largely under their own command – they are in charge of their own destiny and the things that happen to them result from the decisions they make. In contrast, those with an *external* locus of control perceive events as resulting from forces largely beyond their influence. With regard to criminal behaviour, offenders are generally assumed to have a distinct external bias in their personality or specifically more inclined to have an *external locus of control*. Hence offenders will generally put the consequences of their actions, for example being arrested or injured, down to other forces, such as luck or bad timing. Obviously, not everyone who has an external locus of control bias will offend, but Foglia (2000) believes that children who are repeatedly exposed to situations where they only have minimal influence – in particular absent or mentally ill parents – are more likely to develop an external orientation to their being. What results is often an increased risk of delinquency. As with impulsivity, offenders with an external locus of control are unlikely to adequately appreciate the consequences of their actions, but for very different reasons.

Rotter's (1975) theory is widely accepted amongst both criminologists and researchers from wider social science, although the research is inconclusive with regard to providing an adequate overall explanation of many instances of criminal behaviour. Whilst some studies have indicated that many offenders have a high external locus of control, others have not been able to replicate these findings reliably. Indeed some have shown that certain offender populations have a higher internal locus of control than non-offender samples (see Raine 1993). As with many of the discussions on the nature of the 'criminal personality', the inconsistencies in research findings are mostly attributable to being able to adequately define both the concept in question (in this instance locus of control) and what exactly constitutes a 'criminal'. For example, internal and external controls have been shown to deviate within individuals depending upon the subject under examination, such as a job interview vs. a political event (Mirels 1970). Despite these contradictions, locus of control has been argued to be an important predictor of people who are at *risk* of becoming involved in criminal behaviour (Werner 1989). In addition, many cognitive-behavioural rehabilitation programmes delivered in prisons attempt to address offenders' behaviour by questioning such belief systems.

Using the data retrieved from a series of interviews with acute offenders from a Washington secure unit, Yochelson and Samenow (1976) believed that the 'choices' an individual made led to criminal behaviour. These preferences for action were under the person's rational control. What made these people criminal was that they had learned poor and ineffective thinking styles that were at odds with prevailing societal conventions and laws. In particular, criminals' thinking patterns were characterized by a lack of empathy, poor perspective of time, perception of themselves as victims, and general concreteness in their beliefs (Hollin 1989). They identified over 50 of these different 'thinking errors' and these were further separated into three main categories. The first were simple *character traits* that related to overriding needs for power and control (Blackburn 1999). Second, the generalized thinking styles of poor decision-making, lack of trust and failure to honour obligations. The third and final category relates to the judgements directly related to criminal acts. These can take the form of anti-social fantasies, removal or ignorance of deterrents and an elevated sense of optimism. Hence, criminals see nothing wrong with the way they behave and often fail to understand the consequences of their actions. Blackburn (1999) reiterates that Yochelson and Samenow didn't see criminal acts as opportunist but that they were premeditated; if not by actual planning then through general anti-social values and beliefs that instigated offending patterns. From a cognitive perspective, criminals have internalized different ways of thinking about the world and they also fail to understand why they must not behave as they do.

The origins of these 'cognition errors' were believed to begin in childhood, and, like Eysenck (see pp. 91–94), the relationships with parents – both genetic and environmental – were important antecedents to acquiring these flawed thinking styles. As with most criminological research, there were mixed results to support this theory of a general criminal personality, i.e. as a definitive explanation of criminality. Many of the cognition errors identified in the interviews have been found to be present in various criminal populations, but their attempt to produce an all-encompassing theory was flawed in a number of important ways. First, their assumptions were based on a small number (n = 240) of incarcerated offenders with no control group for comparison. This sample is both small and is also curiously flawed in that all the subjects were incarcerated for being 'guilty by reason of insanity'. Hence, to make assertions on the nature of human criminality from these few individuals who quite likely had mental health problems was inappropriate. Hollin (1989) also raises the point that Yochelson and Samenow were labelled as being 'neo-Lombrosian' (see pp. 26–27) because of the way that they define these different types of criminal as being a different 'breed' than other people and without sufficient explanation as to why.

Despite the inherent problems in these approaches, explaining criminal behaviour by way of cognition or flawed thinking styles became an important area of research, particularly because cognitively based theories had less basis in social class or poverty. Two prominent names in the development of this theory have been Ross and Fabiano (1985). They have provided some lucid accounts of how poor upbringing, whether due to general poverty or parental neglect, can hamper the formation of cognitive skills that are appropriate for pro-social behaviour. Ross and Fabiano believe that the way in which people make decisions – their cognitive or 'brain' functioning – will influence future criminality. In contrast to the 'grand' theories which provided elaborate answers to the influence of various factors involved in criminality, the idea that poor thinking patterns could be largely responsible for such behaviour was enduring. The emphasis for the responsibility for committing unlawful acts was also placed firmly with the offender.

Although we talk about flawed cognition in the execution of criminal behaviour, the main emphasis is on social cognition. Social cognition refers to the way in which we think in social situations. For example, if you are in a pub then you are likely to behave differently than when in a church. Similarly, if you are talking to a policeman or teacher then there will be different ways in which you behave towards them and this is all part of social cognition. More specifically, this process is important when considering rules and how to behave. Social cognition amongst criminals is assumed to be flawed, in that they have not learnt socially acceptable ways of thinking. For example, taking drugs or stealing may not be seen by some people to be wrong. There are many different theories about these styles of thinking and how they are acquired. One such example of this is *moral development* (see box 3.4).

BOX 3.4 THE STAGES OF MORAL DEVELOPMENT

Psychologist Jean Piaget and later Lawrence Kohlberg were to develop theories of moral development that consisted of a number of stages that individuals passed through. Whilst it was Piaget who provided the basis of this theory, it would be Kohlberg (1981) who developed this into a consistent and detailed account. As children develop, they begin to learn different ways of behaving. Children begin at Level 1 and then progress through the stages as they grow older. Each person advances at their own pace and doesn't necessarily reach the higher levels, even when they are adults. Essentially, he proposed that there were three levels of moral judgement, each with two separate stages:

- *Level 1: Pre-conventional Morality* (age 9 and below) – In this level, rules are essentially external and self-serving. They are obeyed so as to either avoid punishment or gain rewards. Young children often only see an act as wrong if they are told off or may persist in misbehaving because the rewards are great. A child who eats somebody else's sweets may do so because the consequences may be outweighed by the benefits!
- *Level 2: Conventional Morality* (most adolescents and adults) – The approval of others now plays an important role in moral behaviour in the second level and the perceptions of others are first recognized before embarking on any course of action. Hence, a person may have the opportunity to commit a crime, but desist from doing so as they know that it may have dire consequences for the victim. In particular, they may not want others to think that they are a bad person.
- *Level 3: Post-conventional or Principled Morality* (only 10–15 per cent of adults before age 30) – The two highest levels of moral reasoning are characterized by the broader principles of justice, and they may be surpassed by other obligations. Legally right and morally right become two separate components of behaviour orientation – so although stealing is *legally* wrong, stealing medicine to save someone's life may be seen as *morally* right (as in the famous 'Heinz dilemma').

- Have you ever considered others when deciding what to do – for example, returning a wallet or purse even though you might have wanted to keep the money?
- Have you ever seen or heard about something that made you think that it was unfair and that the law was wrong?
- If you think back, do you see a change in the way you behave now than when you were younger?

There is some debate from within the wider psychological literature as to the way in which people pass through the stages and also some gender and cultural biases in the overall theory (Gilligan 1993). For example, the theory was mostly developed during interviews with Western males, and hence may not apply to the way that females and non-Western people debate moral issues. Nevertheless, the links with crime and social cognition are clearly observable. Kohlberg (1978) believed that criminal behaviour was a direct result of a setback in moral development whereby the individual is 'stuck' reasoning at the lower *pre-morality* levels. These stages are characterized by seeking fulfilment of one's needs, lack of concern for others, and avoiding punishment. The parallels with many descriptions of offenders' behaviour and personality traits are glaringly apparent. The earlier (Level 1) stages are concerned with maximizing rewards whilst avoiding or minimizing punishment. Higher stages (Level 3) are linked with values of morality and less to do with being punished. Criminals are often regarded as thinking within the lower stages of moral reasoning, where they will commit crime so long as the rewards outweigh the potential penalty if they are caught. People who reason at the higher stages may desist from crime as it is at odds with their values of right and wrong; being caught has little significance. Farrington (1992) interviewed many delinquents in his longitudinal studies and revealed that the way offenders thought about crime was quite simple. For some, they only cared about being caught or not, and many didn't care about the victims of their actions. Studies have shown clear differences in the judged acceptability of various offences and behaviour and level of moral reasoning. Some people may regard certain behaviours as reasonable and only care about the chances of getting caught and punished. Others have provided an inclination that lower levels of moral reasoning are symptomatic of individuals nominated as being psychopathic (Hare 1980). Psychopaths generally have little sympathy for their victims and only think about themselves. If they think that they can get away with a crime they generally won't consider the wider implications of their actions, e.g. their victims, and this is similar to people who reason at the first stage or moral reasoning.

Criticisms of this simple explanation of criminal behaviour are significant, and are not just related to the hypothesized relationship. In particular, there are concerns over whether the actual stages proposed by Kohlberg are somewhat arbitrary in that they need not necessarily be passed through in sequential order. Including the gender and cultural biases mentioned by Gilligan (1993), Kohlberg was to himself remove the final stage (Principled Morality) as being largely unattainable and suggested that people could be 'coached' to record higher scores than they probably should. With regard to crime, research has been accused of placing too much emphasis on the *content* of the moral judgements rather than the *processes* involved in attaining these decisions. Similarly to the way in which culture in the non-criminal sense has been found to influence moral reasoning, the 'subcultural' environment that has been argued as a characteristic of criminal fraternities may operate in a similar fashion. By imposing our own moral 'code' by which we judge offenders, we may simply be missing their own values and attitudes that represent different societies. Other theories of morality and its influence on crime have been proposed to confront this anomaly. Bandura (1990) proposed that people could actually become detached from their own moral principles in certain situations. The notion of *moral disengagement* highlights how people can separate themselves from generally accepted morally contemptible decisions by utilizing various psychological 'techniques'. The most common form of disengagement found amongst a cohort of young offenders was to dehumanize the victim. Hence it is not always the offender's own actual moral code that is adhered to, and indeed they can devise justifications for why they offend. For example, people may join gangs to save becoming the actual victim of these groups.

The idea of cognition and crime is closely related to the classical theory of criminology, in that offenders are seen as being responsible for their own behaviour. Psychological explanations of crime see the personality of the offender as having a major influence on their actions; criminal behaviour is regarded as being an almost rational choice that is made by the individual. Although genetic and environmental factors can never be discounted, psychological traits that lead to an offender making decisions to offend can be identified. Cook (1980) believed that offenders conduct a rudimentary cost–benefit analysis when deciding to commit a criminal act. Subsequently if the rewards outweighed the potential negative consequences, it was likely that a crime would be committed. This is generally referred to as the *Deterrence Hypothesis*. These ideas were refined and developed by Cornish and Clarke (1987) into the *Rational Choice Theory* of crime.

The basic premise of this theory is related to the rewards that potential offenders seek from their crimes. This is done by certain decision-making processes that are unique to the individual (e.g. skill) and to the dynamics of the actual situation (e.g. time available). Rational Choice Theory clearly holds that certain crimes are selected by offenders and committed for specific reasons.

QUESTION BREAK

Think of three particular types of crime.

*   What are the rewards gained from committing these crimes?
*   What are the main difficulties and 'dangers' involved in committing them?
*   What generally held moral values have to be 'controlled' to enable people to commit those crimes?

Cornish and Clarke developed a list of such choice properties, which included; technical know-how, resources needed, confrontation with victim and moral evaluation. Although these related primarily to property and offences committed for financial gain, the authors believe that they are easily transferable to violent and sexual crimes. However, despite there being over 15 different reasoning patterns, research has shown that it is the amount of punishment that exerted the biggest influence on whether to offend or not. Hence the relative 'cost' of offending greatly outweighs the 'benefits' of committing the act. In particular, Bridges and Stone (1986) have shown that prior experience of punishment – in the form of prison or other punishment – vastly influenced this equation. So offenders who have been caught and punished for their crimes were able to more accurately evaluate the potential costs more effectively.

BOX 3.5 RATIONAL CHOICE THEORY

Rational choice theories have received increased attention in recent years, and in particular the psycho-geography of crime has seen a resurgence of interest since the early Chicago School proposals. Of particular benefit has been the development of what is termed *situational crime prevention*. Utilizing the theories of criminal decision-making, researchers have shown how simple methods of crime prevention can have dramatic effects on reducing the prevalence of specific crimes. By making the cost of offending greater (for example, making the availability and ease of opportunity for offending more difficult), it becomes less likely for an offender to select a target. Whilst this may sound simplistic, specific models of criminal behaviour have developed.

Routine Activity Theory is one such idea that sees an overlap between criminal and non-criminal behaviour. Cohen and Felson (1979) believed that for a crime to occur, three specific elements must interact: first, the presence of a motivated offender; second, a suitable and accessible target; and third, the absence of any capable guardian. The congruence of these three factors determined when and where crime would be experienced. Support for this theory was, according to Cohen and Felson, shown in the changing type and amount of crime experienced over time. For example, it was discovered that the amount of time people spent away from their home also increased the chance of experiencing a domestic burglary. The empty residence then provided two parts of the crime equation – a suitable target and a relative lack of guardianship. Large increases in the use of crime prevention techniques, such as alarms and CCTV, have indeed impacted on the amount and location of criminal events.

What has emerged as a result of explanations such as these is an increased awareness of how people become victims, and, in particular, how individuals suffer from repeat victimization. For example, Miethe *et al.* (1987) illustrated that people who seldom left the home during the night or day were at the lowest risk of property crime, and naturally the opposite (those often away from home at day and night) had the highest level of victimization. Similarly, Cohen and Felson (1979) identified the increased risk that age makes to the chance of becoming a victim. Older and less 'active' people reported significantly lower levels of victimization. Consequently, it is argued that the more active a person's lifestyle, the more chance they have of coming into contact with suitably inspired offenders and becoming a victim. The importance of absent guardians is also a significant factor. In areas that are characterized by high social disorganization, crime is often high and it may be the lack of neighbours or police patrols that compound this. The opposite may be experienced in areas that have neighbourhood watch schemes and where suspicious-looking people may be reported to the authorities. Although routine activity theory is an attractive and robust explanation of *how* crime can occur, it is less proficient at clarifying *why*.

Researching the social factors of crime

Despite all of the above research, which has focused very much on individual thinking patterns, some psychologists remain committed to the idea that causes of crime are more relational. Many have chosen to look at the social factors in individuals' lives to try to explain why certain individuals become criminals. For example, do people who commit crime come from similar communities? Do they share common occurrences in how they have been raised by their parents? Are they more likely to be found attending certain types of school? The results of the research in this area show that indeed some social factors are commonly seen in the lives of those who go on to commit crimes. However, the research in this area is also surrounded by many 'myths'. For example, we often hear it said that people who have been brought up in violent homes are likely become violent adults themselves. However, the research into the social factors which vary with criminality often shows the facts are not that straightforward, a point we will turn to later on in this chapter.

First, in order to get a feel for how the research in this area has been conducted we shall consider how researchers design studies which enable them to find out which social factors are common in the backgrounds of criminals.

Cross-sectional and longitudinal studies are two examples of research methodologies which can be used to research the social factors of crime. We will look at these examples and suggest some of the main weaknesses with them.

Cross-sectional designs

In a cross-sectional design the researcher takes what is effectively a 'snapshot' of groups of individuals, at a particular point in time. This account is simply a measure of people at that particular stage in their life. When considering social factors, researchers may wish to compare two groups of individuals: one group who are involved in theft for example, and another group who have never committed theft. This method would allow comparisons to be drawn between the two groups (thieves, versus non-thieves) on certain social factors. For example, do those involved in theft tend to come from certain areas? Do they tend to live in crime 'hot spots'? Were they raised by parents who adopted a particular parenting style? Ideally, when using this sort of design the researchers would try to ensure that the two groups were 'matched', i.e. were similar on all criteria other than the one being studied (i.e. theft). This would mean the two groups should be of similar age, class and IQ for example. That way hopefully the only differing variable would be the variable of interest.

WEAKNESSES OF CROSS-SECTIONAL DESIGN

One problem might be that it is very hard to 'match' the two groups effectively. Differences may emerge in that one group might be older, or have a higher level of intelligence, which could add what is known as a confound into the study. Another problem is that often there will be a lot of differences between the two groups, not just, say, the area where they lived, but also other factors such as the size of the family they came from. These factors could also add more confounds to the study.

An additional weakness is that cross-sectional studies do not allow researchers to look at the development of individuals over time, as they are just a one-off picture of a group.

Longitudinal designs

Longitudinal designs differ from cross-sectional designs, in that rather than taking a one-off measure of individuals, they actually look at changes over time within the same person. For example in a longitudinal study the same 'cohort' of participants may be tested once a year for ten years, to see the changes which take place in the group over time. The advantages of longitudinal studies are that they allow researchers to predict later outcomes from information they have when the group is first selected. They also look at the development of the person and can see whether any particular developmental sequences are critical in the person becoming criminal in later life (Loeber and Farrington 1994). There are two different kinds of longitudinal study: retrospective and prospective.

Retrospective designs

In retrospective designs researchers might identify a group of people who they wish to study, for example murderers. They would then analyse existing information on that group, focusing on information from their past (for example their childhood upbringing). Whilst this approach is very useful if you want to study a particular group of people (e.g. people who have already committed a murder), it does have some disadvantages.

WEAKNESSES OF LONGITUDINAL RETROSPECTIVE DESIGNS

One problem is that information may well have been lost over time as the people studied will not have known that in the future they would be asked to be a participant in such a research project. A lot of the information gleaned will be dependent on people's remembered experience which relies upon the human memory processes that we know can be unreliable. None the less the main advantage of this method is when researchers are interested in a rare phenomenon such as murder or arson.

Prospective designs

Prospective designs identify a large sample of people and regularly, over time, test them on various criteria. This overcomes many of the problems with retrospective designs as the measures are taken at various points in time throughout the person's life and so rely less on memory. The researchers can then follow their cohort through their lives and look at who goes on to become criminal, and who does not, and make comparisons between the two groups. An example of a successful longitudinal prospective study would be the Cambridge study of delinquency by Farrington (1995) which looked at the development of 411 boys starting in 1961 and is still in continuation today.

This type of research (due to the amount of testing required) is very expensive, and is often dependent on the same researchers sticking with the project throughout to give continuity to the research project.

One of the things you have probably noticed is that psychologists have come up with several different types of theories which rely on quite different factors as an explanation, ranging from unconscious processes to different learning experiences. And all of these theories are attempting to explain the same thing – why certain people engage in criminal behaviour. This highlights a crucial point in both psychology and criminology; that theorists can come up with quite different theories which can be based on the same sort of evidence. Understanding this point is crucial in developing what are called 'critical evaluation' skills. These skills refer to the ability to look at either theories or research methods and provide critical comments. A good example is the section above on longitudinal and cross-sectional research design. If you had read some research which had been carried out by using one of these methods, you could critically analyse that research by commenting on the weaknesses of such designs, and could comment on whether or not you felt this was the most appropriate design to deal with the topic being studied.

PULLING IT ALL TOGETHER – EYSENCK'S *CRIMINAL PERSONALITY*

Intelligence, impulsivity and locus of control are just some of the more prominent theories that have emerged in an attempt to explain criminal personalities. It can be seen that there are many shortcomings in trying to assign this to any one cause. Consequently, many researchers believe that offending is multi-faceted – it has more than one cause and more than one explanation. For example, just because someone has a low IQ it does not necessarily mean that they will commit crime. Similarly, some offenders might have high levels of impulse control, but choose to offend for entirely different reasons. Because of this, there have been a number of more complete or 'grand' theories that try to show how the interplay between these and many other variables interact and result in criminal behaviour.

Hans Eysenck is perhaps one of the most well-known and widely published psychologists in recent times, and his research interests span many areas from general personality, to intelligence and also criminal behaviour. Eysenck's (1974) theory of crime is a combination theory in that it includes elements of biological antecedents and environmental influences, alongside specific personality traits that are assumed to underpin criminal behaviour. For Eysenck, it was impossible to ignore hereditary and social causes of offending. Instead he believed that poor cognitive or 'thinking' skills were passed down through generations, which then affected the person's ability to effectively deal with external situations and in particular unlawful ones that presented themselves. The interplay between poor social conditioning and inability to comprehend such conditioning subsequently created the 'criminal personality'. Eysenck believed that there were many similarities in the way that a mental illness is acquired and how criminality developed. For example, schizophrenia often runs in families and can therefore be regarded as having a genetic component. However, not everybody will inherit this disorder if they have schizophrenic parents and likewise it is also possible to acquire this disease without any hereditary component. Both genetic (having schizophrenic parents) *and* social factors (e.g. drug taking) can lead to schizophrenia. Hence, in the same way, certain types of personality were more inclined to act in a criminal manner in light of environmental stimuli.

Eysenck's theory of crime essentially explained the criminal personality as resulting from the interaction between three major psychological traits: *Neuroticism* (N), *Extraversion* (E), and *Psychoticism* (P). To begin with, a neurotic can be loosely defined as a person who is suffering from anxiety and appear 'nervous' and 'moody'. However, the manner in which they are defined in Eysenck's theory is not in the strictly clinical meaning; many 'neurotic criminals' would not be seen as suffering from a mental disorder. The second, and perhaps most integral part of this explanation of criminal personality, is the dimension known as *Introvert–Extravert*. Generally introverts are described as being quiet, withdrawn people and conversely extroverts as being outgoing and impulsive. Explanations for this vary, but from within this current theory it is the level of cortical (or brain) stimulation that is important. Extraverts are assumed to have low cortical arousal and seek excitement to maintain levels of stimulation; by contrast, introverts are overly stimulated and avoid stirring situations to avoid becoming over-aroused. Finally psychoticism, which is similar to the more modern term of psychopathy (see Hare 1980), describes people whose personality is characterized by poor emotion, sensation-seeking and general lack of empathy for others. This final variable was added later to the theory, as it was not initially characteristic of all offenders. Later testing did indicate a certain prevalence of this trait amongst many offender groups.

The relationship between these three personality dimensions is for Eysenck the essence of the criminal personality. Specifically, the interplay between these variables is assumed to severely limit the ability of an individual to be conditioned or socialized into a non-criminal way of thinking and behaving. People who were highly neurotic, highly psychotic and are also extraverts epitomized the 'criminal' personality. Alternatively, those who were introverts with low scores on neuroticism and psychoticism were seen to be ideal candidates for social conditioning and less likely therefore to become involved in criminal activity. Interestingly, psychoticism is regarded as being particularly prominent in offenders who display hostility towards others (Hollin 1989). Individual differences relating to the speed and intensity of conditioned responses would therefore explain the correlations between personality dimensions and levels of criminality. An evolution of the separate N, E, and P scales was the amalgamation of the highest scoring items to create the *Criminality* (C) scale (Eysenck and Eysenck 1971). These are the actual statements that best distinguished the criminals from the non-criminals, which were then combined to make this separate scale. This has been reported to be an even greater discriminator in identifying offenders – both adult and juvenile. Interestingly, Eysenck (1987) reports that little in the way of gender differences has been reported, but that high levels of neuroticism are associated with adult offending and extraversion is more prominent in younger offenders. Possible reasons for this included the potential difficulty for adult offenders who had been incarcerated in accurately reflecting the social activity important for assessing extraversion.

CASE STUDY BOX 3.3 CRIMINAL PERSONALITY PROFILING

Criminal personality profiling, or offender profiling, is an investigative technique used by the police to help catch criminals. Many profilers believe that the personality of a criminal is reflected in the way they commit their crimes. One of the first major studies into offender profiling was conducted in the USA by the FBI (Ressler, Burgess and Douglas 1988). They conducted interviews with 36 incarcerated sexual murderers and ascertained a number of significant variables that were features of these offenders. In particular, they were to propose that these offenders could be separated into two main types: the organized and disorganized. By examining the crime scene it was possible to determine which sort of offender had committed the crime. This then gave an indication of the 'type' of person they were looking for. For example, an organized offender was likely to be employed in semi-skilled labour, be married and have access to a vehicle. By contrast, a disorganized offender would be unemployed, live alone and have poor personal hygiene. This information could then be used to prioritize suspects during an investigation. Critics have suggested that this depiction of offenders is too simplistic and further research has produced alternative models. Holmes and Holmes (1996) for example propose a more varied taxonomy, which includes up to six different types of murderer.

Profiling is a useful tool for the police to help identify a suspect from a list of likely offenders, but is not always successful. One of the first cases where a profiler was used in Britain was in the case of the 'Railway Rapist' John Duffy who raped and murdered a number of women in the south of England in the 1980s. A psychologist called David Canter helped the police to identify a number of characteristics of the offender, which led the police to suspect Duffy (Canter 1994). In particular, Canter provided a geographic profile that showed the likely offender would live in a certain area. This was done by analysing the criminal's spatial behaviour and the fact that he had a good knowledge of the railway system – Duffy worked as a carpenter for British Rail and usually offended near stations; hence the name given to him by the media. Other cases that have not been so successful include the murder of Rachel Nickell, who was stabbed as she walked with her young son on Wimbledon Common in 1991. Paul Britton, who was a well-known forensic psychologist, assisted the police and led them to suspect a man named Colin Stagg. When the police set up a trap using an undercover policewoman to try to get him to confess to the crime, Britton guided the operation by telling the police the way in which he believed Stagg would act (Britton 1997). He never confessed to the crime and when they brought him to court the judge refused to hear the case as they had inappropriately used profiling to try to trap a suspect. Another man has since been found guilty of the murder. Profiling can be useful to the police during difficult investigations but doesn't always lead to a suspect and must be used very carefully.

Although Eysenck and his colleagues have continually developed and refined their ideas on the nature of crime and personality, empirical support for its validity has also reported many discrepancies. McGurk and McDougall (1981) found high levels of neuroticism, extraversion and psychoticism amongst a cohort of juvenile offenders. Whilst there were mixtures of the three personality traits amongst these individuals and a control group of non-offenders, only these three variables were *all* present in the offenders. The converse – low-N, low-E and low-P – were only discovered in the non-offending sample. So whilst a mixture of these (e.g. low-N, high-E and high-P) might be present in both offenders and non-offenders, it was the extremes of each variable in combination that predicted criminal behaviour. Others refute these relationships and have reported differing levels of all three variables amongst criminal and non-criminal groups.

Eysenck's theory of crime has been widely reported in criminal research and indeed forms the basis of many discussions on the nature of criminal personality. Despite the inconsistent findings of the high-E, high-N and high-P combinations amongst offender populations, it is generally regarded as too simplistic to define all criminal behaviour in these terms. Further to this there is a wider debate as to whether crime can be explained with reference to psychological factors at all and that the causes of crime are much further reaching. Although Eysenck believed that biological and environmental factors essentially created these personality types, the issue of 'cause and effect' remained largely unanswered. But what did emerge was that criminal behaviour did have a cognitive element, in that it was an individual's thinking style and subsequent behaviour that led to criminal activity. It was a similar notion that drove Yochelson and Samenow (1976) to develop their theory in the study *The Criminal Personality (*see p. 83 above).

QUESTION BREAK: USING SELF-REPORT INVENTORIES FOR ASSESSING PERSONALITY

When researchers attempt to explain and measure criminal personalities, they often use what are called 'self-report' inventories. Generally these are questionnaires that have a number of statements which people respond to. For example, if we were trying to measure impulsivity, we might ask people a number of questions like: *Do you act without thinking about the consequences?* It is usual to give people a Likert-style response option, such as strongly agree, agree, don't know, disagree, strongly disagree. Each choice is then given a score and then all the responses are added up to give a total. Somebody who marks 'strongly agree' to the questions on the Extraversion scale from Eysenck's Personality Inventory would therefore be judged to be an extravert. Psychologists then make judgements about the person on the strength of these scores and for instance, whether they are likely to commit crime. These types of test are widely used in all fields of psychology to measure different types of personality traits and attitudes, such as depression or self-esteem. However, although they can be used to explain why people differ on these personality traits, it is less clear as to why people with different characteristics behave in the way that they do. There is also the question of how they acquire these dispositions.

- Can you think of any problems associated with this method for identifying features of people's personality?
- What other ways might we go about assessing the psychological traits people show?

SUMMARY

This chapter has endeavoured to show that many different psychological theories have all tried to explain the same phenomenon – why people engage in criminal activity. Through a series of question breaks you have had the opportunity to start to think about these different types of theories, and point out both their strengths and also their weaknesses. In so doing you have started to learn how to critically analyse different theories. In addition, you have learned about a number of different methods which psychologists have used to try to research the question of why people become criminal. In learning these different methods you have had the chance to gain an insight into the ways psychologists study human behaviour, and have learned that sometimes, as in any area of social science, these methods seem less than ideal.

There is no doubt that in trying to predict who becomes criminal a whole range of theories and explanations are likely to be at play and it would be naive to expect a simple explanation. Hopefully this chapter has allowed you to come a step closer to formulating your own opinions as to the relative importance of different types of factors.

FURTHER READING

Blackburn, R. (1995) *The Psychology of Criminal Conduct: Theory, Research and Practice* (2nd edn). London: Wiley. Although a little dated, still one of the most comprehensive texts in the area and an excellent in-depth review of the overriding theories on criminal behaviour.

Canter, D. (2008) *Criminal Psychology*. London: Hodder. A useful introduction to the field, along with more specific chapters dealing with the field of psychology as applied to specific crime types, e.g. burglary, domestic violence and victims.

Davies, G.M., Hollin, C.R., and Bull, R. (eds.) (2008). *Forensic Psychology*. London: Wiley. A more focused text arranged around four key areas associated with psychology and crime/law: the *Anatomy of Crime*, *Investigating Crime*, the *Trial Process*, and *After Sentencing*.

Howitt, D. (2009). *Introduction to Forensic and Criminal Psychology* (3rd edn). Harlow: Pearson. A good general introduction to many of the main psychological principles associated with offending and criminal behaviour. Each chapter has a range of useful 'talking points' and interesting case studies. Additional material on the application of psychology in legal contexts and on conducting research.

WEBSITES

http://www.bps.org.uk/careers/what-do-psychologists-do/areas/forensic.cfm – information from the British Psychological Society on qualifications and employment for those interested in pursuing a career in forensic psychology.

http://crimepsychblog.com/ – Psychology and Crime News is a 'blog' dedicated to collating research and reports from around the world, with additional comments from practitioners on current and past cases.

CHAPTER 4

Sociological Explanations for Criminal Behaviour

INTRODUCTION

When we looked at the historical context for crime (Chapter 1), the extent and range of criminal behaviour was emphasized, along with its massive influence on everyday life. Having looked at theoretical explanations from biological and psychological perspectives in the previous two chapters, here we will turn to explanations from sociological perspectives. And as we will see, the divisions between the different 'subjects' of biology, psychology and sociology are by no means obvious or rigid. However, while not seeing non-sociological theories as necessarily 'wrong', sociologists would consider them to offer only partial explanations at best. The emphasis in sociological theorizing is on the social context in which crime takes place – crime and criminals can only be fully understood in relation to the social structure, to specific social conditions and processes. Of course within this broad argument that criminal behaviour can only be explained by social factors, there are a wide variety of specific theoretical positions. As Rock (2007) put it in his recent review of sociological theories of crime: 'sociological theories . . . are wide-reaching: they extend, for example, from an examination of the smallest detail of street encounters between adolescents and the police to comparative analyses of very large movements in nations' aggregate rates of crime over centuries.'

Explanations for criminal behaviour are as old as the types of behaviour themselves – debate and discussion about why people break rules have excited general and scholarly interest throughout history. Indeed most people have their own views as to what are the most likely causes of such behaviour; and these views are all likely to contain some elements of 'truth' without being complete explanations. Inherited defects, overcrowding, inadequate parental supervision and getting in with the 'wrong crowd', for example, have all been proposed as causes of criminal behaviour.

Moreover in looking at theories we should not expect to find some complete explanation or ultimate cause of criminal behaviour. Indeed this behaviour encompasses so massive a range of activities that such an aim is clearly unrealistic. After all, why should one form of explanation or theory be able to explain why some people in well-paid jobs embezzle money and why other people engage in domestic violence and still others get involved in fighting on a night out? To put it another way, is it likely that the criminal identity of a fraudster would be the same as a burglar or a 'professional' armed robber? Furthermore, even if it could be proved that juvenile delinquency was linked to poor parental supervision, it would be necessary to consider why such delinquency occurred amongst some poorly supervised juveniles but not others. Then it would be important to consider why those parents were unable to provide adequate supervision – was it because of their living conditions and, if so, why were they living in such poor conditions? Was this because of government housing policies or a poor employment record? It is clear that we are moving further and further away from explaining the cause of the criminal behaviour. This is not to say it is not important to look for explanations of criminal behaviour; but we do need to be aware that different theoretical approaches and explanations may help explain certain forms of criminal behaviour but not others and that there is no 'ultimate explanation' waiting to be discovered.

Attempting to categorize the wide range of sociological explanations is fraught with difficulty and here we will use an essentially chronological approach to map our way through the different approaches and traditions.

CLASSICAL CRIMINOLOGY

Sometimes known as classical jurisprudence, classical criminology emerged from the period known as the Enlightenment and was developed by penal reformers in the later eighteenth and early nineteenth centuries who wanted to create a fair and legitimate criminal justice system based on equality. The intention was to develop a rational and efficient means of delivering justice in place of previous arbitrary, corrupt and prejudiced forms of punishment. Based on the Enlightenment emphasis on individual rights, rather than the unquestioning acceptance of traditional forms of authority, the core ideas of classical criminology were that the punishment for a crime should be proportionate to the particular criminal act and that it should be seen as a deterrent. As this introductory comment indicates, the focus of classical criminology is very much on the relationship between crime, justice and punishment, rather than with explaining why certain individuals become offenders. Classical criminology was based on the notion that individuals had free will and made rational choices about the way in which they would behave. People, including those who commit criminal acts, have to be considered as rational, and so an individual's behaviour will be based on a rational calculation of the consequences. The major control over a person exercising their free will is, particularly, fear of pain. The fear of pain, in the form of punishment, would, then, deter an individual from criminal activities and act as a control on their behaviour.

Prior to the Enlightenment period, crime was generally believed to be the result of evil and punishments were arbitrary and cruel, based on ideas of revenge or retribution, with torture routinely used to gain confessions. The age of Enlightenment saw the development of formal theorizing about crime and attempts to introduce more rational forms of punishment; and classical criminology can be seen as developing from the general shift from feudal to industrial society (Newburn 2007). The two Enlightenment philosophers most associated with developing this classical approach were Cesare Beccaria and Jeremy Bentham, both of whom aimed to limit the cruel and barbaric nature of the previous systems of justice and forms of punishment.

Beccaria was an Italian university professor who, at the age of only 26, wrote an essay on punishment entitled *Dei Deliti e Delle Pene (On Crimes and Punishment)* that was published in 1764. This book, which was written at a time when severe and barbaric punishments were the norm, caused something of an outcry with its rational approach to punishment – although condemned by the Catholic Church it was widely read and translated into 22 languages. Essentially Beccaria advocated a reformed system of criminal justice that provided a more logical and rational approach to the punishment of crime. Among his ideas were the notion that there must be a proper proportion between crimes and punishment, that to be just and useful punishment should be administered promptly and that one of the greatest curbs on crime is the certainty, rather than the cruelty, of punishment. Indeed one section of his text is entitled 'of the proportion between crimes and punishment'. He starts this section by suggesting the need to classify crimes according to their severity:

> A scale of crimes may be formed, of which the first degree should consist of those which immediately tend to the dissolution of society, and the last of the smallest possible injustice done to a private member of that society. Between these extremes will be comprehended all actions contrary to the public good which are called criminal, and which descend by insensible degrees, decreasing from the highest to the lowest. If mathematical calculation could be applied to the obscure and

infinite combinations of human actions, there might be a corresponding scale of punishments, descending from the greatest to the least.

(Beccaria 1963 (1764))

In elaborating on this he argues that crimes have to be ranked according to the injury done to society:

> Some crimes are immediately destructive of society, or its representative; others attack the private security of the life, property or honour of individuals; and a third class consists of such actions as are contrary to the laws which relate to the general good of the community . . . The first, which are of the highest degree, as they are most destructive to society, are called crimes of leze-majesty (High Treason) . . . To these succeed crimes which are destructive of the security of individuals. This security being the principal end of all society, and to which every citizen has an undoubted right, it becomes indispensably necessary, that to these crimes the greatest of punishments should be assigned.
>
> (ibid.)

And in relation to punishment: 'If an equal punishment be ordained for two crimes that injure society in different degrees, there is nothing to deter men from committing the greater as often as it is attended with greater advantage' (ibid.).

QUESTION BREAK

- In our society which crimes are ranked as most and least serious?
- What factors determine this ranking?
- To what extent do you agree with the way crimes are ranked?
- How does the contemporary ranking of crime relate to Beccaria's arguments?

While the language may sound dated, many of Beccaria's ideas have formed the basis of modern criminological theorizing. In discussing the ranking of crimes within society, Beccaria acknowledges and highlights the relative nature of crime and the social reaction to it – a notion central to the work of the interactionist, labelling theorists whose work became very much in vogue in the Sociology of the 1960s and 1970s (see pp. 121–129):

> Whoever reads, with a philosophic eye, the history of nations, and their laws, will generally find, that the ideas of virtue and vice, of a good or bad citizen, change with the revolution of ages, not in proportion to the alteration of circumstances, and consequently conformability to the common good, but in proportion to the passions and errors by which the different lawgivers were successively influenced. He will frequently observe that the passions and vices of one age are the foundation of the morality of the following . . . Hence the uncertainty of our notions of

honour and virtue; an uncertainty which will ever remain, because they change with the revolutions of time . . . they change with the boundaries of states.

(ibid.)

In particular, Beccaria is known for his advocating of a utilitarian approach to the law and punishment, arguing that although the laws of a society might affect the liberty of a few they would be acceptable if they resulted in the greater happiness of the majority. He believed that human behaviour was essentially rational and based on the pleasure–pain principle. As regards punishment, the pain of punishment should be greater than the potential pleasure resulting from the criminal act – so the punishment should be proportionate to the harm done to society by the crime. Beccaria hoped that making punishment proportionate to the social harm done would limit the arbitrary punishments meted out by judges. This idea suggests that an offender's character and circumstances should not be taken into account when determining and delivering punishment – all offenders should be treated equally, as abstract legal subjects. The essence of Beccaria's argument is illustrated by the concluding remarks he makes in his essay:

From what has been demonstrated, one may deduce a theorem of considerable utility . . . In order for punishment not to be, in every instance, an act of violence of one or of many against a private citizen, it must be essentially public, prompt, necessary, the least possible in the given circumstances, proportionate to the crimes, dictated by the laws.

(ibid.)

In summarizing Beccaria's approach to the prevention of crime, Newburn (2007) highlights three key ideas:

- certainty (how likely is the punishment)
- celerity (how quickly is punishment administered)
- severity (how much 'pain' is inflicted).

In a similar vein, Bentham promoted the utilitarian approach, and argued that punishment should be carefully calculated to inflict pain in proportion to the harm done to the public by the particular crime. This sort of argument was based on the notion that criminals and non-criminals were similar in that criminals were reasoning individuals who had made an error of judgement in committing a crime; and that rational, swift and certain punishment was the best way to stop such behaviour recurring. Influenced by Beccaria, Bentham believed people behaved rationally and would seek pleasure and aim to avoid pain. So punishment must outweigh any pleasure that might be derived from criminal behaviour. Bentham claimed that all law and punishments should be based on the utilitarian principle of 'the greatest happiness of the greatest number' and on calculating degrees of pain and pleasure – so the pain of punishment could only be justified if it prevented more and greater pain. Individuals committed crimes to gain excitement, money or something else that they wanted and criminal justice had to ensure that the pleasure gained from crime was outweighed (but not excessively so) by the pains of punishment. Punishments were basically negative and had to be restricted to producing only the desired outcome and proportionate to the actual crime committed.

Classical criminology certainly seemed to offer a much fairer and more open philosophy and system of punishment than the previous cruel and harsh systems. However, in emphasizing the free will and rationality of individuals, it did not consider issues of social inequality which might encourage certain individuals to commit crime and it assumed there was a generally agreed set of values or goals in society, ignoring the conflicting aims and goals of different groups (as we will see below this is a criticism that is also made of later theoretical positions).

The influence of classical criminology is evident in our legal system today in the way that sentences for crimes are structured, with more severe punishments for more serious crimes – what is known as the 'tariff' for sentences. And the 'just deserts' approach to punishment, that anyone found guilty of a crime should be punished (irrespective of their background – equality before the law) and that punishment must be commensurate (or proportional) to the seriousness of the offence, clearly reflects the classical approach of Beccaria and Bentham.

This form of classical criminology was the dominant approach to thinking about crime until the late nineteenth century when it came under attack from the new developments in the social sciences, notably the development of a scientific approach to studying society and, more specifically, crime.

EMILE DURKHEIM

Of the founding, 'classic' sociological theorists it was Emile Durkheim who wrote most on crime (and on punishment). As the founder of the structural functionalist approach in sociology we will start by briefly setting out his broad theoretical position before examining his application of this to explaining crime.

Durkheim, along with other classic sociological theorists, was interested in explaining how industrial society had come about and how such a complex structure held together. In particular, how was social order maintained in a modern industrial society compared to what he deemed the simpler, pre-industrial society? The 'problem of order' has been seen as a key issue in the development of sociological theorizing. At the time Durkheim was writing (the end of the nineteenth and early twentieth centuries), industrialization and urbanization had led to profound changes in the nature of modern societies and many early social theorists were attempting to understand these changes and their impact on society. Indeed many compared the new modern industrial societies unfavourably with a more communal, pre-industrial form of society. Durkheim, however, interpreted such changes from an evolutionary perspective and considered how societies adapted to the new context, while acknowledging that the transition to modern, industrial societies would cause disruption and disorganization for individuals and for societies in general.

He argued that social order had to be based on a core of shared values which formed the moral basis for what he termed social solidarity. Durkheim believed that without the regulation of society individuals would simply aim to satisfy their own needs and wishes without regard for others. As mentioned above, this regulation would have to be based on shared values which were generally accepted by members of the society. He called these shared, commonly held values the collective conscience of the society, which he defined as 'the totality of beliefs and sentiments common to average citizens of the same society'.

QUESTION BREAK

While phrases such as 'average citizens' and 'common to' raise broad issues of interpretation and definition, the notion of the collective conscience can be clearly related to criminal behaviour and the responses to it.

- Consider a range of different crimes.
- What are the differences in the way that they are responded to?
- Why are there such varied responses to different forms of crime?
- Which values does this suggest to be particularly strongly held by the 'collective conscience'?

So the notion of the collective conscience is central to Durkheim's work – indeed social life, based on social order and solidarity, would be impossible without such collective standards and values. However, in line with his evolutionary perspective on social change, the form or style of social solidarity is not fixed and will adapt to the different, changing forms of society. In his first major work, *The Division of Labour in Society*, Durkheim examined the changing form of social solidarity from pre-industrial to modern, industrial societies. In modern societies, the division of labour serves to integrate individuals who fulfil complementary tasks and roles. He uses the terms 'mechanical' and 'organic' to distinguish the different forms of social solidarity that characterize the two different forms of society. Less complex, pre-industrial societies are characterized by mechanical solidarity, where individuals tend to hold very similar beliefs and emotions and where there is relatively little specialization in terms of occupations. In such situations tradition is particularly strong and collective feelings predominate. By contrast organic solidarity characterizes modern societies, with individuals pursuing a much wider range of different tasks. This leads to a great deal of interdependence – individuals are dependent on others to perform specific tasks and roles. Individuals in such societies pursue different and complementary functions but are still bound together by a strong moral consensus.

Durkheim's theorizing is couched at a very general, abstract level and he did not advocate a simple, straightforward divide between the two forms of social solidarity – for him all societies need a consensus, a collective conscience. However, the strength of this collective conscience will vary from one form of society to another. The mechanical form of solidarity dominates the consciences of individuals more strongly than does the organic form – in modern, industrial societies there is greater scope for individuality and for individuals to express their own feelings and preferences.

Within this general approach to theorizing about the nature of society, crime (and how it is dealt with) were central aspects of Durkheim's sociological analysis. The importance of a collective conscience based on shared values and norms is central to his explanation of crime. Crime is behaviour that breaks or deviates from these shared values and norms. It is also seen by Durkheim as a social fact and must, therefore, perform a social function – along with other social institutions and parts of a society. Given that crime is behaviour that breaks rules it might seem odd to talk about its functions. However Durkheim developed the argument that crime is universal, it exists, albeit to varying extents, in all known societies and must therefore be inevitable. And as well as being inevitable it must also be necessary and useful for society. Put simply, as crime is normal it must also be functional: 'There is no society that is not confronted with the problem of criminality . . . It is a factor in public health, an integral part of all healthy societies' (Durkheim 1895).

Durkheim then explains how crime does have positive functions – first, through encouraging social change and evolution and, second, through helping to sustain conformity and stability. In terms of encouraging social change, criminal behaviour can introduce new ideas into a society and so allow a society to move on and develop. Tierney (2010) calls this the 'adaptive function' of crime – criminals can be innovators who help society to adapt to changing circumstances. Durkheim gives the example of Socrates who was condemned as a criminal in his own time but whose (criminal) ideas benefited Greek society. As he put it:

> According to Athenian law, Socrates was a criminal. However, his crime, namely the independence of his thought, rendered a service not only to humanity but to his country . . . Nor is the case of Socrates unique; it is reproduced periodically in history. It would never have been possible to establish the freedom of thought we now enjoy if the regulations prohibiting it had not been violated. At that time, however, the violation was a crime.
>
> (Durkheim 1964: 67–71)

As regards its role in promoting social cohesion, Durkheim refers to the way in which the sense of outrage that crime can produce helps to reinforce generally held values and beliefs in the majority of people. Tierney (2010) refers to this as a 'boundary maintenance function', reinforcing the boundary between 'good' and 'bad' behaviour. When someone commits a crime, particularly certain forms of generally despised crimes, people often feel closer together through sharing their collective outrage. Through bringing people together crime can thereby have the effect of contributing to social cohesion. The presence of the criminal allows the rest of society to draw together and reaffirm their values; it strengthens the society or social group, and does this by drawing a boundary between acceptable and unacceptable behaviour.

Of course, it is not the criminal actions themselves which draw people together; it is the publicizing and punishing of crime that does that. It is the reaction to crime, evidenced in the way that it is punished, that is of central importance for Durkheim's argument. The public trial of criminals and the media's obsession with portraying crime and criminal trials help to clarify the boundaries of acceptable and non-acceptable behaviour. While the social reaction to and punishment of crime might not always correspond with the extent of social harm done by that criminal action, it does, according to Durkheim, illustrate and express the strength of generally held values and standards. For instance, the extent of social harm done by a specific violent act on a child may be slight compared to the number of people harmed by a company ignoring industrial safety or pollution laws. However the reaction against the child violator will be far stronger than against the offending company. From this viewpoint, the reaction to crime is seen as essentially emotional rather than rational and the demand for punishment as demonstrating a desire to see the offender suffer pain. This emotional reaction is demonstrated by the angry crowds which gather around courtrooms during particularly horrific murder trials. These sorts of responses are best understood if crime is seen as behaviour that offends against strongly held norms and values. Durkheim argued that in order for there to be agreement and social cohesion, people had to be able to react against those who break the shared rules and values and that crime provides such an opportunity. It is this sort of approach to theorizing about crime that allows him to argue that:

> From this point of view the fundamental facts of criminality present themselves to us in an entirely new light. Contrary to current ideas, the criminal no longer seems a totally unsociable being, a sort of parasitic element. On the contrary, he plays a definite role in social life.
>
> (Durkheim 1964: 72)

QUESTION BREAK

- What specific types of criminal behaviour might lead to the introduction of new ideas and social change?
- Can you think of any individuals who were punished for their views but who later became widely respected and looked up to?
- What specific types of criminal behaviour might help to draw people together?
- Consider some recent crimes (and the trials of them) which have attracted media and public attention. How have they helped to promote greater 'social cohesion'?

As well as exploring the functions of crime for society, Durkheim argued that the increased individualism of modern industrial societies and the lesser degree of social cohesion and regulation would encourage a greater degree of social disorganization and lead to a variety of different social problems, including crime. He developed this argument in trying to explain the increase in criminal behaviour in modern industrial societies. During periods of rapid social change, when societies are rapidly modernizing and industrializing for instance, less control is exerted over people's aspirations – as Burke puts it, 'such societies encourage a state of unbridled egoism that is contrary to the maintenance of social solidarity and conformity to the law' (2005: 94). And during such times of rapid change, new forms of control have not developed sufficiently to replace older ones, resulting in societies being in a state of 'anomie', where there is a breakdown in norms and common values and understandings.

Anomie theory has been one of the most enduring and examined ideas in criminological theorizing, even though the term itself is not widely used today (Rock 2007). As mentioned, Durkheim saw anomie as occurring in periods of major social change; so in the transition to capitalist societies, people were forced into specific and limited roles, obliged to work in a society which enjoyed little legitimacy or support. In such a situation moral regulation was weak and there would be less restraint on people deviating and committing crime. Furthermore, when societies face massive and rapid change, the notion of the collective conscience and the semblance of authority and objectivity can founder and people can find it 'hard to live outside the reassuring structures of social life' (Rock 2007). These situations, where formal control and authority are weak or erratic and where there is widespread anxiety and criminal behaviour, can exist at both an individual and a wider, societal level. There are many areas in major cities around the world where there is rampant anti-social behaviour and a lack of informal social control, where personal safety is a concern and where life in general is unpredictable.

THE CHICAGO SCHOOL

Durkheim's early sociological theorizing on crime has been developed in a number of directions by later social theorists and criminologists. Here we will look at the work of the Chicago School on the relationship between increasing social disorganization and criminal behaviour and, in the next section, at the 'strain' theory developed by Robert Merton and linking anomie with criminal behaviour. The notion that modern, industrializing and urbanizing societies would bring with them greater social disorganization and therefore a growth in social problems, including crime, underpinned the work of sociologists at the University of Chicago in the 1920 and 1930s. The approach and theorizing of these sociologists has become know as the Chicago School – Chicago grew at a phenomenal rate in the early years of the twentieth century into a massive metropolis with a diverse population including European immigrants from Ireland, Germany and Eastern Europe and black Americans from the Southern USA. It has been described as a vast social laboratory and it is perhaps no coincidence that the first university sociology department in the USA was established there in 1892.

Based on Durkheim's work, the Chicago School saw crime as a social, rather than an individual, phenomenon. They argued that social life in certain areas and neighbourhoods was chaotic and pathological and that in such situations crime was an expected and normal response. This view was coloured with a degree of optimism in that it was felt such a situation was only temporary due to the rapid social changes brought on by industrialization and urbanization and that in this context a certain amount of crime was inevitable and of no particular threat to the basis of society. A key figure in establishing the reputation of the Chicago School was Robert Park. He believed that in order to study crime sociologists should actually go out into the city and engage in first-hand research – a view that encouraged the development of a number of important and renowned ethnographic research studies by sociologists at the University of Chicago.

Park and colleagues argued that cities should be considered as ecological systems, with different areas and neighbourhoods within them developing at different times and in specific ways. As cities developed and expanded, they argued, there would be a progressive differentiation of area, population and function, with different groupings concentrated in different areas of the city. As Tierney puts it:

> Thus cities such as Chicago had not developed on a random basis, but rather this development was patterned according to 'natural' social processes. The outcome was that cities evolve their own particular types of neighbourhood, each with their own type of social life. Some of these are stable, well organized neighbourhoods, but others are more socially disorganized, and it is here that social problems, including crime, are concentrated.
>
> (2010: 97)

Ernest Burgess, another leading Chicago School sociologist, developed this 'ecological' approach by mapping out the different 'zones' of Chicago which formed five concentric circles covering the whole city; with each of these circles or areas being a zone with a distinct social and cultural life. At the centre there was a business area of banks and offices and outside of this were different residential zones – what was termed the 'zone of transition' just beyond the central business zone, then the zone of workingmen's [sic] homes, the residential zone and the commuters' zone.

The zone of transition was the area where most crime, as well as other social problems, occurred. Clifford Shaw and Henry McKay, two researchers closely associated with the University of Chicago Sociology Department, developed Burgess's approach to examine patterns of juvenile crime in Chicago. In this zone the housing was typically run down and the inhabitants were often new immigrants and others lacking the means to live elsewhere in the city. They found that in this deprived area with a transient population who were unable to put down roots, the values and norms that led to criminal behaviour were most likely to be found.

> The high rates of juvenile crime found in the zone of transition were said to be linked to the social disorganisation in those areas. In the absence of strong normative controls from the family and the community, juveniles were likely to engage in delinquent activities.
>
> (Tierney 2010: 98)

More generally, Shaw and McKay found that the extent of criminal behaviour was inversely related to the affluence of the area of the city, which was reflected in the distance the area was from the central business zone. They showed that crime rates were highest in 'slum' neighbourhoods regardless of who lived in those areas and used these findings to argue that it was the nature of neighbourhoods, rather than of particular individuals or groups who lived in them, that determined the level of involvement in crime. Hence the description of the Chicago School as an ecological approach to explaining criminal behaviour.

ANOMIE – ROBERT MERTON

This notion that crime was linked to a breakdown in social control has been a major influence on a number of later sociological writers who developed the structural functional approach of Durkheim to explain the nature of crime in contemporary society. In particular the link between the notion of anomie and crime was explored and developed by Robert Merton.

Merton's work in this area, known as 'strain' theory or 'anomie' theory, attempts to explain a wide range of forms of deviant behaviour, including crime. As with Durkheim, Merton was not a criminology specialist, he was a key figure in the functionalist school of thought that was predominant in American Sociology from the 1930s to the 1950s. He started his theorizing on crime and deviance from the basic functionalist position that social stability is based on a strong consensus of values, which the majority of people in a society come to share. His most famous statement in this area was a paper entitled 'Social Structure and Anomie', originally published in 1938. The title indicates the influence of Durkheim's concept of anomie, while the term 'strain theory' indicates the basic issue Merton examined – what sort of social conditions and situations lead some people to break rules and act in criminal or deviant ways. Merton rejected individualistic explanations that had tended to dominate criminological theorizing and developed a more sociological approach. He argued that criminal and deviant behaviour came from individuals or groups of people responding in an expected and normal manner to the social situations they found themselves in. In particular it resulted from a disjuncture between the cultural goals of a society and the legitimate means available to achieve those goals. His argument that criminal and rule-breaking behaviour results from 'differentials in access to the success goals of society by legitimate means' has become a classic socio-logical explanation and is worth exploring in a little depth.

Although Merton's work has been criticized (see p. 111), his paper, written over 60 years ago, remains a remarkably prescient view of the nature of contemporary society. Indeed the criticisms often seem to fail to appreciate the vitality and radical aspects of this important example of sociological theorizing on crime and deviance. Merton starts by pointing to the tendency in previous theorizing about crime to focus on biological drives – seeing it as 'anchored in original nature'. He criticizes this view of people being set against society in a 'war between biological impulse and social restraint', suggesting that 'the image of man as an untamed bundle of impulses begins to look more like a caricature than a portrait'. The fact that the frequency and type of criminal and deviant behaviour varies within different social structures questions the role of biological impulses.

In developing a systematic approach to studying such behaviour he aimed to discover how 'some social structures exert a definite pressure upon certain persons in the society to engage in nonconformist rather than conformist conduct'. High rates of deviant behaviour amongst certain groups of people would, he argued, be due to those people responding normally to their social situation and the pressures they faced in that situation. Merton highlighted two specific elements of the social structure which were crucial to his sociological explanation. First, culturally defined goals which are seen as legitimate objectives for everyone – they are things 'worth striving for'. Second there are the acceptable modes of reaching those goals – usually called the 'means' in discussions of Merton's work; he used the term 'institutionalized norms'. These cultural goals and institutional norms are not fixed in a constant relation to one another with the emphasis on one or other varying according to the social context. He describes the two extreme situations between which there will be this variation – on the one hand, a context where 'any and all procedures which promise attainment of the all-important goal would be permitted' and, on the other, a situation where the overall purposes of an activity are forgotten and 'conduct becomes a matter of ritual'. Between these extremes are societies which maintain a balance between emphasis on cultural goals and institutional means; and an effective equilibrium is maintained so long as individuals who conform to the norms achieve the satisfactions and goals they aim for. Merton goes on to argue that 'aberrant (deviant) behaviour may be regarded sociologically as a symptom of dissociation between culturally prescribed aspirations and socially structured avenues for realizing these aspirations'.

Having made these general points, he then considers the particular types of society where the emphasis on goals is especially strong in comparison to the emphasis on institutional procedures. Although all societies have norms that govern behaviour the pressure to attain goals can become predominant, leading to a situation where 'the technically most effective procedure, whether legitimate or not, becomes typically preferred to institutionally prescribed conduct'. In such situations the society becomes unstable and 'develops what Durkheim termed "anomie" (or normlessness)'. The examples Merton used from the world of sport to illustrate this situation – such as illegally 'nobbling' an opponent or using illicit techniques (or substances) to improve chances of winning – will be easily recognizable to anyone even with only a passing interest in contemporary sport.

Give examples of behaviour that illustrates the win-at-all-costs attitude from:
(a) different sports; and (b) other areas of life.

As indicated by the questions above, the notion that it is only success, rather than participation, that can provide gratification is not restricted to competitive sports.

Merton himself lived through the Depression in America in the 1930s and his theory was built on a critique of elements of American culture and the idea of the 'American dream', based on the belief that prosperity and success were available to anyone who worked hard for it (Newburn 2007). This emphasis encouraged some to look for illegitimate means of gaining success, as Merton commented, ' the culture makes incompatible demands . . . In this setting, a cardinal American virtue – ambition – promotes a cardinal American vice – deviant behaviour' (Merton 1957, quoted in Rock 2007). Indeed Merton suggests that 'contemporary American culture appears to approximate the polar type in which great emphasis upon certain success goals occurs without equivalent emphasis upon institutional means'. In particular, he considers how money has become a value in itself, a 'symbol of prestige', and however it is acquired (legally or not) it can still be used to purchase the same goods and services. It is worth remembering that Merton was writing in the 1930s when he stated that:

> To say that the goal of monetary success is entrenched in American culture is only to say that Americans are bombarded on every side by precepts which affirm the right or, often, the duty of retaining the goal even in the face of repeated frustration.
>
> (Merton 1938: 677)

In highlighting the prestige attached to monetary success, Merton provided examples from American business magazines of 'self-made men' whose ambitions drove them to success against all the odds. Of course the corollary of high ambition is that those who do not aspire to success are admonished as 'quitters'.

Individuals have to adapt to the cultural context described by Merton and his explanation of different forms of criminal and deviant behaviour is based around the different responses people make if they are faced with a discrepancy between the aspirations or goals that society has 'taught' them and the ways that they have available to realize such aspirations (their 'means'). On the basis of this explanation, Merton suggested five different ways of adapting to this gap – five different 'modes of adaptation' as he put it. Here we will just provide a brief introduction to each of these modes of adaptation.

First, conformity, which involves the individual accepting both the goals and means. This is the usual form of adaptation – indeed if it were not so societies would become extremely unstable. The majority of individuals will continue to conform in spite of the strain to anomie that Merton highlighted; however, this strain is stronger for certain social groups than for others. The other four modes of adaptation describe ways of dealing with the strain caused by social inequalities. Merton calls the second category or adaptation 'innovation', which involves the adopting of unconventional methods of chasing the goals. These methods could include criminal ways of achieving successes and it is this category which is most relevant to studying and explaining crime. Corporate and white-collar crime, for instance fraud and insider dealing, could be seen as sharing the aims of legitimate capitalist activity while using illegitimate means to attain them. Third, ritualism, where the goals are abandoned but the individual sticks rigidly to the legitimate means of attaining success; Merton's example here was of the typical bureaucrat obsessed with doing things by the rules. Fourth, retreatism, which occurs when both the goals and the means are abandoned, with the individual perhaps 'dropping out' of society altogether. Fifth, rebellion, with the goals and means given up but replaced with new ones, for instance the political radical.

QUESTION BREAK

- Give an example of behaviour, or perhaps an occupation, that would fit each of Merton's five cases of adaptation.
- Think of a particular person (either a 'real' person or a fictional character) who would fit each of those categories.

As suggested earlier, Merton's ground-breaking sociological theorizing has been subject to criticism. In this relatively brief overview we cannot go into a detailed critique but will raise some general points. Although providing a clearly sociological explanation for certain forms of nonconformity, Merton's theory does not adequately explain all types of criminal behaviour. It is difficult to point to the material goals that juvenile delinquents, hooligans or rapists, for example, could be seen as chasing. More generally the theory seems to have a middle-class bias; as well as assuming criminals and rule breakers accept and cherish middle-class goals, the model tends to focus on working-class crime. This is a problem that faces any theorizing based on a consensus views of society – a view that society is held together by common values which are shared by everyone. This bias might be exaggerated by the reliance of Merton on official crime statistics which arguably underestimate middle-class crime and predict too much working-class crime.

In terms of the different types of adaptation forwarded by Merton, there is no real explanation as to why some individuals who are faced with specific situations, perhaps of anomie, conform while others break the rules. Nor does it explain why one particular form of adaptation rather than another occurs – why innovation rather than retreatism for instance.

Having said that, Merton's theory does have certain strengths. It explains crime in terms of the structure and culture of society, rather than individual characteristics. As such it is a structural theory of crime which laid the basis for later theorizing based on the notion of subcultures – the idea that certain groups are more predisposed to break the rules of society than others. Such approaches are introduced below.

DELINQUENT SUBCULTURES – ALBERT COHEN

In his widely cited study *Delinquent Boys*, published in 1955, Albert Cohen provides a different version of strain theory. The influence of Merton is apparent through his focusing on features of contemporary American society that create strains for individuals which eventually lead to delinquent behaviour – in particular the importance of the values which form the 'American way of life'. However, Cohen questions whether criminal and delinquent behaviour is caused by a desire for material goals. Like Merton, he focuses on the working-class delinquency but argues that a large amount of such behaviour is expressive in character and not centred on acquiring money or goods. Delinquency centred on vandalism or violence is a clear example of such behaviour that is not concerned with material gain. So whereas Merton saw deprivation as the major impetus behind crime and deviance, Cohen argued that juvenile delinquents were not searching for material gain or success but for meaning in some other way.

There are clear similarities with Merton's work, but Cohen suggests that competition and frustration around status, rather than anomie resulting from economic deprivation, are the key to understanding juvenile delinquency (Newburn 2007). Cohen's argument is that American society is dominated by middle-class values and norms which are passed on through the education system and mass media. He looks to the education system in particular for his explanation of delinquency. Schools emphasize and embody middle-class values and so working-class boys (he focused on males) are ill equipped to compete with middle-class boys, or 'college boys', and to gain status through education. Such working-class boys, or 'corner boys' as Cohen called them, suffer status frustration at school and respond by attempting to turn the middle-class value system on its head. Anything the school disapproves of the corner boy will see as good, with delinquency seen as a direct denial of middle-class values. Working-class, corner boys reject the values of the school and form groups which emphasize different, essentially delinquent, values – they form what Cohen defined as a delinquent subculture. Faced with status frustration, the 'delinquent boy' joins with others in a similar position. Cohen focused on the delinquency found amongst juvenile gangs; he saw the gang as inverting traditional values and creating an alternative arena within which status could be gained (as Newburn, 2007, points out this is closest to Merton's rebellion adaptation, see p. 111).

BOX 4.1 THE DELINQUENT SUBCULTURE

At the start of *Delinquent Boys*, Cohen provides his definition of the term delinquent subculture, before going on to offer a sociological explanation for how this sub-culture is central to the occurrence of delinquency. Cohen's definition is provided below.

The expression 'the delinquent subculture', may be new to some readers of this volume. The idea for which it stands, however, is a commonplace of folk – as well as scientific – thinking. When Mrs Jones says: 'My Johnny is really a good boy but got to running around with the wrong bunch and got into trouble', she is making a set of assumptions which, when spelled out explicitly, constitute the foundations of an important school of thought in the scientific study of juvenile delinquency. She is affirming that delinquency is neither an inborn disposition nor something the child has contrived by himself; that children learn to become delinquents by becoming members of groups in which delinquent conduct is already established and the 'thing to do'; and that a child need not be 'different' from other children, that he need not have any twists or defects of personality or intelligence, in order to become a delinquent.

In the language of contemporary sociology, she is saying that juvenile delinquency is a subculture . . .

When we speak of a delinquent subculture, we speak of a way of life that has somehow become traditional among certain groups in American society. These groups are the boys' gangs that flourish most conspicuously in the 'delinquent neighbourhoods' of our large American cities. The members of these gangs grow up, some to become law-abiding citizens and others to graduate to more professional and adult forms of criminality, but the delinquent tradition is kept alive by the age-groups that succeed them . . .

Delinquency, according to this view, is not an expression or contrivance of a particular kind of personality; it may be imposed upon any kind of personality if circumstances favour intimate association with delinquent models. The process of becoming a delinquent is the same as the process of becoming, let us say, a Boy Scout. The difference lies only in the cultural pattern with which the children associates.

(Cohen 1955: 11–14)

- What specific social factors do you think would predispose certain individuals to join delinquent subcultures?
- What problems can you think of with explaining delinquent behaviour as a collective, subcultural response?

The stress on delinquency as a collective response is a key aspect of Cohen's sociological theorizing. In contrast to Merton's argument, such behaviour is not an individual response to a failure to achieve middle-class goals. However his approach can be criticized along the same lines as Merton's for its middle-class bias – he assumes that working-class delinquents cherish middle-class status goals such as doing well educationally. Furthermore, the extent to which working-class delinquents do really hold anti-middle-class, oppositional values is certainly debatable. As Tierney (2010) puts it:

> Cohen's theory of delinquency is based upon the assumption that the typical working class delinquent to some degree internalizes middle class norms and values prior to the creation of the subculture . . . the assumption is that middle class culture is widely dispersed and accepted throughout all social classes.
>
> (Tierney 2010: 112)

Both Cohen and Merton see criminal behaviour as resulting from the strains that occur due to the inequality of opportunity that is inherent to modern (in their case American) society. This implies that equality of opportunity would be desirable and have an impact on the extent of criminal behaviour. Tierney points to a basic contradiction in such an approach in that equality of opportunity to succeed implies an equality of opportunity to fail – 'the concept of equality of opportunity presupposes the existence of social class inequality'. And, as we have seen, the structural and subcultural theories of Merton and Cohen see criminal behaviour as an inevitable response to such inequality.

Other theorists have developed variations of subcultural theorizing about criminal behaviour and we will mention some of this work here. Walter Miller (1958), writing a few years after Cohen, suggested that working-class culture (or 'lower class culture' as he put it) was characterized by certain 'focal concerns' and that these concerns – such as toughness, smartness and excitement – encouraged aggressive and often delinquent and criminal behaviour. So just being working- rather than middle-class would predispose individuals towards criminality, with the delinquent subculture seen as one sort of response to working-class life.

A more detailed analysis of delinquent subcultures was offered by Cloward and Ohlin (1960). Cohen had focused on educational failure, whereas Cloward and Ohlin followed Merton's argument in highlighting the anomie that results from the lack of opportunities available to young working class males. They also borrowed from Sutherland's work on differential association (see pp. 120–121) and Cohen's emphasis on the collective, gang response by focusing on how such individuals will find and join up with others facing the same situation as themselves. Cloward and Ohlin argued that an illegitimate opportunity structure (as well as a legitimate one) exists, and that some have greater access to this than others. They then consider different 'illegitimate avenues' for achieving success. They suggest that the potential delinquent may respond to his situation by joining one of three distinct types of subculture – a criminal subculture where delinquency is linked with adult criminality and gangs work essentially for financial gain; a conflict subculture which occurs in areas where links between juvenile and adult criminality are not established and where the main form of crime is likely to be violence; and a retreatist or escapist subculture based around illegal drug use and attracting those who have failed to gain access to either legitimate or criminal (illegitimate) subcultures.

Again a range of criticisms have been levelled at these early American subcultural theories. The sort of delinquent offenders they portray are seen as somehow different from non-offenders and who have been forced into delinquency by circumstances almost beyond their control. Such an explanation seems to ignore the fact that the majority of young males faced with similar situations do not join delinquent gangs. Also, the very notion of offending in gangs is questionable – a lot of juvenile offending is a solitary activity or involves only a small number of individuals. Subcultural theories focus on young offenders reacting against middle-class society and the norms associated with it; however, they offer no explanation as to why such young offenders stop offending as they become older. Most people remain in the same social class after they reach adulthood and are still likely to experience the same lack of 'success'. This raises the question of why their behaviour changes away from delinquency, although, of course, other factors such as increased responsibilities are likely to play a part. Other criticisms include the lack of reference to the role of the authorities, such as the police, in labelling individuals as offenders (see below on labelling) and the assumption that juvenile offending is the preserve of young working-class males with no explanation offered for the offending of young females or of middle-class criminality. In evaluating these theories, Williams (2004) highlights Box's (1981) argument that they suffer from a basic implausibility in that 'lower', working-class boys are seen as being frustrated they cannot attain middle-class goals while also seeming to argue that such boys do not really aspire to such goals anyway. It might be that those boys who just miss out on middle-class goals (rather than those who are miles away from them!) will suffer a greater disappointment and frustration.

CONTROL THEORY – TRAVIS HIRSCHI

The explanations looked at so far have argued that conformity is normal behaviour and criminal behaviour is abnormal in some way; and that it follows that there must be something different, even abnormal, with those individuals who do commit crimes. These differences or abnormalities may be the result of biological, psychological or social factors; but some factor must be present in the individual which encourages their nonconformity.

The central argument of what have become termed control theories is that crime is natural and conformity is the area that requires explanation. As Newburn puts it,

> control theory tends to assume that human conduct is driven by desires and needs and that, therefore, we are all drive to deviance. Social order is maintained by bringing such desires under control. The central concern of control theory is conformity rather than deviance.
>
> (Newburn 2007: 228)

In her introduction to control theories, Williams (2004) suggests that conformist behaviour is the result of particular circumstances and criminal behaviour occurs when those circumstances change or break down. For instance it is not natural to form orderly queues when waiting for tickets yet most people will do so. Indeed throughout our lives, and particularly while growing up, we are learning what behaviour is acceptable and what is not. As Williams puts it, 'Parents at home, teachers at school and other individuals in the community . . . spend a lot of time and effort in controlling each of us'. She sees the essence of control theories as offering explanations for why people conform to rules and accept the social order as it is. Criminal behaviour is, then, the breakdown of the socialization process.

From this brief introduction control theories could be seen to cover a very broad range of explanations; indeed most sociological theorizing, from Durkheim's approach onwards, could be said to include notions of socialization and control. However, this area of theorizing is often connected with the more recent work of Hirschi who, along with Gottfredson in his earlier work, focused on the individual rather than external aspects of control, developing what has been termed a 'social bond' version of control theory. They focused on self-control based on early socialization, and especially on the role of the family. Williams cites two key aspects to their approach – the lack of self-control in an individual and the opportunities for committing crime: 'If the opportunity to commit a crime arises then the person with low self-control will commit it, whereas the person with high self-control will not.' Essentially self-control refers to the degree to which an individual is vulnerable to temptations.

They key issue that Hirschi tries to address is that of why (the majority of) people choose to follow the law. Indeed in his initial, classic study he comments, 'The question "Why do they do it?" is simply not the question the theory is designed to answer. The question is, "Why don't they do it?" (1969). His original argument was that those people who break laws do not have close attachments to others or have aims, aspirations and beliefs that bind them towards law-abiding behaviour. So young people who engage in delinquency do so because they are not strongly tied to the conventional social order – they have less self-control. As Hirschi and Gottfredson put it:

> The theory [of self control] simply stated, is this: Criminal acts are a subset of acts in which the actor ignores the long-term negative consequences that flow from the act itself (e.g. the health consequences of drug use), from the social or familial environment (e.g. a spouse's reaction to infidelity), or from the state (e.g. the criminal justice response to robbery). All acts that share this feature, including criminal acts, are therefore likely to be engaged in by individuals unusually sensitive to immediate pleasure and insensitive to long-term consequences . . . The evidence suggests to us that variation in self-control is established early in life, and that differences between individuals remain reasonably constant over the life course.
>
> (Hirschi and Gottfredson 1994: 151)

In suggesting that law-breaking, rather than law-abiding, behaviour is natural, Hirschi is not restating the 'classical' theoretical position that crime is an expression of free will – people are not born wicked or 'criminal'. However, at birth children do not know what is acceptable and not acceptable and follow their natural desires until they are socialized into the activities of their own community. Socialization is seen as the process by which individuals learn about and consider the consequences of their behaviour. Once they have learnt and accepted this, there is little need for further reinforcement. As suggested above, the key issue or mystery then is how some people are able to ignore the consequences of their behaviour and carry on as if such consequences do not exist. It is very easy for people to steal, for instance, yet self-control will stop the majority of people from doing so. Hirschi also suggests that people are neither permanently law abiding nor law breaking – they may take part in criminal activities at certain periods while following a law-abiding lifestyle at others, depending on the controls that are affecting their lives at particular times.

Williams (2004) highlights four elements that Hirschi sees as vital 'social bonds' that are associated with law-abiding people as 'their attachments with other people; the commitments and responsibilities they develop; their involvement in conventional activity; and their beliefs'. To elaborate on these elements:

Attachments – with other people and institutions in the community. Strong social and psychological attachments make criminal behaviour less likely as they make individuals more aware of and sensitive to the opinions of other people. (Hirschi is aware that strong attachments to criminal groups would have the opposite effect and encourage criminal behaviour).

Commitment – the more an individual has 'invested' in partners, children, education, occupation, property ownership and so on the less likely will she or he risk losing it through law-breaking behaviour. Individuals who do not consider such commitments important or who have less of them are seen as relatively freer to commit criminal acts.

Involvement – refers to the extent that the individual is involved in their legitimate lifestyle/activity; the range of conventional interests they have and pursue. Crime is less likely if being involved in conventional activities is an important part of the individual's life.

Beliefs – in this context Hirschi is referring to things an individual chooses to accept, including the law, rather than deeply held convictions. As these beliefs can be changed (by the individual accepting different arguments, for instance) they need constant social reinforcement.

The presence of each of these elements is seen by Hirschi as helping to prevent criminal behaviour and encourage lawful behaviour.

This theoretical position can be criticized for its generality and vagueness. Socialization is a vast concept and the question is still left as to whether socialization affects some people differently or whether they are differently socialized. It is almost like arguing that one's whole upbringing – interacting with inherited traits – will make the person what she or he is. In similar vein the theory has been criticized for being tautological; it starts from a conception of crime (as acts in which people ignore the consequences of the behaviour) and derives a conception of the offender from this (a person who ignores the consequences of their acts). However, Hirschi and Gottfredson see this as a positive element of their theorizing:

> What distinguishes our theory from many criminological theories is that we begin with the act, whereas they normally begin with the actor. Theories that start from

the causes of crime – for example, economic deprivation – eventually define crime as a response to the causes they invoke. Thus, a theory that sees economic deprivation as the cause of crime will by definition see crime as an attempt to remedy economic deprivation, making the connection between cause and effect tautological.

What makes our theory peculiarly vulnerable to complaints about tautology is that we explicitly show the logical connections between our conception of the actor and the act, whereas many theories leave this task to those interpreting or testing their theory, but again we are not impressed that we are unusual in this regard . . .

In a comparative framework, the charge of tautology suggests that a theory that is nontautological would be preferable. But what would such a theory look like? It would advance definitions of crime and of criminals that are independent of one another.

(Hirschi and Gottfredson 1994: 156)

Control theories have also been criticized for not offering any explanation as to the basis for weak attachment to social bonds or for low levels of belief, two of the key elements of Hirschi's argument. Nor does this approach explain why one form of deviant or criminal behaviour, rather than another, occurs.

In spite of criticisms, Hirschi's central argument that those who engage in crime and delinquency feel cut off from typical societal bonds has been widely and generally accepted.

THE CRIMINAL AS 'NORMAL' – DAVID MATZA

As suggested in introducing social control theories above, most of the theorists looked at so far have examined how criminal behaviour is a response to particular social circumstances and have stressed how, in responding to those circumstances, criminals become distinct from the mainstream, non-criminal population. We will now turn to theoretical explanations which see the criminal as 'normal' and focus on how society defines certain individuals or groups as criminal. These explanations stem from a critique of what is seen as the determinism of structural and subcultural theories. In developing this critique the work of David Matza was of particular importance. While Matza would not have seen himself as a 'control theorist', his approach and arguments did straddle theories of control and anomie and aspects of labelling theory (see p. 122).

The notion of a delinquent subculture implies that working-class adolescents are committed to certain delinquent values. However, Matza points out that delinquents generally conform to certain traditions and values of society and reject others; they are not very different from 'us'. They are not in opposition to or conflict with all aspects of the wider society – indeed they may often be quite conservative in their social and political views. Furthermore, most juvenile delinquents do not engage full-time in delinquent activity and 'give it up' in early adulthood – there are relatively few delinquents aged over 30. In Matza's view, adolescents from time to time act out delinquent roles, rather than becoming committed to permanent violation of the rules of conventional society. He argued that they drift into and out of delinquent activities rather than embracing them as a way of life. His approach is illustrated by the title of one of his major studies, *Delinquency and Drift*.

Matza accepted that adolescents can be part of subcultures whose members do engage in delinquency but did not see such behaviour as a permanent way of life. Indeed he pointed out that individuals could be part of a 'subculture of delinquency' without actually taking part in offending behaviour. As with other explanatory approaches which have criticized 'deterministic' theories of crime, Matza saw the process of becoming an offender in terms of stages. The first stage involves some form of opposition to mainstream values and culture and a desire to be accepted as a member of a group – this is likely to involve some form of criminal or rule-breaking behaviour as a means of gaining acceptance. The second stage comes after these original anxieties about acceptance have been overcome and involves a release from conventional forms of social control which allows the individual to choose to drift into delinquency. During this stage the individual has to adopt what Matza termed 'techniques of neutralization'. He identified five major types of neutralization – a typology that has become established in sociological theorizing about crime:

- The denial of responsibility ('I didn't mean to do it');
- The denial of injury ('I didn't hurt anyone');
- The denial of the victim ('S/he deserved it');
- The condemnation of the condemners ('They're just as bad');
- The appeal to higher loyalties ('I was helping my mates').

While such techniques are basically excuses, Matza argued that they also provide individuals with 'episodic release' from general moral and social constraints and enable the drift into delinquency.

The third stage is when the individual has drifted into delinquency. Such behaviour has been justified and this leads to the acceptance of responsibility for their delinquent and offending behaviour. As Burke (2005: 113) describes it: 'They *know* their activities are against the law. They *know* that they may be caught. They *know* that they may be punished. They probably accept that they *should* be punished. It is one of the rules of the game' (p. 121 – emphasis in the original). As an aside, Burke (2005: 113) highlights how Matza's theorizing has been applied to the study of business crime, where corporate offenders use the same techniques of neutralization to rationalize their illegal behaviour and assuage any feelings of guilt.

QUESTION BREAK

Matza suggests that there are three stages in becoming an offender: (a) opposition; (b) neutralization; and (c) fully accepting their criminality.

Consider how those who engage in the following crimes might fit in with these three stages:

- Robbery
- Terrorism
- Fraud

You might also consider a range of other criminal behaviour and relate it to Matza's argument.

DIFFERENTIAL ASSOCIATION – EDWIN SUTHERLAND

The process of drift and the notion of stages in becoming a delinquent are central to the labelling perspectives on crime that came to dominate sociological theorizing in the 1960s and 1970s which we will consider below. Before doing so it would be useful to refer back to the social learning approach to explaining crime discussed as an example of psychological theorizing (p. 67). Indeed, this highlights the difficulties of dividing theoretical approaches into neat categories – while useful for organizing a textbook it does not acknowledge the overlap and blurring between different approaches. The idea of learning to become an offender was central to the concept of differential association developed by Edwin Sutherland. Differential association explains criminal behaviour in terms of the contact, or association, with particular social groups and environments. It moves away from early theorizing that centred on the individual characteristics of offenders. Sutherland was one of a group of social scientists based at the University of Chicago in the 1920s and 1930s who challenged the individualistic explanations for crime (see pp. 106–108).

Sutherland argued that crime was socially defined by powerful sections of society, but he did not lose sight of the individual and how particular individuals were drawn into crime. He felt that criminal behaviour was learned just as any form of behaviour is. This led to the question of *how* criminal behaviour is learned, which Sutherland answered in terms of differential association; individuals have differential associations with other people who are either more or less disposed to criminality. So, from the different groups people associate with they will learn to deviate from or conform to society's norms. Sutherland's theory is a little more sophisticated than that, in that the different groups people associate with give messages about conformity and deviance. These messages may be mixed but there ends up being a sort of imbalance which leans to or favours one direction or the other – deviance or conformity. Individuals who are exposed to more messages and ideas that promote law-breaking, rather than those that act as barriers to law-breaking, are highly likely to turn to deviant and criminal behaviour. The essence of this approach is that criminal behaviour is learned; the learning occurs through association with other people; learning includes ways and means for carrying out crimes; and so the process involved in learning criminal behaviour is no different from that involved in learning any other type of behaviour. It can be seen from this brief account that Sutherland's theory is both sociological, in its acknowledgement of the power of social forces to define crime, and psychological, with its concern for the individual. And, as with Matza's work, Sutherland applied his theory of differential association to business crime or crimes of the powerful. He argued that white-collar and business crime should also be seen as a normal aspect of business life, and that both white-collar and organized, 'conventional' criminals use similar techniques and hold broadly similar values, in spite of their varying backgrounds.

This emphasis on interactions indicates the influence of the notion of differential association on the labelling explanations that developed from the interactionist (sometimes known as symbolic interactionist) perspective within sociology. The major interactionist theorists were influenced by the Edwin Sutherland, the social psychologist George Herbert Mead and others from the 'Chicago School'. They focused on the key role of meanings in social life and the socially constructed nature of reality – they paid particular attention to the ways that individuals create their world, rather than being just products of it. Social reality, from this approach, is constructed through the interpretation of the meaning of actions (interactions).

INTERACTIONIST THEORIES

Partly in response to some of the problems associated with the structural and sub-cultural theories, a different theoretical approach was developed by the interactionist perspective that became particularly influential in sociology in the 1960s and 1970s. Rather than seeing crime and deviant behaviour as a response of people to their social situation – and a response which established them as distinct from the mainstream, 'normal' population – the interactionist position was that the criminal or deviant can be quite normal. The emphasis, therefore, should be on how society defines certain individuals and groups as criminal or deviant; and the social reaction such individuals and groups engender. As can be seen from this introductory paragraph, interactionists refer to both crime and deviance, and the terms are quite often used interchangeably. Essentially, crime can be defined as action that breaks the criminal law and can be followed by criminal proceedings, while deviance is not used in its literal sense (as anything that is different or deviates from the normal) but taken to refer to any behaviour that is outside the rules of society and that is generally disapproved of. These rules might be legal rules, such as laws, or social and moral rules, such as conventional rules about how people should behave in public, for instance. Below we will usually refer to crime and criminal behaviour when intro-ducing labelling theory.

A major criticism of the earlier theories of crime, from both outside of and within sociology, was their tendency to see such behaviour as relatively straightforward and easily recognizable – as behaviour that breaks the law. Such approaches imply that a general consensus exists within society as to what is right and wrong behaviour. Interactionist work questions this assumption. Numerous studies, plus our common-sense understanding, tell us that most people have broken the law, and that many people do so frequently without ever being recorded as criminals. Given this, it becomes difficult to argue that criminals are somehow different from the rest of society.

QUESTION BREAK

Which of the following crimes have you committed? How often have you done so?

- Taking stationery or similar from the workplace
- Keeping money if you received too much in change
- Keeping money found in the street
- Buying goods that may have been stolen
- Stealing from a shop
- Drinking in a pub while under age
- Taking illegal drugs
- Using a TV without a licence
- Taking 'souvenirs' from a hotel, pub or similar

All of these actions break the criminal law. What would stop you committing those actions?

Labelling

Labelling theory is perhaps the key element of interactionist theorizing on crime and deviance. The focus is on the relationship, or interaction, between the criminal and those groups or individuals who define him or her as such. Essentially, the argument is that the criminal or deviant is an individual who has been labelled by society. The approach is associated with the work of a number of post-Second-World-War American sociologists. Perhaps the most famous and quoted statement defining the labelling approach is found in Howard Becker's collection of essays *Outsiders*:

> Social groups create deviance by making rules whose infraction constitutes deviance and by applying those rules to particular people and labelling them as outsiders. From this point of view deviance is not a quality of the act a person commits, but rather a consequence of the application by others of rules and sanctions to an offender. The deviant is one to whom that label has been successfully applied; deviant behaviour is behaviour that people so label.
>
> (Becker 1963: 9)

This comment indicates that labelling is a process by which individuals and/or groups classify and categorize certain types of behaviour and certain individuals. The focus on labelling raises the obvious question of 'who does the labelling?', with the actions and motives of the labellers being a key concern. Indeed consideration of the labellers highlights issues of who has the power to impose their definitions on others and of the extent to which there is a selective enforcement of the law, a concern articulated by Giddens:

The labels applied to create categories of deviance thus express the power structure of society. By and large, the rules in terms of which deviance is defined, and the contexts in which they are applied, are framed by the wealthy for the poor, by men for women, by older people for younger people and by ethnic majorities for minority groups.

(Giddens 1993: 128)

Becker's famous study included an examination of marijuana users in the USA in the early 1960s in which he describes and explores the notion of the 'criminal career' of marijuana users. This career consists of three main stages – the beginner, using for the first time, the occasional user and the regular user. His study is based on interviews with drug users based on his contacts in the music business (Becker had himself been a professional musician). Becker outlines the steps by which an individual becomes a regular user: learning the technique, learning to perceive the effects and learning to enjoy the effects. However, 'learning to enjoy marijuana is a necessary but not a sufficient condition for a person to develop a stable pattern of drug use' (Becker 1963: 59). The forces of social control still have to be dealt with. These forces include control of supply and access; control through the need to keep the drug use secret; and the control through conventional notions of morality. Of course, Becker's study was conducted over 40 years ago and attitudes to drug use have changed since then; nonetheless his model provides a classic illustration of labelling theory and its application to the study of crime and deviance.

Selective enforcement of the law

Laws and rules are seen as essentially political products that reflect the power some groups in society have; a power which enables them to impose their ideas about right and wrong on the rest of society. Of course it might be pointed out that the criminal law applies to everyone in society, including the rich and powerful, but interactionists would argue that those laws are less frequently and less vigorously applied to some groups and some individuals rather than others.

In his study of the administration of juvenile justice in the USA, Cicourel (1976) looked at the actual process of how delinquency and criminality are defined and applied to certain individuals and groups. His study followed a cohort of juveniles 'from their first contact with the police through their disposition by probation officials or juvenile court'. Essentially, Cicourel found that white, middle-class youths were less liable to be identified by the police and probation officers as having committed or being likely to commit a crime. The police were more likely to react toward those groups and individuals whom they saw as being prone to criminal activity, often labelling them before they actually committed any criminal action. The police, like most people, were seen as having stereotypical views as to the 'typical' criminal or delinquent. In the procedures of arresting and charging individuals and in their treatment in court, Cicourel found clear differences across the middle/working-class divide; and these serve to reinforce the public's (and police's) perception that certain groups are inclined to criminality. For instance he found that probation officers and social workers believed that delinquent behaviour was caused by factors such as 'broken homes', 'poor parenting' or 'poverty' and so juveniles who were seen as coming from such backgrounds 'were seen as the likeliest candidates for a delinquent career and were often, albeit unwittingly, launched upon one' (Burke 2005: 146). In contrasting the treatment of juveniles from different class backgrounds, Cicourel's research included case studies of youths from middle-class backgrounds who had been involved in 'juvenile offences'. In these situations, he found that both law-enforcement officers and family members managed to preserve ideal images of the family unit. The following quote illustrates this differential reaction to young middle-class offenders and Cicourel's argument that certain groups are selected, processed and labelled as criminals:

> When parents challenge police and probation imputations of deviance, when parents can mobilize favourable occupational and household appearances . . . law-enforcement personnel find it difficult (because of their own commitments to appearances – lack of a broken home, 'reasonable' parents, 'nice' neighbourhoods etc.) to make a case from criminality in direct confrontation with family resources and a 'rosy' projected future. Imputations of illness replace those of criminality, or the incidents are viewed as 'bad' but products of 'things' done by 'kids' today.
>
> (Cicourel 1976: 243)

QUESTION BREAK

Cicourel's research on selective law enforcement was conducted over 30 years ago.

- Give more recent examples of how the police and others who work in the criminal justice system might stereotype different individuals and groups.
- What sort of groups and individuals are most likely to 'suffer' from such stereotyping? Why is this?

Consequences of labelling

We have not got the space here to consider the various examples of labelling theorizing; however, in terms of the consequences of labelling for the individual it would be useful to refer to Lemert's conceptualization of primary and secondary deviance and to the notion of deviance amplification. In an early and pioneering work on the labelling of deviant behaviour, Lemert (1951) posed a theoretical distinction between primary and secondary deviation. As he put it in a later paper, he devised this distinction to highlight 'how deviant behaviour originates . . . (and) how deviant acts are symbolically attached to persons and the effective consequences of such attachment for subsequent deviation on the part of the person' (1967: 17). Primary deviance (although Lemert used the term deviation) refers to the initial act, and can be of a very tentative nature and occur in a wide variety of contexts. As such the initial act has only 'marginal implications for the psychic structure of the individual'. As Burke (2005) puts it, 'in short, primary deviants do not view their deviance as central to themselves and do not conceive of themselves as deviants.' It is the social reaction to the primary deviance that can lead to the offender becoming labelled as a criminal or deviant of some sort. In this situation the individual offender is faced with a crisis which, for some, can be resolved by accepting a deviant status and by becoming a secondary deviant, which will lead him or her to 'organise their life and identity around the facts of deviance' (Burke 2005). To use Lemert's own words:

> Secondary deviation is deviant behaviour, or social roles based upon it, which becomes means of defense, attack or adaptation to the overt and covert problems created by the social reaction to primary deviation. In effect the original 'causes' of the deviation recede and give way to the central importance of the disapproving, degradational and isolating reactions of society.
>
> (Lemert 1964: 17)

Lemert sees the distinction between primary and secondary deviation as a key factor in trying to develop a complete understanding of such behaviour. Crime and deviance are seen as the end products of a process of human interaction; primary deviance may or may not develop into secondary deviance depending on the extent and strength of the reaction that it engenders.

> A sociological theory of deviant behaviour must focus specifically on the inter-actions which not only define the behaviour as deviant but also organise and activate the application of sanctions by individuals, groups and agencies. For in modern society the socially significant differentiation of deviants from non-deviants is increasingly contingent upon circumstances of situation, place, social and personal biography and bureaucratically organized agencies of social control.
>
> (ibid.: 17–18)

It is important to bear in mind that the great majority of criminal and deviant acts are never known about or reported and many people who commit such acts may be able to resist ever being labelled for their behaviours. This is why secondary deviation is such a key concept, as Rock (2007) puts it:

> What is significant about secondary deviation is that it may be a symbolic synthesis of more than just the meanings and activities of primary deviation. It may also incorporate the myths, professional knowledge, stereotypes, experience, and working assumptions of lay people, police officers, judges, medical practitioners, prison officers, prisoners, policy makers and politicians.
>
> (Rock 2007: 30)

In terms of what happens to the individual once she or he is labelled as a criminal or deviant, the process by and extent to which the label becomes fixed (its degree of permanence perhaps) is important to consider. Labelling an individual will mark them out and knowing a person has been labelled will be liable to influence the behaviour of other people towards them. Knowing someone has been convicted of theft, for example, might well influence how other people react and respond – keeping a closer eye on their possessions perhaps! Furthermore, the individual who has been labelled will be likely to view him or herself in terms of the label and act accordingly. This leads to what is know as the process of amplification or snowballing – an individual is caught and labelled a criminal, s/he sees her/himself so and acts in that way; as a result the label becomes more widely applied and firmly fixed and the individual more attached to it.

This amplification process can occur on a wider, societal level, as well as at an individual level. Jock Young's work on hippies and the police in London during the 1960s and 1970s illustrated this wider application. Young (1971) found that the harder the police tried to stamp out drug use amongst hippies the more it actually grew. He suggested that the police themselves acted as amplifiers of this illegal behaviour. The police attempted to control drug use through the formation of drug squads; however, this had the effect of spreading and amplifying such drug use. The drug squads discovered more cases of drug use because that was what they were searching for; this led to more police time and money being invested in dealing with it; this led to even more drug use being discovered – in other words there was a 'spiral of amplification'. Furthermore, Young argued that the way in which the police acted against hippies, stereotyping them as dirty, idle, drug fiends and harassing them, helped to unite drug users and led to the development of a sort of group identity and ethos, 'drug taking becomes of greater value to the group as a result of the greater police activity'.

A clear consequence of the labelling process is that once a person is publicly identified as a criminal, once they become 'secondary deviants', it becomes much more difficult for him or her to return, to 'slip back into the conventional world' (Rock 2007). This can be exacerbated by the demand for public recognition of criminals – 'Megan's Law' in the United States requires the names of sex offenders to be publicly advertised, which, although meant to reduce the risk to children, will clearly establish the offender as a secondary deviant. The publicizing of offenders can be related to the idea of 'naming and shaming', which, under the title of 'reintegrative shaming' has been an important new idea in recent criminal justice policy across the Western world. In the United States, in Phoenix, Arizona, for instance, convicted drunk drivers have to wear pink uniforms when undertaking community service such as picking up trash.

John Braithwaite has been the key figure in advocating reintegrative shaming as part of criminal justice policy, and of restorative justice particularly. Braithwaite (1989) suggests that shaming an offender can, in certain contexts, produce a response which enables him or her to become a law-abiding citizen. Newburn (2007) sees this approach and argument as a 'potentially positive version of labelling processes' and as underpinning much of the work on restorative justice (we look at restorative justice in relation to the philosophies of punishment in Chapter 7, pp. 242–243).

The interactionist approach to explaining crime implies that for the purpose of studying such behaviour there is a correlation between being a criminal and being seen to be a criminal. It makes no real difference whether the 'criminal' is innocent or guilty – for the purpose of theoretical explanation such a distinction is essentially irrelevant. In other words, being found guilty has the same consequences for the individual(s) as being guilty. Now of course common-sense would tell us that there is a significant difference between a murderer or bank robber and someone who has been wrongfully convicted of murder or bank robbery. And it could be argued that there is a clear moral and philosophical difference between the 'innocent' and the 'guilty' criminal. However, this difference is not likely to have any effect on the way in which the two 'criminals' are treated. The wrongfully convicted prisoner will be treated identically to any other prisoner by prison officers. Furthermore, protesting one's innocence will be viewed as the kind of thing that everyone does and will gain little sympathy – indeed it may annoy and antagonize prison staff.

So being convicted involves being identified publicly as a criminal and it is in this context that we can say that being found guilty is the same as really being guilty – in terms of how the individual is treated and responded to by others. Thus being known as a criminal is the same as being one. It is these arguments that led inter-actionists to stress how labelling is crucial to the understanding of criminal and deviant behaviour; the labelling process publicly identifies individuals as guilty of criminal acts and leads to the consequences we have considered above.

QUESTION BREAK

- What groups of people are most likely to be labelled as criminals? Why is this?
- How might protesting one's innocence make life more difficult for a prisoner?
- Look up examples of recent miscarriages of justice (examples could include Stephen Downing who served 27 years in prison for the 'Bakewell murder' before being freed in 2001; the Hickeys who were released from prison in 1997 having been convicted of the murder of Carl Bridgewater in 1978; or Sean Hodgson, jailed in 1982 for murdering barmaid Teresa De Simone and released in 2009 after fresh DNA evidence cleared him)
- What led to the uncovering of the miscarriage?
- Did the individual's protesting of his/her innocence have any effect?

BOX 4.2 LABELLING AND MENTAL ILLNESS

Of course the concept of labelling is not limited to criminal and deviant behaviour but occurs in all walks of life. For instance in schools and colleges teachers label pupils and pupils will also label teachers; and once a label is given it is difficult to lose it, for instance once a child is labelled as 'thick' or a 'troublemaker', or indeed positively as 'bright', he or she will tend to be responded to by others in terms of that label. At work bosses label their employees and vice versa, while workers will

continued

similarly label their colleagues in work. In the area of mental health, an area often examined as a form of deviance, the application of labels has been commonplace and a number of studies have examined the effects of this labelling. Such studies have looked at the labelling of particular forms of behaviour as mental illness at different periods of time to illustrate the extent and power of labelling as a process.

For instance, from 1952 until 1980 in the United States, homosexuality was listed and accepted as a mental disorder, and people identified as homosexuals were expected to go for treatment. It was on the Diagnostic and Statistical Manual of Mental Disorders list – the official list of mental disorders. And in the mid-nineteenth century women who expressed their frustrations through anger or crying were regularly classified as suffering from hysteria and confined to their beds for treatment. One particularly famous piece of research was carried out by Rosenhan in the early 1970s in the USA and reported in his paper 'On being insane in sane places'. He persuaded eight 'normal' people to try and gain admittance to psychiatric hospitals by claiming to hear voices in their heads. Once they had done this they behaved as they would usually, and although they tried to get discharged as soon as possible, it took them on average 19 days to be discharged (with one 'pseudo patient' being kept in for 52 days). Indeed their usual behaviours, such as writing notes, were diagnosed as 'exhibiting obsessive writing behaviour'. Clearly the hospital staff assumed the patients were mentally ill and responded to them as such, interpreting all of their behaviour as evidence of their illness.

INTERACTIONIST THEORIES – A BRIEF CRITIQUE

As mentioned above, interactionist theories of crime and deviance, centred around the notion of labelling, became particularly influential in the 1960s and 1970s. The focus on the meanings that such behaviour held for those engaged in it, and specifically the interaction between the criminal and agents of social control, seemed to offer a new direction for the sociology of crime and deviance. These developments attracted a good deal of debate and criticism as well; so much so that in 1973, ten years after the original publication, Howard Becker added an extra, final chapter to his famous study *Outsiders,* entitled 'Labelling Theory Reconsidered', in which he addressed some of the major concerns that had been raised about this perspective.

Labelling theory was criticized for implying that criminals were powerless and passive victims who have just had the misfortune to be labelled criminal and have not been able to do much about it. This seemed to ignore the fact that criminals might often choose to become so – people engage in fraud, smuggling and other crime because they want to. Too great an emphasis is given to the social reaction, thereby minimizing the role of the individual criminal or deviant. Linked with this, labelling theory has been seen as ignoring the origins of criminal behaviour; there is little explanation as to why certain people break laws and others do not. Criticisms, then, highlight what is seen as an over-emphasis on the social reaction and argue that there is no real explanation as to why some actions are made illegal, and of who makes the laws and why.

In 'Labelling Theory Reconsidered', Becker started by suggesting that the term 'labelling theory' was in itself inappropriate. His original work, and that of others, did not warrant being seen as a full-blown theory – a point which critics had, he argued, not recognized. His original position did not attempt to propose solutions as to the origin of criminal behaviour – the etiological question as he put it. Rather he and others had more modest aims: 'to enlarge the area taken into consideration in the study of deviant phenomena by including in it activities of others than the allegedly deviant actor' (p. 179), and 'labelling theory . . . is, rather, a way of looking at a general area of human activity; a perspective whose value will appear, if at all, in increased understanding of things formerly obscure' (p. 181).

He responded to the suggestions that the individual criminals were seen as powerless and passive victims by pointing out that 'the act of labelling . . . while important, cannot possibly be conceived as the sole explanation of what deviants actually do. It would be foolish to propose that stick-up men stick people up simply because someone has labelled them stick-up men' (p. 179). Also:

> To suggest that defining someone as deviant may under certain circumstances dispose him to a particular line of action is not the same as saying that mental hospitals always drive people crazy or that jails always turn people into habitual criminals.
>
> (Becker 1973: 180)

In summary, interactionist approaches concentrate on the specific 'drama' of crime without examining in depth the inequalities of power that underlie the defining and treating of criminal behaviour. It is these issues around decision-making and the distribution of power that are central to conflict and Marxist-based theories of crime which we look at below.

CONFLICT / MARXIST-BASED THEORIES

Marxist-based explanations of crime encompass a range of different approaches with different emphases and nuances, and which have been categorized under various headings including critical criminology, radical criminology, left realism and left idealism. Before introducing some of these developments we will consider the common core underpinning these theoretical explanations and diversions.

Neither Marx nor his collaborator and colleague Engels proposed a full-blown theory of crime; and it has been later social theorists working within a Marxist framework who have developed a Marxist theory of crime. This work has centred on an examination of how crime relates to the power structure of society. From a Marxist perspective crime is largely the product of capitalism, and the relatively high rate of crime in capitalist societies is an indicator of the contradictions and problems that are inherent to such a system. Thus many forms of crime are to be expected under a capitalist system. This is due, in part, to the ability of the powerful to criminalize that which threatens their interests; and to the fact that basic motivations of capitalist societies, such as materialism and self-enrichment, can be pursued illegally as well as legally. In relation to crime one of the crucial questions for Marxists is not 'why does crime occur?' but rather 'why doesn't it occur more often?'

A Marxist analysis of crime cannot be considered in isolation from the broader Marxist analysis of society. In a key example of a Marxist-based, conflict perspective on crime, Quinney (1977) points out that, 'an understanding of crime in our society begins with the recognition that the crucial phenomenon to be considered is not crime *per se*, but the historical development and operation of capitalist society' (p. 39). He argues that understanding crime necessitates an examination of fundamental aspects of capitalism, such as alienation, inequality, poverty and the economic crisis of the capitalist state. In focusing on work, alienation and exploitation – key features of class struggle in the Marxist analysis – Quinney suggests that as work is a central life activity when it is thwarted 'the way is open for activity that is detrimental to self and others'. He goes on to argue that 'activity of a criminal nature becomes a rational and likely possibility under the conditions of capitalism' and that 'crime is a by-product of the political economy of capitalism'.

Later on in his study Quinney (1977) responds to the functional argument of Durkheim that crime is necessary and inevitable. The fact that many people are employed in dealing with crime in one way or another merely demonstrates that crime is generated within the capitalist mode of production. However, even within capitalism this does not make crime functional, 'it results from the contradictions of capitalism, and it contributes further to these contradictions'.

As mentioned, Marxist explanations of crime cannot be considered apart from the broader Marxist analysis of society. This analysis holds that there is a basic distinction between the economic base of society, which determines the organization and structure of society, and the superstructure, the cultural, legal, religious and political aspects of society. These aspects of the superstructure support and reflect the economic base. Therefore, the law will be in line with and reflect the interests of the dominant economic class, and as an instrument of this dominant class, the state will pass laws which support its interests. The various social control agencies of the state, such as the police, courts and prisons, will also perform in a way that is consistent with the interests of the powerful and against the interests of other less powerful groups, particularly the working classes.

So the criminal law is assumed to express and reflect the interests of the powerful. As evidence for this Marxists point out that much of the law is about the protection of property, and highlight the vast increase in the range of behaviour that has become subject to criminal law in capitalist societies. In their introduction to *Critical Criminology*, a key text in the development of Marxist, critical criminology, Taylor, Walton and Young (1975) point out that old laws have been reactivated and new ones created in order to control and contain an ever widening range of what is perceived as socially problematic behaviour. New laws that, for example, regulate industrial dissent and the right of workers to organize can create new criminals who do not fit the picture of the 'typical criminal' – the young working-class male. In view of this, Taylor and colleagues argue that criminological theorizing has to examine rule-making and breaking in relation to the distribution of power in society.

However, power in capitalist societies is not just about formal and institutionalized control and includes the ability to influence the way people think through controlling knowledge and ideas. Marxists argue that there is a dominant ideology from which the standards of acceptable and 'normal' behaviour, and as a consequence behaviour that is problematic and criminal, are defined. An illustration of this is the way in which the law, the media and public opinion would seem to view benefit frauds, 'fiddling the dole', as being more serious and costly than, say, tax evasion, which costs the Exchequer billions of pounds, far in excess of the costs of benefit fiddling. The notion that the law reflects economic interests and protects the dominant classes from threatening or disruptive behaviour, and indeed enables the powerful to get away with exploiting the less powerful without actually breaking the law, is highlighted in Marxist-based studies of white-collar and corporate crime.

Such studies have helped move the focus away from the powerless and marginalized in society. Frank Pearce (1976) has argued that organized crime in the USA is dominated by business; and that the criminal activities of American business corporations involved far more money than did conventional crime. In line with a Marxist argument, Pearce felt that such criminal activity was rarely prosecuted, as to do so would 'subvert the ideology that the bulk of crime is carried out by the poor, and would create a crisis of legitimacy for the capitalist system' (Tierney 2010). In similar vein, William Chambliss (1978), in a detailed study of crime in Seattle, Washington, demonstrated the interconnections between organized crime and the ruling groups in society. Of course the cost of crime is very difficult even to estimate, but a recent survey of 100 major British companies carried out by consultants RSM Robson Rhodes (2004) in conjunction with the Home Office and Fraud Advisory Panel concluded that economic crimes such as fraud and corruption were costing British business £40billion a year, equivalent to about 4 per cent of Britain's gross domestic product – and they suggested this could be just the tip of the iceberg.

Another key way in which the criminal law reflects the interests of the powerful is the assumption that the 'crime problem' refers to working-class crime, often of a relatively trivial nature, and not the more costly area of white-collar and business crime; and that the law is enforced selectively in the interests of the dominant and powerful groups. Put simply, the Marxist argument is that the law, by largely ignoring white-collar/business crime, gives the impression that criminals are mainly from the working classes; and that this serves to direct attention away from 'ruling-class crime'. Examples of the differential treatment of 'conventional' from business crime are provided in the question break below.

QUESTION BREAK

The following extracts describe the manner in which two different types of criminal activity – shoplifting and business fraud – and two different offenders were treated by the criminal justice system in the USA. The first refers to the case of Martha Stewart, celebrity 'lifestyle guru', who was convicted of four counts of conspiracy, obstruction of justice and lying to the government about the sale of shares worth £250,000 in December 2001 and jailed for 5 months in 2004. The second refers to the 'Three Strikes and You're Out Law' in the United States and some examples of the sentences consequent on it.

Martha Stewart starts prison term

Martha Stewart, the US lifestyle guru convicted of lying to federal investigators about a suspicious share sale . . . was sentenced to five months imprisonment in July, after being found guilty of conspiracy and obstruction. Her website revealed that she had started her prison term at a minimum-security jail in West Virginia on Friday. Stewart earned millions from a business empire based on selling domestic items and lifestyle advice . . .

Although she stepped down as chairwoman and chief executive of her firm, Martha Stewart Omnimedia, the domestic icon remains the biggest shareholder in the business. She is expected to resume working for the firm after her release from prison.

(From BBC News, Friday 8 October 2004 (www.news.bbc.co.uk))

'Three Strikes and You're Out'

As violent crime in the United States soared in the 1980s there was a public demand for the lawmakers to do something – the response was the 'three-strikes' law by which anyone convicted of a third felony received an automatic and mandatory (fixed) sentence – some of which were automatic life imprisonment. Felonies did not just mean violent crimes and led to some offenders receiving extremely severe sentences for relatively minor offences.

Below we list some of these cases, starting with a report in the *Guardian* concerning a shoplifter jailed for 25 years in California:

Buried alive under California's law of 'three strikes and you're out'

Brian A Smith didn't know the two women who were shoplifting. They were caught on security cameras stealing sheets at Los Cerritos mall in Los Angeles and received a two-year sentence. But Smith was seen standing near the shoplifters as they committed their crime. Despite having no stolen goods, he was convicted of aiding and abetting them. Under California's three strikes law, which marked its 10th anniversary on Sunday, the 30 year old received a 25-year-to-life sentence.

Smith's crime was to have two previous convictions, one 11 years earlier and the second six years before the shoplifting incident. Those convictions . . . earned him the dubious honour of being one of the first criminals to be sentenced under the California law . . .

Under the three strikes law, 25 years means 25 years: prisoners have no chance of parole. The law was voted for in March 1994, under California's proposition system, in which the electorate votes directly for specific policy initiatives. But unlike the three strikes laws operating in some other states, California's version does not restrict the initiative to violent crimes. Sixty-five per cent of those imprisoned under three strikes in California were convicted of non-violent crimes; 354 of them received 25-years-to-life sentences for petty theft of less than $250.

(From the *Guardian*, 8 March 2004)

Other cases include:

- In Los Angeles, a 27-year-old man who stole a pizza was sentenced to 25 years in prison;
- In Sacramento, a man passed himself off as Tiger Woods and went on a $17,000 shopping spree. He was sentenced to 200 years in prison.
- In California, Michael James passed a bad cheque for $94. He was sentenced to 25 years to life.

(From: Henslin, J. M. (2009) *Sociology: A Down-to-Earth Approach*)

- What factors do you think played a part in the treatment and sentencing of the two offenders?
- How might a Marxist/conflict theory of crime interpret the two extracts?

Strands of Marxist criminology – left realism and left idealism

As we have indicated, Marxist-based explanations do not constitute a unified perspective. In particular, and partly as a reaction to the new Marxist critical criminology of the 1970s, two different approaches or strands developed in the 1980s under the headings of left realism and left idealism.

Left realism developed as a criticism of the Marxist emphasis on crime as a response to class inequalities and to the patriarchal nature of advanced industrial societies – an approach designated by some as 'left idealism'. It is a realistic approach in that the reality of crime for ordinary working-class people is recognized. The fact that victims of crime are overwhelmingly from poor, working-class backgrounds, and that much crime is committed by the working class on the working class, is highlighted. The fear of crime is seen as based on the real experiences of people – as Tierney (2010) puts it, 'it is not the result of false consciousness created by media-induced moral panics'. Critical, 'left idealist' criminologists were seen as concentrating too much on crimes of the powerful and of underplaying the effects of crime carried out by working-class males – and indeed of having a somewhat romantic view of working-class crime as being a fight against the capitalist system. When the working classes reacted in a hostile manner to crime and criminals they were seen as being the victims of some form of false consciousness which turned working people against one another. The crime and criminals that should be focused on and highlighted were the crimes of the rich and powerful.

The left realist position was still 'left' in that it stressed the structural inequalities of class, race and gender in explaining and responding to crime. It involved examining all the basic components of crime – what one of the foremost proponents of this position, Jock Young, has termed the 'square of crime'. The square of crime includes four factors – the state, society, the offenders and the victims – and all need to be included in an analysis of all forms of crime and in any attempt to prevent and deal successfully with crime. This is summarized very clearly by Burke (2005):

> The square of crime is a reminder that crime is the result of a number of lines of force and that intervention to prevent it must therefore take place at different levels in order to be effective. Left realists propose that crime is a function of four factors. First, there is the state, principally through the capacity of its front-line agents to label individuals and groups as offenders. Second, there is the victim who may actually encourage offenders through inadequate defence or may even precipitate crime through his or her life-style or personality. Third, there is society, through which the various sources of social control are exercised. Fourth, there are the offenders themselves (their number, their rate of offending, the type of crime they commit etc) . . . Fundamentally, all crime prevention efforts, of whatever type, involve some relationship between the four corners of the square.
>
> (p. 224)

The belief that crime should be taken seriously led left realists to become involved in research and policy issues, including the development of local victimization studies which asked people directly about the crimes they were troubled by and their views on police effectiveness. Such surveys (for instance the Islington Crime Survey of 1986) highlighted the greater burden of crime on the poor and ethnic minorities. On a policy level, the Crime and Disorder Act of 1998 reflected the emphasis on community safety recommended by left realist theorists (Newburn 2007). Indeed, the need to intervene to do something about crime was a central concern of the left realist position. It stressed the importance of both 'social' and 'situational' crime prevention, supporting effective and practical policing and crime reduction strategies. As Young (1992) himself put it, 'the ultimate task is to make fundamental changes in the social order whilst at the same time intervening on a day-to-day basis to protect the public . . . the central problem is to remain committed to change without being merely utopian'.

Left idealism is often contrasted with left realism – indeed left realism was essentially a reaction to what was felt to be the tendency for Marxist criminologists to idealize and romanticize the working-class criminal and not take enough account of the effect of crime on working-class people and communities. However, a number of British criminologists (including Gilroy, Scraton, Sim and Gordon amongst others) did not accept this left realist argument. They felt that left realism over-simplified the idealist position. Left idealists supported practical action by community groups to change and reform the criminal justice system and supported those who questioned the way the criminal justice system operated. In Britain, they have supported and worked with groups involved in major political issues such as the Hillsborough disaster of 1989 and the inquiry into the death of Stephen Lawrence (Macpherson 1999).

FEMINIST CRIMINOLOGY

Other developments that can be seen as part of a more radical approach to explaining crime have come from feminist theorizing. Until the 1970s the study of crime had been a very male dominated area, but the work of Smart, Heidensohn and others has highlighted the neglect of women in the study of crime. In this section we will not look at the different rates of offending of men and women as this is considerd in more detail in Chapter 5; suffice it to say that however the data is produced, women are less involved in most sorts of criminal behaviour. Here we will provide a brief account of some feminist approaches to the study of crime.

There had been some well known (or perhaps infamous would be a better description) earlier explanations of female criminality. Lombroso, whose somewhat bizarre theories of crime and criminals were looked at earlier (see Chapter 2, pp. 26–27), in a famous study with Ferrero, published in 1885 and entitled *The Female Offender,* offered a physiological explanation for the low rate of female crime, arguing that the physical characteristics that were linked with criminality were much rarer amongst females than males. There were far fewer 'born female criminals'; and women committed far fewer crimes than men because they were less highly developed, and, being more 'primitive', they have less chance to degenerate. They argued that women were 'congenitally less inclined to crime than men' and that those women who did commit crime were not really feminine. Although largely discredited, the biological argument that women are naturally less inclined to crime and that female criminals are in some ways maladjusted has never been fully abandoned. In a variant of the biological explanation, in 1950 Pollak argued that female crime occurred to a much greater extent than crime statistics indicated but that it was much less likely to be detected, in part because of the naturally devious and cunning nature of women which enabled them to successfully conceal their crimes and avoid being caught. Partly as a consequence of what he argued was their mainly passive role in sex, women develop the knowledge and ability to deceive men; and he saw much male offending as being instigated or caused by women. These early biologically based explanations have been criticized by feminists and social scientists more generally. Without detailing these criticisms, it is basically insulting to suggest that the female personality is biologically determined in a way that makes women incapable of rational action.

The feminist explanations in the 1970s came as a relief from these early deterministic theories, with much of feminist criminology being a reaction to established, 'malestream' theorizing. Such explanations have been seen as part of a 'second wave' of feminism – the first having been at the turn of the nineteenth to the twentieth century, encompassing the move to universal suffrage. This second wave of feminism developed a comprehensive critique of the state of contemporary criminology based, according to Rock (2007) around on two themes; on the one hand, women account for a small proportion of offenders and so had received very little attention, and, secondly, when women offenders were considered it was only in a very stereotypical manner based around their supposed biological and psychological nature. Carol Smart's book *Women, Crime and Criminology,* published in 1976, was the first major example of British feminist criminology and highlighted both the neglect of women in the study of crime and the weaknesses, and sexism, of explanations that had included women. This was, according to Newburn (2007), 'the book that has perhaps had greatest impact on (feminist criminology), both in stimulating much of it, and in setting the parameters for many successive arguments'. Heidensohn, another noted British feminist and criminologist, considered why criminological research had been so male dominated. She pointed to the fact that 'the discipline has been dominated by men, which affected such things as access to male gangs, cultural assumptions about masculinity and femininity, and a fascination with the macho, working class deviant' (cited in Tierney 2010: 217). Although the female crime rate is lower than the male rate, explanations for male crime based around structural factors such as poverty, inner city life, the mass media and so on did not explain why females faced with similar experiences apparently committed less crime. Previous explanations centred on labelling or subcultural theories, for example, had little to say about female crime. As Smart (1976) put it, a feminist approach should 'situate the discussion of sex roles within a structural explanation of the social origin of those roles' and criminology has to be 'more than the study of men and crime'.

Since the pioneering work of Smart there have been studies that have looked at the link between structural factors, such as poverty, and female crime. Grover (2008) highlights research by Carlen (1988) and Phoenix (1999). Carlen examined 39 offenders and found some links between crime and material circumstances – 32 of her respondents had been 'poor' (according to standard definitions of poverty) all of their lives but only 12 of them felt their poverty caused their offending. Carlen found four main influences on the offending of her subjects. Poverty was one factor, with the others comprising: being in residential care; addictions; and the search for excitement. The other three factors might, though, relate to poverty; being in care is probably linked with living in deprived material circumstances. The same sorts of themes were apparent in Phoenix's examination of women who were criminalized for being involved in prostitution. Poor work and income opportunities for her 21 subjects were clearly linked to their involvement in prostitution. So feminist theorists have looked at and adapted some of the theories and argument forwarded to explain male criminality. There have been studies of female gangs and subcultures, such as Campbell (1993) and Chesney-Lind (1997), although much of the criminal behaviour examined consisted of fairly minor offences. More recently there has been a growing concern, bordering on a 'moral panic' at times, over girl gangs and their violent behaviour. However, Williams (2004) suggests much of the press reporting of this criminality is misleading and cites Batchelor's (2001) findings that in a survey of around 800 girls none were either in a gang or knew of any other girl who was.

As well as examining female crime and reasons for differing rates of crime between men and women, feminist approaches have also considered issues around criminal justice. These issues include the treatment of women offenders by the criminal justice system (the police, courts and prisons in particular) and the ways in which women working within the system have fared, with regard to working practices, careers and promotions for instance. As regards the treatment of women by the criminal justice system, research and explanations have tended to polarize around the views that women are treated more leniently than men or that they are treated more severely because, as women, they are less expected to commit crime. These contrary views have become referred to as the 'chivalry v. doubly deviant' debate. Just because far more men than women are convicted and the male prison population far outnumbers the female prison population does not necessarily mean women are treated more leniently than men. Lloyd (1995) in her study *Doubly Deviant, Doubly Damned* examined the chivalry argument that women offenders are treated more leniently than males. She found that while this was the case for some women it was not for all. In particular, lenience or chivalry from the police and the courts seemed to be limited to certain types of women. Women who did not conform to a stereotypical picture of how women should behave were treated more strictly and with less understanding than male offenders – they were seen as offending against the law and against conventional notions of 'good women'. Lloyd found that domesticity was a key factor affecting the sentencing of women criminals. The family role and being a good mother was often an important aspect of mitigation pleas and the judiciary seemed to be influenced by the impact of sentencing on children. So 'conventional women', married and mothers for instance, were treated with more lenience than others.

QUESTION BREAK

- What are the benefits for women offenders of being treated 'chivalrously'?
- What disadvantages might such treatment bring?
- List some arguments for and against motherhood affecting the sentencing of women offenders.

A further area where feminist criminology has been important is in highlighting the victimization of women. A major aspect of this area of feminist research has focused on women as victims of sexual crime and domestic violence and the massive under-reporting of such criminality. As Newburn (2007) points out, historically little attention had been given to crimes such as rape and domestic violence, with the private world of the family and what happened within it seen as just that, 'private'. It was only when feminist theorists and campaigners started to investigate such crimes that the victimization of women began to be taken seriously.

This brief overview has considered feminism as a unified approach; however, it is important to point out that feminism has a long history and just as there are variations of feminism in general, so there are different feminist approaches to the study of crime. Daly (1997) suggests two major approaches: one based on liberal theory and one on critical social theory. The former focuses on role differences between men and women and suggests women are denied the opportunities to do the same things as men, including taking part in crime. Critical social theory emphasizes gender power relations and focuses on how gender interacts with class and racial-ethnic differences.

As we have mentioned, these and other aspects of female crime and of feminist criminology are considered in greater depth in an examination of women and crime in Chapter 5.

RECENT DEVELOPMENTS – THE POSTMODERN INFLUENCE ON CRIME AND CRIMINAL JUSTICE

In this chapter we have looked at explanations for crime going back over 200 years. In concluding we will consider some of the recent and current areas of interest in theorizing about crime and consider their possible impact on criminological theorizing.

Changes in the social, political, cultural and economic arenas of life in the late twentieth century led theorists to suggest that Western societies in particular had reached a condition of 'post-modernity'. Some scholars have preferred to use terms such as late modernity or high modernity to describe the rapid transformations of recent years and have debated the extent to which there is a completely new post-modern world or whether there has just been a more rapid development of modernity. However, the different interpretations all highlight the myriad of new freedoms and associated new uncertainties that characterised late twentieth-century society. Some of the basic features of what has become known as postmodernism include a rejection of grand all-encompassing theories – meta-narratives, a consequent acknowledgement that there is no such thing as an absolute truth and an extolling of variety and differences within cultural forms including the media, architecture, art and literature. While modernity is seen as characterized by moral certainty and a belief in the ability of theories to explain problems facing humanity, post-modernity is characterized by moral ambiguity and an acknowledgement that there are a range of truths and discourses that can be legitimate and acceptable at different times and for different people. The influence of postmodernism's rejection of grand theory and the emphasis on diversity of explanations and on the role of the media in contemporary society have impacted on criminological theorizing.

BOX 4.3 GLOBALIZATION AND CRIME

As with postmodernism, globalization is a disputed term. In a limited sense it can be used to refer to the notion of a global economy and world financial markets. It can also be applied in a much broader manner to the blurring of the boundaries between nation states. As regards crime, it can be applied to the increasingly transnational character of organized crime. Technological developments in communication and transportation networks allow criminal operations to develop global networks and alliances. The old notion of crime being a local issue and problem is replaced with the need to understand 'the global contours of crime' (Burke 2005). However, Burke warns against over-romanticizing the past and points out that a good deal of crime in the past also relied on international markets and contacts – including slave and drug trading throughout history. Indeed the adage that 'there's nothing new under the sun' has always had a strong resonance in the study of crime.

Of course drug trafficking and pornography have been transformed by global transport and communications (including the world wide web) and new crimes such as e-piracy have appeared. And old ones have been updated. Piracy is a crime that conjures up images of sailing ships and the middle ages, but such a crime continues with faster speedboats and high tech tracking devices enabling robbery on the high seas to become increasingly sophisticated. Indeed Somali pirates operating off the east coast of Africa have been kidnapping personnel and demanding huge ransoms for the return of ships in recent years. In October 2009 a retired British couple, Paul and Rachel Chandler, who were sailing between the Seychelles and Tanzania were forced to abandon their yacht and were held hostage for over one year while subject to a ransom demand of $7million.

Consider a range of different types of crime – such as burglary, drug dealing, child abuse, fraud, football hooliganism, terrorism. How might developments in global transport and communications affect the form and the extent of such crimes?

Here we will consider how the emphasis on diversity of theories and explanations has impacted on how we think about and respond to crime. One, undoubtedly populist, approach might be to suggest that crime is a reality, a 'truth', to those who are victims and that rather than debating the different 'meanings' of crime the emphasis should be on better prevention of criminal behaviour and harsher punishment of those criminals who are caught. Of course, technological developments in surveillance and private security have enabled some groups to protect themselves from criminal activity to a far greater extent than others. In particular the affluent are able to protect themselves and their property by excluding the poor and marginalized from their areas and from punishing more severely those offenders who are caught. Crime rates in major US cities have certainly declined in recent years but at the cost of a massive increase in the prison population. The number of prisoners in the USA rose to over 2 million in 2002 and the US has the biggest prison population in the world – the highest number of prisoners as a proportion of its population. As a comparison, Russia, with a population of 144 million (compared to 286 million in the US), had a prison population of 920,000 when the US number topped 2 million (in 2003). Indeed the US prison population makes up almost a quarter of all the world's prisoners. And these figures have continued to rise; in the last 25 years the US prison population has almost trebled to 2.3 million in 2008.

Another approach has been to focus on and manage the risks posed by crime and to emphasize the importance of risk management in relation to crime. The idea of a risk society developed by Beck (1992) and others goes well beyond the area of criminality and crime control. However, in the area of crime, the notion that crime is a 'risk' that can be calculated, managed and possibly avoided has been influential. Crime has become a calculable risk for both offender and victim, and for criminal justice agencies. This view tends to see crime as an outcome of normal social interaction, rather than something caused by biological, psychological or social factors that act on specific individuals and/or groups. So risk can be used to refer to decisions about whether to commit crimes and to decisions made by agencies of the criminal justice system. The latter is probably the more common way in which the concept of risk has played a role in criminological thinking. This can be seen in the basing of decisions on information and statistical probabilities about the re-offending of offenders. With or without detailed statistics, risk assessment is also involved in decisions around the security classification of prisoners, pre-sentencing reports prepared for the courts, whether to parole prisoners or keep them incarcerated and so on. Risk in crime goes beyond an application to criminal justice decisions – the design of streets, shopping centres and other community facilities is increasingly organized with risk of crime in mind. Concerns have been raised about the increased focus on risk in criminal justice. In particular that there is a possible net widening effect as people who are potential risks are targeted before they commit offences. Indeed such a focus can increase feelings of insecurity and fear within communities, particularly as those who cannot afford to protect themselves see better security techniques being used by those who can.

In considering recent theoretical developments and the implications of the risk society for understanding crime and the control of it, we will refer to the work of David Garland. His book *The Culture of Control* (2001) is seen by Newburn (2007) as 'arguably the most important and influential book in Western criminology in the past ten years'. He suggests that Western societies are facing a new form and culture of crime control and identifies 12 key indices of this change, adapting Newburn's concise summary, which are listed in Box 4.4 below:

BOX 4.4 THE NEW CULTURE OF CONTROL – DAVID GARLAND

1 The decline of the rehabilitative ideal and of the assumption that people could be 'reformed'

2 The re-emergence of punitive sanctions and retributive justice

3 Changes in the emotional tone of crime policy – a growing fear of crime has led politicians and others to use more emotive terms in talking about crime

4 The return of the victim as a (more) important figure in criminal justice

5 (An increased urgency given to) protecting the public as a central part of crime control

6 Politicization – crime and criminal justice are major areas for political contest and much of the debate is very populist (aiming to gain public support)

7 Emphasis on prison – expanding prison numbers seen as a necessary part of a successful criminal justice system

8 Transformation of criminological thought – emphasis on control theories (see pp. 115–118) – crime viewed as normal and to be expected without suitable controls being in place

9 Expanding infrastructure of crime prevention and community safety – often focused on reducing fear, preventing loss and security

10 Commercialization of crime – a mixture of public and private policing and security provision

11 New management styles – including increasing use of performance indicators and league tables with a stress on cost-effectiveness

12 A perpetual state of crisis with regard to criminal justice

(Adapted from Newburn 2007: 331–2)

Overall Garland suggests that the notion of 'penal welfarism' and the focus on reforming offenders wherever possible has declined and been replaced by an emphasis on control. This new culture of control is reflected in the criminal justice responses to crime, illustrated by the spread of CCTV surveillance, gated communities and private security guards and, especially in the USA, a massive rise in prison numbers.

RECENT DEVELOPMENTS – ENVIRONMENTAL CRIMINOLOGY

Environmental criminology is described by Wortley and Mazerolle (2008) as 'a family of theories that share a common interest in criminal events and the immediate circumstances in which they occur'. This approach looks to explain the patterns of crime in terms of environmental influences; and uses these explanations to help develop and inform strategies that policy makers and criminal justice agencies might use to reduce or prevent crime. As Wortley and Mazerolle point out, this approach differs from other, traditional criminological approaches that focus on trying to explain how the criminal offender is 'created', and once the criminal is created, crime is likely to occur. The environmental approach takes a different stance; rather than focusing on the offender the emphasis is on the 'criminal event' – where and when did it happen, who was involved and what did they do? As Wortley and Mazerolle put it, 'the aim of the environmental perspective is to prevent crime, not to cure offenders'.

The environmental perspective is not based in or on any one academic discipline but draws from a range of areas, including sociology, psychology, geography, architecture and town planning. Wortley and Mazerolle suggest it is based around three key premises: that criminal behaviour is influenced by the immediate environment in which it occurs; that time and space are vital factors – crime will concentrate around environmental features that facilitate criminal activity and will vary according to geographical area and time of day; and that an awareness of these patterns and factors will help the police and others investigate, control and prevent crime.

The roots of this perspective can be traced back to the work of the Chicago School and their ecological approach to explaining crime (see pp. 106–108). Here we will mention some more recent examples of this approach. The modern environmental perspective is generally agreed to have started in the 1970s (Wortley and Mazerolle), exemplified in the work of Ron Clarke on situational crime prevention. Clarke (1980) emphasized the reduction of opportunities for crime as the basis for prevention and he was a key figure in the development of rational choice theory which we consider below. More recently, since the 1980s, there has been a growing interest in examining the geographic distribution of crime. This is exemplified in the work of Bratingham and Bratingham (initially 1984) and crime pattern theory, and the argument that crime is not a random or uniform phenomenon but occurs in highly predictable locations. Indeed with the development of geographic information systems (GIS) improved mapping technology has led to the identification of crime 'hot spots' and geographic profiling of offenders.

Rational choice theory was referred to above and in concluding this section we will refer to the work of Clarke and colleagues in this area (Cornish and Clarke 2008). They argue that at the core of criminal behaviour are concepts of choice and decision-making; the 'desires, preferences and motives of offenders . . . are similar to those of the rest of us'. In highlighting the main elements of this approach they comment: 'while an individual's emotional inheritance and upbringing play some part in delinquency, the major determinants are those provided by the current environment . . . (which) . . . provides the cues and stimuli for delinquency'. Whether an individual commits an initial delinquent act will depend to a large extent on opportunity and the example of others around the individual. Rational choice theory assumes that individuals act rationally and before proceeding with an activity will weigh up the potential profits and benefits against the possible losses (an approach that has its origins in early classical criminology, see pp. 98–102).

Cornish and Clarke (2008) see the rational choice perspective as more a set of working assumptions than a conventional criminological theory and it was conceived and developed mainly to help the development of the situational prevention of crime.

QUESTION BREAK

Rational choice theory focuses on how opportunity, space and time can be used to help prevent crime.

Can you give examples of how architectural design might help reduce:

(a) street violence and assaults; (b) suicides; (c) burglary?

How might products be designed to make theft more difficult?

CRIME AND THE MEDIA – CULTURAL CRIMINOLOGY

A further influence of postmodernism that can be related to theorizing about crime concerns the spread of the media, including the scope this offers for new forms of criminal behaviour and the role it has played in the development of 'cultural criminology'. Particularly associated with the theorizing of American criminologist Jeff Ferrell, cultural criminology emphasizes the importance of image, style and representations and the way these have encouraged a mediated construction of crime and criminal justice. It takes on the postmodern position that 'style is substance' and the meaning of something is based on its representation to suggest that crime can be best understood as part of an 'image driven media loop' (Ferrell 2001). Of the theoretical perspectives on crime looked at so far, this approach is probably closest to that of interactionism, with cultural criminologists emphasizing the symbolic aspect of 'symbolic interactionism', through examining the style of different types of criminal behaviour and the groups and subcultures associated with them. Ferrell (2001) points to a number of areas in which this new theoretical approach has developed. First, crime is seen as a subcultural phenomenon organized around symbolic communication. It also examines the mediated construction of crime and the control of crime; considering the interconnections between the criminal justice system and the mass media, and looking at how certain activities come to be constructed as crimes and other do not; and at the everyday consumption of crime as drama and entertainment. To quote Ferrell (1999): 'The notion of cultural criminology references the increasing analytic attention that many criminologists now give to popular culture constructions, and especially mass media constructions, of crime and crime control.'

A good deal of research in cultural criminology has looked at 'subcultural style', seeing this style as defining the way deviants and criminals characterize their activity and also the way such activities are viewed and constructed from outside. It has also introduced the idea of 'culture as crime', whereby aspects of popular culture become criminalized:

> performers, producers, distributors, and retailers of rap and 'gansta rap' music have likewise faced arrest and conviction on obscenity charges, legal confiscation of albums, highly publicized protests, boycotts, hearings organized by political figures and police officials, ongoing media campaigns and legal proceedings against them of promoting – indeed, directly causing – crime and delinquency.
>
> (Ferrell 1999)

In addition to framing how crime and criminal activities are viewed, the media also frames and determines our perceptions of crime control. With regard to the police, 'reality' policing programmes determine public perceptions of the police and will play a part in officer recruitment. To quote Ferrell (1999) again, 'From the view of cultural criminology, policing must in turn be understood as a set of practices situated, like criminal practices, within subcultural conventions of meaning, symbolism and style.'

The media and cybercrime

As well as cultural criminology highlighting the media as a key contributor to the perception of crime, another important aspect of the link between the media and crime is to examine the way that the media can cause crime. Indeed it could be argued that there has been a 'media revolution' in crime in recent years. This argument sees the media as a cause of an array of new crimes in the sense that it is used to commit criminal activity, such as cyber and internet crime.

Although cybercrime is a term that has become widely used of late, it is not always clear what it actually is. Wall (2004) points to the tendency to call any offence involving a computer a 'cybercrime', and offers a definition that embraces three different forms of such crime, which he suggests are at different positions on a 'cyber-crime spectrum'. In general, 'cybercrimes are criminal acts transformed by network technologies' (Wall 2004); the three different types can be placed at different points on the spectrum. At one end are acts which are called cybercrime but which are basically 'traditional' crimes where the internet has been used to help organize and carry out the crime (e.g. paedophiles). Without the internet the criminal behaviour will still exist using other forms of communication. In the middle are 'traditional' crimes which have 'benefited' from new global opportunities – which Wall terms 'hybrid' cybercrimes (e.g. frauds, global trade in pornography). Such crime would still exist without the internet but on a reduced scale. At the other end of the spectrum are 'true' cybercrimes which only occur as a result of the opportunities created by the internet (e.g. intellectual property theft, 'phishing'). Without the internet these last types of cybercrime would not exist.

We will look briefly at this last type of cybercrime – what Wall terms 'true' cybercrime. The dangers such crime pose are often not immediately obvious. This might be because victims do not regard them as serious or because the danger the pose is as precursors for more serious crime in the future – for instance, identity theft from computers does not become serious until that information is used to harm the person whose identity is stolen. These hidden dangers are apparent in 'phishing' – a word that was coined to refer to scams in which computer hackers 'fish' for passwords for people's accounts on internet service providers such as AOL. In phishing scams, fraudsters target e-mail addresses requesting that the receivers of the e-mail provide personal details. They use very realistic logos and e-mail addresses in doing so, copying as closely as possible those of established banks and financial institutions. The extract below illustrates how phishing scams can and do target major established banks and their customers.

CASE STUDY BOX 4.1 PHISHING ATTACK ON NATWEST HALTS ONLINE SERVICE

By Caroline Merrell and Christine Seib

Tens of thousands of bank customers have been targeted by online fraudsters

One of Britain's biggest banks was forced to suspend some of its internet banking service yesterday after tens of thousands of its customers were targeted by fraudsters.

NatWest banned its one million online customers from setting up any new direct debits or standing orders yesterday in response to an escalating phishing scam, where fraudsters encourage customers to send personal banking details by e-mail.

The move was a recognition of the sharp rise in phishing attacks, and their increasing plausibility. The bank was also responding to comments from the City's chief watchdog, which gave warning last week that banks had to be more preventive in their measures against phishing.

The action by the bank could be followed by others, as it faces an onslaught from criminals who target customers by e-mail, demanding to know personal banking details. The bank said that it had stopped its online customers setting up accounts or servicing third parties to prevent money being switched out of the country . . .

In the phishing scam, fraudsters target e-mail addresses, demanding that the recipients of e-mails provide personal details. The criminals then arrange for money to be transferred out of the country.

(From *The Times*, 18 November 2004)

An example of the way in which the internet can be used to encourage and increase crime is its use by race hate groups. Sutton (2002) argues that the internet has encouraged a growth in the race hate movement in recent years: 'The communications revolution has brought a new dimension to the hate movement. Racist websites provide an enabling environment in which hate can flourish both on-line and off-line in our towns and cities.' He cites the work of Back and his summary of the different ways in which the internet can assist racist activities. Photographs can be used to show and celebrate real instances of racial violence. This can promote an indifference towards victims. The internet provides a vehicle for selling racist paraphernalia and enables the downloading and saving of collections of racist materials. And it enables people to experience and indulge in racism without being directly and physically involved.

Sutton also points to the internet creating a new dimension in hate crime through bringing together a range of distinct racist groups from various countries, which helps create a 'powerful communications medium facilitating the development of neo-Nazi networks'. As well as racist groups using the internet, individuals are able to air and debate their own race hate on newsroom type websites.

CASE STUDY BOX 4.2 PROSECUTING CYBERCRIME

The extracts below highlight some of the issues around prosecuting cybercrime. The first considers difficulties involved in investigating child pornography via the internet; the second and third provide information and comment on the prosecution of computer crime in the UK and are taken from two leading IT news websites.

Prosecuting global cybercrime

Child pornography is illegal in almost every industrialized nation. Just this Saturday, Italian investigators in Italy sought international warrants against almost 1600 individuals worldwide suspected of participating in online child pornography . . . The logistics to enable such a worldwide effort indicate the ferocity that some governments plan to take in regards to cybercrime.

An additional 1030 international warrants are being granted pending the completed investigations of the Italian police. Those additional 1030 international warrants are to be granted as soon as Internet users who entered a website named 'childlovers' are identified.

In no way am I condoning child pornography, but to serve a warrant on someone who entered a site with the ambiguous name of childlovers just doesn't seem entirely fair. The name unto itself is not clearly pornographic in nature.

Your pregnant wife may have done a web search on children and clicked on a link to the childlovers site and I doubt she should qualify as a participant of online child pornography, nor should she suffer the indignity of discovering there's an international warrant in her name. Perhaps that website is clearly pornographic, but I'm not going there to find out.

(From S. Underhill, 'Cybercrime Prosecution is a Nightmare', www.InfiniSource.com, 2 November 2000)

Businesses often shy away from sharing information about cyber crime with the police because they do not want to end up dealing with a public court case, according to an expert. John Harrison, an independent consultant with three decades of experience working for BT, said that companies often don't want to prosecute when they become a victim of cyber crime. Harrison, speaking at the ENISA conference in Greece, said that there was a risk of embarrassment for the business, and that the information coming out in the public domain far outweighed any benefit derived from going ahead with prosecution.

(From A. Wattanajantra, 'Businesses Shy Away from Prosecuting Cyber Criminals', www.itpro.co.uk, 15 September 2009)

Experts have called for more police resources to fight computer crime, after it emerged that only 299 hackers have been charged under the UK's computer crime law over the past four years . . .

Computer Weekly has discovered that only 110 cases involving unauthorised access and virus writing reached magistrates' courts across the country . . . from November 2007 to October 2008, 59 cases reached court in the year to October 2007 . . .

The figures, obtained by CW under the Freedom of Information Act, pale in comparison with the estimated amount of computer crime taking place . . .

The DTI Information Security Breaches Survey showed that 96% of large companies suffered a security incident last year, and 13% of all companies detected unauthorised access on their networks.

(From S. Hilley, 'UK's Poor Record on Prosecuting Hackers Revealed', www. computerweekly.com, 25 February 2009)

- In relation to the first extract, suggest other difficulties that face the policing and control of cybercrime across frontiers.
- What explanations can you offer for the small number of prosecutions of computer crime?

Finally, the media can affect the victims of crime, to the extent of victimizing victims even further. This is not to say that victims of crime are always treated badly by the media; some victims might in fact gain some comfort from seeing their situation getting media attention. As Mulley (2001) points out, the media can give victims the chance to tell their side of the story and 'set the record straight'. Also, people who have been victims of crime or family members or friends of victims often feel that bringing attention to the crime through the media will help to give strength others who have suffered from similar experiences. However, she also highlights how media attention can become a form of secondary victimization. She reviewed research by Victim Support into the concerns and problems experienced by crime victims and witnesses which found that unwanted and intrusive media attention was complained of by 50 out of 80 families interviewed. Victims of the most serious crimes can find media attention extremely difficult, especially if media journalists are particularly persistent and assertive. And Victim Support have also detailed cases where victims have been harassed and intimidated by friends of an offender following media reporting which has provided personal details (anonymity is only legally guaranteed for child witnesses and victims of rape or sexual assault).

FURTHER READING

Hopkins Burke, R. (2005) *An Introduction to Criminological Theory* (2nd edn), Cullompton: Willan Publishing. A very thorough and up-to-date account of criminological theory covering all the major traditions and not limiting itself to sociological theorizing.

McLaughlin, J., Muncie, J. and Hughes, G. (eds) (2003) *Criminological Perspectives: Essential Readings* (2nd edn), London: Sage. There's nothing like the real thing and reading extracts from original sources can give a flavour of the work and writing of key criminological thinkers. This reader contains examples of the core perspectives and early theorists, including Beccaria, Bentham, Durkheim and Becker, and of recent theorizing, including global and cultural criminology. The introductions to the different sections and readings provide particularly helpful guides.

Rock, P. (2007) 'Sociological Theories of Crime', in M. Maguire, R. Morgan and R. Reiner (eds) *The Oxford Handbook of Criminology*, Oxford: Oxford University Press. In the first chapter in the major criminological reference book, the *Oxford Handbook of Criminology*, Paul Rock, himself a key figure in the development of criminology in Britain, provides an insightful and clear summary of the range of sociological theorizing on crime.

Tierney, J. (2010) *Criminology: Theory and Context* (3rd edn), Harlow: Longman. An excellent and accessible overview that explores the history and growth of criminology and examines the major criminological theories that have developed as a result.

WEBSITES

www.crimetheory.com is a site run from the University of Ohio in the USA and includes archives of early criminological texts written or translated in English.

CHAPTER 5

Explaining the Criminal Behaviour of Women

INTRODUCTION

Recent statistics show that women's involvement in crime is rising. In the last decade the number of women in prison has almost doubled, yet their involvement in crime is still minimal compared to that of males. The focus of this chapter will be to discuss the traditional, biological, psychological and sociological explanations for women's involvement – or rather lack of involvement – in crime. Traditional explanations look to religion and naturalistic phenomena. Biological and psychological explanations focus on the individual characteristics and consider, for example, whether female crime is pathological; or whether women are less biologically evolved than men; or does PMT (premenstrual tension) offer a feasible account for most female crime? Sociological explanations look at the structure of society and how it affects individuals or groups. Questions that the sociological approach raises include: are girls socialized differently? does the family make girls passive? has the women's liberation movement led to a generation of 'ladettes' who emulate men even in relation to criminal behaviour? This chapter explores these and other explanations and the associated issues and tries to make sense of women's involvement in crime and how this involvement has changed over time.

In June 2010 the British prison population stood at 85,096 and of this number 4,333 were females (National Offender Management Service data). It is clear that women make up only a small percentage of those imprisoned and there has been a decline in female imprisonment from 5.94 per cent of all prisoners in 2005 to 5.09 per cent in 2010, a trend that, according to predictions, is set to continue. However, the rate of female imprisonment rose by 11 per cent between 2004 and 2008 (Ministry of Justice 2010). This has led to claims by criminologists, the media and politicians alike that society is now faced with a 'new female criminal'; and there has been close to a moral panic surrounding the dawn of the 'ladette' – the violent female girl gang member who can be just as dangerous as her male counterpart.

Feminist criminologists have argued that history has been constructed through a masculine narrative of crime – crime being the province of men and women merely the recipients. The focus, then, has been on women as victims of criminal behaviour. When looking at women as victims the figures remain unusually high. It has been estimated that 70 per cent of female murder victims worldwide are killed by their male partner (WHO 2002) and Seager points out that this amounts to two women per week killed by their partner. In 2002 UNICEF stated that 25 per cent of women in Britain would be punched or slapped by their male partner or ex-partner in their lifetime. The estimated statistics for sexual violence are just as depressing. One in five women will become victims of rape in their lifetime (WHO 1997) and according to UNIFEM (2002) each year 2 million girls between the ages of five and 15 are introduced into the commercial sex market. In the face of such victimization and oppression it would perhaps make more sense to ask the question, 'why don't women commit as much crime as their male counterparts?' Indeed this is an issue that will be returned to later in the chapter.

HISTORY

It is clear that women are capable of, and have been found responsible for, all types of criminal and deviant behaviour. Also, despite recent moral panics around women's increasing criminality, history provides us with information which demonstrates that women's criminality has always existed and is not a relatively recent phenomenon.

Historically the focus for women and crime has centred on arguments around the 'naturalness' of certain behaviours. Female norms pronounce women as biologically predestined and centre on those behaviours deemed 'feminine by nature'. In terms of crime, infanticide, for example, is a female crime that by definition can only be committed by a women and prostitution has in the past been (and still is today) considered to be a crime predominantly committed by women. However, throughout history women have also been capable of crimes which are beyond the realms of supposedly 'natural' female behaviour and, one might argue, have committed what might be labelled 'naturally masculine' crimes. Famous cases include Cleopatra, the last of the pharaohs, who ruled from 69 to 30 BC, and Boadicca, who led the Celts to a glorious but bloody defeat by the Roman Empire between 61 and 63 AD: both were women leaders of great empires who were guilty of crimes against humanity and sanctioned (and in the case of Boadicca took part in) the genocide of innocent people. Mata Hari, a dancer and entertainer, is perhaps the most famous spy of all time – she was executed by the French in 1917 after being found guilty of spying for Germany, although it is claimed that she was a double agent. More recently, the cases of Myra Hindley in the 1960s and Rosemary West in the 1980s involved horrific examples of child abuse and murder.

Those cases of female crime that do fall into the category of being essentially or completely female include prostitution and infanticide, and we will discuss infanticide in some detail as an example of a uniquely female crime.

Infanticide

By definition the crime of infanticide can be committed only by a woman. As a consequence it is not only a heinous criminal behaviour but also a crime which questions female morality and the maternal instinct. The problem of infanticide is not new: throughout history it has taken many guises, from religious and supernatural child sacrifice to a solution for mothers in poverty and to concerns about overpopulation. This type of crime has been attributed to a number of things but for feminist criminologists and social historians alike this crime has been linked to patriarchy and social control over women's bodies.

For example, within the Victorian period (an era renowned for its strict moral sensibility) infanticide reached epidemic proportions and women found guilty were severely punished. Statistics provided in a study by H. R. Jones (1894) show the rate of homicide in England and Wales during the period 1863–87. On interpretation of the data Rose (1986) concludes that children under one year of age accounted for '61% of all homicide victims compared to 2.5–3% of the population'. Partly as a consequence of the growing number of child deaths and partly owing to a sympathetic response from judges, in 1922 the Infanticide Act was introduced to the United Kingdom and was further refined and revised in 1938. The act was introduced partly as a response to the worrying child death rates highlighted above and partly because judges were reluctant to pass the sentence of death on mothers who killed their children, and felt there needed to be a legal means of dealing with such women. As already illustrated, child deaths had reached epidemic proportions in the late nineteenth century and it was believed that this would further be exacerbated by the social and economic problems and conditions that many mothers faced, such as poverty and desertion by the child's father.

The 1922 Act defined infanticide as 'the act of a mother who kills her new born child'. However, the act also stipulated that puerperal psychosis (severe mental disorder relating to childbirth) should be carefully considered. Normally the killing of a child led to the charge of murder and at the time the death penalty; however, the 1922 Act effectively abandoned the death penalty for such cases. As mentioned, in 1938 the Act was refined further; the age range was extended from newborn child to 12 months old and it allowed for a plea relating to the balance of the mind in partial defence for murder. The 1938 Act extended this defence to cases where 'at the time of the act or omission the balance of her mind was disturbed by reason of her not having fully recovered from the effect of giving birth to the child or by reason of the effect of lactation consequent upon the birth of the child'. In 1957 the notion of diminished responsibility was introduced into the British justice system which further allowed for a more appropriate sentence than mandatory life imprisonment for a mother found guilty of killing her infant.

Infanticide, of course, is still a problem for society and has been related to the cultural norms of some societies and the economic and mental health problems of women. Sex-related infanticide is also very common in areas such as China and regions of India where male children are prized over females. Closely related to the problem of infanticide is the rate of abortion. Prenatal sex-determination techniques such as ultrasound have led to an increase in the abortion rates of female foetuses.

In Britain the phenomenon of infanticide has become a major issue as a result of high profile cases of women accused of the crime. Sally Clark (1999) and Angela Cannings (2002) were accused and convicted of infanticide. Both women, like others, later had their convictions quashed on appeal in part because of the 'unscientific and unreliable' evidence and testimony of paediatrician Professor Roy Meadow. In his book *The ABC of Child Abuse*, Meadow establishes and defends the principle that 'two [cases of child death] is suspicious and three murder unless proved otherwise . . . is a sensible working rule for anyone encountering these tragedies'. However, partly as a result of appeals in these high profile cases, it is now widely believed that many cases of what was once thought to be infanticide may be more appropriately attributed to Sudden Infant Death Syndrome (SIDS), more commonly known as cot death, which can help to explain deaths, including multiple deaths, in families.

From a criminological point of view infanticide is an interesting topic for debate as it medicalizes women's criminal behaviour (an issue we will return to when looking at biological perspectives) and furthers the idea that women's crime is related to biology and psychology. For those who are genuinely affected by their biology, and in this case by postnatal depression, the law does seem sympathetic but there is also cause for concern that many women use and take advantage of this notion for their own ends. Second, as indicated earlier, the idea of infanticide may be said to be an example of leniency towards women within the criminal justice system as this form of 'killing' is differentiated from murder (an issue which will be discussed below in relation to the notion of the 'chivalry factor'). Of course the idea of leniency also raises questions about the true level of female crime within the confines of the family. The following extract highlights the current debate around infanticide laws within the judiciary.

CASE STUDY BOX 5.1 SCRAP OUTDATED INFANTICIDE LAW, SAYS JUDGE

Three Court of Appeal judges have called for a review of the 'outdated and unsatisfactory' law on infanticide after upholding the conviction of a mother for the murder of her baby.

They raised concerns that vulnerable, mentally ill women are being given mandatory life sentences for killing their babies when they should have been treated more leniently.

The judges had rejected an appeal by 29-year-old Chaha'Oh-Niyol Kai-Whitewind against her conviction for murdering her 12-week-old baby Bidziil . . .

She was convicted in 2003 of suffocating Bidziil when, the prosecution said, she became frustrated with his refusal to breastfeed and depressed at her failure to bond with him . . .

Ms Kai-Whitewind, who changed her name after adopting native American culture, had told a psychiatric nurse she had thought about killing the baby, who was conceived as a result of rape. Blood was found in the boy's nose and mouth, and his mother had delayed calling an ambulance after he stopped breathing.

But she denied having anything to do with his death, claiming it was from natural causes. She refused to give evidence or plead guilty to infanticide or manslaughter on the grounds of diminished responsibility.

Under the 1938 Infanticide Act, a woman who kills her child when it is less than a year old and 'while the balance of her mind was disturbed by reason of the fact that she had not fully recovered from the effect of giving birth', should not be found guilty of murder.

Of the 49 women convicted of infanticide between 1989 and 2000, only two were jailed; the rest were given probation, supervision or hospital orders.

But because Ms Kai-Whitewind did not admit her guilt and refused to undergo psychiatric reports, she was convicted of murder and given a life sentence.

Giving their ruling yesterday, the deputy chief justice, Lord Justice Judge, sitting with Mrs Justice Hallett and Mr Justice Leveson, said her conviction was 'safe'. But Lord Justice Judge added: 'The law relating to infanticide is unsatisfactory and outdated. The appeal in this sad case demonstrates the need for a thorough re-examination.'

He said a 'particular area of concern' was that the infanticide defence was restricted to a mother being affected by the actual birth and not subsequent events, such as a lack of bonding. He added: 'The second problem arises when the mother who has in fact killed her infant is unable to admit it'.

'This may be because she is too unwell to do so, or too emotionally disturbed by what she has in fact done, or too deeply troubled by the consequences of an admission of guilt on her ability to care for any surviving children. When this happens, it is sometimes difficult to produce psychiatric evidence relating to the balance of the mother's mind'.

'Yet, of itself, it does not automatically follow from denial that the balance of her mind was not disturbed: in some cases it may indeed help to confirm that it was.'

About five infanticide convictions a year are handed down in England and Wales. One in 500 new mothers suffers from puerperal psychosis, a severe form of mania which can result in them harming themselves or their babies. Most cases are now spotted before a tragic incident occurs.

But lawyers say some of the most vulnerable women are still being jailed by the criminal justice system. Helena Kennedy QC, who has defended several women accused of killing their children, said in an interview last year: 'The problem in these cases is that unless a woman says "I did it", you can't mount a psychiatric defence. You can't go behind her back and get a psychiatric report'.

'The problem is that these women can't admit it to themselves, and they certainly can't admit it to their partners. The problem for the lawyer is getting the woman to acknowledge it herself. It's complex.'

Until 1922, the killing of a child was a capital offence, but juries had become so sympathetic to women accused in such cases that the first infanticide law was brought in to cover newborn babies. In 1938, it was extended to the killing by a mother of babies up to a year old.

(From Maxine Frith, *Independent*, 4 May 2005)

- The article argues that 'vulnerable and mentally ill women' who kill their babies should be treated more leniently. What support can you find in the article for this view?

PATTERNS AND TRENDS

Patterns and trends in terms of criminal behaviour suggest that men still commit the majority of crime. In general terms, roughly 80 per cent of those convicted for serious offences in England and Wales are male. Suggested explanations for this gender bias range from exploring the inherently different natures of men and women to focusing on the socially constructed gender roles that play a part in men's and women's lives. Also, it is suggested that statistics do not reflect the hidden nature of women's criminal behaviour; that female crime is allowed to continue unchecked owing to the chivalrous nature of the criminal justice system.

What is clear is that in the last ten years or so more women are being apprehended and charged. Table 5.1 compares female and male offenders found guilty at all courts or cautioned by sex and type of offence at various periods between 1998 and 2008 in England and Wales. The statistics reflect a steady increase in female involvement in crime. During this period women's involvement in crime increased in the areas of violence against the person, robbery, fraud and forgery and criminal damage – crimes which have been more closely associated with males. Men on the other hand (although still committing the bulk of crime) have seen decreases in involvement in the areas of theft and handling of stolen goods, drug offences, motoring offences and 'other' crimes.

QUESTION BREAK

- What are the most 'popular' crimes for males and for females?
- Summarize the changes in the patterns of crime for males and for females between 1998 and 2008.
- Can you suggest any explanations for the patterns and changes?

Apart from new trends in the level of crime there have been some changes in the types of crimes women are prepared to commit (or have been caught involved in). Female crime has traditionally been associated with women's sexuality and gender. The focus has therefore been on what have conventionally been seen as 'female' crimes, such as prostitution and infanticide. Women are still over-represented in terms of these 'feminine crimes'. Statistics for those found guilty reflect this traditional pattern of women's criminality. For example, figures for the year 2003 show that women outnumbered men within seven categories of which four reflect the feminine role – cruelty to or neglect of children, concealing of birth, brothel keeping and offence by a prostitute.

However, the data considered above suggests that a change has occurred and is continuing in terms of female crime. Women have become more involved in what can be described as 'masculine' crime. Analysis of England and Wales Crown Court data in 2003 shows that the two most common indictable (essentially the more serious) offences for women were violence against the person and drug offences. These

Table 5.1 Offenders found guilty at all courts by sex and type of offence, 1998–2008

England and Wales

Number of offenders (thousands)

Sex and type of offence	1998	1999	2000	2001	2002	2003	2004	2005	2006	2007	2008
Males											
Indictable offences											
Violence against the person	33.3	32.1	31.6	31.9	33.9	34.2	35.0	36.5	37.4	37.4	36.6
Sexual offences	4.5	4.3	3.9	4.0	4.3	4.3	4.7	4.7	4.8	5.0	5.0
Burglary	29.7	28.2	25.2	23.7	25.4	24.4	23.0	21.8	21.8	22.7	22.6
Robbery	5.1	5.2	5.4	6.2	6.9	6.5	6.7	6.3	7.2	8.0	7.7
Theft and handling stolen goods	101.2	105.1	102.1	101.2	100.7	93.6	86.6	82.2	79.2	84.9	87.5
Fraud and forgery	14.5	14.7	13.8	13.1	12.9	12.9	12.9	13.0	12.3	13.4	13.6
Criminal damage	10.0	9.9	9.3	9.6	9.8	10.1	10.4	10.4	11.3	11.1	8.5
Drug offences	43.7	43.5	40.1	41.2	44.3	46.1	35.0	34.9	35.7	40.4	47.8
Other (excluding motoring offences)	43.9	42.4	39.3	38.7	42.1	44.6	47.6	46.4	44.1	40.0	34.9
Motoring offences	8.5	7.6	7.2	7.3	7.8	8.2	7.6	6.3	5.6	5.1	4.2
Total	294.4	293.0	277.8	276.8	288.3	284.9	269.5	262.4	259.5	268.0	268.6
Summary offences											
Offences (excluding motoring offences)	353.2	339.2	359.2	325.5	356.8	370.6	386.8	363.6	350.4	338.7	326.5
Motoring offences	586.6	556.2	530.7	509.7	517.5	575.0	612.7	575.7	533.9	519.7	459.2
Total	939.7	895.5	889.9	835.2	874.3	945.7	999.4	939.3	884.3	858.4	785.7
All offences	1,234.2	1,188.5	1,167.7	1,112.1	1,162.5	1,230.5	1,268.9	1,201.7	1143.8	1126.4	1054.3
Females											
Indictable offences											
Violence against the person	3.7	3.6	3.7	3.4	3.8	3.9	4.1	4.5	4.5	4.5	4.7
Sexual offences	0.1	0.1	0.0	0.0	0.1	0.1	0.1	0.1	0.1	0.1	0.1

Burglary	1.1	1.1	1.0	1.1	1.3	1.3	1.2	1.2	1.1	1.1	1.1
Robbery	0.5	0.4	0.5	0.6	0.8	0.8	0.8	0.8	0.9	0.9	0.8
Theft and handling stolen goods	24.5	26.1	25.9	25.8	26.6	25.5	24.0	21.6	19.8	21.1	22.8
Fraud and forgery	5.3	5.6	5.4	5.2	5.3	5.1	5.2	5.5	5.9	6.5	6.0
Criminal damage	0.9	1.0	1.0	1.0	1.2	1.2	1.4	1.3	1.4	1.4	1.1
Drug offences	5.1	5.2	4.6	4.5	4.7	5.1	4.2	4.2	3.9	4.1	4.8
Other (excluding motoring offences)	5.7	5.5	5.3	5.3	5.9	6.8	6.9	6.7	5.9	5.3	4.7
Motoring offences	0.5	0.5	0.4	0.4	0.4	0.5	0.4	0.3	0.3	0.3	0.2
Total	47.3	49.0	47.7	47.4	50.0	50.2	48.4	46.1	43.7	45.3	46.4
Summary offences											
Offences (excluding motoring offences)	109.6	94.4	131.6	116.6	130.4	122.9	136.0	145.2	145.3	152.8	154.2
Motoring offences	78.6	76.6	76.8	73.7	78.3	87.5	95.2	91.4	88.6	91.4	87.8
Total	188.3	171.0	208.3	190.2	208.7	210.5	231.2	236.6	233.9	244.2	242.0
All offences	235.6	220.0	256.0	237.6	258.8	260.7	279.6	282.7	277.6	289.5	288.5

data may go some way to explaining the moral panic surrounding the new violent female and the problems of drink and drugs amongst young women in particular.

It is worth mentioning that any phenomenon subject to statistical analysis must be approached with caution. Crime and female crime in particular is subject to the political, cultural and social context within which criminal behaviour takes place. Therefore perceptions and definitions of crime are socially constructed. Arguably, girls and women are and have been subject to what might be seen as 'stronger' methods of social control – for instance girls are expected to conform to a stricter morality than boys by their parents, and are likely to be allowed less freedom to go out and stay out. Of course, we cannot assume that all girls are more closely controlled and supervised by their parents than boys are. None the less, it seems reasonable to suggest that there is a tendency for this to be the case; and if so this is likely to reduce to some degree the opportunities for girls to become involved with criminal behaviour.

While the patterns and trends of female crime clearly suggest that women criminals are still the minority, there has also been a considerable increase in female crime over the last few years. It is worthwhile here exploring the types of crime that have been traditionally associated with women and compare them with current Home Office statistics which highlight the recent figures in terms of men and women found guilty of indictable and summary offences.

Female crime has also been related to women's position in the social structure and their relationship to the economy. Women tend to be over-involved in 'survival crime', that is crimes which have an economic basis such as theft, shoplifting, prostitution and drug importing – Pat Carlen (1988) stated that this could be attributed to the 'feminization of poverty'. The nature of women's criminal behaviour is highlighted by a recent data from the Ministry of Justice (2010). The publication entitled *Woman and the Criminal Justice System* is compiled each year and details the course of female offending. These statistics found the most frequent offences committed by females who were sentenced to imprisonment in 2008 were theft and handling (2,846), 'other' offences (2,263), violence against the person (1,252), fraud and forgery (904), drug offences (798), burglary (250), motoring offences (221) and sexual offences (18).

So in contemporary society women appear in all categories of crime. It is still the case, though, that certain types of offences are dominated by women more than others. As mentioned, around 80 per cent of those convicted of serious offences in England and Wales are male. And it is still the case that women are particularly likely to be arrested for relatively trivial offences such as theft and handling.

Table 5.2 Offenders found guilty at all courts by sex and type of offence, 1998–2007

England and Wales

Number of offenders (thousands)

Sex and type of offence	1998	1999	2000	2001	2002	2003	2004	2005	2006	2007	2008
All offenders											
Violence against the person	37.1	35.7	35.3	35.3	37.7	38.0	39.1	40.9	41.9	42.0	41.5
Sexual offences	4.6	4.3	3.9	4.0	4.4	4.4	4.8	4.8	4.9	5.1	5.1
Burglary	30.8	29.3	26.2	24.8	26.7	25.7	24.3	23.0	23.0	23.8	23.9
Robbery	5.5	5.6	5.9	6.8	7.7	7.3	7.5	7.1	8.1	8.8	8.5
Theft and handling stolen goods	125.7	131.2	128.0	127.0	127.3	119.1	110.6	103.8	99.0	106.0	110.9
Fraud and forgery	19.8	20.3	19.2	18.3	18.1	18.0	18.1	18.5	18.2	19.9	19.8
Criminal damage	10.9	10.9	10.3	10.7	11.0	11.2	11.7	11.7	12.7	12.5	9.6
Drug offences	48.8	48.7	44.6	45.6	49.0	51.2	39.2	39.1	39.6	44.6	52.9
Other (excluding motoring offences)	49.6	47.9	44.5	44.0	48.0	51.4	54.5	53.1	50.0	45.3	40.1
Motoring offences	9.0	8.1	7.6	7.7	8.2	8.7	8.0	6.6	5.9	5.4	4.5
Total	341.7	342.0	325.5	324.2	338.3	335.1	317.8	308.5	303.2	313.3	316.9
Summary offences											
Offences (excluding motoring offences)	462.8	433.6	490.7	442.1	487.2	493.5	522.8	508.9	495.7	491.5	494.2
Motoring offences	665.2	632.9	607.5	583.3	595.8	662.6	707.9	667.1	622.5	611.1	552.2
Total	1,128.0	1,066.5	1,098.2	1,025.5	1,083.0	1,156.1	1,230.7	1,175.9	1,118.2	1102.6	1046.3
All offences	1,469.7	1,408.5	1,423.7	1,349.7	1,421.3	1,491.2	1,548.5	1,484.4	1,421.4	1415.9	1363.2

The statistics in Tables 5.1 and 5.2 show offenders found guilty at all courts or cautioned by sex and types of offence. Study the statistics and highlight the trends in terms of female and male crime.

- What possible explanations are there for the trends in both tables?
- What possible explanations can you put forward for the increase in violence against the person for women?
- Why has there been a significant decrease in men being cautioned or found guilty of burglary?
- Why has there been a significant increase in men being cautioned or found guilty of sexual offences since 1998?

The social characteristics of female criminals

So who are these women criminals – and especially those few thousand who end up within the prison system? Using prison data as a starting point, in general terms, the majority of women prisoners are likely to be unemployed young women who belong to an ethnic minority group. It has long been established that a rise in the unemployment rate often corresponds with an increase in crime rates; and this has led to the argument that poverty or economic inequality can cause crime. Given that women are especially prone to poverty and/or economic inequality owing to gender bias within society, it would be logical to suggest that women would be particularly prone to crime.

In terms of poverty the social and political situation for women within the last two decades shows an increase in social and economic deprivation. The Prison Service Order, Women Prisoners 2008, found that 25 per cent of female inmates claim never to have had a paid employment and 47 per cent had no educational qualifications, while 33 per cent of sentenced female offenders had been excluded from school (compared to 2 per cent of the general population).

At the very least, such figures indicate that those women convicted of offences serious enough to warrant a custodial sentence are from relatively poor and economically deprived backgrounds.

As regards ethnic background, 26 per cent of women prisoners were from black and minority ethnic background. Twenty one per cent of female prisoners were foreign nationals, of whom 55 per cent would be classified black compared to 9 per cent of British nationals (Ministry of Justice 2010).

CRIMINOLOGICAL PERSPECTIVES

Demonic theory

Historically the origins of criminological thought have focused on religious and supernatural or demonical reasoning. In this context criminal and deviant behaviour is seen as beyond the control of the individual and society. The demonic perspective is therefore a pre-Enlightenment view and focuses on the idea that supernatural forces can control 'man's' behaviour through, for example, demonic possession. This perspective gained its authority and credibility through world religions which promote the idea of dualism – the idea that malevolent powers wrestle for the control of the universe. With regard to Christianity this malevolent power is described as Satan, Lucifer, the Devil etc.

In terms of women, the best example of the use of demonic theory came in the form of the witch craze of pre-industrial Europe in which the majority of those accused were women (Hughes 1965). The notions of demonization and demonic possession explain the fate which befell those women accused of witchcraft, especially during the sixteenth century. These 'witches' were said to be in league with the Devil who, in return for their loyalty, granted them supernatural powers which they used to cause death and destruction within society through illness and disease. In hindsight, different theories have emerged to explain this dark period. Economic and social change, crises within religion, mental illness and the role of King James VI of Scotland and Ist of England and Ireland have been used to explain the actions of the accused and the accusers. Despite the underlying reasons, it is true that those who lived throughout this period (1500–1700) felt a real sense of a malevolent power wrestling with the forces of good for control of the universe.

We may argue that civilization and the rise of scientific reasoning and theory have rendered these ideas obsolete. Since the Enlightenment demonic notions of criminal behaviour have been criticized and superseded by social science. However in terms of human behaviour the religious model is still adhered to by many, and old demonic concepts have survived and are still used and accepted by society as explanation for criminal behaviour (for example the ritual abuse of children and the criminal activities of those who call themselves Satanists). Serious female crime in particular is seen as beyond human comprehension and is often described as 'evil' and 'unnatural'. In particular female child killers, such as Myra Hindley and Rosemary West, have been portrayed as demons.

A clear example of the persistence of demonic perspective in relation to women's criminal behaviour is the case of Aileen Wuornos. Aileen made headlines in Florida in the 1990s for the murder of five men. She was sentenced and was put to death through lethal injection in 2003. The case has been sensationalized using demonic language and was even dramatized in a feature film aptly named *Monster*. Trying to make sense of the crimes herself Aileen stated: 'I pretty much had them selected that they was gonna die. My evil came out because of what I was doing, the hitchhiking and hooking. I'm telling you, you have to kill Aileen Wuornos, 'cause she'll kill again' (Nick Bloomfield documentary *Aileen* (2003)).

Naturalism

Naturalism rejects the notion that behaviour is controlled by supernatural forces and argues instead that events within the natural world explain human behaviour including criminal behaviour. The naturalistic approach developed out of the Enlightenment period of the eighteenth century – often known as the 'age of reason', as it was characterized by a rejection of religious explanations for human behaviour and by greater value given to scientific enquiry. The idea of naturalism is grounded in ancient philosophy; a number of history's most revered scientists and philosophers have incorporated naturalism into their beliefs, including Aristotle (384–322 BC), Thomas Aquinas (1224–74) and John Locke (1632–1704).

In terms of criminology, naturalism requires a more scientific or objective rationale for criminal behaviour, which has influenced both classical and positivist criminology (see Chapter 4). Views of women and their involvement or lack of involvement in crime have in the past focused on common-sense assumptions of female behaviour – and they still do today. From an essentialist (naturalistic) point of view females have a different countenance to men. This naturalistic explanation renders anything that deviates from the female norm as 'unnatural'. The acceptable female norm is closely linked to female biology. For example women are seen to be closer to nature as they give birth and are subject to the menstrual cycle. It is widely assumed then that women are naturally caring, emotional and maternal. As the old nursery rhyme goes, girls are made of 'sugar and spice and all things nice'.

This essentially functionalist and conservative view of women (associated with the work of functionalist sociologists such as Talcott Parsons) has been criticized by many as assuming that what is natural (in their view) is also morally right and desirable. But even more important, especially to feminist thinkers, is the view that these attributes are natural and not socially constructed, that this evolutionary explanation naturalizes and justifies the continuation of sexist attitudes to and perceptions of female criminals. This naturalistic or essentialist approach can be seen to underpin much of more recent positivist theorizing which embraces biological and psychology approaches. Examples of these approaches are considered below.

Biological or physiological views

Lombroso

In the late Victorian period a revolutionary new theory was sweeping Europe which would change the way that 'man' viewed his world forever. Charles Darwin wrote *The Descent of Man* in 1884, which put forward the idea of evolutionary theory as an alternative explanation for 'man's' existence. These ideas influenced many theorists in different philosophical and academic areas. In the field of criminology it was Cesare Lombroso, often described as the founding father of criminology, who utilized Darwin's ideas and related them to criminal behaviour (see pp. 26–27).

Lombroso's ideas stem from the idea of atavism, which is based around the theory of evolution. Whilst most humans evolve, it was Lombroso's contention that criminals or deviants devolve, in other words they become primitive or atavistic.

Criminals according to Lombroso were marked and identified by their atavistic stigmata. Atavistic stigmata may be reflected in the physical features or characteristics of a person, for instance the size of cranium, hands or ears.

The Female Offender (1895) was the first scientific text ever written on women and crime. Analysing data on female crimes throughout Europe and searching their anatomy for 'atavistic' elements, Lombroso (with Ferrero) deduced that women in general failed to reach the evolutionary progress of European males. On his scale white men were at the pinnacle of evolutionary progress and black women at the base. Normal women were amongst 'others' included in a group that held criminals, savages, and children in terms of their lack of evolutionary progress. Women had failed to evolve their moral senses; they often lied – a 'fact' deduced from the fact that women masked menstruation from men and sexual intercourse from children (*la donna delinquente*); they were unusually cruel and politically inept. Indeed the female offender was described by Lombroso to be like 'a man arrested in his intellectual and physical development'. In relation to their anatomy, Lombroso suggested that between European women there was a low degree of differentiation; and for him this strengthened the idea of the atavistic women. It was precisely the 'normality' of woman that pointed to her degeneracy – no variation pointed to a lack of progression.

So, if 'normal' females were less evolved, how could the idea of atavism be used to understand female criminality? Even at this time in history it was generally agreed that women were less involved in crime than their male counterparts, so how could this be reconciled with the idea that women were as primitive as criminals – why was their behaviour less criminal? If all women were evolutionary degenerates (as were criminals) shouldn't they be committing as much crime, as if not more crime than, their male counterparts? The answer to this question was seen to lie in atavistic stigmata.

The idea of stigmata was very important within Lombroso's study of women. Analysing criminal and non-criminal females in Sicily, he deduced that stigmata relating to female criminals manifested itself in a number of ways. The female born criminal was described as being short, with dark hair, moles and masculine features. It was noted by Lombroso that 'normal women' had a small cranium, which made them less intelligent and less passionate. On the other hand criminal women had a larger cranium which made them more like men. 'Normal' women were less intelligent than criminal women which lowered their capacity for reason. In place of natural female traits criminal women had 'strong passions and intensely erotic tendencies, much muscular strength and a superior intelligence for the conception and execution of evil' (Lombroso and Ferrero 1895: 150–2). They were 'born criminals' and 'monsters' who 'belong more to the male than to the female sex, combining the worst aspects of womanhood – cunning, spite, and deceitfulness – with the criminal inclinations and callousness of men' (ibid.: 152–3).

Further, Lombroso argued that sexual deviancy was the female equivalent of male crime – which is why women feature most heavily within the area of prostitution.

To Lombroso, then, female offenders were dangerous because they lacked womanly qualities such as maternalism. He went so far as to describe female offenders as 'excessively erotic, weak in maternal feeling, inclined to dispassion, astute and audacious' (1895: 101). It has been argued that Lombroso's ideas on crime and female criminality in particular did not make a lasting impression on British criminology – the idea that there was a distinct 'criminal type', and his use of Social Darwinism and atavism to 'prove' this, was criticized by Lombroso's contemporaries. Today, Lombroso's work is still heavily criticized, particularly by feminist writers (Rock 2007).

Pollak

In 1950 Otto Pollak published *The Criminality of Woman*. He emphasized the link between female biology and criminal behaviour. According to Pollak, women's crime was related to the biological phases that women endure during their lifetime, for example menstruation, pregnancy through to the menopause. These biological phases undermine women's inhibitions and can therefore influence female participation in criminal behaviour. Menstruation led to feelings of irritation and forced women to reflect upon their subordinate position in society; pregnancy led to emotional and physical imbalances; and the menopause left women feeling insecure about their status within their marital relationships. All, according to Pollak, can lead to female offenders being what he described as 'deceitful, vengeful and unemotional'.

It would seem then that women are emotionally unbalanced for the most part of their lives. This raises the question as to why, according to the statistics of that time as well as today, female crime statistics are so low in comparison to men. Pollak suggests that the reason for a lack of crime could be related to the nature of crimes committed and the deceitfulness of women. First, women did not appear within the statistics as they preferred to be involved in professions that rendered their crimes relatively undetectable. Traditionally female occupations focused upon jobs which were relatively private and isolated. He claimed, for example, that women prefer professions like maids, nurses, teachers and homemakers so they can engage in undetectable crime. In hindsight it is quite naive to state that these occupations were preferred; they were more likely to have been taken through necessity.

Not only were these types of crime 'undetectable' but they were also made invisible because women had superb skills of deceit and concealment. Pollak again attributed this to female biology. Deceit and secrecy were skills acquired through social reinforcement but which had their roots in female biology. To explain further, women's crimes are masked by their art of deceit and this stems from their concealment of menstruation and ability to fake orgasm. Society, in particular male society, has therefore encouraged and allowed women to be deceitful, even in terms of the personal and biological.

W. I. Thomas

W. I. Thomas's early work highlighted the biological biases of the time at which he was writing – the early twentieth century. In *Sex and Society* (1907) he states, 'Morphologically the development of man is more accentuated than that of woman. Anthropologists . . . regard women as intermediate between the child and the man.' Therefore his early work pointed to the idea that women were biologically inferior to men. As his work progressed Thomas studied early matriarchal society and concluded that social rather than biological change had left women subject to male domination.

> In the earliest period of a society under the maternal system the woman had her own will more with her person; but with the formulation of a system of control, based on male activities, the person of women was made a point in the application of the male standpoint.
>
> (Thomas 1907: 158)

Thomas examined the problems of monogamy and, he argued, its resulting boredom, writing that 'It is psychologically true that only the unfamiliar and not-completely controlled is interesting' (1907: 56). Explaining the growth in female crime, Thomas argued that traditional society was going through what he considered 'social disorganization'. The social control of women had lessened and the deviant or criminal woman was emerging. Thomas understood this in terms of pathology rather than biologically inherited traits. Focusing on juvenile girls in *The Unadjusted Girl* (1923), he claimed that women committed crime out of 'wishes' for excitement and new experiences. These new experiences manifested themselves through women's sexuality. Confined under monogamy women's pent-up sexual energy was released in criminal acts.

Thomas's approach to theorizing was the basis of what later became known as symbolic interactionism – in examining the phenomenon of female crime he adopted a 'micro level' perspective. In order to understand deviant behaviour more fully Thomas developed the notion of 'definition of the situation', meaning that a situation is constructed through the context of the interaction and the consequences of the situation. The understanding or meaning of a situation is derived from contact between members of a group and the overall definition of the situation. However, a group defines the norms of particular situations and this determines whether or not a reaction to a situation is considered deviant. In one of the most sophisticated sociological analyses then available, he stated that women's behaviour was a function of definitions of the situation that were socially and culturally derived.

Contemporary applications

Despite the fact that many of these theories have been criticized for oversimplifying, generalizing and 'pathologizing' women, there has been a resurgence of biological theory in understanding the female offender. The idea that hormones affect behaviour has been with us for many years. High testosterone levels in men, for example, are said to lead to aggressive behaviour. For women hormone levels are said to fluctuate during pre-menses, postnatal and menopausal stages. Premenstrual syndrome, in particular, is said to cause irritability and mood swings in many women. Trimble and Fay (1986) point to the fact that the symptoms of PMS were noted by the ancient Greeks. The philosopher Simonides for example warned: 'One day she is all smiles and gladness. A stranger in the house seeing her will sing her praise . . . But the next day she is dangerous to look at or approach: She is in a wild frenzy . . . savage to all alike, friend or foe' (cited in Trimble and Fay 1986: 183).

Criminological studies into female crime have supported the idea that PMS can contribute to the female crime rate. Indeed, Lombroso and Ferrero (1895) concluded that, of 80 women arrested for 'resistance to public officials', 71 were menstruating at the time, pointing to menstruation as a catalyst to deviant behaviour. In 1961 Dr K. Dalton (who coined the term premenstrual syndrome with Dr Raymond Greene in 1953), found that, of 156 British women imprisoned for theft, prostitution and public drunkenness, half the offences had been committed during paramenstruum (four days prior to bleeding and the first three days of menstruation). Similarly Ellis and Austin (1971) found that 41 per cent of female inmates who had committed violent acts when in a North Carolina prison had been within the paramenstruum stage at the time. More recently Moiré and Jessel (1997) suggests that there is a link between suicide or aggressive behaviour in women and PMS. However, in the modern medical community there is no consensus upon the origins or indeed existence of PMS.

In terms of criminal behaviour PMS has been used successfully within the courts in mitigation of crimes such as shoplifting and murder. One of the most famous cases of a successful plea was the case of R v Craddock 1980 and R v Smith 1981 (Craddock and Smith are the same person). Craddock, a barmaid with 30 previous convictions, killed a co-worker. In court it was successfully argued that Craddock suffered from acute PMS and the judge accepted PMS as a mitigating factor. Probation and progesterone treatment were recommended. The following year (and on a reduced level of progesterone) Craddock (now Smith) attempted suicide and threatened to kill a police officer. Again the judge accepted PMS as a mitigating factor. Since this case, PMS has been raised successfully within the British court system both civil and criminal.

Despite this many legal experts argue that PMS should not be asserted as a complete defence but rather a mitigating factor. Some feminist arguments go further and suggest that when used as a defence some women may be treated with greater leniency, but that this will also perpetuate stereotypes around female criminal behaviour.

Psychological approaches

In terms of women and crime Freud believed that all humans had criminal tendencies that were part of the natural human drives and urges. In the 'normal', these drives and urges were suppressed through the process of socialization, in which the individual developed 'inner controls'. Improperly socialized, however, a child will develop personality disorders and indulge in anti-social behaviour, which displayed inwardly would become neurosis and outwardly criminal. The genesis of criminal behaviour, then, could be traced back to early childhood trauma using psychoanalysis, and the most common cause according to Freud was faulty identification with parents. Psychological approaches overlap with the physiological theories looked at earlier. Indeed, Thomas's work (p. 164) embraces psychological and sociological factors as well as physiological. And Freud's early work was a major influence on the work of Pollak (p. 164).

Freud's analysis of women as criminals was built around the premise that women are anatomically inferior to men. As with many of the theories discussed above, in terms of women and crime Freud saw the cause of female criminality as sexual in nature. The criminal woman is motivated by sexual neurosis. This idea is derived from what is commonly and famously known as 'penis envy'. According to Feud, as a female child develops she becomes aware that her sexual organs are incomplete and inferior to her male counterparts; as a result envy ensues and leads the girl to feel revengeful. 'Normal' women will, through socialization and 'inner controls', deal with these feelings and emotions. However, the result will be a strong need for male love and approval which such women will gain through narcissism and exhibitionism, often resulting in an obsession with being physically beautiful. In a patriarchal society where male law takes precedence, females adhere to their given social roles as flouting them would mean the removal of male affection and love and protection.

According to Freud, however, criminal or deviant women reject this 'forced' passivity. They are driven by the desire to gain a penis – ultimately this type of woman longs to be a man. Of course this want of a penis is futile and as a consequence the woman becomes neurotic and aggressive in a way which will predispose her to criminal behaviour.

Sociological and feminist perspectives

Introduction

Within traditional theories of criminology the focus has been on male offenders. To some extent this has been a rational response to the statistical evidence showing men as the overwhelming perpetrators of crime. Those theories discussed so far have been criticized for providing a one-dimensional view of female criminality and, particularly, making parenthetical reference to women and crime. Traditionally explanations for female crime (or lack of it) have their roots in the 'natural state of women'. Woman is caring, emotional and maternal and attached unequivocally to the private sphere – incapable practically and emotionally of committing serious crime. When she does move into the criminal arena, the woman is degenerate, failing to reach the same evolutionary stage as her male counterpart. Historically then, explanations have centred upon women's inferiority to men and the sexual nature of her deviance or crime.

The 1960s and 1970s saw rapid social change within society. Older and traditional theories around human behaviour seemed out of touch with the reality of late twentieth-century life and in terms of criminology new theorists began to develop their ideas around the social construction of crime (for example, Becker 1963, Goffman 1968 and Foucault 1977). These ideas challenged traditional notions of how crime was defined and explained.

In general terms, the private and public arenas of women's lives were subject to accelerated economic, social and medical change. This led to the challenging of traditional definitions of and explanations for female behaviour. There was a need to re-evaluate the way in which criminal and deviant women had been researched and theorized. Feminist criminology in its various forms (given that feminism is not just one generally agreed position, with different categories or types of feminism including liberal feminism, socialist feminism and black feminism) placed gender at the heart of its investigations into criminal or deviant behaviour. Patriarchal ideology within society led to a male power base which led to differentials in equality affecting men and women in their experience of crime, both as the offender and the victim. This affected not only the likelihood of criminal behaviour but the way in which the criminal justice system was likely to respond to that behaviour.

This section aims to explore the various feminist viewpoints and go some way towards rectifying the misrepresentation and exclusion of women and girls from traditional criminological theory. There is no doubt that feminist criminology has 'grown up' since the late 1960s. This has reflected the fact that the feminist experience has moved through stages, from the search for gender inequality and its removal from society to a realization that the concern may lie in the importance of epistemology in producing knowledge and truths (here the work of Foucault has been particularly important). For feminist criminologists, the general focus of research into criminality has fallen into two camps. There are first those who investigate the lack of female criminality compared to male and second, those who seek to answer the question of rising female crime statistics.

QUESTION BREAK

- What changes in the private and public areas of women's lives might affect the extent and type of female crime?
- How well do you think these changes explain the rise in the number of women committing crime?

So far our discussion has focused on the biological and psychological differences between men and women as being an important part of the explanation for women's relative lack of involvement in crime. From a feminist perspective the key lies in the social construction of gender identity and how this affects behaviour. Therefore male and female identity or characteristics are not the result of biological differences but the product of social and cultural processes. In 1972 Ann Oakley challenged the notion that men and women were two separate and distinct biological categories. Oakley stressed the difference between sex and gender – sex being defined by the anatomical and physiological characteristics which determine maleness or female-ness, and gender referring to the socially constructed notions of masculinity and femininity which are learned behaviours picked up through imitation of family and society in general (primary or secondary socialization). Behaviour patterns, then, are not universal; rather they will depend upon the society that the individual belongs to, as different societies vary in the ways that they define the social, cultural and psychological attributes of men and women.

The study of conformity and deviance is central to the exploration of criminal behaviour. How individuals react to social constraints and regulations is of great importance to the criminologist. For feminist researchers, gender and the rules and regulations attached to gendered identities can help to explain female crime patterns.

A key question within criminology is: what is it that makes one person go through life relatively crime-free compared to someone who immerses themselves within a criminal subculture? The answer, according to Hirschi (1969), lies in control theory (see pp. 115–118).

According to Heidensohn (1996), women's behaviour is much more closely monitored than that of males and this control begins within the immediate family in early childhood. Expectations of behaviour begin at an early age. Boys are expected to conform to society's view of masculinity – they should be tough, independent and strong, whereas girls are expected to be emotional, passive and domesticated. These ideas are similar to the expected roles of men and women within the family put forward by functionalist sociologists such as Talcott Parsons (1951).

Ultimately the gender socialization process of females affords them fewer opportunities for exploration than boys. According to Smart (1976) a particularly important aspect is the fact that restrictions are placed upon girls' freedom in adolescence. For boys these restrictions are less stringent and their freedom of movement may aid in the discovery of delinquent behaviour. Girls on the other hand lack the opportunity to witness, learn about and engage in delinquency. Thus, this social control prevents women from entering the criminal arena as they lack such exposure and access to it. Therefore, from this feminist viewpoint the patriarchal male-dominated society controls women more effectively than men – these controls also operate within the public arena through work and leisure. Here controls are often in the form of invisible structures which prevent female freedom of movement and expression. Privately, women are physically and mentally controlled through domestic violence but it is the threat of public violence towards women which forms a much more subtle form of control. Fear through the media's portrayal of 'stranger danger' keeps women physically off the streets and confined to their homes especially after dark. Over the last 20 years the media have concentrated on women as victims rather than perpetrators.

Conformity is learned behaviour, and owing to their differential socialization women tend to conform to the 'norm' more than men. Conformity in women brings praise and rewards. According to Carlen (1988) women are controlled by two mechanisms in modern society: home and work. The socialization process in early childhood and the conformity impressed on them mean that the rewards of this conformity remain psychologically important to women. Hence the rewards of employment are more prized than entering the criminal arena. For women there are more moral sanctions attached to criminal behaviour; not least the threat to the stability and happiness of the family unit which prevents many women from turning to crime.

Of course not all women conform, a fact which is reflected in the rising female crime statistics. Conformity in women and girls may depend on a number of things. First the structure of the family is an important indicator of the level of future conformity. Hagan (1990) points to changes in the family structure to explain levels of female crime. Since the late 1950s family style and structure have been changing.

The patriarchal family was once the norm within society and was characterized by the father as the controlling influence and occupying the traditional 'breadwinner, head of the family role'. Mothers on the other hand occupied the domestic realm and were subordinate to their husband's position. Daughters, then, were closely supervised by mothers and expected to follow the female pattern of entering the 'cult of domesticity'. Therefore girls were socialized away from risk-taking behaviour, whilst boys were encouraged to 'experiment'. However, changes in family structure (single parents, reconstituted families) and parenting styles have produced what Hagan calls the egalitarian family, which stresses greater fairness between the sexes and in turn greater independence for women, thereby providing a greater propensity for risk. Hagan further argues that female delinquency may have a class dimension. In terms of the egalitarian family Hagan argues that middle-class aspirations (such as autonomy, success and mobility) dominate and that children of both sexes are encouraged along these lines. The conclusion drawn is that daughters and sons now have the same (or at least getting close to the same) propensity towards delinquent behaviour.

Siegel (1992) suggests that:

> Middle class girls are more likely to violate the law because they are less closely controlled than their lower class counterparts. And in homes where both parents hold positions of power, girls are more likely to have the same expectations of career success as their brothers. Consequently, siblings of both sexes will be socialized to take risks and engage in other behaviour related to delinquency. Power control theory, then, implies that middle class youth of both sexes will have higher crime rates than their lower-class peers.
>
> (Siegel 1992: 207)

Of course this idea cannot explain the fact that the vast majority of women within the prison system are working class or 'underclass'.

Second, Heidensohn (1997) points to the fact that girls and women do not always live up to gendered stereotypes and therefore do not always conform to the social norm even if this was the expected behaviour within their family unit. Girls may resist and resent controlling techniques. After all if social control theory was to be an unflawed theoretical position, society would have no female crime!

Emancipation and crime

It was in the 1960s and 1970s that women began to emerge from their traditional roles of mother and housewife. Owing to social and economic changes women were no longer slaves to their biological make-up. The advent of the contraceptive pill allowed women to make their own choices regarding pregnancy and family size, affording them a new independence. As a result women began to enter the public arena which had previously been dominated by men. In terms of the employment sector, the growth of women in employment began under the first wave of feminism in the early twentieth century when the Suffragette movement began to gain momentum. In what has become known as the 'second wave' of feminism, the 1960s and

1970s, the Equal Pay Act (1970), the Sex Discrimination Act (1975) and the Employment Protection Act (1975) helped to establish women's social and legal rights as equals of men. During the period 1951–79 women's employment rates doubled (Reid and Wormald 1982). It seemed at this time that the women's liberation movement was beginning to gain ground in the fight for equality.

During this period female crime statistics had also shown a significant rise and it was not long before a link was made between rising female criminality and the 'new found' emancipation of women and their increased economic opportunities. The relationship between rising crimes and women's emancipation was the focus of Adler's major work *Sisters in Crime* (1975). In terms of equality and crime Adler wrote that 'women have lost their chains. For better or worse they have lost many of the constraints which kept them within the law' (p. 24). Figures in her book stated that between 1969 and 1972 national arrest rates in the USA for major crimes showed a jump for boys of 82 per cent and for girls of 306 per cent.

> During the twelve-year period between 1960 and 1972 the number of women arrested for robbery rose by 277 per cent, while the male figure rose 169 per cent. Dramatic differences are found in embezzlement (up 280 per cent for women, 50 per cent for men), larceny (up 303 per cent for women, 82 per cent for men), and burglary (up 168 per cent for women, 63 per cent for men).
>
> (Adler 1975: 16)

Rita Simon (1975) added to the debate through focusing on women's access to blue- and white-collar crime through their extended employment opportunities. She wrote: 'Women's participation in financial and white collar offences (fraud, embezzlement, larceny, forgery) should increase as their opportunities for employment in higher status occupations extend.'

Therefore the social control that women had been subjected to began to break down and, as they entered the workforce, their access to criminal subcultures increased. For instance, it is the case that more women are now involved in the higher echelons of big business, so providing more opportunity for fraud and embezzlement. One high profile recent case was that of Martha Stewart. The American ex-stockbroker turned style guru was accused and charged with insider dealing in 2001. The case related to the sale of $225,000 of shares in the biotech firm Implone the day before it was announced that federal regulators had turned down a review of the cancer drug Erbitux (produced by Implone). Stewart's case was well publicized and she was sentenced to five months in prison in July 2004 for obstructing a federal securities investigation. Having served her sentence, Martha Stewart was soon back in the media spotlight with her career seemingly little affected by her imprisonment (see also p. 132).

The emancipation thesis does not relate only to women's position within the world of legitimate business. There is also an argument that we are now entering an era of the new 'liberated female criminal'. Some theorists have gone as far as to suggest that female behaviour is becoming 'masculinized'. Women now have greater parity with men and are increasingly likely to engage in behaviour once deemed inappropriate for females. In recent years women's prominence within the underworld has been felt.

Within the mafia, for example, as fathers and brothers are murdered or sent to jail, the women within the families are taking control. This situation has become known as the Godmother phenomenon and is considered in the question break. In terms of street crime there is now an acceptance that young females in particular are engaging in behaviour that was once the remit of males. As the statistics we looked at earlier suggest (see Table 5.2, p. 159) there has been an increase in females perpetrating violence against the person and robbery; and media headlines over the last 15 years have focus on the rise of female gangs, female binge drinking and 'ladette' culture.

QUESTION BREAK

Read the articles on 'mafia godmothers' and 'female violence' below.
In what ways might the articles be used to:

(a) criticize the emancipation thesis?
(b) support it?

Mafia Godmothers Seize Control: Arrested at Dawn in Curlers and Pyjamas
Anti-Mafia police arrested mafia chieftain Concetta Scalisi after bursting in on her hideout on the slopes of Mt Etna in Sicily this week.

Having been on the run for eight months, Concetta is facing three murder charges, but more chillingly, she's one of a growing breed of Godmothers, who are proving as ferocious and cold-blooded as their male counterparts.

Cornered in a house where she was being harboured by two other females, Scalisi, whose sartorial style is as strict as her alleged control over the mob – no make-up, lipstick, earrings or other jewellery, white shirts, dark suits – greeted police by slashing her hands and stomach with a piece of glass, apparently in an attempt to be sent to hospital, rather than directly to prison. Her ploy failed. Though it wasn't exactly what you'd have expected of Al Capone, its suddenness and Scalisi's rare ferocity of purpose left the officers shaken.

'To all intents and purposes,' said Inspector Alvaro Cavazza of the police in Catania, who arrested her at the end of a probe involving a mixture of old fashioned detective work and electronic eavesdropping devices, 'Concetta Scalisi is a man. Her gestures, way of acting and of talking are typical of the male Mafioso.'

It is not surprising. She took up the reins of her murdered father Antonio's clan following the arrest in March 1997 of a nephew who had been minding the shop . . .

Gone are the days when the place of a mobster's wife was in the cucina, rattling the pots and pans and daily making fresh pasta all'uovo, while her husband was busy refining heroin, collecting the pizzo or protection money and killing. Now, more and more often, it is the women who are forced to step in to run the 'firm' when their husbands or brothers are sent to jail or are killed by Mafia rivals.

The Godmother phenomenon first came to light a few years ago in Naples, where Rosetta 'Ice Eyes' Cutolo, the sister of the jailed former *capo dei capi* of the city Raffaele Cutolo, heads a line-up of feared Godmothers now behind bars. Clutching her handbag and often seen in the company of a priest, 'Ice Eyes' evaded the law for 13 years until her arrest in 1993, running her brother's criminal empire as he languished in jail doing seven life sentences . . .

In Sicily, Catania and its lawless environs are proving to be the most fertile ground for the growth of the phenomenon of the 'Woman of Honour'. The area's, and Sicily's, first Godmother was arrested four years ago: although only 26 at the time, Maria Filippa Messina was accused of having taken over her husband Antonio's clan two years earlier, when he was jailed for 21 years for murder. The clan ran prostitution, drugs and extortion rackets.

Messina was arrested with seven men after they were overheard plotting the massacre of six members of a rival clan. She is now breaking stones – the only woman in Italy subject to Law41/BIS, which metes out extra harsh prison conditions for the most serious Mafia offenders.

(Adapted from the *Daily Telegraph*, 19 April 1999)

Teenage girls driven to violence by feuds, drink and jealousy

Two court cases last week sparked debate about the growth of violence among young women. Here, teenagers talk about the aggression and bullying that is part of their lives.

Sitting on a cold concrete step by a north London canal, dressed in pink and black with swinging plastic earrings, thick eyeliner and hair intensively straightened, the girls look like any other teenagers on any other British street.

In a week where two court cases involving vicious assaults by teenage girls ignited fears over a growing trend towards violence among young women, these two 17-year-olds are adamant that there is no such phenomenon as girl gangs, just groups of mates who look out for each other. 'If someone's been talking about you behind your back and saying things that aren't true, or if she's been making threats, then you can front her up, and if it gets mean, then you might end up giving her a slap. You can't just go around being bullied,' explains Tish. 'But that's not violence, that's self-defence. [If] you are a bully, then you deserve whatever you get. Violence is stabbing and a proper beating. I don't hang out with girls that carry knives.'

Jozee raises her eyebrows and starts laughing. In March, egged on by her friends, who claimed her stepbrother had been spreading malicious rumours about her, Tish attacked him with a hunting knife. The bottle of vodka she had drunk beforehand made sure she didn't inflict any serious damage, unlike an incident when she was 15 and broke another girl's nose. 'I didn't start that fight, she was bullying me and thought she could turn all my mates against me. She deserved that.' . . .

While young women aged 16 to 24 still have the highest risk of becoming victims of aggressive crime in this country, recent statistics show that there has been a significant rise in the numbers turning to violence themselves. Youth Justice Board figures for last year show that, while overall crime rates are falling, there is a 50% rise in violent crime committed by young women.

From 2004–5 to 2007–8, there was a 71% rise in the numbers of young women being electronically tagged and a 25% rise in offences committed by girls aged 10 to 17. It means girls are now responsible for around 21% of offences that reach the courts. At the Old Bailey on Wednesday Hatice Can, a 15-year-old runaway from Belvedere, Kent, and Kemi Ajose, 17, from London, were found guilty of causing the death of Rosimeiri Boxall, a 19-year-old whom they tormented and bullied before encouraging her to leap to her death from a third-floor window in May last year.

After delivering the verdict many of the jury were visibly distressed as Can, only 13 at the time of the killing, broke down in tears and hugged her mother.

Last week it was revealed that a hairdresser, Ashleigh Holliman, had rammed a pint glass into another young woman's face in an unprovoked pub attack. Holliman, from Croxley Green, Hertfordshire, admitted causing actual bodily harm to Jennifer Wilson, 20, who helped track her down via Facebook, one of the social networking sites blamed for facilitating a rise in cyberbullying by girls. . .

The trend towards violence by girls is not just happening in Britain. Other western European nations report upward trends in female crime, while research findings reveal that over the past 10 years the rate for violent offences involving adolescent girls in Canada has increased at twice the rate for boys.

In America violence by young women has been rising steeply for 15 years. Among the first to look at the trend, US psychologist Richard Felson said it challenges the deeply held assumption that violence against women is different from violence against men because it is promoted by sexism or hatred of women. He says the motives for violence are the same for all genders – to gain control or retribution and to promote or defend self-image. But women are still far more likely to be victims of gun crime than perpetrators in the US, although in the UK, by August this year, more girls had been caught carrying guns than in the whole of last year.

In Scotland, where the lord advocate Elish Angiolini last year told the Scottish parliament of an increase in 'appalling acts of murderous torture' by women against women and in the number of young girls using knives, officials are linking the rise to binge-drinking and an increase in 'ladette' behaviour.

'This can be gang-related or it can just be that there is someone in a group who is quite persecuted by the gang leader or their cohorts,' said Angiolini. 'That is the kind of machismo behaviour that hitherto we would only see from a male offender.' She put the blame firmly on 'the rise in consumption of alcohol'.

But researchers and psychologists point out that the picture is, they believe, more complicated than that.

Dr Susan Batchelor of Glasgow University has written several academic papers on the subject and she points out that, while the figures for serious assault by girls rose by 138% in Scotland in the 10 years from 1997, violence was involved in just 2% of all the offences committed by young women.

In her latest, soon to be published report, Batchelor questions whether more girls getting arrested or charged over violence was really 'the dark side to girl power' or whether in fact it was just an 'invisible minority' being held up to be used as a scary example of social change for the worse.

Dr Val Besag, an international educational psychologist who works with the anti-bullying charity Kidscape, said both alcohol and shifting aspirations were key to the rise in female violence.

'Girls traditionally were heavily socialised to be nice to each other and to be ladylike,' said Besag. 'We would say to girls who fall out "go away and be friends". You say to a boy "fight back" or "keep away from them". We socialised girls to stay in horrendous marriages, to work harder.

'But actually, despite all that cultural and emotional pressure, evolutionary science tells us girls are just as violent as men but they are much, much slower, it takes much more, for much longer, for us to get aroused to anger – we procrastinate. But if you throw in drink and drugs, then you shortcut that. And you can't expect to say to young women: "Here, we've lifted the glass ceiling. Go out to work but just have a small sherry while your male colleagues are knocking themselves senseless with drugs and drink." But, of course, women's bodies can't process alcohol terribly well.'

'All these horrendous cases we are seeing of girls killing or bullying other girls will have drink or drugs involved. You only have to come across a crowd of drunken girls on a dark night in Newcastle to see the potential for violence.'

(Adapted from the *Observer*, 22 November 2009)

Since Adler's and Simon's studies many feminist criminologists have vehemently criticized the emancipation thesis. Chesney-Lind (1997) has argued that there is no evidence to suggest that emancipation in terms of criminal behaviour has occurred.

As indicated earlier by the data on the under-representation of women offenders, women's criminal behaviour is, on the whole, still marginal compared to that of men. Theoretically the emancipation thesis was born of liberal feminism and its emphasis on equality. This has led to framing criminal behaviour in gender-neutral terms, which assumes an equality and masks the patriarchal structures within which female crime occurs. For example in terms of female violence 'women's violence is profoundly threatening for a patriarchal society because it challenges the naturalness of the gender binarism on which that society depends' (Boyle 2005: 100).

During the 1980s researchers and theorists such as Naffine (1987, 1997) and Steffensmeier and Allan (1996) have rejected the idea that there has been a gender convergence in terms of criminal behaviour. Indeed Steffensmeier and Allan (1996) argue that between 1935 and 1990 the increase in female crime has actually been modest with the exception of larceny, fraud and embezzlement. Moreover increases in these crimes are in line with traditional gender roles. For example statistics for larceny probably relate to increases in shoplifting and fraud and embezzlement figures for women are dominated by welfare and credit card fraud.

Some have argued that the changing rate of female crime is related directly to the demise of 'chivalry' within the criminal justice system (see below). Chesney-Lind (1989, 1997) believes that women are now treated more punitively than men within justice agencies such as the police and the courts. Of course this leads directly to arguments that the increase in the female crime rate is simply due to the fact that more women are being apprehended and charged than in previous years, that the 'dark figure' of female crime (crimes that remain hidden from public view and are not recorded in official crime statistics) is being illuminated by new policy and changing attitudes towards women and crime.

The chivalry hypothesis

Pollak, whose work we looked at in relation to biological explanations (see p. 164), argued that women do commit (much) crime yet the true level is masked by the existence of chivalry within the criminal justice system. The chivalry hypothesis – in contrast to the emancipation theory – argues that women have not achieved an equality with men in terms of crime or punishment. On the contrary this line of thought points to the chivalrousness of a patriarchal society permeating a criminal justice system that is prepared to treat women more leniently compared to men and so masks their true level of criminal behaviour.

The chivalry argument affects woman in different ways. The idea of paternalism in the criminal justice system permeates all other explanations; women are viewed as submissive or passive and are therefore in need of a caring attitude. This paternal attitude also tends to view women as naive, which has ramifications for the way they are responded to – they will be seen as capable of being misled or of not understanding the gravity of the crime. This naivety also leads criminal justice personnel to believe that women are less dangerous and less capable of committing crime compared to men.

Moreover the chivalry hypothesis points to the argument that chivalry may affect the type of punishment that women receive. On a practical and moral level judges may be reluctant to imprison women with children as incarceration leads to additional expense and upheaval when placing children in adequate care as well as long-term emotional or psychological turmoil that might affect the offender and her children.

As mentioned, these ideas emanate from Pollak's biologically based arguments which today have been criticized for being rather crude and without real evidence. One line of criticism suggests that a chivalrous response is afforded only to women who closely relate to the socially acceptable feminine traits. Ann Lloyd (1995), for example, agrees that chivalry does exist but only in respect of those who are seen to conform to gender stereotypes; in other words those women who engage successfully in female heterosexual behaviour. She goes as far as to argue that those who do not fit or refuse to fit gender norms are often treated more harshly, as not only do they commit crime but they also transcend female norms. As the title of her book, *Doubly Deviant, Doubly Damned*, suggests, these women are seen to be doubly deviant and doubly damned. Indeed, Farrington and Morris (1983) were among the first to point to the fact that a female offender's background, such as marital status, was deemed important when sentencing women.

QUESTION BREAK

- To what extent do you think that factors such as child care should influence the sentencing of women (and men)?
- Find some recent press reports of criminal trials which involve male and female defendants. Can you find evidence for the chivalry thesis?

Evidence shows that different factors interact to produce different experiences for women within the criminal justice system. Pat Carlen for example points to the effects that class and race can have on a women's apprehension and eventual punishment and suggests that while 'women who break the law come from all kinds of backgrounds . . . Those who land in prison are much more likely to have come from the lower socio-economic groups than from the higher ones' (Carlen 1985).

The marginalization thesis

Most contemporary research into women and crime has argued that a more plausible explanation for a rise in the female crime statistics is women's economic marginalization; that is the idea that women have suffered increased financial deprivation compared with men. In terms of crime, poverty – absolute and relative – has forced women into the criminal arena. As mentioned earlier it is the case that the most popular and fastest growing area of female crime can be termed 'survival crime'; this refers to crimes which are characterized by the need for financial gain, such as prostitution, shoplifting and acting as drug mules. In 2008 the most popular offences for which females were imprisoned were theft and handling of stolen goods (see p. 000).

This raises the question of to what extent women turn to crime through reasons of economic marginalization rather than through an increased liberation from economic and social inequality.

Steven Box was one of the first criminologists to claim a link between economic marginality and female crime. Analysing unemployment rates over the period

1951–80, he concluded that the rate of female employment had some bearing on female crime statistics. For instance, Box argued that:

> although some upper middle-class women have made inroads into formerly male professions, the vast bulk of women have become increasingly economically marginalised – that is, more likely to be unemployed, or unemployable, or if employed, then more likely to be in insecure, lower paid, unskilled, part-time jobs, where career prospects are minimal . . . [and] the welfare state, on which proportionately more women than men depend, has tightened its definition of who deserves financial assistance and at the same time has become increasingly unable to index these payments in line with inflation.
>
> (Box 1983: 197)

Feminist researchers (particularly those adopting a Marxist or conflict perspective) have referred to the 'feminization of poverty' thesis to explain women's position more specifically. That is, that women represent a disproportionate percentage of the world's poor – women globally own the least property and work the longest hours for the least pay. And this trend is expected to continue in developed and underdeveloped worlds alike. Pat Carlen (1988), for example, focused on the policies of the Thatcher government in the 1980s to explore this notion of the feminization of poverty. Her study followed the criminal careers of 39 women and, in her conclusion, she argued that Thatcherite policies on employment, tax and social security benefit had had the effect of criminalizing women who found economic survival under such policies virtually impossible.

In recent years there has been an increase and improvement in women's position within the employment sector. However, while it may be true that women occupy a higher percentage of the employment sector than ever before, they still exist in disproportionately large numbers in low-paid, part-time positions which are more often than not lacking the protection of trade unions. For example, much of the increase in the number of women in paid work can be accounted for by the rise of part-time work. Between 1971 and 1993, 93 per cent of the total increase in women's employment was in part-time work (Court 1995).

The Equal Opportunities Commission states that although 46 per cent of women are now part of the labour market, 44 per cent of women workers are in part-time employment compared to only one in ten male workers. Hourly earnings for women in full-time employment are 18 per cent lower than for men in equivalent employment, and for women in part-time employment the figures are significantly lower, at 40 per cent that of men.

This argument does not suggest that all women have become economically marginalized. However, some have suggested that those who have gained from the women's liberation movement are middle-class white women – often in professional-type occupations. In terms of female criminality, such changes need to be related to the picture of the typical female criminal, who is not a mid-twenties to thirties professional worker.

Women offenders tend to be poor members of minority groups with truncated educations and spotty employment histories. These were precisely the women whose lives were largely unaffected by the gains, such as they were, of the then white, middle class women's rights movement (Chesney-Lind 1997).

THE MEDIA REPRESENTATION OF FEMALE CRIMINALS

In the final section of the chapter we will look at how gender influences the way the media represent crime. In particular we will examine the media portrayal of female criminals. In this relatively brief discussion our focus will be on how the media reports violent women offenders, and particularly women found guilty of murder.

It is clear that men commit the vast majority of crime (and always have done so) – as we saw earlier (p. 155), in general terms roughly 80 per cent of those convicted of serious offences in England and Wales are male. However, about a third of violent crime stories in the media are about female offenders. This raises the question as to why the media seem to be more interested in female offenders than males.

As we have seen, views of and explanations for women and their involvement or lack of involvement in crime have ranged from exploring the inherently different natures of men and women to focusing on the socially constructed gender roles that influence men's and women's lives. There has often been (and still continues to be) a widely held acceptance of 'common-sense' assumptions of female behaviour. From an essentialist (naturalistic) point of view, females have a different countenance to men. This naturalistic explanation renders anything that deviates from the female norm as 'unnatural'. The acceptable female norm is closely linked to female biology. For example women are seen to be closer to nature as they give birth and are subject to the menstrual cycle. It is widely assumed, then, that women are naturally caring, emotional and maternal.

This view of women has been criticized by many as assuming that what is natural is morally right and desirable. But even more important, especially to feminist thinkers, is the view that these attributes are accepted as natural and not socially constructed and, importantly, that this 'evolutionary' explanation naturalizes and justifies the continuation of sexist attitudes to and perceptions of female criminals (see pp. 162–165).

In recent years the media have helped in the formation of strong biological interpretations of female behaviour which have found their way into explanations for female criminality, for example premenstrual syndrome, battered women syndrome, post-natal depression, infanticide. This has resulted in more sympathetic treatment by the media and the criminal justice system as it denotes a form of diminished responsibility. As an example of this, premenstrual syndrome (PMS) has been used successfully in courts as a mitigation for crimes varying from shoplifting to murder. A famous case we referred to earlier was that of R v Craddock in 1980 and R v Smith in 1981 (Craddock and Smith being the same person – see p. 166) where it was successfully argued that Craddock suffered from acute PMS. Since that case, PMS has continued to be used as a mitigating factor in the British courts.

However, by rooting offending women's behaviour within biological and psychological explanations we are in danger of creating an over-simplistic view of female criminality. To recap, interpretations of female criminality that have focused on biological and psychological differences between men and women have also been used to explain women's relative lack of involvement in crime. However sociological and feminist-based explanations emphasize the social construction of gender identity and how this influences behaviour, including criminal behaviour. So, for instance, girls and women have fewer opportunities for crime as girls tend to be more constrained and regulated by their families when growing up.

Common-sense assumptions about gender roles and the 'appropriate' behaviour for men and women are reflected in the way the media report crime and criminals and their use of these stereotypical views of women. The language or discourse used by the media is a key factor here. Discourse is an important concept when discussing the media portrayal of the female offender. Indeed Foucault argued that, 'Social control depends on language. Discourses of sexuality, sanity and criminality are transformed into a technology of power formulated in terms of the law' (1978: 87).

The narrative within the media is in essence a form of story telling. Within news media, items are often referred to as 'stories'. This is most apparent within newspapers and TV crime news in which journalists construct news stories which can be evaluated easily by the audience. News and the selling of newspaper then is reliant on a number of 'stock stories' which follow a well established path. The idea of the stock story within mainstream journalistic portrayals of female offenders has been much documented during the last 20 years. Often these stock stories come in the form of binary classifications steeped in gothic story telling, for example the virgin or vamp (see Benedict 1992). On the one hand is the Lady Macbeth figure (the unnatural monster and manipulator) or the Pygmalion; on the other hand is the dupe, the woman who is willing to do anything for love and resorts to killing as a way of cementing her relationship with a man (see Cameron and Fraser 1987). Other narratives focus on appearance and contrast the ugly duckling with the femme fatale. Finally are those stories that focus on women's biology and psychology and emphasize the mad and the bad, which gives recourse to the so called link between femininity and madness and evil (see Frigon 1995).

Bronwyn Naylor (2001) examined the reporting of violence in the British print media and found significant differences in the intensity and nature or the reporting of violent male and female offenders. Again narratives used in female accounts pointed to the emotional and irrational nature of female crime whilst male violence was presented as 'normal' and 'natural'.

The male gaze

The concept of the 'male gaze' was first introduced in media studies by Laura Mulvey in the 1970s to describe how the audience is forced to view women through the eyes of the heterosexual man. Although first used in film theory the concept is often applied to other kinds of media, for example advertising and journalism. The male gaze points to the fact that images of females within the media are framed for the benefit of the 'male', therefore images stress the importance of physical attractiveness. This idea can be seen in the way that when female offenders are portrayed, the offender's physical appearance rather than the offence itself often become the focus of attention.

In their book *Media and Body* image, Wykes and Gunter (2004) argue that the media are guilty of socially constructing femininity. Powerful messages which are unrealistic yet persuasive are used within the media to encourage women to fit the feminine stereotype. For example women are encouraged and expected to be forever slim, youthful, feminine and heterosexual. In terms of female offenders their appearance, unlike their male counterpart, is subject to intense scrutiny.

Physical appearance becomes an important aspect in the reporting of female offenders. Rather than the offence being described, the female offender becomes the central focus. The male gaze becomes an important tool when analysing the content of newspaper articles. Most reports of female offenders are dichotomized into those who fit the male gaze, those who are physically attractive and those who are the opposite and physically unattractive. This dichotomy is popularly reflected in the contrasting images of the ugly duckling and the femme fatale.

QUESTION BREAK

The extract below is adapted from an article by Dawn K. Cecil entitled 'Looking Beyond Caged Heat: Media Images of Women in Prison' (2007).

Media Images of Women in Prison

Images of prison life are gendered. Most feature men in prison and highlight the violent nature of these institutions, and when they concentrate on women, the imagery is sexualized (Britton 2003). These images of women in prison are found in all facets of the media; however, most of the literature on the representation of female prisoners focuses on the entertainment media.

The most common and damaging of these images are produced by Hollywood. Rafter (2006: 175) states, 'Until recently, if one wanted to see a film about women in prison, there were only two choices: *I Want to Live!* and soft pornography,' the latter of which are commonly referred to as 'babes-behind-bars' or 'vixens in chains' films. Films such as *Big Doll House* (1971), *The Big Bird Cage* (1972), and *Caged Heat* (1974) are notorious for their highly sexualized images of women in prison. Very little factual representation is contained in these films. It is Hollywood, after all; they do not necessarily seek to educate – instead they aim to titillate: 'These tales of vulnerable young things navigating a harsh prison are largely vehicles for money shot-style images that are the films' raison d'être: a roomful of women being hosed down by their sadistic warden as punishment (1971's *Big Doll House*) . . . or a young reform-school inmate gang-raped with a plunger by her roommates (1974's *Born Innocent*)' (Clark 2005: 37–8).

Images of women in prison are not limited to Hollywood representations; television producers also focus on these women in entertainment programs as well as in educational and news programs. In terms of entertainment television, not many dramas focus on prison life, let alone women in prison. Two women-in-prison dramas have been aired on British and Australian networks. In an attempt to educate viewers on the perils of women in prison, an Australian production company created *Prisoner Cell Block H*, also known as *Prisoner*, which aired in the 1970s (see Wilson and O'Sullivan 2004). Although it was intended to be a serious drama about women in prison, Wilson and O'Sullivan (2004) comment that it quickly became 'archetypical camped-up cliché' (p. 123), thereby losing its ability to educate and inform viewers.

The second program is *Bad Girls*, which is currently in its eighth season on British television. Set almost entirely in a fictitious women's prison in South London, it is said to be a combination of soap opera, cult TV program, and drama (Wilson and O'Sullivan 2004). According to Wilson and O'Sullivan (2004), *Bad Girls* is popular because it plays to the audience's desire to be entertained, while at the same time making a conscious effort to bring prison issues to the forefront. In doing so, the program 'generally concludes that, as far as women are concerned, for a surprising proportion of prisoners prison is not an appropriate response to their problems, or their offending behavior' (Wilson and O'Sullivan 2004: 130). However, this program does not completely diverge from its film predecessors in that sexuality is a key issue. Although less common than images presented on the silver screen, those presented in these television dramas offer a more comprehensive look into the lives of female prisoners, which is probably due in part to the serial nature of these programs. One must remember, though, that the images are still fictionalized, thereby limiting the accuracy of the information presented.

- Using recent TV soap operas and films how do they portray the female prisoner?
- Cecil states that these sexualized images of women in prison are damaging. Why might this be the case? Do you agree?

FURTHER READING

Renzetti, C. M. (2011) *Feminist Criminology*, Routledge. Feminist criminology grew out of the Women's Movement of the 1970s in response to the neglect of women by, and the male dominance of, mainstream criminology. This important book traces the development of feminist criminology and assesses its impact. It considers the development of feminist theoretical perspectives and empirical research in criminology. The book also includes an extensive bibliography covering the wide body of feminist criminological literature.

Walklate, S. (2004) *Gender, Crime and Criminal Justice* (2nd edn) Willan Publishing. This text provides a thorough overview of explanations as to why women do (and do not) commit crime and on the treatment women offenders receive from the criminal justice system. It considers women both as offenders and as victims; and also examines in some depth issues around the fear of crime and sexual violence.

Feminist Criminology is a journal published quarterly by Sage Publications. The journal focuses on current research related to women and girls and crime within the context of feminist critique of criminology. It also provides a forum for discussion of the different contexts within which women and girls come into contact with crime and the criminal justice system including as victims, prisoners and as workers within the system.

WEBSITE

www.methodist.edu/criminaljustice/index.htm. This website is a general criminology one which contains a wealth of information on criminological theorizing. It discusses the work of many of the theorists we have looked at in examining the criminal behaviour of women, including Alder, Hirschi and Lombroso.

Explaining the Criminal Behaviour of Ethnic Minorities

▌ INTRODUCTION

The idea of 'black crime' and more generally the relationship between race and crime are seen as recent phenomena, and, while our focus will be on explanations for current patterns of ethnic minority crime, it would be appropriate to start with a brief reminder that this is not a new issue. 'Scientific' approaches to the notion of racial differences and hierarchies are seen as originating at the time of the Enlightenment – with Enlightenment philosophers associating civilization with white European peoples and regarding other cultural and racial groups as less rational and moral than these white populations. Phillips and Bowling (2002) refer to Gobineau's 1853 essay on *The Inequality of Human Races* in which 'negroes' are described as having mental faculties that are 'dull or even non-existent' and as killing 'willingly, for the sake of killing'. Later in the nineteenth century, Lombroso (whose theorizing is examined more fully below) argued that there was a clear link between race and crime: 'many of the characteristics found in savages, and in the coloured races, are also to be found in habitual delinquents'.

Such theories and arguments legitimated ideas of white supremacy and practices of slavery. British merchants and traders sold their goods for black slaves from Africa, who were taken to the West Indies to work in the British colonies there. Although slavery was abolished in the nineteenth century, the notion of the superiority of the white race and, in particular, the British Empire has left a legacy of racist thinking. And such thinking was brought to the fore in the 1950s and 1960s when immigration from the British colonies was encouraged as a result of the labour shortage in Britain. While there was a clear need for immigrant workers in Britain, their arrival still encouraged racist sentiments and worries around the 'racial degeneration'. There was widespread hostility to the influx of 'coloured' immigrants to particular areas of Britain, the best-known example being Enoch Powell's 1968 speech predicting 'rivers of blood' on the streets of Britain as a result of immigration from Asia and the West Indies. Although Powell's comments were widely condemned, when Margaret Thatcher became Prime Minister in 1979 her sympathetic comments over white fears of being ' swamped' by 'alien cultures' reflected similar sentiments. In the early 1980s the inner-city disorders in many parts of Britain, most notably Brixton, Bristol, Liverpool and Manchester, lent support to the stereotype of black youths as disorderly and criminal. This stereotype still exists today, fuelled by right-wing political parties such as the British National Party (BNP) and evidenced in the relative success of the party in recent years – as the following comment from the BNP manifesto for the 2010 election illustrates: 'Immigration has had a dramatic effect on Britain's rising crime rate. According to official figures, over 77 per cent of adult black males between the ages of 18 and 35 are on the police's DNA database.' However, when these supposedly 'official figures' are examined, their reliability is brought into question. For instance, everyone who is arrested has their DNA taken meaning that many people are on the database without ever being convicted of a crime; and as some people are arrested more than once they might well be double counted.

Reports of the disorders of the early and mid-1980s highlighted the deprived social and economic conditions of the areas where there were high concentrations of ethnic-minority groups. Ethnic-minority groups were shown to be concentrated in the most deprived and depressed neighbourhoods; Afro-Caribbean boys, in particular, were over-represented in exclusions from schools; and unemployment rates were consistently higher among ethnic-minority groups than for the population as a whole. None the less, the basic link between crime and certain ethnic-minority groups was never far from media and public thinking. And, as we have indicated, this link has a long, undistinguished history. The rest of this chapter looks at the evidence and explanations for the link between race and crime. In recent years terrorist crimes have been committed by many different ethnic-minority groups in many countries including Britain. However, the focus of this chapter is on the criminal activities of black ethnic minorities in Britain.

THE EVIDENCE – PATTERNS AND TRENDS

QUESTION BREAK

Before reading this section consider the following questions and return to them later.

- Which crimes are commonly perceived as committed by Afro-Caribbeans or Asians?
- Which crimes do you associate with Afro-Caribbeans or Asians?
- Where have your ideas come from?

It is a common stereotype that young males, and especially young ethnic-minority, and particularly black, males, are especially prone to criminal behaviour. And a range of crimes are widely seen as typically committed by young black males. Since the 1960s, for instance, drug use and supply and 'mugging' or street robbery have been popularly associated with black people and more recently car-jacking and gangland violence have been characterized in a similar way. Illegal immigration and asylum seeking have also been associated with ethnic-minority groups, although this has tended to be characterized as Asian and/or Middle Eastern rather than black. Indeed this highlights the danger of lumping all ethnic-minority groups together when examining 'race and crime' – a point we will reiterate throughout this chapter.

Before looking at the official data and statistics on ethnic-minority involvement in crime, we will consider this characterization of certain types of crime as typically the preserve of 'black' or other ethnic-minority groups. In the mid-1990s, the Metropolitan Police Commissioner Sir Paul Condon controversially stated that the majority of muggers in London were black. It is well established that black people are more likely to be stopped by police than whites, with one of the most senior black officers in the Metropolitan police, Chief Inspector McConney, making the point that too many police officers acted on hunches and stereotypes, so that in the 1960s black people in cars were seen as ponces, whereas in the 1980s and 1990s they were seen as drug dealers (Hyder 1995). However, a closer and more historically informed look makes it clear that mugging – essentially street robbery – is neither a new nor a particularly 'black' crime. Histories of crime highlight the panic over street robberies such as garrotting in the mid nineteenth century and the criminality of the first officially named 'Hooligans' of the later nineteenth century (Pearson 1983). The media of the time helped to fuel a moral panic over the 'new' crime of garrotting; as Pearson commented: 'Panic swept through respectable London in the winter of 1862 about what *The Times* (10 June 1863) would eventually describe as a "new variety of crime" and "this modern peril of the streets [that] created something like a reign of terror"' (pp. 128–9). Of course highway hold-ups and robbery are a part of our folklore; and, while it is easy to romanticize the exploits of 'stand and deliver' highwaymen such as Dick Turpin, the truth is probably less glamorous. Indeed Dick Turpin, born in Essex in 1708, was a cattle thief who fled into the countryside when caught trying to steal two oxen and, rather than being a lone highwayman, was a member of the Essex Gang who invaded isolated farmhouses, terrorizing and torturing the female occupants into giving up their belongings.

Similarly, there has been recent comment and concern about the upsurge in gangland violence and shootings in British cities which have been associated with black people, even by politicians who tend to be seen as sympathetic to ethnic-minority groups and issues. For instance, Lee Jasper, a race campaigner and leading adviser to the former Mayor of London Ken Livingstone, blamed the recent upsurge in shootings and car-jacking on a moral vacuum inhabited by many black people, saying that 'young men have been sucked into a multimillion pound economy of drugs and guns which subverts mainstream morality and social responsibility' (*Guardian*, 17 February 2002). More recently, Nicholas Clarke, known as Ratty, was one of many black youths killed in London in 2008 (*Guardian,* 19 March 2010) However, again, gangland violence and shootings are not new phenomena – there were vicious gang fights in major British cities in the 1920s and 1930s and, to quote from Pearson's historical account again, 'razor gangs, race-course roughs, violent bag-snatchers, vice rackets and motor banditry were integral features of the crime picture in the interwar years, and feuds between armed mobsters were not unknown' (1983: 38). This was a period of violence and criminality in the United States as well – with Prohibition and the 'reign' of gangsters such as Al Capone.

The notion that illegal immigration is linked with 'black crime' is further exposed by a glance at the data on asylum seekers. As well as the number of asylum seekers going down in recent years – the number of asylum applications in 2009 was 24,250 down from a peak of 84,130 in 2002 (National Statistics Online) – the top six applicant nations were Afghanistan, Zimbabwe, Iran, Eritrea, Iraq and China, and not nations associated with Afro-Caribbean criminality.

Having explored and debunked some of the popular perceptions, or myths, about race and criminality, we must look at the official data; and these data need to be set in their historical context.

Like many, if not all, nations with a long history, Britain has always been culturally heterogeneous. Indeed immigration is a common feature in the development of all 'advanced' Western societies and this was particularly so across Europe in the 1950s and 1960s in the aftermath of the Second World War. However, the British situation during this period was different from other Western nations in that migrants to Britain had an automatic right of entry; they were British passport holders living in British or ex-British colonies around the world. And these migrants to Britain were also different from many of the 'guest workers' who entered other European nations because of the colour of their skin – because they were non-white. More specifically, in the 1950s and 1960s there was a massive increase in immigration to Britain from the New Commonwealth, and in particular from Asia and the West Indies. This sudden and large influx of immigrant groups soon encouraged concern if not panic among sections of society and led to new and major restrictions on immigration being introduced in the 1970s and since. However, it is now almost two generations on from the 1950s and 1960s and the majority of children in ethnic-minority groups in contemporary Britain were born in the country.

As we highlighted in the introductory comments above, partly as a result of the rapid increase in immigration and therefore ethnic-minority group numbers and partly as a result of the high visibility of black ethnic-minority groups, public concerns about immigration grew in the 1960s and 1970s. One area of concern was the supposed link between ethnic background and criminality – a concern which prompted sociological research into the relationship between race and crime. In their major study of delinquency published in 1983 Rutter and Giller reviewed such studies and research on race and crime. An early study by Lambert (1970) concluded that first-generation immigrants were no more delinquent than the indigenous white population. However, ethnic-minority immigrants tended to live in areas which had high rates of crime; and while the reasons for this were economic (not being able to afford housing in 'better' areas) such an association would encourage a 'misleading impression in the public image that black immigrants were themselves delinquent'. Rutter and Giller suggested that up to about 1970 rates of crime and delinquency for the black and Asian populations were comparable to, or below, those of the white population. And while the younger members of these groups were no more delinquent than their peers, West Indian boys were found to be more disruptive at school and tended to have a higher rate of features associated with a higher risk of delinquency, such as low educational attainment, being part of large families and admission into care.

Since then some studies have suggested that second- and third-generation ethnic-minority youths have developed distinctive subcultures which can encourage criminality and delinquency. However, there is little evidence that this joining of subcultures was more evident amongst black youth than young people in general and Rutter and Giller suggested there was also evidence which suggested that many black teenagers appeared to be more committed to education than their white peers. With regard to different ethnic groups, Stevens and Willis (1979) found that Asian crime rates were substantially lower than white rates and found that Asian communities (at this time anyway) were generally law-abiding. By contrast, arrest rates for black groups (and especially West Indian) were much higher than for the white population for both adults and juveniles. In concluding their review, Rutter and Giller highlighted three distinct findings. First, the delinquency rates for Asians had been and remained equal to or lower than those for the white population. Second, although the arrest rates for blacks in the 1950s and 1960s were similar to those for whites, they had risen substantially above that during the 1970s. Third, most of the violent crime that did occur was between people of the same skin colour. Since the late 1970s and Rutter and Giller's study the position regarding Asian criminality has altered. The notion of young Asians as being essentially 'conformist' has been challenged by groups of Asian youths defending 'their territory' from racist white youths. As Phillips and Bowling (2002) comment, the idea of the 'Asian gang' was 'brought to the fore in 1994 by the murder of Richard Everitt in King's Cross by a group of Bangladeshi youths, the disorders in Manningham in Bradford in 1995, and again in the summer of 2001 with disorders in Oldham, Burnley and Bradford'. More recently, Pakistani and Bangladeshi groups have been portrayed as increasingly violent and disorderly and as a source of Islamic terrorism – a portrayal that was cemented by the London bombings of July 2005, perpetrated by Muslim and British citizens (Phillips and Bowling 2007).

More generally, what is the situation almost thirty years on from Rutter and Giller's work? Official Home Office statistics on race and the criminal justice system are produced annually under section 95 of the Criminal Justice Act 1991, which states that 'The Secretary of State shall in each year publish such information, as he considers expedient for the purpose of . . . [avoiding] discriminating against any persons on the ground of race or sex or any other improper ground'. These statistics provide a wealth of information across a range of areas including stop and search rates, arrest rates, prosecutions and imprisonment, as well as detailing the numbers and proportions of ethnic minority practitioners working in the different criminal justice agencies. The Ministry of Justice report of April 2009 refers to figures for 2007/8 and covers England and Wales. As regards the percentage of the population from different ethnic groups, the 2001 census figures are used, with 2.8 per cent of the general population Black, 4.7 per cent Asian and 1.2 per cent 'Other'. These proportions need to be kept in mind when looking at the proportions of different ethnic minority groups involved with crime and criminal justice. There were 1,035,438 stop and searches recorded by the police in 2007/8, of which 13 per cent were of Black people, 8 per cent of Asian, 3 per cent of mixed ethnicity and 1 per cent of Chinese or 'other' ethnic origin. So relative to the general population figures, Black people were 8 times more likely to be stopped and searched than White people, and Asian people twice as likely. Of just under 1.5 million arrests for notifiable offences, 7 per cent were recorded as being of Black people, 5 per cent Asian, 3 per cent of mixed ethnicity and 1 per cent Chinese or 'other', with Black people almost four times more likely to be arrested than White people. The report also breaks down these arrest figures for different offence groups, which show that the main differences between ethnic groups was a greater tendency for White people to be arrested for burglary and criminal damage, Black people for robbery and fraud and forgery and Asian people for fraud and forgery. Table 6.1 provides a summary of information on the ethnic background of those who come into contact with the criminal justice system at different stages.

Table 6.1 Percentage of ethnic groups at different stages of the criminal justice process compared to the ethnic breakdown of the general population, England and Wales, 2007–08

| | Ethnicity | | | | | | |
	White	Mixed	Black	Asian	Chinese or Other	Not stated/ Unknown	Total
General population (aged 10 & over) @ 2001 Census	91.3	1.3	2.2	4.4	0.9	0.0	100
Stops and searches[1]	68.1	2.5	13.1	8.1	1.2	7.0	100
Arrests[2]	79.3	2.8	7.4	5.1	1.4	4.0	100
Cautions[2][3]	82.5		6.5	4.6	1.4	5.0	100
Youth offences	84.8	3.5	5.8	3.0	0.4	2.5	100
Tried at Crown Court[3][4]	73.5		14.0	8.0	4.4	*	100
Court ordered supervision by probation service[5]	83.6	2.5	6.3	4.6	1.2	1.8	100
Prison receptions[6]	79.1	2.9	10.6	5.9	1.2	0.2	100

Note: Figures may not add to 100% due to rounding.

(1) Stops and searches recorded by the police under section 1 of the Police and Criminal Evidence Act 1984 and other legislation.

(2) Notifiable offences.

(3) The data in these rows is based on ethnic appearance, and as such does not include the category Mixed ethnicity (the data in the rest of the table is based on self-identified ethnicity).

(4) Information on ethnicity is missing in 19% of cases; therefore, percentages are based on known ethnicity.

(5) Commencements

(6) Sentenced.

Summarize the information in the table and try to offer explanations for the over-representation of the different non-White ethnic groups at the different stages of the criminal justice system.

The proportions of ethnic-minority groups in prisons are massively greater than would be expected by the general population figures. Data from the Ministry of Justice report of April 2009 showed that at the end of June 2008, 27 per cent of the prison population of 83,194 were from BME (Black Minority Ethnic) groups. Black and minority ethnic groups accounted for 27 per cent of the male prison population (15 per cent Black, 7 per cent Asian and 5 per cent Mixed, Chinese and Other) and 29 per cent of the female prison population (19 per cent Black, 3 per cent Asian and 7 per cent Mixed, Chinese and Other). However, these figures included foreign nationals, who made up 14 per cent of the male and 23 per cent of the female prison populations. Even looking only at British nationals, there were more than five times more Black people in prison per head of the population than White people.

- How could you account for the massive discrepancy in prison figures between Black, White and Asian populations?
- Why do you think almost a fifth of female prisoners are Black?

Finally, with regard to people working in the criminal justice system, the most obvious finding is the under-representation of ethnic-minority groups. While these figures do not relate to Black and non-White people committing crime, they are worth mentioning in relation to the treatment and perceptions of treatment of ethnic-minority groups by the criminal justice system, and to the related issue of bias (or not) within the system. In 2003–4 the proportion of Black and ethnic-minority officers with the 43 police forces in England and Wales was 3.3 per cent; however, the figure dropped to 2 per cent for those at Inspector or Chief Inspector level. None the less this was an increase on previous years, and a similar increase was found in the number of Black and ethnic-minority prison officers, with 4.1 per cent from Black and ethnic-minority backgrounds. However when it comes to the judiciary, the proportion of non-White people reaching the more senior positions is virtually negligible. Of the 105 High Court Judges and 36 Lord Chief Justices none was from ethnic-minority backgrounds; amongst the 564 Circuit Judges, one was Black and three Asian (*Statistics on Race and Criminal Justice System*, London: Stationery Office, 2004).

So far we have considered the data and patterns around race and crime. The next section turns to the theoretical explanations for the links between ethnic group background and criminal behaviour.

EXPLANATIONS

There are two basic explanations for the heavy over-representation of ethnic-minority groups in the crime statistics: first, that ethnic minorities, and especially black people, do commit more crime than the white population and the reasons for this 'fact' need to be explored and established; second, that ethnic-minority groups do not commit any more crime than the rest of the population but the criminal justice agencies, such as the police and courts, work in a way which is biased against them so that they are more likely to be recorded as committing crimes. This second line of explanation examines issues of racism within the criminal justice system. First, though, we will look at black crime as a social reality. This basic division – which suggests a sort of either/or in terms of whether ethnic-minority populations commit more crime than the white population or whether such groups face discriminatory treatment by the criminal justice system and so are over-represented in crime statistics – has been criticized by recent commentators (Phillips and Bowling 2002). Such a distinction, it is argued, ignores or underplays the experience of ethnic minorities as victims of crime. While acknowledging this is an important issue, the focus in this chapter is on why particular groups of people do or do not commit crime and in order to keep this focus we will consider different explanations under the two basic explanations for the disparity in crime statistics between the black and white populations suggested above.

Black crime as social reality

We have been using the terms 'ethnic minority' and 'black' and it is important to be aware that such terms cover very broad categories that need to be broken down when looking at explanations for criminal behaviour. The stereotypical black criminal has been based around African or Caribbean groups, who have been seen for centuries as having characteristics that predisposed them to criminality. In contrast, Asian criminality has been viewed in a very different way; the popular image of Asian communities has been one which has not highlighted criminality, but rather passivity, family-centredness, tradition and conformity. Although this image has been challenged in recent years, with examples of Asian youths turning to criminal and violent behaviour, the basic stereotypical division remains (see p. 188).

Biological explanations

The earliest criminological theorizing that attempted to explain the link between crime and race offered individualistic solutions – focusing on the biological and/or psychological characteristics of offenders. These approaches, which emerged in the nineteenth century, adopted the methods of the natural sciences and were particularly influenced by the work of Charles Darwin and other 'Darwinists'. Cesare Lombroso is generally regarded as the most influential of the early scientific criminologists and as the 'founder' of modern criminology. In his book *L'uomo delinquente* (The Criminal Man), published in 1876, he developed a complex description of what he called the 'born criminal', who could be recognized by a variety of physical characteristics, in particular facial characteristics – for example large jaws and high cheek bones. In the medical faculty at the University of Rome there are portraits of splendidly ugly delinquents who were used by Lombroso to illustrate his theory. For Lombroso criminals were throwbacks to an earlier evolutionary form of species. To use his own language:

> Thus were explained anatomically the enormous jaws, high cheek bones, prominent superciliary arches, solitary lines on the palms, extreme size of the orbits, handle-shaped or sessile ears found in criminals, savages and apes, insensibility of pain, extremely acute sight, tattooing, excessive idleness, love of orgies and the irresistible craving for evil for its own sake.

Lombroso believed there was a clear link between racial origin and criminality. As he put it, 'many of the characteristics found in savages, and among the coloured races, are also to be found in habitual delinquents'. Among these common characteristics were thinning hair, receding foreheads, darker skin, curly hair and large ears. By contrast the white race were the most evolved species and 'represent the triumph of the human species'.

Lombroso's ideas were developed in Britain and the United States and played a part in the eugenics movement and its advocating of selective policies to improve the human race – through, for instance, encouraging elite groups to have children and discouraging the less intelligent. Although Lombroso's work has been widely criticized and rejected by social scientists, the attempt to identify biological explanations for crime and to link this with race has continued and will be explored briefly here.

While most advocates of biologically based theories do not express themselves in the same bizarre language and style as Lombroso, such approaches to explaining crime are not merely historical relics that died with Lombroso. In a major study of institutionalized delinquents in the USA in the 1950s, Sheldon and Eleanor Glueck found that delinquent boys were twice as likely to have a mesomorphic build – a chunky muscular physique – compared to non-delinquent boys. Similarly, Herrnstein, writing in the 1990s, concluded that mesomorphic people were more likely to become criminals. With regard to the links between criminal behaviour and inherited characteristics, other theoretical explanations have suggested an association between criminality and personality. Such approaches might be termed 'psychological positivism' and see the most usual psychological 'cause' of crime to be low intelligence, as measured by IQ tests. Again, the work of Herrnstein (1995) has been at the forefront of such theorizing, arguing that the fact that criminals have lower IQs is 'among the prime discoveries of criminology'. Herrnstein and Charles Murray (see next section) wrote *The Bell Curve*, which, as well as being a best-selling book, excited massive controversy in the scientific community. It explored the role of intelligence in understanding social problems in America, the term 'bell curve' referring to the bell-shaped graph that a normal distribution of IQ scores would show. Herrnstein and Murray argue that there has been a rise of a 'cognitive elite', a stratum of highly intelligent people who have the greatest chance of success in life. However, the book became (in)famous for its discussion of the links between race and intelligence and its examination of the role IQ plays in determining the social and economic differences between ethnic groups. The authors argue that intelligence is largely inherited and that genetic differences in intelligence are increasingly contributing to social and economic differences among individuals. The claims that white ethnic groups had more (natural) intelligence than other ethnic groups attracted the most controversy, with the subsequent debate and defence largely centred on the work and ideas of Murray, as Herrnstein died in the early 1990s before *The Bell Curve* was published. Indeed the debate around the book led the American Psychological Association to set up a task force to investigate the claims made in it. Essentially its report was non-commital, stressing that there was no definite evidence that the black–white differences in test scores were due to genetic differences between the groups. It concluded that 'the question (as to whether there were genetic explanations for differences in intelligence) has no scientific answer'.

QUESTION BREAK

- If it could be proved that the causes of criminal behaviour could be found in physical (bodily) or mental characteristics that some people were born with, what sort of policies might be suggested to deal with crime?
- What problems or dangers could you foresee if such explanations were widely accepted?

Look also at the discussion of biological explanations in Chapter 2.

These biological and psychologically based theories do not focus solely on race; however, it is never far from the surface and is regularly linked with crime through its association with supposedly inherited characteristics such as intelligence or extraversion. A major problem faced by approaches that suggest a link between genetic make-up and criminality is the difficulty of separating genetic and environmental effects. While genetic influences certainly exist, just what is inherited is very difficult to measure.

Cultural explanations – the importance of economic and social conditions

Moving away from the individualistic, physiological explanations for criminal behaviour, cultural theories take a sociological approach to explaining crime. Crime cannot be considered apart from its social context; crime and the criminal can be understood only in relation to the social structure and to the social conditions and opportunities that impact on individuals' lives. Sociological explanations for crime were considered in Chapter 4, and in this section we will try to relate these sorts of theoretical approaches to the issue of race and crime. Cultural theories focus on the lifestyles of different groups within society – and offer different perspectives on them. Bowling and Phillips (2002) suggest three major variants of cultural theory – conservative, liberal and radical – which we will introduce briefly here.

Conservative cultural theory offers a right-wing approach that suggests there is an 'underclass' whose poor position, in terms of poverty, is largely its members' own fault and a result of their own inadequacy and lack of drive. Although the notion of an 'underclass' has been around for many years (with the 'dangerous classes' regularly referred to in the eighteenth and nineteenth centuries) Charles Murray 'rediscovered' and applied the term in the 1980s and 1990s, suggesting that in modern Western societies there was a growing group of people who inhabit a 'different world' to the decent and respectable majority (1990). He saw crime as heavily focused in underclass neighbourhoods where young males are socialized from an early age to seeing crime as a normal activity. Although it is not just a 'race' issue, conservative, 'underclass' theorists see ethnic-minority groups as not assimilating into the majority white culture but rather as holding on to their own values and norms, and have argued that there is a strong tendency for ethnic-minority communities, especially black communities, to fit into the 'underclass'. Such an approach, which essentially sees criminal behaviour as a matter of choice, takes no real account of the ways in which individuals' and groups' life chances are structured by social and economic forces that are largely beyond their own control.

Liberal cultural theory suggests that crime (and, more generally, disorders such as riots) is a collective demonstration of despair by those who are marginalized in modern society. Crime, then, is largely a result of social position, with class and ethnic background being key factors that affect such position. With regard to race, the Chicago school of social researchers, writing between the 1920s and 1940s, noted the tendency of ethnic immigrant groups to become concentrated in poorer inner-city areas. The Chicago researchers defined 'zones of transition' in the city in which immigrant groups were particularly likely to settle. Some groups managed to move out of these 'zones' and become assimilated into the wider cultural life of the city. Others were not able to escape these socially disorganized areas which were characterized by crime and poverty. These ideas were applied in a famous study of race and class by Rex and Moore (1967) to Britain and the settling of immigrant groups in the Sparkbrook area of Birmingham in the late 1960s. This approach sees black groups as prone to criminality because of their poor economic, social and geographical position within white society. In response to the conditions they face, deviant and criminal subcultures are formed, and black and Asian groups have been seen as particularly likely to form such subcultures as a way of coping with what they perceive as a hostile wider society. As Lea and Young (1984) put it, 'the economic alienation of young black people gives rise to a culture with a propensity for crime' (quoted in Bowling and Phillips 2002).

Radical or critical cultural theory does not see crime as basically a part of black culture. Rather it focuses on the conditions which drive black people to commit crime. Social and economic conditions encourage black cultures to develop which challenge their oppressed position. The law, both immigration and criminal, discriminates against black groups and, indeed, serves to 'criminalize' them; and the police response to black youth and black crime is seen as exacerbating the sense of oppression felt by such groups. One response to this situation, for black youth in particular, has been to turn to illegitimate avenues for economic and social fulfilment.

QUESTION BREAK: THE UNDERCLASS

Read the following extracts and consider the questions below.

There are many ways to identify an underclass. I will concentrate on three phenomena that have turned out to be early-warning signals in the United States: illegitimacy, violent crime, and drop out from the labour force . . . I begin with illegitimacy, which in my view is the best predictor of an underclass in the making.

Illegitimacy and the underclass

Why should it be a 'problem' that a woman has a child without a husband? . . . Why is raising a child without having married any more of a problem than raising a child after a divorce?

. . . Illegitimacy has been sky-rocketing since 1979 . . . From the end of the Second World War until 1960 Britain enjoyed a very low and even slightly declining illegitimacy ratio . . .

The sharp rise is only half the story. The other and equally important half is that illegitimate births are not scattered evenly among the British population . . . The increase in illegitimate births is strikingly concentrated amongst the lowest social class . . .

'It's mainly a black problem.' . . . The statement is correct in this one, very limited sense: blacks born in the West Indies have much higher illegitimacy rates – about 48% of live births is the latest number – than all whites.

Crime and the underclass

Crime is the next place to look for an underclass for several reasons. First and most obviously, the habitual criminal is the classic member of an underclass. He lives off mainstream society without participating in it . . . To the extent that many people in a community engage in crime as a matter of course, all sorts of the socializing norms of the community change, from the kind of men that the younger boys chose as heroes to the standards of morality in general.

Unemployment and the underclass

If illegitimate births are the leading indicator of an underclass and violent crime a proxy measure of its development, the definitive proof that an underclass has arrived is that large numbers of young, healthy, low-income males choose not to take jobs . . .

My hypothesis . . . is that Britain is experiencing a generation gap by class. Well-educated young people from affluent homes are working in larger proportions and working longer hours than ever. The attitudes and behaviour of the middle-aged working class haven't changed much. The change in stance toward the labour force is concentrated among lower-class young men in their teens and twenties. It is not a huge change. I am not suggesting that a third or a quarter or even a fifth of lower-class young people are indifferent to work. An underclass doesn't have to be huge to become a problem.

(Murray 1990)

Zones of transition

As we saw above, the idea of a zone of transition comes from the Chicago School of sociologists and specifically Ernest Burgess. It was a zone from his division of the city into a series of concentric circles or zones which had differing usages. The zone of transition was an area between the central business unit and the outer rings of working and middle-class residence; it contained run-down housing which was gradually being displaced as the business areas of the city moved outward. The zone was largely inhabited by the poor and by ethnic minority groups (with the two often overlapping of course). In modern cities the term inner city is roughly what Burgess referred to as the zone of transition. Such an area has a shifting population with little sense of community and a high crime rate.

- How might Murray's notion of an underclass be particularly applied to ethnic-minority groups?
- What criticisms can you make of Murray's argument and hypothesis?
- Think of your region, town or city – can you recognize a 'zone of transition'? How closely does it fit the Chicago School's idea?

These different explanations have been introduced only in a very sketchy manner to highlight the structural and cultural approaches. A problem with such arguments is that they take little account of human agency – of the way in which structure is mediated by the role of the individual. The tendency to see poor, oppressed and marginalized people as almost forced into criminality seems to ignore the fact that there are massive differences in how particular marginalized, ethnic groups respond to their situations. This indicates a more obvious point about over-generalizing, which is illustrated by the fact that one member of a family may engage in theft or violent crime while another, in a similar environment, will not.

Race, crime and bias – black crime as over-exaggerated by the crime statistics

The criminal justice system and racial bias

The argument that the various agencies of the criminal justice system work in a manner that discriminates against ethnic minorities is potentially a major reason for the higher number of ethnic minority offenders. In looking at patterns and trends in criminal statistics earlier, we saw that members of ethnic-minority groups, and especially black people, were more likely to be stopped and searched, arrested and end up in prison than the white population. Here we will consider evidence and arguments that there is bias against ethnic-minority groups. It is important to bear in mind that bias can, and perhaps most often does, result not from deliberate discrimination but through unconscious prejudice and stereotyping. As Cavadino and Dignan put it: 'Bias can operate at any and every stage of the criminal process, stages which include investigation and charge by the police, prosecution decisions by the Crown Prosecution Service, bail decisions, court verdicts and sentencing decisions' (2002: 309). In this brief review, we will look at bias and the potential for bias in the three major criminal justice agencies – the police, the courts and prisons.

First we will consider the extent to which the greater likelihood of black and Asian people being stopped and searched and arrested than white people (see p. 189) is evidence of prejudice and/or discrimination within the British police. This raises the question of whether police culture and practice is racist. Various studies (Smith and Gray 1983; Reiner 2000; Holdaway 1996) have found that police culture is inherently conservative. In part this is because of the nature of police training and practice; the whole process of becoming a police officer happens in a very institutionalized manner, with probationers at the bottom of a rigid hierarchy that emphasizes discipline and following orders. Probationers are placed under the guidance of experienced officers from whom they pick up the 'real' world of day-to-day policing and the common-sense discourse on crime and criminals. Indeed the nature of police work involves developing methods for recognizing certain types of people as 'typical' criminals and encourages the adoption of stereotypes. Furthermore, the nature of police work encourages a distrust of the outside world and a feeling of 'them versus us' expressed in terms such as 'the thin blue line' to describe the police as guardians of respectability against the forces of crime and disorder. The police, then, are likely to feel a sense of isolation from society owing to the special nature of their job (enforcing the law) and this encourages a strong degree of solidarity within the police; and such solidarity helps breed a strong internal working culture.

One element of this essentially conservative culture is racism. As we saw earlier, there are relatively few black police officers, especially in the more senior ranks; this in itself does not mean there is a racist element to police culture, but it may be indicative. The Policy Studies Institute report, *Police and People in London* (Smith and Gray 1983), examined the work of the Metropolitan police force in London and, when published in 1983, was the most detailed study of a British police force yet produced. In looking at the relationship between the police and people in London it provided a good deal of information on police culture and racism. It found that racist language was used in a casual and almost automatic way, even over radio links that were picked up by all officers. For instance, the researchers heard an inspector say, 'Look I've got a bunch of coons in sight.' It is, of course, debatable whether people who use racist language behave in a racist manner. One young officer told the researchers, Smith and Gray, 'I know that PCs call them spooks, niggers and sooties, but deep down the majority of PCs aren't really against them, although there are some who really hate them . . . I call them niggers myself now but I don't really mean it.'

The PSI report found that there was some racism within 'the Met' but that it did not lead to black people being treated in a biased or inferior way, although there was some evidence that the police tended to link crime and black people and so be more suspicious of ethnic-minority groups. In general terms the report found that a lack of confidence in the police was quite widespread among Londoners, and especially amongst young black Londoners, with almost two-thirds (62 per cent) of black

QUESTION BREAK

One aspect of policing that the PSI report referred to above considered was the relationship between the police and black people. Read the brief extract below and answer the questions after it.

> Police officers often use racialist language (among themselves) for effect, but it is the more casual and automatic use of such language that is most telling . . . racialist language is quite commonly used over the personal radio. For example, JG [J. Gray] heard the inspector of the relief with which he was working say over the personal radio, 'look I've got a bunch of coons in sight'. The inspector was standing in a public place at the time, and of course this message came up over the radios of all police officers on the Division . . .
>
> Although the terms by which police officers refer to black people are in common use in various other social contexts, they seem to be more commonly used within the Met than in most other groups: there can be few other groups in which it is normal, automatic, habitual to refer to black people as 'coons', 'niggers' and so on . . .
>
> (From Smith and Gray 1983: 111–15)

- What effects might this language have on black people's view of the police and the law?
- Should police officers be disciplined for using racist language?

(More generally, you might consider whether police officers should have to follow more stringent rules of behaviour than other people in society, given their unique position of authority.)

15–24-year-olds thinking the police often used threats or unreasonable behaviour. However, while this demonstrated a degree of criticism of the police, the vast majority of young black people also said they wanted a police force and did use its services like anyone else.

So, to what extent are the PSI findings relevant almost thirty years on? The Macpherson Inquiry report (1999) into the murder of the black teenager Stephen Lawrence in 1993, highlighted the continued existence of 'institutional racism' within the Metropolitan police. It concluded that the Met operated an 'unwitting' form of racism. In gathering its material, Macpherson took evidence from the Chief Constable of Manchester, David Wilmot, who accepted that institutional racism existed in his force, saying 'we have a society that has got institutional racism. Greater Manchester Police, therefore, has institutional racism . . . and it is our responsibility to try and make sure it is eradicated.' And in a follow-up survey to these remarks, the *Independent* (16 October 1998) found that 'twelve police forces admit racism', with the Chief Constable of Sussex, Paul Whitehouse, for example, stating, 'Yes, there is institutional racism within Sussex police.'

One of the recommendations of the Macpherson Report was to step up efforts to recruit more ethnic-minority officers. Cashmore (2001) considered the issue of under-recruitment in examining the experiences of ethnic-minority officers in Britain. Since the 1960s the British police have been encouraged to recruit more officers from ethnic-minority backgrounds; indeed in 1965 there were only three such officers in the whole British police force. In 1981 the Scarman Report into the Brixton disorders urged more ethnic-minority recruitment to the police. However, the lack of success in this regard was shown by the fact that the Macpherson Report almost twenty years later was again highlighting the police's failure to recruit enough ethnic minorities. Cashmore's research, which was undertaken in the twelve months after the Macpherson Report was published (February 1999), investigated this persistent failure to recruit through interviewing already serving ethnic-minority officers to try to understand their experiences. One area he focused on was the extent to which racism in the police service might explain the under-recruitment. The notion of institutional racism raised by Macpherson was felt by Cashmore to emphasize 'institutional aspects' of police work and ignore the everyday talk and banter which seemed part and parcel of police life. Ethnic-minority officers referred to racist talk which they felt they had to accept, almost as if they were being tested to 'see if they could take a joke'. Other studies of the police's occupational culture have suggested that the day-to-day racism within the police is due to the nature of their work (Chan 1997; Holdaway 1997). Indeed as one officer interviewed by Cashmore said: 'I've got colleagues who subscribe to the philosophy that, if you see four black youths in a car it's worth giving it a pull, at least one of them is going to be guilty of something or other.' And if the police are under pressure to get arrest figures, the officers will be tempted to perform more searches based on their stereotyped views as to who is likely to be a 'good arrest'.

As to why this sort of racist talk is not challenged, the nature of police work necessitates black and white officers working as a team, which can lead to a reluctance to 'rock the boat', and for ethnic-minority officers to avoid 'getting a reputation'. Police work is a potentially dangerous occupation and ethnic-minority officers will want their (white) colleagues to be 'there when they need them'. As one Asian officer put it: 'If I call for assistance that means I need somebody there now, not in ten minutes . . . If I've taken somebody to task for a racial remark or whatever, months or weeks later that somebody might be the one who's called out for me . . . it would put some doubt in your mind.' In concluding, Cashmore suggested that ethnic-minority officers don't challenge racism because of their career ambitions and orientations and, particularly, because of the special nature of police work which can, unlike most jobs, involve life-threatening situations.

In the context of considering the careers of black and ethnic-minority police officers, Britain's most senior black officer and the first black chief constable is Mike Fuller, who began his career with the Met police force in 1975 and became chief constable of Kent in 2004. As part of a BBC *Panorama* documentary broadcast in October 2008, 'The Secret Policeman Returns', looking into the issue of racism in British police forces, Fuller commented that ethnic-minority police officers have to work harder than their white colleagues to succeed: 'BME officers have to work twice as hard to be recognised and really to compete with their peers and that is a big concern'. In producing the documentary, *Panorama* surveyed BME police officers and staff and found many felt that to complain about racism would increase the risk of them being subject to internal investigation. It also sent Freedom of Information requests to all the British police forces asking for data on the number of internal investigations of BME and white officers. The programme found that officers from ethnic minority background were five times more likely to be investigated than white officers in Strathclyde and two and half times more likely in the Met (London).

In relation to institutional racism, the Runnymede Trust carried out an independent review entitled 'The Stephen Lawrence Inquiry 10 Years On' and published in 2009. It concluded that the police remain institutionally racist and that relationships between the police and ethnic minority groups had not improved significantly in the ten years since the Macpherson Inquiry. Also, that the police service was continuing to experience difficulties in recruiting BME officers and had not reached the target set by the Home Secretary, Jack Straw, ten years previously; and that retention of BME officers remained a problem, with disproportionate numbers of these officers leaving the service after two years' service compared with their white colleagues (Runnymede Trust 2009).

There is less research on race, racism and the courts and prisons than with regard to the police. However, one of the most startling of all criminal justice statistics is the massive over-representation of ethnic-minority populations who are sentenced to prison. Although making up just over 6 per cent of the British population, ethnic minorities account for a much higher proportion of the prison population. Data gathered by the Institute of Race Relations showed that in June 2000 ethnic minorities accounted for 19 per cent of the male prison population and 25 per cent of female prisoners (Institute of Race Relations 2002). Since then there has been an increase in the proportion of both male and female black prisoners – Ministry of Justice statistics on race and the criminal justice system (see p. 190) show that in June 2008, 27 per cent of male prisoners and 29 per cent of female prisoners were from black and minority ethnic groups. As well as the basic population figures, there are differences in the length of imprisonment for different ethnic groups – for both young and adult sentenced prisoners. For example 67 per cent of adult Black prisoners were serving a sentence of four years or more, compared to 54 per cent of White adult prisoners; and while overall 13 per cent of sentenced prisoners were serving a sentence of less than one year, 9 per cent of Black prisoners were (Ministry of Justice 2009).

The question such figures raise is whether the differences can be explained by a higher crime rate among ethnic-minority groups or whether other factors, including bias in the system, can offer an explanation. One point to bear in mind is the high number of foreign nationals who are imprisoned for drug smuggling – a factor which skews the female prison figures as a high proportion of such prisoners are black. In addition demographic and social factors will have an influence, such as the lower average age of the ethnic-minority population and the tendency for Afro-Caribbean groups in particular to have other characteristics associated with higher offending, such as higher unemployment, lower educational attainment and living in areas with high crime rates.

However, these points do not tell us if the court system works differently for the different ethnic-minority groups it deals with. Differential treatment in court is likely to occur as a result of the tendency for black offenders to plead not guilty. For example 48 per cent of young black offenders plead not guilty in crown courts, compared to 30 per cent of young white offenders. And as offenders are given heavier sentences if found guilty after not guilty pleas (as a consequence of the discount on sentence given for pleading guilty), this can lead to more black offenders being imprisoned, and for longer.

Hood's study for the Commission for Racial Equality (1992) examined and tried to explain the over-representation of ethnic minority prisoners. In considering whether ethnic minority offenders were sentenced according to the same criteria as white offenders a number of relevant factors were highlighted. A higher proportion of black people were charged with offences that were deemed to be more serious and that could be dealt with only by the crown court. For instance, many more were charged with robbery and, although robbery is a nasty crime, it could be questioned whether it is any more serious than housebreaking or grievous bodily harm (GBH), both of which can be dealt with summarily by magistrates' courts if both parties consent. As regards the classifying of offences, black offenders were disproportionately charged with supplying drugs – and the insistence that offences involving trading in small or moderate amounts of cannabis should be committed to crown court is also likely to influence the rate of imprisonment for black offenders. As well as being more likely to plead not guilty (see above), black defendants were found to be more likely to be remanded in custody by magistrates: a factor which can, again, lead to a greater likelihood of a custodial sentence.

Hood's research suggested that ethnic-minority, and particularly black or Afro-Caribbean, defendants were subject to forms of indirect discrimination at least. The implications of a practice that favours so strongly those who plead guilty and the ways in which different offences are ranked in terms of where they should be tried, for example, would seem to work against the interests of ethnic-minority offenders. Hood acknowledges that it is a complex issue but on the basis of the detailed sample of almost 3,000 crown court cases it would seem that some discrimination does occur in courts.

More recently, Hood, along with Shute and Seemungal, has examined the extent to which ethnic minorities get a fair hearing in the criminal courts (Shute *et al.* 2005). The focus of the study was on perceptions of unfair treatment, which, it is argued, can be as important as unfair treatment itself – if people are treated fairly they will have positive perceptions and increased confidence in the system. The research examined how defendants and witnesses experience their treatment, and was based on a very detailed interview schedule carried out in 2001 and 2002, with defendants, witnesses, court staff, solicitors, magistrates and judges interviewed. All in all 1,250 interviews were carried out by the team of researchers (including ethnic-minority interviewers). As with the police, but even more so, there is massive under-representation of ethnic-minority people in judicial and court positions, and especially amongst the higher ranks of the judiciary (see p. 190). Shute *et al.* found that the proportion of black and Asian defendants who felt they had been treated unfairly owing to their race was lower than expected, with one in five black defendants feeling their treatment had been influenced by racial bias. However, amongst those black and Asian defendants who thought they had been given a heavier sentence than others, more than half put it down to their ethnicity rather than what they had done or said in court; and they seemed to believe that there was a sort of institutional racism present. As a 19-year-old Caribbean male who had lived in Britain all his life said after being sentenced to five years in prison: 'If I was a different colour a light sentence would have been given . . . the judge wanted to take another black face off the street . . . I was treated as a black offender.' To summarize their findings: the majority of defendants did not think they had been unfairly treated in court; however, of the minority who did feel unfairly treated, more than half attributed this to racism, and it was black defendants in crown courts who were most likely to feel they had been treated unfairly. It could be argued that even if only a minority hold this view, it is not satisfactory that most of this minority come away from court feeling they have been subject to racial bias.

Finally, we turn to what happens in prison and whether ethnic-minority prisoners receive differential treatment from white prisoners. We saw above the massively disproportionate numbers of ethnic-minority groups, and especially black people, in prison in Britain; here we will focus on what happens within prison.

There has been long-standing concern over the treatment of ethnic-minority prisoners, particularly since studies of racist attitudes amongst prison staff in the 1970s and 1980s (Phillips and Bowling 2002). Genders and Player's (1989) widely cited research in the 1980s found clear evidence of racial discrimination in prisons, and this seemed to affect the sort of prison jobs such prisoners were given and the extent to which they were allocated to open prisons. Black prisoners were also found to be more likely to be placed on disciplinary charges than white prisoners (McDermott 1990). A Home Office survey in 1994 found that prison officers held stereotypical views on ethnic-minority prisoners, describing them as arrogant, hostile to authority and as 'having a chip on their shoulders'.

The issue of racism within prisons is still high on the agenda. The murder of Zahid Mubarek by his cellmate Robert Stewart, a known and violent racist, at the Feltham Young Offenders Institution, West London, in 2000 and the subsequent investigations into it have highlighted the extent of such racism. Mubarek died seven days after he was beaten in his cell by his cellmate Stewart, who has since been sentenced to life for murder. The investigation into Mubarek's murder has uncovered damning evidence of continuing racism within prisons. In his comments to the Inquiry, Duncan Keys (Assistant General Secretary of the Prison Officers Association) said that warders at Feltham youth jail 'thought it would be funny to see what would happen when they put a young Asian lad in with someone who wanted to kill Asians'. He claimed that Mubarek died because he was placed in a cell with a white racist psychopath for the 'perverted pleasure' of officers. He referred to a game of what officers called 'Gladiator' which involved pitting inmates against one another and betting on who would win in a fight. White inmates would routinely be placed with black prisoners and bullies would be placed together to try to spark a conflict.

The investigation showed that the Mubarek case was not an isolated incident. The Prison Service's first race equality adviser, Judy Clements, told the inquiry that racism was rife at Feltham, saying she had heard numerous reports of ill-treatment of black and ethnic-minority prisoners. In a statement cataloguing racist abuse throughout the system, she said, 'In most areas, prison staff and management were . . . in complete denial that prisoners were subjected to any form of racism'. In every prison she visited, she found that black and ethnic-minority prisoners were 'disproportionately over-represented in the prison discipline regime'. Looking beyond Feltham, the prison service's own internal report found racist language and jokes to be widespread. At Portland jail a staff member told a black member of the investigating team that 'we're being overrun by you lot'.

Since Mubarek's murder evidence of racism amongst prisoner staff continues to be uncovered. Two prison officers were suspended in July 2001 for allegedly intimidating black staff. They were kept on full pay for three years after Nazi memorabilia, neo-fascist literature and 'nigger-hunting licences' were found in police raids on their homes, where one room was decorated as Hitler's bunker. In July 2004 a Home Office Inquiry finally admitted that it was not acceptable for prison officers to keep such items on display and recommended that both officers be charged with serious unprofessional conduct. More recently, Ministry of Justice complaints data show a rise in alleged racist incidents across the prison service of England and Wales. The data, released to the *Guardian* under the Freedom of Information Act, reveal that prison officers are more than twice as likely to be reported for racism as prisoners. In commenting on the findings, the Chair of the Prison Officers Association, Colin Moses, expressed concern about the growing extremist and racist tendencies amongst a minority of staff: '(Officers) are coming forward and saying they openly want to be members of the BNP. The National Offender Management service has forgotten that prison can become a feeding ground for white nationalists as well as Islamic extremists' (*Guardian,* 7 February 2010).

QUESTION BREAK

Earlier we asked you to consider whether police officers should be dismissed for using racist language. Read the following extract from the BBC News below and consider the following questions.

Muslim Inmates in Racism Claims

Despite claims that the prison service has been making progress on tackling racial inequality in prisons, Muslim inmates at a young offenders' institution have told the BBC that they have been verbally abused by staff. In an interview with a documentary team at the Glen Parvu institute in Leicestershire, one man said: 'I've been called a terrorist just because I grow my beard . . . or stupid Muslim. I had so many problems in this joint I can't tell you. This is the worst prison I've been to . . . more racist than others' . . . Another prisoner, Mohammad, said the prison staff, when they were letting them out of their cells, would say 'it's bhangra boys coming'. 'Other days they'd say "terrorist" or "al-Qaeda" . . .'

Last October, the Chief Inspector of Prisons, Anne Owers, warned of a growing 'disaffection and distance' between Muslim inmates and the prison system following a report about Whitemoor high security jail in Cambridgeshire. She said the growing situation 'urgently' needed addressing, but her annual report in January said efforts to 'tackle racial inequality were improving. Glen Parvu is the largest young offender institute in Europe and of 800 prisoners, 46 are British Asian, all but two of them Muslim.'

(From BBC News 21 March 2009 (www.news,bbc.co.uk))

- Do you think prison officers should be dismissed for racist language? Give reasons for your answer.
- To what extent do you think that the studies and evidence looked at above support the argument that there is racial bias in the criminal justice system? What points might be made to argue against that view?

In concluding this section and as a final comment on racism within prison, we will refer to the report from the Commission for Racial Equality on 'Race Equality in Prisons' (CRE 2003). This report looked for evidence of racial discrimination other than that which related to Mubarek's murder (on which a separate report has been published); it examined three prisons – Brixton, Parc and Feltham. The evidence found ranged from acts of intimidation and serious racial harassment to issues to do with whether prison meals fitted particular dietary requirements. The investigation found many areas of 'failure' with regard to race and equality, which are too numerous to list here. The two general overall findings the Commission highlighted were, first, that prisoners from ethnic-minority backgrounds were not provided with equivalent protection (to white prisoners) from racial violence and, second, the prison service failed to provide race equality in its employment or custodial practices. In 2008, the Prison Service published their Race Review which reported on progress made since the CRE report of five years previously – indeed it was launched on 16 December 2008, exactly five years after the CRE report. The Prison Service Review highlighted the progress made in delivering race equality in prisons in terms of establishing systems and processes to effectively manage race equality in prisons. It also acknowledged that, in spite of such changes, the experiences of BME prisoners and staff had not been transformed. The Director General of the National Offender Management Service, Phil Wheatley, commented that:

> In moving forward, the report does not call for a raft of new initiatives but for a more common sense, ordinary understanding of race, where right relationships are the key to progress and where good prison officers, good managers and good leaders are the means of achieving that.

Some of the key problems and issues raised by the CRE report of 2003 and the Prison Service Review of 2008 are detailed in the box.

CASE STUDY BOX 6.1 SUMMARY OF FINDINGS OF CRE REPORT *RACE EQUALITY IN PRISONS* (2003) AND HM PRISON SERVICE REPORT *RACE REVIEW 2008: IMPLEMENTING RACE EQUALITY IN PRISONS – FIVE YEARS ON*

The General Atmosphere in Prisons

Prison 'culture' among prison staff meant race equality procedures could be ignored, staff operated in a discriminatory way, and racist attitudes and behaviour were tolerated. Racist abuse and harassment and the presence of racist graffiti were persistent features of prison life for many staff and prisoners.

Treatment of Prison Staff

Ethnic minority staff had to work in an atmosphere of racist taunting and intimidation. Ethnic minority staff who spoke up about these matters were subsequently victimized.

Treatment of Prisoners

Complaints of racial discrimination raised within the prison by prisoners were often not investigated.

Access to Goods, Facilities and Services

Meals provided for prisoners and goods available in prison shops often did not meet the needs of ethnic-minority prisoners.

continued

Discipline for Prisoners

Prison statistics clearly suggested a consistent over-representation of black male prisoners in the prison disciplinary system.

Access to Work

Allocation to prison jobs (or in some cases work outside prison) tended to be at the discretion of individual officers, and was a long-standing source of complaint by black prisoners.

Black and Asian prisoners were consistently under-represented in work parties at Brixton and Feltham.

Protection from Victimization

Prisoners who made race complaints were punished or victimized for making the complaint.

HM Prison Service Race Review 2008 (Extracts from the Executive Summary)

Following several findings of unlawful racial discrimination, in December 2003, the Prison Service committed itself to a five-year partnership for reform with the CRE . . . As we approached the end of the five-year period, we embarked upon a wide-ranging review, with the assistance of partners from external organisations, to assess the progress the Service has made against the CRE failure areas and action plan . . . The review report highlights the significant progress made in putting the systems and processes in place that are the foundation for the effective management of race equality in prisons. However, despite considerable investment in procedural changes, the experience of BME prisoners and staff has not been transformed . . .

At a national level, structures have been put in place to enable the effective management of race equality. A detailed and comprehensive Race Equality Action Plan (REAP) has been developed. This sets out all the high-level actions that the Prison Service is taking on race equality, including those to address the recommendations of the Zahid Mubarek Inquiry . . . A Programme Management Board . . . oversees implementation of REAP. This reports quarterly to the NOMS Management Board . . . To co-ordinate and lead the Service's work in this area, a 25-strong Race Equality Action Group (REAG) was created at NOMS headquarters. The Group is led by the Race Advisor who plays a key role in ensuring that issues of equality contribute to all Board discussion and decisions . . .

As well as putting management structure in place, huge progress has been made in implementing systems to manage race equality effectively. A revised national policy on race equality was issued (and an) accompanying Prison Service Standard non Race Equality.

FURTHER READING

Bowling, B. and Phillips, C. (2002) *Race, Crime and Justice*. Harlow: Longman. This is a comprehensive text that focuses exclusively on racism and the criminal justice process. It examines and discusses theorizing on the link (or not) between race and crime and issues around the treatment of ethnic-minority groups by the criminal justice system – including the police, courts, probation and prison service.

Shute, S., Hood, R. and Seemungal, F. (2005) *A Fair Hearing? Ethnic Minorities in the Criminal Courts*. Cullompton: Willan Publishing. This is an interesting and readable example of a piece of first-hand research that looks into a little-researched area of criminal justice – the treatment of ethnic minorities by the court system.

WEBSITES

www.homeoffice.gov.uk The Home Office website provides masses of statistical information on crime in general and accessing the section on crime and victims and narrowing the search to race provides a wealth of data relevant to our examination of ethnic-minority criminality.

www.nationalbpa.com This is the National Black Police Officers Association site which aims to ensure equitable treatment for all staff, and particularly the BME staff it represents.

PART 2

EXPLORING AND EXPLAINING CRIMINAL JUSTICE

CHAPTER 7

Why Punish? Philosophies of Punishment

INTRODUCTION – STUDYING PUNISHMENT

The basic question that this chapter will be considering is 'why should offenders be punished?' In addressing this question it will look at the aims and justifications for punishment and at the philosophies that lie behind them; and will consider what type of punishment, and how much of it, will satisfy these aims and justifications. Before doing this and by way of an introduction, some general points about the sociological study of punishment will be raised.

The sociological study of punishment examines the relationship between crime, punishment and society. It looks at punishment as a social phenomenon and, in particular, the role of punishment in social life. While punishment occurs in a variety of different contexts, in the home, at school and at work for instance, the focus here is on the legal punishment of offenders. This legal punishment is a complex process that involves the making of laws, the trial, conviction and sentencing of offenders and the administration of particular penalties. Given this complexity it is not surprising that legal punishment can have various aims. However, it is likely that a majority of people would see the reduction or containment of crime as the major purpose of punishment, with punishment seen as a means to an end – that of controlling crime. Although crimes still occur and in ever increasing numbers it would perhaps be unfair to say that punishment has therefore 'failed'; rather it is arguably an unrealistic aim and expectation of punishment that it control rates of crime.

Until comparatively modern times there was little attempt to use punishment to reform wrongdoers and there was little pity wasted on law-breakers, with punishments tending to be quick, harsh and public. The history of crime and punishment (examined in detail in Chapter 3) demonstrates that there have been attempts to reform criminals but they have not detracted from the general motif of punishment as needing to be severe and exemplary. Reform and rehabilitation as 'aims of punishment' gained perhaps their widest support in the late 1950s and 1960s, providing a different sense of purpose for punishment and leading to a general optimism about the possibilities of punishment. This was reflected in various new methods of punishment introduced in Britain and elsewhere in this period, including parole, suspended sentences, community service orders and day training centres. The optimism of the 1960s soon gave way to a more sceptical perspective; rising crime rates and high rates of re-offending led to criticisms of the new methods of punishment as being too soft. The emphasis moved away from reform, with senior politicians advocating a hard-line approach to punishment that was reflected in 'short, sharp, shock' sentences being introduced in the early 1980s, and more recently the introduction into Britain of policies influenced by American 'boot camps' and 'three strikes and out' policies.

However, these newer, harsher initiatives have, similarly, had little effect on the size of the prison population or on rates of recidivism. Without going into great detail, some overall figures will help illustrate the pressures on the prison system in Britain and provide a context for considering the different philosophies of punishment. The prison population in Britain has continued to rise steadily over the last few decades, with over 83,000 people in Prison Service establishments in January 2010 (Ministry of Justice, Nation Offender Management Service, Prison Population and Accommodation briefing 22 January 2010). The number of people given immediate custodial sentences in 2005 was over 100,000 compared to just under 80,000 in 1995 (Ministry of Justice, Criminal Statistics for England and Wales: 2007). (The reason the number of people sent to prison each year is greater than the prison population reflects the fact that most prisoners are sentenced to short sentences of less than one year and so not all would be in prison when the annual figure is calculated.) As regards repeat offenders, it would seem that a relatively small number of offenders are responsible for a large proportion of offences. In 2000, 65 per cent of prisoners had at least five previous convictions, while only 15 per cent of all prisoners sentenced had no previous convictions (Rose 2003).

In commenting on re-offending rates, the current (2011) Deputy Prime Minister, Nick Clegg (when he was Liberal Democratic Shadow Home Secretary) argued that: 'Reoffending rates are arguably the most reliable gauge of the efficacy of a criminal justice system. Put simply, if criminals who come into contact with a criminal justice system are not turned away from further crime, the system is failing' (2007).

These kinds of figures and comments, and the obvious concerns they highlight about justice and punishment, raise questions about the aims and philosophies of punishment which we will now turn to.

QUESTION BREAK: 'HARD' AND 'SOFT' APPROACHES

In the introduction above reference was made to the support for 'hard-line' approaches to punishment in response to criticisms of newer, reformative approaches to punishment as being too 'soft'. The terms 'hard' and 'soft' are routinely used to indicate polarized positions in the debate about punishment.

Former Home Secretary and leader of the Conservative Party, Michael Howard has been a strong advocate of the 'hard position', and is particularly renowned for his 'prison works' comments:

> 'Prison works . . . it makes many who are tempted to commit crime think twice . . . This may mean that more people will go to prison. I do not flinch from that.'

> (Conservative Party Conference, 1993)

While Howard's predecessors as Home Secretary (including Kenneth Clarke, Kenneth Baker, David Waddington and Douglas Hurd) as well as key figures involved in running the criminal justice system (including Lord Woolf, former Lord Chief Justice) have favoured a reduction in prison sentences, for minor offences at least, the hard-line approach tends to be popular with the wider public and certain sections of the mass media. In contrast, any perceived 'soft-ness' on crime tends to be seen as a sign of political weaknesses; and when we hear of horrific crimes occurring it is easy to see how a hard-line, 'hang 'em high' approach will gain considerable sympathy and support.

It is not surprising, then, that the hard-line approach has been regularly advocated by politicians. Former Prime Minister John Major (commenting in 1993 on the supposedly lenient treatment of juvenile offenders) said that 'we should understand a little less and condemn a little more'. The Labour government that replaced him in the late 1990s immediately promised to be 'tough on crime and tough on the causes of crime' and to give 'zero tolerance' to crime and criminals. In a similar vein are the comments made by David Cameron, currently Prime Minister (2011), after the trial and sentencing of two brothers, aged 10 and 11, who had tortured and left for dead two other youngsters in Edlington, South Yorkshire in 2009. Cameron talked of 'evidence of a broken society' and said that the case was not 'an isolated incident of evil' which must lead people to asking 'deep questions' about social breakdown.

The 'debate' between the 'hard' and soft' positions can be illustrated by the comments made by the Lord Chief Justice, Lord Woolf, in December 2002 when he told judges and magistrates that burglars facing a sentence of up to 18 months should not go to prison, but be given a non-custodial sentence, and even where a prison sentence was imposed it should be no longer than necessary. This 'soft' position prompted the leader of Britain's Chief Constables, Sir David Phillips, to say that such a move would undermine the morale of the police who had successfully focused on burglary for a number of years; an attack on Lord

Woolf's proposals that was supported by the Police Federation, who represent rank and file officers, who felt such comments would only encourage burglars. More recently in 2007, when John Reid, as Home Secretary, appealed to judges to lock up fewer criminals in the face of ever rising prison numbers, leaders of junior and middle-ranking police officers said he had 'let down' officers who had 'worked hard to catch crooks' (Ford 2007).

Further examples of the 'hard' versus 'soft' approaches to punishment can be seen in the way the press report and comment on prison life in contemporary Britain. The following four headlines are taken from different newspapers over the last couple of years and illustrate quite contrasting views of prison life as either brutal and demeaning or easy and even privileged:

'Now Prisoners get to Watch TV to Save Distress'
(*Daily Express*, 2 July 2007)

'"Jail is Just Like Being on Holiday" Killer Boasts from his Prison Cell'
(*Daily Mail*, 18 February 2009)

'Killer's Jail Life is Piece of Cake'
(*Sun*, 24 December 2009)

'Portland Youth Prison "Unfit for Use" Says Chief Inspector'
(*Guardian*, 18 November 2009)

'Scotland's Only Women's Prison in "State of Crisis" Says Inspector'
(*Guardian*, 27 January 2010)

- Why do you think that: (a) the reformative approach might be unpopular with the general public; and
- (b) a tough approach may be more popular?

THE AIMS OF PUNISHMENT

While punishment and the institutions associated with it are generally accepted to be a necessary part of any orderly society, that does not mean it is unproblematic. As Garland puts it:

> The modern institutions of punishment are especially prone to conflicts and tensions that tend to undermine their effectiveness and legitimacy as instruments of social policy. These conflicts – between condemnation and forgiveness, vengeance and mercy, the sanctity of the law and the humanity of compassion, social defense and individual rights, the urge to exclude and the dream of reha-bilitation – set up complex, ambivalent sentiments that colour the day-to-day

experience of those caught up in penal relations, whether as administrators and officers, inmates and clients, or as members of the public.

(Garland 1999: 5)

Given these and other tensions it is of little surprise that the history of punishing offenders has been one of 'reform and reaction, of false dawns and disappointed optimism' (Garland 1999). Garland also points to the ambitious expectations held for our modern criminal justice system. It is not just viewed as being about 'doing justice' through law enforcement and punishing offenders, but also as having a wider remit to reduce crime through reforming offenders and deterring others from offending. And as the expectations of reducing crime have not been met, so issues about the aims and success of punishment become a focus for public concern.

It is not surprising, then, that various different aims of punishment have been advocated or that different commentators adopt different ways of categorizing these aims. And the philosophies that underpin the reasons for punishing offenders are an important area to consider, perhaps at the most basic level because punishment will involve some form of compulsion (forcing something on someone) which, typically, involves hardship. Decisions to punish inevitably raise fundamental issues of moral justification, of what are the reasons for doing it. Walker (1999) suggests that the reasoning that underpins decisions about appropriate sentences, and whether to exercise mercy or make them harsher, is based on retribution, utility, expediency or humanity (issues we return to after the question break below). More formally, the Criminal Justice Act 2003 set out the 'matters to be taken into account in sentencing' – which are worth setting out in full:

Purposes of Sentencing

Any court dealing with an offender in respect of his offence must have regard to the following purposes of sentencing –

- the punishment of offenders
- the reduction of crime (including its reduction by deterrence)
- the reform and rehabilitation of offenders
- the protection of the public, and
- the making of reparation by offenders to persons affected by their offences.

(Criminal Justice Act 2003, Section 142)

Before considering the major aims of punishment, the following exercise asks you to reflect on what you think the justification for punishment should be.

Read the two brief fictional case studies and then answer the question at the end.

Case 1

James has been found guilty of fraud. Over a number of years he embezzled funds from the city bank at which he worked – he opened false accounts and used them to finance a lifestyle way beyond what would have been possible on his regular salary. As well as a large country house in Britain, he owned a small villa in Spain and an apartment in New York. He justified his wealth to his colleagues by claiming he had been left money by a rich spinster aunt which he had invested successfully. The court heard that he stole over 2 million pounds between 1977 and 1999.

Case 2

Paul has been found guilty of burglary. He broke into a house while the residents were at work and stole a VCR, a number of CDs and videos and cash – to the value of some £500 in all. He had one previous conviction for burglary, for which he had received a six-month probation order, which he had successfully completed.

As a judge you have to punish the two offenders. For both James and Paul (separately) decide which of the following approaches would be your personal motivation in determining the appropriate punishment. (You can choose only one.)

(a) The punishment must be unpleasant enough to discourage James/Paul from committing another crime.
(b) The punishment must be in line with the punishment others would get for a similar crime and be of sufficient severity to match the crime.
(c) The punishment must provide opportunities for James/Paul to make better choices in the future so that he is unlikely to want to commit another crime.

Discussion

Consider what your answer tells you about your 'philosophy of punishment' – did you lean to punishment as a deterrent (answer a), or as retribution (b), or rehabilitation (c)?

Probably the requirement to choose only one answer restricted you. Often there will be more than one philosophy at play; and the philosophy that guides your own decisions may well change if you get to know more about the circumstances of the offence, the characteristics of the offender and so on.

The exercise above illustrates the point that there are various plausible justifications for punishment, and that difficulties can arise for sentencers because these justifications can and do conflict with one another. In particular, and as the comments from Garland illustrated, there is a basic tension between protecting the rights of offenders not be punished more than they deserve and protecting the rights of the public not to be victims of crime.

In the rest of this chapter, we will examine the major aims of punishment and, as we mentioned earlier, there are different ways of listing and categorizing these aims. Hudson (2003) suggests two basic groupings – those aims that are concerned with preventing future crimes and those with punishing already committed crimes. Those focused on future prevention could be seen as utilitarian, as having a certain degree of 'usefulness' for the wider society. Thus if a punishment deters someone from re-offending or discourages others from offending or 'reforms' offenders so that they do not offend again its utility is clear. These future-oriented aims of punishment have been called reductivist or consequential by some commentators as their aim is to reduce crime (Cavadino and Dignan 2007). Past-oriented aims and approaches to punishment are known as retributivist (and sometimes non-consequentialist) in that their focus is on exacting retribution from offenders, the blame is placed squarely on the offender and the future conduct of that offender is not seen as the major issue; punishment is essentially about blame and repayment. In general terms, utility has always been a major aim of law enforcement but in modern times retribution has come to the fore. Retribution is based on the notion that there is a right and even a duty to punish offenders because of their culpability – because they are to blame (Walker 1999).

QUESTION BREAK: CRIMINAL RECORDS

There is clearly a conflict between these two broad aims of punishment. As Hudson (2003) comments:

> if a person is assessed as likely to commit a further offence, should s/he be punished more severely than someone who commits the same offence but is not assessed as likely to reoffend? Conversely, should someone who commits an offence and has a record of previous offences be punished more severely than someone committing the same offence for the first time?
>
> (Hudson 2003: 5)

- What priority do you think should be given to someone's criminal record and what to the actual offence? Give reasons for your answer.
- We will come back to this important issue when considering some of the factors affecting sentencing decisions later in the chapter (pp. 228–232).

DETERRENCE

This is a future-oriented aim in that the intention behind it is to reduce crime. It could also be seen, therefore, to have a utilitarian rationale. As mentioned above, 'utility' would be apparent if a punishment deterred an offender from re-offending or if it discouraged others from offending in the first place. This comment indicates that there are two basic ways in which deterrence can work, either at an individual or general level (Cavadino and Dignan 2007). Individual or specific deterrence involves the punishment showing the offender that her/his action was undesirable because it brought her/him more pain than pleasure; so the fear of punishment would prevent the individual from repeating the offence. General deterrence works by showing others who may consider a criminal act that they will suffer painful consequences if they commit the offence. General deterrence depends on convincing potential offenders that they are likely to be caught and convicted (which criminal statistics suggest is probably not the case); it is, though, perhaps more likely to influence potential offenders than actual offenders (who probably have a fair idea of the likelihood of getting caught).

Before trying to assess the effectiveness of deterrence as a basis for punishment, it would be useful to explore the relationship between the utilitarian philosophy that underpins deterrence and punishment. While utilitarian approaches to punishment are not exactly synonymous with reductivist approaches, recent theories of punishment that focus on crime-reduction are clearly linked with the theorizing of the Enlightenment thinkers Cesare Beccaria (1738–94) and Jeremy Bentham (1748–1832), the classic exponents of utilitarian theory. Essentially, the utilitarian argument is that actions are moral if they are useful and so punishment can only be morally justified if the harm and suffering it prevents is greater than the harm it inflicts on offenders; and unless punishment reduces future crime then it would add to rather than reduce the sum of human suffering. When Beccaria published *Essay on Crime and Punishment* in 1764 he advocated a system of justice and punishment as much as an explanation of crime and, in a similar vein to the British philosopher Bentham, proposed that punishment should be used to achieve some greater good for society – with a reduction in crime being a clear of example of such a good. Beccaria proposed that a graduated system of penalties with the particular punishment appropriate to the crime would work as a deterrent. Prior to the move to democratic, constitutional governments (as opposed to monarchies) in Europe in the eighteenth and nineteenth centuries, punishment was often arbitrary and down to the whims of the nobility and monarchy. Bentham developed what has become known as the 'classicist' penal code based on the classic ideas of the Enlightenment. He stressed the importance of human reason rather than notions such as the divine right of monarchs as a means of governing. As regards punishment, he argued that this should be rationally based. Bentham saw the criminal as an individual with free choice who could therefore be deterred by the threat of future punishment. He also argued for a strict link between crime and punishment – once a crime was committed it should be punished accordingly with no room for mitigating circumstances to be taken into account. For both theorists, then, the crime issue was basically the punishment issue; and punishment should be rational, fair and just. They argued that excessive and violent punishments were barbaric and not worthy of civilized nations and that each particular form of punishment must impose just enough pain and suffering to outweigh the pleasure that may come from committing the specific crime.

In summarizing Bentham's approach, Hudson (2003) highlights three ways which he suggests can deter an individual from re-offending. First, through taking away the individual's ability and power to offend; second by taking away the individual's desire to offend, and third by making the individual afraid to offend. The first of these would involve some form on incapacitation, the second refers to a reformist or rehabilitative approach which we will consider later, while the third, deterring someone through fear of the potential punishment, is the meaning that is conventionally attached to deterrence.

Now an obvious way in which deterrence might work would be to have very draconian punishments that were so severe that people would be bound to be put off committing crimes. This sort of approach could not really be called utilitarian in that there is no attempt to limit the amount of pain as there would be no limit on the severity of punishment. While life imprisonment for driving over the speed limit or for shoplifting might lead to a dramatic reduction in those offences, and while 'get tough', 'hard' approaches to punishment may be attractive to politicians because of their appeal to the wider public, the notion of very severe punishment for any but very serious crimes would be held by most to be unacceptable from a human rights point of view. A compromise position is the notion of passing 'exemplary sentences' – sentences that are more severe than would usually be given for a particular offence because they aim to get over a message that such behaviour is being taken especially seriously. The notion of such 'exemplary' penalties raises the interesting point that for punishment to work as a general deterrent it is not necessary that only guilty people are punished. And while the punishing of innocent people would, hopefully, be rejected by all ethical systems, there may be some justification, in terms of general deterrence, for punishing people for something they have not yet done but may be likely to do in future. This raises the philosophical question of whether punishing a person known to be innocent could ever be said to be justified. In considering this issue, Walker (1999) cites an academic scenario from Ten (1987) in which a sheriff in a small community is faced with a situation where a black man had (allegedly) committed a rape. If someone was not convicted there would have been lynchings and a likely riot. In order to prevent this should he consider convicting an innocent person? However, as Walker comments, most, including utilitarians, would agree that such a situation would be intolerable.

The focus of the deterrence philosophy is, essentially, on frightening people into not offending; and it is, therefore, generally associated with more severe penalties such as long prison sentences. One problem with this notion is that what one person may feel to be severe might be viewed by another as mild. Another is that for general deterrence to be effective, the punishment has to be severe, and painful, enough to outweigh the potential pleasure that the particular offence might give the offender – a difficult assessment to make. It is also necessary that there is adequate publicity so that would-be offenders are aware of the particular punishments meted out. Indeed any publicity that leads to an increased awareness that many crimes are not being solved or that highlights an increase in what are seen as lenient punishments can work against the effectiveness of deterrent punishments.

It seems fair to say that there is little evidence that deterrence 'works' and we will conclude this section with a brief assessment of the effectiveness of deterrence as a justification for punishing offenders.

It might seem reasonable to suppose that offenders who had received a harsh punishment would be less likely to re-offend than offenders who had received a less severe punishment. However, there is little evidence that this is the case. The figures on repeat offenders that were given at the start of the chapter certainly raise questions about the deterrent effect of punishment, while young offenders who served custodial sentences under the stricter regimes of detention centres in the 1980s were just as likely to re-offend as those who had not been subject to such regimes.

This does not mean that harsh punishments never deter, but does indicate that the basic notion of deterrence is difficult to measure and assess. Walker (1991) points out that individuals can be deterred from committing offences at certain times and in certain places, but merely commit that (or another) offences elsewhere, and that such 'displacement' of offences hardly constitutes deterrence. He also points to the effectiveness of 'on the spot' deterrents which pose practical difficulties for would-be offenders, but which again may only serve to 'displace' offences. Furthermore, deterrence can work 'at a distance'; for instance the potential 'stigma' of being known as a shoplifter might put many people off from even considering such an offence. These sorts of examples indicate that the likely form of punishment is certainly not the only possible consequence that will influence a would-be offender.

Deterrence, then, involves would-be offenders weighing up a range of possible consequences of future offending. For it to have an effect, individuals have to be tempted to offend in the first place; deterrence cannot be applied to a person who is not tempted to offend. However, it can 'work' in an indirect way – refraining from committing an offence because the individual would reproach themselves at some future date demonstrates a deterrent effect. Walker (1991) argues that the crucial factor in assessing the effectiveness of deterrent punishments is that the individual believes in the deterring consequences, even if they are not very likely to occur. For instance, many people stopped buying and eating British beef in the 1990s because of the remote possibility of contracting the human form of 'mad cow disease'. Furthermore, the deterrent effect will vary as an individual's state of mind varies; people who would not normally consider breaking the law may become undeterrable and commit offences when they are influenced by drink or drugs or when driven to do so by anger or jealousy, for example.

It may be that people are just not that rational and calculating; and if their behaviour is not determined by free will but rather by biological, psychological or social factors then they are not going to be deterred by the potential punishment. We have highlighted the difficulties with applying and assessing the notion of deterrence not to dismiss the notion but to question the extent to which the type or severity of punishment influences how effective it is. Some people would be unlikely to commit any offence however harsh the punishment attached to it might be – the fear of being caught and stigmatized would be enough to deter them. For others, the punishment may be accepted as part of the risk, 'if you can't do the time, don't do the crime'. This is not to say that punishments cannot have a deterrent effect. As mentioned earlier, and slightly tongue-in-cheek, massively severe penalties for relatively minor offences would have a general deterrent effect and significantly reduce those offences. However, aside from extreme examples, there is little evidence that the type or severity of punishment has much influence as a general deterrent. This argument is supported by a case that is often referred to whereby a Birmingham youth received a 20-year detention sentence for a mugging offence in 1973. Although this exceptional punishment was given widespread media coverage, comparisons of rates of mugging before and after this 'exemplary' sentence found it had no effect on the rate of such offences (cited in Cavadino and Dignan 2007). However, this does not mean that exemplary sentences never work; it may be that muggers do not follow the news closely.

QUESTION BREAK: EXEMPLARY SENTENCES

Suggest (a) some positive benefits and (b) some negative consequences of 'exemplary sentences'.

- List any crimes that you have committed or have considered committing. What would deter you from committing them again (or in the first place)?
- Why do you think that young offenders who have been subject to a strict punishment regime might be more likely to re-offend?

There is a danger that deterrence can outdo itself as a justification for punishment, with too severe a punishment for a relatively minor offence pushing the offender into committing more serious ones – 'might as well be hanged for a sheep as a lamb'. And while offenders do always run the risk of being caught, the chances of getting away with an offence (chances which are often pretty good given the estimated amount of unrecorded and unsolved crime) will greatly weaken the deterrent effect of any punishment.

In concluding, then, it would seem fair to suggest that deterrence is a rather limited basis for penal policy. As the White paper which preceded the 1991 Criminal Justice Act put it:

> Much crime is committed on impulse, given the opportunity presented by an open window or unlocked door, and it is committed by offenders who live from moment to moment; their crimes are as impulsive as the rest of their feckless, sad or pathetic lives. It is unrealistic to construct sentencing arrangements on the assumption that most offenders will weigh up the possibilities in advance and base their conduct on rational calculation. Often they do not.
>
> (Home Office 1990)

Impulsive offences are clearly a problem for a penal strategy of deterrence and it could well be argued that many, if not most, crimes are not rationally premeditated.

If it were possible to measure the crime rate accurately and if there were a reduction in crime according to the statistics, it would still be difficult to relate this to the effect of particular punishments. Hudson (2003) uses driving with excess alcohol to illustrate this point. This might seem an offence which could be targeted by deterrent sentencing; and it is clear that sentences have become much harsher for this offence, with fewer fines and more prison sentences (and this has not just happened in Britain). It would also seem to be the case that less driving with excess alcohol now occurs, with the common, and police, view seeming to be that only a hard core of drunk drivers remain. However, Hudson questions whether this change in behaviour is due to the increased punishments, because as well as tougher penalties there has also been an extensive educational and moral campaign highlighting the dangers of drink-driving. She suggests that 'there seems to have been a change in public consciousness about the activity, rather than, or as well as, a fear of tougher penal consequences'. More recently, there have been similarly hard-hitting television advertising over the dangers of speeding and it will be interesting to see if this has an effect on the public view of breaking the speed limits and on the extent of that offence.

The difficulties we have highlighted with the notion of deterrence as a justification for punishment have lent support to the argument that the probability of conviction is the one deterrent factor that is likely to have any great effect. Offenders' own estimates of whether they will 'get away with it' would seem to be the crucial influence on whether an offence is committed. The actual punishment would seem to have less deterrent influence than offenders' own estimations of the likelihood of detection.

QUESTION BREAK

As well as the difficulties with the notion of deterrent sentencing that we have highlighted above, there are also moral objections, including that the offender might be punished in excess of what is deserved by the offence and that this approach would allow for the punishment of offences which have not been committed on the grounds that they may be in the future.

Make a case for and against an approach that would allow for some people being overly (or wrongly) punished on the grounds that this may prevent more future crime?

In concluding this overview of issues around the notion of deterrence as an aim of punishment, Walker (1999) suggests that all that can really be said is that: '*some* kinds of penalty, of *some* degrees of severity, will for *some* lengths of time deter *some* kinds of people from *some* sorts of behaviour in *some* situations' (p. 19 – italics in original). He goes on to suggest a number of points to consider when assessing the effectiveness of deterrence as a basis for punishment which we will summarize here before looking at the retributive approach to and aim of punishment:

- an increased probability of detection and conviction seems more effective;
- some offenders will not be deterred due to their strong beliefs and motivations (e.g. terrorists);
- law-abiding people over-estimate the risks of being detected and convicted (and so punished);
- few people actually remember what sentences have been passed (except for some exceptional crimes);
- the stigma of being convicted is feared by some (but less so by those already stigmatized as offenders);
- some offences don't stigmatize those who offend (e.g. football hooligans);
- when an offender stops offending how can we be sure he has really stopped?
- even if someone has stopped offending, why has he? It may be that it was not the punishment but the way it was administered – for instance, one probation officer may handle things differently to another and/or 'get through' to some offenders but not others.

(Adapted from Walker 1999: 19–20)

RETRIBUTION

In contrast to the future-oriented, utilitarian emphasis of deterrence, retribution as a philosophical justification for punishing offenders is clearly based on the past. The retributivist approach is based on the revenge motive, expressed in supposed the logic of 'an eye for an eye and a tooth for a tooth'. Historically retribution was related to the paying back of a debt (with the Latin word *retributio* meaning repayment), while in the penal context it has referred to the idea of deserved punishment. It is obvious that it is often seen as the most important aim of punishment. Certain offences deserve certain punishments and if offenders did not receive their 'proper', deserved, punishment then surely law and order would break down? Linked with this basic notion of retribution is the belief that punishment should also demonstrate a society's condemnation of particular offences and of particular offenders; and that those offences that excite the strongest condemnation merit the most severe punishments. While it is accepted that a punishment cannot undo the harm done by an offender, it can have the potential to make victims of crime (including indirect victims such as families and friends of victims) feel better and can perhaps enable people to make sense of the senseless (in cases such as child abuse, for example).

Retributivists emphasize the denunciation aspect of punishment. The passing of a sentence acts to denounce the particular offence and can be seen as a public statement of disapproval, with the severity of the punishment demonstrating the degree of this disapproval. And it is only by pronouncing a proper and proportionate penalty that the offence can be given the disapproval that it merits. Punishing offenders is also seen as the best way of connecting them to the values of their society; and even if it does not have a good effect on the offender it will, at least, send a message. However, as Walker (1999) asks, how can punishment show that an offender has flouted such values? The retributive position would suggest that the offender has done to him (or her) what he did to the victim, or the nearest thing to it – in other words punishment is 'talionic' (of the same kind). This is a position that raises a number of difficulties and issues as we shall discuss below. For instance, if someone attempts (and fails) to commit a crime, what sort of punishment is appropriate and what sort of compensation can the offender make?

QUESTION BREAK: PUBLIC PUNISHMENT?

The emphasis on revenge and public condemnation and disapproval suggests a case for public punishments, which used to be commonplace in previous times. As well as public hangings and other forms of physical punishment, offenders following community orders are sometimes named and shamed by being made to undertake their community sentence in public and wearing clothing that shows the wider public who they are. For instance, convicted drunk drivers in Phoenix, Arizona are made to wear pink t-shirts while collecting rubbish from the streets.

What arguments can you suggest for and against public punishments?

Before considering some of the issues around the retributionary justification for and philosophy of punishment, we will refer to the way in which retribution has come back into vogue and manifested itself in recent years. For much of the twentieth century, and certainly up to the 1970s, as the study of crime and the discipline of criminology developed and spread, retribution was seen as being rather an unprogressive approach to punishment that was largely based on vengeance. The emphasis of criminal justice policy and practice during this period was on doing something positive to rehabilitate and re-integrate offenders. During the 1970s there was a return to the old retributive ideas and by the 1980s a new sort of retributionary approach, under the banner of 'just deserts', became the most influential aim of and justification for punishment. In part this was due to a feeling that the rehabilitative initiatives and efforts of the previous decades had been too lenient and partly to the concern that the indeterminate sentencing approach associated with rehabilitation (giving offenders a custodial sentence which they were only released from when they had demonstrated that they had been 'reformed') was making a mockery of sentencing (issues surrounding indeterminate sentences are returned to when looking at rehabilitation later, see p. 240). This indeterminate sentencing, although no doubt based on admirable intentions to reform offenders, meant in practice that some offenders convicted and sentenced for relatively minor offences ended up spending excessively long periods in custody, often longer than much more serious offenders who managed to play the system and demonstrate that they were 'reformed'. Hudson (2003) highlights how the disparity in sentences, resulting from the discretion that those working in the criminal justice system had to decide when offenders were, or were not, 'reformed', led to a strong 'back to justice' movement in England, Wales and elsewhere.

The emphasis on rehabilitation and reform of offenders in prison had an unsettling effect on the running of prisons. The fact that prisoners did not know when they would be released, and their consequent dependence on 'experts' saying that they were fit to be released, increased the tensions in prisons, particularly in the USA where indeterminate sentences were used as a matter of course in the 1950s and 1960s.

So, by the 1970s there was a situation where 'rehabilitative' punishments were seen by some, perhaps the more critical, commentators as overly oppressive and by others, more politically to the right, as soft and ineffective. All of this helped a swing against rehabilitation and reform and towards retribution in the 1970s and beyond. As Hudson puts it:

> the primary principle of new retributivism is that punishment should be commensurate to the seriousness of the offence . . . the modern version interprets commensurate as *proportionate*. What is required is that there should be a schedule of punishments in which the most serious is reserved for the most serious offences, and that penalties should be graduated throughout the scale according to offence seriousness.
>
> (Hudson 2003: 40)

This retributivist approach is known as *tariff* sentencing and in practice usually involves bands of sentences. For instance the 'band' may be between three and five years, depending on the particular circumstances of the offence.

This emphasis on the relationship between seriousness of offence and form of punishment leads to the obvious question: how should offences be ranked in terms of seriousness? In attempting to grapple with this issue, the 1991 Criminal Justice Act set out three broad divisions of seriousness: so minor that a discharge or fine is appropriate; serious enough to warrant a community punishment; and so serious that only a custodial sentence was appropriate. The Act attempted to bring proportionality into sentencing so that sentences should be 'commensurate with the seriousness of the offence'.

QUESTION BREAK: 'JUST DESERTS'

While it may not be so hard to agree on those offences which are 'so minor' and those which are 'so serious', it is perhaps more tricky to rank those of medium seriousness. After all, most of us would be happy to rank rape as more serious than shoplifting, but would be less sure of ranking burglary in relation to embezzlement.

- What do you think should be the key factors that determine the seriousness of an offence?
- Try to devise a scale to indicate the appropriate punishment for different offences. What difficulties do you find in trying to do this?

Although there are different retributive approaches to punishment, there is a general agreement that punishment has to be backward looking in important respects and that the infliction of suffering through punishment is justified because of what the offender has already done. Retribution as a justification for punishment requires that the amount of punishment must fit the wrong done and, therefore, that the offender should get no more than their 'just deserts'.

Walker (1991) sees retribution as offering the certainty that the deterrent and utilitarian approaches cannot provide. Punishments that are based on retribution will at the least ensure that offenders get what they deserve. However, while the retributive justification for punishment is clearly based on what an offender has done, it does not follow that it is unproblematic. As we have discussed above, the idea of deserved punishment implies that there should be an equivalence between the seriousness of the offence and the penalty received. In particular, the gravity of the offence, measured in terms of the amount of harm done, is generally regarded as they key factor in determining the severity of penalty. Harm done, though, is not a clear-cut determinant. It is conventionally accepted that the extent to which harm was intended is a variable that should affect the sort of punishment received, so that an accidental killing is not punished as if it were murder even though the end result may be the same. In many cases the amount of harm done is a matter of luck. Speeding or dangerous driving, for example, may result in accidents which cause a great deal of harm or very little harm, raising the question of whether the punishment should reflect the likely effect or the actual effects (Walker 1999). Furthermore, there are offences that might cause only a minimal degree of harm yet would be generally seen as meriting severe punishment; while an attempted murder or unsuccessful terrorist attack may not do any actual harm, such offences would be seen as deserving a punishment almost as severe as a successful murder or attack. As Walker (1991) eloquently puts it, 'incompetence does not mitigate'. However, consequences can have an effect and so murder and attempted murder are treated by the criminal justice system as different offences; and it is likely that the vast majority of people would want a driver who has killed someone to be convicted of a more serious offence than one who had not.

Although few would argue that some harms are clearly greater than others – injuries that cause permanent disabilities are obviously distinguishable from minor cuts or bruises, for instance – harm is not just a physical concept. The psychological harm that is caused to victims is less easy to quantify. While it may be possible to 'rank' thefts in terms of the amount of money involved, this will not necessarily relate to the harm felt by the victim. Someone who loses all of their savings, however limited these may be, is likely to suffer more than better-off victims who lose a similar amount in real terms; and in a similar vein, stealing from a large shop or company is liable to cause very little in the way of personal suffering. As well as it being difficult to quantify the harm experienced by the direct victims of offences, a by-product of punishment is that other 'innocent' people can unintentionally suffer from the punishment of an offender. Imprisonment will often cause hardship and distress to the innocent partners and/or children of an offender; and fines may lead to the dependents of offenders suffering perhaps to an even greater extent than the offenders themselves. This also raises the question of whether some offenders suffer more than others when punished. For instance a prison sentence given to a Muslim wife was reduced as the courts felt she would suffer more than most in prison (cited in Walker 1999).

So harm is a difficult concept to categorize. We have suggested above that most people would support a less severe penalty for a criminal attempt which fails rather than one which succeeds. However, if the unsuccessful attempt is due to bad luck or incompetence, Walker (1999) suggests that the retributivist could argue that the intention is what counts and the (would-be) offender is just as culpable (as in the case of a failed terrorist bomber). Yet he points out that the penalties in sexual crimes are much less for attempted unlawful sexual intercourse than for completed ones. And in deciding on appropriate retributive punishments, should factors such as losing one's job play a part? Again, Walker (1999) cites a case where two soldiers were found guilty of assaulting a police officer and were sentenced to prison. At their appeal they told the court that imprisonment would mean automatic discharge from the army. One of the soldiers had an exemplary military record and his sentence was commuted to a fine; the other had a previous conviction and his appeal was turned down (even though his wife and children would lose their home). The question break below asks you to consider what factors should or should not be taken into account when sentencing offenders.

QUESTION BREAK: MITIGATING FACTORS AND SENTENCING

Although failing to succeed in committing a crime through incompetence would not normally be seen as a mitigating factor that should lessen the severity of a punishment, there are other factors which are taken into account when sentencing offenders.

Give examples of the sort of factors which you feel should be taken into account when punishing offenders, and explain why you feel they should affect a sentence.

You might consider factors that relate to (a) the offender; (b) the victim; and (c) the offence itself.

We have tried to highlight some of the difficulties with applying the retributive approach to punishment and with the notion that certain crimes deserve certain punishments. Before moving on to examine the idea that punishment can be used to reform or rehabilitate the offender, we will consider a more general concern about and criticism of retribution – that it is nothing more than vengeance.

Both retribution and vengeance share what Nozick (1981) has termed 'a common structure'. They both involve dispensing harm and/or deprivation for a reason. He does, though, distinguish between the two in that retribution is done in response to a crime or some other wrongdoing while revenge can follow something that is not necessarily intended (e.g. an accidental injury). Also, there is usually some limitation placed on the extent of retribution, while revenge can be unlimited; retribution involves punishment but also offers protection from over-punishment through the just deserts model. Retribution could, then, be thought of as a sort of vengeance, but one which is bounded by a notion of proportionality and of the rights of the individual. In a similar vein, retribution should involve impartiality and should lack the personal element often implied in revenge. This personal element might even involve gaining pleasure, or at least satisfaction, from the suffering of the 'wrongdoer'.

Before concluding this overview of the retributory approach to punishment we will consider some of the main factors that might be taken into account in finding an appropriate and 'deserved' punishment. This summary is based on Walker's discussion of aggravation and mitigation in sentencing decisions (1999), and is essentially a list of possible factors and the key questions or issues they raise.

Aggravating factors

These factors might lead to a more severe penalty than could have been imposed.

Previous record

In the question break earlier (p. 218) we asked you to consider what account should be taken of an offender's previous criminal record in deciding on the sentence. It might be argued that failure to respond to a previous sentence indicates the need for a more severe one, although this could be said to be punishing someone twice for the same offence – the offender had already been punished for the previous offence so why should he be punished for it again? And should an offender be given even more severe punishments if it is a third, fourth or more offence?

Sacrilege

Lying in court (perjury) after swearing on the Bible is seen as worse than giving a false written statement.

Offending on bail

This could be viewed as a breach of trust and so meriting a more severe penalty.

Premeditation

Is a deliberate and premeditated offence worse than a spontaneous and unpremeditated one?

Prevalence

The issue here is whether a spate of criminal offences in an area would justify a longer sentence for offenders caught (perhaps due to the alarm that is present in those areas).

Victims

The extent to which the vulnerability of victims (for instance their age, or the fact they were victims in the course of doing their job such as police officers) should influence the sentence given.

Abuse of trust and/or hospitality

Sexual offences by teachers, or doctors, tend to be seen as 'worse' due to their position of trust. In a similar vein, refugees who commit an offence after have been given permission to stay in the UK could be seen to be abusing the hospitality offered to them.

Lack of remorse

Although a difficult factor to assess, the absence of remorse is likely to be taken as indication that the offender is likely to re-offend and so will lead to a more severe penalty.

Professionalism

The implication here is that a 'professional' criminal has been skilled in avoiding detection for a length of time (and that a more severe penalty is needed to compensate for this).

Tactics

The tactics of a defendant in court, which might include submitting victims to long and unnecessary questioning, can be used as an aggravating factor. Walker (1999) refers to a case in 1997 where a rapist dismissed his counsel and subjected two victims to lengthy and intimate questioning, which probably contributed to a very long 16-year sentence.

Mitigating factors

These factors might lead to a less severe penalty than could have been imposed. The extent to which these factors are taken into account is usually based on a judgement that the offender is not as culpable (or as much to blame) as the nature of the offence would suggest. They can also be used to reward an offender's co-operation; indeed according to the Criminal Justice Act of 1991 'any such matters as in the opinion of the court are relevant in mitigation of sentence' can be taken into account.

Pleading guilty

This is a factor which the courts are obliged to take into account, with the stage of proceedings at which the guilty plea is made being important in that the earlier the plea, the more time and money is saved. There are fairly clear guidelines to the courts on this, with the suggestion that there is a reduction of a third for a timely guilty plea.

Exceptional circumstances

This is quite a subjective factor and might include the mental or physical state of the offender, or responsibility for a dependant. It can also relate to quite unique situations. Walker (1999) refers to a case where a research student supplied a friend with Ecstasy but avoided a prison sentence as he was engaged in valuable research work designed to reduce angina.

Motivation

Although usually used to justify a more severe penalty, sometimes motivations can be used in mitigation; for instance when an offender cites her (usually) love and devotion to a co-offender. Or offenders may be treated more leniently if the judge sympathizes with their grievance (Walker refers to a case where a group of drivers felt their employer was making excessive deductions from their pay and responded by stealing some of the fares they received from passengers to make up for this).

Entrapment

This is usually taken into account in sentencing if an offence only occurred because the offender was enticed into it, perhaps by journalists or police officers.

Incompetence

Although this is not usually a mitigating factor (see p. 227), some criminal attempts are so incompetent that they are treated leniently. Walker gives the example of an alcoholic faced with a large debt who set his carpet alight and went to bed drunk. Subsequently he had to be rescued by the fire brigade and was charged with arson. However his sentence was reduced by a year on appeal as his attempt 'was not a calculated, cleverly planned attempt to defraud an insurance company . . . (but) was one . . . doomed to failure'.

Necessity

This might involve having to break a law (for instance driving dangerously) to escape from would-be offenders.

Absence of dishonesty

The example provided by Walker is of someone who found that a £20 note he had received in change was forged and who tried to use it himself. His sentence was halved as it was accepted he had not acquired the note with a view it using it dishonestly.

Intoxication

This tends to be less usually accepted as an 'excuse' in courts than it was in the past.

Good character

This is a very imprecise factor, Good character may just mean the offender has no previous convictions, or that he has a job, or it may refer to something more 'special' such as a brilliant record of voluntary service.

Meritorious conduct

As examples of good character, offenders have had prison sentences reduced or suspended because of their military service record, or, in one case cited by Walker, where someone on bail saved a drowning boy at risk to his own life.

Assisting law-enforcement

Co-operating with the police through providing information or evidence. While the police cannot promise a particular sentence they can stress how helpful offenders have been and such factors would usually be taken into account.

Remorse

Sentencing guidelines typically suggest that remorse should be taken into account. It is usually seen as more credible after impulsive violence, for example, rather than a planned sexual or other offence.

QUESTION BREAK: THE DARK FIGURE OF CRIME

Consider each of the aggravating and mitigating factor listed above. To what extent should each of these factors be taken into account in deciding on the appropriate sentence for an offender?

It is apparent that mitigation can be based on a wide range of factors, and in addition to this already quite lengthy list of examples provided above, there are a number of other reasons for judges and magistrates to show leniency when sentencing. Here we will refer to age and mental disorder in relation to 'deserved punishment' and retribution.

Youth is one of the oldest reasons for showing leniency in dealing with offenders. The age at which children can be deemed to be capable varies over time and from place to place, with the Latin phrase *doli incapax* (incapable of guile) applied to children under a stated age. In the UK it remained at seven until 1932, when it was raised to eight and, then, to ten in 1963. In terms of old age, maturity can, on occasion, be an aggravating factor (as in 'they should know better'). On the other hand, the Crown Prosecution Service might take old age into account when deciding whether it is the public interest to prosecute. In deciding on the length of a custodial sentence, a long sentence will deprive an old person of a larger proportion of his/her remaining life.

As regards mental illness, the notion that insane offenders should not be punished goes back to ancient history. Marcus Aurelius argued in the second century that the insane are 'punished enough by their madness' (in Walker 1999). Indeed in the UK those sentenced to capital punishment up to its abolition were examined to see whether they were insane, as it was held that a person must not be executed while insane. Insanity is rarely used as defence nowadays and has been almost completely replaced by 'diminished responsibility'.

In finishing our discussion of retribution and factors affecting the punishment of offenders, we will refer to revenge and provocation. Revenge is usually seen as a factor that would lead to a more severe penalty but it can also be used in mitigation; for instance in cases where offences are committed against someone who has attacked or injured a family member. A different sort of example cited by Walker (1999) is when a person who had had acid thrown in his face later threw acid back at his attackers and was treated leniently as the act was seen as 'delayed provocation'. Indeed the idea of revenge being treated sympathetically goes back a long way, with a famous judgement of 1707 listing four situations where provocation might lead to violence: suffering a physical insult, learning of an assault on a friend/kinsman, witnessing a person being wrongfully deprived of liberty, and finding one's wife committing adultery. Violence in such cases was seemingly justified in terms of 'outrage' and an attack on one's 'honour' (for instance, the idea of fighting a duel to avenge an attack on honour). Essentially, though, revenge involved some degree of premeditation whereas provocation involves a loss of self-control. This raises the issue as to whether loss of self-control has to be sudden or whether there can be a slow loss of control, an issue that has been highlighted in cases where women (usually) have killed their partners after having suffered over a period of time. This was illustrated most famously in the case of Sarah Thornton, who had previously talked of killing her partner, who had sharpened the knife beforehand and stabbed her partner when he was asleep. She was convicted of murder in 1990, her first appeal failed in 1992 but at a retrial in 1995 she was acquitted of murder and convicted of manslaughter and immediately released from prison.

Deterrence, retribution and capital punishment

Arguments over the effectiveness or otherwise of deterrent sentences have been a central element in the debate over capital punishment. Advocates of capital punishment have argued that the death penalty would have a deterrent effect and would, as a result, lead to a reduction in serious crime, and at a simple, common-sense level many might feel that it would be a better deterrent than any other penalty. However, this view presupposes that the potential murderer rationally calculates the advantages and disadvantages of murder and would be deterrable if the disadvantages were believed to be sufficiently strong. A problem with this view is that many, if not most, murders are not planned or calculated but are committed on impulse, perhaps during a fight or while in a fit of rage, and would probably be little affected by the threat of capital punishment. And even the supposedly rational murderer, the terrorist or the person who kills in the course of a robbery for instance, is not necessarily easily deterrable. In most cases such would-be murderers will believe they have a good chance of getting away with their crime.

These problems with justifying capital punishment on the grounds of its deterrent potential do not mean that such a punishment has no deterrent effect – there is, though, a lack of reliable evidence of just when deterrence might work and there is little evidence that long-term imprisonment would be a weaker deterrent than capital punishment. However, there are other arguments concerning capital punishment that have nothing to do with its deterrent potential, and these arguments relate to the retributionary aim of punishment. Indeed capital punishment can perhaps more easily be justified in terms of retribution – someone has killed and so deserves to be killed themselves. In his examination of arguments over capital punishment, Wolfgang (1998) questions whether any real equilibrium would be achieved by the 'life for a life' approach to such punishment. Retribution could be said to require an equal pain being inflicted on offenders which raises the question of how the state could inflict an equal kind of pain. The sort of torturous executions that happened in the past would be out of line with modern, Western ideas (in the USA for instance the killing of offenders is done clinically and under medically protective circum-stances). Taking this argument further, Wolfgang asks whether societies would tolerate other punishments of the body in response to what offenders have done. For instance, stabbing or throwing acid in the face of people convicted of assault-type offences would be considered completely inappropriate, which, he argues, would seem to question a retributionary rationale for the death penalty.

Of course, the 'just deserts' retributionary approach does not mean the punish-ment should be exactly like the crime but that there should be equivalencies or seriousness of punishment. In Britain, equivalencies of pain in kind are looked for; and the common commodity of pain is deprivation of liberty measured in lengths of time spent in prison. And in terms of pain, it would be argued that death ends all pain and the pain of imprisonment is greater, with the lingering reminder of deprived liberty providing a more enduring pain, a point made by the famous Enlightenment thinker Beccaria in the eighteenth century: 'the death penalty expends its total influence in a single moment [and] may look on death with a firm and calm regard . . . [however in prison] the evildoer begins his sufferings instead of terminating them' (cited in Wolfgang 1998).

Wolfgang finishes his discussion by highlighting a comment made by Sister Helen Prejean after her eyewitness account of the death penalty, where she says, 'you could say "they deserve to die", but the key moral question is "do we deserve to kill them?"'

The death penalty is perhaps the most obvious example of a retributionary punishment that clearly meets the desire for revenge – if someone has killed then it can be argued that they deserve to be killed themselves. And murder is a crime totally condemned by society and so generally seen as requiring the severest possible punishment. However, the retributionary argument is not generally put forward as the most important reason for the re-introduction of capital punishment; in spite of the uncertainties over the deterrent effect of punishment, it is this issue that has tended to be the focus of the death penalty debate.

- List the philosophical arguments for and against capital punishment and consider which of the aims of punishment they most closely relate to.
- What other arguments are there for and against this punishment (e.g. you may consider practical rather than philosophical points).
- To what extent have your views on capital punishment altered since you started studying criminal justice?

REHABILITATION

As with deterrence and in contrast to retribution, rehabilitative aims of punishment can be seen as future oriented and, therefore, having a utilitarian rationale and appeal. The rehabilitative approach is based on the belief that people can change and that they are never beyond reform. Thus offenders can be taught how to be 'normal', law-abiding citizens; and punishment can be organized so that they will be less likely to re-offend. In these brief introductory lines the terms rehabilitation and reform have been referred to and in the rest of this section those terms will be used regularly and, to a certain extent, interchangeably. Strictly speaking, however, the terms refer to different approaches and processes. Reform relates to an individual offender being given the opportunity and space and persuaded to change him or herself, while rehabilitation involves a more planned, regulated and imposed treatment, perhaps in the form of a supervisor overseeing an offender pursuing a training or employment programme and monitoring his or her progress. Thus reform has some similarities with deterrence in that it works through the will of the individual offender, whereas rehabilitation implies that the offender is not acting from his or her own free will but is expected to respond to attempts from outside to change him or herself. Indeed in order for rehabilitation to have a chance of succeeding those involved need to be active and willing participants – apart from in some of the rather extreme examples of rehabilitation portrayed in the classic novels (and subsequent films) *A Clockwork Orange* (Burgess 1962) and *One Flew Over the Cuckoo's Nest* (Kesey 1962). A difference that both these approaches have from the aim of deterrence is that reform and rehabilitation aim to make the offender a more useful, productive and 'better' member of society, whereas deterrence is primarily concerned with whether the offender commits further offences.

In general terms, the focus of these approaches and philosophies is on how punishment can be used to 'correct' an offender's behaviour, and Walker (1991) uses the term 'correction' in preference to either rehabilitation or reform; as he puts it, 'correction is a very non-committal word, very wisely adopted by penologists in the United States'. Here, though, we will stick to the more conventional and generally used terms of reform and rehabilitation. In their summary and critique of the scientific approach to offender rehabilitation, Ward and Maruna (2007) start by referring to the lack of a general public approval for and interest in offender rehabilitation; indeed the first chapter of their study is entitled 'How did rehabilitation become a dirty word?'. They highlight what they term the 'vaguely preachy and evangelical . . . notion of rehabilitation', and comment that 'even offenders hate rehabilitation'. While offenders may talk about changing themselves or 'going straight' they tend to be suspicious of structured and psychologically based rehabilitation programmes.

Given that the prison population has risen massively in recent years and that the vast majority of these ever increasing numbers of prisoners will return to society, issues around rehabilitation are still vital. Although terms like 're-entry' and 're-settlement' are more in vogue, Ward and Maruna argue for a 'return to basics' and for the 'recasting of rehabilitation as a way of helping people who want to go straight' and they make the point that 'the old-fashioned term rehabilitation will suit our discussion just fine'.

The broad aim of rehabilitation became of increased importance in our penal system in the late eighteenth and early nineteenth centuries. In this period of the industrial revolution and the move from absolutist to more democratic forms of government in Europe, there was a growing demand for labour (particularly in the new factories of early industrial Britain) and so punishments which equipped offenders with self-discipline and a desire to work were popularly advocated. It was around this time that the notion of imprisonment as a punishment developed, with the prison changing from being a place that just held people awaiting trial or deportation toward being a method of punishment in its own right, as an alternative to the death penalty, transportation and other sentences. Since the Middle Ages local jails had performed this holding function – including holding debtors until they were able to pay their debts, as well as those awaiting trial or exile. These jails were privately run with deplorable conditions the norm, particularly for those who could not pay for their jailers for services. There was no segregation of women and men or of tried and untried prisoners, with racketeering and extortion rife (see Chapter 13, pp. 434–44 for a fuller discussion of the history of imprisonment).

In the face of the appalling conditions and abuses, the authorities were persuaded that 'a well-ordered, disciplined, clean and properly managed form of confinement was required' (Mathews 1999). This led to the development of new, refurbished prisons in the early nineteenth century and to a different view of the purpose of imprisonment.

Sentencing offenders to a period of imprisonment was seen as offering the potential for reform as well as being purely punishment. This contrasts with the contemporary view that sees 'reformative' punishments such as community orders and probation as 'alternatives to prison', with the implication that reform and imprisonment do not go hand in hand. The prisons built in the major industrial cities in Britain and elsewhere in the nineteenth century were designed to reform as well as incarcerate. It was believed that this reform would occur through a combination of work and solitary contemplation and the model for these prisons was based on a sort of monastic ideal, with individual cells allowing time for reflection and penance after the prisoner had finished a hard day's labour in a prison workshop.

The monastic style of the new prisons was one element of the strong religious influence on the methods and forms of punishment; and this influence has usually emphasized the reform of the offender. However, the early, religiously motivated attempts to reform often caused as much hardship for prisoners as they had faced under the previous, corrupt prison regimes. The early Victorian reformers, for instance, felt that prison should be a place where the offender might became a reformed and God-fearing person. Thus they advocated long periods of solitary confinement during which time the prisoners could examine their souls and consciences, spend hours in prayer, read (if they could) the Bibles that were made available in all cells and emerge purified.

The differing interpretations for the development of prisons and imprisonment at this period will be considered later (in Chapter 13); however, it would be useful to say a little about the early prison reform developments here. The work of John Howard, who examined and then described and catalogued the state of prisons in the late 1700s, was a major impetus for prison reform. His detailed account of prison life painted a graphic picture of squalid, disease-ridden conditions and led him to recommend sanitary and separate accommodation for prisoners, the introduction of useful labour and the banning of alcohol in prisons. Howard's pioneering survey of prison conditions was a major influence on the sort of new prisons that emerged in the nineteenth century. As Priestley puts it:

> In order to understand why so many Victorian prisoners were locked up in these gloomy rooms and forced to endure absolute solitary confinement that might last anything from a few days to eighteen months . . . it is necessary to look back at what went on in the unreformed prisons of the late eighteenth and early nineteenth centuries.
>
> (Priestley 1985: 33)

QUESTION BREAK: VICTORIAN PRISONS – THE SEPARATE SYSTEM

Read the extract from Priestley's study *Victorian Prison Lives* and consider the questions below.

The 1835 Select Committee on Gaols and Houses of Correction closely questioned the governor of Newgate about stories that 'there was gambling carried on all day long' . . . and that prisoners were 'boasting of their former robberies, some cursing and swearing, telling of obscene stories, and some singing vile songs. . . . Here and there these ribaldries were lubricated with quantities of beer . . .

It was a desire to remove these sources of corruption that led the 1835 committee to propose fundamental changes in the English prison system. Their views were not in the least revolutionary; their origins can be located in a tradition that predated the work even of John Howard . . . Condemnation of these evils (of prison life) was so widespread as to constitute an almost unanimous expression of enlightened opinion in the early part of the nineteenth century . . .

The recommendations of the select committee started with the proposition that 'One uniform System of Prison Discipline be established in every Gaol and House of Correction in England and Wales' . . . As to the nature of the 'uniform system' the committee wished to see established, the intellectual climate of the time presented them with 'two principal plans . . . the silent and the separate' . . . Under the Silent System the prisoners are collected in masses for work and other purposes, but are forbidden to speak or hold any intercourse; under the Separate System they are precluded from intercourse, by being kept not only in silence, but separation at all times . . .

The Separatist plan 'won' . . . with a decision to construct a new national penitentiary at Pentonville along 'separate' lines . . . The design of the new penitentiary was entrusted to Captain Joshua Jebb . . . In his eyes, the virtue of the separate system was that 'in depriving a prisoner of the contaminating influences arising from being associated with his fellow prisoners, all the good influences which can be brought to bear upon his character are substituted for them' . . .

One of the reasons for the immediate success of the 'separate' system was its capacity to appeal simultaneously to different and often conflicting constituencies of interest.

(Priestley 1985: 33–7)

- What do you think the 'different and conflicting constituencies of interest' that Priestley refers to in the final sentence of the extract might be?
- How might the 'separate' system (a) help reform offenders; (b) work against such reform?

More recent advocates of the rehabilitative philosophy of punishment have promoted a treatment, rather than a spiritual, model of reform. Alongside the establishment of the 'human sciences' of psychology and sociology as reputable academic subjects in the late nineteenth century, the new and distinct discipline of criminology emerged. This reflected a greater interest in studying the reasons why particular people offended and in the classifying of offenders into various categories and types. This new scientific knowledge could then be applied for the purpose of reforming such offenders. The work of Cesare Lombroso, generally agreed to be one of the key founders of the science of criminology, was particularly important in assessing and creating typologies of criminals. Lombroso was an Italian army physician who argued, in his famous study *L'Uomo Delinquente* (1876), that criminals were 'born so' and claimed his research proved that the criminal was a throwback to primitive, aggressive human types who could be recognized by their physical characteristics, particularly facial characteristics like prominent foreheads, large jaws and ears and shifty eyes. Lombroso's work, and his rather bizarre descriptions of criminals, have been criticized and dismissed by modern theorists, and his method of examining only those offenders who were in prison and then basing a general theory of crime around this evidence is clearly methodologically flawed. However, the growing development of a science of criminology and the growing role of doctors and psychiatrists in diagnosing and treating offenders illustrated the move to a treatment model of reform and rehabilitation and away from the old religiously motivated and driven approaches. As Mathews (1999) put it, 'Crime, like madness, was seen by many medical professionals as arising from a lack of self-control, and as a deviation from the path of reason.'

The development of the 'new' punishment of imprisonment along with the growth of the scientific study of crime provided a strong impetus for the introduction of more constructive and humane punishments both within and outside of the prison. The prison rules that were established in the early prisons invariably required that prisoners be engaged in useful work. While the extent to which the work was useful might be debated, there was a clear commitment to instilling in prisoners the discipline of regular work; so much so that where productive and useful labour was not available, a range of 'work for the sake of it' practices and schemes were devised and introduced. The treadmill, for instance, was widely used in nineteenth-century prisons. It was attractive to prison authorities because, as Mathews (1999) points out, 'it provided a form of exercise that could be used by the uneducated, while the pace and resistance of the wheel could be controlled'. The lack of skill and education of prisoners did, though, cause difficulties in providing useful work, as did the fact that many prisoners were sentenced to relatively short spells of imprisonment. According to Mathews nearly two thirds of those sentenced by magistrates in the 1860s were given terms of a month or less.

Although short sentences and the lack of skills training of the prison population are still evident, even if to a lesser degree than in the mid-nineteenth century, the impetus towards more constructive forms of punishment has continued and has gained strong support from important and influential pressure groups such as Amnesty International and the Howard League, who have campaigned against unjust and inhumane punishments in more recent times. However, in spite of the promotion of rehabilitation and reform, revenge and deterrence as justification for punishment are still widely supported and public anxiety and panic is easily aroused over any supposed 'softness' in modern punishments. Whenever there are moves to release, or even discuss the release of, widely condemned prisoners there is invariably and immediately a massive, media-orchestrated public outcry. Before her death in November 2002, any consideration of parole for Myra Hindley, the Moors murderess, caused so much public and media anger that it is unlikely any Home Secretary would have contemplated it. There have also been cases in which the sentences given by the courts to very young offenders (whom might be considered to be more open to rehabilitation and reform) have been attacked by the public and media for being too lenient. The two boys found guilty in 1993 of murdering two-year-old James Bulger in Bootle, Liverpool were initially sentenced with a recommendation that they serve a minimum term of eight years. The *Sun* newspaper led a popular campaign, which included petitioning the then Home Secretary Michael Howard and persuading him to extend their sentence to a minimum of 15 years (although this was later deemed unlawful and the killers, Jon Venables and Robert Thompson, were released on licence in 2001, after serving 8 years). A more recent example is the response to the sentence of indefinite detention, with a minimum of five years, passed in January 2010 to two young brothers who beat and tortured another pair of boys in Edlington, South Yorkshire. This has led to similar criticism, as the following headline illustrates: 'Campaigners call for Edlington attackers to spend 10 years in jail: Child Welfare campaigners are to demand the attorney general doubles the sentence for the brothers who tortured boys' (*Guardian,* 23 January 2010).

It would seem to be the case that rehabilitation is associated by many with softness, which in turn is associated with political weakness, and which arguably has not given it much of a chance as a philosophical underpinning for punishment. Below we will consider briefly some of the criticisms of the rehabilitative aim of punishment.

First, there is a danger that offenders are dealt with in a degrading, or at the least patronizing manner, almost as if they are animals to be trained. Given that the medical or treatment models of rehabilitation are based on the idea that criminal tendencies can be 'cured' by changing the personality of offenders, and in particular by restricting or taking away their capacity for moral choice, it is hardly surprising that such methods can appear to be demeaning. Although treatments based on behaviourist techniques, such as aversion therapy, as well as more clearly medically based approaches, such as chemically reducing the libido of offenders, might be provided in the name of treatment and so for the offender's own good, they can still be criticized as inhumane.

As well as the sort of approaches mentioned above, which might be seen as 'assaulting the personality' of offenders, the rehabilitative approaches to punishment invariably involve indeterminate sentences. These are open-ended sentences where the length of time that is spent in custody is dependent on the judgement of prison administrators and other experts. Here the punishment is less closely related to the particular offence committed but more about deciding if and when the offender is rehabilitated and so harmless, or at least able to be returned to 'normal' society. Although more a feature of the system of criminal justice in the United States, there are elements of this approach in the way the parole system works in Britain, with prisoners released on licence ahead of their expected release date on the advice of professional experts. A danger with these sorts of sentences is that they can encourage offenders to 'play the system', to do all they can to show those who decide on release that they are reformed – with there being an obvious temptation for such offenders to be less than honest and trying to create a false impression that they are reformed.

- To what extent do you think that an offender's behaviour during a sentence (for instance while in prison) should determine when s/he is released?

- Suggest arguments for and against the used of indeterminate sentences.

Of course, it is extremely difficult to assess how effective rehabilitative approaches are. It is clear that there are some successes but the 'success' of a programme or initiative for a particular offender can never be guaranteed; something may work for some offenders but not others. Ward and Maruna (2007) make the point that when an offender does not 'go straight', it is typically the offender who is blamed rather than the help or rehabilitation that has been given. While this may often (and even usually) be the case, it could also be that the help provided was not enough or needs improvement; or that the help provided was fine but the offender simply chooses to re-offend.

We will look at initiatives in 'restorative justice' as an example of rehabilitation below, after a general comment on the way in which the policies adopted towards the punishment of offenders have demonstrated a balance or see-sawing between reform/rehabilitative and retributivist themes. One or other of these broad themes or approaches has tended to become fashionable and dominant at particular times. In the 1950s and 1960s, for instance, the rehabilitative model was in vogue and a range of new, reform-based approaches to dealing with offenders were introduced, including parole, suspended sentences and community service orders. However, there was no hard evidence that these 'reformist' initiatives were any more effective in reducing re-offending than more obviously punitive measures. By the late 1970s the notion of rehabilitation had become discredited with the emphasis on policy moving away from reform, a move reflected in the hard-line approach to punishment advocated by politicians and government ministers and characterized by the introduction of 'short, sharp, shock' sentences in detention centres in 1980 and, more recently, the support for adopting hard line initiatives from the Unites States such as 'Boot Camps' and 'three strikes and you're out' legislation.

The concern in the 1970s in particular about the extent to which rehabilitation was 'working' led to the emergence of what has been termed the 'justice' or 'just deserts' model of punishment. As mentioned above, rehabilitative, treatment-based approaches had led logically to indeterminate sentences, based on the notion that when a treatment had been shown to 'work' the punishment could end. This was seen as giving too much discretion to 'experts' working in the criminal justice system and the justice model argued that punishment should be based on the seriousness of the offences, so that all offenders received their 'just deserts'. In addition, the rehabilitative approach was seen as inherently unfair in that it treated offences of similar seriousness in very different ways. For instance, two offenders could be found guilty of the same offence (indeed they could be co-defendants for the very same case) and end up receiving quite different sentences and, in some cases, spending widely differing lengths of time in custody. As evidence of the impact of the justice model on penal policy in Britain, Cavadino and Dignan (2007) highlight the abolition in 1982 of indeterminate borstal sentences for young offenders (who were released after any time between six months and two years according to how they had 'responded' to their punishment) and its replacement with fixed-term sentences.

Restorative justice

In recent years there has been a revival of rehabilitative approaches, but according to Cavadino and Dignan the claims made for them are now more modest. The idea that methods of punishment could work almost independently of the offenders has been replaced with an emphasis on how a particular punishment can be used to help offenders improve their behaviour. These newer approaches often include confronting offenders with the consequences of their behaviour in the hope that they will choose to change both their behaviour and their attitudes towards offending. These ideas characterize the notion of restorative justice which we will consider here as an example of newer rehabilitative initiatives. Restorative justice is most closely associated with the principal of reparation, based on the notion that crime affects communities and victims, who should therefore have a part to play in administering justice. As mentioned, this approach usually involves the offender being brought face to face with someone they have harmed and thereby confronting what they have done. When serving as Chief Constable of Thames Valley Police, Charles Pollard introduced a community conferencing scheme which gave victims 'a part to play in the system' and was a strong advocate of restorative justice. He saw the Thames Valley initiative as:

> a hugely powerful thing . . . This is about coming face to face with the harm they have caused, and that has the impact of shaming the offender. But what's important is that it is private and is what we call reintegrative shaming which means that once that person has really understood the impact they have had on others they are very ready to really think about how they are going to change their behaviour in future. They are ready to think about the damage to the people they have harmed whether by compensation, certainly by apologising, maybe doing some work for them.
>
> (Pollard 1998)

Pollard goes on to point out that the criminal justice system does not have a mechanism for people to apologize for their behaviour; and that an apology should be the first and most important part of any reparation. However, since the pioneering work of Pollard and Thames Valley Police, many more police forces have adopted some form of restorative justice. Most approaches target juvenile offenders, although Cheshire Police have a scheme which is aimed at first or second offenders of all ages and every officer in their force has been trained in restorative justice. This does seem to have had some effect, with the re-offending rate of first-time offenders having fallen by 60 per cent (www.itv.com/newstonight 11 February 2010).

With regard to compensation more generally, it would seem to be logical to try to compensate the injured party and for the offender to do that in some way, If there is no clearly identifiable or individual victim, then the community can be compensated through some sort of community service undertaken by the offender or by a fine paid into public funds. This notion of reparation or compensation is not always easy to apply. Offenders may not have the means to repay the victim; and the extent to which parents should be responsible for compensating for the behaviour of their children is debatable. However, such an approach can be appropriate in certain situations. In many offences the offender and victim will know one another and if they are brought together to reach a settlement it can be better for all parties, as well as cutting down on court workloads. It is an approach that is probably particularly suited to minor crimes rather than a cure-all for crime generally, but, like other new approaches to punishment, is not likely to gain favour with the general public or the popular media who will see it as too soft a response to crime.

This sort of critical response to new, rehabilitative approaches to punishment highlights a basic problem that is faced by any penal system; the lack of success of harsh, retributive punishments might encourage reform measures, but in turn these are liable to be felt by many as not a 'proper' response to the harm caused by offenders. As a result, there tends to be the see-sawing between reform and retributive based punishments that we referred to above (p. 241).

In assessing the extent to which rehabilitation 'works', Walker (1991) points to the difficulty of ever being sure why a particular offender ceases to offend. There are all sorts of possible reasons: the stigma of being caught, the unpleasant memory of the punishment, the influence of family, friends or social workers. Even offenders who appear to have changed their behaviour may well still be involved in offending but are better able to avoid detection. The difficulty with assessing these approaches to punishment does not mean that 'nothing works', but rather that there are no guarantees that particular punishments work as they are intended to and that some approaches may work with some offenders but not with others. The rehabilitative approach, and the difficulties with assessing it, is illustrated by the methods used at Grendon prison, the only prison in Europe that operates solely as a therapeutic community and the only prison in the UK that has been proven to reduce re-offending rates. The boxed insert below looks in more depth at Grendon prison and its approach to rehabilitation.

QUESTION BREAK: HMP GRENDON – BRITAIN'S MOST SUCCESSFUL PRISON?

HMP Grendon is a category B adult male prison that was opened in 1962. It takes prisoners who are felt to be dangerous and difficult, most of whom have been convicted of crimes against the person and will have been sentenced to four years or more. All inmates will have volunteered to come to Grendon and are held in an environment quite different from that in other prisons – it is run as a therapeutic community with a focus on group work. So it has twin roles as a prison and as a therapeutic facility for severely personality-disordered offenders. We will include comments and extracts from reports that have looked at the effectiveness of Grendon prison. In terms of its reconviction rates, a Home Office study in 1997 considered the reconviction rates within four years of release of prisoners who went to Grendon between 1984 and 1989. It found that even though prisoners sent to Grendon tended to be high risk offenders they had lower reconviction rates than would have been expected had they not gone there; and time spent at Grendon was closely related to reconviction in that prisoners who stayed at least 18 months had reductions in reconviction rates of around 20–25 per cent (Home Office 1997). Extracts from more recent commentaries are included below:

Low Levels of Assaults and Drug Use at Grendon

About 70% (of Grendon's inmates) are serving life sentences . . . a significant proportion are sex offenders or paedophiles . . . By consenting to serve their time at Grendon, these prisoners are signing up for an intensive programme of therapy. Each wing of up to 40 men has is own psychologist and psychotherapist and every day inmates are asked to sign up for one of a selection of group therapy sessions . . . Grendon's daily therapy regime is highly intensive . . . Group sessions are psycho-dynamic in nature, and although they are very open, they tend to focus on past events that prisoners believe may have triggered their offending behaviour . . .

Of course, therapy does not work for everyone. Grendon's drop out rate is about 20%, but the majority of those leave during the 12 week induction programme . . . For the majority of prisoners at Grendon, however, this intensive therapeutic regime seems to be working. As one prisoner puts it: "Being held accountable to my group and my peers has given me the strength to be accountable to myself. Coming here makes you face up to your actions." . . .

Grendon's success shows up in numbers as well as anecdotes. As well as reducing the chances of reoffending, Grendon experiences the lowest number of assaults of any prison in the UK. It also has some of the lowest rates of drug use and self harm in the prison estate . . .

With such positive results, you'd be forgiven for thinking that Grendon was phenomenally expensive, but this is not the case. The institution's £42,000 per prisoner per year may be higher than most category B prisons, but it's substantially lower than the £250,000 per head charged by therapeutic hospitals . . .

So why aren't more prisons run like Grendon? The real problem is not so much results, economics or impracticalities, but politics. The political tide has turned against such liberal initiatives, and a growth in penal populism has left politicians thinking that support for Grendon will be paid for in political points . . . After serving 18 months at Grendon, prisoners are 10% less likely to commit another offence.

(Davies 2008)

Is this Britain's Most Successful Prison?

(Grendon) remains an anomaly in Britain's overcrowded prison estate, which is perpetually under threat from Ministry of Justice bureaucrats who favour 'Titan' jails run by private contractors where inmates are stacked high and costs kept low, but (it) has just picked up the annual Longford prize as, in the judges' words, 'a beacon of hope for the Prison Service because of it proven track record in cutting reoffending and promoting the principles of rehabilitation'. . . .

Successive academic studies have shown that reconviction rates among 'Grendon graduates' are lower than across the prison population as a whole. When you bear in mind that Grendon is often dealing with some of the most serious and damaged offenders in the system – for whom every other option has failed and who might otherwise have been sent to secure mental institutions at a cost to the taxpayer of £250,000 per year – its track record is nothing short of remarkable.

(Stanford 2009)

A Weekend Behind Bars Showed Me Why This Prison is Precious

The majority of Grendon inmates are lifers, comprising some of the most dangerous and disruptive men in the system . . . Latest research shows that for prisoners who stay here for more than 18 months, the reconviction rate within two years of release falls to 20%, compared with almost 50% for those serving in conventional prisons. Just as significant, the number of drug and violence related offences is close to zero, compared with 120 annually for every hundred inmates elsewhere . . .

Grendon doesn't work for everyone, but, for those who survive it, the results are astonishing . . . Grendon is the one place in the country to practise this most dangerous and magical of beliefs – that bad and broken men can redeem themselves.

(Brooks 2009)

- Why do you think Grendon has been more successful than other prisons?
- What problems might there be with extending the sort of regime at Grendon across more prisons?

Other aims of punishment

In this chapter we have focused our discussion under the three main headings of deterrence, retribution and rehabilitation and in doing so have included issues that might have been looked at under additional headings. In particular, some studies refer to incapacitation and denunciation as distinct 'aims of punishment' and we will say a little about them here.

Incapacitation

This means that the offender is prevented, usually physically, from re-offending due to the punishment given. So, at the extreme, capital punishment means that the offender could never offend again. Imprisonment would normally mean the offender cannot commit a range of crimes while serving the sentence; and disqualification from driving should prevent motorists from repeating their offences. Other examples of incapacitation include the physical prevention of sexual offenders committing offences through castration (surgical or chemical), although this is not part of the criminal justice system in the UK. Incapacitation has no interest in rehabilitation, reform or even retribution, it is about protecting (the rest of) society. As imprisonment is the most severe penalty available to our criminal justice system, we will focus on its incapacitation effects. While there will certainly be some period of incapacitation in relation to a wide range of crimes (such as burglary or car theft, for instance), Cavadino and Dignan (2007) suggest that the 'incapacitation effects of imprisonment are only modest' – most "criminal careers" are short and by the time offenders are imprisoned they may be about to give up or reduce their criminal behaviour. Furthermore it is difficult to prove with any degree of accuracy which offenders are particularly likely to reoffend. None the less, this approach and justification has been important in recent years in both England and the USA, for example policies such as the 'three strikes and you're out' law in the USA, whereby repeat offenders are automatically given a life sentence for a third offence are clearly linked with the notion of incapacitation.

Denunciation

The emphasis here is that punishment is used to show society's condemnation of an offence and that this can be seen as a justification for punishment. Cavadino and Dignan (2007) highlight different reasons behind the idea of denunciation. Instrumental denunciation is related to the reductivist approach and suggests that it can be used to reduce the amount of crime. This can be related to the idea put forward by the early social theorist Durkheim (see Chapter 8, pp. 252–257) that punishment sends out a moral message to society that the offence is abhorred and therefore morally wrong. Expressive denunciation suggests that punishment is justified irrespective of whether it educates the public and reduces crime; punishment is just the expression of a society's abhorrence of the particular crime. As Cavadino and Dignan argue, this 'looks suspiciously like a knee-jerk retributivism' cloaked in reference to the community or society. On the other hand they point out that focusing on the moral gravity of an offence can help provide an 'acceptable principle of distribution for punishment'.

SUMMARY

In this chapter we have considered some of major aims and philosophies of punishment and the issues and debates they have raised. Perhaps not surprisingly this discussion has uncovered a great deal of uncertainty as to what works and how; and perhaps it is unrealistic to hope to find one approach to punishment which will be generally seen as just and effective and so widely supported. A basic reason for why punishment poses such dilemmas is because it involves treating other people unpleasantly. We have seen that there are a number of grounds and justifications that can be put forward for punishing offenders, including to deter others, to denounce, because it is deserved and to reform or rehabilitate. It is this last one, the focus of the final section of this chapter that is especially tricky because it is seemingly for the benefit of offenders yet still involves forcing them to do something – and something which will be inconvenient and probably not chosen voluntarily (pursuing some form of treatment programme or undertaking work for no financial reward, for instance). This ambivalence is particularly illustrated when attempts are made to rehabilitate offenders within custodial institutions.

So there are no clear answers to the question of 'why punish?' Punishment involves using legal authority to do things which would otherwise be morally wrong; and with no guarantee that those things will achieve what they are intended to. The basic justifications we have considered here both contradict and overlap with one another. Retribution looks back and aims to punish in proportion to the offence committed; deterrence and rehabilitation look forward and aim to reduce future offending. These different rationales can exist together within particular punishments, so that a prison sentence can be passed with the intention of being retributionary, of deterring offenders and of offering rehabilitation.

QUESTION BREAK: THE *OBSERVER* CRIME AND JUSTICE DEBATE

Tough on crime, tough on the causes of crime. But that was only half of it. Tough on criminals – there's the full story. Lock them up (71,000 of them). Make sure the good-for-nothings are so far from home and family that regular visits are near impossible or, at least, financially crippling. Cut the training and education budget, so that their spell inside will really brand them second-class citizens incapable of holding any job apart from sweeping streets or washing cars . . .

Mete out this kind of treatment to the average healthy Anglo-Saxon, and you'll find they develop a bit of an attitude problem; but about half of prisoners have the reading skills of an 11-year-old, and more than 70 per cent suffer from a least two mental disorders: when these people come out after a spell inside, is it any wonder that, in two out of three cases, they are re-convicted of another crime within two years?

This is a primitive, short-sighted prisons policy, as Cherie Booth warned in *Inside Time*, the newspaper for prisoners . . . Today's prisoners will one day sit next to you on the Tube, or fix your car. If their time inside has offered them nothing but hardship and humiliation, how will they view you?

Given the certainty that prisoners will be recycled in our society, Cherie Booth's warning should be heeded. But in Britain's culture of retribution . . . [it] is sure to give rise to cries of horror . . . They're guilty, aren't they? Let them rot in hell. They've been tried and convicted: we've done our duty by them . . .

This indifference to the prisoner's future is shown in our failure to invest in programmes or schemes that can enable inmates to turn their lives around.

A few work apprenticeship schemes exist . . . but our failure to reproduce such schemes throughout the prison system, or to protest the repeated budget cuts that have shrunk education programmes behind bars, have reduced rehabilitation to an empty word, and turned every prison sentence into the first step in a campaign of retribution . . .

It's an eye-for-an-eye mentality that betrays how, beneath the civilised arguments of defence and prosecution, an Old Testament heart beats within the body of British justice. It's an attitude betrayed by the hysterical headlines every time the debate about Myra Hindley's release resurfaces; and by the row over the freeing of James Bulger's murderers, when threats to the boys' lives prompted police to move them and their families, and issue them with new identities. No-one believed in their redemption: no matter how many years Myra languished inside, no matter how young Robert Thompson and Jon Venables had been when the perpetrated their crime. Given their faith in this tough and unforgiving philosophy, can we really expect people to lobby for more schemes to train prisoners? Can we hope for a more generous budget for education behind bars? Once you've been convicted, it would seem, you've forfeited all rights to our concern.

(Christina Odone, *Observer*, 7 July 2002)

- What evidence is provided to demonstrate the popularity of the retributive mentality?
- Why do you think that rehabilitation does not easily gain public support?
- What might be done to change the public's attitude to rehabilitation?
- How might retribution and rehabilitation co-exist within a criminal justice system?

FURTHER READING

Hudson, B. (2003) *Understanding Justice: An Introduction to Ideas, Perspectives and Controversies in Modern Penal Theory.* This is the second edition of a very successful text that summarizes the major philosophical ideas of retribution, rehabilitation and incapacitation and discusses their strengths and weaknesses.

McLaughlin, E., Fergusson, R., Hughes, G. and Westmarland, L. (2003) *Restorative Justice: Critical Issues.* This edited collection traces the development of restorative justice (which was introduced in the discussion of rehabilitation in this chapter) and includes examples of current practices and policies from around the world.

Walker, N. (1991) *Why Punish?* Oxford: Oxford University Press.

Walker, N. (1999) *Aggravation, Mitigation and Mercy in English Criminal Justice.* These two books highlight the conflicts and issues both within and between the major aims of punishment. The first is a short, thought-provoking book that considers the different justifications for and aims of punishment, grappling with the moral issues and dilemmas that they raise. The second considers the sentencing of offenders and issues of proportionality – and the considerations that persuade courts to pursue the aims of punishment with either leniency or severity.

The journal *Punishment and Society: The International Journal of Penology* was launched in 1999 and is an excellent source of recent research and theorizing that is relevant to the topics examined in this chapter and in Chapter 2 on theories of punishment.

Theories of Punishment

INTRODUCTION

In this chapter the focus moves from the philosophical justifications for punishment to a consideration of some of the theoretical explanations for punishment. In particular, we will examine what social theorists have said about the nature and the role of punishment in society.

While moral and legal philosophers have examined the different aims or justifications for punishment, social scientists have centred their explanations on the relationship between particular societies and the forms of punishment – or penal system – that characterize them. In considering this issue, the major social theorists have tried to explain a movement from physical punishments (punishments of the body such as execution and mutilations) to punishments of the mind and soul (especially, forms of custodial punishment). They have explored the role and purpose of punishment in relation to the forms of authority prevalent in different societies, an approach which has involved a consideration of the law and legal authority. As we will see later, early, classic, social theorists such as Durkheim and Weber emphasized how punishment and the law helped to hold societies together, while Marx and Marxist scholars have seen it as supporting and maintaining the interests of the powerful.

Hudson (2003) points out that the philosophical approaches to punishment have not concerned themselves with:

> why, in different places or at different times, societies use different kinds of penal strategy. Why, for example, did punishments such as ducking stools and stocks

go out of fashion? Why have so many industrial democracies given up capital punishment? Why has imprisonment become such an important form of punishment?

(Hudson 2003: 95)

It is questions such as these, about penal strategy, that are the central concern of sociological theories of punishment. And social theorists have tried to relate these questions and the attendant issues to some of the philosophical justifications for punishment considered in the previous chapter. Why, for instance, has retribution seemed to fit the mood of the day at certain times, while at other times rehabilitation has been favoured? Why at some periods in history has there been a greater tolerance and optimism while at other times vengeance has come to the fore?

Although the theorists mentioned above are not solely sociologists, in this chapter we will look at what are generally taken to be the major sociological theories of punishment. The approaches we will look at can be grouped under three headings:

- The role of punishment in promoting social solidarity – the work and influence of Durkheim and Weber.
- Punishment as a part of a class-based process of economic and social control – the Marxist approach.
- The relationship between punishment, power and regulation – Foucault.

These theoretical approaches examine punishment in social terms, rather than as a mechanism for the control of crime. In his comprehensive discussion of theories of punishment, Garland (1990) points out that the specific forms and institutions of punishment, such as prisons or community service orders, are social artefacts that reflect particular cultural standards and styles. And just as styles of building or music cannot be explained solely in terms of their obvious purposes – of providing shelter or entertainment in the cases of building and music – so punishment has to be considered in a historical context and as a cultural and social phenomenon.

What the sociology of punishment shows us is that penal policies and goals have to be seen in relation to other areas of social life, such as the economic system of society or the form of government that has evolved. As Hudson puts it:

Sociological writing on punishment has been focused on penal change and development; on the relationship between punishment and other aspects of social life; on the functions punishment performs for various sections of society; and on the ideas and expectations people have of punishment.

(2003: 96)

It is important to keep these general notions and points in mind when considering the theories of punishment that have been developed by social theorists. The work of Durkheim, Foucault and others has to be seen as part of a more general interest in and question about the ways in which order and authority are maintained in society. Indeed, questions of social order, and how it is maintained and transmitted from one generation to the next, have always been at the core of sociological theorizing in general.

THE ROLE OF PUNISHMENT IN PROMOTING SOCIAL SOLIDARITY – THE WORK AND INFLUENCE OF DURKHEIM AND WEBER

Emile Durkheim (1858–1917) is one the key founding figures in sociology. He was one of the first scholars to differentiate sociology from other branches of social and political philosophy. In particular he played the leading role in establishing sociology as a respectable academic discipline in his native France. Although none of Durkheim's major works focused solely on crime and punishment, he wrote more on these areas than any other of the early, classic social theorists. A brief overview of his general sociological perspective and an introduction to some of the key terms he used in his work will help provide some background and context for discussing his analysis of punishment. His approach to understanding society was to look at how it had an existence and a reality apart from the individuals who made it up. For instance, he looked at how social rules and relationships influence the behaviour of the individual members of society, at how people behave in accordance with social rules (even when no one is observing them), and at how the existence of social rules forms a culture which gives each society its distinctive character. These general points illustrate the central idea behind Durkheim's sociology and, therefore, his theorizing, that the individual is born of society, rather than the society of individuals. For Durkheim, then, the society has primacy over the individual. This can be seen in his emphasizing the priority of the whole over the parts and his argument that individual phenomena had to be explained by the state of the collectivity (or society).

In looking at the nature of modern, industrial society, Durkheim focused on the moral basis of social order and stability – the basis of what he termed social solidarity. He argued that without the regulation of society, individuals would attempt to satisfy their own desires and wishes without regard to their fellows. This societal regulation had, he believed, to be based on a set of shared values; and a working society required that the individuals within it accepted these common values. Durkheim called this common set of values the collective conscience, which he defined as 'the totality of beliefs and sentiments common to average citizens of the same society'.

For Durkheim, the achievement of social life among people, the existence of social order and social solidarity, is ensured by collective standards of behaviour and values. Such social solidarity is crucial for the existence of society. However, the particular form of solidarity is not fixed and will vary with the changing forms of society. Durkheim explored the changing nature of social solidarity from early, pre-modern societies to complex, modern ones in his first major study, *The Division of Labour in Society*.

Within this general approach to theorizing about the nature of society, crime and punishment was one of the central objects of Durkheim's sociological analysis. (Durkheim's theoretical approach to crime and its role and function in society was considered in Chapter 4, pp. 102–106; here we will focus on his analysis of the role and function of punishment, although there is some overlap between the two areas.) He saw punishment as representing the collective conscience of society at work, and a detailed examination of it would, he argued, provide an insight into the moral and social life of the particular society. Durkheim focused on punishment because he felt that the ways in which a society chooses to punish would provide an important indicator to that society's culture – punishment was viewed as one of the key indices of a society's culture. He was also interested in the functions that punishment might fulfil for the maintenance of social order and for the reinforcement of the culture of a society. The punishing of law breakers, then, was not just, or even mainly, about controlling crime.

So, for Durkheim, social order was based on a core of shared values and moralities; and punishment provided a clear illustration of this moral nature of social order. These ideas about social order and punishment were first elaborated by Durkheim in *The Division of Labour in Society* (first published in 1893), with changes in the nature of punishment seen as reflecting changes in the nature of social morality and social solidarity. His analysis of the relationship between the punishment of crime and the maintenance of moral and social order begins by looking at crime and, although our focus is on theories of punishment, it is useful to consider briefly his discussion of crime. Crimes are acts which violate the society's collective conscience; they violate its moral code and this violation produces a punitive reaction. To put it another way, crimes are seen as moral outrages which lead to a demand that they be punished. In Durkheim's words, 'crime brings together upright consciences and concentrates them', it provides the occasion for the collective expression of shared moral feelings.

Crime, then, can only be understood in relation to the particular social context; it is simply an act that is prohibited by the collective conscience of the particular society. And the relative nature of crime means that it can only be defined in terms of the state of the collective conscience of the society in question; as Aron (1970) points out, the fact that an act which one society called a crime might seem quite innocent to observers several centuries after the event, or observers belonging to a different society, is of no importance to Durkheim.

> Sociologically, to call someone a criminal does not imply that we consider him guilty in relation to God or our own conception of justice. The criminal is simply the man in society who has refused to obey the laws of the city.
>
> (Aron 1970: 28)

Durkheim's approach to crime and the collective conscience of society are considered in the question break below.

QUESTION BREAK: CRIME AND THE COLLECTIVE CONSCIENCE

> In the first place crime is normal because a society exempt from it is utterly impossible. Crime consists of an act that offends certain very strong collective sentiments . . . Imagine a society of saints, a perfect cloister of exemplary individuals. Crimes will there be unknown; but faults which appear venial to the layman will create there the same scandal that the ordinary offense does in ordinary consciousness. If this society has the power to judge and punish,

it will define these acts as criminal and treat them as such. For the same reason, the perfect and upright man judges his smallest failing with a severity that the majority reserve for acts more truly in the nature of an offense . . .

Crime is, then, necessary; it is bound up with the fundamental conditions of all social life, and by that very fact it is useful, because these conditions of which it is a part are themselves indispensable to the normal evolution of morality and law . . .

Crime itself plays a useful role in this evolution. Crime implies not only that the way remains open to necessary changes but that in certain cases it directly prepares these changes. According to Athenian law, Socrates was a criminal. However, his crime, namely, the independence of his thought, rendered a service not only to humanity but to his country . . . Nor is the case of Socrates unique, it is reproduced periodically in history. It would never have been possible to establish the freedom of thought we now enjoy if the regulations prohibiting it had not been violated. At that time, however, the violation was a crime . . . From this point of view the fundamental facts of criminality present themselves to us in an entirely new light. Contrary to current ideas, the criminal no longer seems a totally unsociable being, a sort of parasitic element. On the contrary, he plays a definite role in social life.

(From E. Durkheim, *The Rules of Sociological Method*, 1964, pp. 67–72)

- What positive and useful functions of crime are suggested by Durkheim?
- Suggest any other social functions that crime might perform.

To return to Durkheim's analysis of punishment. The existence of social morality and social solidarity makes punishment inevitable and necessary, in that it reaffirms and strengthens the moral and social bonds. Of course, punishment is not the only process that does this; religion, education and family life all help to strengthen the collective conscience and to promote social cohesion. However, formal punishment is given a special place in Durkheim's analysis.

So far, we have considered Durkheim's general approach to punishment and its role without relating it to particular societies and the notion of social change. Durkheim acknowledged that the nature and to some extent the importance of punishment would change as society changes. In general terms, he saw punishment as being more important as a means of reinforcing moral and social order in less complex societies with a less developed division of labour. However, while methods of punishment change over time, the essential functions of punishment remain constant. Although the collective conscience of a society changes over time and people are outraged by different activities, punishment as a social process has an unchanging character.

In contrasting simpler societies based on what he termed mechanical solidarity with modern societies based on organic solidarity, Durkheim suggested that the former were characterized by more severe and intense forms of punishment. To elaborate on this a little, in *The Division of Labour in Society* Durkheim described simpler societies as having a mechanical sort of social solidarity whereby individuals would, he argued, feel the same emotions, hold the same values and the same things sacred and where, essentially, there would be little differentiation between them. In contrast more modern societies would have an organic form of social solidarity characterized by increased differentiation between individuals; there would still be a collective conscience but of a slightly weaker nature.

In comparing the forms of solidarity and consciousness in these two types of society, Durkheim examined the role of the law and legal phenomena and distinguished between two kinds of law, each of which was characteristic of one of the basic forms of social solidarity:

- *Repressive law* was found in simpler forms of society which exhibited mechanical solidarity, and the punishments associated with it revealed and reflected the force of common sentiments.
- *Restitutive law* was typical of more advanced societies, where the focus was not just to punish but to re-establish the state of things, in accordance with justice (Aron 1970: 29).

Durkheim goes on to suggest that the intensity of the collective conscience of society (indicated by the form of social solidarity) is reflected in the intensity of punishment. In more modern, advanced societies, collective sentiments are less demanding and there is more scope for diversity and interdependence. In those societies punishments for violation of the collective conscience (and more specifically the law) are consequently more lenient. So Durkheim argues that as the intensity of punishment reflects the strength of the collective conscience, then as a society develops the severity of punishment will diminish. In *The Division of Labour*, he points to a progressive decline in the degree of repression as mechanical solidarity recedes and organic solidarity advances.

The link between punishment and morality is perhaps the key element of Durkheim's sociology of punishment. Punishment is seen as an important and necessary part of the moral order of society. It helps prevent the collapse of moral authority and demonstrates the strength of moral commands. For Durkheim, the primary function of punishment is the reassertion of the moral order of society. From this analysis, punishment is not an instrument of deterrence that aims to prevent the repetition of a guilty act; the threat of the unpleasant consequences of particular punishments are just practical problems that might stand in the way of the criminal's desires. Rather it is a means of conveying moral messages and of indicating the strength of feelings that lie behind those messages and the common consciousness. In practical terms punishment may have to be unpleasant but in terms of the role of punishment in society Durkheim sees that as incidental – the essence of punishment is the expression of moral condemnation.

- List the crimes that excite the greatest moral repugnance. Why do they?
- In what ways can punishment express this moral condemnation and repugnance? (Think of punishments in a range of different societies.)

In introducing Durkheim's work on punishment we have focused on the arguments and points he made in his first major work, *The Division of Labour in Society*. Durkheim elaborated on his theory of punishment in an article published some years later in 1901, 'The Two Laws of Penal Evolution'. In this article he developed his argument that punishments become less repressive in modern compared to traditional societies and built this into his 'two laws'. The first law relates to the 'intensity' of punishment which is seen as 'greater in so far as societies belong to a less advanced type – in so far as the central power has a more absolute character'. In developed, modern societies collective sentiments exist but they are constituted by the laws rather than enshrined in religion, and the law is seen as a human rather than a divine construction. As a consequence, crimes are seen as transgressions against fellow humans rather than offences against a god or gods and so do not arouse the same outrage and indignation. Also, there is likely to be more human sympathy for offenders as the punishment does not have to be undertaken to appease the god or gods. Durkheim argued that in the more modern forms of society, retribution is tempered by mercy. The evidence for this first law can be found, Durkheim argued, in the changes in the forms of punishment over time. In particular, he refers to the decline of aggravated capital punishment where death was accompanied by rituals of mutilation and torture. As examples of this greater leniency, he contrasts the barbarity of imperial Rome and of pre-revolutionary France, with the more democratic, republican regimes that followed them.

The second law also relates to the 'lesser intensity' of punishment as society develops and as imprisonment becomes the main means of punishment. 'Deprivation of liberty and of liberty alone, for periods of time varying according to the gravity of the crime, tends increasingly to become the normal type of repression.' Durkheim saw this second law as dependent on the first.

These laws, and Durkheim's theory of punishment, led him to consider why it is that punishments become milder as societies move from less to more advanced types. His explanation centred on the relationship between punishment and crime and in particular the changes in the ways in which collective sentiments respond to crimes. This point is explained by Lukes (1973) in his detailed study of Durkheim's life and work. Durkheim classified crimes into two basic categories: those directed against 'collective things, such as religion, tradition and public authority', and those directed only against individuals. The first he called 'religious criminality' and the second 'human criminality'. As societies evolved, so the religious crimes declined and crimes against the individual gradually took their place. The former, often seen as sacrileges, inspired greater passion and fear and left little room for pity for the criminal.

However, when the individual was the object of the crime collective sentiments were less aroused and less fearful. As a consequence, as crime became less religious and more human, so punishment became less severe.

Another variable in Durkheim's discussion of crime and punishment is that of political power, which he refers to in the first law of penal evolution in claiming that as governments become more absolute so the collective sentiments become stronger and more imbued with 'religiosity'. Absolute governments, he suggested, treated political offences as sacrilegious and repressed them with greater violence.

To summarize, Durkheim explained punishment and changes in penal practice in terms of the changes in collective sentiments and beliefs that occurred with the evolution of societies and social practices and institutions. Durkheim also emphasized the necessity for punishment; it would not disappear as societies evolved further. As Lukes puts it, 'the penal system was ultimately a function of the moral beliefs of society, and it was fair to predict that the list of human crimes would lengthen, and they would be punished less severely, but punished nonetheless' (1973: 262).

QUESTION BREAK: THE RITUALS OF PUNISHMENT

In seeing punishment as a means of conveying moral messages and fostering social solidarity, Durkheim emphasized the importance of the rituals associated with the punishment, rather than the actual details of the particular punishment. With the decline in public punishment such as floggings or executions, these rituals tend nowadays to centre around the courtroom. They include the wearing of wigs and gowns and the process of the trial and the passing of sentence. There are rituals associated with particular punishments; in his famous study of total institutions, Goffman highlighted the initiation rituals that helped to 'mortify the self', including the shaving of heads of prisoners and the restrictions on contact with the outside world (Goffman 1968). These rituals, however, are undertaken for an internal audience rather than the general public. As a consequence of the decline in public punishment, the focus of public and media interest tends to be on the courtroom drama and the trial of offenders – on 'who gets what' rather than on the detailed workings of the processes of punishment.

- Consider some recent criminal trials that have received detailed media coverage.
- How would you describe the media reporting of these trials?
- To what extent might such trials and the reporting of them help to strengthen the 'collective conscience'?
- Court cases and punishments can provide a range of other responses as well as social solidarity. What other responses might these recent trials have provoked?

Durkheim and punishment – comment and criticism

Durkheim described these historical changes in very general and sweeping terms which have been criticized as over-simplistic. His description of simple societies, characterized by a mechanical form of solidarity, and advanced societies, characterized by organic solidarity provides no real account of the range of intermediate possibilities. Garland (1990) suggests that the historical transition from simpler societies with more severe forms of punishment to advanced ones with more lenient punishments is assumed by Durkheim rather than actually demonstrated in any sort of detailed historical account.

In a similar vein, Garland also raises questions about Durkheim's application of the notion of the collective conscience. The fact that there is a certain degree of order and agreement in society does not necessarily mean there is a generally held commitment to shared moral norms. People follow rules and laws for a variety of reasons some of which might be purely practical (to avoid punishment for instance) rather than because of any deeply held moral commitment. This raises the issue as to whether violations of the criminal law do really break genuinely held moral sentiments. Of course, there is some link between popular sentiment and the law; laws protecting a person's safety or property, for instance, are widely and generally supported. However, while there may be general agreement that rape, burglary and so on are morally repugnant, there is much less agreement over what should be the 'proper' punishment for such behaviour. And there is even less agreement over criminal offences which do not offend such strongly and widely held moral sentiments – crimes such as drug use, tax evasion or infringing copyright laws do not excite the same sort of general, moral repugnance (and are viewed differently by different groups of the population). It would seem that it is those punishments which deal with the most shocking and serious crimes, such as child murder, that provoke the sort of collective moral outcry that Durkheim described. This is not to say that punishment of crime does not produce emotive responses – the general fascination with crime and criminals evidenced in the popularity of films, books, magazines and TV programmes on serial killers, for instance, demonstrates that. However, crime and criminal behaviour and the punishment of it perhaps covers too broad a spectrum to be generalized about with the confidence of Durkheim.

This raises the question of the extent to which punishment is functional for society. There is likely to be little disagreement with the argument that it performs some functions – that it legitimates some forms of authority and restrains some types of behaviour. However, what is functional from one point of view or for one group in society might prove to be dysfunctional for others. This sort of criticism can be applied to the work of Durkheim, and to the general functionalist perspective that developed from his work. It takes issue with the idea that there is a general agreement over what is functional or not and what should and should not be valued and appreciated in society. As regards punishment, there are dysfunctional consequences as well as functional ones. In this context Garland refers to Mead's argument that the passions and emotive responses engendered by crime can encourage societies to direct their energies to denouncing certain individuals, rather than to doing anything about wider social conditions that might give rise to crime. The directing of anger at particular evil perpetrators might also encourage the scapegoating and consequent harassment of certain groups.

The emphases given to the notion of a collective conscience and a general moral agreement also take little account of the obvious power differentials involved in the business of maintaining order in society. Is the law reflective of general interest or rather the interests of those who are in positions of power and authority? Durkheim's work seems to underplay the fact that individuals are members of groups that can and do have opposed interests; it neglects the conflict between interest groups. This point raises questions as to the extent to which Durkheim's theory is relevant to modern, advanced societies with complex divisions of labour and where the moral order is not necessarily universal.

In spite of these critical comments, Durkheim's work has highlighted and encouraged a detailed examination of the social processes of punishment; his work explored the symbolic and emotional elements of the punishment process, rather than just then narrow technical side of it. And in his arguing that punishment was necessary and functional for society, Durkheim was well aware that it had only a limited ability to control criminal behaviour. It is this apparent contradiction – that punishment was politically and socially functional yet had little effect on actual criminal behaviour – that illustrates, for Garland, the crucial characteristic of punishment: 'This sense of being simultaneously necessary and also destined to a degree of futility is what I will term the tragic quality of punishment' (1990: 80).

Max Weber: rationality and punishment

Before moving on to the second major sociological approach to punishment, theoretical work influenced by the writings of Karl Marx, we will look briefly at another of the classic, founding theorists in sociology, Max Weber (1864–1920) in terms of his contribution to the sociology of punishment. Although Weber did not study or write about crime or punishment specifically, his work was wide-ranging and covered areas that can be applied to them. In particular, he examined and categorized different forms of authority in different types of society and argued that modern advanced societies were increasingly characterized by more rational and formalized social structures and institutions.

In his study *Economy and Society* (published in 1920), he examined the social institutions of modern capitalist societies and described the forms of authority and rational organization associated with them. Weber distinguished authority from power in terms of the extent to which consent was present. Power he saw as the ability to get things done or to compel others to comply with demands, whereas authority also involved the ability to get things done but in contexts where the particular order is seen as legitimate and accepted by those to whom it is applied. So authority is legitimated power or power by consent, in contrast to power exercised through coercion. Power and authority are closely related concepts but for Weber the notion of legitimacy is the important distinguishing feature. Having made this initial distinction, Weber then defined and classified three types of authority which were based on different types of legitimacy. These three types were traditional, charismatic and rational-legal authority and these were, he argued, found in one degree or another in all forms of society.

With traditional authority there is an unquestioning acceptance of the distribution of power. The leader has authority by virtue of the traditional status of the office that she or he holds and legitimacy is believed because it has 'always been so'. Charismatic authority is based on commitment and loyalty to a leader because of that leader's exceptional qualities. In this situation, the word of the leader is seen as all important. This form of authority tends to be unstable, as it depends on a leader keeping the loyalty and support of the masses and because it is difficult to pass on from one generation to the next (why should the successor of a charismatic leader have the same exceptional qualities?). Furthermore, the authority of the charismatic leader tends to become routine over time; she or he will almost inevitably have to involve other staff as the job of leader extends and evolves. Rational-legal authority is based on a legal framework which supports and maintains the distribution of power amongst different groups in the society. This form of authority is characterized by bureaucracy where there is an emphasis on rules rather than on the individual qualities of the leader (charismatic) or the customs of the society (traditional).

In broad, historical terms, Weber believed that the third form of authority was the most appropriate form of rule for modern industrial societies. Traditional and charismatic forms of authority which were common in earlier, pre-industrial societies would become redundant as a general rationalization occurred (by this Weber means the increased application of scientific thought and the influence of science in behaviour). Authority, then, would become increasingly rational-legal, based on formal rules – specifically the law. And in practice, the most typical form of rational-legal authority would be bureaucracy; which was, for Weber, the characteristic form of administration in modern society, not just confined to the political arena but common across all areas of society, including education, religion and, as regards our concern in this discussion, crime and punishment. Bureaucracy he saw as a system of authority based on proceeding according to strictly laid down rules and with individuals following clearly defined roles. We won't go into the details of Weber's definition of bureaucracy here, but consider how it relates to development in penal practice and policy.

QUESTION BREAK: BUREAUCRACY AND PUNISHMENT

- Consider the sort of punishments that are typical of modern societies such as Britain. To what extent are they based on the idea of rational-legal authority?
- Look up Weber's definition of bureaucracy (in a sociology dictionary or introductory textbook). In what ways is the punishment of offenders bureaucratized?

Weber's general argument about the increasing rationalization of society can, then, be applied to punishment. Indeed, there can be instances when the public criticizes any move away from a rule based, bureaucratic approach to punishment. Hudson (2003) refers to the concerns and criticism made of judges who pass individualistic sentences that seem to be based on their own views and beliefs rather than according to the facts of the case and the rules of due process.

It would certainly seem to be the case that over the last two hundred or so years punishment has become increasingly rationalized and bureaucratized, and the make-shift, ad hoc punishments of the past have been replaced by a centrally administered system of punishments. In part this has been due to the population growth since the eighteenth century along with the rising rates of crime. In general terms this has led to a greater uniformity of punishments and to the development of a penal infrastructure. Garland (1990) has argued that these developments have led to a 'professionalisation of justice', with a range of professional groups now working in the area of punishment, including social workers, probation officers, psychiatrists, police and prison officers. With the increasing complexity of punishment, different approaches to the treatment of the punished, and of prisoners in particular, have been instituted. At the same time those who are professionally involved in the penal system have come to see offenders in different terms; to see them as either good or bad inmates on account of their institutional behaviour, rather than as evil or wicked on account of the crimes that they are being punished for. These changes, Garland suggests, have taken the emotion out of the punishment of offenders, with punishment being administered by paid officials rather than the general public or even those personally affected by the offenders' actions. All of this affects the form (and length) of punishment, for example how an inmate behaves in prison will affect the length of time they spend in prison.

The rationalization and professionalization of justice has clearly altered the meaning and the practices of punishment in modern society. The institutions of punishment have become less accessible and more secretive as specialized professions have taken a greater role. This trend toward rationalization would seem to run counter to Durkheim's emphasis on the emotional nature of punishment – on punishment as reflecting an outrage to the moral sentiments of a society. The lack of involvement of the public in the day-to-day business of punishing offenders may help to explain why the public do from time to time vent their anger and frustration at the closed nature of the penal system, as evidenced in the outrage of hostile mobs of people who gather to hurl abuse at those involved in crimes against children, or by the campaigns to ensure that the child killers of toddler James Bulger remained in prison, or the massive opposition to any suggestions that Moors murderer Myra Hindley be considered for early release on parole (prior to her death in November 2002). A more general example of media and public outrage was illustrated by the campaign led by the News of the World in 2000, in response to the murder of eight-year-old Sarah Payne, to 'name and shame' scores of people it said were guilty of sex offences against children. With headlines such as 'Join our Campaign: Sign here for Sarah' and 'If you are a Parent you Must Read this: Named Shamed', the paper had some success in mobilizing public and political opinion to support stricter monitoring and sen-tencing of sex offenders. Ten years after his campaign, the News of The World claimed they had won 'a huge victory in the fight to protect our children from paedophiles' – under the heading 'Success for Sarah's Law' they commented, 'Today we announce a massive victory in our Sarah's Law campaign . . . A scheme to alert parents to dangerous child molesters – which has already saved at least 24 KIDS from the clutches of perverts – is to be rolled out across the WHOLE of England and Wales' (*News of the World*, 23 January 2010).

QUESTION BREAK: PUBLIC OUTRAGE

The sort of public outrage described above was graphically illustrated in summer 2002 after the arrests of Ian Huntley and Maxine Carr for the murders of ten-year-olds Holly Wells and Jessica Chapman in Soham, Cambridgeshire. Crowds gathered outside Peterborough Magistrates' Court as Maxine Carr was remanded in custody.

Hate fills the air as public vents feelings

Explosion of rage outside court as Maxine Carr is remanded . . .

It was the mothers who led the ugly chorus, jeering and shouting at a woman they could not see . . .

"I've never done anything like this before," said Nicola Warrener, a 24-year-old hairdresser from Peterborough . . .

She added: "I didn't know I could feel like this . . . but I'm actually shaking with rage. I have been thinking of starting a family, but now I am not so sure. I think I would be too afraid to leave them with anyone."

(From the *Guardian*, 2 August 2002, 'Hate fills the air')

Into the gauntlet of hate

Mob hurls abuse and eggs at caretaker's girlfriend after court appearance

As the vehicles swept by, the boos rose up, turning into a feverish caco-phony of screams. Eggs were thrown as young mothers with crying children yelled obscenities. Accusations of "sick cow" and "murdering bitch" were hurled at Ms Carr. A banner proclaiming "rot in hell forever" summed up the mood.

Earlier, television crews from across the world had tried to catch a glimpse of a woman who in just a few days has become a figure of hate . . .

(From: the *Independent*, 22 August 2002, 'Into the gauntlet of hate')

More recent examples of widespread media and public outrage include:

(a) the responses to the trial and sentencing in January 2010 of two young brothers who attacked and tortured two other young boys in Edlington, South Yorkshire as illustrated by the following headlines:

'Evil in Edlington the system could not handle – but terrifyingly it could happen anywhere'

(From the *Daily Mail*, 8 September 2009)

'Reaction of shock to Edlington torture attack'

(BBC News online, 22 January 2010)

and

(b) the *Sun*'s comments on what it felt should be done to paedophiles:

'British paedos should be castrated . . . like us' (referring to the castration of four Czechoslovakian sex offenders)

(From the *Sun*, 19 May 2009)

- How do these sorts of reactions relate to the work of (a) Durkheim and the collective conscience, and (b) Weber and the increasing rationalization of punishment?

PUNISHMENT AS PART OF A CLASS-BASED PROCESS OF ECONOMIC AND SOCIAL CONTROL – THE MARXIST APPROACH

The practices and institutions for the punishment of offenders were not analysed or written about in any detail by Marx, or his collaborator Engels. Neither did they write much on crime or criminals and they did not develop a theory of crime and punishment in the same manner as Durkheim. So we have to look at the writing of later Marxist-influenced writers to provide us with a Marxist analysis and theory of punishment.

As with Durkheim, the context and background for the Marxist approach to punishment comes from Marx's general theoretical writing and analysis. This analysis sees the economy as the key locus of power in society, with the economic system determining all other areas of social life, including, in this context, the legal system. Those groups who have economic power are able to ensure that social institutions work in a way that is consistent with their own interests. Thus the various institutions of the law and punishment come to reflect and represent the interests of the dominant economic groups. Consequently, a Marxist analysis of punishment has tended to focus on the way in which elements of the superstructure (essentially the rest of society, apart from the economic base) support the powerful, ruling groups in society.

How, for instance, the law works in the interest of some groups more so than others; an analysis that is reflected in the adage, 'there's one law for the rich and one for the poor'.

The Marxist approach argues that market relations, and in particular the economic relations that involve some groups in society exploiting and others being exploited, condition all other social institutions, including the laws but also other institutions such as the education system, the mass media and the family. As Hudson puts it:

> All social institutions, according to Marxists, have as their prime function the maintenance of the capitalist system. Laws will protect rights to property necessary for capital accumulation; families reproduce workers, and give workers motivation to work for wages; education gives potential workers the skills that are needed in the workforce, and instils attitudes of respect for authority.
>
> (Hudson 2003: 114–15)

As regards the social institution of the law, it is seen by Marxists as performing functions that are either *regulatory* (mechanisms for keeping the system working effectively), or *repressive* (imposing penalties on those who do not accept and keep the rules of the capitalist system), or *ideological* (ensuring that the workforce and the population in general believe that society and social arrangements and differences are fair and work in the interests of everyone).

Punishment, and more generally the law, are seen from a Marxist perspective as serving all three of these kinds of function. Legislation concerning health and safety or the rights of employees, for instance, might seem to be specifically serving the interests of workers and thereby acting as a sort of curb on capitalist exploitation. However, such legislation can have a regulatory function that works in the interests of capitalism; it might help prevent individual capitalists from damaging the overall system, and so help maintain the smooth running of capitalist economies.

QUESTION BREAK

Think of other areas of legislation – for example, laws regarding fraud and forgery or illegal drug use – and consider how they might fulfil regulatory, repressive and ideological functions.

As regards the repressive function of law and punishment, the Marxist analysis of punishment centres on the notion of class struggle and the ways in which the relationship between social classes determines the form of punishment present in any particular society.

These brief introductory comments have presented what is basically the orthodox or classic Marxist view. Garland (1990), among others, has highlighted the work of Rusche and Kirchheimer as the clearest example of this Marxist interpretation of punishment. Rusche and Kirchheimer's major text, *Punishment and Social Structure*, was first published in 1939 but was not widely referred to by western theorists until its reissue in 1968. Since then their work has been taken up by Marxist criminologists and become much more widely known and referred to.

Rusche and Kirchheimer provide a detailed history of punishment which emphasizes how the economy and, in particular, the labour market influences the methods of punishment adopted by different societies. They suggest that the severity of punishment is influenced by the value in which labour is held. Its value is higher when labour is scare and, as a consequence, punishments become relatively more lenient; by contrast when there is a surplus of labour punishments tend to become more severe. They illustrate their argument in their account of the development of punishments such as galley slavery, transportation and hard labour. These emerged as 'new' punishments in the sixteenth and seventeenth centuries alongside the early developments of a capitalist economic system. At this time, labour power was increasingly seen as a vital resource and the harsh physical punishments, such as whipping, branding, mutilation and execution, were replaced by punishments that involved some form of productive, hard labour; and particularly work that 'free' people would be less willing to undertake.

Transportation demonstrates this shift in the emphasis of punishment. At this period there were vast amounts of land in the colonies that needed to be worked and the penalty of transportation was introduced to help develop these areas. It was initially offered as a commutation of capital punishment but by the early 1700s was regularly used as a specific sentence for a range of quite minor offences. As an indication of its popularity, around 30,000 people were transported to the American colonies between 1718 and 1775. With the move towards American independence (the American War of Independence ran from 1775 till 1783), the transportation of convicts to America declined; and without an adequate English prison system, an alternative punishment was to develop convict labour through the confinement of offenders in old vessels, known as hulks. Offenders punished in this way were given hard labour to do in the daytime, dredging the Thames and other rivers for instance, and returned to the vessels at night to eat and sleep. However, concern over the conditions in these hulks was such that they did not figure as a major method of punishment for long and transportation to Australia came to the fore (see boxed insert).

BOX 8.1 TRANSPORTATION TO AUSTRALIA

After American independence and the consequent ending of transportation there, the focus of transportation shifted to Australia, with the first fleet of ships setting off for Botany Bay in 1787. There were differences with the earlier transportation to America which had relied on free settlers buying convicts and using them as labourers, a system which did not cost England anything once the convicts had landed and been sold. By contrast, there were no free settlers in Australia to buy the convicts and so their upkeep had to be paid for by the English government (and,

continued

of course, Australia at the time was more remote and less well known than America had been). However, many thousands of convicts were transported to Australia; 736 went on the first fleet in 1787, all coming from England and having been sentenced to a range of property crimes, including some very minor ones, including Elizabeth Beckford, a seventy-year-old woman who got seven years' transportation for stealing 12 pounds of Gloucester cheese. Conditions on the ships taking the convicts to Australia were appalling and the death rate was as high as 25 per cent. In all, the government sent 825 ships from England and Ireland to Australia with the peak period being between 1831 and 1835 when 26,731 people were transported.

By 1852 transportation to Australia and Tasmania (Van Diemen's land) was finally abolished, with a 'ticket of leave' scheme offered in place of it to convicted offenders (a scheme which foreshadowed the development of parole as a means of punishment). There were a number of reasons for this form of punishment to be abolished. There was a decline in the number of crimes that led to hanging (which was regularly commuted to transportation to Australia) and an extension of the English prison system (in particular the Prison Acts of 1835 and 1839) enabled the government to be in a position to keep its criminals in the country. Also, there was growing prosperity in the colonies that led to the decline in this form of punishment. Those people who emigrated of their own free will to Australia and elsewhere were not too happy about convicts and criminal labour undercutting their wages, while the authorities felt that the punishment of transportation was becoming less of a deterrent to criminals.

(The above information adapted from R. Hughes 2003)

So for Rusche and Kirchheimer, the severity and the form of punishment were related to the value of labour, and they examined the link between demand for labour and forms of punishment in different periods of history. In the medieval period around the thirteenth century, the labouring population was small in relation to the land that had to be utilized for production; as a result punishments that limited labour power were not common practices, with fines or doing penance being more popular penalties. As we have seen above, in the early days of capitalism (in the sixteenth and seventeenth centuries) demand for labour led to more 'productive' punishments, such as transportation and workhouses. By contrast, when there was a surplus of labour, and it was no longer necessary to employ offenders, the punishments tended to leave them with nothing to do. This, Rusche and Kirchheimer argue, raised a dilemma as to the purpose of imprisonment and brought the repressive and deterrent side of punishment and imprisonment to the fore. In England and elsewhere, hard labour within prisons was introduced as a form of punishment rather than as a means to increase productivity or engender profit; and moral arguments were used to justify this sort of punishment within a punishment – the argument that hard labour was good for moral improvement and discipline, for instance.

Prison labour, then, became a method of punishment after the Industrial Revolution of the late eighteenth century and when there was a large industrial reserve army of labourers; being sent to prison was not the complete punishment, punishment also happened within prison. Indeed the authorities became pretty adept at inventing new forms of prison labour, including prisoners carrying huge stones from one place to another and then back again, or treading water mills which just sent water round in a circle with no useful purpose. The treadwheel was a sort of 'everlasting circle' that might be used to grind corn or might just grind nothing, and was widely used because it was a cheap and easy means of forcing prisoners to work and one that might also deter any who might feel prison was a place of potential refuge and rest.

Rusche and Kirchheimer argued that the move to incarceration and prison labour fitted in with the aims of a capitalist economy. It would help to create a submissive and regulated workforce, would contain working-class unrest and teach habits of discipline and order. Although humanitarian principles and ideas were advocated, the Marxist interpretation saw this as merely rhetoric. Prison conditions remained deplorable in the nineteenth century, characterized by meaningless and degrading work. Rusche and Kirchheimer saw the expansion of imprisonment resulting from a combination of population increase and the emergence of industrial capitalism creating a depressed labouring class; the aim of the prison was, then, to teach the discipline of labour and to encourage the poor to accept whatever conditions were imposed on them by their employers. It was taken as evident that conditions in prisons had to be worse than those faced by even the worst off 'free' workers, and as a result prisons developed and intensified the punishments they imposed on their inmates, based around forms of hard labour as illustrated above.

Put simply, the 'Marxist thesis' is that during the Industrial Revolution the rationale for punishment changed from being directly economic (a need for productive labour) to being something much more repressively punitive, with prisons being used as a means for inflicting control and intimidation.

In his discussion of the work of Rusche and Kirchheimer, Garland summarizes the key points that they make (see boxed insert below). He highlights the most quoted sentence in their study *Punishment and Social Structure* as, 'every system of production tends to discover punishments which correspond to its productive relationships'. In modern industrial societies, the 'corresponding punishment' is clearly imprisonment. Garland considers why Marxists such as Rusche and Kirchheimer argue this. For them, prison was a source of labour and therefore became the dominant mode of punishment at a time when the emerging capitalist system produces an almost insatiable demand for labour. This, though, raises the question of why imprisonment has persisted when the economic need is less obvious, given that the number of 'free' people who are able to work does not need to be supplemented with that of convict labour. The answer for Rusche and Kirchheimer and others is to emphasize the role of the prison in creating a regulated and submissive workforce.

GARLAND'S SUMMARY OF RUSCHE AND KIRCHHEIMER'S THEORETICAL APPROACH

- Punishments have to be viewed as historically specific phenomena that appear in particular forms at different periods. This principle of historical specificity distinguishes Marxist accounts from Durkheim's view of punishment as something that performed essentially similar functions in all societies.
- The mode of production is the major determinant of specific penal methods in specific historical periods. Different systems of production will produce different methods of punishment.
- The particular forms of punishment are, therefore, social artefacts or constructions.
- Penal policy is one element within a wider strategy for controlling the poor. Punishment is seen almost exclusively as aimed at the control of the 'lower orders'. Rusche and Kirchheimer suggest that there were clear similarities between the way criminals were treated and the policies aimed at controlling the labouring masses. In the early industrial period the regime and organization of prison life was similar to the way workers were treated in factories and beggars and vagrants in workhouses.
- Punishment is a mechanism deeply implicated within the class struggle: 'the history of the penal system is the history of the relations between the rich and the poor' (Rusche 1933).
- Although punishment is generally and conventionally seen as an institution which benefits 'society as a whole', for Marxists, in reality it supports the interests of one class against another. Punishment is (another) element and example of control that is hidden within ideological veils.

(Adapted from D. Garland 1990: 90–2)

In a similar vein to Rusche and Kirchheimer, and relating the form and extent of punishment to the labour market, it would be useful to refer briefly to the Marxist sociologist Pashukanis who suggested a link between crime, punishment and wage labour (1978). Waged labourers are paid according to the hours they have worked, which Pashukanis sees as related to the way in which crime and punishment are treated in capitalist societies, with punishment being the work and the benefits of crime being the wage. Time is the commodity that is traded in the crime and punishment relationship (and punishment is measured in terms of time) just as it is in the work–money relationship. As Hudson (2003) puts it, Pashukanis points to 'a correspondence between receiving reward for labour by the hour and paying for crime by "doing time"'. In developing this argument, Melossi and Pavarini (1981) argue that imprisonment is the typical and flagship form of punishment in modern capitalist societies both because of the time–money relationship mentioned above, and because imprisonment and factory work and production share a common emphasis on and requirement for discipline. Just as wage labourers are not free and equal to the capitalists who buy their time and labour, so convicts have to accept the disciplinary regimes they face in prisons. Imprisonment as a punishment, then, fits the classic Marxist view of the forms of social and economic relationships under capitalism.

So far, we have referred to the regulatory and repressive functions and role of punishment and prison; below we will consider the role of *ideology* in the Marxist approach to punishment. In the context of Marxist theory, an ideology refers to a set of ideas which influence and govern people's perception of the world. In capitalist societies, ideas which support the capitalist relations of production are seen by Marxists as essential for ensuring the continuation of that form of society. Here we will look at how the Marxist approach to punishment and the law relates to this notion of ideology.

The law, and punishment for breaking it, is important to the maintenance of capitalist society in that it seems to express values of equality and thereby give credibility to the state's claims that it is ruling in the interests of all citizens, rather than just one group or class. Althusser, for instance, sees the law as one part of what he terms the Ideological State Apparatus, working along with the education system, the mass media and so on to ensure the continuing domination of the ruling, capitalist class. As Hudson (2003) puts it, 'Law and institutions of punishment are part of a series of ideological subsystems which produce in the non-capitalist class the necessary attitudes for acceptance of the discipline of the factory and of the legitimacy of ruling-class power' (p. 123).

The penal system itself (the institutions of justice and punishment such as the police, courts and prisons) is seen by Althusser as part of the Repressive State Apparatus, as it enforces the law by coercion when 'ideological control' fails.

The law, then, is seen as functioning at both the ideological and the repressive levels. Marxists point to the large, symbolic prisons built in working-class areas of the major towns and cities as capitalism developed, serving as a stark reminder to everyone that if the discipline of the factory was ignored or rejected, workers might face an even more austere and rigid discipline within the prison. The differing levels of importance given to either the ideological or the repressive role of punishment are essentially a difference in emphasis for Marxists; punishment is seen as having both an ideological and a repressive role and function.

In recent years, and particularly since the 1970s, Marxists criminologists have tried to explain the rise of a 'law and order' ideology, which has seen prison numbers grow and grow while there has been a cutback on social welfare institutions. In part, this has been explained as a mechanism of social control, and a way of creating specific groups to blame for economic downturn and depression – illegal immigrants, welfare scroungers and criminals, for example. Concerns and fear over economic recession become less urgent in the face of fear of crime. It is debatable whether economic depression does lead to any increase in crime; however, Hudson argues that:

> what is not debatable is that in times of recession the vocabulary of justice becomes harsher . . . Blame is attached to individuals, and social responsibility for crime

is denied; lack of investment in areas of high unemployment is blamed on crime rates rather than on the flight of capital.

(Hudson 2003: 125)

In such a climate, theories of justice will emphasize punishment rather than treatment; incapacitation rather than deterrence or rehabilitation will come to the fore. Policies of containment of persistent offenders will gain support and influence, with the rights of offenders of less and less concern. Hudson refers to the 'three strikes' laws passed in California, whereby a third offence of any sort can lead to an immediate 25-year term of imprisonment with no parole, as illustrative of this development in penal philosophy and strategy.

The Marxist approach – comment and criticism

The priority given to economic explanations by Marxist writers such as Rusche and Kirchheimer has been criticized for understating the importance of non-economic factors. Political, religious and humanitarian influences on the development of punishment are only accorded secondary importance for example. Furthermore, the emphasis given to class and class relationships tends to ignore popular attitudes to punishment. There is widespread support among the working classes for harsh punitive policies and little evidence that the working classes are any more sympathetic towards criminals than other social groups, points which Garland (1990) suggests cast doubt on a simple class conflict approach to analysing punishment. However, these comments do not necessarily refute the Marxist argument of Rusche and Kirchheimer that economic relationships and the labour market can exert an important influence on penal policy and that the institutions of punishment can be seen as part of a wider strategy for managing the poor and working classes.

The essence of the Marxist argument is that the approach to and form of punishment is influenced by the strategies that the dominant, ruling groups adopt towards the working classes. Punishment is not just determined by the extent and pattern of crime but by the perception of the working classes, and particularly the poor, as a social problem. Rusche and Kirchheimer argue that the working classes have little commitment to the law or to the dominant moral order in general and that it is therefore important that the criminal law and the punishments attached to it do all they can to ensure that crime does not pay. For this reason, punishments have to be severe and institutions of punishment such as prisons have to be unpleasant; and certainly more unpleasant than the conditions that the general working population are able to live in.

QUESTION BREAK

Think of recent criminal cases that have received a lot of publicity – consider different sorts of crime – for example:

The murder of Holly and Jessica in Soham in August 2002;

The attack and torture of two young boys in Edlington, South Yorkshire in 2009 by two other young boys who lived in a family of seven brothers, a drug-addicted mother and a violent alcoholic father;

The conviction and jailing of millionaire novelist Lord Jeffrey Archer for perjury in 2001;

The trial and imprisoning for 150 years of one of the most powerful Wall Street financiers, Bernard Madoff, in June 2009, for a $65 billion fraud that affected thousands of investors, depriving many of their life savings.

- In terms of these and other criminal cases, how big a part do you think class plays in public reaction to crime and criminals?
- To what extent do you think it is fair for Rusche and Kirchheimer to suggest that the working classes have little commitment to the law?

In contrast to Durkheim's view that punishment expresses the interests of the society as whole, the fairly basic review of the Marxist approach to punishment that we have presented here sees punishment as only expressing the interests of the dominant, ruling groups. Although the criminal law and punishment does provide protection for the working classes as well as the ruling classes – protection against assault and burglary, for instance – it does not, according to Marxists, 'protect' against economic domination and oppression.

Marxism, gender and punishment

The Marxist approach to punishment emphasizes how it works in the interest of some groups more than others and, in particular, how punishment is imposed on and directed against the working class and, more specifically, sections of the working class. The argument that punishment can reflect the interests of some sections of society more than others should, Hudson (2003) suggests, encourage an examination of the treatment of groups other than the working class and lead to a 'recognition of the significance of gender for the sociology of punishment'. In this context feminist approaches have been concerned with the penal treatment of women, although such work has tended to remain 'on the margins of penology and criminology'. We have seen how the traditional Marxist approach highlights the relationship between the labour market and methods of punishment. In relating this to the issue of gender and punishment, women have been seen by Marxists as part of a 'reserve army of labour' encouraged into the workplace at certain periods and discouraged at others. Adapting the Marxist argument, there should, then, be a link between rates of imprisonment of women and the labour market situation of women. Hudson points to the limited research in this area, which does, however, emphasize women's importance to the capitalist system as reproducers of labour power, both in the biological and the sociological sense (in terms of their socializing and educating roles). Research on the imprisonment of women has shown that having a family to look after does encourage leniency in punishment (Eaton 1986 cited in Hudson 2003); this is in line with the Marxist notion of the family as reproducing a disciplined and essentially submissive workforce. In the context of the relative penalties given to women and men, an issue which the Marxist approach does not really address is that of why women offenders are more liable to be seen as mad rather than bad, and punished accordingly (see pp. 161–167 for fuller discussion of this point).

QUESTION BREAK: *RICH LAW, POOR LAW*

The sociological study of business crime lends support to the Marxist argument that the extent and severity with which the legal system is applied varies between different social groups. In *Rich Law, Poor Law* Dee Cook (1989) examined the different responses to tax and supplementary benefit fraud. She cited the following examples of judicial responses to defrauding the public purse by two different means: defrauding the Inland Revenue by evading tax and defrauding the DHSS by falsely claiming supplementary benefit:

> Two partners in a vegetable wholesalers business admitted falsifying accounts to the tune of £100,000. At their trial the judge said he considered they had been 'very wise' in admitting their guilt and they had paid back the tax due (with interest) to the Inland Revenue. They were sentenced to pay fines. A chartered accountant who defrauded taxes in excess of £8,000 was sentenced to pay a fine as the judge accepted, in mitigation, that his future income would be adversely affected by the trial.
>
> An unemployed father of three failed to declare his wife's earnings to the Department of Health and Social Security (DHSS). He admitted the offence and started to pay back the £996 he owed them by weekly deductions from his supplementary benefit. He was prosecuted a year later and sentenced to pay fines totalling £210, also to be deducted from his benefit. Magistrates told him that 'this country is fed up to the teeth with people like you scrounging from fellow citizens'. A young woman defrauded the DHSS to the tune of £58: she served three months in custody as magistrates said she 'needed to be taught a lesson'.
>
> (Cook 1989: 1)

In looking at why the law does not treat white-collar crime in the same way as conventional crime, Hazel Croall (1992) points out that white-collar crime is subject to different regulatory arrangements and these tend to be more lenient than those of the criminal justice system – regulatory bodies are less worried about securing convictions and more keen on settling disputes with a minimum of fuss and, often, publicity. Burglars, for example, are more likely to be prosecuted and imprisoned compared to fraudsters whose offences usually involve much larger sums of money. This point is supported by Steven Box's comments on the deterrents for would-be corporate criminals:

> For the most part corporate crimes are not/do not fall under the jurisdiction of the police, but under special regulatory bodies . . . In the UK, there are numerous inspectorates, commissions and government departments.
>
> Corporate executives contemplating the possibility of being required to commit corporate crimes know that they face a regulatory agency which for the most part will be unable to detect what is going on, and in the minority of cases when it does, it will have no heart and few resources to pursue the matter into the criminal courts . . .
>
> Criminal laws designed to regulate corporate activities tend to refer to a specific rather than a general class of behaviour . . . they focus purely on the regulation broken and not on the consequences of that broken regulation. Thus the company responsible for the hoist accident at Littlebrook Dee power station were not prosecuted for the fact that five men died, but for the fact that the machinery was not properly maintained or inspected. For this they were fined £5000. In conventional crime . . . a person is charged with the consequences of his/her action; if someone dies as a consequence of being stabbed, the assailant is more likely to be charged with a homicide offence rather than 'carrying an offensive weapon'. The point of this fracture between the regulation broken and its consequences is that it facilitates corporate crime; executives need only concern themselves with the likelihood of being leniently punished for breaking regulations.
>
> (Box 1983: 44–58)

White-collar offenders are usually better off and can use their superior resources to avoid detection, prosecution and severe punishment. They can emphasize that they are respectable business people who have made one mistake and don't deserve severe punishment. The law itself encourages such compliance strategies and allows for out-of-court settlements.

The two extracts above highlight some important differences in how the criminal justice system treats different types of criminal activity. Before considering the questions below you might also look at the extracts in Chapter 4 (pp. 131–133) which provide more recent examples of the way in which different crimes (burglary and business fraud) were treated by the criminal justice system in the USA.

- What are the key differences between corporate and conventional crime?
- To what extent do you think that they provide a justification for the differential treatment of white-collar and business criminals?

PUNISHMENT, POWER AND REGULATION – THE WORK OF MICHEL FOUCAULT

Foucault (1926–84) was a French philosopher whose major works were published in the 1970s. His writing focused on issues surrounding knowledge, power and the human body, and was not confined to the area of crime and punishment. However, as regards our interest here, his emphasis was on the emergence of 'crime' in the early nineteenth century. The turn of the nineteenth century was the period of the industrial revolution and the aftermath of the democratic revolutions in France and the USA. It was a time of hectic social change that was accompanied by a widespread concern over the threat to social order that would result, it was feared, from an emerging industrial working class who would be less likely to respect traditional hierarchies. It is not surprising that this period also excited a great deal of comment and analysis from social and political theorists, philosophers and other commentators. Indeed the attempt to understand the significance of the changing nature of the new industrial society of the nineteenth century led to the emergence of sociology as a new area of study and discipline.

Although writing a hundred or so years after the key founding social theorists such as Karl Marx, Max Weber and Emile Durkheim, Foucault also examined and analysed the social changes brought about by the emergence of modern industrial society. In this context, his main theme and focus was that of the 'disciplinary society', of the pervasive nature of social control and of the struggle of individuals against the power of society. In his detailed study of the prison system that was established in the early nineteenth century he emphasized that the methods of dealing with criminals in the modern penitentiaries of that time were part of a wider process of control and regimentation in society. The criminal was no longer viewed just as a law breaker who should be punished, but rather was seen as a pathological individual who required close surveillance and expert supervision in order to be returned to 'normality'.

Discipline and Punish (1977), one of Foucault's later works, focused on what he saw as the 'problem' of knowledge and power, and has become one of the key texts in the sociology of punishment. It is arguably Foucault's most important and lasting study and demonstrates most clearly his major theme of power and domination, and how the elite dominate and control the rest of society. In it, Foucault examines and explains why the penal system evolved into its current form and how it works to control the masses in society. Foucault saw punishment as a system of power and regulation which is imposed on people; an analysis that overlaps with the Marxist approach considered above and contrasts with Durkheim's argument that punishment is embedded within collective sentiments and therefore conveys moral messages.

Where Foucault differed from both of these 'grand theories' was in his methodological approach. He focused on the specific working of penal institutions, on how they were organized and structured and how they actually imposed and exercised control. This approach moved away from an examination of society as a coherent whole that could be analysed by structural methods, and to that extent Foucault's work could be described as phenomenological rather than structural, or Marxist. To elaborate on this point, as with the other social theorists we have looked at, such as Durkheim and Rusche and Kirchheimer, Foucault was also concerned with the historical transition in the forms of punishment, from the harsh physical penalties of pre-industrial societies to the more regulated sanctions of industrial capitalist societies. So, *Discipline and Punish* followed the same broad themes as other social histories of punishment but differs in the methodological approach that is used. Foucault did not adopt the grand theory, 'top down' approach that characterizes the work of Durkheim, Marx and other classic social theorists, but developed his theoretical argument on the basis of a detailed examination of specific penal practices. This building of theoretical explanations from the detailed descriptions of specific things and events and patterns that emerge from such descriptions illustrates the phenomenological approach of Foucault. To a certain extent, then, and as Garland (1990) argues in his discussion of Foucault's work, it is not so much the originality of Foucault's themes but rather the method that he used in examining and analysing them that is perhaps his major contribution to the sociological study of punishment.

To return to Foucault's study, the historical issue that he set out to explain in *Discipline and Punish* was the disappearance of punishment as a public spectacle of violence and the emergence of the prison as the general form of modern punishment; indeed the subtitle of *Discipline and Punish* is *The Birth of the Prison*. This change in the basic form of punishment took place between the mid eighteenth and early nineteenth centuries when, Foucault argued, the target of punishment changed; the emphasis moved towards changing the soul of the offender rather than just the body; towards transforming the offender, not just avenging the particular crime. Foucault saw these developments as reflecting the way power operates in modern society, with open physical force and the ceremonies and rituals associated with it being replaced by a much more detailed regulation of offenders, and with troublesome individuals being removed from their society and, hopefully, re-socialized, rather than being broken and destroyed. In prisons, discipline could be used to instil and impose useful, social qualities into convicts so that on release they would be less likely to re-offend and be better prepared to lead a useful and productive life.

In trying to explain why imprisonment so quickly became the general method of legal punishment, Foucault considered the developing role of the human sciences. The prison practice of isolating and monitoring inmates encouraged the idea that they should be responded to and studied as individuals with their own characteristics and peculiarities. To an extent, then, prison was seen as leading to the discovery of the 'delinquent' (a person distinct from the 'normal', non-delinquent) and, according to Foucault, to the rise of the science of criminology. Foucault also argued that the 'creation' of delinquency has been a useful strategy of political domination that encouraged divisions within the working class, and enhanced and guaranteed greater powers to the police. Delinquency itself generally consists of relatively minor attacks on authority and is not a particular political danger and so can, within limits, be tolerated by the authorities. In addition it produces a group of known, habitual criminals who can legitimately be kept under surveillance. This benefits the ruling, powerful groups by marking out troublesome members of society as separate from the rest of the 'lower class', thereby helping to render them politically harmless.

As regards his history of punishment and the basic change in punishment between the eighteenth and nineteenth centuries, Foucault described the punitive phenomena which, he argued, characterized each period – public execution (and specifically aggravated capital punishment) in the eighteenth century and the timetabled regime of a modern nineteenth-century young offenders' institution. These descriptions are used to start his book *Discipline and Punish*; the two types of punishment that are detailed define particular 'penal styles' and have to be seen in relation to the different social contexts in which they occurred. First, the public execution of the *ancien régime* in pre-revolutionary France and second, the new prison system characteristic of modern industrial capitalist society. For Foucault, the overthrow and passing of the *ancien régime* is also the passing of public execution and the emergence of the industrial factory society is the emergence of the imprisoning society.

QUESTION BREAK: *DISCIPLINE AND PUNISH*

Read the edited extract from the start of Foucault's *Discipline and Punish* and consider the questions at the end of it.

On 2 March 1757 Damiens the regicide was condemned 'to make the *amende honorable* before the main door of the Church of Paris', where he was 'taken and conveyed in a cart, wearing nothing but a shirt, holding a torch of burning wax weighing two pounds'; then, 'in the said cart, to the Place de Grève, where, on a scaffold that will be erected there, the flesh will be torn from his breasts, arms, thighs and calves with red-hot pincers, his right hand, holding the knife with which he committed the said parricide, burnt with sulphur, and, on those places where the flesh will be torn away, poured molten lead, boiling oil, burning resin, wax and sulphur melted together and then his body drawn and quartered by four horses and his limbs and body consumed by fire, reduced to ashes and his ashes thrown to the winds . . .

'Finally he was quartered', recounts the *Gazette d'Amsterdam* of 1 April 1757. 'This last operation was very long because the horses used were unaccustomed to drawing; consequently, instead of four, six were needed; and when that did not suffice, they were forced, in order to cut off the wretch's thighs, to sever the sinews and hack at the joints . . .

It is said that, though he was always a great swearer, no blasphemy escaped his lips; but the excessive pain made him utter horrible cries, and he often repeated: "My God, have pity on me! Jesus, help me!" . . .

Bouton, an officer of the watch, left us his account: 'The sulphur was lit, but the flame was so poor that only the top skin of the hand was burnt, and that only slightly. Then the executioner, his sleeves rolled up, took the steel pincers, which had been especially made for the occasion, and which were about a foot and a half long, and pulled first at the calf of the right leg, then at the thigh, and from there at the two fleshy arts of the right arm; then at the breasts. Though a strong, sturdy fellow, this executioner found it so difficult to tear away the pieces of flesh that he set about the same spot two or three times . . .

After these tearings with the pincers, Damiens, who cried out profusely, though without swearing, raised his head and looked at himself; the same executioner dipped an iron spoon in the pot containing the boiling potion, which he poured liberally over each wound. Then the ropes that were to be harnessed to the horses were attached with cords to the patient's body; the horses were then harnessed and placed alongside the arms and legs, one at each limb.

Monsieur Le Breton, the clerk of the court, went up to the patient several times and asked him if he had anything to say. He said he had not; at each torment, he cried out, as the damned in hell are supposed to cry out, "Pardon, my God! Pardon, Lord." . . .

The horses tugged hard, each pulling straight on a limb, each horse held by an executioner. After a quarter of an hour, the same ceremony was repeated and finally, after several attempts, the direction of the horses had to be changed, thus: those at the arms were made to pull towards the head, those at the thighs towards the arms, which broke at the joints. This was repeated several times without success. He raised his head and looked at himself. Two more horses had to be added to those harnessed to the thighs, which made six horses in all. Without success . . .

After two or three attempts, the executioner Samson and he who had used the pincers each drew out a knife from his pocket and cut the body at the thighs instead of severing the legs at the joints; the four horses gave a tug and carried off the two thighs after them, namely, that of the right side first, the other following; then the same was done to the arms, the shoulders, the arm-pits and the four limbs; the flesh had to be cut almost to the bone, the horses pulling hard carried off the right arm first and the other afterwards.

'When the four limbs had been pulled away, the confessors came to speak to him; but his executioner told them that he was dead . . .

Eighty years later, Leon Facher drew up his rules 'for the House of young prisoners in Paris':

Art. 17. The prisoners' day will begin at six in the morning in winter and at five in summer. They will work for nine hours a day throughout the year. Two hours a day will be devoted to instruction. Work and the day will end at nine o'clock in winter and at eight in summer.

Art. 18. *Rising.* At the first drum-roll, the prisoners must rise and dress in silence, as the supervisor opens the cell doors. At the second drum-roll, they must be dressed and make their beds. At the third, they must line up and proceed to the chapel for morning prayer. There is a five-minute interval between each drum-roll.

Art. 19. The prayers are conducted by the chaplain and followed by a moral or religious reading. This exercise must not last more than half an hour.

Art. 20. *Work.* At a quarter to six in the summer, a quarter to seven in winter, the prisoners go down into the courtyard where they must wash their hands and faces, and receive their first ration of bread. Immediately afterwards, they form into work-teams and go off to work, which must begin at six in summer and seven in winter . . .

Art. 27. At seven o'clock in the summer, at eight in winter, work stops; bread is distributed for the last time in the workshops. For a quarter of an hour one of the prisoners or supervisors reads a passage from some instructive or uplifting work. This is followed by evening prayer.

Art. 28. At half past seven in summer, half past eight in winter, the prisoners must be back in their cells after the washing of hands and the inspection of clothes in the courtyard; at the first drum-roll, they must undress, and at the second get into bed. The cell doors are closed and the supervisors go the rounds in the corridors, to ensure order and silence.

- How would you describe the aims of the two styles of punishment?
- What might the likely effect of those punishments be on the rest of the society?
- What, if anything, do you think the style of punishment can tell us about a society?

In both the forms of punishment characterized by Foucault, the body of the offender remains central, but in the second example the body is incarcerated rather than mutilated and the soul of the body becomes the focus for reform. There is a change in the objective of punishment – away from being a display of the awful consequences that accompany a crime against the crown and toward instilling discipline and ensuring that the offender's body and soul function in a regular manner that helps the smooth running of the prison. So the modern prisons regulated their inmates by detailed control of all activities so as to ensure standardized, uniform conduct. The constant supervision and discipline would break the will of criminals and turn them into 'docile bodies'.

Foucault was critical of the likelihood of prisons being able to do anything to reduce crime: 'Prisons do not diminish the crime rate . . . (indeed) detention causes recidivism; those leaving prison have more chance than before of going back to it.' However, he did believe that the prison system was very effective at achieving other goals such as continuing the subjugation of the lower classes and, through the segregation of criminals, rendering them politically and socially harmless. Individuals could either resist the discipline of society and be criminalized and imprisoned, or accept it and lose their own identity.

To return to the history of the different forms of punishment, Foucault did not propose a simple theory of historical progress; and he was well aware that there was not a sudden change from one form of punishment to another in all societies at a specified time. He stressed the discontinuities and complexity of historical change – the ending of public execution, for instance, was not a single event but a series of changes and counter-changes brought in as governments became more or less punitive at different periods between the mid eighteenth and nineteenth centuries.

Foucault's major concern was with power and in particular power over the body. Public execution is a clear demonstration of the application of this power. Foucault also tries to show that the imposition of punishment in modern societies illustrated the differences and asymmetries of power just as much as it did in the *ancien régime*, even though infliction of physical pain was rejected and replaced with punishments that involved the suspension of rights, through the deprivation of liberty and control over the individual's time and space. The modern forms of punishment might even involve withdrawal of the right to live, in situations where societies still use the death penalty for instance. However, in these situations the death penalty is administered in a medicalized and closed sort of way – through lethal injection, gas chamber and the like – and there even tends to be a good deal of concern over how to ensure the capital punishment avoids any unnecessary agony for the executed.

Although Foucault did not develop a 'grand theory' in the manner of classic social theorists such as Karl Marx, his work shares a Marxist appreciation of the importance for capitalism of labour power. In the context of punishment he considered how methods of punishment could be used to turn rebellious subjects into productive ones. For instance, in charting the emergence of prisons and prison regimes in the nineteenth century, he emphasized how they produced a new kind of individual 'subjected to habits, rules and orders'. This investigation of the development of prisons in the early nineteenth century was utilized by Foucault to help him explore the general themes of domination and how that is achieved and of how individuals are 'socially constructed'.

Foucault saw an extension of power and domination occurring through the methods of surveillance that were part of the design of the new prison buildings of this time. The panoptican designed by Jeremy Bentham was a prison building constructed so as to allow for the constant observation and monitoring of 'progress' of all its inmates. Essentially it was a circular building built around a central axis that allowed the guards to observe the inmates without themselves being observed. The aim of this design was to induce in the inmates the belief that they were under constant surveillance and although that classic sort of panoptican was never fully instituted, the ideas and basic approach behind it were integrated into the architecture of the new nineteenth-century prison buildings. Foucault, then, saw the prison as illustrating the basic principle of punitive and disciplinary power:

> The perfect disciplinary apparatus would make it possible for a single gaze to see everything constantly . . . the major effect of the panoptican: to induce in the

inmate a state of conscious and permanent visibility that assumes the automatic functioning of power.

(Foucault 1977: 173–201)

To elaborate on this a little, the 'panoptican principle' is the principle of disciplinary regulation and for Foucault this is the fundamental principle of social regulation in modern society. He sees society as a 'carceral archipelago', essentially a chain of institutions with all members subject to an overarching disciplinary regulation, including being liable to the suspension of their rights across all aspects of their lives. While such disciplinary regulation is most obviously and fully realized in the prison, it is also dispersed out from the prison to other areas of society. There are, of course, many other social institutions and organizations that regulate us and that could also be said to be in the business of surveillance. As well as obvious examples such as the police and security companies, schools and colleges monitor our educational progress, the Inland Revenue checks to see whether we have paid our taxes and social service agencies keep records on citizens' uptake of services, to name a few. And all of these forms of checking and surveillance have been massively helped by advances in video and computer technology that have extended the range and the ease with which information from people can be gained, stored and utilized (further examples of the increased surveillance in contemporary society are included in the question break below).

It is this argument that disciplinary regulation underpins the whole web of social interaction and relationships – and that prisons, factories, schools and other institutions differ only in the degree to which they are permeated by such disciplinary regulation – that is perhaps Foucault's most controversial claim. Foucault's analysis dissolves the differences between punitive and non-punitive institutions and presents a view of society that is a mesh of disciplinary relationships, as he puts it, citizens of modern society as 'inhabitants of the punitive city within the carceral archipelago'. The prison is just one end of a continuum in which regulation and surveillance are normal. As mentioned above, the very term 'carceral archipelago' implies a chain of institutions that stretches out from the prison; and Foucault's whole argument conjures up images of totalitarianism and a 'big brother' society that does not sit easily with our notion of Western, liberal, democratic values. Indeed this critical edge to Foucault's work perhaps explains why he has become so much in vogue in academic circles over the last few decades.

QUESTION BREAK: DISCIPLINARY OBSERVATION

The extract below from *Discipline and Punish* illustrates Foucault's analysis of how 'disciplinary power' works by using a series of simple instruments, including what he termed hierarchical observation. He describes how architectural planning can be used to help the surveillance of individuals in a wide range of social institutions, including hospitals, schools and working-class housing estates. He discusses how the power of observation operates in a more insidious and subtle manner than conventional means of exercising power, such as the use of force.

Hierarchical Observation

The exercise of discipline presupposes a mechanism that coerces by means of observation: an apparatus in which the techniques that make it possible to see induce effects of power and in which, conversely, the means of coercion make those on whom they are applied clearly visible. Slowly, in the course of the classical age, we see the construction of those 'observatories' of human multiplicity for which the history of the sciences has so little good to say . . .

These 'observatories' had an almost ideal model: the military camp – the short-lived artificial city, built and reshaped almost at will . . . In the perfect camp, all power would be exercised solely through exact observation; each gaze would form part of the overall functioning of power. The old, traditional square plan was considerably refined in innumerable new projects. The geometry of the paths, the number and distribution of the tents, the orientation of their entrances, the disposition of files and ranks were exactly defined; the network of gazes that supervised one another was laid down: 'In the parade ground, five lines are drawn up; the first is sixteen feet from the second; the others are eight feet from one another; and the last is eight feet from the arms depots . . . All tents are two feet from one another. The tents of the subalterns are opposite the alleys of their companies. The rear tentpole is eight feet from the last soldiers' tent and the gate is opposite the captain's tent . . .' For a long time this model of the camp, or at least its underlying principle, was found in urban development, in the construction of working-class housing surveillance. The principle was one of 'embedding' (*encastrement*). The camp was to the rather shameful art of surveillance what the dark room was to the great science of optics.

A whole problematic then develops: that of an architecture that is no longer built simply to be seen (as with the ostentation of palaces), or to observe the external space (cf. the geometry of fortresses), but to permit an internal, articulated and detailed control – to render visible those who are inside it; in more general terms, an architecture that would operate to transform individuals: to act on those it shelters, to provide a hold on their conduct, to carry the effects of power right to them, to make it possible to know them, to alter them . . . In this way the hospital building was gradually organized as an instrument of medical action: it was to allow a better observation of patients, and therefore a better calibration of their treatment; the form of the buildings, by the careful separation of the patients, was to prevent contagions; lastly, the ventilation and the air that circulated around each bed were to prevent the deleterious vapors from stagnating around the patient, breaking down his humors and spreading the disease by their immediate effects. The hospital –which was to be built in the second half of the century and for which so many plans were drawn up after the Hotel-Dieu burnt down for the second time – was no longer simply the roof under which penury and imminent death took shelter; it was, in its very materiality, a therapeutic operator.

Similarly, the school building was to be a mechanism for training. It was as a pedagogical machine that Paris-Duverney conceived the Ecole Militaire, right down to the minute details that he imposed on the architect, Gabriel. . . . The very building of the Ecole was to be an apparatus for observation; the rooms were distributed along a corridor like a series of small cells; at regular intervals, an officer's quarters was situated, so that 'every ten pupils had an officer on each side'; the pupils were confined to their cells throughout the night; and Paris had insisted that 'a window be placed on the corridor wall of each room from chest level to within one or two feet of the ceiling. Not only is it pleasant to have such windows, but one would venture to say that it is useful, in several respects, not to mention the disciplinary reason that may determine this arrangement.' In the dining room was 'a slightly raised platform for the tables of the inspectors of studies, so that they may see all the tables of the pupils of their divisions during meals'; latrines had been installed with half-doors, so that the supervisor on duty could see the head and legs of the pupils, and also with side walls sufficiently high 'that those inside cannot see one another'. This infinitely scrupulous concern with surveillance is expressed in the architecture by innumerable petty mechanisms. These mechanisms can only be seen as unimportant if one forgets the role of this instrumentation, minor but flawless, in the progressive objectification and the ever more subtle partitioning of individual behaviour. The disciplinary institutions secreted a machinery of control that functioned like a microscope of conduct; the fine, analytical divisions that they created formed around men an apparatus of observation, recording. And training. How was one to subdivide the gaze in these observation machines? How was one to establish a network of communications between them? How was one so to arrange things that a homogenous, continuous power would result from their calculated multiplicity?

The perfect disciplinary apparatus would make it possible for a single gaze to see everything constantly. A central point would be both then source of light illuminating everything and a locus of convergence for everything that must be known: a perfect eye that nothing would escape and a center toward which all gazes would be turned.

(From M. Foucault, 1977, pp. 170–7)

- Consider the institutions that you have come into contact with (such as schools/colleges, places of work, leisure centers, hospitals etc.). To what extent does their design and architecture help to impose discipline and control?
- What do you think are the main strengths and weaknesses of Foucault's argument that observation can be used as a means of regulation and control?

Foucault – comment and criticism

There is no disputing the fact that Foucault's much broader approach to the analysis of power and domination has changed the way in which social scientists think about those concepts. Foucault placed power at the centre of social life and has encouraged an examination of how power operates no longer through a centralized body, such as the state, but as a network without a centre. Power is invested in all of the relationships that make up social life. However, in spite of the importance of these general ideas, the emphasis on 'hierarchical observation' and disciplinary control have raised concerns and been subject to specific research that has questioned some of Foucault's arguments.

In a paper that he entitled 'What would it matter if everything Foucault said about prison were wrong?', Alford (2000) drew upon research that he undertook in a maximum-security state prison in Maryland, USA to contrast Foucault's account of how power operates within prison with his own experience. Although Foucault emphasized the ways in which surveillance, categorization and classification and regimentation characterized the disciplinary nature of prisons, Alford did not find this to be the case in his research. Not only were those disciplinary practices absent, but he found almost the opposite to exist. The prison authorities in the prison he was based in did not spend their time constantly observing the prisoners because they didn't have to. As long as the entrances and exists were controlled there was no need to constantly monitor what was happening inside. As Alford points out, this approach is hardly new and is captured in the populist sentiment, 'lock 'em up and throw away the key'. So rather than excessive supervision, he found an absence of supervision to be the norm in American prisons. Close surveillance and supervision might still occur in the wider society but not within prisons, as Alford puts it, 'The panoptican might be a bad way to run a prison, but a good way to run a society, at least from the perspective of knowledge/power'.

Real power, for Alford, would involve not having to bother to look; indeed having to look is a sign of the limits of power, 'if you have to look, you do not really control. If you are in control you do not have to look.' What is important in controlling inmates within prison is the count – one inmate is exactly like another and all that needs checking is that none have escaped, 'the count is the ultimate in human superfluity, each inmate's like every other. But the count is not unique. It finds its tally in everyday life in bureaucracy.' Alford coins the term 'nonoptican' rather than panoptican as best describing what goes on in prisons. It is not that guards have a greater respect for the prisoners' privacy; rather they don't care, and one aspect of this not caring is the lack of concern with how prisoners spend their days and nights – as long as there is no trouble what they do is immaterial. He argues that there is nowhere where time is less structured and people more idle than in prison.

While increased surveillance in general and the growing use of CCTV specifically can be and is criticized as attacking individuals' civil liberties and privacy, research into the use of CCTV inside police stations has produced some interesting findings that seem to offer 'support' for such monitoring from inmates and offenders themselves. Newburn and Hayman (2001) evaluated the use of CCTV within custody suites by the Metropolitan Police. Cameras have been introduced into booking areas and cell corridors as well as a small number of cells for 'vulnerable' prisoners. Newburn and Hayman found the major worry that the inmates felt about the use of cameras was the invasion of privacy, with the filming of their use of the toilet a particular concern. They also found that the officers in the police stations were bothered about the constant filming. As well not being able to switch off images of people they had detained going to the toilet, they were concerned that the films might be used to check up on their behaviour also. However, the inmates did see some benefits from the use of cameras in police cells. They felt it increased their safety from physical threats, particularly those who had been assaulted when in custody previously. As one of the detainees said to Newburn and Hayman, 'They [police officers] wouldn't risk beating you up if they knew there were people watching the camera. The cameras are there for my benefit rather than theirs. I'm less likely to get a kicking.' So the detainees were aware of the benefits as well as being concerned about the intrusive nature of the cameras. Newburn and Hayman conclude by arguing that CCTV can be both a means of social control and a means of safeguarding individuals' rights, and can do these two things simultaneously. Individuals may face a loss of privacy but they may also feel that they are better protected.

More generally, it could be argued that Foucault's theorizing overstates the extent people are disciplined and controlled in everyday life. While we as individuals are not free to do what we like when we like, and while we all have to follow rules and laws, this is not necessarily the same as being in a prison. Also, while the laws and legal system may favour the powerful groups more than other groups in society, there are laws which protect, rather than enslave, individuals; and without them the weaker members of society might be more vulnerable to the powerful.

QUESTION BREAK: SURVEILLANCE – BOON OR BANE?

In considering the spread of surveillance and CCTV in relation to Foucault's discussion of disciplinary observation, some benefits as well as dangers were highlighted. These issues are illustrated in the following extracts from recent media accounts.

Plan to monitor all internet use

Communications firms are being asked to record all internet contacts between people as part of a modernisation in UK police surveillance tactics . . . The new system would track all e-mails, phone calls and internet use, including visits to social networking sites . . .

Announcing a consultation on a new strategy for communications data and its use in law enforcement, Jacqui Smith (then Home Secretary) said:

"Advances in communications mean that there are ever more sophisticated ways to communicate and we need to ensure that we keep up with the technology being used by those who seek to do us harm. It is essential that the police and other crime fighting agencies have the tools they need to do their job . . ."

(BBC news online, 27 April 2009)

Police mapping out mission to count every spy camera

CCTV is almost completely unregulated and there is pressure on the Government to introduce controls . . . It is impossible to know how many CCTV cameras there are. The Information Commissioner does not know, the Home Office does not know, the police do not know . . .

Many people question whether these systems are worth it. Yet pictures from CCTV provided police with valuable information at the time of the terrorist attacks in London in July 2005. They also led to the capture of Brixton nail bomber David Copeland. However, looking for the right image can be a time-consuming exercise. In the case of Copeland, police spent 4,000 hours viewing 1,097 CCTV tapes . . .

CCTV reduced crime in car parks and shops but was less successful in cutting disorder and anti-social behaviour in public spaces . . .

There is no statutory or legal obstacle to installing CCTV cameras. The only obligation on those who install them is that they must meet the terms of the Data Protection Act in areas such as handling, storage and processing of the images obtained.

(From R. Ford, *The Times*, 7 March 2009)

Big Brother is watching

The government is backing a project to install a 'communication box' in new cars to track the whereabouts of drivers anywhere in Europe . . . Under the proposals, vehicles will emit a constant 'heartbeat' revealing their location, speed and direction of travel. The EU officials behind the plan believe it will significantly reduce road accidents, congestion and carbon emissions. A consortium of manufacturers has indicated the router device could be installed in all new cars as early as 2013. However privacy campaigners warned last night that a European-wide car tracking system would create a system of almost total road surveillance . . . enabling cars to be tracked to within a metre – more accurate than current satellite navigation technologies . . .

Roads in the UK are already subject to the closest surveillance of any in the world. Police control a database that is fed information from automatic number plate recognition (ANPR) cameras, and are able to deduce the journeys of as many as 10 million drivers a day. Details are stored for up to five years.

(P. Lewis, the *Guardian*, 31 March 2009)

High-teach solutions to low-tech crimes?

The effort to combat terrorism with technology has been stepped up since 9/11, but there is broad public concern that surveillance strategies designed to identify potential terrorists are being employed in more insidious ways to spy on the population at large, with the result that civil liberties are being undermined and personal privacy is a thing of the past . . .

In the wake of 9/11, the climate of political and public acceptability has become more favourable to the idea of surveillance. For example, many governments – our own included – are trying to gain public support for mandatory 'smart' ID cards.

(Y. Jewkes 2005)

- To what extent do you agree with Foucault's emphasis on surveillance creating disciplinary control that dominates our everyday lives?
- What do you consider to be the major advantages and disadvantages of increased use of CCTV and other forms of surveillance?

SUMMARY

The sociological theories of punishment we have considered have tried to explain the form and role of punishment in society and to relate this to the changing nature of society. In introducing our discussion of these theories we referred to Garland's (1990) argument that styles and institutions of punishment have to be studied as social constructions. We will finish this overview of such theories by considering the concluding comments that Garland makes in his more detailed study.

In spite of the hopes and claims that inevitably accompany the introduction of new forms of punishment, it is clear that no form of punishment has ever managed to control crime or to achieve high rates of reform of offenders. And Garland argues that it is unrealistic to expect anything else. Punishments are bound to 'fail' because they can never be much more than a back-up to the mainstream processes of socialization. Acceptable standards of behaviour have to be learned; they cannot be forced on people. As Garland puts it: 'Punishment is merely a coercive back up to those more reliable social mechanisms, a back up which is often unable to do anything more than manage those who slip through these networks of normal control and integration' (1990: 289).

He suggests that maybe we should expect less from policies on punishment, which, while sometimes necessary, is inevitably beset by contradictions and tensions:

However well it is organized, and however humanely administered, punishment is inescapably marked by moral contradictions and unwanted irony – as when it seeks to uphold freedom by means of its deprivation or condemn private violence using a violence which is publicly authorized.

(Garland 1990: 292)

It is appropriate to finish the chapter by referring to Garland's work as he is arguably the key modern commentator on theories of punishment and in his work he has tried to move away from the tendency for one or other theoretical position to be the current 'flavour of the month'. While Foucault is understandably a major force in the area, Garland argues that we need the insights of all the major theorists for a fuller understanding of punishment. From the Marxist approach and from Foucault we can gain complementary but distinct appreciations of the relations between social institutions and the power dynamics of society; Durkheim's arguments demonstrate how punishment and the law are both part of and help to make up the moral character of a society; and Weber enables us to see the processes and policies of punishment in relation to broader issues concerned with the rationalization of modern society.

FURTHER READING

Cavadino, M. and Dignan, J. (2007) *The Penal System: An Introduction* (4th edn). Although this is a general introductory text that examines the workings of the contemporary criminal justice system, chapter 3, 'Explaining Punishment', provides a clear and accessible introduction to the main sociological theories of punishment.

Garland, D. (1990) *Punishment and Modern Society: A Study in Social Theory*. This is a comprehensive introduction to the sociological study of punishment, which critically examines punishment as an instrument of ideology and as a means of class control. It includes a detailed assessment of the work of Durkheim, Foucault and of Marxist analyses.

Valier, C. (2002) *Theories of Crime and Punishment*. While there are plenty of texts introducing criminology and criminological theory, this book provides a critical introduction to the main theories of both crime and punishment from the late eighteenth century to the present day.

The journal *Theoretical Criminology* is an interdisciplinary, international journal that focuses on the theoretical aspects of criminology, including research and comment that relates to the philosophies, theories and history of punishment.

CHAPTER 9

The History of Crime and Justice

INTRODUCTION

The historical development of a state's criminal justice system (CJS) can be viewed simply as a series of rational responses to 'criminality', as variously defined by successive governments through time. Alternatively, the CJS can be described as the policies of a political executive (be it monarch, chief minister, Council or Parliament) that happened to hold power during the period under review. Yet these are inadequate attempts to understand the meaning of criminal justice and punishment through the ages and they disguise rather than examine the underlying structural issues. They are particularly weak as explanations of policy because they fail to indicate the central importance of the theoretical models that historians and sociologists of state punishment have used to understand the development of a CJS, its administration, and the impact on governors and governed alike. This chapter will select a variety of state initiatives in penal policy from the medieval to the modern period and show how their development can be explained in their historical context.

This theoretical approach will consider two related themes: first, sociological theories that are central to the interpretation of past policies on crime and punishment and, second, some of the contemporary theories of government, authority and punishment which conditioned policy action in the periods under review here. Consequently, this chapter builds on the discussion of the theories of Marx, Durkheim, Weber and Foucault introduced in Chapter 2. They will be used to explain major policy changes and modern writers, such as Ignatieff, Cohen, E. P.

Thompson, Hobsbawm, Sharpe and Ballinger, will be used to show how modern research has developed earlier theoretical paradigms. This chapter seeks to understand the history of crime and punishment in terms of the nature, structure and power matrices of the governments and societies responsible for such policies.

Of course it is possible to deny or at least play down the existence of crime in the past. The 'common sense' view is that crime is more prevalent in modern society. Pearson (1983) has shown how every generation feels threatened (especially by its youth) and looks back, erroneously, on a 'golden age' in which crime was not such a problem. In this past utopia all front doors remained open and 'everyone' was secure in the knowledge that the felons simply did not exist who would dare disturb a peace to which all subscribed. Such folk memories are not empirically verifiable yet popular perceptions of criminality are an important area of analysis. Pearson (1983), and Cohen (1980), have used the idea of the 'moral panic' to show how perceptions of threat, which have little basis in fact, can have a real impact on the legislative process and produce important changes in the criminal law and penal policy. There are many examples of 'deviancy amplification' as a moral panic spirals out of control sufficiently to legitimize the increased severity of a state's punishment regime. Examples range from mediaeval Christian concern about schismatic sects, Protestant reactions to 'popery' after the Reformation, nineteenth-century fears of 'Outcast London' and the garrotting panic of the 1860s. More modern crises include 'mods and rockers' (Cohen's classic work on the 1960s) and the threat of the black mugger in the 1970s. The concept of moral panic is important in assessing not just popular assumptions (i.e. 'bottom-up' understanding) but also the reasons for initiatives in state policy carried by governing elites ('top-down' action).

When complemented by state concern for the unity and stability of society and the security of the political system, moral panics are part of a significant force for the extension of punishment. This was especially recognized by Durkheim (see pp. 252–257) as he saw punishment as central to the establishment of the moral authority of the state and its social solidarity in order to preserve what he termed the 'conscience collective'. Of course the 'moral authority' is imposed with greater force when a new institution of power has captured the state apparatus and the policies of theocratic states in the medieval and early modern periods show this.

QUESTION BREAK: RELIGIOUS JUSTIFICATIONS FOR PUNISHMENT

The supporters of [religious] coercion looked to the writings of St. Augustine who had done more than anyone else to legitimise the use of force in religion. [H]e wrote a series of famous letters justifying the persecution of the Donatists [who] were a purist sect, schismatic sect who had separated from the Catholic church. His arguments carried the day, or rather the millennium, for his position became the established orthodoxy of Western Christendom, both Catholic and Protestant. . . . Elizabethan bishops, mid-seventeenth-century Puritans and Restoration Anglicans all justified their drive for uniformity by referring their readers to Augustine's famous epistles against the Donatists . . .

[I]n the next two centuries the capital punishment of heretics was to become widespread across the continent . . . The medieval Inquisition was established to counter the threat of these groups and the fourth Lateran Council of 1215 codified the theory and practice of persecution. The greatest medieval theologian Thomas Aquinas summed up the standard medieval position when he declared that obstinate heretics deserved 'not only to be separated from the church but eliminated from the world by death.' The condition of the Jews also worsened dramatically in these years, as massacres occurred in a number of areas of Europe, and vicious anti-semitic stereotypes developed. Eventually, in 1478, an Inquisition was established in Spain which aimed to destroy all remnants of Jewish faith in the land. Finally, from the mid-fifteenth century, we find the first outbreaks of the witch-hunts that were to claim more than 30,000 lives over the next three centuries.

The sixteenth-century Reformation did little to end these persecutions. Indeed, by presenting a new and more powerful threat to the unity of Christendom than medieval heresies, the Reformation served to intensify persecution by Catholic regimes . . . [They] fully embraced Augustine's vision of the coercive role of the Christian magistrate, and many shared Aquinas' belief in the legitimacy of the death penalty for heresy.

Yet the theorists of uniformity were not just concerned about religious truth and church unity, but also about political order . . . [They were] much more concerned with political power and the preservation of stability . . . There can be no doubt that defenders of uniformity were convinced that religious pluralism would have disastrous political consequences.

Most early modern Englishmen assumed that some form of religious uniformity was absolutely essential for the unity of the nation . . . To tolerate different religions, therefore, was to commit political suicide . . .

Those who supported persecution constantly stressed the seditious character of religious deviants. Sir William Cecil [in Elizabethan England] was emphatic in his assertion that Catholics were only executed for sedition, not for their religion.

(From J. Coffey 2000: 22–38)

- Summarize the views of St Augustine and suggest why they had such a significant impact on state punishment policy.

- Explain the severity of state punishment for 'religious deviants' in this period.
- Why did Catholic regimes 'intensify persecution' during the Reformation?
- Why do you think the toleration of different religions might be seen as 'political suicide'?

EARLY HISTORY – BEFORE THE 'BLOODY CODE'

Therefore punishment in the medieval and early modern state was a direct function of concern by elites for political and social stability. It also represented a clear endorsement of the dominant religious and political beliefs of the day. There were elements of a 'moral panic' in the reactions of state authority to religious diversity in the period. Of course there were fundamental challenges to religious orthodoxy and it is not the intention here to relegate the Reformation to a moral panic. However, it is equally clear that politico-religious authority at this time was exceptionally sensitive to any group or movement that seemed to constitute an alternative faith, new intellectual paradigm or political threat. As in all the cases considered in this chapter, the correlation between the actual, as opposed to the perceived, threat is variable but the impact on penal policy is consistently demonstrated.

The role of the prison in the early modern period illustrates how penal policy reflects closely the changes in dominant discourses of social and political correctness. Peters (1998) refers to the 'prison before the [modern] prison' and he describes the increase of imprisonment as a complement to forms of penality such as mutilation, the wheel, the rack and other forms of execution. Peters emphasizes the custodial role of prisons as pre-trial holding stockades rather than the punishment itself:

> When Henry II issued the Assizes of Clarendon in 1166, he ordered that sheriffs should build jails in each county to hold those accused of felonies until they could be tried by itinerant royal justices.
>
> From the 1270s on, the number of prisons in England and of imprisonable offenses increased rapidly. By 1520 there were 180 imprisonable offenses in the common law.
>
> (Peters 1998: 31)

The increase in such offences and the extension of state punishment were a feature of the Tudor period in England. The high point of judicial excess was reached in the reign of the Catholic Mary I. 'Bloody Mary' ensured that over 300 Protestant heretics were burned alive in three years (1555–8). Elizabeth I sentenced over 700 to death for supporting the Northern Rebellion and it is estimated that there were over 1,000 executions a year in the Tudor period (1485–1603) and 75,000 died in the period 1530 to 1630. If such a rate of judicial slaughter was replicated today in the USA it is estimated that executions would run at 46,000 per annum (Coffey 2000; Jenkins 1986). Such executions were public, didactic theatre and often required that victims be disembowelled before death. Imprisonment, transportation (to America and Australia) and torture, especially the rack, were also used, not only against religious deviants but also those convicted of treason (which was usually closely linked to the heretical) and indicted for a felony (homicide, highway robbery and burglary for example).

An increase in severity was also a central feature of Caroline and Puritan punishment regimes in the seventeenth century as Charles I's attempts to impose his royal authority on Parliament led eventually to the outbreak of Civil War in England, and his execution in 1649. Religious militancy once again determined criminal justice policy and was sufficiently important to revolutionize the constitutional and political structure of the country. Yet this was not before the destruction of both consensual government and socio-economic stability proved to be the context for the imposition of more vicious forms of punishment as supporters of one side or another suffered the consequences of their misplaced loyalties.

After the traumas of the Civil War and the Restoration of the monarchy under Charles II (1660) state punishment operated in a new context and there were significant changes which occurred in its nature and incidence. For example, it is clear that from the mid-seventeenth century the rate of execution in England shows a significant change with imprisonment increasingly favoured as punishment (see Table 9.1 below).

QUESTION BREAK

Table 9.1 Capital punishment inflicted for felony: Palatinate of Chester 1580–1709

1580–08	91
1600–09	62
1620–29	165
1640–49	12
1660–69	18
1680–89	24
1700–09	10

Source: Sharpe, J. A., *Crime in Early Modern England, 1550–1750* (Longman, 1999), p. 91

[T]he crucial issue is clear enough: in the century before 1640 English society was, and felt itself to be, under pressure.

By the 1660s this pressure had waned, and the late 17th century and early 18th centuries experienced a period of relative social stability. Changes and conflicts still occurred, of course, but they did so within the constraints of a new equilibrium. For the historian of crime, the most important component of this equilibrium was the emergence of the poor as an institutionalized presence. The poor were not now the occasional beggar . . . nor were they the sturdy beggars of Elizabethan trauma. They were that third or so of the population who were unlikely to be able to support themselves from week to week without assistance. The propertied, however much they grumbled over the poor rates, and however much they despised the labouring poor, had learnt to live with them, and to fit them into their concepts of how society functioned. In such a context the poor house or the house of correction was a handier means of controlling the poor than . . . frequent executions . . .

Disorder and division were still present, but they were less menacing than they had been – and above all they were perceived as being less menacing by contemporaries. Most arguments on this point have revolved around elite culture and elite reactions: [and here] is an image of a "settled and relaxed world" in the 18th century. The falling off of prosecution . . . and the drop in executions . . . must be regarded as symptoms of this massive shift. Behind it all . . . there lies an unconscious psychological reaction as the wave of demographic expansion levelled off.

(Sharpe 1999: 264–6)

- How does the passage explain the trends in the figures shown in Table 9.1?
- What social factors does Sharpe link to the changing rate of execution?
- How had perceptions of criminality changed by the 1660s and why did this have an effect on the rate of execution?

Sharpe also shows that the percentage of felons receiving the death penalty fell dramatically in this period. In the mid-sixteenth century about 25 per cent of cases brought the death penalty. By the early eighteenth century this was around 10 per cent. Also the rate of acquittal rose. By the first decade of the eighteenth century about 40 per cent of those accused were released: comparable figures a century earlier were about 25–27 per cent. In the first half of the eighteenth century there was also a rise in the numbers transported with up to 20 per cent of criminal convictions leading to transportation. According to Sharpe these figures illustrate a clear shift in state punishment policy.

There is another important question that needs to be addressed. Why did the use of the prison increase so? In England, a form of the prison called a 'House of Correction' was used from the mid-sixteenth century and its increase has also generated debates about the origins and purpose of such institutions. The 'House' represented an important change in the nature of state punishment in England. Sharpe believed that it 'provides an almost unique example of an institution which has been universally regarded as marking a new departure in such matters. The House of Correction, of which the London Bridewell was the prototype, constituted an important shift in punishment policy' (1999: 256). The 'new departure' was the use of the prison for the reform of the criminal and to impose the discipline of labour. Inmates were put to work, in textile manufacture usually, and their output could be sold to generate profit for the institution. Given the regard for reform and rehabilitation, the House of Correction can be seen as the ancestor of the modern prison whose development is treated more fully below. Explanations for such shifts in penal policy include the important Marxist interpretation of the rise of the prison found in Rusche and Kirchheimer's classic *Punishment and Social Structure* that was published in 1939 (see pp. 264–268). It is a key Marxist interpretation of the history of incarceration and its development up to the modern day. Marxists look at the rise of the prison (indeed all criminal law) as the product of economic forces and the needs of an emerging capitalist mode of production. The prison, it is argued, is vital to the mature, capitalist economy because it retains and disciplines the labour force, secures adequate social control of labour units and perpetuates the exploitation of the workers in the interests of the bourgeois elites. The bourgeoisie thus remain the controllers of the 'means of production, distribution and exchange'. This is of particular importance to any analysis having nineteenth-century British economic growth as its context. Writers such as Ignatieff (1978) have shown, using concepts of the 'carceral society' developed by the French post-structuralist, Michel Foucault, how prisons developed into 'total institutions' designed to strengthen the rigorous social control that elites thought the labouring, or 'dangerous' classes required.

QUESTION BREAK: THE RISE OF THE PRISON

Rusche and Kirchheimer . . . argue that far from being motivated by humanitarianism, the establishment of houses of correction [and later prison regimes] reflected a growing demand for a regulated and disciplined labour force in the days of emerging agrarian capitalist and mercantile societies. In reviewing changes in forms of punishment from the late Middle Ages to the 1930s, they contend that:

Transformation in penal systems cannot be explained only from changing needs of the war against crime. Every system of production tends to discover punishments which correspond to its productive relationships. . . .

The rationale for the houses of correction . . . lies in the fact that they were primarily factories turning out commodities at a particularly low cost due to their cheap labour. Their use burgeoned . . . because the relative labour shortage in the general population coincided with the development of mercantilism [commercial expansion]. In short, to secure the development of an emerging capitalism, the labour of prisoners was to be exploited . . .

It was the conditions of the local labour market which frequently determined . . . [that] valuable, able-bodied workers tended to be confined in houses of correction for as long as possible.

(From J. Muncie 1996: 161)

- What forms of emerging capitalism did the Houses of Correction resemble?
- Given that the Houses emerged in the sixteenth century and that their inmates were often vagabonds, army deserters and petty criminals, how might the Marxist link between imprisonment and capitalism be criticized?
- Criticize the view that such Houses were the direct forerunners of the modern prison.

THE EIGHTEENTH CENTURY AND THE 'BLOODY CODE'

The eighteenth century was a period of considerable social, economic and political change. Population growth was spectacular. Stimulated by industrialization it doubled from about 5 million to over 10 million. Urban growth and migration became features of Britain's development: in the period 1700 to 1750 London attracted about

½ million migrants and as early as 1700, 25 per cent of the population of England lived in towns. The period saw political upheaval and rebellion as the succession to the throne remained controversial following the removal of the Stuarts. Great political disturbances shattered notions of an ordered society. Violence seemed endemic in politics and society and the British were regarded as 'an ungovernable people'. Governments became acutely concerned about the preservation of social stability and the defence of property. They perceived the masses as increasingly dangerous and fear of crime began to reach the dimensions of a moral panic.

Historians of criminal justice identify a direct connection between social upheaval, economic instability and depression and increases in crime and perceptions of its threat by political elites and other propertied classes. Heightened perception of criminality leads to a more vigorous application of the criminal code and a strengthening of agencies responsible for crime and punishment. Certainly, the economic trends discussed above increased social polarization and tension and historians such as Douglas Hay and E. P. Thompson see the criminal justice system in this period as an ideological instrument preserving class hegemony or at least, as V. A. C. Gatrell believes, securing the social hierarchy in the interests of the powerful and propertied. Debates about this and the eighteenth-century 'Bloody Code' are discussed below but it is clear that eighteenth-century law had the role of legitimizing both the political system that produced it and the distribution of political power and property upon which it was founded. The following example illustrates this important point.

In 1723 Parliament passed the 'Black Act'. It created about 50 new capital offences immediately and was passed by the Commons without any debate. The initial reason for the legislation was the sharp rise in attacks on cattle, deer and rabbits in Windsor Forest by thieves and poachers whose faces had been blackened to avoid detection. The list of offences was extended to include acts of arson and the cutting down of trees. The historian of the 'Black Act', E. P. Thompson (1985), has shown how it enforced the Whig political ascendancy (Whigs had displaced Tories as the ruling party after the removal of the Stuart kings in 1688) and generalized the protection of property rights at a time when Whigs felt insecure in the face of their enemies the Hanoverians (who supported the new king George I). Popular ideas that the masses had legitimate access to land and its product were also destroyed. The Act demonstrated the contrast between 'normative', or popular notions of right and wrong, and the more powerful legal definitions imposed by law.

QUESTION BREAK: THE 'BLACK ACT'

Thompson saw this law as an instrument of class power:

[The Black Act] is clearly an instrument of the ruling class: it both defines and defends these rulers' claims upon resources and labour-power. It says what shall be property and what shall be crime – and it mediates class relations with a set of appropriate rules and sanctions, all of which confirm and consolidate existing class power. Hence the rule of law is only another mask for the rule of a class . . .

But this is not the same thing as to say that the rulers had need of law in order to oppress the ruled, while those who were ruled had need of none. What was at issue was not property, supported by law, against no property; it was alternative definitions of property rights: for the landowner, enclosure – for the cottager, common [land] rights; for the forest officialdom, 'preserved grounds' for the deer; for the foresters, the right to take turfs.

(From E. P. Thompson 1985: 259–61)

- Suggest reasons for the great number of capital offences established.
- In what sense can the Black Act be seen as an 'instrument of the ruling class'?

The eighteenth century was also the era of the 'Bloody Code'. The English criminal law was one of the most savage in Europe. The flow of capital statutes was the product of contemporary fears that a supposed criminal class was increasing its assault on respectable society. Governments indicated that harsh penalties were required to defend a society under attack. Yet here too there is debate. Many of these statutes, such as the 'Black Act', were passed without serious examination by the House of Commons and considered by its members as a conventional response to the subversive masses. It was the defence of property and the state that was at the heart of such legislation and the 'Bloody Code' was administered by political and social elites in their own interests to impose a measure of social control over the masses. From the 1750s there seemed ample confirmative evidence for those who felt that the collapse of civil society was imminent in the face of great increases in crime and civil disorder. Sir Henry Fielding, Chief Magistrate at Bow Street in London, suspected the idle masses were increasingly a threat to 'respectable classes' and dangerously attracted to seditious schemes and treasonous designs. This was the time of the creation of the Bow Street Runners (the 'Thief-Takers') and Horse Patrol and the increases in the establishment of watchmen and stipendiary magistrates. Fielding's brother, Sir John Fielding demanded increases in the efficiency of magistrates across England.

Such panics were reinforced by dramatic outbreaks of civil disorder. London riots were provoked by support for John Wilkes' campaign for increased political representation (the cry was 'Wilkes and Libert') in 1768 and the Gordon Riots of 1780 provoked a week of destruction in the capital as fears of uncontrolled popery ran wild. The powers of government were further placed in doubt by the loss of the American colonies by the mid 1780s and the unending, or so it seemed, list of strikes and food riots that increasingly challenged the coherence of the state and its powers to keep the peace. Even elements of the armed forces refused to comply, in 1783, when ordered to defend the American colonies in the final stages of the war of independence. By the 1790s, an age of unreason seemed to threaten. The excesses and upheavals of the French Revolution appeared ready to cross the Channel. For treason, the Code indicated hanging, drawing and quartering: women murdering their husbands were burned at the stake. Persons found guilty of a felony (murder, theft, robbery, rape, forgery and burglary for example) were hanged. In the late seventeenth century there were 50 capital offences. By 1800 this number had risen to over 200.

The period demonstrates an increase in the number of convictions, and the percentage of felons convicted. Pardons were increasingly refused and the numbers of felons hanged rose to heights not reached in a century. In the 1780s the proportion of those condemned to death that were actually hanged leapt from a previous average per annum of 30 per cent to over 60 per cent and in 1787 it is known that the figure reached 80 per cent. This seems to support traditional views of the impact of a 'Bloody Code' targeted by later nineteenth-century reformers as a barbaric and shameful expression of the arbitrary power of the criminal law in an unenlightened era. It also seems to support the view that the 'Bloody Code' was a piece of 'class legislation'.

Revisionist historians have a different view. Gatrell (1994), Langbein (1983) and Emsley (2005), for example, have rejected the view that a harsh and 'bloody' eighteenth-century criminal code was the result of the self-regarding action of an identifiable, coherent and unified governing class committed to the manipulation and control of an equally distinct and identifiable class of the labouring, poverty-stricken and criminally-inclined. Rather, they see the law providing for the resolution of disputes within and between a range of competing groups and they reject the polarized model of social conflict indicated by left-wing historians such as Hay and colleagues. According to this alternative explanation the many capital statutes provided an alternative, lesser sentence that was left to the discretion of the judge. Transportation, under the Act of 1718, is such an example and until the American War of Independence it was used increasingly as an alternative, secondary punishment for a growing list of property offences. Revisionists emphasize that many of the eighteenth-century capital statutes were in fact never used and that most convictions were achieved using older legislation. Gatrell argues that over 90 per cent of convicted felons were actually pardoned. Revisionists therefore argue that Parliament was not really concerned about any perceived threat to the social and political fabric (there was little debate about such issues of criminal justice when Parliament sat) and the 'Bloody Code' has been misinterpreted.

QUESTION BREAK: THE 'BLOODY CODE'

Argue the case for and against the view that the 'Bloody Code' was a clear piece of 'class legislation'.

THE BIRTH OF THE PRISON – THE LATE EIGHTEENTH CENTURY AND BEYOND

The late eighteenth and early nineteenth centuries represented a turning point of great importance in punishment practices in Britain. Capital punishment declined in incidence and public displays of hangings and ritual disembowelment were abandoned after centuries of practice. The public assault on the body of criminals was traditionally accepted as necessary to display the power and majesty of the socio-political system and especially to broadcast the limitless capacity of the monarchy to exercise ultimate control over life and death. This theatre of punishment had the most serious objective: the social control of the masses by example. Yet the plan could misfire. Folk heroes on the scaffold could invite attempts at rescue or give a volatile crowd the opportunity to express opposition to the very forces of law demonstrated there. More frequently, the executions were occasions for the mixing of people from all walks of life and the melodrama of death was often reinforced by impassioned speeches from the condemned. They attributed their downfall to drink, women or their own idleness and misfortune and expressed their regret and penitence whilst warning others who might be tempted to follow in their footsteps. A successful scaffold oration brought public acclamation to the condemned and a 'good end' was applauded and remembered in ballad and broadsheet. Copies of famous 'last words' were very popular and sold widely in the eighteenth century.

Yet by the late eighteenth century public execution as a spectacle was being questioned. By the 1820s, after much debate, punishment was rationalized and was moved behind closed doors. It was a period of the rise of the modern prison, the establishment of the 'new' police and debates about the role of incarceration rather than execution dominated contemporary debate. The issues were given greater urgency by the disappearance of the option of transportation as the American colonies gained their independence and rising concerns about the cost of maintaining a penal colony in Australia led to the eventual abolition of transportation. Imprisonment in hulks tied in southern coastal waters was increasing by the 1790s as the transportation option receded. This in fact unwittingly constituted the first phase in the move over to incarceration as a major feature of public penal policy. Although the abandonment of transportation was not to be official policy until 1868, opposition to transportation had been mounting for some time as concerns over the efficacy of such punishment were added to the financial issues. This is discussed later when the philosophy of punishment in the emergent modern state of the nineteenth century is considered.

Calls for the reform of punishment, a less severe penal code and a more humane and rational system of punishment appeared in the historical literature. In particular, the origins of modern criminology can be traced to Cesare Beccaria's *Essay on Crimes and Punishment* published in 1764. Beccaria attacked uncontrolled use of execution as misconceived. For him, the severity of punishment should be governed by the nature of the crime rather than the criminal and punishment should be sufficient for deterrence and based on rational grounds comprehensible to the public. The assumption in this 'Classical Theory of Criminality' was that crime was the result of individual, rational choice and that the best policy was crime prevention rather than arbitrary and severe punishment. Such prevention would best be achieved by condemning the offender to hard physical labour in order to deter future offenders. Such theories were very much part of the period known as the Enlightenment and Beccaria's rational approach to these issues was in keeping with the views of English reformers like William Eden, Samuel Romilly, John Howard and Elizabeth Fry (who attempted to reform conditions facing women prisoners in Newgate). It was Howard, campaigning in the 1770s and 1780s, who was responsible for the spread of the idea for the penitentiary as the preferred alternative to execution and the rise of the modern prison dates from this period of debate and reform. A follower of Beccarian philosophy was Jeremy Bentham whose utilitarian approach to punishment involved the prison as a means of constant surveillance. His Panopticon of 1791 was a plan for such a prison and, although never built, it represents the changing nature of the debate about appropriate punishment. Of importance for the new philosophy was Bentham's proposal that new prisons be financed by the labour of prisoners who, it was hoped, would calculate that it was wiser to avoid offending rather than submit to such a prison regime. (See also pp. 218–219.)

Traditional interpretations of the rise of the prison in the nineteenth century (Radzinowicz 1968, and more recently McGowan 1998) as a departure from the barbarism of earlier punishment regimes are described as 'whiggish' models of explanation. Here the prison is seen as the result of humanitarian reform and part of a whole package of advances in social reform that would lead to the greater welfare reforms of the twentieth century and the concept of the modern welfare state. Such an approach does not really withstand critical, or historical, scrutiny. Howard's reforming zeal and the ideals of Elizabeth Fry were not confirmed by subsequent policy and the ideal of the humanitarian reformation of the prisoner remained a theoretical ideal to those responsible for administering Victorian prisons. Ignatieff (1978), in particular, has critically assessed the work of the 'humanitarians' as merely an alternative method of securing a more effective control. Regulated prisons were a more efficient means of securing offenders.

French philosopher Michel Foucault has provided a radical interpretation of these developments. His major work in this area is *Discipline and Punish: The Birth of the Modern Prison*, published in 1977. Foucault suggests that a 'carceral society' was being established and that it required that punishment be moved away from the public arena. The change occurred gradually but the public ritual of execution was replaced by the greater subtleties of institutionalized punishment. For Foucault, the prison was one of many institutions created in the nineteenth century in order to develop a matrix of control that transmitted and circulated discourses of conformity and power that were internalized by the masses. Here the focus is on imprisonment but as well as penitentiaries, mental institutions, hospitals, workhouses, night refuges, monitorial schools and factories were, for Foucault, part of a complex that ensured the control of the body and the subjection of the mind in what are called 'power–knowledge' matrices that manipulated the masses. For Foucault, prisons demonstrated power over the mind and body and were concrete representations of social division and the normalizing of incarceration as a means of social control (see pp. 274–282).

Foucault's analysis includes what at first seems the odd claim that the prison, as it developed in the nineteenth century, actually failed to achieve its goal of reforming offenders. Foucault, however, claims that this failure was actually a central part of the state's penal strategy. In effect tolerated recidivism would mean the continued recycling of offenders through prison and back to society. The state prison would be publicly legitimized as the defender of the community as it acted to incarcerate the 'dangerous classes'. The masses, therefore, could be 'provoked' (a key Foucauldian concept) into obedience. In this way the Victorian state, officially bounded by liberal principles of laissez faire and the ideology of the minimalist nature of state intervention into the lives of its citizens, could extend the administration and rationalization of the emerging prison system.

Foucault does not identify a specific source of power and control. Marxists (Rusche and Kirchheimer for example), however, regard the prison as a function of industrialization with the precise aim of controlling the labour force in the interests of the capitalist class. In this view capitalists created the prison as a factory of repression to hold a reserve army of labour ready to be used as the business cycle dictated. Thus the prison was part of an apparatus of social control and discipline that preserved the dominance of the bourgeoisie. Indeed, the CJS, as an institution, was part of the 'superstructure' of society used by the bourgeoisie to ensure control and support of the masses as a defence of industrial capitalism. Here too, however, the failure of the prison to eradicate crime completely was not necessarily catastrophic as fear of crime and recidivist (working-class) criminals would divide the working classes as they feared for their own security. Thus they would become more dependent than ever on the paternalist bourgeois state. It is central to Marxist thinking that the criminal justice system is required to endorse a capitalist social structure. Criminal justice is designed to protect property, control the labouring masses and preserve the class hierarchy.

Michael Ignatieff explained the coming of the modern prison as a new disciplinary strategy emerging in the early nineteenth century following disillusionment with the effectiveness of traditional rituals of public punishment. Ignatieff's is not a Marxist perspective but he does see the prison as a successful exercise in social control as elites responded to fears of crime waves and social disruption in a period of dramatic economic, social and political change between 1780 and 1850. Ignatieff feels that the prison was not just an attempt to control crime. There are links with ideas of class power and discourses of social control but Ignatieff adopts a revisionist stance in that he avoids Marxists notions of determinism and focuses on the process of reform in its social context.

> The persistent support for the penitentiary is inexplicable so long as we assume that its appeal rested on its functional capacity to control crime. Instead, its support rested on a larger social need. It had appeal because the reformers succeeded in presenting it as a response, not merely to crime, but to the whole social crisis of a period, and as a part of a larger strategy of political, social and legal reform designed to re-establish order on a new foundation. As a result — the penitentiary continued to command support because it was seen as an element of a larger vision of order that by the 1840s commanded the reflexive assent of the propertied and powerful.
>
> (Ignatieff 1978: 210)

The transformation of punishment policy in Britain was extensive. The 1779 Penitentiary Act began the building of new prisons in London and Millbank Prison with a capacity for 1,000 inmates was opened in 1816. Peel's Gaol Act of 1823 attempted to impose uniform standards of administration and inspection across the country and to improve the health and treatment of prisoners. The culmination of reform was the opening of Pentonville in 1842 (see p. 436). As we have seen, such reform can be explained as the result of the efforts of social reformers such as John Howard and William Eden and the humanitarian impulses of the day. However, Ignatieff's explanation is more radical. He dismisses Whiggish notions of humanitarian reform and emphasizes the importance of social control theories. Ignatieff places his explanation for the rise of the prison firmly in the context of nineteenth-century social and economic upheavals. Social peace and stability were perceived by both traditional, landed elites and the new-rich factory owners and capitalists to be endangered. Such powerful opinion makers, including many middle-class property owners, saw what they felt to be the critical balance of classes that had once secured social stability directly threatened. The spread of industrialization, increased population growth and movement, growing urbanization, the impact of faster travel as the railways were laid from 1830, changes to the labour market and the increase in the volatility of labour relations were forces that posed new questions about social control. There were transformations in the social structure as the period saw what the social historian E. P. Thompson has called 'The Making of the English Working Class'.

Other social historians have also used the concept of Social Control to explain the transformation in penal policy as the product of the tensions between social classes. Garland (1985) explains penal policy in the Victorian period to 1890 as the outcome of a growing concern of the state, and those classes who directed it, to control a mix of targeted communities. Such groups were the stuff of innumerable Victorian panics throughout the period and included the working classes, the poor, the criminal, the 'alien' (Irish especially), the prostitute, the unemployed and the itinerant. Garland sees the incarceration of such groups as an example of social control policy founded upon contemporary ideas of a moral divide. Those classes beneath respectability were morally bankrupt at best and criminally dangerous at worst. The respectable part of the working class could be saved by the Methodist Mission, The Savings Bank, Mechanics' Institutes and Samuel Smiles' gospel of 'self-help'. Those beneath constituted an underclass requiring control and incarceration. Garland writes:

> [There was] a definite gulf between 'respectable' and 'rough' elements of the working classes, a separation clearly understood by the individuals involved . . . This division, and the respectable life-styles, responsible opinions and respectful attitudes that it upheld, were the major achievements of the forces of discipline and moralisation. The practices of penality, the poor law, the charities and so on ensured that these divisions were maintained by the threat of punishment or pauperisation for those who traversed the moral divide. But this separation once established, was by no means secure. . . . There was thus a continuing problem of containment and quarantine. Once concentrated in this small class, criminality and its related vices had to be kept there, within its fixed and manageable bounds.
> (Garland 1985: 39)

Clearly, the prison and the 'new' police as they developed from 1830 represented the strengthening of the power of the modern state and its legal-rational, legitimate force.

The state was equipped with the power to control its own population in the interests of social stability and the defence of the constitution.

THE POLICE AND THE EMERGENCE OF THE CRIMINAL JUSTICE SYSTEM

The creation of the police was a major development in the evolution of the nineteenth-century Criminal Justice System. Robert Peel's Metropolitan Police Act of 1829 is often seen as a seminal act in the formation of the modern penal system. The state's 'legitimate force' registered the strength of what Max Weber, the pioneering German sociologist, termed its 'legal-rational authority'. The historians of the 'new police' (Emsley 1996a and Phillips 1983) have shown there is debate about its significance. For the traditional school, the police were a legitimate response to the growth of urban unrest and the criminal tendencies of the masses during an era of revolutionary economic and industrial change. There was also the danger of political revolution after the end of the Napoleonic Wars in 1815. These are the views of Whiggish, conservative historians who celebrate the development of institutions of state control as evidence for the growth of Britain's 'civilized society'. Representative of this view is the work of Charles Reith and Leon Radzinowicz. Peel was lionized as the man who had brought efficiency and control to an outdated system reliant on part-time parish constables and aged watchmen. Such an interpretation is also linked to triumphalist views of the police as the guarantor of the British constitution and its ability to guarantee freedom and democracy. Revisionist work (for example, Robert Storch, 1975), suggests a different story. Here the police are seen as the representatives of economic elites who are determined to control the masses in the interests of the existing power relations. Storch quoted contemporary, working-class views of the new police as a 'plague of blue locusts' determined to enforce new laws which restricted not only the political radicalism of the masses but also their cultural and sporting 'excesses' in the interests of the preservation of a subservient labour force. E. P. Thompson (1985) has written persuasively of assaults by elites on the 'moral economy' of the English crowd. This meant that the authorities were determined to remove the right of demonstration that had been a tradition in working-class communities when grievances (in Thompson's research it was outrage at high grain prices) were considered important enough for public display. Hobsbawm (1964) refers to the expression of working-class industrial grievances using 'collective bargaining by riot'. The police, in effect, were an ideal instrument of class hegemony, acting as 'domestic missionaries' as they tightened supervision of the unruly. This view has been endorsed by Marxists, who saw the police as no more than the agents of a coercive, bourgeois state. However, ideas of 'hegemony' and social control are by no means unproblematic. There is no real evidence of a coherent, identifiable elite class acting to extend police control over town and village in their own class interests. Indeed, there was hostility to the police as 'continental despotism' amongst the middle and professional classes. In many provincial areas widespread resistance to the 'new police' meant that a force was not established until decades after Peel's metropolitan experiment. Neither is there unequivocal evidence of consistent and united working-class opposition to the police as 'blue locusts'. Again, this is not without debate; while Emsley (1996a) does accept that violent clashes between policemen and working class communities occurred with frequency, he also points out that:

> it would be wrong to conceive of the relationship between the working class and the police in the second half of the 19th century as entirely one of mutual hostility. Many members of the working class also sought respectability and desired orderliness and decorum. It is probable that . . . the appearance of the police on the streets increasingly led members of the working class to believe that they too had the right to freedom from the annoyance of crime and public disorder.
>
> (Emsley 1996a: 80)

QUESTION BREAK

- Why would members of the working classes fear the 'new police' as a 'plague of blue locusts'?
- How convincing are the views of orthodox historians of crime and justice who see the 'new police' as no more than a justifiable response to the rise of illegality in a society increasingly out of control?
- Summarize the main different schools of thought on the creation of the 'new police'.

The twentieth century witnessed the growing centralization of the administration of the police force as local watch committees and police authorities found themselves by-passed as the technical and financial demands of policing escalated. The advent of the motor car and the steady rise in crime after the Second World War were just two factors which enforced rationalization and central control. The Desborough Committee of 1919 was a significant step towards rationalization and the process was strengthened by the demands of the wartime emergency from 1939 to 1945 and perceptions of threats to social order in the post-war period represented by growing trade union militancy and urban unrest.

For the sociologist Max Weber, the nineteenth century was a period in which the modern state developed and he pointed particularly to the role of bureaucracy as evidence for the emergence of modern state apparatuses and the extension of legitimized state powers. Social control, and its agencies in the police and criminal justice system, has been the subject of a series of important studies by historians and criminologists (see Stanley Cohen and Andrew Scull 1985, Michael Ignatieff 1978 for example). Whilst acknowledging that simplistic notions of a crude 'class hegemony' or polarity of classes do little to further understanding the complexity of nineteenth-century society, they defend the concept of social control as an important element driving public penal policy.

The work of Gareth Stedman Jones has reinforced the social control model. His *Outcast London* shows how the authorities responded to what was perceived by the

1880s as a floodtide of dangerous classes, a social residuum before which civilized society faced destruction. This is a recurrent theme in a period which, as discussed above, witnessed the triumph of the coercive and retributitive ideal. As Stedman Jones explains:

> (i) The social crisis of London in the mid-1880s engendered a major reorientation of middle class attitudes towards the casual poor. In conjunction with the growing anxiety about the decline of Britain's industrial supremacy, apprehensions about the depopulation of the countryside and uncertainty about the future political role of the working classes, fear of the casual residuum played a significant part in the intellectual assault against laissez faire . . . in the 1880s.
>   (ii) The counterpart to the wooing of the respectable working class . . . was the espousal of a more coercive interventionist policy towards the 'residuum'. The residuum was far too great a threat to be left to natural forces and the poor law . . . At a time when the residuum might overrun London, this policy of laissez faire was dangerous.
>
> (Stedman-Jones 1986: (i) 296–7, (ii) 303)

The Poor Law Amendment Act of 1834 (the 'new' poor law) and the Prisons Act of 1865 (the most important Act determining prison policy in the nineteenth century) provide good examples of official sanctions given to the principle of 'less eligibility'. Workhouses and prisons were to be institutions where the regime was to be made worse than the conditions experienced by the lowest-paid labourers outside. In prisons, the dominant penal option, the regime was dominated by the control of time, silent routines, solitary confinement and meticulous controls over diet, medical treatment, clothing and movement. Repetitive work having no ostensible value or outcome was a requirement. The treadmill and the endless 'oakum picking' (separating the strands in large pieces of old, thick, rope) were to impress upon the prisoner the value of obedience and of a disciplined and rigorous use of time. Such a measure of control over body and mind, frequently endorsed by the prison chaplain using the exhortations of the Christian religion was, nevertheless, regarded as a means of correcting the inmates. The focus was on the 'micro-control' of the individual who was to be treated the same as everybody else. Penality was certainly not individualized but the 'disciplinary gaze' (as Foucault put it) of the institutions of control established a process of 'individuation' as each prisoner was wrapped in the total embrace of the penal institution.

The mid-nineteenth-century state made no commitment to provide comprehensive, universal social support or provide for the rehabilitation of prisoners. The philosophy was summed up in an important government investigation of the prison system in 1863 when the Carnarvon Commission stressed the value of deterrence over any ideas of rehabilitation or reformation of the prisoner. It was this philosophy that was to dominate penal policy until the end of the century. As Carnarvon put it:

> The large majority of criminals were low and brutish 'mainly swayed by self-gratification and animal appetite'. It followed that such brutes must be managed physically: 'the enforcement of continuous labour, which the true criminal abhors,

and an uninviting diet which is unquestionably the odious penalty in his eyes . . .
Self-gratifying instincts should be foiled by withholding all indulgences and diver-
sions such as secular books, slates [i.e. writing materials], hammocks and the like.
(Comments of the Earl of Carnarvon, quoted in
McLaughlin and Muncie 1996: 186)

The Prison Act of 1877 secured the control of the prison service in the hands of
central government and finally removed the vestiges of local autonomy in the penal
practice. As such it was an important recognition of the powers of the emergent,
modern state apparatus. Also in 1877 the new Prison Commissioner was Edward
Du Cane and this appointment firmly removed the rehabilitative ideal from British
prison policy and replaced it with the harsh reality of 'discipline and punish'. Penal
policy remained the perfect complement to ideas of economic liberalism, free trade
and the minimalist free state so idealized by followers of laissez faire principles. The
criminal was seen as an individual freely deciding to adopt criminality as a way of
life. The prison was in place to reprocess the individual, to re-establish his (prisoners
were predominantly male) contract with society. Crime was a product of an individual
pathology and not something to be seen in a social, economic or cultural context. This
is very much like the neo-liberal sentiments expressed in government circles during
the Thatcher administrations of the 1980s and which are still a central part of 'right
realism' or 'rational choice theory' in the criminology of today.

The strength of the retributive school was also explained by popular reaction to a
series of moral panics. There were concerns about the behaviour of veterans recently
returned from the Crimean War and in 1862 the garrotting of an MP in London
brought immediate legislation in the form of the 'Garrotter's Act' of 1863 which
brought back flogging and introduced tougher sentences for robbery. The *Cornhill
Magazine* wrote of a great 'public dread [that] has almost become a panic' and some
historians have used such evidence to accept without question that a substantial
increase in crime occurred that justified such a legislative response. Tobias, for example, wrote that 'The streets of London were dangerous places, day and night . . . and
many people carried arms. . . . Though London was the main centre of the criminal
class, it was by no means the only one' (1967: 139–40).

QUESTION BREAK

Read the following extracts and consider how they can help to understand the
development of the prison and/or penality in the nineteenth century. Try to
relate them to the theoretical perspectives considered in the previous section.

Extract 1: Wormwood Scrubs, 24 September 1860

Shaving Prisoners. Ordered: That no prisoner should be allowed to shave
himself. He must be shaved by an officer, or, by another prisoner in the

presence of the officer. With regard to prisoners for trial or under remand GREAT CARE must be taken by the officer that the appearance of the prisoner be not altered by such shaving.

E. J. Jonas. Governor.

Extract 2: The Misconduct Book, Pentonville Prison, 24 June, 1863

Name: Edward Hughes

Offences for which reported: Receiving a Communication in Chapel [i.e. talking in the prison chapel]
    Continually laughing and talking at exercise after being cautioned, and calling the officer a liar on leaving the Governor's office.
    Having thread in his possession
    Persistent talking in his cell
    Remarks [i.e. Punishment] Exercise in Round Yard and 6 days on bread and water.
    Dark Cell/Close Confinement [i.e. Solitary Punishment Cell] and forfeit badges [i.e. privileges]. All remission lost. To be sent to Dartmoor.

Extract 3: Licence Papers, 19 October 1853

Name: ——————————— William Young
Licence: ——————————— No. 23
Complexion: ————————— Fresh
Hair: ——————————————— Light
Eyes: ————————————— Grey
Height: ———————————— 5 feet 2½ inches
Scars, Cuts, Moles
And Marks on Body and Limbs ——————————— Round Full Face, Feet Flat
Description ——————————— Moderately Stout
Received at Wakefield 2nd May 1850
Removed from Wakefield 13th March 1851
Received at Portland Prison from Wakefield 14th March 1851
Received at York Hulk from Portland 20th May 1852
Removed to Portsmouth Prison 13th May 1853 from Sterling Castle hulk
Portsmouth Prison 13th May 1853
Licenced [sic] 19th October 1853

Extract 4: Examples of Sentencing

(i) 5th September 1855: Edmund Dowding charged with stealing dried cut grass worth 2 pence. Punishment 10 days' hard labour in the County House of Correction (Wiltshire)

(ii) 2nd January 1845: At Maidstone Quarter Sessions, Thomas Groves charged with stealing clothes. Punishment 7 years.

(iii) 27th June 1831: Joseph Clayton alias Cary charged with stealing an ass sentenced in Nottingham to 7 years. Character bad. Been convicted before. Connexions indifferent.

(iv) 26th January 1874: Ellen Berrett, aged 13 years, charged at Trowbridge with stealing a pig's foot from a bakehouse. Sentence 14 days' hard labour in the Common Gaol and 2 years in a Reformatory School.

(v) 25th January 1873: James Leadbetter ('Aged 11 years, 4 ft. 1 3/4 inches tall, brown hair and eyes, single and without occupation. Scar on forehead and on right shoulder') charged with stealing celery and convicted. Sentence: imprisonment for 4 days with hard labour. Previously convicted for stealing pears and given 7 days' hard labour.

Extract 5: The Reverend Sydney Smith, c. 1840

We should banish all the looms in Preston jail and substitute nothing but the tread-wheel, or the capstan, or some species of labour where the labourer could not see the results of his toil, – where it was monotonous, irksome, and as dull as possible, – pulling and pushing, instead of reading and writing, – no share of the profits – not a single shilling. There should be no tea and sugar – nothing but beating hemp and pulling oakum and pounding bricks, – no work but what was tedious, [and] unusual.

Extract 6: Contemporary Views of the London Working Class as Threat c.1867

No-one who lived in the suburbs could help feeling that they were in circumstances of considerable peril. (Thomas Beggs)

What could a force of 8,000 or 9,000 police be against the 150,000 roughs and ruffians, whom, on some sufficient exciting occasion, the Metropolis might see arrayed against law and order? (The Reverend Henry Solley)

Extracts 1–4 are taken from D. T. Hawkings, 1992.
Extract 5 is from U. R. Q. Henriques, 1979, p. 169.
Extract 6 is from G. Stedman-Jones, 1984, pp. 242–3.

TWENTIETH-CENTURY DEVELOPMENTS

By 1895 the fears of a social crisis had reached boiling point and the regime of deterrence and harsh sentencing imposed by Du Cane was being seriously questioned. There was concern that the disciplinary approach was not working and the 'dangerous classes' remained a serious source of anxiety. The middle classes especially felt that the state had not removed the threats to social stability represented by the 'casual poor' and 'criminal classes'. A change of philosophy was to be registered by the 1895 Gladstone Committee on Prisons. This endorsed a more rehabilitative system that would seek to treat prisoners as individuals in need of some support. Deterrence was not completely abandoned but it was to be complemented by treatment and a degree of consideration for the individual. This was a radical move away from the tenets of laissez faire and the traditional belief that offenders should be classified as rational beings who deserved to be subject to a strict, attritional control regime in prison. These changes were also the result of far-reaching developments in Britain's economy and society. Uncertainty followed the realization that UK economic growth was in decline and that rising foreign competition, principally from Germany and the USA, endangered traditional export markets upon which depended the core of the country's industrial structure and employment. The long-term decline in profits during the 'Great Depression' (1873–96) and the growth of unions for the unskilled that adopted militant and socialist tactics seemed to threaten social stability. Large-scale industry and the appearance of monopolies and cartels meant the end of the classical free market based on free trade and competition. The shocking extent of poverty and the appalling living conditions in Britain's cities revealed by the social investigations of Booth and Rowntree at the end of the nineteenth century (they showed that over 30 per cent of urban dwellers existed beneath the lowest of poverty lines) added to the sense of impending disaster. In such circumstances there had to be an attempt to treat the social crisis. The inner city as a site of criminality and 'deviant', transient communities had received particular focus in the researches of the Chicago School of Sociology from 1892. Under its pioneer director Robert Park the School a singled out the centre of cities (research was carried out in Chicago itself) as run-down 'zones of transition' as a source of criminality. Such was the first experiment in 'environmental criminology' (see pp. 106–108).

The exposure of such urban degradation led to an increasing acceptance that the state should intervene more directly and tackle social problems. More directly, social reform was also the product of the realization by politicians that any retention of political power required extensions to social policy in order to assuage the demands of a growing electorate that could be attracted by socialism and the new political parties and groups on the left. Additionally, there were continued concerns over racial degeneration. Social policy, including criminal justice, was strongly influenced by the new, now discredited, science of eugenics. This meant that legislators felt it necessary to improve the 'quality of the race' by more careful state intervention in the interest of health, welfare and, as far as criminal offenders were concerned, rehabilitation. Lloyd George, the politician identified with 'New Liberalism' and the introduction of National Insurance, felt that 'you can't run an A1 empire with a C3 population.' Of the recruits for the British Army about to fight the Boer War in 1900, one in three were rejected as medically unfit. This was at a time when the army, in the absence of conscription, was not over-fussy about its recruits' physical capabilities. The investigation was significantly called 'The Report of the Committee on Physical Deterioration' (1904). In an age of increasing international tension and economic competition, 'national efficiency' was an important watchword.

There was particular concern over the failure of the prison to solve the problems of criminality. The prison itself had become a source of the problem of recidivism. Novice offenders could emerge from prison as hardened criminals who had benefited from contact with experienced, career inmates. In 1880, Sir William Harcourt, Home Secretary, wrote to the Queen. Using what must be the earliest reference to what was to become labelling theory, he referred to a group of boys (one was a 'small, delicate boy who can neither read nor write') and girls between 10 and 13 originally imprisoned for innocuous offences such as 'damaging grass by running about in the fields' or 'bathing in the canal'. Harcourt wrote:

> Protracted imprisonment in such cases has an injurious effect both upon the physical and moral nature of children of tender years. The child who has been guilty of only some . . . thoughtless prank which does not partake of the real character of crime finds himself committed with adult criminals guilty of heinous offences to the common gaol. After a week or a fortnight's imprisonment he comes out of prison tainted in character amongst his former companions, with a mark of opprobrium [scorn] set upon him, and he soon lapses into the criminal class with whom he has been identified.
>
> (Harcourt quoted in Hawkings 1992: 34)

Given such concerns, there was, at the end of the nineteenth century, a redirection of penal practice. The transformation in policy was assisted by changes in the intellectual climate as Positivism began to dominate social thought and research. Important new theorists in the late nineteenth century such as Lombroso, Ferri and Garofalo showed that crime was not the product of individual choice but determined by forces within the offender and in society that were beyond the control of individual offenders. Durkheim had made similar breakthroughs in his classical study of suicide. Accepting the sociological and scientific context meant that 'criminals' could be 'cured' once they had been scientifically identified, weighed and analysed. Lombroso classified offenders according to physical characteristics and tried to show that certain human beings were 'throw-backs' to earlier, and less mature and sophisticated, human types and thus were 'born criminals'. His science was therefore based on the confirmation of atavistic tendencies in humans. If the science is controversial, Lombroso can, nevertheless, be called the father of modern criminology, and the founder of the most important developments in British penal practice in the twentieth century because of his concern to establish the understanding of criminality on scientific grounds. The policy implications were not at first clear. Lombroso's ideas of biological determinism and the eugenicist focus on the dangers of atavism led to calls for the cauterizing and isolation of criminals as a racial 'infection'. This would mean that the primary, and only, aim of punishment should be the removal of offenders from society and the 'gene pool'. Prisoners would be stockpiled and quarantined. However, in Britain the result of the positivist revolution was not to reduce the range of treatment but quite the opposite. It led away from the punitive to the emphasis on rehabilitation. It was here that the growth of alarm about the failures of the prison and the impact of the 1895 Gladstone Report had their effect. The Report stressed the need to classify inmates according to their needs. They should not be treated as an amorphous crowd of 'criminals' to be incarcerated and controlled. It had an important impact on criminal policy. Wiener (in 'Reconstructing the Criminal', 1990) has shown how the focus turned to rehabilitation and treatment and away from the traditionally punitive approach. Garland (in *Punishment and Modern Society*, 1990) has also emphasized how policy therefore moved away from Du Cane's harsh regime.

Instead of treating all offenders alike the penal system now introduced discrimination and special categories of prisoners were given separate treatment. An early example was the removal from general prisons of juvenile offenders. The Borstal Schools were made part of the state apparatus in 1908 and the Industrial Schools, which acted as a kind of reformatory for juveniles, were also incorporated in a centralized system that attempted to remove the vulnerable from the general prison and meet their particular needs. Thus education became an important part of the rehabilitative process before the First World War. Probation was accepted as a further sentencing option (The Probation of Offenders Act 1907) which was to be made more sensitive to the needs of the individual offender, and underpinned by the notion of rehabilitation. Similar reforms before 1914 led to the removal of the mentally ill into special hospitals such as Broadmoor and Rampton. The first prison specifically for women had been Brixton (opened in 1853) but the incarceration of women in large, mainstream prisons was discouraged by the beginning of the twentieth century. This has led one historian, Lucia Zedner, to suggest that the 'decriminalization of women' was occurring (1998). However, Zedner does agree that the movement of women into specialist institutions did not reduce their vulnerability to the controls imposed on them by a society dominated by male power brokers who accepted contemporary notions of female instability and dependence. Given dominant, patriarchal views of women's 'rightful' place in the home, their peripheral role in industry and the subsequent increase in surveillance and control, the reduced presence of women in the criminal statistics can be explained. It has been suggested that the criminal records do not reveal the true extent of the criminalization of women. Property offences involving women were often not considered in higher courts and Zedner has shown that if crimes of violence alone are examined, women were in fact the subject of one in three prosecutions.

Penal policy in the post First World War period saw the development of such 'new liberal' and progressive sentiments and the treadmill became a thing of the past. However, many writers, such as Rawlings (1999) and Muncie (1996), have rightly warned that classical theories of deterrence and punishment were not completely forgotten and that many institutions did not necessarily take the new philosophies of punishment to heart. In large public enterprises, policy could be dictated from the top but implemented in terms of deep-rooted local and traditional practice. Du Cane's successor as Chairman of the Prison Commission, Sir Evelyn Ruggles-Brise, worked until 1921 to implement the progressive policy but he ensured it was balanced by the retention of older, classical ideas of proportionality (i.e. make the punishment fit the crime) that had roots back to Beccaria. Penal strategies also retained their punitive element with the introduction of indeterminate sentences for offenders, which were based on the capacity of the prisoner to respond effectively to treatment. However, the issue here was the individual prisoner, not the offence.

Social reformers were unhappy with what they felt to be the limited impact of the Gladstone Report and the work of Ruggles-Brise, which, for radicals such as the Webbs, R. H. Tawney and Fenner Brockway, had not gone far enough. Alexander Paterson, a reforming member of the Prison Commission after the retirement of Ruggles-Brise, led prison policy between the wars and worked to establish more liberal and rehabilitative regimes. The 'separate system' was finally abandoned in favour of prisoner association and specialists were introduced, such as psychologists, probation officers, health and welfare specialists, to provide a framework of support for prisoners. As a result the prison was no longer as dominant in the Criminal Justice system as had been the case in the last 75 years of the nineteenth century. A whole raft of penal and non-penal experts had been brought in on the strength of the positivist revolution. Sentencing policy had been overhauled to reduce the severity of imprisonment (e.g. the concept of the minimum security or 'open' prison was established) in order to provide such support for prison inmates. The time in prison was now to be constructively used by the prisoner and the focus was moved to training, education and psychological strategies that would improve the chances of offenders making a successful return to the outside world.

Of course there are many interpretations of the changes Paterson and others brought in. Whig historians, we have seen, would view such changes as a tribute to the strengthening humanitarian impulses of the age, as the barbarities of the past were overcome by the more sophisticated and civilized procedures of the more informed modern era. This looks like an attractive model but unfortunately it is not good history. Apart from the assumption that the present is always superior to the past, it does not really show an understanding of historical change. Change is the subject of contradictory forces, and simplistic linear views of unimpeded progress are naive. Alternative approaches would see the rehabilitative ideal as no more than the evolution of a disciplinary society strengthened and disguised by its liberal façade. Foucault, Ignatieff and Marxist commentators have such a view, with the 'carceral society' and/or bourgeois control and manipulation of the masses seen as compelling features of modern society and reform and rehabilitation dismissed as cosmetic.

After 1945, there was a reinforcement of progressive agendas in many areas of social policy. The Beveridge Report of 1942 led to the Labour government's social democratic 'welfare state' being ready to use its resources to resolve social problems in the interest of all. These had their counterpart in the reforms of the criminal justice system. The Criminal Justice Act of 1948 finally abolished imprisonment with hard labour, extended the successful Borstal experiment and gave young offenders a further opportunity to avoid imprisonment when attendance centres were set up. In fact such centres were sites of retributive justice and what was later to be called the 'short, sharp shock'. However, by the mid-1960s, the progressive era inaugurated by the Gladstone Report in 1895 was coming to an end. The 1960s brought further changes, including the decriminalization of homosexuality, divorce and abortion law reform, the abolition of capital punishment and attempts to further distance young offenders from conventional prison sentences through the extension of care facilities. However, there were signs that the progressivism did not enjoy unqualified acceptance, as laws against drug taking were strengthened and immigration was increasingly the subject of restriction.

Classical theories of penalty based on notions of deterrence and rehabilitation were set for a renaissance because, despite the millions spent on welfare reform and the widespread belief that the economy was improving living standards, the crime statistics for the post-war period climbed and climbed. As the 1960s closed it became clear that once more society was threatened by economic problems, a decline in British power and authority in the world and increasing social unrest at home. Classical theories of deterrence were always beneath the surface and they now seemed justified as the research into criminality seemed to show the inability of progressive policies to reduce crime. The welfare state had not secured social democracy and 'freedom': instead its right-wing enemies saw it as producing a dependency culture funded by excessive public spending which in turn failed to address problems of rising crime. There were moral panics in the 1970s about black criminals and street muggings, race riots, 'wildcat' strikes, drugs, prison unrest and, in the 1980s, what seemed to be unprecedented outbursts of civil disorder in Britain's cities. The scene was set for a lurch to the right as the Thatcher and Major administrations of 1979–97 followed a populist course, reimposing traditional understandings of crime and the state's right to retributive justice. Thatcher famously summed up this attitude stating, 'A Crime is a Crime is a Crime' and calls for the harsh treatment of 'criminals' became a regular manifesto reference. Successive Conservative Home Secretaries claimed that prison was effective (Michael Howard in 1993 declared 'Prison works!') and the numbers incarcerated climbed annually. Calls for the return of capital punishment and longer prison sentences were annual events at Conservative Party conferences and were notably endorsed by Home Secretary Waddington in 1990. Here was a 'crisis of penology' as criminologists seemed at a loss to explain rising crime and progressive agendas were overtaken by populist rhetoric. Important sociologists and criminologists such as Jock Young were, by 1986, lamenting the 'failure of criminology' as they noted the rise of right-wing, conservative penal agendas in Britain and the USA that had resulted from the campaigns for punitive justice successfully carried out by Margaret Thatcher and President Reagan. Young felt that 'The demise of positivism and social democratic ways of reforming crime has been rapid, [ensuring] "a silent revolution"' (Young 1996: 442).

Certainly, in the 1990s regular Criminal Justice Acts (1991, 1993, 1994 and 1997) dismantled enlightened policy as prison sentences were increased and non-custodial sentences (tagging, Community Service) were either increasingly neglected or underfunded. A large programme of prison building was started. The Labour Party attracted electoral support as it too showed its adoption in 1997 of the retributive ideal with the slogan 'Tough on crime and tough on the causes of crime'. Edmund du Cane would have been pleased. From 1946 to 1999 the prison population quadrupled from 15,000 to 60,000. In 1993, the average prison population was 44,570. By 2000, it was over 64,500 with Britain having the second highest incarceration rate in Europe at 124 per 100,000 population. (Portugal had the highest at 127.) In 2010, the prison population was projected as 85,700 (Home Office Statistical

Directorate). Overcrowding has become a serious issue that has led to prison riots. It seemed that by the end of the twentieth century conservative, populist policies of retributive justice had become irresistible to all parties.

QUESTION BREAK

- Why do you think the rehabilitative ideal failed to survive in the post-war period?
- Examine the reasons for the 'unprecedented' rise in the prison population in the last years of the twentieth century.
- Identify the similarities and contrasts evident between the repressive regimes of the pre-1895 era and the more punitive Criminal Justice System of the late twentieth century.

GENDER

State-centred studies of the changing administration, philosophy and ideology of punishment ignore the ways in which different groups of the population are affected by the criminal justice system, and can lead to neglect of the important issues of gender and ethnicity. A central premise of the British criminal justice system, and one that has been maintained for centuries, is that women represent a special pathological case. Female 'deviance' had been the reason for the vicious attacks on women accused of witchcraft in sixteenth- and seventeenth-century England. Ecclesiastical courts and state legislators particularly identified women who refused to respect contemporary norms of gendered behaviour that required them to be submissive and confined to their 'domestic' duties. For Keith Thomas (1978), in his study of witchcraft, the real discourse the 'witch' was attacked for was her nonconformist behaviour in highly structured and gendered rural communities where eccentricity was considered unacceptable. He writes:

> She [the witch] was the extreme example of the malignant or non-conforming person against whom the local community had always taken punitive action in the interests of social harmony . . .
>
> The old woman who had taken recourse to malignant threats in her extremity was therefore liable to pay a high price for the consolation they afforded her . . . Quite apart from the risk of prosecution the suspected witch might be ostracised [shunned] by her neighbours [and she] . . . was also liable to informal acts of violence. The 94 year old Agnes Fenn alleged in 1604 that after she was accused of witchcraft, Sir Thomas Gosse had punched, pricked and struck her, threatened her with firebrands and gunpowder, and finally stabbed her in the face with a knife.
>
> (Thomas 1978: 632–3)

What Thomas does not consider is that the use of violence and legal sanctions against women classed as witches was the product of a patriarchal society's demonization of women. Witchcraft provided church, parish and state with the ideal opportunity to legitimize male bastions of power and use women as an 'alien other' against which patriarchy could strengthen and prevail. When disaster occurred, 'Women's bodies were the instruments for exorcising political and social evils, establishing the power of institutions, and for the symbolic marking of boundaries of appropriate female behaviour' (Dobash *et al.* 1986: 18).

Discourses, or unquestioned assumptions about what was 'right and proper', held that women were subordinate creatures whose roles were prescribed by their ability to produce the next generation and act in the domestic sphere as wives, cooks, cleaners and mothers. Women who attempted to reject these roles were targeted as dangerous and in need of further control and restraint. Accusations of sorcery and witchcraft were ideal ways to enforce the discourse of male superiority.

Assumptions of female dependence and inferiority have become institutionalized within the criminal justice system. Examples over the last three hundred years can illustrate this. Women were often held in houses of correction that were required to instil in them subservience to their parents or husbands. Women caught stepping out beyond their 'domestic' role were dealt with sharply. They were assumed to be either insane or potential prostitutes. Female thieves, murderers and beggars could expect harsh sentences and it was common for such women to be hanged, transported or incarcerated for long periods. The exception was where the offence was in some way excusable as a desperate attempt by a woman to maintain her given station in life.

BOX 9.1 WOMEN CRIMINALS IN THE EIGHTEENTH CENTURY

Case 1

Anne Flynn Convicted of Robbery in 1750. She had stolen a shoulder of mutton but the court was affected by her defence that her husband was desperately ill and her two infant children starving. The Court recognised she had already been confined for 2 weeks, fined her one shilling. The jury decided to pay the fine!

Case 2

Mary Young (or 'Jenny Diver') was charged with pickpocketing and hanged in 1740. Mary had been a thief for years and had twice escaped execution when transported. The nickname 'Jenny Diver' was slang for prostitute. Most women indicted were assumed to be prostitutes as well.

Case 3

Hannah Webley convicted in 1794 for the murder of her infant son. She was hanged. She was unmarried and aged 16 years. The judge said:

> Hannah Webley, you have been convicted of a most cruel and unnatural murder. So far were you led on by fear of a discovery of your shame, as first to curse and then deprive an helpless infant of life: by this wicked act your own life is forfeited . . . You must now suffer a severe punishment for your crime . . . [which] dreadful as it is will be an instructive lesson to the female part of creation, and convince them that those who swerve from the paths of virtue will be tempted to the commission of the worst of crimes. I also hope that your punishment will be a lesson to those young men who artfully endeavour to seduce young women from the paths of virtue.

(The cases are taken from the Newgate Calendars and reprinted in Moore (2000) pp. 112, 101–2 and 56–8 respectively.)

In cases 2 and 3 above the accused woman had 'swerved from the paths of virtue' and had become targeted as particularly dangerous therefore. In case 1 the woman was attempting to look after her family and this was seen as an attempt to continue to conform to the prescribed role of the female as home-maker so leniency was the result. Interestingly, poor Hannah Webley's death was to act as a lesson for men who were responsible for the damage to that essential guarantee of society's stability: women securely committed to the 'paths of virtue'.

In the eighteenth and nineteenth centuries, courts were reluctant to convict women for infanticide. Research has shown that at Surrey Assizes one such offence was tried every 18 months in the eighteenth century. However, juries were not so ready to convict. The reason is unclear unless a heightened sympathy for such women as the 'weaker sex' is the explanation. Juries often sympathized with women in severe distress whose poverty was a major factor in the death of a child. Cases of infanticide fell considerably in the nineteenth century. Modern sentencing of women is certainly affected by such stereotypical ideas of women as naturally caring beings, unlike the strong, aggressive male. Unfortunately, for Hannah Webley, no such notions affected her treatment by the courts.

The execution of women in the twentieth century in Britain has been the subject of some interesting research by Annette Ballinger who studied the execution of 15 women for murder in Britain between 1900 and 1955 (2000). It is clear from her work that if the reluctance to execute women for infanticide persists into the modern era, by contrast women guilty of murdering an adult were more likely to be hanged than men who had committed a similar offence. The reason is that such women demonstrated an unsuitability for the 'motherly', caring image that men demanded. As Ballinger notes:

The mere fact that a woman has broken the law ensures that she will be regarded as someone who has failed to fulfil gender role expectations, and if this is overlaid by a refusal to demonstrate her commitment to conventional female roles in her personal life, especially in the areas around sexuality, respectability, domesticity and motherhood, she can expect to find herself at the receiving end of the full force of . . . 'judicial misogyny'. [i.e. hatred of women] [Women murders] fell victim to cultural misogyny in general and judicial misogyny in particular.

(Ballinger 2000: 3)

Outside of murder and judicial execution, public, physical punishment of women classed as 'scolds', 'slanderers' or responsible for the cuckolding of their husbands included the stocks, the ducking (or 'cucking') stool and ritual, communal shaming. Men subjected to nagging and shrewish or disobedient wives, or those dominated in any way by their spouses, could take comfort in local custom, often reinforced at law, which would reimpose the male sanction. The wearing of a bridle or mask in the seventeenth century was the lot of women certified as beyond the proper control of their husbands.

The disappearance of such public rituals and the penal revolution of the late eighteenth and early nineteenth centuries which moved punishment away from public scrutiny, have been discussed above in terms of the models applied by Foucault, Ignatieff and Garland. But much of this work on this period has ignored the implications for women swept into the new 'carceral society'. The emerging ideas of 'power-knowledge' and control of the body began when punishment was withdrawn from the public gaze but there were also profound implications for women. These new institutions of control acted as agencies for the strengthening of patriarchal discourses and they gave opportunities for tightening control of women in industrial society. The imprisonment of women was transformed as separate prisons were set up in which the supposedly unique character of the female could be treated. In such institutions women could experience the most degrading conditions and exploitation of all kinds. The standard work on the imprisonment of women (Dobash *et al.* 1986) is a revisionist account of women's treatment in gaols that reject 'Whiggish' or humanitarian interpretations that focus on the work of reformers such as Elizabeth Fry and their responsibility for the supposed improvement in the conditions of imprisonment for women in the nineteenth century. Fry's work at Newgate and elsewhere, from 1816 to the 1830s, was important but limited in its effect. It continued the stigmatization of women and the application of male assumptions of female pliability and submissiveness.

Apart from sexual exploitation and abuse, historians such as Rafter (1983) have found that the female inmate faced appalling neglect, in poor, insanitary conditions and was invariably put to work cooking, washing and cleaning. This was the accepted view of her proper role in life and one to which she had to be reconditioned. The aim was to enforce the stereotypical gendered division of labour and produce the conforming female. Any ideas of rehabilitation, even those discussed after the revolution in punishment strategies signalled by the Gladstone Report of 1895, remained theoretical. However, nineteenth-century reform did provide for the separate confinement of women. After months of solitary confinement followed by domestic work in the prison, women were placed in secure refuges and reformatories often after they had served their sentences. The regulation of women in prison does seem to be more rigorous than that experienced by men. Women were subjected to the humiliation of constant surveillance and supervision and a work regime that reinforced their gendered destiny as dependent members of society. Such prison regimes were reinforced by strict disciplinary systems, punishment practices using reduced diets ('B & W' or bread and water), handcuffs and other restraints, solitary confinement in darkened cells and the exhortations of prison chaplains who shared without question the belief in male superiority.

Research by modern feminist historians has revised thinking about the control of women in penal institutions dominated by the male discourse. They have found that the marginalization of women is neither confined to the past nor restricted to the two areas of discrimination often chosen for study: the state prison and the family. Intermediate between the two, a whole range of 'intermediate' or 'semi-penal' and 'semi-formal' institutions was established, which extended the female carceral system. The nineteenth and twentieth centuries have witnessed an increasing institutionalization of women in this way. Such 'half-way houses' have been examined by Barton (2001) who found that many private organizations replicated official anti-female ideologies, and were able to strengthen acceptance of women's 'abnormal' behaviour as a 'deviance' in need of containment. Many charitable and religious foundations ran houses for 'fallen women', female 'inebriates' and 'lunatics' in what was a thriving 'voluntary sector'.

QUESTION BREAK: CONTAINING WOMEN

Foucault stressed that institutions of discipline rested on the unwitting internalization or acceptance by inmates of discourses of obedience, subservience and dependence. They accepted labelling as insecure and maladjusted. Although it was not written about women Foucault's analysis shines through the extract below from Barton's work on a range of half-way houses such as the 'Lock Hospitals' for sexually deviant women and prostitutes, Magdelene Homes for girls with VD and houses for 'delinquent' girls and 'mad' women. Read the extract and consider the questions the follow it:

Women had to be consenting, compliant and co-operative in order for these establishments to function effectively, as being non-statutory they had no power to confine women against their will. However, . . . women were frequently pressured into giving their consent for a period of residence through a network of influence which included family, friends, reformers, charity workers, police, court officials, clergy and prison staff. . . . Women would agree to be admitted to these institutions, and consequently conform to their regimes, because the alternatives presented to them were so appalling. Young women labelled as 'immoral' might be willing to submit to a period of semi-penal confinement as they would be made well aware that if they were to become pregnant they stood a fair chance of being forcibly admitted, as were many unmarried mothers, to a lunatic asylum as a long-term inmate.

(Barton 2001)

- Why was it important that such women be removed from society?
- Why do you think young unmarried women would be sent to a 'lunatic asylum'?
- Why did dominant male thinking require that particular efforts were made to get prostitutes into such places?

Two categories of female 'deviancy' illustrate the continuation of the patriarchal assumptions of the criminal justice system: the prostitute and the suffragette. Prostitution was often the recourse of women who found it impossible to earn money to survive and many working-class women were forced into it during times of depression. Victorian sensibilities were predictably outraged and saw the prostitute as a danger to moral standards, the family and the quality of the race. 'Fallen women' were incapable of taking their place as wives and mothers and were thus targeted as asocial elements to be removed from society. The Contagious Diseases Acts of 1864 and 1866 (CDAs) were used indiscriminately in public against women who were suspected, often on the flimsiest of grounds, of being prostitutes. Josephine Butler worked courageously in the 1880s for the abolition of the CDAs which notoriously classed all women as potential prostitutes and gave them little redress when a case was brought against them by the, obviously male, police. Once again women were stigmatized by men who made decisions about what was, and what was not, acceptable female behaviour. Simply put, women were a source of infection and had to be legally contained. Male sexual licence, however, was accepted as a natural expression of a man's make-up: such 'double standards' reinforced the exploitation of women in the criminal justice system. Ironically, many of Butler's supporters turned their energies to campaigns for 'moral purity' and the repression of prostitution. The historian of Victorian prostitution shows how strong traditional ideas of female separateness were even among the campaigners against the CDAs.

This attack on patriarchy and male vice [i.e. on the CDAs] involved no positive assertion of female sexuality. It was still couched within the terms of a 'separate spheres' ideology and assumed that women were essentially moral, 'spiritual' creatures who needed to be protected from the essentially animalistic, 'carnal' men.

(Walkowitz 1982: 256)

The prostitute and the erring mother threatened that bastion of Victorian social stability and respectability, the patriarchal institution of the family. Female transgression was also feared as a potential threat to the quality of the race and women who refused the gendered stereotypical roles as subservient domestic dependants within the family were considered both 'mad and bad'. It must be said that working-class women who were prostitutes continued to be considered the danger. Butler's reform movement was avowedly middle class and it did little to improve the position of working-class women stigmatized within the legal system as prostitutes in particular or as 'wayward women' in general. Women who failed to conform were not classed as witches by the end of the nineteenth century but they were increasingly the subject of medical discourses that classified them as insane. The 'hysterical woman' was a standard character in Victorian fiction and the incarceration of women on such grounds increased as the psychiatric profession established its professional presence. Asylums were, like prisons, institutions where 'female maladies' and 'lunacies' could be affirmed and controlled as an exercise in patriarchy.

Suffragettes were spectacular victims of the late nineteenth-century criminal justice system as Acts were passed confining such 'dangerous women' who affronted men with their demands for the suffrage. Mrs Pankhurst's WSPU (Women's Social and Political Union) used violent tactics to bring the issue to the public. These included setting fire to pillar boxes, breaking the windows of West End clubs, the dynamiting of a cabinet minister's country house and violent interruption of political meetings in and outside the Commons. Such violence was an affront to the received view of the 'proper' place and behaviour of the female and the full force of the law led to them being force-fed using steel 'gags' that wrenched open the mouth in order to insert tubes down the prisoner's throat. They caused extensive injury. The prisoners then had liquid food poured into them. There were cases of prisoners dying following such assault. The following is a description of this treatment meted out to suffragette prisoner Constance Lytton at Walton Gaol in Liverpool in 1910.

> The pain of it was intense and at last I must have given way for he [the prison doctor] got the gag between my teeth, when he proceeded to turn much more than necessary until my jaws were fastened wide apart, far more than they would go naturally. Then he put down my throat a tube which seemed to me to be much too wide and was something like 4 feet in length. The irritation of the tube was excessive. I choked the moment it touched my throat until it had got down. Then the food was poured in quickly; it made me sick a few seconds after it was down and the action of the sickness made my body and legs double up, but the wardresses instantly pressed back my head and the doctor lent on my knees. The horror of it was more than I can describe. I was sick over the doctor and the wardresses, and it seemed a long time before they took the tube out. As the doctor left he gave me a slap on the cheek.
>
> (Lytton 1988 [1914]: 269)

The so-called 'Cat and Mouse Act' was passed in 1913 so that suffragettes on hunger strike in prison could be released if they were seriously ill so that they could be rearrested after their recovery to complete sentence. Contemporary medical opinion saw such women as mentally unbalanced because of the nature of their menstrual cycle and 'exceptional' physiology. In short, such 'unladylike' behaviour was explained by (male) doctors as the result of their inability to conform to the stereotypical image of the meek and dependent, 'caring' female; they must be mad and treated accordingly.

The twentieth century saw the disappearance of reformatories and 'half-way houses' and the female prison population fell steadily. There had been 33,000 women in prison in Britain in 1913, nearly half for drunkenness, but by 1960 there were only 2,000 (see p. 443). Women's wings in prisons across the country were closed and hostels, which had proved expensive to run, had a questionable ability to rehabilitate their inmates. Similarly, in this more liberal-progressive period, the sentencing of women to prison was not regarded as appropriate and alternatives to custody (suspended sentences, fines) were created. Where imprisonment was recommended, women were now sent to specialist prisons such as Holloway in London. It was not until the post-1960 period when female criminality appeared to be on the increase that 'specialist treatment' in newly designed prisons (Holloway was largely rebuilt) was recommended for female inmates. Significantly, given the history of the treatment and classification of women in the criminal justice system over the centuries, it was now believed that women who offended needed medical and psychiatric treatment as well as exceptional support and guidance before being readmitted to society. So, the discourse of the 'errant' female as pathological has proved impossible to remove even after three hundred years of criminal justice. As Zedner has commented:

> Holloway has developed much more like a 'conventional prison' than its originators intended. Yet its specialist facilities for mentally disturbed prisoners are a testament to the continuing view of criminal women as mentally ill or inadequate. The view that a proportion of the female prison population was mentally retarded now seems to have spread to envelop the female prison population as a whole.
>
> (Zedner 1998: 321)

ETHNICITY

Perhaps even stronger has been the fear, contempt and hostility aroused by members of ethnic minority communities targeted by the forces of criminal justice. The focus here is primarily, but not exclusively, on black communities yet similar views have been expressed about Irish immigrants, Jewish communities, Russians, Poles and German 'fifth columnists' in the past, and there are moral panics today about asylum seekers. Of course racist discourses are of ancient lineage, but in the seventeenth and eighteenth centuries the British legal system was required to establish its position on the question of the place of the black community. The country deepened its involvement with the slave trade and the growth of commerce with West Africa, the West Indies and North America had led, by 1760, to questions about the legality of this trade. Abolition of the British trade came in 1833 but it was preceded by a vigorous debate about whether the 'negro' was a human being. For those involved in the trade, this commodification of racism was an unexceptional part of everyday business. Racialized discourses were prevalent and they have survived in strength to the modern day. They have influenced how black people have been treated in the criminal justice system over the centuries. The trade had been endorsed by numerous Acts of Parliament and black slaves were classed as cargoes. As such they were property, but the legal system was presented with many problems concerning the status of slaves and their right to hold property and to gain freedom. The most famous example was the Somerset Case of 1772 which, after Lord Mansfield's judgment, granted slaves a defence against illegal, indefinite imprisonment and abolished a master's right to remove slaves from England against their will. However, an attack on slavery in England was not an attempt to remove it in the colonies and there was little legal redress for those unfortunate enough to travel the 'middle passage' on Liverpool slave ships. The criminal justice system was oblivious to the barbarities and murders, which were commonplace on the trip across the Atlantic. Walvin (2001) gives the example of the Liverpool slave ship Zong on which 132 Africans were murdered in 1781. The only legal outcome of this outrage was an application by the ship owners for insurance compensation for their loss of cargo.

The issue of the black presence in Britain was given urgency after the loss of the American colonies when large numbers of freed black slaves, and those still enslaved to British loyalists, came to Britain and established a black community. The size of the black presence is a matter of debate but the rise in the numbers of blacks among the poor and beggar classes in London meant that fears of a threatening 'dangerous class' were deepened as they took on a racialized perspective. Black people were subjected to casual violence, arbitrary arrest and imprisonment; they were typically classified as primitives compared to the civilized and enlightened, white Englishmen. Elites reinforced their feeling of superiority with racialized views of the animalistic blacks who were beneath classification as humans. They were in fact mere anthropological curiosities. New social, political and legal structures reinforced such views. If criminality was seen as an inevitable characteristic of Britain's working-class residuum of paupers and vagabonds, the black was permanently associated with alien and dangerous forces. 'Alien' and immigrant communities were always assumed to have higher rates of criminality than 'English' people.

QUESTION BREAK: 'UN-ENGLISHNESS'

The identification of law with national interests, and of criminality with un-English qualities, dates from this process of state formation and has a long history which remains relevant to the analysis of 'race' and crime today.

Anxiety about the criminal predisposition and activities of the immigrant population inspired demands for the introduction of immigration controls in the first years [of the 20th century]. When the issue of alien criminality was debated in Parliament, [in 1902] the settlement of Russians, Rumanians and Poles in the East End of London was described by Tory member . . . in military metaphors no less potent than those chosen by Enoch Powell. . . . He concluded: 'I should have thought we had enough criminals of our own . . .'

(Gilroy 1987: 92–3)

- What were the 'un-English' characteristics which supposedly confirmed 'alien criminality'?
- Why might such views becoming prevalent at a time when the British Empire was at its peak?

It is clear that race has had a distinct impact on the operation of the criminal justice system. Research by Hood (1992) and extended examination of policing in the twentieth century and after have indicated that racial minorities are subjected to discriminatory treatment. The great increase in the black community since the Second World War particularly has extended ideas of racialized inequality and this has been reinforced by stereotypical images of such communities as hotbeds of crime. When considering the current context, it is important to remember that the criminalization of ethnic minorities has been a long-standing feature of the criminal justice system. Post-war racism was not unique; rather it was the continuation of discriminatory practices that had been tolerated for decades. Simplistic views of a racial hierarchy had been given credibility in the nineteenth century by the pseudo-science of eugenics and the legal system perpetuated racist discourses as police operated a casual and institutionalized racism that passed without public comment. Studies of the policing of the British Empire (such as Anderson and Killingray 1991) reveal, for example, the unquestioned assumption of racial superiority which ensured that only white, British men were considered officer material and no black policemen would dare to attempt to arrest a white man. Black criminality, however, was taken for granted and there was more severe punishment for the 'inferior race'. Colonial administrators had operated racist criminal justice across the empire for decades and their return to Britain strengthened such views among governing elites. Race riots had occurred in Britain after the First World War in seaports like Liverpool, Glasgow, East London, Cardiff and Tyneside where West Indian seamen were concentrated. The lodgings of black seamen and their families were ransacked and some were killed in the disturbances. Police forces and the courts were not conspicuous in their defence of such communities. The so-called alien races in Britain were considered part of the residuum, with little chance of anything other than dismissal as a racialized and criminalized other.

In Britain after 1945 the rapid increase in immigration fuelled fears of racial degeneration and criminality. Stories of black criminality contained lurid images of sexual perversion, pimping and the 'racial contamination' of the white race. That black pimps were assumed to be earning vast sums living of the earnings of white prostitutes further generated the moral panic. In the late 1950s, after race riots in Notting Hill and Nottingham had attracted huge publicity, the catalogue of crime attributed to black criminals was extended to include drug trafficking and brothel keeping. The demonization of the black criminal was to reach hysterical proportions in the 1970s mugging 'crisis' that associated violent street robbery with black criminality. Stuart Hall and others (1978) produced the definitive study of this moral panic and showed it to be the product of police manoeuvres designed to increase the resources delivered to a particular force. The invention of the crime wave was to deepen suspicion of blacks. This is similar to the revelations of Howard Becker, in his *Outsiders* (1963), that explained the criminalization of marijuana in the USA between the wars as produced by the need for the FBI Narcotics Bureau to justify its existence and attract greater Federal funding. Becker sees 'rule creators' as 'moral entrepreneurs' strengthening their careers at the expense of those thus victimized by the extension of the criminal law. The mugging crisis is a good British example. Here the victims were the demonized, racialized 'alien' black community. It led to the great increase in the incidence of police 'stop and search' which meant that in some areas blacks were ten times more likely to be stopped by the police on suspicion than a white person.

Police focus on black people, through 'stop and search' for example, picked up more criminality, naturally, than in other cases not so strictly policed. Thus the stereotypes of black, or 'alien', criminality which had been central to the perception of racial difference since the era of the slave trade were continued within a criminal justice system which has in modern times been considered institutionally racist. The accusation of 'institutionalized racism' was also levelled at the police during the Macpherson investigation into the murder of teenager Stephen Lawrence in 1999 (see pp. 396–397).

This chapter has endeavoured to show how, historically, dominant ideological, economic and cultural forces have driven criminal justice policy. The historians of crime discussed here have focused on matters of ideology, class, economic change, social control theories, gender, ethnicity and developments in criminological theory to explain the trends in punishment policies that have characterized the history of criminal justice.

FURTHER READING

Dobash, R. P., Dobash R. E. and Gutteridge, S. (1986) *The Imprisonment of Women*, Oxford: Blackwell. Chapters 1–5 are particularly recommended as an historical study of the punishment of women which emphasizes the imposition of patriarchal assumptions of female criminality and the implications for punishment strategies. The book has a comparative theme and analyses developments in Britain and the USA through the last two centuries.

See also Godfey, B., Farrell, S. and Karstedt, S. (2005) 'Explaining Gendered Sentencing Patterns for Violent Men and Women in the late Victorian and Edwardian Period', *British Journal of Criminology* 45(5): 696–720.

Emsley, C. (2005) *Crime and Society in England 1750–1900* (3rd edn), Harlow: Longman. A most useful analysis of the period that includes chapters on the origins and development of the police, class perceptions of criminality, issues of gender and the changes in punishment.

Hay, D., Linebaugh, P., Rule, J. G., Thompson, E. P. and Winslow, C. (1975) *Albion's Fatal Tree. Crime and Society in Eighteenth-Century England,* Harmondsworth: Allen Lane. A classic, historical analysis of the use of the criminal law as an ideological weapon. It focuses on the manipulation of the 'bloody code' by 'an astute ruling class in their own interests'. Hay's essay on 'Property, Authority and the Criminal Law' is particularly recommended as a study of eighteenth-century capital punishment.

Ignatieff, M. (1978) *A Just Measure of Pain. The Penitentiary in the Industrial Revolution*, London: Macmillan. A path-breaking, incisive interpretation of the development of the prison as a 'total' institution in the context of industrialization and the perceived need for the social control of the masses that it provoked.

Morris, N. and Rothman, D. J. (1998) *The Oxford History of the Prison,* Oxford: Oxford University Press. This provides a comprehensive coverage of the history of incarceration from ancient times to the modern day. Examples are drawn from Britain, continental Europe and the United States.

Sharpe, J. A. (1998) *Crime in Early Modern England 1550–1750* (2nd edn), Harlow: Longman. An excellent, wide-ranging analysis of crime, criminality and punishment in the early modern period. Especially useful are Chapters 3 and 4 on measuring and controlling crime. Chapter 5 is a valuable study of offenders that includes a useful section on gender. Other areas covered include popular attitudes to criminality and elite perceptions of crime and threat.

Wiener, M. J. (1994) *Reconstructing the Criminal. Culture, Law and Policy in England 1830–1914*, Cambridge: Cambridge University Press. This is a major study of nineteenth- and early twentieth-century crime and criminal justice policy in their social and cultural contexts. Penal policy is examined as it developed from its reliance on the punitive to the later regard for welfare and treatment.

Victimology

INTRODUCTION

It goes without saying that any criminal justice system will be preoccupied with the behaviour, the punishment and the rehabilitation of the criminal. The behaviour of the criminal has been the particular focus of criminology, although work in this area overlaps with a number of academic disciplines, including sociology and psychology. As regards the punishment of offenders, the different aims of and justifications for punishment, whether they be essentially retributive or reformative, have sparked continued philosophical debate. However, this academic obsession with the criminal has been at the expense of detailed consideration of the victim. Indeed, the victim often seems to be added to criminological theorizing and debate merely out of politeness or political correctness. The consequences of this omission are important. The lack of academic interest has left the victim in the dark – a situation that has led to a good deal of public policy making not being informed by the needs, wants and status of the victim within the criminal justice system.

This neglect has been recognized in recent years, so much so that the status of the victim within the criminal justice system and within the academic discipline of criminology has become a controversial and important issue, especially in the wake of the 'Victim's Charter'. This was introduced in 1990 under a Conservative government and revised in 1996; it was replaced by the Victim's Code of Practice as a result of the Domestic Violence, Crime and Victims Act of 2004. Essentially, the Victims' Code is a recognition of victims' rights as consumers of the criminal justice system.

The purpose of this chapter is to trace the origins and the emergence of victimology as an academic discipline and to discuss how this has contributed to the status of the victim as a significant actor in the criminal justice process. In order to do this, it is necessary to critically analyse the theoretical and conceptual frameworks that have developed as a consequence of the different 'types' of victims and their very different treatment within the criminal justice system. It is equally important to identify and define those who are victims of crime and to understand those social factors which may render them 'victim prone' or contribute to their victim status.

The chapter starts with a brief consideration of the range of victims of criminal behaviour before looking at the emergence of victimology as a distinct discipline and at the major theoretical positions within it. The rest of the chapter then focuses on examples of victims of private and public crime – in particular, victims of domestic violence and of corporate crime.

WHO ARE THE VICTIMS?

The trend in victimology has been to divide victims of crime into two crude camps: the victims of 'conventional' crime and victims of 'corporate crime'. Conventional crime may be defined as 'street' or 'public' crimes. As such victims are easily identifiable; the extent of victimization is relatively easy to quantify. Corporate crime, by contrast, can be defined as crimes committed within a legitimate formal organization as a result of either deliberate decision-making or negligence. Corporate crime is by nature diffuse; therefore it is difficult to identify the extent of corporate victimization. It is no wonder that the corporate victim is often rendered 'invisible'.

The purpose of the following discussion is to outline the difficulty of these divisions and to demonstrate that victims of crime cannot be categorized so easily. How, for example, can the above definitions cater for victims of child abuse, domestic violence or state-sanctioned violence?

Historically, the term 'victim' originally referred to the sacrifice of a person or animal in the name of religion. Of course, today the term refers to those who have experienced loss, hardship or injury due to any cause. In relation to the study of crime the cause is a criminal act.

Victims can be categorized as primary or secondary. Primary victims are those who experience the act or its consequences at first hand; for instance a child who is the victim of a hit and run driver. Secondary victims are those who suffer the effects but are not immediately involved; for instance the relatives of that child who suffer anguish and grief. To define the victims of crime is not an easy task; and it would be helpful here to outline very briefly some of the major examples of victims of crime to highlight this difficulty.

Victims of violence

It has been argued that victims of violence can be defined as victims of 'conventional' crime. However, there are problems with this category. The official construction of violent crime fails to acknowledge *other* forms of violent crime. For example, Stanko argues that 'the hegemonic image [is] that "real" violence and crime is something that occurs on the street, in public, and is committed by strangers' (1990: 94). According to Home Office criminal statistics, violent crime can be categorized as 'crime against the person, sexual offences and robbery' (Colman and Moyniham 1996).

Missing from official categorization is state-sponsored or state-sanctioned violence, which according to McLaughlin (1996) includes the atrocities of military dictatorships and totalitarian regimes, such as the Nazi Holocaust against the Jews and political dissidents, mass political killings in Timor and Uganda, apartheid in South Africa and ethnic cleansing in Bosnia. Scraton *et al.* (1991) have also noted that it can include situations 'where liberal democratic states employ unreasonable force, act negligently, and tolerate miscarriages of justice'. This therefore allows the inclusion of events such as the investigation into the murder of Stephen Lawrence in 1993 and the police handling of the Hillsborough tragedy in 1989. Scraton *et al.* (1991) state of the Hillsborough case:

> There is no simplistic jump here which suggests that the senior officers' actions were comparable to the tortures in Pinochet's Chile or South Africa's apartheid regime, but the political-ideological processes of explanation and denial, their associated techniques of neutralisation and disqualification, are strikingly consistent.

The Lawrence case and the Hillsborough case have highlighted the plight of victims of the criminal justice system, and there have been numerous high-profile cases of victims of miscarriages of justice over the past 20 years, including the Birmingham Six (who were released in 1991), the Guildford Four (1989), the Bridgewater Three (1997) and the cases of Stefan Kiszko (1992), Sally Clark (2003), Barry George (released in 2008 after facing two trials for the murder of TV presenter Jill Dando) and Michael Shields (pardoned by the Home Secretary, Jack Straw, in September 2009). Taylor (1999) has outlined the responsibilities the state should have towards these cases. He argues that:

> the state's responsibility in relation to wrongful conviction should not, and does not, end with the quashing of such a conviction. But on the other hand such recompense does not arrive quickly and neither can it compensate for the horrors that have been endured by defendants and their families.

Other victims of violence include victims of domestic violence and victims of child abuse – victims who have until recently remained largely within the private arena. However, feminist arguments have highlighted the patriarchal attitude that sees women and children as the property and responsibility of the man, and have argued that domestic violence and child abuse is no longer a private worry but a public issue (to use C. Wright Mills's (1970) famous distinction).

Victims of child abuse

Child abuse has been described as any form of adult behaviour which (intentionally or otherwise) causes harm to a child. Kempe and Kempe (1981) identify four possible types of abuse: physical violence, physical and emotional neglect, emotional abuse (such as being continually terrorized, berated or neglected) and sexual abuse. Child abuse is an area that for a long time was ignored, if not tolerated, in our society. However, today charitable organizations such as the NSPCC and government projects such as Childline have highlighted the need for the protection of children. High-profile cases, such as the crimes of Myra Hindley and Ian Brady in the 1960s, Fred and Rosemary West in the 1980s and the murders of Victoria Climbié and Baby P in 2000 and 2008 respectively, are a reminder to society of the threat of child abuse. And the successful prosecution of celebrity figures such as Jonathan King and Gary Glitter is a reminder that child abusers do exist, exist in all walks of life, and are punished regardless of their status.

Victims of domestic violence

Domestic violence is often described as the exclusive domain of female victims; official statistics state that nine out of ten recorded incidents are of domestic violence upon women. However, according to the BCS (British Crime Survey) of 2009, men now make up 40 per cent of domestic violence victims. Victims of domestic violence can suffer from a number of types of abuse, including physical violence, psychological, emotional and verbal abuse, social abuse (enforced isolation), economic abuse (total control of finances) and sexual abuse (rape and coercion into sexual acts).

Victims of corporate crime

Corporate victimization is complex, as it is often indirect and diffuse; therefore there is difficulty in identifying victims. However, the recognition of corporate victims has been established within law with the introduction of the Corporate Manslaughter and Corporate Homicide Act (2007). Victims are generally described as workers, consumers and the general public. Victimization ranges from corporate manslaughter to fraud, pollution, medical blunders and health and safety issues. High-profile cases include the collapse of the US companies Enron and of Worldcom, which led to massive losses for shareholders.

This brief introduction to some of the main examples of victims of crime (and victims of domestic violence and of corporate crime will be examined in greater detail later in the chapter) indicates that the amount and extent of victimization relate to a number of variables. As the examples given demonstrate, victimization may relate to age, class, race, gender, or area of residence. These factors often work in combination with one another. One form of victimization may be compounded by another, which means that some individuals or groups may be more vulnerable to victimization. For example, ethnic minority groups are over-represented in lower socio-economic groups, which may affect their area of residence, forcing them to live in high-crime areas, which leaves them more vulnerable. This is also compounded by the fact that they are susceptible to institutional racism and racially motivated crime.

QUESTION BREAK: VICTIMS OF HATE CRIME

In recent years there has been a rise in what might be called hate crime which although traditionally associated with racism has now broadened its definition to include victims of homophobia, islamophobia, anti-semitism, xenophobia and so on. Croall and Wall (2002) argue that hate crime can be defined as crimes against those who are different, such as 'ethnic groups, the gay community, vulnerable women, different religious groups and those such as travellers whose lifestyles are perceived to be different'.

Disability hate crime is an area which over the last few years has gained greater public and media attention. The Criminal Justice Act 2003 defines disability hate crime as

a criminal offence motivated by hatred or prejudice towards a person because of their actual or perceived disability. It is also a criminal offence in which immediately before, after or during the offence the perpetrator demonstrates hostility towards a person because of their actual or perceived disability.

(See s.146 Criminal Justice Act 2003)

In December 2009 the EHRC (Equality and Human Rights Commission) announced that it was to launch a formal inquiry into disability-related harassment in England and Wales and how public authorities such as the criminal justice system are protecting disabled people's human rights. This announcement follows the tragic deaths of Fiona Pilkington and her daughter Francecca Hardwick. Read the following extract about this case and consider the questions below it.

Incident diary reveals ordeal of mother who killed herself and daughter

A vulnerable single mother who killed herself and her disabled daughter after years of harassment wrote about sitting in darkness in her house as youths yelled abuse outside, an inquest was told.

Extracts from a 'harassment diary' Fiona Pilkington, 38, kept for her local council were read to the hearing at Loughborough town hall. She kept the diary for a short time about six months before her death in November 2007.

An extract from May 12 read: 'They were shouting outside the window from 11.30pm until it went quiet at 2.30am.' Pilkington had opened the living room curtains to see if she could scare away the gang, who regularly gathered outside her 1930s semi-detached house in Barwell, Leicestershire. This failed and she turned off the light. The entry ends: 'Sat in the dark until 2.30am, stressed out.'

. . .

The last entry was written late at night on June 2, another Saturday. Youths had pelted the house with stones. 'They then went [next door] to number 57, lit a fag and then tried to set fire to fences between the houses. Really cheesed off. Can't they just walk down the street without doing anything? It seems impossible.'

Little more than six months later, after she had abandoned recording the incidents of abuse or, apparently, informing the council about them, Pilkington drove her blue Austin Maestro to a layby on the nearby A47 and set it alight. Inside, fire crews found her severely burned body and that of her 18-year-old daughter, Francecca.

An inquest has been told that the ever-changing gang of around 16 local youngsters seemed unable to leave the family in peace because they were perceived as different and vulnerable, and fair game . . .

Yesterday it also emerged that the council failed to pick up on the family's vulnerability, or share information with local police, even though both organisations knew the identities of the children behind the harassment, most of whom lived on the same street.

Tim Butterworth, a community safety officer for Hinckley and Bosworth borough council, sent Pilkington the diary after visiting her at her home in February 2007, and he read the extracts to the inquest. His only other recorded contact with her was a 10-minute phone call in April . . .

Had he known the family's situation, Butterworth said, he would have treated the matter as a suspected hate crime and pursued it far more vigorously.

(From the *Guardian*, 24 September 2009)

- What do you think are the key factors that lead to hate crime?
- What are the main similarities and differences between hate crime and other crime?

THE EMERGENCE OF VICTIMOLOGY

Victimology as a separate academic discipline has sought to highlight the plight of the victim. Although it is generally still studied as a sub-discipline within the realm of criminology in the past half-century or so there has been an increasing interest in establishing victimology as a distinct discipline in its own right. The intention of this brief overview of the history of and background to victimology is to trace its development from its academic emergence in the 1940s through to the present day. This historical review and analysis will also take account of the changing theoretical debates within victimology.

However, before we consider the different victimological perspectives, it is important to set the emergence of victimology in its historical, social and political context and to do this by addressing the issue of how (and why) the victim has become the focus of much (greater) intellectual inquiry.

The devastation of two world wars played an important part in encouraging an acceptance of the notion of the victim. The effect of the Second World War was especially noticeable during the 1950s, when the growing emphasis on social rights was an important element in the establishment of the welfare state. It was a short step from the notion of social rights of citizens to include the right of victims. Victims of (conventional) crime, victims of racial discrimination and victims of war all helped to propel the concept of the victim into academic circles and political policy. The post-war settlement was a time of consensus and reparation which fostered a climate that allowed victims to begin to organize themselves in pressure groups and demand some recognition and status within the criminal justice system. The importance of the British prison reformer Margaret Fry (1874–1958) in this process cannot be over-estimated. She played a key role in the creation of the Criminal Injuries Compensation Scheme, which emphasized the contractual nature of post-war Britain. Although the scheme did not materialize until 1964, after her death, her ideas made a significant impact upon criminal justice debate and policy. In referring to her role, Rock points out that

> In her last formulation of the problem, compensation would represent a collective insurance provided by society. All tax payers would be regarded as subscribers. All tax payers were at risk of becoming victims. Since the state forbade citizens arming themselves it should assume responsibility for its failure to provide protection.
>
> (Rock 1990: 66)

Fry highlighted the injustice of a criminal justice system that emphasized the criminal and displaced the victim. Most importantly, she championed the politicization of the crime victim (Miers 1978), which led to the beginnings of the victim movement and helped to set the agenda for the next decade.

The 1960s saw the establishment of a victims' movement that was especially active in the United States. However, this movement did not develop a united front but was fractured by a range of interested parties each with their own group interests, motives and perspectives. Feminists, black rights activists, consumer victims and victims of war (and in the United States, particularly the Vietnam War) all claimed the title of victim and each saw the criminal justice system as prioritizing the needs of the criminal. The demand for restitution and compensation became increasingly difficult to ignore. The demise of the rehabilitative method in the 1970s and the rise of a neo-classical ideology that advocated just deserts gave the victim movement a legitimate, political voice. As Smith stated, 'It was not until the conflict between the rehabilitative ideal and the resurgence of classicism in the 1970s that public indignation over the forgotten victim began to appear' (1985).

The 1970s saw the efforts of earlier campaigners come to fruition. Concern for the neglected victim led to the establishment of a number of voluntary organizations and social policy changes within British and US law. Victim Support was founded in Bristol in 1974 and has grown to play an important role within the criminal justice system. The organization has over 400 community-based services and is in touch with more victims and witnesses than any other agency, contacting over 1.5 million victims in 2008 (Victim Support Annual Reports and Accounts 2008). By the 1970s the feminist movement had matured and had played its part in the formulation of equal rights campaigns and policy, culminating in the Equal Pay and the Sex Discrimination Acts of 1975. Moreover, the feminist movement allowed and encouraged radical feminists to set up women-only organizations, which have flourished not only in Britain but also in the United States, such as Women Against Violence Against Women (WAVAW), the National Coalition Against Sexual Assault (NCASA) and the National Organization of Women (NOW). The success of NOW is significant, as the organization participated in the drafting of the Violence Against Women Act (VAWA II), which was first introduced to Congress in 1998 and which expanded the protections first won in the 1994 Violence Against Women Act VAWA I. This new, dynamic feminist movement promoted the official recognition not only of crime against women and children such as rape, domestic violence, sexual abuse and child abuse, but also of those crimes produced by patriarchal institutions and a sexist society, such as discrimination, poverty and prostitution.

The influence of the feminist movement began to be felt within British social policy in the 1970s and was largely influenced by two women's groups: the National Organization for Women and Women's Political Causes (WPC). In 1972 the first women's refuge opened in Chiswick, London and the first rape crisis centre in London in 1974 (Mawby and Walklate 1994). In the late 1980s Victim Support also acknowledged the rights of women by establishing the Victim Support Working Party on domestic violence. Today, the government has in place a multi-agency response to domestic violence and the Domestic Violence, Crime and Victims Act (2004) has established victims' rights in law. The prominent Zero Tolerance campaign launched in 1992 advocating the prevention of male violence against women and children has kept the issue of domestic violence and child abuse in the public's consciousness. However, despite the influence of the feminist movement, women's status as victims still tends to be marginalized – a factor that will be discussed in more detail later in the chapter (pp. 344–345) when considering critical victimology.

In a different vein, right-wing political and economic ideology of the 1980s radically changed the status of the victim. Consumerism permeated the institutions of Britain, and the criminal justice system was no exception. Jefferson and Shapland (1990) have gone as far as to argue that 'The idea of consumers of the criminal justice system is one of the more important initiatives of the 1980s. Agencies for the first time are being enjoined to care about lay people who are using their services.'

Developments in business culture in the 1980s, including the growing importance attached to the market and market forces, also encouraged new theoretical debates among academics concerning the question of the corporate criminal. This in turn highlighted the invisibility of many of societies' victims and allowed a much broader-based discussion. Prominent cases in the 1980s such as the Maxwell case involving pensions fund fraud and the widespread fraud in the US savings and loans (S&L) industry in 1989 raised in the public's mind the rights of the consumer. The publicizing of the corporate criminal also allowed the voice of the corporate victim to be heard within politics, the media and criminological debate.

Dramatic economic changes that affected the structure of society also affected the nature of corporate crime. As the traditional industrial base shrank, so the service/financial industry began to grow, and the relationship between corporate crime and the state altered: 'While manufacturing crimes tend to advance corporate profits and thus follow the logic of capital, financial fraud undermines that logic, jeopardizing the stability of the financial system and/or institutional survival' (Calavita and Pontell 1994).

In this context, it becomes more important for the state to prosecute corporate criminals, which in turn highlights the plight of victims, especially in fraud cases. The work of the victim surveys in the 1980s (such as the British Crime Survey) also highlighted the amount of pain that was wrought by crime – both conventional and corporate.

More recently, the position of the victim has become much more central to government policy and has led to a gradual transformation of the criminal justice system. The Labour Party's electoral manifesto pledged to make the victim of crime a high priority and the formulation of the second victims' charter (1997) has had a considerable effect on the treatment of victims in the Criminal Justice System. As mentioned in the introduction to this chapter, in 2006 the Victims' Charter was replaced by the Victims' Code of Practice which emerged from the Domestic Violence, Crime and Victims Act (2004) which has given victims much-sought-after statutory rights for the first time. The Code was put in place to enhance the experiences of victims of crime within the criminal justice system; and criminal justice agencies, such as the police and probation services, are bound by the Code's stipulations. The Code put forward a number of requirements which deal with the physical, emotional and financial rights following a crime. There is now an expectation (enforceable by law) that court officials be sympathetic towards the victim's ordeal, especially in rape and sexual offences trials. Again the Victims' Code can be seen as an ideological document that underpins the notion of consumerism. As Paul Rock puts it, 'the first Victims' Charter talked of the rights, the second of 1996 of standards of service' (1999).

The government are at present introducing The Coroners and Justice Bill which aims to create a separate office of Victims and Witnesses Commissioner. In January 2009 Sara Payne, mother of the Sarah Payne murdered in 2000, was appointed Victims' Champion 'to learn with and from Victim Support'. Her post is based in the Ministry of Justice. This appointment was initially announced at the Labour Party conference of 2008 when Gordon Brown stated, 'In consultation with Victim Support we will create an independent commissioner who will stand up for victims, witnesses and families – the people the courts and police exist to serve' (*Daily Telegraph*, 26 January 2009).

The establishment of policies around human rights has enabled the victim to be heard. On both a global and a local level, human rights became a philosophical issue that dominated much of the 1980s and 1990s. Cohen states:

Whatever the concept of human rights means, it has become a dominant narrative. Arguably, with the so-called death of the old meta-narratives of Marxism, liberalism and the Cold War, human rights will become the normative political language of the future.

(Cohen 1996: 491)

The 1990s also saw the maturing of the Green movement, which has been influential in creating new pressure groups and successfully lobbying and arguing for laws and control. This further widened perceptions of the range of corporate crime and therefore corporate victimization. The regulation of corporate crime is a direct response to the suffering of victims who have had to live with and deal with the effects of environmental pollution, such as that of contaminated water, and climate change. Ecological movements and prominent politicians worldwide have drawn attention to the problems. In 2006, the former US vice president Al Gore released the film *An Inconvenient Truth*, which focused on trying to educate society about the problem of global warming. It is no longer a question of saving socialism or capitalism but rather that the whole of humanity is existing on a threatened planet. To that extent, then, ecological groups have emphasized the victim as being humanity itself and have considerably broadened the concept of the victim.

An awareness of the large numbers of victims of race and sex discrimination has also grown out of the era of human rights. One particular landmark case was that of Stephen Lawrence, who was murdered on 22 April 1993. This case highlighted the plight of victims of racial violence in society and, according to the subsequent Macpherson Report (1999), the extent of institutional racism within the Metropolitan Police Force. In the last decade there have been a number of Acts and regulations incorporated into British law and relating to equality – such as The Race Relations (amendment) Act 2000, the Disability Discrimination Act 2005 and the Equality Act 2006.

The first years of the new millennium have to some extent consolidated the position of the victim. In 2001 the opportunity for victims to have their statements read out in court was introduced. And in March 2002 the Labour government unveiled plans to provide victims of crime with a Bill of Rights, to appoint a commissioner for victims and to establish a government advisory panel which would consist of victims of crime and their relatives. David Blunkett, the then Home Secretary, stated:

Victims of crime are still too often treated with indifference or with disrespect. I am not having that. These are the very people the criminal justice system should protect and defend, the very people who should be cared for and considered at every stage and by every element of the justice process.

(*Independent*, 22 March 2002)

However, the success of victims of crime in establishing their rights through the Victims' Charter has been limited. The Charter, for example, does not take account of victims of 'workplace crimes' – something that the TUC has taken issue with in recent years:

[T]he TUC believes that if the Victim's Charter was extended to cover workplace injury and illness, it would signal the importance of such crimes (which are all too often seen as mere technical breaches of regulations, or only accidental, leading to injury or illness).

(Trades Union Congress, *Rights for Victims of Workplace Crime*, 26 May 2001)

All these 'new' victims represent different periods in history and provide victimology with new areas to research. As a consequence, new perspectives have emerged which have broadened the theoretical debates around the status of the victim in contemporary society. The theoretical debates within victimology, beginning with its academic genesis in the 1940s and the focus on positivist principles, now face a challenge from radical and critical victimology. In a post-modern era, traditional epistemologies within victimology are subject to criticism. In highlighting the increasingly recognised and important role of the victim, Howarth and Rock argue that:

Additions to the roster of victims of crime can have a very real usefulness to criminology. They can illuminate the complexity of crime, the abundance of the groups it affects and creates, the multiple consequences that it inflicts, the diversity of the responses that it elicits, and the concomitant intricacy and scale of the social structures it generates. Crime has diffuse and proliferating repercussions which are now only beginning to be (mis)understood.

(Howarth and Rock 2000: 59)

Restorative justice

Victims of crime have also become more involved in the actual criminal justice process due to the rise in restorative justice techniques. In 2003 the Home Office put together a restorative justice strategy, the aim of which was to 'build in high quality restorative justice at all stages of the Criminal Justice System'.

Restorative Justice takes on a number of different forms, including victim offender mediating, group conferencing, family conferencing and indirect mediation/reparation. But the main tenet and principle of restorative justice is to bring together those involved in the actual offence committed; in other words the stakeholders. This may involve the offender, the victim, members of the community etc. It is seen as a chance for reflection, apologies and reparation.

Restorative justice has probably been most successful in the area of youth crime. Restorative Justice practice was introduced into the area of youth justice under the Crime and Disorder Act 1998. Particularly prominent in this area has been the work of the Thames Valley Police. In 1994 Thames Valley Police experimented with restorative justice cautioning in Milton Keynes – this involved a police officer inviting all those who have been affected by an offence to engage in a conference in which the offence and its ramifications are discussed. This procedure is now widely used in other police forces around the country (Hoyle, Young and Hill 2002).

Although restorative justice has been welcomed by victim groups it has yet to make the impact hoped for. Any claims of the success rate of Restorative Justice techniques and programmes with regard to the victim must be approached with caution as the variety and volume make it difficult to evaluate the impact on the victim. Many theorists in the area also criticize Restorative Justice for focusing on the shaming and reintegrating of the offender and the effect on re-offending rates (recidivism) instead of focusing on victim related concerns. (For a discussion on the inherent problem with Restorative Justice, see Dignan 2007).

QUESTION BREAK: CHANGES IN VICTIMIZATION

In the section above, we have highlighted how different times and eras have led to the emergence of new and different groups of victims.

- What groups of victims became particularly recognized in each of the following decades: the 1960s, 1970s, 1980s, 1990s and 2000s?
- Why did these victims emerge at those particular times?
- What sort of 'future victims' do you think might emerge over the nest few years?

THEORIES AND METHODS OF RESEARCH IN VICTIMOLOGY

The intention of this section is to set out and examine the major theoretical perspectives within victimology and the methodologies that underpin them.

The term 'victimology' was first coined by Frederick Wertham (1949), who called for a 'science of victimology'. However, as regards theorizing about victimology, it can be argued that Mendelsohn and von Hentig are widely recognized as the 'founding fathers' of the sub-discipline. Both have been profoundly influential in establishing victimology as an academic discipline, but in very different ways. Von Hentig's work is closely linked to criminology in that its concern and focus is with the victims of crime, so victimology is analysed as a part of criminology. In contrast, Mendelsohn's victimological theorizing is very much related to the philosophy of human rights, and victimology is seen as, essentially, an independent discipline. As Mendelsohn himself states,

> We must point out a fundamental difference between the points of view of Professor von Hentig and Professor Ellenberg on the one hand and of ourselves on the other hand. The former consider the study of the victim as a chapter of criminology, whereas we consider it as a separate science, which because of its structure and its aim should be independent.

(Mendelsohn 1963: 241)

This division, and Mendelsohn's views in particular, help explain why victimology has been able to incorporate those who are best described as 'unconventional victims' – a particular area that has been crucial to the development of both radical and critical victimology.

However, despite these differences, both theorists are proponents of what has become widely known as positivist or conventional victimology. The key characteristics of positivist victimology can be described as 'the identification of factors which contribute to a non-random pattern of victimisation, a focus on interpersonal crimes of violence, and a concern to identify victims who may have contributed to their own victimisation' (Miers 1989). Miers, therefore, draws upon a number of influences which underpin positivist victimology, including a concern with the patterns and regularities of victimization and the development and application of the key concepts of 'victim precipitation', 'victim proneness' and lifestyle.

Arguably the first systematic study of the victims of crime was von Hentig's book *The Criminal and his Victim*, published in 1948 (of course, the use of the male term was even more the norm in the 1940s). The importance of this study cannot be overestimated. It transformed criminology from a one-sided study of the offender. Indeed, Fattah (1986) went so far as to argue that 'Since criminal behaviour is dynamic, it can only be explained through a dynamic approach, where the delinquent, the act and the victim are inseparable elements of a total situation which conditions the dialectic of the anti-social conduct'. Von Hentig proposed a dynamic approach which discussed how the offender and the victim were involved in an interaction, thereby challenging the concept of the victim as passive. *The Criminal and his Victim* includes a chapter dealing with victims entitled 'The Contribution of the Victim to the Genesis of the Crime' in which the concept of victim proneness – the notion that some individuals might be more susceptible to victimization than others – is discussed. In order to operationalize this concept, von Hentig developed his now famous typology of victim proneness. It is worth listing it in full: the young; the old; the female; the mentally defective; immigrants; members of minorities; dull normals; the depressed; the acquisitive; the wanton; the lonesome and heartbroken; the tormentor; and the fighting victim. People in each of these categories were said to be victim-prone owing to their social and/or psychological state. In other words, these are characteristics which may have precipitated the offence through which they were victimized.

QUESTION BREAK: CATEGORISING VICTIMS

While we may question von Hentig's use of certain typologies – such as the dull, normal or the lonesome – it is worth considering whether these categories tell us anything about our own personal risk of victimization.

- How many of the typologies do you fit into?
- How and why would they make you more victim-prone in today's society?

Mendelsohn (1963) on the other hand developed a sixfold typology of victims which reflected their culpability: in other words, the extent to which the victim was responsible for her or his victimization. According to Mendelsohn, certain victims of crime were more or less culpable – an obvious example of greater culpability being the aggressor who through the fault of his own actions is killed. While both of these approaches tend to overemphasize notions of blame and vulnerability, they nevertheless provided the impetus for further research within the discipline of victimology. Furthermore, the idea of the blameworthy victim was to form the basis for theories of victim precipitation.

Wolfgang (1958) subjected von Hentig's ideas to empirical testing in his study of criminal homicide in Philadelphia. As a consequence, he developed the term 'victim precipitation', which refers to situations in which the victim is a direct precipitator of the offence. He argued that:

> The term victim precipitation is applied to those homicides in which the victim is a direct, positive precipitator in the crime. The role of the victim is characterised by his having been the first in the particular homicide drama to use physical force directed against his (usually) slayer. The victim precipitated cases are those in which the victim was the first to show any use of a deadly weapon to strike a blow in altercation – in short the first to commence an interplay or resort to physical violence.
>
> (Wolfgang 1958: 24)

The idea of victim precipitation and culpability also feed into the criminal justice process. Terms such as reasonable and appropriate behaviour are often used when apportioning blame or dealing with a victim's case. In other words there is an assessment using a supposed 'objective standard' to find out if due care and foresight were present in a person's behaviour. Contributory negligence is also a premise that is often used within court proceedings especially pertaining to a victim's behaviour prior and during a criminal offence. This may be loosely defined as a victim failing to take the socially optimal level of precaution; the legal thinking behind this being that victims (or claimants in the case of a financial claim) are often able to avoid or reduce the severity of their injury by taking more care. Later in the chapter we will discuss the inherent problems with, and consequences of, the concepts of victim precipitation and culpability.

The risk of being a victim

In recent years the notion of a risk society has become very much in vogue in academic thinking (Beck 1992). However, over 20 years ago, positive victimologists were using similar ideas for understanding the risk or chance of being a victim. It has been argued that a much more realistic approach would be to try to understand victimization in terms of risk. This can be related to the concept of lifestyle, which was introduced to victimology by Hindelang, Gottfredson and Garofalo in 1978 and takes us beyond the individual victimizing event, instead emphasizing the constraints and impact of structure on the individual. In other words, variables such as occupation, status, daily routine and leisure outside the home can compound one another, giving rise to increased chances of victimization. In relation to occupation, for example, it has been documented that hospital workers are at increasing risk of attack during their working hours from violent, often drunk, patients. This theory has been adapted by Laub (1990) in developing 'routine activities theory', which attempts to predict the risk of victimization according to lifestyle, behaviour and demographic characteristics. The risk of becoming a victim of crime varies as a function of demographic characteristics, such as gender, age, race or socio-economic class. It is a fact that men, and particularly young men aged between 18 and 24, have a higher risk of assault than women (with the exception of sexual assault and domestic violence); yet they also have higher rates of assaultive behaviour than any other group. These characteristics are further complicated by the fact that residential location and exposure to potential assailants vary as a function of lifestyle. For example, if a person's lifestyle or routine activity places that person in considerable contact with young men, then it would follow that his or her risk of victimization is high.

As a result, the concept has been praised for shifting the focus away from victim blaming and emphasizing instead the importance of the individual's daily routine.

Positivist methods and victimology

In considering positivist victimology it is important to keep in mind that it relies on positivist methodology (research based upon the logic and methods of scientific inquiry). In its embryonic stage this viewpoint led to the development of typologies (in the work of both von Hentig and Mendelsohn, for example) and, more recently, large victimization surveys which claim to have identified 'victim-prone' personalities and victim precipitation – the argument that some victims actually cause their victimization.

For some time, information about crime was gathered from official police records. In response to the criticism that crime statistics recorded by the police are an inadequate tool and do not measure the 'dark figure' of crime or the experiences of victims, positivist victimology developed the victim survey. The victim survey was first developed in the United States in the 1960s as a consequence of a 'war on crime' initiative. The first British victimization survey was published by Sparks and colleagues as *Surveying Victims* in 1977. The British Crime Survey was produced by the Home Office in 1981 and the results were published by Hough and Mayhew (1983), whose findings referred to the likelihood of victimisation – for instance it showed that:

> A statistically average person aged 16 or over can expect a robbery once every 5 centuries (not attempted), an assault resulting in injury (even slight) once every century, the family car to be stolen or taken by joy riders once every 60 years, a burglary in the home every 40 years.

The methodology used to develop the British Crime Survey has allowed the differences in risk, in terms of, for example, age, sex, race, to be highlighted. The survey also raises victims' issues and provides evidence of levels of crime, public attitudes to crime and fear of crime. It includes crimes which are not reported to the police and has become an important alternative to police records. It provides evidence of how victims are treated by the police and what they want in the way of police attention. However, there are various weaknesses in the methodology which create a number of limitations. Such limitations include *non-response*, whereby some groups are omitted or under-represented. These include those in institutions, the homeless, victims of corporate crime and young people (especially victims of child abuse), although the British Crime Survey did extend its population to include the under-16s in January 2009 and there is further work being undertaken to examine victimization of the homeless and those living in institutions. *Response bias* is also a problem, as respondents may not give accurate answers to questions: they may have difficulty recalling the incident, or in some cases may fabricate information. There is also the problem of forward and backward telescoping, with people mistaking the length of time since an event occurred (Mirlees-Black *et al.* 1996). And the range and extent of offences such as domestic violence and sexual offences are likely to be poorly measured because of their delicate nature.

However, it is important to acknowledge that in spite of these legitimate criticisms, the victim survey has developed from positivist victimology and has helped to place criminal victimization firmly on the political agenda, perhaps most notably through the British Crime Surveys, which have been produced annually since 2001 and which are seen as an authoritative source of data by criminal justice agencies, the media and academics.

QUESTION BREAK: CRIME SURVEYS

The British Crime Survey 2008/2009 interviewed 46,000 people over the age of 16. It asked adults in private households about their experience of victimisation in the last 12 months.

- What victims might be excluded from the British Crime Survey?
- Explain how the survey can be improved in order to take account of these victims.
- How could the data from the chart help the police to improve their service?

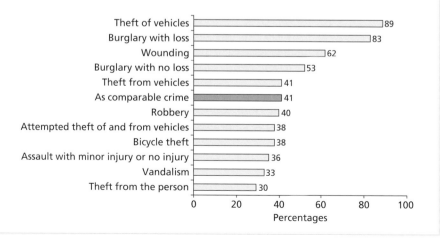

Critique of positivism

As well as there being difficulties with positivist methods, positivist ideas have led to a great deal of debate and have been strongly criticized, not least because of their attempts to cite the victim's role as a causal effect in his or her victimization. The use of the notion of victim precipitation and its connotations of victim blaming is highly controversial, but still remains a prominent feature in the formulation of explanations and reasons for crime which are employed by various agencies within the criminal justice system. However, a major limitation of the concepts of victim precipitation, culpability and proneness is that they are heavily focused on the individual 'victimization event'. As a consequence of this, victimology as a discipline has received strong criticism. Clark and Lewis (1977), for example, argued that 'In the social sciences, victim blaming is becoming an increasingly popular rationalisation for criminal and deviant behaviour . . . over the past few years, victim blaming has become institutionalised within the academic world under the guise of victimology.' This scathing attack on victimology and specifically on positivist victimology echoes the sentiments of feminist criminologists in particular. According to feminists, victimology became a weapon of ideology used to further the view of a patriarchal society and legitimize physical and sexual dominance of the male over the female. As Clark and Lewis put it:

> The male researcher finds his escape in victimology. He seeks the problem's cause in the behaviour of its victim, and goes on to persuade himself and the public at large that by changing that behaviour the problem can be controlled. In this way the study of victimology becomes the art of victim blaming.
>
> (Clarke and Lewis 1977: 29)

The controversial nature of victim precipitation has been highlighted in relation to rape, and in this context has received a great deal of media attention over the past 20 or so years. In some of the most publicized cases, there has been a clearly negative portrayal of women who have been raped and a tendency for their ordeals to be trivialized, with a consequent 'blaming of the victim'.

In particular, feminists have rejected the operationalization of the concept of victim precipitation provided by Amir, who used the concept to investigate patterns of forcible rape. Amir studied 646 reports of forcible rape in Philadelphia between 1958 and 1960 and concluded that 19 per cent of the rapes were precipitated by the victim. According to Zedner, Amir's definition of the concept of victim precipitation in relation to rape (Amir 1971: 262) could be defined as follows:

> The victim actually, or so it was interpreted by the offender, agreed to sexual relations but retracted . . . or did not resist strongly enough when the suggestion was made by the offender. The term also applies to cases in which the victim enters vulnerable situations charged sexually.
>
> (Zedner 1992)

As mentioned earlier victim precipitation and victim culpability have been equated with 'victim blaming'. These factors have helped in the formulation of laws citing contributory negligence as providing an understanding of a victim's role within a crime (and also the use of 'victim blaming' as an understanding of rape crimes can be related to the conviction rates and occasional comments made by judges and barristers).

The scientific basis of positivism relies upon that which can be objectively observed and measured; therefore positivist victimology has a tendency to focus on the public rather than the private. Dichotomies like public/private have always been criticized by feminists because of their invocation of a scientific objective rational reality, which ignores natural, subjective and emotional accounts of victimization. Until recently this had allowed certain crimes (in particular those that occur behind closed doors, such as rape and domestic violence) to be under-reported and therefore rendered invisible.

More fundamental to the feminist position, however, is the use of traditional epistemologies which, they argue, have promoted a view of sociological (and general) knowledge as androcentric. Therefore the methods, theory and patriarchal academic modes of production used to study victims are seen as illegitimate, as they are based upon partial knowledge. Indeed, many would argue that the theories and methods of sociology derive from the visions of the social world that men have. This line of criticism will be returned to below when we examine critical victimology.

Radical victimology

In response to some of the criticism lodged against positive victimology, the radical victimological perspective emerged in the late 1960s and 1970s. As mentioned, radical victimology can be traced back to the work of Mendelsohn and his argument for a victimology of human rights that allows for exploration of the role of the state in defining who 'legitimate' victims are and, more importantly, how the criminal justice system is implicated in the 'construction' of victims and criminals. As a consequence, radical victimology acknowledges, in particular, those victims who have been rendered invisible. And of course without the co-operation of the victim in reporting crime, finding evidence, identifying the offender and acting as witness in court, most crime would remain unknown.

These victims have been best described by Quinney (1972) as 'victims of police force, the victims of war, the victims of the correctional system, the victims of state violence, the victims of oppression of any sort'. It is evident, then, that the effect of the victim movements of the 1970s and 1980s have been instrumental in placing radical victimology on the theoretical agenda within victimology. In essence, radical victimology questions and criticizes the tendency of positive victimology to concentrate upon conventional victims rather than 'unconventional' victims. Radical victimology's holistic approach towards the victim allows issues relating particularly to women, such as rape and domestic violence, to enter the public arena. Moreover, the emphasis on the role of the state in the production of victims gives the corporate/white-collar victim a legitimate status. The concern to expose human misery and the role that the capitalist state has in the distribution of this misery has been outlined in the work of Box, particularly in his study *Power, Crime and Mystification* (1983), in which the identification and extent of victims of corporate crime is graphically documented.

What might be termed conventional radical victimology has, then, helped to expose the limited structural basis of victimization and therefore the problems facing the poor and the powerless. However, it did not contribute in any meaningful way to empirical research. And, as implied above, although positivist victimology generated much invaluable data, its research was based upon conventional constructions of crime and therefore neglected sexual and racially motivated crime and victims of corporate crime.

It is within radical left realist victimology that the issue of reliable and valid research has become paramount. Theoretically, radical left realism has developed from the left realist perspective within criminology, typically associated with the work of Lea and Young (1993). It therefore acknowledges the role of the state in what Young has called the 'square of crime' (Young 1997) and argues that in order to fully understand crime in all its dimensions, all four corners of this 'square' – offenders, victims, the community/ public and the state – and the interrelationships between them have to be fully investigated.

In relation to methodology, radical left realists have argued for more locally based victim surveys which show the geographically and socially focused distribution of criminal victimization; furthermore, local crime surveys tend to be explanatory rather than descriptive (as with positivist examples such as the British Crime Survey). Variables such as age, gender, ethnicity are taken into account during the sampling process and, as a consequence, local surveys have challenged the view that crime is a rare occurrence, have helped to uncover the social characteristics of the victim and have highlighted the problem of intra-racial, intra-class and gender issues around crime. Valuable data have emerged from such surveys – Jones et al. (1986), for instance, uncovered high levels of racially and sexually motivated crime through the Islington Crime Survey. Other local crime surveys include those carried out in Edinburgh and Merseyside (Kinsey 1984; Anderson et al. 1990). Also, victim surveys have included questions on commercial and health and safety at work offences, which has allowed victims of corporate/white-collar crime to be given a voice (Pearce 1990). Local authorities and crime prevention organizations have adopted the local victim survey in order to assist in the development of policy. As Young has argued, in order to make the plight of the victim real, it is essential to develop 'an accurate victimology understanding problems as people experience them' (1986: 23–4).

Local surveys have helped to dispel the view that crime affects few people and have highlighted those people faced with specific difficulties and at particular risk (of domestic violence or racism, for example). However, as with positivist victimology, the radical left realist approach relies on victimization surveys and therefore focuses on patterns and regularities rather than trying to understand the underlying mechanisms which contribute to the victimization process. A critique that has been lodged against the methods of radical theorists is that local crime surveys assume a harnessing of the democratic process – in other words, they assume that the community participates in the decision-making process and its members understand their rights as a citizen and the obligation of the state. In a similar vein to radical victimology, the critical theorists (who are discussed in the following sub-section) would also ask whether people are aware of their social reality and whether it is safe to assume that the state is neutral in its response to crime and victimization.

Critical victimology

Partly as a response to the shortcomings of other victimological perspectives and partly to build on the insights of feminism and left realist approaches, a new, 'critical' victimological approach has emerged in recent years. As with radical victimology, with which it overlaps in a number of ways, it is based on an essentially interpretivist, 'micro' approach to theorizing about social issues – in the context of victimology, to theorizing about victims of crime. Critical victimology looks to include the 'hidden' victims of crime in its analysis and to consider and highlight the role of the state in perpetuating inequalities in the 'production of victims'.

This more interpretive approach to victimology can be illustrated by the emphasis given to labelling and, as Miers (1990) suggests, the focus on 'who has the power to apply the label'. It is well established that labelling and the interpretivist perspective of interactionism provide a massive input to (and led to a change of direction in) the sociology of deviance in the 1960s and 1970s. Equally, though, this perspective attracted a good deal of criticism from critical criminologists of the period. In a similar vein, the emphasis on the 'label' in critical victimology has been seen as doing little to help us understand the structural formations that underpin our definitions and interpretations of the victim.

The early critical victimological approach has been criticized and developed by Walklate (1989, 1990) among others. In particular, she has advocated a critical victimology that takes seriously the need for the (sub)discipline to be based on empirical, objective research and to take close account of the structural context in which it is operating, but at the same time to do this without losing the real insights and strengths that can be offered by an interpretive understanding.

A key issue here seems to be the need to define what is 'real' and to examine the processes which help provide an understanding of everyday reality. This issue is highlighted partly to take account of the fact that it is quite possible for victims not to know about their victimization and, therefore, the causes of it. It is for this reason that critical victimology advocates the need to examine the processes which 'go on behind our backs' in the context of defining victims. Mawby and Walklate (1994) make the point that this emphasis on hidden processes has also been a major concern of feminist work (and its attempt to ensure that women – and in this case women victims – are recognized as occupying both the public and the private domains).

Critical victimology problematizes the relationship between the citizen and the state: it does not see the state as neutral; rather, the state's mechanisms contribute to those victims we see and those we don't see. It is therefore not objective but self-interested and self-motivated. This, according to critical victimology, raises problems in relation to race, gender and class and how they are articulated in policy terms.

Idealistically, the notion of the citizen as consumer maintains the citizen and state as neutral entities. However, the inextricable link between citizenship and con-sumerism gives the impression that citizens' social rights are being catered for, yet

The rights of citizenship are a reality only for those who have belief in their authenticity and the skills needed to exercise them. Indeed, if rights are to exist in a real sense, it is essential that those entitled to social services know what their rights are and that they are able to lay claim to them.

(Barbalet 1993: 54)

In a similar manner, if that state in question is a patriarchal one, the question arises of whether we are all awarded the same rights, as the notion of the 'citizen/consumer' would have us believe. Mackinnon states that 'The liberal state coercively and authoritatively constitutes the social order in the interests of men as a gender through its legitimating norms, forms, relation to society, and substantive policies' (1989).

The reduction in the role of the state during the Thatcher era, in response to what was seen as a dependency culture and the notion of the nanny state, created what has been termed possessive individualism. This has also affected the idea of victimization. As Young puts it, 'Everyone is a victim, then everyone has a part to play in the struggle against crime. More strongly everyone has a duty: it is part of the offices of the citizen to minimise the risk of becoming a victim' (1996: 56).

Critical victimology, then, can be seen as a theoretical perspective that examines the wider social context. In modern industrial societies, this context has tended to focus on the ways in which capitalism and patriarchy influence how victims are perceived and responded to. In doing this it emphasizes the key role of the state and of the law but at the same time acknowledges the importance of the micro level of analysis – in other words, of agency as well as structure.

This theoretical approach to or refinement of critical victimology, developed by Mawby and Walkate (1994) among others, draws upon Giddens's (1984) theory of structuration in highlighting the importance of both macro- and micro-analysis – of structure and agency, as Giddens terms it. Structuration (as emphasized throughout critical victimology) allows the victim a voice. Critical victimology highlights the importance of people's ability to fight for themselves against their structural constraints, and quite often with surprising results. Examples of successful 'voices' include Greenpeace, the Hillsborough campaign (especially in boycotting the *Sun* newspaper in Liverpool), Rock against Racism and anti-capitalist protests against the World Trade Organization, as well as centres that have been established to support victims of domestic violence.

Critical victimology has developed partly as a response to the methodological flaws within positivist and radical victimology. It does not deny the worth of the criminal victimization survey, but stresses the importance of considering historical, social and political processes. At an empirical level, critical victimology argues that comparative and longitudinal studies need to be employed, although there is no uniformity in its methods. That said, it could be argued that critical victimology is an approach that has attempted to incorporate a critical understanding of the role of the law and the state in the victimization process as well as recognizing the important role of human actors in influencing the conditions under which they exist. It has also been informed by the work of feminism and has brought feminist thinking into the mainstream of victimology.

Zemiology

In recent years there has been a rise of the new concept of Zemiology – or social harm/social injury. This concept was originally used in order to criticize criminology's focus on 'conventional crimes'. Zemiology is an emerging area of study that is attempting to move beyond conventional legal notions of crime and draw attention to social harms (financial , physical, social and psychological) which have a profound impact. Social harms can include environmental pollution, medical malpractice, criminal miscarriages of justice, global economic fraud and so on.

Critical victimologists have long argued that radical left realism and positivist victimology are inadequate theories as they are trapped by legal definitions of crime. As Hillyard and Tombs suggest, 'the definitions of crime in the criminal law do not reflect the only or the most dangerous of antisocial behaviours' (2004). As a consequence critical victimologists in particular have been quick to adopt the ideology of zemiology and apply it to the study of victims; and as the notion of social harm is not bound by legal interpretation this expands the parameters of victim status.

VICTIMS OF PRIVATE CRIME

As discussed earlier, positivist victimology has been the most prominent theoretical mode of study of victims and has concentrated on victims of 'public' or 'conventional' crime. As a consequence, victims of private and or 'unconventional' crime have until relatively recently been rendered largely invisible within academia. Such victims may include victims of domestic violence, victims of child abuse and victims of corporate crime. This public/private dichotomy has always been found problematic by feminist writers, and it is for this reason that critical and to some extent radical victimology are of paramount importance in placing the victims of private crime (for example, domestic violence and child abuse) on the social and, more crucially, political agenda. We will now look at domestic violence as a specific and major example of private crime.

Victims of 'private' crime: domestic violence

Violence in the home has become recognized as a major issue and concern, and society is now more aware than at any other time in history of the nature and extent of such victimization. The civil rights movements of the 1960s and 1970s (especially those relating to women and children) highlighted oppression and violence within the home. As a consequence, violence in the home has been legally and politically recognized, which has successfully led to *some* awareness within the criminal justice system (with the instigation of domestic violence and child protection units and protective laws) and the voluntary sector (which has provided refuges and self-help groups) of the extent of the problem.

This increased focus on violence within the home (which can range from sexual to physical to mental abuse) gives the impression that this is a new phenomenon that contemporary society has to deal with. However, feminist theory in particular has highlighted that this problem was 'institutionalized' during the Victorian era; in other words, given credence through the norms and values which governed everyday life and legalized through the criminal justice system. This was an era when the phrase 'An Englishman's home is his castle' meant just that. The father/husband was the ultimate ruler and could legally chastise his wife and children in any manner he saw fit. This, however, is not to deny the involvement of women in violence in the home.

The Home Office's definition of domestic violence is as follows: 'any violence between current and former partners in an intimate relationship, wherever the violence occurs. The violence may include physical, sexual, emotional and financial abuse' (www.homeoffice.gov.uk). Definitions by the ACPO (Association of Chief Police Officers) and the CPS (Criminal Prosecution Service) also includes abuse by 'other' family members.

These definitions have to some extent alleviated the concerns of many feminist researchers who argued that definitions of domestic violence used by agencies of the state (the police, the courts, etc.) were much too narrow, either not dealing with the forms that violence was likely to take or projecting domestic violence as a heterosexual problem, omitting those victims who suffer domestic violence within same-sex relationships. However, for many the term 'domestic violence' is in itself problematic. Most violence in the home is perpetrated by men towards women – the term 'domestic violence' hides the gender of the perpetrator (Morley and Mullender 1994). Similarly, the term 'violence' has been criticized for being too narrow. The term should be broadened to include verbal abuse, intimidation, physical harassment, homicide, sexual assault and rape.

Domestic violence may, then, be defined as the actual or threatened physical, economic, psychological, verbal, sexual or social abuse of an individual by someone with whom they have had or are having an intimate relationship. There are many ways in which each criterion may manifest itself, and this will to some extent depend on the victim's (the survivor's) social status and support network. So domestic violence can be actual or threatened abuse, which allows for an understanding of the victim's fear and intimidation, often cited as the most upsetting ordeal a victim will go through, worse than the eventual attack or row.

This definition implies that domestic violence is not necessarily restricted to physical abuse; it can include anything from punching and kicking, to sleep deprivation and even murder. It is also sexual: any sexual act against the woman's wishes (in the vast majority of cases it is a female who is the victim), which can be anything from rape to forced prostitution. Economic abuse is an often overlooked but important area as it is often the main reason why women stay in violent relationships. Regardless of the fact that there are more women within the workplace than ever before, many women are still financially reliant upon their husband/partner. Economic abuse may take the form of the perpetrator making the victim beg for money or withholding money, even in some cases for basics such as food and sanitary towels.

Psychological or emotional abuse is often the cruellest form of abuse as it breaks down the victim's defence strategies and destroys the image they have of their 'self'. This can be achieved through constant criticism: they are 'ugly', they are a 'bad' person, no one else would want or love them. Social abuse is closely linked to psychological abuse in that it also breaks down self-esteem. It is often the case that social abuse involves behaviour that is based on an approach of divide and conquer, thereby removing the victim from any support systems that he or she may have. The victim may be isolated from friends, forbidden to see family members and allowed out only at specific times.

QUESTION BREAK

Think of other examples of abuse/domestic violence that have not been discussed here. Try to think of examples of the different forms – including psychological, emotional and social abuse.

Explaining domestic violence

Although it is not the purpose of this section to investigate in any great depth the causes of domestic violence, it is worth briefly outlining the major perspectives that have developed over the past thirty or so years. Biological and psychological explanations are related to the extent that they argue that such violence is a result of specific, individual factors. The medical world, for instance, has focused on human DNA in order to explain a range of behaviour, including homosexuality, mental illness and violence. It has been argued that violence can be attributed to having an extra Y chromosome. Socio-biologists have even argued that violence within the home has the function of helping the 'fittest to survive' (Draper and Burgess 1989). The psychological approach also aims to understand domestic violence through individual factors such as personality traits, mental illness and internal defence mechanisms. For instance, Snell *et al.* (1964) claimed that it was a wife's masochistic personality that caused her to be abused by her husband and, by implication, that victims of domestic violence actually enjoyed experiencing pain and thus wanted to be abused. Erin Pizzey (1974) argued that male perpetrators were psychologically maladjusted and had often grown up in abusive families themselves – a process that encouraged a 'cycle of violence'. These ideas have been criticized because of their assumption that victims are culpable in part for their victimization, that all women who are abused within a relationship are in some way 'crazy', and that men who abuse are psychologically maladjusted and come from violent homes. Strauss (1980), for example, found that men who abused their partners did not have an uncommonly high rate of psychological disturbance. More importantly, these theories ignore issues around power and raise the question of why, if perpetrators of domestic violence are psychologically maladjusted, do they not beat their bosses, friends and fathers rather than wait until they are in the privacy of their own homes before engaging in violence?

From a sociological perspective, domestic violence is investigated in relation to structure, and feminist approaches have tried to shift this focus from victim as individually culpable to an analysis of the socially constructed political, economic and cultural contexts within which violence against women flourishes. Domestic violence (especially against women) is explained in relation to gender, in particular the subordination of women by men in society (patriarchy). Gender relations are characterized by power, and in relation to domestic violence, men dominate women through abuse whether it be physical, psychological, social or economic. Domestic violence is seen as understandable within a historical sociopolitical context that relates to family life and marriage (Dobash and Dobash 1998). Feminists argue that these institutions have been dominated by men through the years and that this has been allowed by a patriarchal society. The social construction of masculinity and violence allows men to produce and maintain their authority over women and children. Within Victorian society, for example, the criminal justice system sanctioned men's rights to control women and children through abusive means if necessary.

In a similar vein, sex-role theory argues that sex-role socialization can explain why violence in general and more particularly within the family is perpetrated by men. Throughout primary and secondary socialization, girls are socialized into the victim status: they are taught through play and observation that they are to be passive and yield to the control of men. Similarly, boys are taught that they should display strength and control. Sexual childhood socialization (or 'sex scripts', as Strong and DeVault (1995) put it) also teaches children the required behaviour within relationships: boys are taught to be the sexual aggressor and girls to be submissive. Moreover, the socialization of girls and women in society forces them into accepting patriarchal values, which leaves them open and vulnerable to abuse.

So the earlier theories of domestic violence, in particular biological and psychological ones, emphasized the role of the individual, whether the perpetrator or victim. By contrast, sociological theories, notably feminism, have looked beyond the individual and analysed the social and political structures which have allowed domestic violence to continue. One of the most significant of these structures has been the criminal justice system.

Victims of domestic violence and the criminal justice system

The criminal justice system is not an institution in isolation; many areas of life may affect its response to certain phenomena. In particular, contemporary dominant discourses (e.g. patriarchy), political movements, government policy, pressure groups, public opinion, and the media have all (whether we like it or not) affected the response of the criminal justice system. As an example, we will consider how the police respond to victims of domestic violence.

As stated earlier, the victims' movement of the 1970s highlighted issues of social rights, and domestic violence became a prominent area, no longer a private issue, the victims of which suffered in silence. Since this politicization of domestic violence, the government has recognized that this form of violence deserves state intervention and the status of 'real' crime; yet the criminal justice system has responded slowly and at times inconsistently to this status.

Up until 1975 the police service's role in relation to domestic violence had been negligible. The attitude had been to avoid arrest and prosecution, and to observe the notion that such behaviour was a private affair between spouses and that intervention (except in relation to particularly violent episodes) was to be discouraged. In 1975 the first public policy on domestic violence outlined the serious nature of this type of crime and detailed the role that the police should play in relation to arrest. Following this report, various government acts and recommendations were put into place which aided the police in performing their role, including the Domestic Violence Act 1976, the Domestic Violence and Magistrates Act 1978 and the Matrimonial Homes Act 1983. Further, Home Office Circulars of 1986 (no. 69) and 1990 (no. 60) urged the police to improve services to victims and to treat domestic violence in the same way as any other serious crime, and encouraged forces to keep accurate statistical records.

Despite the new rules, regulations and initiatives (the high-profile Zero Tolerance campaign being an example), the public still seem to be reluctant to involve the police in domestic violence incidents. Twenty-nine per cent of those who took part in a BBC survey stated that they would be reluctant to involve the police in an incident of this sort (*BBC News*, 11 February 2003). Conversely, the police are often still reluctant to intervene, despite governmental and public pressure.

So what reasons are there for the lack of public faith in the police and for the apparent police apathy towards incidents of domestic violence?

Public faith in the police is often drawn from experience – either direct or indirect. In relation to domestic violence, the police are often criticized for their apathetic reaction to it. Studies have shown that victims often feel that response to their situation has been inadequate. Grace (1995), for example, found that police failed to deal with incidents of domestic violence seriously or sensitively. The feeling was that domestic incidents are low on the list of priorities for an overburdened police service and that time could be better spent looking for 'real' criminals rather than wasting time on another 'domestic'. Victims also feel that the police cannot offer effective support once the incident has been reported (Hoyle 1999). Drawing on victims' experiences, many feminist theorists have highlighted the misuse of discretionary powers available to the police when dealing with incidents of domestic violence. Decision making is influenced by the police culture, which can be patriarchal by nature, therefore individual judgements may often be based upon stereotypes and bias (Edwards 1989).

However, people's perception of the police do not always match the reality, and it is clear that dealing with domestic violence is often problematic for the police. Police work is subject to the organization's bureaucratic structure, and the police decision-making process is reached via a number of considerations. Obviously, evidence is of the utmost importance when trying to bring a domestic violence case to court and needs to be substantial enough for the Crown Prosecution Service (CPS) to consider prosecution. Hoyle (1999) explains this phenomenon as being partly due to the importance afforded to the 'victim's preferences'. Although a victim is not allowed to withdraw charges (this is within the remit of the police and the CPS), the victim often withdraws her or his statement for a number of reasons, both personal and practical. Also, despite the efforts by the police to set up domestic violence units and recruit domestic violence officers, such officers regularly complain that they feel marginalized and that their area of work receives low priority and status.

Recently a new effort has been made by the Metropolitan Police to deal with domestic violence incidents more effectively. The 'golden hour' is a new initiative that lays emphasis on the importance of gathering evidence from the scene of a domestic dispute within an hour in order to gain the best chance of conviction of the offender. Community Safety Units have also been put in place to advise all victims of hate crime (including domestic violence).

Victims of domestic violence have various ways in which to access the criminal justice system. There are a number of laws that serve to protect victims of domestic violence. The Protection from Harassment Law (the 'stalkers' law') is unique in the fact that this is the first law to protect from behaviour that is not specifically criminal. The Harassment Act 1997 criminalizes the psychological nature of domestic violence. The Youth Justice and Criminal Evidence Act 1999 has also put in place measures to provide protection for victims and witnesses, including victims of domestic violence. The Domestic Violence Crime and Victims Act 2004 is the most all-encompassing piece of legislation regarding domestic violence ever passed in this country. The Act puts in place a number of reforms to police and court procedures. For example the circumstances under which non-molestation orders can be imposed has been extended to include same-sex couples and cohabiting couples. The Act also paved the way for the Code of Practice for Victims (2006) which, as we have seen, gives statutory rights to victims of crime and sets out services and rights that victims of crime could expect.

After the initial police report and arrest, the next stage that the victim of domestic violence must endure is the court process. The majority of domestic violence cases, and crime cases in general, are tried at the magistrates' courts, so it is crucial that the attitudes of magistrates towards domestic violence are free from bias. The implementation of the Code of Practice for Victims (2006) outlines that victims at court must be treated sympathetically, leading to the Magistrates Association calling for an examination of magistrates' approaches to domestic violence cases.

Despite this reflective mood, Gilchrist and Blisset (2002) uncovered evidence that there remains differential treatment and punishment towards crimes involving public and private violence. Their results found that 32 per cent of those accused of assault within the home were given a custodial sentence, compared to 37 per cent of those accused of assaulting a stranger. Moreover, explanations for the perpetrator's conduct were discussed more openly and deemed more 'important' in domestic violence cases than in stranger assaults. As Gilchrist and Blisset put it, 'This type of discussion mirrored the language and explanation commonly heard in domestic violence perpetrator programmes: excusing the man, minimizing the assault and blaming the victim for the perpetrator's behaviour' (2002: 360).

It would seem that despite the structural measures taken to protect victims of domestic violence and punish the perpetrators, there is always danger of individual bias from a particular magistrate or judge – and this is an area that it is very difficult to monitor effectively and deal with.

QUESTION BREAK: UNCOVERING DOMESTIC ABUSE

Read the following extract and answer the questions that follow.

ICM interviewed a random sample of 1020 adults aged 18+, face to face in January 2003. Interviews were conducted across the country and the data has been weighted to the profile of all adults.

One in four adults in Britain has experienced domestic violence, a poll for the BBC suggests. In the survey of more than 1,000 people, a quarter said they had been involved in violence, either as the victim or perpetrator.

The research by pollsters ICM covered all the relationships from short term to marriage. More than a quarter of the women who were questioned (27%) said they had been physically abused. The corresponding figure for men was 21%. Of those who had been involved in domestic violence 37% of women had reported an incident to the police, compared with 19% of men.

More than a third of the sample said they knew someone who had experienced domestic violence but women were much more likely than men to tell a friend or go to the police.

Yet the issue of whether the police should intervene in domestic violence remains contentious. Nearly three out of 10 people surveyed said they thought the police should always be called. But twice as many feel they should not be routinely involved. Seven out of ten people said they thought the police were more likely to give priority to dealing with an incident between people in the street than a disturbance between a man and a woman in their own home. Almost half the respondents thought that it was up to the people concerned to sort it out behind closed doors. Only 29% thought that the police should always be called in such cases.

The extent of domestic violence has always been difficult to measure because many people are reluctant to talk about their own experiences. This survey confirms that it is still a major problem that affects people of all ages and social classes, right across the country.

(*BBC News*, 11 February 2003)

The survey revealed that a majority of people still feel reluctant to involve the police in cases of domestic violence. How could you account for this attitude?

The survey suggests that 'the extent of domestic violence [is] difficult to measure'. Explain the reasons why people might be unwilling to divulge information about their experiences of domestic violence.

Corporate crime and its victims

The plight of victims of corporate crime rarely features in discussions of criminology or victimology. Here we will attempt to identify the diverse nature of corporate victims, illustrated by case studies involving employees, consumers and general citizens. The discussion devotes some space to the physical and emotional effects upon the victims and then considers some of the problems affecting the legal treatment and status of the victims of corporate crime within a capitalist society.

The writer generally associated with placing the corporate crime on the criminological agenda is Edwin Sutherland. Sutherland's book *White Collar Crime* (1960) is arguably the first text that gives credence to the fact that corporate crime creates many victims. His study demonstrated that corporate crime was widespread and virtually endemic within contemporary national and transnational corporations. Sutherland dealt with the economic impact of corporate crime in a comprehensive manner. His contribution in relation to corporate victimization rests upon his analysis of the difficulties in recognizing and giving status to the corporate victim. He argued that this stems from the fact that many corporate offences are less readily definable as crime than are other types of offence, in part because of the rippling effect of corporate crime, which may involve only a small loss to individual victims but enormous gain to the perpetrators. For that reason, there tends to be a lack of deep public resentment towards corporate crime, as there seems to be no identifiable victim.

Corporate crime is often seen as part of the broader concept of white-collar crime, and is defined by Croall (1992) as 'the abuse of a legitimate occupational role which is regulated by the law'. This includes occupational crimes committed by employers and corporate crime in which business or corporations exploit consumers and workers. Our interest here is to draw attention to the way in which the corporate organization promotes certain types of activity or inactivity resulting in victimization rather than to consider the way in which individuals negotiate their own activities within an organizational framework.

Using radical criminology, Box argued that most crimes are committed by powerful multinational corporations, the government and the police. He argued therefore that we must reconceptualize the definition of serious crime. Box acknowledges the real suffering of what he terms 'conventional victims', but feels that it is imperative that criminology look at the victims of corporate crime.

> Murder, rape, robbery and assault . . . Maybe they are only *a* crime problem and not *the* crime problem. Maybe what is stuffed into our consciousness as the crime problem is in fact an illusion, a trick to deflect our attention away from the other, even more serious crimes and victimising behaviours, which objectively cause the bulk of avoidable death, injury and deprivation.
>
> (Box 1983: 3)

Consequently, Box provides an illuminating commentary on 'intention' versus 'indifference' (to harmful consequences), thereby comparing the status of the corporate victim with that of the conventional victim. Moreover, Box's concept of 'avoidable harm' should be carefully considered when analysing the status of the corporate victim in relation to current legislation pertaining to the corporation.

Since Box's classic study, the plight of the corporate victim has captured the attention of a number of theorists (e.g. Pearce and Tombs 1998; Croall 1992; Levi 1992). However, it would seem that there has been less systematic exploration of victims of corporate crime than of victims of 'conventional' crime, which has led to a tendency within victimology and criminology to emphasize the victims of 'conventional crime'. Two reasons contribute to this lack of attention: the problems of measuring victims of corporate crime and the way in which the corporate victim is rendered invisible.

Until recently, corporate crime has been viewed as a 'victimless' crime, with those who suffer from it being seen rather as victims of disasters or accidents, not really as victims of criminal activity. Indeed, Fattah states:

> Despite the scope of white collar crime and despite the fact that its depredations far exceed those of conventional crime it is totally left out of victim campaigns. Moreover, other socially harmful actions such as pollution of the environment, the production of hazardous substances, the manufacture and sale of unsafe products, and so on, cause more death, injury and harm than all the violent crime combined.
>
> (1986: 5)

Whereas the liberation movements created an academic breeding ground for victimology which challenged the legitimacy of the legal system and directed attention to the crimes of the powerful, in legal and social terms the victim is still largely invisible. This problem occurs as a result of lack of 'victim awareness': within the criminal justice system there is a lack of established legal concepts or definitions that take account of the victims of corporate crime. Similarly, there is a lack of any substantial empirical evidence (through a lack of effective measurement) to raise awareness of the growing number of such victims.

There are difficulties involved in offering any accurate measurement of corporate victimization. For the impact of crime to be measured, the victims first of all must define and recognize the behaviour or activity affecting them as criminal. This is especially difficult in relation to corporate crime. Corporate victims are not always aware that a crime has been committed or that the behaviour or activity affecting them holds any criminal consequences. This is what Geis (1967) has called 'victim responsiveness'. He argues, 'It is particularly notable, first of all, that people do not react vigorously, deep with outrage to most forms of white collar crime' (Geis uses the term 'white-collar crime' in a similar sense to corporate crime). In a similar vein, Levi states (in relation to fraud), 'Fraud then is an unusual type of crime because the fraudster gets the victim to part with his money voluntarily albeit under false assumptions about the transaction' (1987: 24).

Walklate (1989) has argued that the notion of 'victim responsiveness' is related to the victim's state of mind, and this appears to include an unwillingness to report incidents to the relevant regulatory bodies. This may be due to the fact that victims feel foolish for being taken advantage of or that they do not know what the relevant bodies are and the extent to which corporate victimization exists.

The neglect of corporate crime by both criminologists and victimologists is not due to a lack of interest within the area but more to the fact that there are many difficulties to be overcome in researching this area. Collating and comparing statistical information in relation to corporate victimization proves difficult owing to the sheer number of agencies and departments involved in regulating corporations. In relation to fraud, for example, Levi points out:

Consumer frauds (including restrictive trade practices) may be dealt with by the Trading Standards offices or by the Office of Fair Trading: bankruptcy, liquidation, banking, and investment frauds are within the remit of the Department of Trade and Industry; and tax frauds are dealt with by the Inland Revenue or the Customs and Excise departments.

(1987: 24)

Moreover, data from official agencies can only reveal prosecutions and not sanctions or settlements that may be reached; obviously this reveals only a partial picture concerning the victims of business activities. Therefore, given the difficulties of using official sources to construct a measure of corporate crime, there are even more difficulties in using these sources as indicators of levels of corporate victimization.

Criminal victimization surveys are also of little use in measuring victims of corporate crime. Hough and Mayhew (1983) point out that 'They can only discover crimes which have clearly identifiable people as victims, they cannot easily count crimes against organisations (such as fraud, shoplifting or fare evasion).' Therefore, criminal victim surveys rest upon clearly identifiable people as victims, which causes a problem in regard to corporate crime, especially when considering concepts of 'victim responsiveness'.

Identifying the victims of corporate crime

Whether as consumers, workers, investors, passengers, residents or employees, most people will become victims of corporate crime. Here we will concentrate on victims of corporate crime in relation to workers, consumers and the citizen, and to illustrate the seriousness of corporate victimization will refer to Stuart Hills's concept of 'corporate violence':

actual harm and risk of harm inflicted on consumers, workers, and the general public as a result of general decisions by corporate executives or managers, from corporate negligence, the quest for profits at any cost, and the wilful violations of health and safety and environmental laws.

(1987: 7)

Hills aims to heighten awareness of the respectable business people who impersonally maim and kill for profit. The solution to corporate victimization, according to Hills, is to develop a broad-based democratic political movement that may bring about structural changes.

Consumers

The growth of the consumer society has brought many practices which adversely effect us as consumers. Consumers as victims of corporate violence are not a new phenomenon. Dowie (1977) documents the case of the Ford Pinto and its dangerous petrol tank. On discovering that the Ford Pinto had a design fault with its tank, it was decided by Ford's board of directors that it would be more economical to pay out insurance upon any future deaths or injuries rather than recall the Pinto and redesign the tank. Dowie claims that between 500 and 900 burn deaths resulted from the ensuing explosions.

Fifty years on, it is still just as difficult to gain convictions for corporate manslaughter cases involving transport. Successful manslaughter cases are difficult to bring, and high-profile attempts at prosecution often fail (for example, the 1997 Southall rail crash which killed seven people and injured 139 and the 1987 Zeebrugge ferry disaster, which killed 192 people). Another (in)famous case related to the Dalkon Shield contraceptive, which killed several women, left many childless and caused enormous suffering to countless others (Perry and Dawson 1985).

Such cases have occurred over the decades, and the cases of consumers as victims have become ever more complex. Consumers throughout the developing world can be the victims of corporate violence through exploitation by multinational corporations. For example, Nestlé has been accused of promoting a product (milk formula) that resulted in the death of hundreds of thousands of babies in developing world countries. It has been argued that through promotional campaigns the company claimed that its product was more nutritious and healthier than breast milk. The result was that mothers were encouraged to pay extortionate prices for a product that they could not afford and did not need.

As medical knowledge and the use of drugs has expanded over the past 20 years, so the consumer's safety within the medical world has become an issue. John Braithwaite, now a Trades Practices Commissioner, provided a devastating exposé of the pharmaceutical industry in his study *Corporate Crime in the Pharmaceutical Industry* (1984). International bribery and corruption, fraud, negligence in the testing of drugs, and criminal negligence in the unsafe manufacture of drugs demonstrated that the pharmaceutical industry had an appalling record of lawbreaking. Evidence of such malpractice was also evident in the thalidomide case – a drug which after years of extensive animal testing was marketed as a perfectly safe tranquillizer for pregnant mothers. The end result was that more than 10,000 grossly deformed babies were born. During the trial of the manufacturers in the 1970s, numerous court witnesses, who were all animal experimenters, said under oath that the results of animal experiments are never valid for human beings. However, the incredible reaction to the thalidomide tragedy by the pharmaceutical lobby was that it was an exception and that it emphasized the need for more animal testing, not less.

As technology advances and more high-tech gadgets invade the market, consumers of these manufactured goods are at risk of becoming victims of a new type of corporate crime. The Department of Trade and Industry has highlighted the danger of unscrupulous firms who are using computers, mobile phones and fax machines to market their product. Ambiguous promotional messages are being sent via e-mail and text messages, and to answer these messages may cost the consumer a premium-rate call. For most of us, mobile phones and computers have become essential and part of everyday life, and also a new way in which we can be victimized. The question break below considers new forms of victimization.

QUESTION BREAK: OFT TARGETS ONLINE TICKET SCAMS

OFT (Office of Fair Trading) research reveals almost one in 10 buyers has been ripped off by a bogus site . . . Victims lost an average of £80, but in more serious cases fans have been fleeced for hundreds of pounds.

Music fans have recently suffered from an explosion in the number of fraudulent gig ticket websites, with fraud experts estimating that 30,000 people in the UK were ripped off last year . . .

Many people are buying tickets that never arrive. One firm that left music fans high and dry was SOS Master Tickets whose website was taken down after it took money for tickets for the 2008 V Festival that never arrived.

The OFT's Just Tick It campaign, being launched today, offers a checklist on the government's Consumer Direct site to help ticket buyers differentiate between bogus and legitimate websites.

Research by the OFT shows that more than four in 10 (44%) people who had fallen victim to a scam had been anxious to secure tickets. Almost a third (32%) were tricked by the legitimate and professional appearance of the websites. And after realising they had been duped, one in five were then too shy to report it . . .

Mike Haley of the OFT said: 'We're working hard with other law enforcement agencies to crack down on these types of crimes and consumers can help themselves to avoid falling victim by knowing how to spot a scam site.'

Many of the bogus sites tend to be hosted outside the UK, with Hungary a favourite safe haven. In many cases the Metropolitan Police has written to the web-hosting companies and domain registrars to ask them to pull the plug, but these requests are often refused . . .

Bogus sites often carry all the official branding, stolen from legitimate sites, and have plausible web addresses, which is often enough to fool people into thinking they are real.

Last weekend, a number of fans of rock band Muse were turned away from the group's two open-air shows in Teignmouth, Devon, after buying tickets from museboxoffice.com which either never arrived or never existed. The website is still live and offering tickets for the band's forthcoming European shows. But it gives no contact number or postal address (people can only get in touch via email) and hides behind a US company called InvisiHosting.

(From the *Guardian*, 10 September 2009)

- What other 'consumer scams' can you think of?
- What groups in society do you think are most likely to be the victims of 'high-tech scams'?
- What do you think the impact of such crimes would be on the victims?

Workers

Employees have long been exploited within the workplace in relation to low pay, long hours and unsafe conditions. In Britain a large number of deaths and injury within the workplace result from the failure to comply with safety regulations. Reports carried out by the Health and Safety Executive in the 1980s indicated that in at least two-thirds of fatal accidents, managers had violated the Health and Safety at Work Act (Tombs 1990). Workers not only are affected by safety regulations but can die as a result of diseases contracted at work, most notably from asbestos poisoning (mesothelioma) but also from lung disease and occupationally related cancers.

The Health and Safety Executive revealed some disturbing figures in their annual report of Health and Safety Statistics 2008/2009:

- **1.2 million** people who worked during the last year were suffering from an illness (long standing as well as new cases) they believed was caused or made worse by their current or past work.
- **180** workers were killed at work, a rate of **0.6** per 100 000 workers.
- **131,895** other injuries to employees were reported under RIDDOR (Reporting of Injuries, Diseases, and Dangerous Occurrences Regulations), a rate of 502.2 per 100 000 employees.
- **246,000** reportable injuries occurred, according to the Labour Force Survey, a rate of 870 per 100 000 workers.
- **29.3 million** days were lost overall (1.24 days per worker), 24.6 million due to work-related ill health and 4.7 million due to workplace injury. (www.hse.gov.uk/statistics)

As the industrial base of the nation has shrunk and modern service work increased, so the nature of corporate violence against employees has changed also. This may lead to health and safety issues being less visible; for example, it has been proven that CRTs (computer monitors) can seriously affect the health and safety of employees. Exposure to radiation in chemical plants and dangerous materials in laboratories and hospitals also illustrates the point that victims of corporate crime are often those employees who are in low-level, low-paid, non-unionized jobs and are the victims of poverty that corporations create in their pursuit of maximizing profit. An example of this involves the sports retail giant Nike. In November 1997 in a document that had been leaked to Corporate Watch (the watchdog on the Internet), it was alleged that Nike was running Vietnamese sweatshops where workers (the majority of whom were women) were low paid and mistreated, working in appalling conditions. It was only through media attention that Nike eventually pledged to end child labour, follow the occupational health and safety standards, and allow non-governmental organisations (NGOs) to participate in the monitoring of its Asian factories (Corporate Watch Website 1998). Similarly Primark, the clothes shop that prides itself on affordable clothes, was voted least ethical retailer by *Ethical Consumer Magazine*. This followed an exposé by the BBC current affairs programme *Panorama* entitled 'On The Rack' in June 2008. The documentary revealed that some of Primark's clothing suppliers in India were subcontracting labour to children from refugee camps in southern India.

The real impact of crime within the workplace is rarely considered. Medical costs in the event of injury, counselling in the event of mental abuse and higher prices of products due to theft affect a number of people. Gill (1999) states:

> If staff are affected by the crime they may need counselling and time off; if they leave there are additional recruitment and training costs in addition to the impact this may have on the image of the company from staff, customers or the community at large.

To be a victim of corporate crime one need not be either an employee or a consumer. Fraud such as tax evasion and large-scale embezzlement can affect the finances of every one of us as taxes are increased to compensate the Treasury. New technology, especially the Internet, is generating what has become known as 'cybercrime'. Wall (1999) has identified four areas of such activity: cyber-trespass (hacking), cyber-thefts (fraud, appropriation of intellectual property), cyber-obscenities (pornography, sex trade) and cyber-violence (stalking, hate speech). He has also highlighted the problem of defining the victims of cyber-crime – owing to the fact that victims can be individuals or social groups and the harms done may range from actual to perceived: 'In cases such as cyberstalking or theft of cybercash, the victimisation is very much directed towards the individual. However, in other cases the victimisation is more indirect as with cases of cyberpiracy and cyberspying/terrorism' (1999).

Citizens are also threatened by noxious emissions from factories, by chemicals in water supplies and by pollution of beaches and rivers. The victims of such pollution have gained a higher profile recently as a result of the heightened awareness of pollution through EU regulation. Richard Mills, the secretary of the National Society for Clean Air, stated that 'even on a conservative estimate, air pollution is killing 10 times more people than road incidents every year' (*Guardian*, 5 December 2002). The Environment Agency has for many years argued that the penalties for companies that pollute should be increased considerably to avoid such companies regarding pollution and the court action that might result from it as an acceptable 'business risk'. In 2009 the European Union announced that it planned to take the UK to court for flouting air pollution laws. The Commission stated: 'we have started infringement proceedings against the United Kingdom for failing to comply with the EU's air quality standard for dangerous airborne particles known as PM10. These particles can cause asthma, cardiovascular problems, lung cancer and premature death.'

Although both men and women can, of course, be victims as consumers, workers and citizens, it is still the case that a neglected area of victims of corporate crime is that of women as victims. The invisibility of these women victims in current criminological research is attributed to the paternalism within society and the focus on causal rather than structural explanations of criminality. Examples of the corporate victimization of women include women working in sweatshops, men-only occupations, the pharmaceutical industry and work-related diseases. Gerber and Weeks (1992) argue that feminist theories sensitive to the gendered nature of human existence are required to analyse female corporate victimization adequately.

Unlike many issues related to women's health, the recent controversy of silicone breast implants did create a great deal of public interest. Rybrant and Kramer (1995) use the feminine gaze to place the silicone implant dispute within the larger theoretical framework of corporate violence. Their case study of the historical development of this debate illustrates: duplicity in the chemical industry; the power of special interest groups; the importance, and the complicity, of governmental regulatory agencies; and the vital impact of cultural perceptions of beauty on women. The issue of weight and the idea that the super-skinny size zero is an ideal image of the female in contemporary society has lead to a multi-million pound industry in diet and dietary supplements and anorectics. Fen-phen was an anti-obesity medication which was used and prescribed mainly to females in the 1980s and 1990s. The drug led to the death of a 30-year-old women in 1997 and medical trials reported that the drug caused valvular heart disease and pulmonary hypertension primarily amongst women users. Following recommendations of the FDA (The Food and Drug Administration in the USA), Fen-phen was removed from the market in 1997. Thousands of lawsuits have been filed by Fen-phen victims in recent years. Cultural perceptions of women may also affect the treatment that they receive in the criminal justice system. In litigation surrounding the Dalkon Shield contraceptive case, women were blamed for being promiscuous, and, similarly, women who received silicone breast implants for cosmetic as opposed to medical reasons have been awarded lower damages (Finlay 1996).

The physical and emotional effects of corporate crime

The physical effects of corporate crime are self-evident: disease, illness, deformity, accidents and death can and do occur as a result of corporate malpractice. The emotional aspects of corporate crime are less visible and as a consequence have received very little academic attention. This is especially true of victims of financial fraud, although such victims share many of the same devastating outcomes as their counterparts who have suffered serious violent crime. Indeed, certain white-collar crime victims may suffer more emotional distress. Wells (1989) argues that some of the effects include guilt, shame, disbelief, anger, depression, sense of betrayal and loss of trust. These emotional repercussions are often misunderstood by law enforcement, criminal justice and victim service providers, as well as the community at large; indeed, the victim is often doubly victimized by this dynamic. As Walsh and Schram have described,

> People who have lost money to white collar criminals (like swindlers and con artists) often encounter scepticism, suspicion and contempt when they seek help. This negative treatment leaves them feeling guilty and ashamed. The double standards used in handling white collar offenders and their victims has been attributed to the status of the accused perpetrators, the difficulty in establishing criminal intent in such cases and the belief that imprisonment is not the cure for this kind of stealing.
>
> (1980: 33)

Another factor is the largely ambivalent attitude towards, and negative images of, these victims held by the public and by the criminal justice officials. A number of aphorisms are used to blame these victims: 'fraud only befalls those of questionable character' or 'an honest man can't be cheated'. The stereotypical response to cheated parties is that they have disregarded the basic rules of sensible conduct regarding financial matters. Their stupidity, carelessness or complacency undermines their credibility and makes others reluctant to activate the machinery of the criminal justice system on their behalf so as to formally punish those who harmed them, and to validate their claims to be treated as authentic victims, worthy of support rather than as mere dupes, losers or suckers who were outsmarted (Karman 1990).

Victims of financial crime often describe a tremendous violation of their personal integrity, using phrases such as 'It was like being raped' and 'I have lost all of my sense of trust.' Because the psychological wounds are not perceived in the same way as wounds to the body, nor as generally understood as the emotional scars of a sexual assault, the effects on victims of corporate crime are often, and inappropriately, minimized. Wells notes that victims of corporate crime, unlike the victims of violent physical crime, have 'wounds' that 'are not always easy to see and most often internal rather than external' (1989: 26–7). However, he goes on to support the notion that victims of corporate crime have a similar sense of violation and often require 'psychological first aid'.

Victims of corporate crime and the criminal justice system

Thus corporate victims suffer physically and emotionally. Despite this, the criminal justice system does not have the necessary mechanisms in place to support or protect corporate victims. This type of victimization is often described as 'an accident' or 'a disaster', which minimizes the serious nature of such crimes.

Crimes committed by corporations for the most part do not fall under the jurisdiction of the police; they are the remit of regulatory bodies. The fact that this type of crime is regulated rather than policed tends to create the impression that the victims' case is less urgent than in those cases that involve 'conventional' crime. Monetary support for those agencies that deal with corporate crime tends to be very low compared to other criminal justice agencies.

Unlike victims of more conventional crime, victims of corporate crime have not benefited from the victim-centred reforms that we have seen over the last decade. They have been excluded from the Victims Code of Practice enacted under the Domestic Violence, Crime and Victims Act (2004) and its predecessor, the Victims' Charter in the 1990s (which was put in place to improve victims' experience within the criminal justice system). The exclusion of corporate crime means that victims do not benefit from the safeguards that the Victims' Code of Practice may provide. Victims of corporate crime are exempt from the Criminal Injuries Compensation Scheme and rely on charitable non-profit organizations for support and advice such as CCA Centre for Corporate Accountability. The Trades Union Congress has been particularly outspoken and critical of the government's 'victim centred' approach and has pressed for it to be extended to cover the victims of workplace crimes. Moreover, the Victims Code of Practice points to Victim Support as an agency that can be contacted to help victims with their ordeal. However, this organization does not deal with corporate victims, leaving the victims of corporate crime in a vulnerable situation.

For many years law surrounding corporations and companies has been criticized for being unfair and ineffective. In particular, in relation to corporate manslaughter there remained many limitations to early legislation. Directors or managers, not companies, were held responsible; schools, police forces and other unincorporated organizations could not be prosecuted; and third, Crown immunity meant that Crown and government organizations were above the law and therefore exempt from accountability. This old common law on manslaughter, and in particular the idea of Crown immunity, were criticized for being biased and working upon the premise of outdated concepts which allowed government agencies to commit criminal offences. The Corporate Manslaughter and Corporate Homicide Act put in place in 2007 has been a significant improvement. The Act now applies to corporations, government departments, the police service, partnerships and trade unions that employ staff. In 2008 the CPS brought its first charge of Corporate Manslaughter against the company Cotswold Geotechnical Holdings for the death of a young geologist in September 2008 (at the time of writing in 2010, the case had still to be heard).

Clearly, this new offence will help victims of corporate offences gain some credibility within the justice system. However, as Hills argues,

> Until there is great public understanding of the relationship between corporate decision making and human suffering – indeed until there is a sense of public sensibility that provokes moral outrage at this corporate indifference, the far reaching structural reforms that could make a major and lasting difference are unlikely to occur.
>
> (1987: 202)

QUESTION BREAK: CORPORATE KILLING OR MANSLAUGHTER?

- What would be the advantages of a statute that recognized 'corporate killing' rather than 'corporate manslaughter'?
- How difficult would it be to enforce such a law?
- Read the comment from Hills above. Why is it so important for the status of the corporate victim that there is public moral outrage against corporate crime?

Victims of fraud do have limited success in the criminal justice system. The Serious Fraud Office (SFO), for example, was created by the Criminal Justice Act in 1987 to investigate major fraud. The Director of the SFO is Richard Alderman and he is accountable to the Attorney General. In April 2010 the SFO declared a particularly high rate of prosecution for the previous year. The conviction rate, measured as defendants convicted over the number tried, has risen from 78 per cent the previous year to 91 per cent. At the same time the agency achieved a 100 per cent success rate in trials where at least one defendant was convicted. The previous year this was measured at 94 per cent (www.sfo.gov.uk).

However, during the early and mid 1990s a number of high-profile cases collapsed or failed, earning the office the title 'seriously flawed office'. The chronology of failed cases includes the following:

- the collapse of the 'Guinness case' against Lord Spense and Roger Seelig (£10 million fraud charge) in 1992;
- the sentence of Roger Levitt to 180 hours' community service for a £358 million fraud charge in 1993;
- the 1994 acquittal of George Walker (head of Brent Walker) of £164 million fraud charges;
- in 1996, the clearing of Kevin and Ian Maxwell of fraud charges following the loss of £440 million in pension funds.

This section has explored the relatively hidden nature of corporate victimization. Far from being a 'victimless' crime, it is now evident that all of us will at some stage become a victim of corporate crime, whether within our public or our private lives. Despite this, the victims of corporate crime have remained relatively invisible. This is due in part to the diffuse nature of this kind of victimization, but the main contributing factors are inadequate legal sanctions and ineffective law enforcement. It is evident that corporate victimisation is not a priority in the criminal justice system.

QUESTION BREAK

Positivist victimologists measure risk of victimisation in terms of individual social charateristics or lifestlye (see pp. 339–342).

- How does (a) gender, (b) age, (c) economic situation/occupation, (d) geographical location affect the likelihood of becoming a victim of each of the following corporate crimes: cyber-crime; health and safety lawbreaking; medical blunders; pollution?

FURTHER READING

Croall, H. (2009) *Corporate Crime,* London: Sage. This three-volume set focuses on the issues around health and safety, consumerism and globalization. It discusses the problems regarding the definition and extent of corporate crime and also gives depth to the theoretical argument through using relevant case studies. Part 1 looks at definitions and problems with them; part 2 at the criminological study of corporate crime; and part 3 at the controlling of this form of crime.

Hoyle, C. (1999) *Negotiating Domestic Violence*, Oxford: Clarendon. This is a study of police response to domestic violence based on interviews and observation. It examines police culture and its effect on police structures, training and practice and outlines the very difficult position of the victim of domestic violence.

Walklate, S. (ed.) (2007) *The Handbook for Victims and Victimology*, Abingdon: Willan Publishing. This book brings together leading scholars who discuss the recent debates and issues within victimology. It provides an overview of theoretical perspectives within victimology, discussion around the different types of victims, including corporate victims and domestic violence victims, and analyses the criminal justice response to such victims.

Punch, M. (1996) *Dirty Business: Exploring Corporate Misconduct. Analysis and Cases*, London: Sage. This book explores corporate misconduct in some detail. Part 1 reviews the literature on corporate deviance (with case studies); part 2 explores cases of corporate crime in some depth; and part 3 draws on the literature review and case studies to offer some conclusions.

The International Review of Victimology is an international peer-reviewed journal. It covers theoretical and empirical research that focuses on a number of areas including victim and offender relationships; reparation and restitution; and the victim and the criminal justice system.

WEBSITES

The home page of the Home Office for the UK – www.homeoffice.gov.uk (and specifically the Victims of Crime Index)

Centre for Corporate Accountability – www.corporateaccountability.org

The International Victimology Website – www.victimology.nl

Police and Policing

▌ INTRODUCTION

In this chapter the main issues that we will be addressing are the reasons for the emergence of modern policing at the beginning of the nineteenth century and how policing has developed since then.

In his detailed political and social history of the English police, Emsley (1996a) argued that since the middle of the nineteenth century there has been a growing centralization of the police in England; and that this cannot be explained in terms of some sort of conspiracy but is rather due to a number of particular pressures that have moved policing in this direction.

First, there has been what Emsley describes as 'a rationalizing of the police in the interest of what has been seen as economy and efficiency', a process that has involved legislation to reduce the differences between different police forces and a limiting of the authority of police committees of local government. Second, during periods of national emergency closer contact between local police forces and central government was established, in periods of war and widespread strike activity, for instance. And while these may have only been intended as temporary centralizing measures, they set precedents. Third, as the police began to be seen as professionals in handling crime and public order so government ministers and civil servants began to communicate directly with the experts and to by-pass amateur local police committees; and this growth of professionalization led senior police officers to discuss and decide policy with one another, again marginalizing local committees.

Emsley suggests this sort of centralization of policing in England was strengthened by the fact that its constitutional structure has been pretty stable for over two centuries

– there haven't been serious challenges to its legitimacy and it has had no need to reconstitute itself as a result of defeat in war.

Early institutions of law enforcement

Although the modern form of policing is generally seen to have emerged in the nineteenth century, the history of law enforcement stretches back many centuries. There were codes of law in Anglo-Saxon England (a period of roughly 600 years after the end of Roman Britain and up until 1066 and the Norman conquest) which basically supported the authority of the monarchs. These codes of law tended to place obligations on the local community to deal with law-breaking and, more generally, wrong doing. Rawlings (2003) refers to the 'hue and cry', which involved neighbours banding together to pursue, catch and punish law breakers such as thieves. This sort of communal policing developed and flourished under feudalism; however by the late fourteenth century the feudal system was decaying, the economy was stagnating and poverty and famine were rife. These factors encouraged law enforcement to move away from the involvement of the whole community and into the hands of local and parish officials – and towards a more formal regulation of the labouring people by such officials. So by the medieval period (the 1350s onwards) high constables of the hundreds and petty constables of the manors were well established official positions. The latter were sort of parish constables, and were usually men appointed from within the community. One of their tasks was to report to the local courts about 'felons, miscreants and nuisances'. Although locally appointed, they did acquire royal authority and were given responsibility for maintaining the King's peace in their district.

Another early agent of local law enforcement was the watchman – a position which was made obligatory by legislation (the Statute of Winchester) in 1285, with all towns and boroughs having to provide a number of watches. As well as guarding the entrances to towns, watchmen were expected to patrol the streets and maintain order. London, for example, was divided into 24 wards each of which had to have a watch of six men supervised by an alderman. By the seventeenth century, justices of the peace were expected to ensure that night watches were kept in their towns from sunset to sunrise. Although watch duty was not always popular, the system was well established by the 1700s and by the nineteenth century some places had established clear guidelines and regulations over the qualifications, pay and discipline of watchmen (Rawlings 2003).

Justices of the peace were constitutionally superior to constables and watchmen in the law enforcement pecking order of medieval England. This position originated from Richard I's reign (1195) and the first justices of the peace were also the social superiors of constables – indeed, they were often lords of manors; and they presided at the courts to which petty constables brought cases. Justices of the peace were appointed by the Crown, through the offices of the Lord Chancellor, with patronage playing a big part in the appointments. The office of justice of the peace was well established by late sixteenth century and the holders became key figures of local government. The workload of justices of the peace varied, often according to the particular individual's inclination. They didn't have to attend quarter sessions, for instance, and some were more dedicated than others.

The emergence of the modern police force

The period of the later eighteenth and early nineteenth centuries saw a radical transformation in Western societies. It was a period of rapid industrialization and of the growing influence of capitalism. The shift from traditional occupations and lifestyles to the new practices of the industrial factory system saw massive migrations of rural populations to the centres of industrial production and the rise of a new urban, industrial class. This period also saw the great ideological revolutions in the USA (1770s) and France (1789) which encouraged a questioning of traditional forms of authority. Such changes were accompanied by a concern about increases in crime and disorder. The concerns which promoted a development and extension of the early institutions of law enforcement were driven to a large extent by fear of property crime from the better-off sections of society. These developments were evidenced in the improvements in the watches in London and elsewhere. Small regular patrols of watchmen were organized for the streets of London; by 1824 these consisted of 24 men divided equally into day and night patrols. As well as in the City of London, similar patrols were set up in the districts outside the City such as Westminster. As early as the 1790s an armed patrol of about 70 men had been established at Bow Street to watch the main roads into the centre of London and by 1828 this consisted of a Horse Patrol, Night Foot Patrol and Day Foot Patrol. In 1785 the then Prime Minister, Pitt, had proposed the establishment of a centrally controlled police for the entire metropolis which had led to the London and Westminster Police Bill and the setting up of nine police divisions.

These brief examples illustrate the beginning of organized, modern policing. Such developments led almost naturally to Robert Peel, appointed as Home Secretary in 1822, introducing legislation for the creation of the Metropolitan Police; with 1829 seen as the official commencement of beat patrols of uniformed Metropolitan Police officers. Initially this legislation was kept to London as he seemed to feel that the creating of a large, centralized police force for all England was not appropriate.

Metropolitan Police of London

Prevention of crime was seen as the first duty of the new Metropolitan Police constables, and beat patrols (a sort of natural follow on from parochial watchmen) were designed with that in mind. Although efforts were made to ensure the police did not look like soldiers, a good deal of early criticism focused on the military nature and style of the new police. In addition there was also some concern about the costs of the new police who were to be paid out of local rates – as had been the case with the watches.

In spite of some early criticism, within a decade or so the Metropolitan Police came to be seen by London's property owners as a fairly effective preventive force. By the

1830s Metropolitan Policemen began to appear elsewhere in country at the request of local authorities – for instance, supervising race meetings or acting as stewards at public disturbances (such as Anti-Poor Law demonstrations). Robert Peel's Metropolitan Police acted as a model for provincial police reformers during the 1830s and 1840s, with a Royal Commission set up in 1836 to enquire into the best means of setting up a rural constabulary.

Essentially, then, the new forms of policing of the late eighteenth and early nineteenth centuries came from the growing concerns about the consequences of an increasingly industrialized and urbanized society. As indicated, a major driving force behind these changes was Robert Peel. However, it is important to bear in mind that police reform (as with other major social changes and reforms) is invariably a slow process involving experiment, debate and compromise; and the debates and experiments over policing continued through the nineteenth century and beyond.

So why did the modern police force emerge at the beginning of the nineteenth century? Until then the threat to individual liberty had been used as an argument against organized policing. However, the coming of industrial capitalism led to large numbers of impoverished workers – unemployed or poorly employed – moving to the expanding urban centres. This, along with the general population growth, led to a fear of the new industrial proletariat – in short, to a fear of the 'dangerous classes'. This line of argument suggests that it was class interest which accounted for the emergence of the modern police. In addition, it could be argued that the previous, locally based form of policing was uncoordinated and unpredictable whereas modern, public policing was a way of promoting the greater efficiency and order needed for the smooth running of industrial capitalism.

It should be borne in mind that even after establishment of the 'new police' other groups and individuals continued to do 'police tasks'. Private watchmen and gamekeepers were still employed by those who could afford them; and the docks maintained their own police, as did the railways until nationalization in 1948. More recently, of course, there has been a massive rise in the private security industry.

So from its very inception, the police force has been subject to a sort of creeping centralization. This was inevitable, in part at least, because of the Home Office influence through the Treasury Grant it provided for police forces. It was also encouraged by the tendency for police forces to work together to police major events, such as big industrial disputes or political demonstrations.

QUESTION BREAK: THE EMERGENCE OF A POLICE FORCE

Of the two main theoretical explanations for why an organized police force emerged in the early nineteenth century, the first is the argument that saw this development as, essentially, reflecting a progressive view of history, with the emergence of the new police reflecting a need for a more efficient organization to deal with the (perceived) increased crime and disorder at that period. This view has been termed the traditional Whig history which sees social progress as developed by far-sighted individuals and, in this context, assumed the Metropolitan Police were an important advance on what had existed before (an approach evidenced in the writings of Reith, see Emsley (1996a and 2003)).

The second is the Marxist argument which focused on the new police as an element in a broader strategy of control of the labouring classes. This approach, known as the revisionist history, saw the new police as a means for controlling and disciplining the growing urban, industrial working classes (see Storch, 1976, cited in McLaughlin and Muncie (eds), 2001).

Read the extract below and suggest how it relates to those different explanations.

> The shift in opinion which enabled (police) reforms began in the late eighteenth century – the key moments being the Gordon Riots in 1780 and, for the rural gentry, the Swing Riots in 1830, although the feeling that there was a pervasive climate of disorder among the labouring classes was, perhaps, more important. Towns like London and the rapidly growing cities of the industrial north represented a new and vibrant engine of wealth, but they seemed out of control. That impression appeared to be confirmed by increasing crime and radicalism, both of which seemed to be spreading into the countryside.
>
> It was not that disorder was new . . . rather it was that there was a growing lack of tolerance among the ruling classes born of a sense that old structures of authority, which depended on paternalism and deference, had at last broken down. The ruling classes realized that the connection . . . between themselves and the labouring classes had no foundation. The reaction of some was to seek to shore it up, while others assumed that the problem lay in the moral degeneration of the labouring classes and that liberty and property could only be protected from the consequences of this moral decline by intervention from local and central government.
>
> (From P. Rawlings 2002: 144)

The early developments in establishing a national policing structure were formalized with the passing of Grey's Bill for Police Reform in 1856. This led to an Act that made the formation of police forces obligatory for local government at Borough and County levels. It also established Inspectors of Constabulary who were expected to make annual inspections of every force in the country and to present a certificate of efficiency which was necessary for a particular force to get their Treasury grant. However and in spite of these moves toward a centralized police force, local police forces still remained unequivocally under local authority control with there being obvious differences from one local area to next. For instance the uniforms and colours of local forces varied, a legacy that has continued to the present day with different forces using different colours on their cars for example. However, the dominant style of policing was based on the metropolitan model, and this became the pillar of the constitutional and legal structure of Victorian England, characterized in the notion of the English 'bobby'. Although the new police were criticized when they failed to prevent offences or solve particular, and significant, crimes (such as the panic around garrotting in the 1860s and the Jack the Ripper murders of 1888) there was general support from both the public and the press of the day.

While there was some affection for English bobby, the early police officers were also regularly assaulted by public and in some of the rougher working-class areas police officers had to patrol with cutlasses. Indeed certain areas were virtually left to themselves, with police numbers being insufficient to provide any effective form of crime control. Early complaints of police corruption and about police brutality in dealing with crowds exacerbated the negative view of the new police held by many. While the police were intentionally kept as distinct from the military (with the uniform, for instance, purposely avoiding military colours), it was widely felt that there was a strong link between the police and the armed forces. Indeed as Rawlings (2002) points out the denunciation of the police as a military force was common. The colloquial term for the new police of 'Jenny Darbies' was a corruption of the French 'Gens d'armes', a symbol for the English of despotism. Concern over the cost of the police was also apparent, with *The Times* suggesting, 'their pay constitutes a very serious tax on the London householder' (*The Times* 19 August 1830, quoted in Rawlings 2002). Criticisms over the police peaked in November 1830 with Vine Street Police Station besieged by thousands of demonstrators. And opposition to the police was not limited to London, with rural areas seeing them as agents for enforcing unpopular government policies; they were seen by some as a sort of invading army who were liable to destroy local lifestyles, recreation and working practices.

Policing at the turn of the twentieth century

As indicated, there was some opposition to the new policing of the Victorian period, with working-class communities not liking what they felt to be police interference in their areas, which probably contributed to the feeling of many working-class people that there was one law for the rich and one for the poor. However, as Emsley points out this did not mean that 'the relationship between the working class and the police in the second half of the nineteenth century [was] one of mutual hostility' (1996a: 80). And certainly a very positive view of the British police was held by 'respectable' society and the 'establishment' by the turn of the century, with *The Times* in 1904 describing the police as 'a great human mechanism, perhaps the greatest of its kind'. Rawlings refers to contemporary sources in suggesting that,

> By the early twentieth century, [the police] had become 'the nurse of national morality' and the defence against an invasion of 'vice and crime', while the 'romance of Scotland Yard' involved nothing less than 'the building up . . . of a vast, ingenious machine which has become one of the greatest instruments of civilisation the world has ever seen'.
>
> (Rawlings 2002: 152–3)

As regards the management and control of the new police there were different kinds of authority. The Metropolitan Police were answerable to the Home Secretary, county police were responsible to local standing committees and borough police to watch committees. However, the idea that there was a particular and peculiarly British style of policing seemed to have taken a hold, with the beginnings of a corporate identity for the police helping this development – as illustrated by the creation of the Chief Constables Association in 1893. The inspectors of constabulary, introduced after the 1856 legislation referred to above (p. 369), also helped to introduce a greater uniformity across the local and provincial police institutions through establishing what activities were proper for the police and how police efficiency should be measured (Rawlings 2003). Local police forces were also encouraged to provide mutual support and aid to each other in cases of popular disturbances, including cases of industrial unrest in the early twentieth century such as the South Wales coal strike of 1910–11 and the rail strike of 1911.

Another manifestation of the developing corporate identity of the police was police unionization. Trade unionism was emerging elsewhere, of course, and to begin with police organization was on a pretty ad hoc basis – the police weren't seen as skilled craftsmen which were the areas where unionism developed significant strength initially. Police union organization occurred most notably in urban areas; with the fact the police in those areas often lived in barracks helping nurture feelings of solidarity. This was particularly the case in London with agitation over pay, pensions and conditions apparent at end of the nineteenth century in the Metropolitan Police. Although the attempt to establish a police union in 1890 didn't succeed, the idea did not die and received some support and coverage in the journal for police officers, the *Police Review*. Indeed the development of a trade press for the police helped develop a national awareness among officers (Rawlings 2003). This was also illustrated in the strike by the Metropolitan and City of London Police forces in 1918 following the dismissal of an officer for his 'union activities'. Indeed the Desborough Committee, established by the government after the strike to look into police pay and conditions, recommended standardization across the country as well as better pay for the police.

Early police recruitment

Sir Robert Peel's 'vision' was that the Metropolitan Police officers should come from the working classes and should be able to rise through the ranks through their own efforts. In contrast the managers within the Met, the commissioners as they were known, would be 'gentlemen'. A similar approach was adopted by provincial police forces and most police recruits from the 1840s through to the 1940s were from the working classes and usually with semi-skilled or unskilled backgrounds. Indeed many joined because they were unemployed and often had little idea what the job involved. Large numbers of these initial recruits came to loathe the discipline, the night work and other elements of the job and there was a very high turnover in the early days.

Although the majority of early police recruits were from working-class backgrounds there were obvious differences between policing and most working-class jobs

Summarize these differences.

What sort of issues or problems might these differences raise for the working-class police officer?

There were constraints on the early police officers that marked the job out from other working-class occupations. Police officers had to follow a military style of discipline and were subject to a detailed intervention in all aspects of their lives; in particular, there were much closer and more explicit expectations of and controls over their private lives. Up until the Second World War police officers had to ask permission to marry and prospective wives had their characters investigated to ensure they would be 'suitable' as policemen's wives. During the nineteenth century police wives were not allowed to be in paid employment and were expected to act as sort of auxiliaries to their husbands (taking messages and suchlike).

While the job of the early police officers had its unpleasant side, there were also clear advantages over other working-class occupations. Police officers were provided with good health provision for themselves and their families, there were rent allowances and a pension scheme. The nature of the job in the early days was hard and there was a real danger of assault, and this helped a tough masculine culture to develop, with an emphasis on 'being able to look after oneself in a fight' an element of this. It also encouraged a strong occupational solidarity. The nature of police accommodation, particularly the police barracks, further encouraged this group solidarity among officers, especially in London. And there was a clear feeling of togetherness that did lead to a pride in the job – a pride and consciousness that was fostered by the *Police Review* journal.

As regards the recruitment of women police officers, the First World War boosted the demand for women to serve in the police. Rawlings (2003) highlighted the pressure placed on the police by the First World War. As well as police numbers being depleted, there was also a concern that the large numbers of soldiers living in garrisons and towns away from their homes would encourage prostitution. These sorts of concerns led to the use of women police for the first time. Voluntary Women Patrols began in the days of the war and by 1916 some of these volunteers were made full-time members of the Metropolitan Police force. Initially, women police were employed to patrol women working in large numbers in munitions factories. In an attempt to open up policing to women, some women of 'higher' social class backgrounds with suffragette and feminist leanings enrolled as police officers. However, women officers were not given equal treatment within the police and while some chief constables kept women on after the war, others were keen to dispense with them and it was not until 1949 that the Police Federation agreed to accept women as full and equal members.

Indeed by 1939 there were only 226 women police officers in England and Wales, with over half of them based in London, and with their duties largely restricted to dealing with women and children.

In this brief historical overview we have considered the new emergent police as one body. There were, however, divisions within the organization, most notably between beat officers and detectives. According to Rawlings:

> The beat constable represented the idea of preventive policing; the detective's existence demonstrated the failure of that project. The beat constable was meant to be in the public eye . . . The detective, on the other hand, was secretive, his ability to melt into the community was a matter of pride . . . The separation between the branches became more pronounced as detection came to be represented as dependent on the acquisition of special skills.
>
> (2002: 186–7)

This division became even more pronounced in the twentieth century with the CID tending to see itself and act as an elite and separate organization.

QUESTION BREAK

To what extent do you think that the nature of the job encouraged the development of a tough masculine police culture? (Or is the job of policing likely to attract people who have those sort of attitudes?)

Policing since the Second World War

Although there is a danger of generalizing, the British police were, on the whole, respected and reasonable well regarded by the early years, and through the first half, of the twentieth century. Arguably, this essentially positive view changed in the latter decades of the last century. A brief review of some of the background and historical factors that have played a part in the changes of attitudes to, and styles of, policing from the 1960s will help to establish a context from which to consider contemporary policing. Although many of these factors overlap, as a starting point it is helpful to attempt to categorize them in some way. To that end, we will group them under the following headings: changes in police organization and practice; police–public relations; and general social changes.

Police organization and practice

A new technology of policing, extolled in particular by Harold Wilson's Labour government of the 1960s, was embraced with enthusiasm by the police and Home

Office. The new technology was a key factor in the development of the Unit Beat System of policing. This developed out of experiments in the Lancashire constabulary to cope with the large new town of Kirby on the outskirts of Liverpool. The use of special patrol cars (rather than 'bobbies on the beat') had begun in 1958 and was popularized in the TV series *Z Cars,* set in a town modelled on Kirby. By 1965 policing in Kirby had been completely reorganized with mobile beats with radios replacing all other beats; this soon spread and by 1968 the Unit Beat System covered two thirds of the population in England and Wales. These developments distanced the police from the public they were policing, with police officers in cars less approachable than the police officer on a foot patrol.

Meanwhile, there were growing concerns, especially in the late 1960s and 1970s, over police corruption and scandals. In an account written in the 1970s Cox, Shirley and Short (1977) refer to the 'fall' of Scotland Yard between 1969 and 1972, when many London detectives were jailed and hundreds more left the force in disgrace. These developments undermined the myth of the British police and led to a led to a major inquiry into the Metropolitan Police. In particular, into allegations of widespread corruption amongst detectives working in the vice world of Soho, London, which eventually led to the trial and jailing of the two most senior officers ever brought to justice – Commander of the Flying Squad, Kenneth Drury and Head of the Serious Crime Squad, Wallace Virgo. In 1972 Robert Mark was appointed as Commissioner to the Metropolitan Police and set out to cleanse the detective side of the force. He set up a department to investigate complaints against police officers, moved detectives from one department to another and put some back on the beat. In his five years as Commissioner 500 men were dismissed or required to resign. Robert Mark's work in this direction was followed up by his successor David McNee (who set up Operation Countryman to investigate the robbery squad). Although scandals and corruption were not a new phenomenon, what was a revelation in the 1970s was that it was 'systematic and widespread', with some of Scotland Yard's most senior officers found guilty and jailed. And this was not just the case within the Met; in 1989, for example, the entire West Midlands Serious Crime Squad was disbanded amid allegations of corruption.

The pressure on the police to solve crimes has led to rule-breaking and corrupt behaviour in dealing with suspects who are being detained and questioned – this has been termed 'noble cause corruption', in that the 'ends' were to solve crimes and convict criminals. It came to the fore in the attempts to solve the bombing campaigns by the IRA in the 1970s and the release of supposed terrorists such as the Birmingham Six and Guildford Four, due to concerns about police fabricating evidence and allegations of police violence and intimidation. These high-profile miscarriages of justice led to a Royal Commission on Criminal Procedure and, in 1984, the Police and Criminal Evidence Act (PACE), which introduced safeguards to ensure the police did not and could not abuse their power when interrogating suspects.

There have been more recent examples of police corruption, including that of Scotland Yard Commander, Ali Dizaei, the most senior police officer to be convicted of corruption offences in over 30 years. He was jailed for four years in February 2010 after abusing his position to arrest and frame an innocent man, and then telling a series of lies to cover up his abuse of office (other examples are included in the question break below).

QUESTION BREAK: POLICE CORRUPTION

In spite of the efforts of Commissioners such as Robert Mark and David McNee in the 1970s, there are still regular examples of police corruption and malpractice. Read the extracts below and consider the questions that follow.

Met suspends nine police officers in corruption inquiry

Vikram Dodd

Scotland Yard suspended nine detectives over corruption allegations. The nine are based in the north London borough of Enfield and face allegations concerning stolen flat-screen televisions, computers and other consumer electrical goods. Anti-corruption detectives have been investigating claims that electrical goods were taken from criminal suspects.

(From the *Guardian*, 17 February 2009)

Corrupt officers jailed for leaks

Two former Nottinghamshire police officers have been jailed after pleading guilty to corruption charges. Charles Fletcher, 25, and Phillip Parr, 40, admitted at Birmingham Crown Court to separately passing data on serious inquiries to suspected criminals. Fletcher, a trainee detective, was jailed for seven years and Parr, a former PC, was sentenced to 12 months. The 25-year-old leaked details of investigations including the murder of Nottingham jeweller Marian Bates. Fletcher also admitted two charges of conspiracy to pervert the course of justice . . .

The court heard Fletcher trawled police computer data bases to find information that he supplied to criminals over a two-and-a-half-year period between December 2002 and June last year . . . In return for his service, the 25-year-old received discounts on designer suits from a Nottingham fashion store.

(BBC News 26 October 2006, www.news.bbc.co.uk)

Yard detectives jailed over drug racket

Stewart Tendler, Crime Correspondent

Five Scotland Yard detectives were in jail last night after a female supergrass helped to uncover one of the worst cases of police corruption for over 30 years.

The officers, who seized drugs during police raids which were then passed on to criminals to sell on the streets, were last night branded a 'disgrace' by Scotland Yard.

The exploits of the elite drug squad, nicknamed the 'Groovy Gang' ended when Evelyn Fleckney, an underworld drugs queen known as 'chairman of the board', gave evidence against some of the corrupt officers . . .

(From the *Guardian*, 5 August 2000)

- What might lead police officers to engage in corrupt practices?
- How might police work encourage corruption and malpractice more than other occupations?

It is, of course, difficult to assess the extent of police corruption and malpractice. However a recent assessment into the scale of corruption within the British police, the Serious and Organised Crime Agency (SOCA) has suggested that today's police are more vulnerable to being targeted by criminals and abusing their powers than ever before (Laville 2010). In particular, SOCA points to evidence that officers at all ranks are vulnerable to being exploited by criminals in three new areas – social networking sites; bodybuilding gyms (where officers are known to take steroids); and because of the increased access police officers have to confidential information in IT systems (which they can leak for financial gain). More generally, in a major study of police corruption, Punch (2009) looks at how the very nature of police work encourages what he terms 'organisational deviance'. He suggests that people do not join the police aiming to be corrupt and deviant (indeed most recruits are probably motivated to abide by the law and become good officers); however, every officer will face some departure from rules and a variety of opportunities for deviance. These can vary from free meals and discounts on goods to attempts to achieve justice by 'noble cause corruption'. Punch points out that police corruption is invariably group rather than individual behaviour, and behind every 'bent cop' there will always be others involved. Indeed the 'social cement' of corruption is the code of silence amongst officers, and the emphasis on fitting in and not 'rocking the boat' (points that we consider further in looking at police culture later in the chapter, pp. 387–399).

Police–public relations

During the 1960s public attitudes to the police became characterized by a growing dissatisfaction with and concern over police behaviour. This was fuelled by the policing of public mass demonstrations such as CND marches and, later in the 1960s, rallies and demonstrations over the Vietnam war and apartheid. In these and other instances, there was strong criticism of the police for being too heavy handed; and increased media coverage served to sharpen such criticism.

As well as the policing of civil and political demonstrations, the way the police handled industrial disputes excited similar concern and criticism. For instance, the policing of the 1972 miners' strike , the Grunwick trade union dispute of 1977, the steel strike of 1980 and, most dramatically, the miners' strike of 1984/5. As regards that last event, in one sense it could be argued that the police 'won' in that coal supplies continued. However, the policing of the strike was very confrontational (most graphically illustrated by the 'battle of Orgreave') and polarized the police from people who they could not easily label as 'radicals' – from 'ordinary' miners and their families. This miners' strike was seen as 'politicizing the police', who became seen as 'Thatcher's army'.

The inner-city rioting and disorder of 1980/81 in Brixton, Toxteth, Moss Side and elsewhere and of the mid-1980s in Handsworth (Birmingham) and Broadwater Farm (London) reflected an increased alienation between the police and sections of the population. In all of these events, the police played some initial part, through arresting black youths or raiding public places such as cafés that were predominantly used by black youths, and then were patently unable to prevent the full-scale mayhem and disorder that followed.

Related to this and an important factor in police–public relations and the crisis of confidence therein is the issue of race. The disorders referred to above reflected a massive deterioration in police relations with black communities; and race is an issue we will return to in looking at police culture below.

Sanders and Young (2000) make the point that successful policing depends on information and cooperation from the community. However community support for the police cannot be assumed and appears to be diminishing. They highlight findings from the British Crime Surveys that indicate that the proportion of the public who think the police do a 'very good' or 'fairly good' job declined from 92 per cent in 1984 to 82 per cent in 1994 and the proportion who thought they did a 'very good' job from 43 per cent to 24 per cent.

Read the extract from Waddington, Jones and Critchers's discussion of the policing of the 1984 miners' strike and consider the questions at the end of it.

The picketing of Orgreave, May–June 1984

Pickets began arriving at Orgreave very early in the morning (of 29 May). By about 7 a.m., two large groups had been formed . . . about thirty minutes later, those pickets opposite the gate were charged by police officers – some on horseback, some on foot, and others with dogs. The pickets responded angrily. Some objects, mostly pieces of wooden fencing, were thrown in retaliation . . .

The pickets were frustrated. They were being effectively prevented from carrying out any form of picketing at all . . .

The police's immediate response to this situation was to spread a line of riot officers, equipped with white crash helmets and body-length perspex shields, right across their ranks . . . Some pickets were provoked, others panicked. Many started to throw stones . . . Very soon this pattern, of pickets throwing stones and the police charging in on horseback, became routine . . .

Analysis

The public image of Orgreave was of an orgy of violence, endorsed by the police view that a hooligan element the worse for drink had taken over . . . The ingredients of this view are familiar and seem to figure in most police accounts of public disorder. Violence is attributed to a combination of drink, irresponsible leadership and outside agitators. There seems little evidence of the influence of the latter . . .

[We suggest that there needs to be] a deeper level of analysis . . .

Orgreave seems to have been identified by the police as the show-down with the miners, the outcome of which would indicate the future progress of the whole strike.

As for the events at the scene itself, there is still no clear picture. The miners' account is that they were deliberately provoked by the police . . . For them, throwing stones was largely a defensive measure . . .

The police explained their own conduct as equally defensive . . . they acted against the pickets only when, provoked . . .

The use of mounted police seemed to have the effect of heightening the crowd's anger . . .

This and other moves do appear to have been premeditated. As subsequently became clear at the trial in Sheffield of fourteen pickets charged with riot at Orgreave – all of whom were acquitted – the police tactics used there mainly followed closely those recommended in the secret manual 'Public Order Tactical Options' drawn up by the Association of Chief Police Officers (ACPO) in the wake of the riots of 1980–1. They included the charging of the crowd with truncheons and the incapacitation of ringleaders. Their effect was wholly provocative, as was the rhythmic beating on shields – recommended by the manual – which greeted the return of the mounted police.

The events of 18 June indicate that the police used the opportunity to vent all the feelings of resentment accumulated over the previous three weeks

. . .

The events at Orgreave were removed from a local context, with its potential for locally negotiated agreements between police and pickets, and inserted into a national arena of irreconcilable conflict. Orgreave was not seen as a local picket during an industrial dispute but a trial of strength in a politically charged struggle . . . The confrontation between the South Yorkshire police and the area NUM had been transformed into a confrontation between the state and the 'enemy within'.

Summary

In our discussion of Hadfields (where a mass picket occurred during the 1980 steel strike) we noted a number of factors which helped to account for the relatively low level of police–picket violence. These included the definition of the dispute, the liaison between picket organizers and police, the organization of the police, their attitude to minor breaches of the law, and the extent to which police and pickets shared a definition of behavioural norms. On all these criteria Orgreave was different.

(From D. Waddington, K. Jones and C. Critcher 1989: 84–92)

- What criticisms could you make of the policing of the picketing at Orgreave?
- What reasons could you offer for the police's actions?

General social changes

The supposed growing affluence of society in the late 1950s/1960s, illustrated by the comments from Harold Macmillan, the prime minister at the time, that we had 'never had it so good', led to an increase in car ownership and the consequent extension of police work into traffic duties. This increased the potential for antagonistic encounters between citizens and the police ('they should be catching criminals, not bothering law-abiding folk like me' is a widely held attitude). Of course, there has been widespread debate within sociology over the 'meaning' of this increased affluence (in terms of perceptions of class position, for instance), and notions of consumerism and the consumer society have been used to suggest that modern societies are increasingly characterized by and organized around patterns of consumption. The ownership of more consumer goods can lead to more frequent opportunities for encounters with the police; in particular cars with all the attendant legislation surrounding their ownership and use – speeding, parking, taxing and so on.

The style of policing in Northern Ireland has also impacted on attitudes to the police across the UK. The image of the police there is of a force that is routinely and heavily armed in a way not seen on an everyday basis on the mainland; again helping to further undermine traditional notions of police.

Although these factors played a part in changing the public's attitude to the police and policing in Britain, encouraging a much more critical and negative view amongst sections of the population, it is important to bear in mind that alongside such criticism there was and is still a great deal of sympathy and support for the police. While the post-1960s, modern policing adopted a much tougher approach and style than that associated with the old image of *Dixon of Dock Green*, the police were still seen as, essentially, upholding the cause of right against wrong – *The Sweeney*/Jack Regan image popular in the 1970s was of tough, macho officers whose hearts were in the right place but who were prepared to kick out against the bureaucracy that got in the way of catching 'real' criminals.

The statement of common purpose and values that was publicized in 1990 and displayed on notice boards across all London police stations evidences the concern the police had about their image:

> The purpose of the Met is to uphold the law fairly and firmly . . . to protect, help and reassure people in London: and to be seen to do this with integrity, common sense and judgment.
>
> We must be compassionate, courteous and patient, acting without fear or favour or prejudice to the rights of others . . .
>
> We must respond to well-founded criticism with a willingness to change . . .

The anxieties, revelations and events of the recent past were clearly a driving force behind these kinds of mission statements.

As indicated, all of these historical, contextualizing factors signified (and encouraged) a move away from traditional notions of policing and the image of the local bobby to a sort of state role for police. In the miners' strike of 1984/5, for example, the Association of Chief Police Officers (ACPO) told all its chief constables in writing that they had the Home Secretary's assurance that resources for policing the miners' strike would not be a problem; in other words they were given a blank cheque, perhaps further evidence of the 'politicizing of the police' mentioned above.

So where has this left policing today? In the last 30 years or so, two major threads or developments of policing have become apparent. There has been a dual emphasis on crime prevention and crime detection which has pulled the police in quite different directions. On the one hand there has been an emphasis on targeting serious offenders and on crime detection. This has encouraged a more strong-arm, militaristic approach with greater us of guns, CS gas, surveillance and so on. On the other hand, crime prevention has been the key motif, with the involvement of community and other public services emphasized. This 'softer' approach has supported greater citizen participation, more police patrols and developments such as juvenile liaison schemes and Neighbourhood Watch.

Faulkner (2001) argues that there is no inherent contradiction between the two styles of policing and that both are needed. Attempts to reduce crime can be made through partnership, community-based methods of policing while the police also enforce the law more vigorously against those who are suspected of breaking the law. However, 'soft' policing focusing on preventive work in the community involves different policing skills and different relationships with the community than 'hard' policing and an emphasis on finding and convicting criminals. And the application of 'hard' policing can get in the way of successful community policing, particularly if the two approaches or styles of policing are adopted in the same place at the same time. Faulkner points out that it is usually community policing that suffers: 'because the inputs and outputs (though not the outcomes) of 'hard' policing are easier to measure than those of 'soft' policing, the process may tend to promote 'hard' rather than 'soft' police methods' (2001: 260).

These different approaches to and styles of policing highlight a contrast between *reactive* policing with all the technology and gadgetry and *proactive* policing aiming to foster closer police–community partnerships. Below we will consider where this history has taken contemporary policing and how the different styles of policing are accommodated in the modern police service

THE POLICE ROLE TODAY

Waddington (2000) describes policing as 'morally ambiguous'. The police occupy a unique role in society in that they are allowed to exercise coercion over other citizens and to act in ways that would not be tolerated if done by anyone else. As he puts it:

> police officers may legitimately intrude into the privacy of others: it would be quite abnormal for anyone other than a police officer to approach strangers in a public place and to demand (however politely) that they give an account of themselves.
>
> (2000: 156)

This moral ambiguity is perhaps highlighted by the fact that much police work is not about fighting crime (an activity that is generally strongly supported by the public). Certainly, the popular image of police work as being, essentially, about fighting crime does not seem to be the reality. A great deal of police work might be called 'relief' policing in that it is responding to whatever happens during a shift 'on the beat'; and is largely instigated by calls from the public (Newburn 2007). Analysis of calls to the police shows how relatively little time is spent on crime matters compared to matters of 'plight', such as being locked out of one's home (Waddington 1993). Waddington's research found that only 6 per cent of calls from the public led to arrests, with another 12 per cent leading to crime reports that might be followed up in the future. Indeed it would seem that any generally held notion that most police involvement with the public occurs when people contact them to report serious criminality is not really the case. The ACPO estimates suggest that typically only 18 per cent of calls for help are about crime and they take about 30 per cent of police time, while the other 70 per cent of police work consists of reassuring the public, giving advice and assistance, regulating problematic personal/interpersonal situations and dealing with a miscellaneous range of other problems.

As Morgan and Newburn put it when describing 'the police function':

> The police frequently are the only 24 hour service agency available to respond to those in need. The result is that the police handle everything from unexpected childbirths, skid row alcoholics, drug addicts, emergency psychiatric cases, family fights, landlord-tenant disputes, and traffic violations, to occasional incidents of crime.
>
> (1997: 79)

QUESTION BREAK

- What do you think would be the most common reasons for calling the police?
- What response do people expect when they call the police?
- Why do people think that calling the police will help?

Aside from the need to get a crime number for insurance purposes, it would appear that the police provide a symbolic and visible representation of the rule of law and present the public with a reassuring appearance of authority. When, for instance, burglary victims report a crime they don't really expect the burglar to be caught, yet calling the police is an almost automatic thing to do, it helps to re-establish the 'order' of things. And it is not only victims who see the police as symbolically representing order; the presence of police in public places provides reassurance. Even if they're not doing anything the public feel safer, at events such as football matches, for instance.

As Waddington (1993) suggests this point arguably goes to the heart of policing. It is commonplace to hear comments about 'more bobbies on the beat', and images of golden law-abiding days, without any real evaluation of what those bobbies are actually going to achieve. In fact, there is plenty of evidence which shows they're unlikely to prevent or detect crime. For example victim surveys such as the British Crime Survey point out that an average beat control might pass within 100 yards of a burglary every 11 years (and then not necessarily know it was happening!). As well as reassurance, perhaps what is behind the demand for 'bobbies on the beat' is the idea of ordinary police officers who are approachable and non-threatening, who provide the public with the feeling that order is being maintained. And if this is the case, it makes it pointless to try and measure the success of foot patrols in terms of crime and detection rate, or to be unduly panicked by statistics demonstrating increases in rates of known crimes. This is not to say that the officer on the beat is just an expensive public relations exercise, but that she or he is likely to have little effect in terms of winning the 'war on crime'.

Although the majority of police work, especially for uniformed officers, might consist of public reassurance and relief, the police do also engage in proactive policing. The police role does involve criminal investigation, particularly for police detectives, who account for about 15 per cent of police resources (Newburn 2007). As mentioned above, the popular, and media, image of police work tends to centre around criminal investigation and forensic work. Forensic work in policing tends to focus on collecting evidence from the scene of crimes, such as fingerprint and DNA evidence. We will not go into forensics here but it is worth highlighting that while it lends a sort of scientific respectability to criminal investigations, forensic evidence is not foolproof. Newburn (2007) highlights the wrongful convictions of Sally Clark and Angela Cannings for murdering their own children and suggests that the strength of such evidence can be 'overestimated and over-stated'. Sally Clark spent three years in prison from 2000 until 2003 based on the flawed evidence of a pathologist and a paediatrician, Professor Roy Meadow – who committed suicide in 2007. Angela Canning spent 18 months in prison after being convicted in 2002, also on the evidence of Professor Roy Meadow (who was subsequently struck off the General Medical Council).

The police's role in maintaining public order

It has been argued that one reason the police can't really do much about crime is that crime control is not their real function; their main role is to support the authorities through dealing with threats to political order such as demonstrations, strikes and riots. The emphasis here is on public order policing, which has always been a very sensitive role for the police. If the police use excessive force to suppress popular dissent then they are likely to be seen as a 'state' rather than a 'public' police and will lose both public sympathy and therefore some legitimacy.

Up until perhaps the 1970s there was a general feeling that maintaining public order wouldn't be a massively controversial aspect of policing in Britain because Britain was a democracy that allowed for disagreement, because public protests would be orderly, because the police would use minimum force and so on. However, as mentioned above in reviewing policing since the Second World War, there were increasingly bitter conflicts – industrial disputes, urban riots, political demonstrations – in the 1970s and 1980s; and in some of those events the police seemed to 'lose' control of the situation (for instance, the miners' strikes of the early 1970s, the inner-city disorders of 1980/81). These situations led to the police reshaping and rethinking their strategies for maintaining order. Local forces established public order units, with more police officers being trained in the new public order tactics and strategies. Of particular importance for the future of policing, the National Reporting Centre was strengthened and allowed to deploy police from different parts of the country. In the 1984/5 miners' strike, for instance, police were bussed in from all over the country to counter mass picketing.

An important question to consider here is the extent to which such developments have signalled a move to 'paramilitarization' of the police. Two opposing responses to that broad question are introduced below.

Jefferson (1990) argues 'yes' and suggests that this has been an insidious development. New tactics might well start as something exceptional and temporary to deal with particular instances of disorder, but they soon become normal and institutionalized police responses. And ordinary officers who have been mobilized in such riot situations are likely to find it difficult to readjust to normal duty; the 'mindset' of officers becomes locked into such tactics. In addition to this new, elite squads are developed and the policing of mass events tends to become seen as a science, with certain groups within the police recognized as the experts in it.

The other side of the 'paramilitary' argument is forwarded by Waddington (1991). He argues that we need the police to maintain a democratic social order; the police give us a sense of public security in various situations where public order is important such as football matches, rallies, marches, rock festivals. In reality the police spend a great deal of time informally negotiating with groups and offering advice to avoid confrontation and trouble and Waddington goes on to make the point that most public order situations do pass off peacefully. Police officers at every level try to avoid confrontation because they know that media images of violence lead to calls for public inquiries and don't help the police in winning support and approval from the wider public.

He also makes the point that there are people and groups in Britain who will hijack public events and 'have a go' at the police and that society has a duty to provide its police with adequate protection from extremist elements. Essentially Waddington is arguing that the police are not really responsible for any 'paramilitarization' in their approach, rather they have had to react to the situations of violence that they have been faced with.

The police's role in maintaining order brings them into contact with groups of people who are not criminal and who can claim to be acting out of a sense of citizenship; pickets and protesters are usually acting in what they see as a principled manner and on behalf of a wider community. Waddington suggests that protesters and pickets can 'claim to be the moral equals of the police with a degree of success rarely achieved by criminals' (2000: 157). He illustrates this point by referring to the confrontations over the export of live animals to Europe in 1995. The animal rights protest at the small Essex port of Brightlingsea gave the police a difficult public order situation. The protesters were made up of a wide cross-section of society and their concern about the export of animals in cramped crates clearly had a moral justification. The exporters demanded that the police protect their right to trade lawfully at to use the Queen's highways to do so. The protesters took the direct action of lying in front of trucks that were carrying calves and this willingness to suffer discomfort as part of the protest encouraged a great deal of sympathy for them and made the police's actions in trying to remove the protesters more 'morally dubious' as Waddington put it.

▌CASE STUDY BOX 11.1 MAINTAINING PUBLIC ORDER

The extract below could be compared with that on the policing of the miner's strike in 1984/85 (pp. 378–379) and, as with that extract, it raises issues concerning the police–public relations.

Riot police thwart animal welfare protest

At least 250 police, some wearing riot gear, pulled around 500 people from the main street of the town where residents had successfully halted the first attempt to land lambs on Monday.

The scenes came as operators who had planned to fly calves from Swansea to the Continent pulled out after receiving death threats. Protesters had set up a round-the-clock vigil at the airport to prevent the exports . . .

Assistant chief constable Geoffrey Markham described the operation as a success, with only two arrests and no serious injuries. But he added: 'I would have thought it would have been a frightening experience for young children to see that number of police officers deployed in that fashion.'

He also blamed sheep exporter Roger Mills for the size of the police action . . . Mr Markham said: 'the exporter Mr Mills informed me that he intended to move his vehicles in Brightlingsea with or without police support. I considered that if he went on his own with those large vehicles, that in the interests of public safety, that would have been an extraordinarily fraught situation.'

He added: 'I am sorry that we caused any upset to the people of Brightlingsea because that is the last thing we wanted to do.' He conceded that no more than 60 of the demonstrators were 'hardline outsiders'.

Rock Morgan, Brightlingsea mayor, praised the protesters and criticized the police, saying: 'I saw nothing but a peaceful protest and the level of police response in my opinion was over the top and completely unjustified.'

Clifford Brown, a retired carpenter, said: 'I have never before been in a demonstration and could not believe these police with truncheons and visors looking every bit like storm troopers.'

Heather Dewdney, a 16-year-old childminder, said: I was sitting in the road showing no violence when I was dragged across the road on my back. We then

(continued)

saw a man being beaten by a policeman and when I asked for his number he punched me extremely hard between my breasts' . . .

Maria Wilby, of the pressure group Brightlingsea Against Live Animal Exports, said she was shocked by police tactics and said dozens of people had been injured. 'There were mothers with toddlers here today and some were pulled out by their hair.'

(From J. Erlichman, the *Guardian*, 19 January 1995)

- Describe the 'moral ambiguity' that the police may have faced in policing the demonstration at Brightlingsea.
- As with the Orgreave demonstration (see p. 378), what reasons can you offer for the police actions?

This case illustrates the distinction and contradictions between the police's roles of crime fighting and order maintenance. Public order maintenance, according to Waddington, is the maintenance of 'a particular order' and although the police may be enforcing the law, if that law is seen as unjust then their enforcement is also tainted; illustrating his argument about the 'morally ambiguous' nature of public order policing.

Before looking at how the role of the police has influenced the development of a distinctive police culture, it would be useful to say a little about the way policing is organized across England and Wales. There are 43 separate police forces, including the Metropolitan Police and the City of London Police (Scotland has eight regional forces and Northern Ireland one). These forces vary considerably in size – the Metropolitan force has around 31,000 officers plus 14,000 civilian staff, while some of the smaller forces, such as Suffolk and Cumbria, have fewer than 1,000 officers (for more detail see Newburn 2007: 598–9). As the figures from the Metropolitan Police indicate there are a significant number of civilians working within the police. These are not just as administrative support workers but include Police Community Support Officers, introduced in 2002, and special constables. The Community Support Officers are able to patrol but do not have full police powers; however, they can detain suspects, stop vehicles and issue fixed-penalty notices. Special constables are volunteers who work with police officers and who wear uniforms that are very similar to other police constables.

As well as the increase in civilian staff in recent years, there has also been a growing number of private security companies performing policing functions in the UK. Private security firms have no official powers, but they can and do charge residents to patrol streets and deter troublemakers – for instance residents in Darlington pay between £2 and £4 a week to have their homes patrolled and to receive an instant response if they need help (BBC News, 14 November 2009). More generally, in recent years shopping centres and pubs and clubs (and the streets outside them) have increasingly been patrolled by private security staff. Indeed Westmarland (2010) shows that the number of private security 'police' is almost double the number of sworn police officers and although there is a regulatory body (the Security Industry Authority) it is not compulsory for all types of security staff.

POLICE CULTURE

The solidarity of the police as an occupational group was highlighted in our brief look at the early history of policing. This solidarity has encouraged the development of a distinct occupational culture within the police – termed 'cop culture' by Reiner (2000) who defined it as 'how police officers see the social world and their role in it'. Although sometimes seen as a single, monolithic culture, Foster (2003) stresses that there are differences within and between various police subcultures, such as 'street' cops and 'management cops', and uniformed officers and detectives. In looking at this police culture, an interesting question to start with is that of whether police officers have a distinctive set of personality characteristics that set them apart from the public.

It could be argued that because of the nature of their work a police career attracts recruits of a particular psychological disposition. However, a more sociological/cultural approach would stress it is group socialization and institutional routines that generate a particular working personality and a strong occupational subculture – what is commonly termed a 'canteen culture'. The whole process of becoming a police officer happens in very institutionalized manner, with probationers at the bottom of a hierarchical structure and quasi-military bureaucracy that emphasizes command, discipline and following orders. Probationers are placed under the guidance of experienced officers from whom they pick up the real world of practical policing: the folk-lore, the common-sense discourse on crime and so on. New recruits quickly learn that policing can be difficult and challenging and that to 'survive' their work they need to be part of a team (Foster 2003). New officers also develop a sense of knowing when something or someone is not right. They learn when to use conciliation and when to use the full force of law; they learn how to identify and classify offenders and suspects.

Having said that, police officers do have considerable autonomy, which in practice serves to strengthen the internal police culture. Law enforcement is a complex activity and officers have to exercise *discretion* in all sorts of situations. As they translate written law into law in action they make key decisions all the time. A patrolling officer ignores a large number of offences and potential offences every day (prostitutes soliciting, illegal parking) and when action is taken this takes up a lot of time which inevitably means that nothing is done about other offences. The way in which this discretion is exercised reflects the general occupational culture. New recruits, for instance, will almost inevitably pick up and apply the practices of the more experienced officers whom they are placed with when learning the day-to-day realities of policing.

There are bound to be different views and approaches to their work held by officers in any organization as large as the police, and, as mentioned, the occupational culture of the police cannot be described as a 'monoculture'; however, there are particular characteristics that are perpetuated through the way new members are selected, trained, socialized and accepted by their colleagues. These characteristics include isolation and solidarity, but also a sense of mission, suspicion, machismo, intolerance, prejudice and conservatism (Reiner 2000). Police officers tend to be isolated from previous friends, the community and even their families. Their work encourages a tendency for them to become suspicious of everyone and the authority vested in them furthers a sense of isolation. This isolation encourages a 'them–us' world view and, on the face of it, leads to a strong degree of solidarity between police officers. Indeed solidarity seems to be a basic police cultural value and one that is encouraged by a tendency for police officers to socialize together as well as to count on one another for support. As we will touch on later, police solidarity can have both and negative effects on policing practice.

The nature of police work requires the police to develop methods for recognizing certain types of people as 'typical' criminals; they are likely to have a picture of stereo-typical villains. Through acquiring 'conventional wisdom' they know about criminals, how to recognize them and where to locate them – in 'bad' neighbourhoods, for example. As a consequence of this, the police tend to concentrate on street crime such as robbery, burglary and assault with a consequence that the population on whom they concentrate are liable to feel 'picked on', which leads to sense of injustice that will in turn affect police–public relations. In addition to this the nature of police work makes it likely that they will experience some *depersonalization* in their work; they may be viewed by members of the public not as people but as faceless officials – 'filth' or 'pigs', for instance. In a similar vein and in order to do their job police have to depersonalize the public by stereotyping them – as 'rough', 'respectable', 'toe-rags', 'slags'.

In terms of what's been done to change elements of police culture that encourage this sort of 'them v. us' attitude, there are difficulties for senior officers. Police officers place great value on group *solidarity* and will 'close ranks' to keep working routines as they would prefer. This can be frustrating for senior officers who find themselves not being able to prevent a sort of action-based police culture whereby officers tend to persist in rushing from incident to incident and show less interest in the proactive business of fostering links with the community. This is partly due to the well documented subcultural emphasis on 'action and excitement'. Emphasis on the exciting and dangerous nature of police work is reflected in the image of policing portrayed by the media and the image probably held by the public in general. In contrast to this image, police patrol work is invariably boring and somewhat aimless. Foster (2003) refers to Banton's ground-breaking, 1964 study of the police in Britain which suggested police officers are peace-makers more than law-enforcers and that many aspects of their work are routine and boring – as she comments more than forty years later these points remain resonant. The extract below taken from the Policy Studies Institute report into the Metropolitan Police in the 1980s highlights the potential conflict between the image and reality of police work and the way this impacts on police behaviour.

Read the extract below from the PSI report *The Police in Action* based on a participant observation study of the Metropolitan Police by David Smith and Jeremy Gray:

> A considerable amount of police behaviour can best be understood as a search for some interest, excitement or sensation. An officer on foot will often spend a whole shift without doing any police work, and without talking to anyone except to greet them and provide simple information . . . Even officers in cars with mainsets can spend several hours without responding to a call and without finding something to do on their own account. Of course, there are times when a car rushes straight from one call to another, but overall these are definitely unusual except in very restricted areas.
>
> The importance of boredom and aimlessness is very much obscured by most popular treatments of police work, whether in fictional or in documentary style. They naturally concentrate on the interesting bits, and, so, of course, do the police themselves . . .
>
> Most constables would like to have a reasonable number of dramatic or at least interesting crimes to deal with. One PC complained at length to a sergeant that the 'ground' where they both worked had become much quieter; he looked back with nostalgia to the old days when the ground was much 'harder' and ' you could literally be strolling past a pub and a bloke would come staggering out with a knife in his back . . .'
>
> A considerable number of stops are carried out mainly for something to do. When DJS [David Smith, one of the researchers] spent a whole night walking with a probationer who could find nothing at all to do, the probationer eventually waited on a main road where there was virtually no traffic and stopped the first two cars that came by. Both were young men on their way to work, and both said they were frequently stopped by police at about 5 am as they went to work.
>
> (From D. J. Smith and J. Gray 1983: 51–5)

- Aside from shift workers, which groups of people do you think are most likely to be stopped and questioned by the police?
- How might this affect police relations with such groups?

Solidarity is emphasized in most studies of police culture and practice and although it is by no means unique to the police – all occupational groups will have it to some degree – it is particularly apparent within the police. While it can encourage the covering up of errors, group solidarity can also be a positive feature when it comes to helping out colleagues. Chan (1997), for example, has highlighted how police culture can be functional for police officers in an occupation that is unpredictable, alienating and can be dangerous. Police solidarity offers reassurance and is not just a result of isolation; there is a need to have colleagues who can be relied on in tight spots. As Newburn and Reiner (2007) put it: 'Solidarity is knitted from the intense experience of confronting shared dangers and pressures, the need to be able to rely on colleagues in a tight spot, and the bonding from having done so' (p. 918).

The fact that the police's occupational culture and police working practices place great emphasis on solidarity and mutual support arguably benefits those who are part of that culture. However, as we will examine in the next two sections, those officers who do not belong to the majority social categories in the police (essentially those who are not male and white) are placed at a distinct disadvantage by this occupational culture.

Sexism, homophobia and racism

In looking at police culture it is useful to focus on some specific elements of it, in particular the extent to which it is sexist, homophobic and racist. As Foster has commented:

> Despite changes in policy, and recruitment, the police service remains a largely male, white and heterosexual organization, where those who are perceived to be 'different' by virtue of their race, gender or sexuality have reported significant problems in gaining acceptance, and in some cases recognition or legitimacy for their experiences.
>
> (2003: 213)

Here we will highlight a few issues and questions that might be explored in relation to these aspects of police culture.

Sexism and homophobia

One of the most obvious and consistent factors shown by criminal statistics is that very few criminals are women. This does not necessarily mean that women suspects are treated favourably or chivalrously by the police. However it does seem that women are responded to by the police and the criminal justice system more generally in terms of how closely they correspond to a conventional imagery of 'good women'. As Newburn and Reiner put it women tend to be viewed either as 'whores' or 'wives' (2007).

As regards women who work in the police, the data on female (and ethnic minority) officers shows that there is far from equality in respect both of number of officers and promotion to top positions within the police (see Table 11.1 opposite). Although the proportion of female officers has risen in recent years, women still occupy very few of the most senior posts and it was not until 1995 that the first woman chief constable was appointed – Pauline Clare as chief constable for Lancashire Police.

While the percentage of women officers is rising, the dominant attitude in the police still amounts to what is essentially a cult of masculinity. Until the 1975 Sex

Table 11.1 Police officer strength:[1] by rank and sex, 2006–07

Great Britain	Numbers		
	Males	Females	All
ACPO[2] ranks	217	30	247
Chief superintendent/superintendent	1,592	170	1,762
Chief inspector	1,929	255	2,184
Inspector	7,043	1,024	8,067
Sergeant	20,802	3,646	24,447
Constable	90,302	31,599	121,902
All ranks	121,884	36,724	158,608
Police staff	32,471	49,792	82,263
Police community support officers[3]	7,706	5,791	13,497
Traffic wardens[4]	625	406	1,031
Designated officers[3]	960	657	1,617
Total police strength	163,646	93,370	257,016
Special constabulary[3]	9,327	4,694	14,021

1 At 31 March 2007. Full-time equivalent figures rounded to the nearest whole number. Includes staff on secondment to NCOs (Non-commissioned officer in the armed forces), central services, and staff on career breaks or maternity/paternity leave. See Appendix, Part 9: Police.
2 Police officers who hold the rank of Chief Constable, Deputy Chief Constable or Assistant Chief Constable, or their equivalent.
3 England and Wales only as these are not available for Scotland. Headcounts for special constabulary.
4 Excludes local authority traffic wardens.

Source: Home Office; Scottish Government

Discrimination Act discrimination within police forces was open and institution-alized, with different departments for female and male officers. Although this is no longer the case, the police as an institution is still seen by many commentators as essentially and strongly masculine and there is still plenty of evidence of discrimination against and harassment of women officers. In what Foster (2003) terms the highly gendered and pressurized environment of policing, women officers often struggle to find acceptance and are forced to choose between embracing the male culture or sticking to the traditional expectations of their role. There are various 'common-sense' reasons for the continuing 'macho' culture within the police – male officers feeling that women colleagues do not have the necessary physical strength, that their presence in violent situations would put male officers at risk and that their domestic commitments would come before commitment to their police career.

As indicated by the figures in Table 11.1, women officers have fared badly with regard to promotion to senior positions A particular *cause célèbre* was the case of Alison Halford who in 1990 was Assistant Chief Constable in the Merseyside Police

Force and the highest ranking woman officer at that time. Halford brought a sex discrimination case against the force on the grounds that further promotion for her was being turned down while male officers with less experience and qualifications were being appointed. Her decision to go public led to a very public and bitter dispute with the Chief Constable and the police authority on Merseyside. She accused senior officers of ingrained hostility to women officers, of patronage to male colleagues and of tapping her telephone in an attempt to undermine her position. In turn, she was suspended and was accused of being promoted beyond her ability for reasons of political correctness, of not being a team player and of irrational behaviour. In 1992 after the police authority was found to have acted unfairly in the opening disciplinary proceedings against her, Alison Halford took an out of court settlement and so the case was never dealt with officially.

In terms of the generally sexist nature of police culture, a masculine cult would seem to be apparent within the police force. The PSI report into the Metropolitan Police in the 1980s (see pp. 388–389) found the emphasis on masculinity was particularly strong in the CID; this macho image was associated with drinking which for CID officers seemed to be an integral part of their working lives. While drinking in pubs, CID officers were often 'on duty' or 'working overtime' and as they had a legitimate reason for being in pubs it was difficult for them, or anyone else, to regulate the amount of time they spent there. The PSI report goes on to suggest that CID officers who did not drink with colleagues would be seen as a bit odd; as one office put it 'in the department drinking is a way of life'.

Another aspect of the male code is the ability to handle squeamishness. As a young officer dealing with his first death told the PSI researchers,

> Soon after I went on district I had to deal with a fatal accident with an old PC who was a real devil. The bloke had the top of his skull knocked off and his brains were spilling out. I was not too happy about it all. When we got back to the police station, the old devil took me to the canteen and deliberately ordered spaghetti Bolognese and sat there eating it in front of me.
>
> (Smith, D. J. and Gray, J. 1983: 74)

Although the proportion of women police officers is increasing, the dominant attitude in the police seems to have changed relatively little from what the PSI report referred to as a 'cult of masculinity'. This exerts a strong influence on attitudes towards female officers. The PSI report found that, as with other male-dominated groups such as the army, a certain pattern of talk about women and sex is almost expected, with male officers adopting the sort of values and responses that they think are normal within groups of men. However, in spite of the culture of male domination, male officers have to work closely with women as colleagues and most of the women officers interviewed by the PSI researchers felt that male officers were prejudiced against them, that the importance of physical strength in police work was greatly over-emphasized and that they were regularly excluded from some of the more interesting areas of police work. Many women officers seemed to accept, or at least accommodate, these attitudes. One recounted how an inspector at her training school had said to her, 'Why don't you admit it, you're only here to get a husband, aren't you? Why don't you resign and save us a lot of time and money?' She had stayed cool and let it 'run off her back'. Complaints made by women officers about their treatment were supported by the observations of the PSI research which found many drivers trying to avoid working with women .

More recent research indicates that the macho elements of police culture have by no means disappeared. Carol Martin (1996) examined the day-to-day experiences of women police constables in her research with the Sussex police. The participants in her research were all from one division (of 105 officers) within the Sussex police and she interviewed 9 female officers and 13 male officers with a range of experience and length of service as police officers. A number of the women officers interviewed had worked in the Special Enquiry Unit (SEU), undertaking work that had traditionally been handled by the old Police Women's Section. While the unit dealt with all sexual crimes, the vast majority of its work consisted of dealing with women and child victims. The SEU was staffed entirely by females with one male, a detective sergeant, as their supervisor. When asked why there was this preponderance of women working in that field, one officer commented:

> The work is considered very much 'women's work' . . . The status of the work is low because it's women that do it. We don't have detective status and yet we are investigating what we consider, after murder, to be the most serious crimes there are: rape, buggery, serious sexual abuse, serious indecent assault. One supervisor (a man) is a DS though.

Martin found that the women officers involved with the SEU were very committed to their work but felt that there was no reason why it should be seen as a predominantly female posting. Some did acknowledge that there was a demand from the public for female officers to be available to deal with female and child victims; however, it was clear that several women officers felt that the preponderance of women in the unit contributed to its low status among other officers, in spite of the fact that its work was largely investigative – and such work is normally accorded higher status within the police. As one male officer put it: 'I know some colleagues who would have been interested if there hadn't been the sort of stigma attached to it that it was girls only.'

In looking at how gender impacted on their careers as police officers, two major issues were highlighted by Martin's respondents – sexism and family responsibilities. As regards the latter, having a career and having children was still seen as problematic:

> I believe this is the hardest job to come back to. They treat you as if you've got a disease as soon as you are pregnant, you're immediately off the section and there's no guarantee you will go back to the same division or job.

While Equal Opportunities policies might be able to deal with issues of sexual discrimination, women officers in this study certainly felt indirect discrimination was widespread in that they felt they effectively had to choose between career and family. Women officers who returned after maternity leave found that child-care problems were exacerbated by shift work and that they were virtually confined to nine to five office-based police work (often not the reason they had joined the police in the first place).

All but two of the nine women officers interviewed by Martin had experienced sexual harassment of a physical nature, and all these incidents had occurred when they were either on probation or newly in service. In spite of this startling figure, only one had complained and the 'aggressor' had received a warning. Two others had responded physically (for example 'a knee in the groin') and while this may have ended the particular harassment it had left those officers resentful. 'Blaming the victim' was felt to be a real issue in this context and although the women knew of the grievance channels most felt an incident would have to be very serious to go through such channels. The other side of sexist treatment was the chivalrous attitudes shown to women officers. While this may have its pleasant side, Martin found a clear feeling that it undermined the position of women officers and compromised their capabilities as police officers through perpetuating a 'weak link' argument in situations of potential danger and violence.

QUESTION BREAK: THE DARK FIGURE OF CRIME

Suggest ways in which a chivalrous attitude might work against the career prospects of women police officers.

All the officers in this study were aware of the 'canteen culture' although most denied it was excessively macho or sexist. There was agreement by male and female officers that there was an element of coarse language and sexist joking but it was stressed that 'the girls give as good as they get'. Although harassment has been identified by others as the greatest problem faced by women in the police (Heidensohn 1998), these officers, both male and female, believed that issues around maternity leave and child-care were the key ones that worked against female officers. And although the sexism of the canteen culture was acknowledged, most of the women officers did not appear personally threatened by it, or at least had found strategies for coping with it.

In a comment on women in policing, Heidensohn (1998) points out that while there is a trend for increased recruitment of women to the police, the deployment of those women within the police and the promotion of them remains a contentious area, with the most prestigious and high-profile positions still mainly restricted to males. She suggests that the main barrier to real equality within policing remains the sexist nature of the internal police culture. She does, however, highlight some positive developments and a general acceptance, by senior managers in the police at least, that the skills needed for success in the job are no longer those of the traditional macho officer. The achievements of individual women officers who have risen to senior positions have also had a significant impact. She concludes by commenting that, 'It is difficult to argue that old style cop culture still plays a useful role in present day policing. Eradicating it in favour of a more inclusive organizational style would be a worthy aim for the 21st century police.'

Another aspect of the macho aspect of internal police culture can be seen in relation to attitudes to sexuality and, specifically, homosexuality. With regard to this, strenuous heterosexuality seems to be the basic order of the day in police culture, and this emphasis on masculinity can increase the likelihood of homophobia. Emsley (1996) refers to a book written by a homosexual police officer, Daley, in which he talks about how he was victimized because of a lack of interest in women and also because of an interest in books and music.

There has been much less debate and research on issues of sexual orientation and policing than with regard to sexism or racism. While data can be found on female and black police officers, the numbers of homosexual or lesbian police officers can only be estimated. In terms of how the police respond to issues of sexual orientation, Walklate (2000) points out that while forward-thinking and liberal sounding statements can be made, the influence of the strongly heterosexual, macho police occupational culture ensures that the reality of the work experiences of gay and lesbian police officers is similar to that described by Daley above. She argues that the experiences of gay and lesbian police officers are the most invisible and least debated aspects of equality within police culture. The formation of the Lesbian and Gay Police Association in 1990 might have been expected to lead to greater confidence among gay and lesbian officers; however, the furore and negative publicity that have surrounded the establishment of this organization provides a clear example of the deeply rooted negative attitudes to homosexual and lesbian officers (as well as homosexual and lesbian people in general). Brown (1997) argues that in spite of police equal opportunities policies with regard to sexual orientation, there is still a real and distinct gap between policy and what happens 'on the ground'. As Foster (2003) comments, 'it seems that the dominant culture is as staunchly heterosexual as it is racist and sexist', a comment that was supported by the Home Office report by Foster, Newburn and Souhami (2005). The report aimed to assess the impact of the Macpherson Inquiry on police culture and practice and found that by focusing on the issue of race, sexism and homophobia remained widespread. It found a tolerance of sexist and homophobic language in all areas of police work:

> Further, while the police service has focused very successfully on eliminating racist language among its staff, sexist language remains widespread and many women and minority officers and staff continue to feel marginalized and discriminated against.

Racism

As with female officers, but more so, there are relatively few black police officers. The proportion of officers in England and Wales from an ethnic minority group has increased from 2 per cent in 1999 to 4 per cent in 2008, although only 2 per cent of Chief Superintendants were from an ethnic minority (Home Office, Social Trends 2008) and the highest ranking ethnic minority officer was an assistant chief constable in Lancashire (Walklate 2000). Almost 30 years ago the Scarman Report (1981) highlighted the need to recruit more ethnic minority police officers and, given the figures above, the recruitment strategies since then do not seem to have been very successful. Walklate suggests that reasons for this include the negative image of policing held by ethnic minority, and especially young black, groups and the fact that ethnic minority officers face difficulties both from their own communities as well as from within the police force. This lack of black officers does not in itself mean that there is a racist element to police culture although it may be indicative of the attitudes within the police and of the attitudes held by the black population of the police. As with gender, discrimination on grounds of race is against the law, although this does not ensure equal treatment of black police officers. Brown (1997) points out that black officers experience racial prejudices and discrimination from both the public they police and from their fellow officers.

Again, the PSI report into the Metropolitan Police (Smith and Gray 1983), even though over 20 years old, is still a major source of information here and a useful starting point in looking at the extent of racism in the modern force. One area the report particularly looked at was the relations between police and black people in London (it is interesting to note that in the early 1980s when the research was conducted the term 'coloured' was used throughout, a term now considered inappropriate in referring to black people). It found that racist language was used in a casual and almost automatic way within the Met, even over the radios that were picked up by all officers, as well as anyone else listening in. For instance, the researchers heard one inspector say, 'look I've a bunch of coons in sight'. Whether the use of racist language means that the people who use it behave in a racist manner, or even hold racist attitudes, is an issue that was considered by Smith and Gray, the report's author. They cite one young officer telling them, 'I know that PCs call them spooks, niggers and sooties, but deep down the majority of PCs aren't really against them, although there are some who really hate them . . . I call them niggers myself now but I don't really mean it'. In their overall conclusions, the PSI report found that there was some racism in the Met but that it did not lead to black people receiving greatly inferior treatment from the police. While this interpretation may be correct it could be argued that it is difficult if not impossible to prove it. The findings on stopping and arresting suspects provided some evidence that black people (although not Asians) were more likely to be stopped and that the police did tend to link crime and black people and so tended to be more suspicious of black people. Without going into the findings on police public relations in great detail, the report did highlight a widespread lack of confidence in the police among the London population, and especially amongst young and young black Londoners – 62 per cent of young blacks (15–24 years of age) thought the police used threats or unreasonable behaviour.

The PSI research was conducted almost 20 years ago and raises the question as to what extent such findings are still relevant.

In 1993 black teenager Stephen Lawrence was murdered in London by a gang of white youths. The judicial inquiry, led by Sir William Macpherson, into the Metropolitan police investigation of this murder is a very useful source for considering evidence concerning racism within the police (Macpherson 1999). In particular the inquiry considered the issue of institutional racism and the extent to which it applied to the police. The inquiry (also) made recommendations for reforms in many areas of policing, including recruitment, the investigation of racially motivated crimes and the relationship between the police and black and Asian people.

Institutional racism had been considered before Macpherson and indeed was rejected by the Scarman report into the inner-city disorders of the early 1980s. Scarman was aware that 'unwitting racism', as his report put it, could exist and that some officers no doubt held racist attitudes, but stopped short of describing the Metropolitan Police as institutionally racist. In contrast, in giving evidence to the Macpherson inquiry a number of Chief Police Officers acknowledged that institutional racism was still widely prevalent within the police and this view was confirmed in the report itself which accepted that there was institutional racism and defined it as:

> the collective failure of an organization to provide an appropriate and professional service to people because of their colour, culture or ethnic origin. It can be seen or detected in processes, attitudes and behaviour which amount to discrimination through unwitting prejudice, ignorance, thoughtlessness, and racist stereotyping which disadvantage ethnic minority people.
>
> (Macpherson 1999)

In his evidence to the inquiry, the Chief Constable of Greater Manchester, David Wilmot, accepted that institutional racism existed in his force:

> We have a society that has got institutional racism. Greater Manchester Police, therefore, has institutional racism. Some of it is not of the overt type; it's that which has been internalized by individuals and it's our responsibility to try and make sure that it's eradicated.
>
> (quoted in the *Guardian*, 14 October 1998)

In response to these comments a survey undertaken by the Independent newspaper found that two other chief constables, from Sussex and West Yorkshire, also accepted the existence of institutional racism within their forces, while ten chief constables admitted that their forces had racist officers in their ranks – although they were keen to point out that this did not mean all their officers were racist. As Paul Whitehouse, the Chief Constable of Sussex, put it, 'Yes, there is institutional racism within Sussex police but that does not mean that Sussex Police is an inherently racist service' (quoted in the *Independent*, 15 October 1998).

Although not a government report or what might be termed academic research, it is worth referring to the documentary for the BBC by journalist Mark Daly entitled 'The Secret Policeman'. This programme was commissioned by the BBC in the aftermath of the Macpherson report and broadcast in October 2003. It involved Daly trying to discover the extent of racism in the police by working under cover as a policeman in Manchester; after undergoing the training programme for five months he spent eight weeks as a fully operational police officer. While most of the people who he worked with did their job professionally and ethically, he covertly filmed evidence of quite extreme racism from some officers. Much of his information was got at the Police National Training Centre in Warrington, where he found racist abuse, such as 'Paki' and 'Nigger' commonplace amongst trainee officers. The programme, which led to the suspension and disciplining of a number of officers, found first-hand evidence of appalling racist comments – one was heard to say 'Police are racist mate, police are racist'; and he added he would stop a member of the public because they were black or Asian saying, 'I'm stopping him because I'm fucking English. At the end of the day mate, we look after our own' (cited in Allison 2003). Daly was arrested after seven months of undercover reporting but in the end not charged. Five years after the original documentary, Daly made a follow-up documentary, 'The Secret Policeman Returns'. This included a survey of black police officers and showed that although some progress had been made, the problem of racism in the police was still apparent. In particular, black minority ethnic officers still felt sidelined and victimized, with 72 per cent saying they had experienced racism at work and 60 per cent feeling their careers had been hindered by their ethnicity.

As well as the issue of whether the police are institutionally racist, concern about the way in which the police use their powers to stop and search has been an issue of particular concern and controversy. Bowling and Phillips (2002) make the point that it would certainly seem to be the case that young black and Asian men, in particular, see the inequitable use of stop and search as the most obvious example of the police abusing their powers in a racist manner.

They then go on to consider explanations other than racism for the differing stop rates of black people. The stopping of young black people may reflect the age and class profile of the black population in Britain. Another explanation is classified by Bowling and Phillips as 'subject availability' and refers to the fact that most stops occur in the afternoon, evening and night and, because of their higher levels of unemployment and school exclusions black people are more likely to be 'available' for stopping on the streets at those times. This can also be linked to lifestyle factors such as going out more frequently in the evenings.

In concluding their examination of racial discrimination in policing, Bowling and Phillips categorize the range of different explanations under four broad headings which it would be helpful to introduce here. First, the 'bad apple' argument, that racial prejudice and discrimination in the police service is apparent in the attitudes and behaviour of a small number of racist police officers. This explanation was favoured by the Scarman report into the inner-city disorders of the early 1980s and is reflected in the view that the 'solution' is to locate and remove the 'bad apples' and then to prevent any more getting in. Second, the 'reflection of society' argument suggests that as the police service is a cross-section of society it is inevitable that some police officers will hold racist views. This is not to condone such views or discriminatory actions but to see the police service as no exception to wider society where racial discrimination is endemic. These explanations can be criticized for not taking any account of the way in which prejudices are part of the police organizational culture. The 'canteen culture' explanation sees racism as one of the core elements of police culture (see the discussion on the PSI research above), along with conservatism, machismo and solidarity with other officers. Linked to the view that racist attitudes are a part of police culture, though not, of course, held by all officers, is the view that there is an inevitable clash of cultures between the white population and ethnic minorities. This clash of cultures is reflected in the stereotypes held about different minority groups and the view common among many white people that 'their' white culture was being rejected; as Bowling and Phillips put it, 'the failure to "accept"

Englishness, made ethnic minorities at once threatening and vulnerable to attack'. The final possible explanation, of 'institutional racism' was highlighted above in our consideration of the Macpherson Inquiry into the Stephen Lawrence murder.

Of course, many elements of police culture and working practices are by no means unique to the police and are probably common in many male work organizations. But in the context of policing, people are perhaps bound to wonder what the general public, including the female, gay and black, can expect if this is how the police treat their own female, gay and black officers.

Suggest other occupational subcultures which might demonstrate similarities with the police's 'canteen culture'.

Bearing this in mind, to what extent do you think we should expect 'higher' standards and different cultural norms in the police? To put it another way, should the police be 'better' than the general population or should they be representative, with all that that entails?

- Considering police culture in general, how do you think it might influence (a) police–public relations; and (b) how police officers carry out their job?

FURTHER READING

Newburn, T. and Reiner, R. (2007) 'Policing and the Police', in M. Maguire, R. Morgan and R. Reiner (eds) *The Oxford Handbook of Criminology* (4th edn). This chapter examines some of the key issues that relate to public policing in the twenty-first century, in particular issues around police management and governance that we were not able to examine in detail, including how to measure and assess what the police do, police partnerships with other agencies, transnational policing; and police accountability.

Emsley, C. (1996) *The English Police: A Political and Social history* (2nd edn). This provides a comprehensive coverage of the history of the English police, from the earliest agents and institutions of law enforcement to the increasingly centralized, state-regulated, role of the police in the 1990s.

Leishman, F., Loveday, B. and Savage, S. (eds) (2002) *Core Issue in Policing* (2nd edn). This edited collection includes chapters from academic researchers and practitioners who provide different approaches to examining the context and functions of the police and to considering the future.

Rowe, M. (ed.) (2007) *Policing Beyond MacPherson: Issues in Policing, Race and Society*. An examination of the impact of the Macpherson Report into the Lawrence murder and the extent it has led to changes in policing in modern Britain.

Newburn, T. (ed.) (2008) *A Handbook of Policing* (2nd edn). This is a comprehensive text (running to over 900 pages) that provides a detailed overview of policing in Britain. It is divided into four sections – comparative and historical perspectives; the context of policing; doing policing (how the police operate in specific areas such as drugs, terrorism and organized crime); and themes and debates (including chapters on race, gender, ethics and restorative justice).

WEBSITES

The following Home Office website includes information on police powers, recruitment, training and resourcing (and also provides a link to the website for the HM Inspectorate of Constabulary): www.homeoffice.gov.uk/crimpol/index.html

www.policefed.org is the website for the Police Federation, established in 1919 as the staff association for all police constables, sergeants and inspectors. The website for chief police officers and other senior staff is www.acpo.police.uk

The website for the Centre for Crime and Justice Studies (www.kcl.ac.uk) provides information on events, research and publications in the criminal justice field. The Centre for Crime and Justice Studies is a charity based at King's College London which aims to inform and educate about all aspects of crime and the criminal justice system.

CHAPTER 12

The Courts, Sentencing and the Judiciary

INTRODUCTION

A glance at the newspapers, television schedules or cinema listings on any particular day will demonstrate the fascination, some might say obsession, we have with crime and criminals – with what crimes are committed, with who commits them and with what happens to those criminals who are caught. It is this last aspect that provides the focus for this chapter. Questions such as 'should all murderers get life imprisonment?', 'what should life mean?' and 'should burglars go to prison?' excite widespread interest and debate, evidenced by the front page headline in *The Times* (20 December 2002) which announced that the 'Lord Chief Justice tells courts not to jail burglars'. Indeed the media interest with crime and criminals is largely based around what happens to offenders who are caught – with who gets what within the criminal justice system. What happens in the courtroom forms the basis for much media reporting of crime for local and national newspapers and broadcasting; and the courtroom drama is regularly used to boost audience figures in soaps and as the basis of storylines in films and other productions.

In covering the 'who gets what' of criminal justice the chapter will start with an overview of the structure of the courts in England and Wales, the role of the Crown Prosecution Service and some of the key principles that inform the sentencing of offenders. The issue of impartiality in sentencing will be considered by looking at the extent to which race, gender and class, and in particular the race, gender and class of offenders, influences sentencing. The final part of the chapter examines those people who have the power to pass sentence on offenders – the judiciary; it considers the background, training and appointment of magistrates and judges.

THE STRUCTURE OF THE COURTS

The court structure we have in England and Wales (there are differences in the Scottish and Northern Irish criminal justice systems) is the result of hundreds of years of development, with some parts of it dating back over 900 years. It is based on a clear and recognizable hierarchy at the top of which sits the Supreme Court as the 'highest court in the land' (until 1 October 2009, the House of Lords was the highest court, although the supremacy of this court could be questioned as British laws are now subject to the European Court in Luxembourg). However, there is not a straight-forward pyramid structure; perhaps not surprisingly given its ancient origins there are all sorts of deviations and historical idiosyncrasies that affect the court structure.

There is, though, a basic dividing line between the criminal and the civil courts. On the criminal side, prosecutions are generally brought by the state against those whose behaviour has broken the criminal law. If found guilty the individual is pun-ished by the state. By contrast civil cases are between private interests and involve one party suing another, usually for some harm caused or money owing. The police are not usually interested in such cases unless the behaviour also amounts to a crime. Different standards or degrees of proof are required in criminal and civil cases; in criminal cases there is a conviction only if the case is proved 'beyond reasonable doubt', whereas civil cases are won on the 'balance of probabilities' – in other words a slightly lesser degree of proof is required. In addition the titles and names used by the people involved in the different courts differ; for instance the term plaintiff, for the person bringing an action, is only used in civil cases.

Another general and fundamental principle underlying our criminal justice system is that what happens in (adult) courts should be open and public; and apart from a few exceptions, for instance where there is felt to be a national security risk, any member of the public can see what goes on in court. Table 12.1 below lists the main courts and their functions.

Table 12.1 The modern English court system

Court	Criminal functions	Civil functions	Number of courts	Caseload	Composition
Magistrates' Courts	Minor crime	Very limited	Several hundred	Vast	Part-time lay JPs, a few full-time stipendiary magistrates in large cities
County Courts	None	Extensive case load	260	Approx 2 million cases started each	Circuit and district judges

Table 12.1 continued

Court	Criminal functions	Civil functions	Number of courts	Caseload	Composition
				year – of which about 5% come to trial	
Crown Courts	All	Limited	Technically one court with 90 locations	100,000 plus cases	Circuit judges and recorders
The High Court:					
Chancery Division	None	Trusts, tax law, wills, property etc.		Approx. 700 trials	17 High Court judges
Family Division	None	Family law in general		2–3,000 defended cases	15 High Court judges
				1,500–2,000 trials	63 High Court judges
Queen's Bench	Some appeals from tribunals	All civil law apart from above – especially contract and tort			
Court of Appeal:					Lord Chief Justice and Master of the Rolls
Criminal Division	Most criminal appeals	None		6–7,000	Sits in benches of 1 or 2 judges from Court of Appeal and judges from Queen's Bench
Civil Division	None	Appeals from High Court, County Court and tribunals		about 1,500	Sits in benches of 3 judges
House of Lords	Appeals from any court in England and Wales on any matter (and from Scotland and N. Ireland in many cases)			50–60	Benches of 5 from the 10–12 Lords of Appeal under the Lord Chancellor

Source: Adapted from I. Budge *et al.* (1998) pp. 476–7.

Magistrates' Courts

The 460 or so magistrates' courts are the first layer of our court structure and can be found in most towns. Each of these courts has a 'bench' which is staffed by magistrates who are, in the main, part-time, unpaid lay persons. There are about 30,000 lay magistrates, known as Justice of the Peace (JPs); and the fact that the vast majority of criminal cases are judged by non-professional, part-time members of the community provides a unique aspect to the criminal justice system of England and Wales. In addition to JPs, there are a small number, around a hundred, of paid, legally qualified magistrates; now known as District Judges, until 2000 these professional magistrates were called stipendiary magistrates. District Judges are full-time members of the judiciary who have the same powers as benches of two lay magistrates. They usually sit in the bigger, urban courts with particularly heavy case loads and tend to hear the lengthier and more complex cases that come before magistrates' courts. As well as District Judges there are also Deputy District Judges who sit in magistrates' courts not as full-time professionals but on a fee-paid basis, and who can apply to be District Judges after serving for a minimum of two years or 40 days in court. It is likely that there will be pressure to extend the professional magistracy in the future (an issue we will return to when looking at the appointment and background of the judiciary later in the chapter). However, in spite of this it is important to remember that the vast majority of criminal cases in magistrates' courts are heard by a lay, part-time judiciary.

The main task of magistrates' courts is to deliver 'summary justice' to people charged with less serious crimes and to decide which cases are serious enough to be sent for trial by judge and jury in Crown Court (or for sentencing in Crown Court if the offender has pleaded guilty). Having to send more serious cases to a higher court does not mean that magistrates have little power; they are able to send offenders to prison for up to six months (or twelve months when there are two sentences that are to run consecutively). Furthermore although they only deal with less serious crime, the huge bulk of crime is of a relatively minor nature, which means that the vast majority of all criminal cases (something in the region of 98 per cent) start and end with the magistrates' courts. The great majority of defendants who come before magistrates' courts plead guilty, with the magistrates then having to pass sentence (or, as mentioned above, to send them to the crown court if the offence merits a more severe punishment than magistrates can give). Those defendants who plead not guilty have the choice of trial by magistrates with no jury or of going to crown court for a jury trial – although there have been recent government moves to abolish the automatic right for a jury trial (an issue we look at in the question break on pp. 405–408).

As with all courts, there is a good deal of variation in sentencing practices across magistrates' courts and to try to ensure there is as much consistency as possible, each magistrates' bench is advised by a justice's clerk. These clerks are qualified lawyers with specialist training and as well as advising magistrates on legal procedures they are also responsible for training them. They also have a big role in pre-trial proceedings, including determining legal aid applications and organizing court timetables. As regards sentencing in all the courts, offenders can appeal against their sentence, although in English law it is normal for sentences to commence straight away after they are given even if the offender is going to appeal. The appeals process is so slow that those serving short sentences are likely to have finished or almost finished them by the time any appeal is heard (this and the fact that crown courts can now increase sentences which offenders have appealed against makes appealing a high-risk strategy for offenders).

Apart from their role as judges and sentencers, magistrates have also to decide whether to grant defendants bail or remand them in custody to wait for trial; and they have a wide range of powers in family matters (for instance in decisions over maintenance to separated partners) and over decisions to grant drinks and opening hours licences.

Crown courts

Crown courts deal with the more serious criminal cases – the few per cent that get beyond the magistrates courts – and are based at over 90 locations in England and Wales. In theory the crown court in England and Wales is one court that sits at various locations. The cases heard at crown courts are ranked according to seriousness, with the most serious heard by senior judges and the majority of (slightly less serious) cases dealt with by more junior judges – either circuit judges or recorders. Where there is a plea of not guilty crown court trials involve a jury who decides on the outcome of the trial. Cases come to the crown court by different routes; from a magistrates' court for either trial or sentence or if a defendant has appealed against the verdict or the sentence given at magistrates' court. Crown courts deal with criminal cases and their equivalent on the civil side of the court system are county courts which deal with matters of civil law, so they are not the focus of our interest here in looking at the criminal justice system. There are around 260 county courts which hear cases for, among other things, recovery of money, and most of these cases lead to settlements out of court.

The crown courts hear in the region of 120,000 cases per year, about a quarter of which have the defendants pleading not guilty. The most famous crown court is the Central Criminal Court or Old Bailey in London.

QUESTION BREAK: JURY TRIALS?

Jury trials in England and Wales date back to the twelfth century and the reign of Henry II, when 12 'free men' were assigned to arbitrate on disputes over land. In the crown court of today they are the body which determines guilt or innocence. However, the effectiveness of the jury system has been the subject of some debate in recent years. On the one hand they are seen as upholders of democracy in our legal system, on the other as unwieldy and unprofessional.

Eligibility to serve on a jury has been extended over the years (it used to be restricted to property owners for example) to include all adults aged 18–70 years with some exceptions, including members of the judiciary, the mentally disordered and ex-prisoners.

As research and investigation into the effectiveness of juries is not allowed and jury members are not allowed to discuss their deliberations, relatively little is known about their workings or effectiveness (there have been moves to loosen this restriction and some important research has been undertaken in recent years, as the extracts below illustrate).

It has been a basic principle of our criminal justice system that defendants pleading not guilty would have an automatic right to trial by jury. However the Criminal Justice Act of 2003 allowed crown court trials without juries in the more lengthy and complex fraud cases – a measure that was due to be extended by the Fraud (Trials without a Jury) Bill of 2006, but which was delayed by opposition in the House of Lords.

The extracts below highlight some of the issues surrounding jury trials. Read them before considering the questions below.

Ground-breaking research finds juries are fair and effective

Are juries fair? by Cheryl Thomas, Professor at the Centre for Empirical Legal Studies at University College London, is a two-year survey of more than 1,000 jurors at crown courts and a separate study of over 68,000 jury verdicts. In the report, sensitive issues about jury decision-making have been tackled for the first time. It reveals that:

- all-white juries do not discriminate against defendants from black and minority ethnic (BME) backgrounds
- juries almost always reach a verdict and convict two-thirds of the time
- there are no courts where juries acquit more than convict.

It also shows that:

- jurors want more information about how to do their job
- some jurors use the internet to look for information about their case
- some jurors find media reports of their case difficult to ignore.

Professor Thomas said:

"This research shows that juries in England and Wales were found to be fair, effective and efficient – and should lay to rest any lingering concerns that racially-balanced juries are needed to ensure fairness in trials with BME defendants or racial evidence."

(Ministry of Justice, www.justice.gov.uk 17 February 2010)

Jury trial: Case dismissed

Research published yesterday by the Ministry of Justice ought to stop most of this campaign dead in its tracks. For many years, there were plenty of opinions but very few facts about how this country's jury system works. This landmark research remedies that omission in a comprehensive way. It has analysed over 68,000 jury verdicts and has looked in depth at dozens of cases in much greater detail. At the end of it, the researchers have come up with a ringingly reliable answer to the question posed in their own publication's title, *Are Juries Fair?* Their answer, quite simply, is yes, they are.

On almost every count, the verdict on the jury is positive – even on issues where juries are popularly thought to be failing. Juries make their minds up properly. They convict more than they acquit, even at courts with a reputation for leniency. They are most likely to convict in cases of deception, drugs and theft, and least likely to do so in cases of non-fatal offences against the person (though even there they convict in most cases). They take much care in considering a defendant's state of mind. Juries convict more than they acquit in rape cases. Even all-white juries do not discriminate against ethnic minority defendants. Women jurors change their minds more than men.

Proper concerns remain. Not enough jurors understand judges' legal instructions. Too many jurors surf the internet for help. In high-profile cases, media reporting infects the process. These, though, are solvable problems. In most respects the jury is not guilty as charged.

(*Guardian* Editorial, 18 February 2010)

Does the jury system still work?

Jury service is carried out by an average of 390,000 British citizens a year. It is an important civic duty; but it is not an easy task, involving hours of waiting to be called; starting to hear a trial, only for it to be aborted; or hours of legal argument. It can also involve the most gruesome of crimes, or highly technical and complex evidence. The responsibility is huge: jurors must be sure "beyond reasonable doubt" that the defendant committed the crime, knowing that a loss of liberty may result. So it is no surprise that they may be traumatised. Worse, if they experience distress or doubts, they cannot talk about it — because they are prohibited in law.

(*The Times* Online, 30 June 2009)

Debate on the jury

Arguments for retaining the jury

- Juries represent a cross-section of the population so the accused is tried by his or her peers
- Juries enable the public's view of the criminal justice system to be reflected
- Juries ensure that unpopular or 'unjust' laws cannot be enforced
- There is no acceptable alternative
- Jury members are not 'case-hardened' and are more likely to have an open mind.

Arguments against retaining the jury

- Juries are not representative of society as a whole
- Juries are not able to handle complex issues
- Juries are subject to prejudice and irrationality
- Juries prolong the length and therefore the cost of trials
- Juries are too ready to believe the prosecution evidence
- Juries are naïve and unaware of courtroom tactics to manipulate information

(adapted from Davies *et al.* 2005)

- What criticisms of the jury system are raised in the extracts?
- What positive aspects of the system are highlighted?
- Which of the arguments in the last extract 'Debate on the jury' do you feel to be most persuasive?

The High Court

Above the Crown Courts is the 'legal elite'. The High Court, which handles the most difficult and complex cases, is the most senior civil court. The High Court is a generic term which covers three separate kinds of courts, each with separate functions and each dating back hundreds of years. The three courts or divisions are: the Queen's Bench, headed by the Lord Chief Justice and the main civil court for disputes and wrongs; the Chancery Division, which deals with financial issues including trade and industry disputes; and the Family Division, which hears all cases involving children and matrimonial issues.

The Court of Appeal

Appeals against convictions or sentences given in a lower court are heard by a higher court. Anyone convicted and sentenced by a magistrates' court can appeal to the crown court; and anyone convicted and sentenced by the crown court can appeal to the Court of Appeal. The Court of Appeal is staffed by the most senior judges, and the decisions these judges make influence and form the law of the country. There are two divisions within the Court of Appeal – the Criminal Division, headed by the Lord Chief Justice, and the Civil Division, headed by the Master of the Rolls. The Criminal Division hears around 8,000 cases a year, most being appeals against sentence, and the Civil Division over 1,000, generally appeals from decisions of the High Court and certain tribunals (e.g. industrial tribunals). The Court of Appeal is unlike the lower courts in that it does not hear from witnesses except in exceptional cases; the decisions it makes are based on documents and transcripts from the particular case in question, occasionally supplemented with arguments from barristers.

The Supreme Court (previously the House of Lords)

As mentioned earlier this is the highest court in the country. In this context, and up until October 2009, the House of Lords referred to the Judicial Committee of legal members of the House of Lords – 12 Law Lords who have reached the very summit of the legal profession. It was not the same as the parliamentary House of Lords. Since then, as a result of the Constitutional Reform Act of 2005, the Law Lords have become Justices of the Supreme Court, reflecting the fact that they had no effective political role. The Supreme Court started work on 1 October 2009 and, as its name suggests, is the highest court and the final arbiter of justice in this country (strictly speaking this relates to English, Welsh and Northern Irish Law and Scottish Civil, but not Criminal, Law). It is independent of Parliament and hears the most important legal cases. However there is no automatic right of appeal to it, with the right to appeal granted by The Court of Appeal. It only handles cases which are felt to have important implications for the impact of law on society.

There are other, more specialized courts and tribunals which relate to specific areas of the law – such as Coroners' Courts and Employment Appeal Tribunals – but which we will not go into here. In addition there are the two European courts which have a role to play in our criminal justice system. The decisions of the European Court in Luxembourg and the European Court of Human Rights in Strasbourg are theoretically superior even to those of the Supreme Court. However, the extent to which the British government takes notice of and responds to their decisions is debatable. The European courts cannot be approached directly; all cases go to the European Commission first and few ever reach the courts.

THE CROWN PROSECUTION SERVICE

The Crown Prosecution Service (CPS) was established by the Prosecution of Offences Act of 1985. It takes over cases when the police have decided to prosecute and is therefore responsible for most public prosecutions in England and Wales. If the CPS does not agree with the police that the case should be prosecuted, it can be dropped, the charges can be changed or more evidence required. The CPS was set up to be an independent service – independent from both the police and the government so as to provide suspected offenders with an extra layer of protection from both these institutions. Although a national body, the CPS is organized into local areas which closely match up with the areas covered by regional police forces.

Rather than go into the organizational structure of the CPS, we will focus on how it decides whether or not to prosecute the cases that are handed over to it. Essentially this involves following what is known as the Code for Crown Prosecutors. As the code says in its introduction, prosecuting an individual or body is a serious step and so has to be as fair and effective as possible. The general principles guiding the CPS are that it ensures the right person is prosecuted for the right offence and that it acts in a fair, independent and objective manner. In deciding whether to prosecute or not the CPS applies what are know as the 'twin tests' – the evidential test and the interests of justice test.

The evidential test is the first stage of the decision to prosecute and essentially means that a prosecution should only be introduced and continued with if there is a realistic chance of conviction. If there is not then the evidential test is not passed and the prosecution should not go ahead. In deciding on how realistic a chance there is of conviction the CPS considers what the defence case might be and how this is likely to affect the prosecution and, then, whether a jury or magistrate (as the case may be) is more likely than not to convict the defendant or defendants. It may have to consider matters such as whether evidence that will be used in the case is reliable or not.

If the particular case does pass the evidential test then the CPS has to decide that a prosecution would be in the public interest. In cases of any seriousness a prosecution is usually expected unless public interest factors are particularly critical, and generally speaking the more serious the offence the more likely it is that a prosecution will be in the public interest. The sorts of factors which may lead the CPS not to prosecute in relation to the public interest test might be if the offence is only likely to attract a very small penalty, if the offence was committed as a result of a genuine mistake or if there has been a long time lag between the offence and the date of the trial. However, and as mentioned, none of these factors would be considered if the offence was serious enough – so, for instance, murder cases are often dealt with years after the offence as a result of new evidence coming to light. Other public interest factors considered include the age and health of the defendant and the effect that a prosecution may have on a victim's health.

We have not got the scope here to assess the effectiveness of the CPS. However, and as mentioned above, the decision to prosecute is a fundamental one and it is important to bear in mind that the issues that the CPS has to weigh up provide scope for the different treatment of offenders and for the favouring of some interests rather than others.

TRIALS AND SENTENCING: PRINCIPLES AND ISSUES

Criminal liability

It is a fundamental principle of criminal law that a person should only be punished if they have committed the act in question and if they are blameworthy – in other words the offender has to have committed the act and be responsible for it. This requirement for there to be an action and intention is expressed in the legal terms *actus reus* (a Latin phrase meaning guilty act) and *mens rea* (guilty mind). While this might seem clear enough in theory, there are some crimes which do not involve or require a guilty mind, where there is not the same level of blame as in offences that are clearly intended. These might include certain driving offences, such as speeding for example. And although the most serious offence, murder, clearly involves intention, the law recognizes that deaths can be caused in many circumstances which do not involve the same degree of intent and blame. So there are various categories of homicide that include manslaughter as well as murder; and murder charges can be reduced to manslaughter if, for instance, the offender was provoked or under pressure, or was suffering from diminished responsibility. What the criminal justice system is trying to do is to ensure that the law reflects the extent of moral blameworthiness. However, in doing so difficulties can arise. Among other examples, Davies and colleagues (2005) refer to careless driving which can kill innocent people but which in many instances has no adverse consequences or only very trivial ones. They ask what offence careless drivers should be charged with and what punishment they should be sentenced to when their actions kill other people.

Mitigation

After an offender is found guilty or has pleaded guilty, factors of mitigation can be offered in defence to suggest that s/he is less blameworthy than might appear, or to suggest that the offence itself was perhaps not as serious as it might have been. So factors of mitigation may relate to the personal circumstances of the offender – they had lost their job or been deserted by their family, for instance – or to the offence itself – the offender was provoked or led into it. This aspect of the criminal justice process allows a convicted person an opportunity to argue for a more lenient sentence than they might otherwise be given. Issues around mitigation and the relevance of various mitigating factors are considered in some detail in Chapter 7 (pp. 228–232).

Establishing guilt

The criminal justice system in England and Wales is adversarial, which means there are two sides, the defence and prosecution, who argue their case as best they can within certain ethical and, of course, legal limits. Rather than seeking to find the 'truth', each side aims to win its case by persuading the magistrates, judges or juries (depending on the particulars of the case) to find in their favour. Within this context, the rules surrounding court proceedings aim to protect the innocent from unfair conviction. This means that in theory the onus of proof is on the prosecution and that the defendant should be treated fairly. However, in the day-to-day practice of the court it is easy to assume that those who are accused (the defendants) are likely to be guilty, and to assume that the police must be pretty sure to bring them to court anyway. Given this tendency to assume that defendants have 'done something wrong', it is often a high-risk strategy to plead not guilty. If a defendant is found guilty after pleading not guilty the sentence received will tend to be longer (for instance, it will be felt that the defendant has wasted the court's time and has subjected witnesses and victims to unnecessary pressure through cross-examination). In general terms, the Court of Appeal has indicated that a discount of between one quarter to one third of the expected sentence is appropriate for a guilty plea. Furthermore if a defendant is found guilty it becomes more difficult to provide convincing mitigation to be taken into account in the sentence given (it is difficult to plead not guilty and then, if found guilty, to say, 'I'm sorry and I won't do it again'!).

A key decision facing a defendant is to whether to plead guilty or not. And a decision to plead guilty can be affected by many considerations (as well as the 'truth'). A defendant may feel that to plead not guilty would protract the case, or that they did not commit the offence but it is only their word against the police, or that they are likely to get a lighter sentence if they plead guilty (which as mentioned above is the case). A guilty plea, then, involves weighing up a range of factors and may following a bargaining process involving legal representatives. And while not formally advocated, plea bargaining can save the expense of a contested trial, can avoid the risk of a defendant being convicted for a more serious offence, saves police time, and reduces the uncertainty of the outcome following a not guilty plea. Thus both sides could be said to benefit – the defendant is assured the penalty is not too harsh and the police and prosecution are assured of a conviction.

QUESTION BREAK: GUILTY OR NOT?

The above section considered the decision to plead guilty or not. The two extracts below highlight other issues involved in determining guilt or innocence.

First, the comment from Lord Donaldson, Master of the Rolls from 1982–92, makes the point that when defendants are acquitted it does not necessarily mean that they are innocent.

Second, it is a basic, almost sacrosanct, feature of court proceedings that what happens in discussions among jurors should be kept absolutely secret.

Read the two extracts and consider the questions below.

A 'guilty' verdict means that in the view of the jury the accused undoubtedly committed the offence. It is not only the innocent who are entitled to a 'not guilty' verdict. They are joined and, in my experience, are heavily outnumbered by the almost certainly guilty. This is as it should be because, as every law student is taught, it is far better that ten guilty men (sic) go free than that one innocent man be convicted.

(Lord Donaldson, Letter to *The Times*, 19 August 1994)

Imagine you are an Asian man on trial for arson, facing the prospect of years in jail if found guilty. Your fate is in the hands of 12 men and women chosen at random from the electoral roll. But what if some of those jurors are racist? Suppose they make disparaging remarks in the jury room about your appearance, your accent, your poor English and your business integrity . . .

That's what happened during Sajid Qureschi's trail at Mold Crown Court in October 2000, according to one of the jurors who convicted him by an 11–1 majority and sent him down for four years . . . In a letter to the court six days after his conviction, she claimed that some of her jurors seemed to have already decided their verdict from the start, that one juror fell asleep during the evidence . . . and that some tried to bully others. Enough, you might think, to raise serious doubts about whether Qureschi had a fair trial.

But not enough for the Court of Appeal . . . (which) refused him permission even to launch an appeal. The stumbling block was the Contempt of Court Act 1981, which bans anyone – and that includes judges – from inquiring into the secrets of the jury room.

(From C. Dyer, 'Jurors Behaving Badly', the *Guardian*, 25 June 2002)

- What arguments could be made against Lord Donaldson's conclusion?
- What are the arguments for maintaining the absolute secrecy of jury deliberations?
- Do you agree with them?

Types of sentence

Before listing the different sentences available to the court, it is worth bearing in mind that the passing of a sentence only occurs in a relation to a small proportion of the actual crimes that are committed. Aside from the massive amount of crime that is never reported, of those crimes that are reported, many are never recorded by the police as crimes and even when they are recorded never get 'cleared up' or solved. And much of the estimated 5 per cent of all crimes that are 'cleared up' are not followed up by any official action; it may be that the offender is too young or that there is not enough evidence to proceed, for example. On top of this, about one third of offenders are cautioned rather than prosecuted so that it is maybe only something like 2 per cent of all offences that lead to a conviction and a sentence from the court. This is not to say that sentencing is of no importance, and it certainly has strong symbolic importance, but such figures do highlight the need to be wary of expecting sentencing policy and practice to do much about altering the patterns of behaviour of criminals.

There are a number of basic forms of sentence available to the courts and they can be grouped under four basic categories. First there are discharges. These can be absolute, where the conviction is recorded but nothing will happen to the offender, or conditional, where the offender will receive no further punishment if s/he is not found guilty of any other offence for a certain period of time (a three-year conditional discharge, for example). If sentenced for another offence during that period the offender can additionally be sentenced for the offence for which they were originally discharged. So the discharge is a sort of denunciatory sentence that does not seek to actually punish but does have a deterrent effect in that if the offender offends again s/he will be punished.

Second, the most common penalties are financial. These are subject to a maximum (of £5,000) in magistrates' courts, while there is no limit in crown courts. As well as financial penalties in the form of fines, there is also compensation that has to be considered by a court when cases involve personal injury or damage to property and costs, which can be awarded against offenders. In terms of priority and order of payment, compensation has to be paid first, then fines and finally costs, with compensation to the victim taking priority.

QUESTION BREAK: THE DARK FIGURE OF CRIME

- What punishment should be given to someone who does not pay a fine?
- Should persistent non-payment lead to imprisonment? Suggest reasons for and against such a course of action.

Third are community sentences. Theses were first introduced in law in 1907 for the 'probation' of offenders and have undergone various changes in form since then. Until the Criminal Justice Act of 2003 there were three main types of community sentences that were supervised by the Probation Service. These were Community Rehabilitation Orders (until recently known as Probation Orders), Community Punishment Orders (previously known as Community Service Orders) and Community Punishment and Rehabilitation Orders (a combination of the other two). For these sentences to be imposed, the offence had to be sufficiently serious and, usually, the offender has to agree to the particular order. As a result of the Act, these were replaced by a single, general community order which enables the courts to choose different elements from a range of possible requirements; the aim being to choose the right mix of punishment, programmes and supervision for the particular offender. The courts can choose any combination of the following 12 different requirements:

- compulsory unpaid work;
- participation in specific activities (such as literacy or numeracy education);
- programmes aimed at changing behaviour (such as anger management);
- prohibition from certain activities (such as attending football matches);

- curfew (often monitored with an electronic tag);
- exclusion from certain areas:
- residence requirement;
- mental health treatment (with the consent of the offender);
- drug treatment and testing (with the consent of the offender);
- alcohol treatment (with the consent of the offender);
- supervision (regular meetings with a probation officer);
- spending time at an attendance centre.

As these brief comments and the list of possible requirements indicate, community sentences can be seen to meet some of key aims of punishment discussed earlier in Chapter 7. Community orders are rehabilitative, with offenders hopefully acquiring new skills while following them; there is some denunciation if the community work undertaken is public and visible; and there are elements of reparation, if not always to the individual victim, then to the community.

Custodial (prison) sentences are the fourth main form of penalty and are imposed for the more serious offences. Shorter custodial sentences can be suspended if there are 'exceptional circumstances'; these suspended sentences were introduced (by the 1967 Criminal Justice Act) to encourage the diverting away from prison of offenders. However they did not succeed in lowering the prison population with some courts seeming to use such sentences when they may not have passed a custodial sentence in the first place, rather than as intended as a substitute for custody. Initially sentences of up to two years could be suspended, but as part of its overview of the sentencing of offenders, the Criminal Justice Act of 2003 stated that a suspended sentence should only be used where the court would have passed a custodial sentence of less than 12 months. The sentence could be suspended for between six months and two years and during that time the offender can be required to undertake one or more of the requirements of the community order (listed above).

Although there are not fixed lengths of custody for particular offences, there are certain rules and guidelines that judges and magistrates have to follow. There is a mandatory life sentence for anyone guilty of murder (although the actual length of time a murderer spends in prison varies, with a minimum period recommended by the courts) and there are discretionary maximum sentences for other serious crimes. The sentence imposed by the court is the maximum amount of time the offender will spend in custody with different release arrangements depending on the sentence given and when the offence was committed. There is also a sort of 'going rate' or tariff for different offences that has built up on the basis of decisions made by the Court of Appeal. The starting point for deciding on length of sentence for serious offences is the time that a murderer would be expected to spend in prison. In the mid 1970s, for instance, the Lord Chief Justice, Lord Justice Lawton, took as a starting point that a murderer would spend 15 years in prison, which would be the equivalent of two thirds of a 22-year sentence (there was a third remission from prison sentences in the 1970s). What he termed 'wholly abnormal' offences such as political kidnapping and bomb attacks were placed just beneath this 22-year guidance, with armed robbery next 'down' at 18 years. Thus the Court of Appeal has developed 'guideline judgments' for different offences that take into account the likely remission that prisoners would receive from their initial sentences. In May 2003 the then Home Secretary David Blunkett advocated changes to the way murderers would be sentenced. He said that he intended to ask Parliament to approve a much tougher sentencing framework. This would include 'whole life' prison terms for cases involving child sex, terrorism and multiple murder and a second tier of a minimum 30 years for contract killers, racist murder and those who kill police officers, compared to the current minimum of 20 years. These proposed changes were attacked by lawyers and the judiciary for interfering with judges' independence. The Bar Council, which represents barristers in England and Wales, said the plans were 'constitutionally a leap in the dark', with the Home Secretary accused of 'trying to institutionalise the grip of the executive around the neck of the judiciary . . . (in a manner that) will erode the separation of powers, which is something which has for hundreds of years been seen to be something which is a strength in our democracy' (quotes from *The Times*, 7 May 2003).

Although there have been various attempts through legislation to cut back or at least restrain the growth of custodial sentences, the prison population continues to grow (recent trends in the prison population are examined in Chapter 13, pp. 440–443). New release arrangements were introduced in April 2005. Prisoners serving custodial sentences of 12 months or more serve half of the sentence in custody and the second half on licence in the community (and during the period of the licence the offender can be recalled into custody if they commit another offence or break the conditions of their licence). Those serving sentences of less than 12 months again only spend half of their sentence in custody but are not on licence for the second half. For offenders deemed to be 'dangerous' who are serving longer and indeterminate sentences for public protection the release arrangements are different (this includes the new Imprisonment for Public Protection sentence introduced by the Criminal Justice Act 2003 for those convicted of a serious violent or sexual offence). Such offenders are not released until the risk they pose is assessed by the Parole Board and seen as manageable (and if the risk is not acceptable they may never be released).

Sentencing procedure

There are various stages between establishing guilt and the passing of sentence. The sentence is not usually imposed immediately, unless the offence is of a very minor nature or if it is murder where life imprisonment is the mandatory, automatic sentence. The guilty defendant may ask for other offences to be taken into consideration, perhaps to indicate that a clean breast of past offences is being made. The defendant may personally or through legal representation put forwarded mitigation (see p. 411). And the court may wish to look in more detail at the offender's circumstances, including mental and physical health. In addition the court will consider reports from appropriate bodies such as the Probation Service and personal character references. So there are a whole range of factors that are liable to influence the decision as to what sentence should be given, including the seriousness of the offence and the offender's previous record. In spite of the sentencing guidelines mentioned above, this leaves those who assign sentences – the judiciary – with a good deal of discretion;

certainly compared to other places which have much more precise rules determining the passing of sentence. In the USA sentencing guidelines have been established for more than a quarter of a century and have had a major influence on sentencing policy and practice. By introducing greater consistency into the sentencing process, guidelines have made it easier to predict sentencing outcome and the costs of these sentences. In most examples of these guidelines, two criteria are used to prescribe the punishment: the seriousness of the crime and the criminal history of the offender. Different states in the USA have their own guidelines, and they can be extremely detailed. North Carolina, for example, uses a matrix that separates its sentences into three categories: active punishments, including total confinement to prison; intermediate punishments, that might include sentences with elements of electronic monitoring or intensive supervision; and community punishments, that include probation, community service and fines. After an offender is placed within a range in the matrix, two further ranges are also used to take account of any aggravating or mitigating factors.

QUESTION BREAK

What factors do you feel should guide magistrates and judges in determining an appropriate sentence? Why should they?

SENTENCING AND SOCIAL DIVISIONS

This section will consider the question of who gets sentenced – in particular, the influence that the ethnic, gender and class background of offenders has on the sentence they receive.

Race and sentencing

One of the most startling statistics regarding court sentences is the massive over-representation of ethnic minority populations who are sent to prison. Although BME (Black and Ethnic Minority) groups make up just under 9 per cent of the population of England and Wales (as at the last UK census, 2001), in June 2008 BME groups accounted for 27 per cent of the male prison population and 29 per cent of the female prison population (Ministry of Justice 2009). This over-representation is even more noticeable for specific ethnic minority groups. Of the 27 per cent of male prisoners, 15 per cent were classified as Black (largely Afro-Caribbean), 7 per cent as Asian, 3 per cent as Mixed and 2 per cent Chinese or Other; the respective figures for the female prison population were 19 per cent Black, 3 per cent Asian, 4 per cent Mixed and 3 per cent Chinese or Other. These figures are particularly striking in that only around1.8 per cent of the population is classified as Black. The question this raises is whether these figures reflect a much greater propensity to commit crime among ethnic minority groups or whether they can be explained by other factors. Other factors that affect the prison statistics include the fact that the very high figures for Afro-Caribbean women is in part explained by the relatively large number of foreign nationals who are imprisoned for drug smuggling; plus the fact that women who are first-time offenders are more likely to be imprisoned than male first-time offenders. Demographic factors include the younger average age of the ethnic minority, and especially the Black Afro-Caribbean, population; young people are more likely to offend (or be caught at least) than older people. In addition to this, Black Afro-Caribbean males are more likely to have other characteristics associated with higher offending rates, such as higher unemployment, lower educational attainment and living in areas with higher crime rates.

However, as regards sentencing practices, these points do not tell us whether the court system itself works differently for the different ethnic minority groups it deals with. Differential treatment in court is likely to occur as a result of black offenders being more likely to plead not guilty – for instance 33 and 48 per cent of black defendants plead not guilty in magistrates' and crown courts respectively, compared to 21 and 30 per cent for white defendants and 24 and 41 per cent for Asian defendants (Barclay and Mhlanga 2000). One effect of this is that offenders are given heavier sentences if found guilty after a not guilty plea – as a consequence of the discount given for guilty pleas (see p. 412 on 'establishing guilt' above). Pleading not guilty can also influence the extent to which mitigating factors are taken into account in passing sentence. Pre-Sentence Reports (PSRs – previously known as SERs) are prepared by the Probation Service and provide the courts with information on the circumstances of offenders. Pleading not guilty may affect whether an offender is provided with a PSR and the recommendations made in such a report. It might be that pleading not guilty is interpreted as not facing up to one's guilt, which might influence the sort of sentence advocated in the report.

One of the largest and most detailed studies on sentencing in this country was undertaken by Roger Hood (1992) for the Commission for Racial Equality. This study examined and tried to explain the over-representation of prisoners from an Afro-Caribbean background. The key issue Hood investigated was whether ethnic minority offenders are sentenced according to the same criteria as white offenders. Although it was difficult to pinpoint exact answers to that question a number of relevant factors were highlighted. A higher proportion of black people were charged with offences that were deemed to be more serious and that could only be dealt with by the crown court. For instance, many more were charged with robbery and although a nasty crime it could be questioned whether it is any more serious than housebreaking or grievous bodily harm (GBH) both of which can be dealt with summarily by magistrates' courts if both parties consent. As regards the ranking of offences in terms of seriousness, black offenders were disproportionately charged with supplying drugs, and the insistence that offences involving trading in small or moderate amounts of cannabis should be committed to crown court is also likely to influence the rate of imprisonment for black offenders. As well as being more likely to plead not guilty (see above), black defendant were found to be more likely to be remanded in custody by magistrates; a factor which can, again, lead to a greater likelihood of a custodial sentence – it is difficult to prove one has behaved well for a period of time after the offence if kept in custody.

Hood's research suggested that ethnic minority, and particularly black/Afro-Caribbean defendants were subject to forms of indirect discrimination at least. The implications of a practice that favours so strongly those who plead guilty and the ways in which different offences are ranked in terms of where they should be tried, for example, would seem to work against the interests of ethnic minority offenders. Hood acknowledges that it is a complex issue but on the basis of the detailed sample of almost 3,000 crown court cases it would seem that some discrimination does occur in courts. And as Reiner (1993) argues it does seem to be the case that with so many factors and people involved in decision-making in our criminal justice system, even small degrees of ethnic bias and/or differential treatment could have a very large cumulative effect.

More recently Roger Hood and colleagues were involved in further research into the treatment of ethnic minority groups in the criminal courts that was published in 2005 (Shute *et al.* 2005). This study focused on the perceptions of unfair treatment held by ethnic minority people who had come into contact with the courts – how defendants and witnesses, for example, felt about their treatment, as compared with white defendants and witnesses. With regard to perceptions, the Macpherson report (1999), although focused on the police, concluded that the criminal justice system in general was perceived by ethnic minorities to be biased against them. Shute and colleagues' study explored the subjective experiences and interpretations held by ethnic minorities about their treatment and the extent to which this affected their trust and confidence in the criminal courts. The research was extensive, involving about 1,250 interviews with defendants, witnesses and also solicitors, court staff, judges and magistrates. With regard to the defendants themselves, one in five black defendants felt their treatment had been influenced by racial bias (a proportion lower than the research team had expected). However, a number of black and Asian defendants thought they had received a heavier sentence than others because of their ethnicity. For example, a 19-year-old Afro-Caribbean male who had lived in Britain all his life commented, after being give a five-year prison sentence, 'If I was different colour a light sentence would have been given . . . The judge wanted to take another black face off the street . . . I was treated as a black offender. I've been in prison (on remand) for three months. I've seen white people with shorter sentences for more serious crimes. And a 37-year-old Afro-Caribbean sentenced to four months' imprisonment was critical of the pre-sentence report. 'The probation officer should be investigated . . . he is there to see me as a person . . . He had written down crap "He's going to be high risk" . . . I've completely changed . . . It's got to be nothing else apart from I'm a blacky.' Overall and in summary, the findings of this more recent study from Shute and colleagues found that the majority of defendants did not think they had been unfairly treated in court, but of the minority who did feel unfairly treated more than half attributed it to racism, with the main complaint being about excessive and unfair sentences (rather than racist language and attitudes of the judges and court staff).

Another study of the treatment of black defendants throughout the prosecution process was commissioned by the Crown Prosecution Service (CPS). The research examined almost 13,000 files and was published in 2003 (John 2003). It found that Afro-Caribbean and Asian defendants were more likely to be acquitted, or have the cases against them discontinued, suggesting they were being unnecessarily charged. Also, that the CPS was more likely to object to bail for Afro-Caribbean defendants as compared to white defendants. The study examined in depth 46 cases with a race element and commented on how they had been handled by the police and the CPS. It found a general failure of the police and CPS to properly acknowledge and/or record racial aggravation in almost half of the cases, even when there was clear evidence of such; and in 19 cases the police failed to recognize racial aggravation even when there was evidence of it from the victim. One of the report's recommendations was that specialist prosecutors should be appointed to deal with racist and religious crime.

Gender and sentencing

The vast majority of prisoners in England and Wales are male. In June 2008 males accounted for over 94 per cent of the total number of prisoners – 78,689 out of a total of 83,194 prisoners (Ministry of Justice 2009). The fact that such a massive proportion of prisoners are male might help to explain the common assumption that women are treated more leniently than men in the criminal justice system. This assumption is often referred to as the 'chivalry thesis', given that most criminal justice decision-makers are male. A different interpretation sees the criminal justice system as treating women in a discriminatory and sexist manner which leads to women offenders being doubly punished – for breaking the law and for breaking from traditional expectations of gender role behaviour. This 'debate' will be introduced in this brief section.

Statistics seem at first sight to offer strong support for the chivalry notion. Even though the female prison population is the fastest growing of the whole prison estate, as mentioned above, many more men than women are given custodial sentences and longer ones as well. Similarly males outnumber females in terms of crimes committed. In 2007, 1.41 million offenders were sentenced for indictable and summary offences in England and Wales. The great majority of these were male. The peak age for men being found guilty of, or cautioned for, indictable (more serious) offences was 17, with 6 per cent of men aged 17 being found guilty or cautioned, compared to 1 per cent of women of that age (Social Trends 2009).

Such figures do not, however, mean that women are necessarily dealt with more leniently than men, just that they are dealt with differently. In her study *Doubly Deviant, Doubly Damned* Ann Lloyd (1995) examined the chivalry argument that the criminal justice system deals with women offenders in a more lenient manner than male offenders. She found that this might be the case for some women but not for all. In particular chivalrous treatment from agencies such as the police and courts seemed to be limited to those women who were felt to conform to stereotypical views of how women should behave. In contrast those women offenders who did not fit such a picture were treated with (even) less understanding than male offenders – they were seen as offending against the law and against generally held notions of 'good women'. Domesticity would appear to be a key issue as regards the sentencing of women; the family is often an important aspect of mitigation pleas and the judiciary seem to be influenced by the impact of sentencing on children, although whether this influence works to the same extent for male as for female offenders is debatable.

QUESTION BREAK: WOMEN AND THE CRIMINAL JUSTICE SYSTEM

The extract below is taken from Ann Lloyd's study referred to in the previous section.

> The leniency or 'chivalry' argument is that women are treated more leniently by the courts simply because they are women. My argument is that while chivalry may well be extended to some women – those who conform to approved stereotypes – leniency will not be shown to 'deviant' women.
>
> 'If a woman conforms to a judge's idea of what is appropriate for a woman he will have trouble convicting her', Helena Kennedy told a conference at St. George's Medical School in 1991. 'Chivalry exists but it is very much limited to those women who are seen to conform.' She added that a woman who showed anger would be viewed as threatening by the court, which puts women who've been violent at particular risk of being treated more harshly than women who are perceived as conforming to notions of what constitutes proper womanhood. . . .
>
> Another point to bear in mind when analysing statistics of conviction and sentencing rates is the influence of conventional stereotypical ideas and assumptions about women . . .
>
> Farrington and Morris noted that some factors (notably previous convictions) had an independent influence on sentence severity and reconviction for both men and women . . . others only had an influence for one sex. In particular, marital status, family background and children were more important for women than men . . .
>
> Working lawyers I've spoken to agree with these findings, and tell me that chivalry is very much limited to those women who are seen to conform. The criminal lawyer, the probation officer and the psychiatrist all know how the system works: judges and magistrates make decisions based on a division of 'good' and 'bad' women, so the defence team tailor what they do and say to try to ensure their clients approximate to that stereotype as closely as possible.
>
> Lawyers may well be aware that these strategies are locking women into traditional stereotypes and may even question what they are doing to women in general. But their job is to do their best for the client. Helena Kennedy discusses these methods with women clients, trying to give them choices about what they want to do, telling them that if they turn up in a broderie anglaise blouse or a nice Marks and Spencer's dress they will be dealt with in a rather different way than if they turn up in bovver boots, sporting a spiky hair-do . . .

[Also] where women can be shown to be mentally and emotionally unstable, they are likely to be treated more sympathetically than men. This viewing of women as unstable, though it may be advantageous to individual women, is a high price for all women to pay insofar as it is premised on a belief in women's inherent instability *per se*. It also raises questions about the unfairness of treating men as if they had no inner lives and therefore of denying psychiatric help to men who could benefit from it.

(From A. Lloyd (1995) *Doubly Deviant Doubly Damned: Society's Treatment of Violent Women*, pp. 56–70)

- Why do you think that Lloyd suggests that while treating women offenders in terms of stereotypical views might benefit some women, 'it is a high price for all women to pay'?
- To what extent should factor s such as child care influence the sentencing of women (and men)?
- Look at recent press reports of crimes which involve both male and female defendants. Can you find any evidence for the chivalry argument?

Class and sentencing

As well as race and gender, it is important not to lose sight of the importance of social class background on justice received. However, social class is such a broad variable, and includes a whole cluster of factors such as housing, income, wealth, status and power, that its influence is perhaps even more difficult to measure than race or gender. Issues around class and punishment were raised in examining theories of punishment (Chapter 8) and particularly arguments that there is 'one law for the rich and one for the poor'. In that context, class was considered in terms of the power some groups have to influence how certain types of behaviour are interpreted and defined as criminal. Having said that, social class position is conventionally determined by occupation and we can raise a couple of points here with regard to its possible effect on sentencing.

Although attitudes toward unemployment may have changed as a result of mass unemployment in the 1970s and 1980s in particular, and while those passing sentence are probably more aware that unemployment is commonplace and not the individual's 'fault', traditional attitudes that 'people can find work if they really wanted to' might still be influential. There is a possibility that middle-class judges and magistrates (as the vast majority are) might see an employment record as evidence of stability and character and see unemployed people as lacking characteristics such as self-discipline and motivation. Furthermore, offenders who have jobs are likely to use their employment as a factor in mitigation and it might seem sensible for sentencers to take account of the effect that losing a job would have on an offender (and his/her family) should s/he be sent to prison. And if having a job is seen as a positive thing that might be used in mitigation, those who are unemployed might be deemed to have less to lose and therefore be sentenced more severely; while it is also more difficult to fine offenders who are not in work so reducing the options available to sentencers.

QUESTION BREAK: CLASS IN COURT

Consider the following two cases:

The theft of £500 goods from a shop.
The embezzlement of £500 from a company's funds by a director.

- How is each case likely to be dealt with?
- How might this relate to social class?
- Do you think that position in the community or 'respectability' should affect the sentence an offender receives?

(Adapted from McLaughlin and Muncie 2001: 144)

THE JUDICIARY

In this section we will look more closely at the appointment and background of the judiciary and at their role in the criminal justice system. There has been a massive increase in the number of judges and significant changes in the role of judges in the last 30 years or so, and certainly since the creation of the crown court in 1971. There are various different categories within the judiciary forming a hierarchy at the top of which are the Lords of Appeal and High Court Judges, then circuit judges, recorders, district judges and Magistrates. Before looking at the senior judges who sit in the crown courts and higher courts we will consider the judiciary who sit in the magistrates' courts.

Magistrates

As was detailed above (p. 404) the judiciary in magistrates' courts is dominated by lay magistrates, known as JPs; as of April 2009 there were 29,270 lay magistrates with a fairly even balance between males and females (14,472 males and 14,798 females). These magistrates are supported by around 100 full-time, professional magistrates, known as District Judges. There has been a movement in the direction of a more professionalized magistracy in recent years, partly as a result of the increasing workload of magistrates' courts and the difficulty of recruiting enough lay magistrates. Although the number of District Judges serving in magistrates' courts is relatively small, there have been concerns that in due course they will undermine the 'local' character of our justice system. In assessing the impact of stipendiary magistrates (the name given to professional magistrates up to 2000 when the term District Judge was introduced), Seago *et al.* (2000) found that they had had little impact on the work cultures or procedures in magistrates' courts. They dealt with cases more quickly than the lay magistrates although this was due in part to the fact that as they sat alone in court there was no need to confer with other magistrates and as they were legally trained professionals they had less need for advice from justice's clerks. Seago and colleagues argue that any wholesale replacement of lay magistrates by professionally trained magistrates would 'dilute the fundamental principles of citizenship and democracy', as well as being much more expensive.

QUESTION BREAK: LOCAL JUSTICE

A Light on the Lay Magistracy

> In writing . . . about the magistracy based on my own experiences in north London and visits to other parts of the country, I have come to the view that the system works pretty well. JPs strike me on the whole as conscientious, thoughtful folk, whose fair-mindedness may be judged from the fact that only a very small proportion of their decisions, around 4 per cent, are taken to appeal . . . (Any) imperfections are easily outweighed by the merit of involving ordinary, independent-minded people at the very heart of the judicial process.
>
> (From T. Grove 2002: 25)

Apart from being more expensive, suggest the advantages and disadvantages of a more centralized and professional rather than local and 'lay' magistracy.

Magistrates have traditionally been appointed in the name of the Queen by the Lord Chancellor, although more recently this role has been taken over by the Ministry of Justice, which is advised by almost 100 local Advisory Committees whose membership has traditionally been secret so as to prevent canvassing by would-be magistrates. In recent years this secrecy has been reduced with successive Lord Chancellors having tried to broaden and democratize the ranks of magistracy. There have been occasional advertisements in the press to encourage a wider range of candidates; however, personal recommendations from existing magistrates or locally respected organizations still play a major role in determining who is appointed. The selection process is, though, rigorous, with local Advisory Committees conducting interviews and turning down about three quarters of applicants, often in the interests of getting a more balanced bench. While lay magistrates do undergo some training, it is not intended to turn them into professionals; indeed magistrates are not encouraged to sit too often (or too infrequently), so as to prevent them from becoming 'case-hardened'.

Certain groups of the population are better suited to fitting in with the working patterns of lay magistrates than others in that not everyone can spare the time, or risk the financial loss, to sit as magistrates. As a result, groups who tend to be well represented on the bench include retired people, housewives with adult children and the more senior teachers. Having said that, the ranks of JPs have broadened and include people from many different backgrounds and occupations.

Compared to the senior judiciary, there has been less research on the background and attitudes of magistrates. One study which did focus on the ideology of magistrates and how this influences their 'performance' in court in terms of their sentencing of offenders was undertaken by Parker *et al.* (1989) and is considered in the case study below.

BOX 12.1 DECIDING THE SENTENCE

In their study *Unmasking the Magistrates*, Parker and colleagues (1989) examined the factors that influence the way in which magistrates sentence offenders. Based on first-hand research across a number of magistrates' courts, they considered how magistrates sift and evaluate all the information they are presented with in court and how they arrive at a particular decision. Social Enquiry Reports (now called Pre-Sentence Reports) seemed to be treated with some misgivings by magistrates – an attitude that stemmed from an implicit criticism of the social work profession, based on very stereotypical views and illustrated by comments such as:

> Some social workers are very put out if you don't accept their recommen-dations, but they're often not realistic, recommending conditional discharges all the time. The best social workers have been lost to early retirement. The new breed of whiz kids go to Keele for two years, have their brains removed, get a plastic card with their picture on it and think they're a social worker.
>
> (Parker *et al.* 1989: 95)

and

> I can remember that probation officer hitch-hiking round Europe with a guitar and a little rucksack. He had hair down to his shoulders and a beard to his navel. People of that kind are likely to take a lenient view of crime (ibid., p. 95).

While possibly tongue-in-cheek, such comments from practising magistrates indicate rather narrow-minded and conservative attitudes. By contrast, school reports were generally well received by magistrates and seen as more reliable. In a similar vein to social workers, defence lawyers were not seen as trustworthy and as being too much on the defendant's side.

As well as information from reports, there is also an element of assessment of the defendant's appearance and demeanour; with magistrates feeling they have the ability to assess a defendant's character almost at first sight. As one of the interviewed magistrates said, 'that girl had no intention of going to school . . . she had her story off pat . . . then when she turned away and I saw her split skirt and high heels, I thought, "you'll be on the game in a year or two"' (p. 102).

continued

While many factors interact and combine to determine a sentence, in particular the seriousness of the offence and the previous record of the offender, what is surprising is the weight magistrates gave to their own moral assessment of defendants. Parker and colleagues concluded that it is no wonder sentencing patterns are so difficult to explain. Although on one level it is true that 'every case is different', magistrates seemed to resist the principle of treating cases alike and those interviewed in this study seemed to think that being consistent was being too rigid. The magistrates appeared to view sentencing as something of an art rather than a science and were very sceptical of sentencing guidelines.

Judges

Although the judiciary, and especially the 'senior' judiciary, is an institution heavily steeped in tradition and very protective of its independence, the growth in the number of judges in recent years has helped to encourage a greater openness and democracy. In her examination of the effects of this expansion on the appointment, training and monitoring of what she terms the 'new judiciary', Malleson (1999) points out that, 'the recent introduction of public advertisements, interview panels and job descriptions would have been almost unthinkable 30 years ago' (p. 2). In spite of these changes and the fact that judges are more subject to media scrutiny and are more willing to engage in public debate, there is also a great reluctance to depart from traditional practices. In 1992, for instance, the Lord Chief Justice proposed the abolition of wigs – a suggestion that was swiftly defeated by opposition from other members of the senior judiciary. Such unwillingness to change is likely to reinforce the image of the judiciary as an archaic institution. In this section we will follow Malleson's approach and consider the appointment, background, training and accountability of judges.

Appointment and background

The appointment of judges is in the government's hands, and has traditionally been the task of the Lord Chancellor's (a member of the government) Department. However from April 2006 the Judicial Appointments Commission has taken over this responsibility, although it only selects candidates who still have to be confirmed and appointed by the Lord Chancellor. The Commission has 15 members including judges and lay members and has introduced a much more formalized system for selecting candidates for the judiciary. For instance applicants have to fill in a lengthy application form and write a 1,500-word self-assessment as well as being interviewed. As well as having the final responsibility for appointing judges, the Lord Chancellor also has to agree and formally ratify which barristers are awarded the coveted title of Queen's Counsel (QC); and the great majority of senior judges are appointed from the ranks of QCs. Before recommending the appointment of a judge or a QC, the

Lord Chancellor's Department will consult judges and senior legal figures for their opinions on the suitability of prospective candidates. These consultations are known as 'secret soundings'. This informal process originates from the time when the Lord Chancellor would personally know all the applicants because of the small group from which selection took place. So in spite of the recent expansion of the judiciary, the increase in part-time appointments and the consequent growth in promotions within the judiciary and the key role of the Judicial Appointments Commission, the appointment process is still typified by a degree of informality and secrecy.

With the increase in the number of judicial appointments (and the introduction of application forms), interview panels have become much more widespread and occur for all the 'lower' appointments, so district judges, assistant recorders, recorders and circuit judges all attend interview panels, although these panels are only one part of the appointment process and only make recommendations. In attempting to broaden the spread of applicants, advertisements have also become more common and there have even been adverts for High Court Judges since 1998. Again this has only been seen as a supplement to other information and not as a replacement for the traditional system of 'secret soundings' whereby likely candidates are asked to apply.

The appointment process has been criticized for encouraging self-replication amongst the judiciary; and in spite of the changes mentioned above, judges are still overwhelmingly white, male barristers over the age of 50 and having had a private education followed by Oxbridge. The choice of senior judges is limited by the fact that they are invariably chosen from the most experienced barristers. This severely restricts access to the judiciary as training to be a barrister has conventionally involved having to have a private means of funding for the early years of practice. However, it is becoming easier for newly qualified barristers to earn an adequate income which should help encourage a less exclusive recruitment, as well as opening up access to the judiciary to solicitors as well as barristers.

The judiciary, and particularly the senior judges, remain a very privileged and atypical group. Of the first 85 judges appointed since the Labour Party's election to power in 1997 only seven were women and only one of these made it to the High Court bench. This imbalance seems set to continue. As of April 2009 of the 109 High Court Judges only 15 were women (under 14 per cent) and of the 38 Lord Justices of Appeal only three were women (under 8 per cent). With regard to ethnic minority judges, none of the 38 Lord Justices of Appeal were from minority ethnic backgrounds and only three of the High Court Judges were (3.5 per cent) (data from www.judiciary.gov.uk). In terms of social background, in 2004, three quarters of judges and more than two thirds of barristers at top chambers had been educated at private schools, while 81 per cent of judges had been to Oxford or Cambridge Universities. Furthermore, judges earn high salaries that have increased relative to average pay rises in recent years. In November 2007 the Lord Chief Justice, for instance, saw his salary rise by over £5,000 to £230,400. There were similar rises for other senior judges, with Appeal Court judges getting £198,700, High Court judges £165,900 and circuit judges £123,200. It has been argued that these salaries and pay rises are necessary to attract suitable recruits to the judiciary given that it is possible for top legal experts to earn substantially more money in other forms of legal work;

and judges would argue that senior positions in other walks of life are also very well paid. Nonetheless, the restricted social background from which senior judges come and their high salaries do raise issues as to their understanding of and empathy with the wider population.

Of course when looking at the senior judiciary it should be borne in mind that the same comments about background and exclusivity could be applied to the upper echelons of other key institutions in Britain, such as the army, church and civil service. As regards judges, it is clear that the appointments system lacks transparency and helps to perpetuate a white, male judiciary drawn from a narrow social group. This has led to pressure for some form of judicial appointments committee, which led in turn to the establishment of the Judicial Appointments Commission in 2006 (as part of the reforms introduced by the Constitutional Reform Act of 2005). Judicial appointments commissions are used in a number of countries and do appear to generate greater public confidence in the appointments process and in turn in the judges themselves. However, senior judges have spoken out against these changes to the appointments system. In 1999 the Lord Chief Justice, Lord Bingham insisted that this system was 'as good as any to be found anywhere in the world' and dismissed arguments for a more transparent selection procedure with candidates being sifted by a judicial appointments commission. He described the present system as 'extraordinarily thorough and comprehensive and extraordinarily successful', adding that a system of selection which produces 'a high quality product cannot be as bad as suggested' (quoted in the *Guardian*, 1 June 1999).

QUESTION BREAK: BECOMING A QC

Read the extract on how to become a QC

Smoothing the way to silk

- Applicants must be a barrister or solicitor with rights of advocacy in the higher courts. Should have at least 10 years' experience.
- Candidates should pay a fee of £720 and fill in a form which includes self-assessment and the names of up to six 'nominated consultees'.
- Details of all applicants sent to 300 automatic consultees – senior judges and leading members of the legal profession. All are asked to comment on the applicants' suitability.
- Officials from the Lord Chancellor's Department hold meetings with senior judges, leaders of the bar's circuits and officers of the Bar Council to obtain their views.
- Applications sifted by a senior official, who identifies candidates worthy of the Lord Chancellor's consideration, divided into an A list (strong support) and B list (less strong support but warranting consideration). Most candidates do not make it on to either list.

- Lord Chancellor is given a briefing on applicants on A and B list.
- Lord Chancellor discuss briefings with heads of the high courts divisions, attorney general and solicitor general before deciding on the successful applicants.

(From the *Guardian*, 8 October 2002, 'Judge selection found to lack transparency')

- What effects will this process have on the make-up of the judiciary? (Try to consider both beneficial and less beneficial effects)
- Does the social background of judges matter? If so, why? (You might consider whether you think it will affect their interpretation of the law)
- What difficulties might there be in trying to widen the social background of judges?

Training

As the judiciary has grown and become (slightly) more open, so there have been developments in judicial training. Until around 30 years ago training for judges was non-existent; it was felt to be unnecessary and a threat to the independence so valued by judges. Since the introduction of the Judicial Studies Board in 1979 training has become much more established and accepted. The Board is chaired and run by judges with some academic input and has become generally well regarded by judges. However, the amount of training undertaken by judges is still limited. crown court judges' training, for instance, amounts to a four-day residential course and the shadowing of an experienced judge for another ten days.

Malleson (1999) found that courses run by the Judicial Studies Board were generally felt to be of high quality and that judges were aware and supportive of the need for training, given the growing complexity of their jobs. The range of training has also needed to expand given the speed of changes to the law and the growing diversity of the population – advice and training on matters of race are provided by the Board, for instance. There has also been a massive increase in the amount of guidance and advice from the Ministry of Justice (and in the number of publications offering advice) that is available to the judiciary at all levels. And as from April 2010 a new Judicial College will start offering lessons in judging in an attempt to boost the training of judges. The College will oversee judges acting out trials and then being judged on their performance by their peers; it will include the filming of judges to enable them to see themselves in action and to get feedback on how well they manage courts. Although this training will not be based at their own college, judges would use a university for their courses. Lord Justice Maurice Kay, chairman of the Judicial Studies Board, commented that this development 'marked a radical shift away from that old system to a more practical training' and would help ensure that judges are sensitive and aware of those in court (Gibb 2009).

Accountability and independence

Judges have not been subject to the sort of accountability found in virtually all other professions and applied to senior officials in other spheres of public service. This has been due to judges (in particular) arguing that accountability would threaten their independence. The principle of judicial independence is based on the notion that there should be a clear separation of powers between the executive (government), the legislature (Parliament) and the judiciary. This separation, it is argued, ensures that judges are able to balance competing interests and that they will not feel under pressure from the government, for example, to come to particular decisions because they fear their position may be threatened. Malleson (1999) argues that in practice this separation of powers is by no means clear cut, with the government appointing and paying judges and with all senior judges being members of the House of Lords.

Like any powerful group, the judiciary has a vested interest in maintaining its independence and avoiding critical scrutiny. This does not necessarily mean they have anything to hide and judges would argue that they are bound to make unpopular decisions; therefore there is always a danger of improper interference in their decision-making processes. Judges themselves might say that they are not free to express their views; that they are bound by precedent and duty. However, the law is often not clear and judges do have a fair degree of discretion in terms of how it is interpreted. It is likely, and hardly surprising, that judges, like anyone else, will make decisions on the basis of their own values. And in the case of judges, given their backgrounds and training, these values are likely to be conventional and conservative. This is not to say that judges deliberately attempt to impose their views when judging, but does raise the question of whether there can ever be a 'neutral' decision, as any choice will represent some set of values.

Although there may be a general level of respect for judges, confidence in them seems to have fallen in recent years and criticisms of judges for being too lenient or too harsh have encouraged a closer scrutiny. As with the appointing and training of judges, there have been moves towards greater openness with regard to judicial practice. And again as with these other areas, the introduction of greater accountability has mainly applied to the lower ranks of the judiciary, with the way they are 'appointed, trained and monitored significantly different from that of the higher judiciary' (Malleson 1999: 233).

However, apart from extreme misconduct, judges are still virtually unaccountable for how they behave when acting as judges and the removal of a judge from office is almost impossible. As well as dismissal being extremely rare, the Lord Chancellor is able to admonish a judge with a public rebuke – again an extremely rare occurrence. There have been changes in what judges can say in court with rudeness and intolerance, for instance sexist or racist behaviour, no longer acceptable. It remains the case, though, that 'judges remain almost immune from the consequences of all but the most extreme forms of misconduct or incompetent behaviour' (Malleson 1999: 230).

In an attempt to increase the openness and scrutiny of the judiciary, the *Guardian* newspaper challenged the fact that the government and judiciary were able to conceal the names of judges who had been disciplined, and the reasons for their disciplining. However, in June 2009, the Freedom of Information tribunal ruled against the

Guardian, arguing that such a move would undermine judges' authority in the court-room. The current situation (2011), which the tribunal supported, leaves the Justice Secretary, Jack Straw, and the Lord Chief Justice, Igor Judge, in charge of deciding how to punish judges. The Ministry of Justice publishes details on the number of times judges have been disciplined and the broad categories of misconduct, such as 'inappropriate behaviour', but does not give details of individual cases.

QUESTION BREAK: JUDICIAL ACCOUNTABILITY

Incompetent judges do not get the sack

Judges enjoy the privilege of being almost entirely unaccountable for poor work . . .

Judges enjoy this immunity from the normal hazards of employment because of their constitutional position. Security of tenure underpins judicial independence and ensures that judges can rule against ministers or governments without an eye to promotion.

High Court judges can be removed from office only by the Queen after a vote by both Houses of Parliament and none ever has. Circuit judges can be dismissed for incapacity or misbehaviour by the Lord Chancellor.

That hardly ever happens. Only one, Judge Bruce Campbell, has been sacked this century, after pleading guilty to a smuggling offence.

(Adapted from F. Gibb, 'Incompetent judges do not get the sack', *The Times*, 9 July 1998)

- Suggest the advantages and disadvantages that might come from greater judicial accountability.
- What arguments are there for judges being 'above the law'? Do you agree with them?

A changing judiciary?

The size and influence of the judiciary has grown enormously in the last 30 or so years. In concluding her account of the developments that have taken place in the appointment, training and accountability of judges as a result of these changes, Malleson (1999) suggests that:

Thirty years ago the judiciary was a largely self-selecting, self-regulating and self-taught body which operated its own informal rules almost entirely free of external scrutiny . . . The consequence of pressure for changes has been that the elitism, secrecy and amateurism which were traditionally the hallmarks of the judiciary are slowly being replaced by diversification, openness and professionalism.

(p. 233)

This change to a more open and accessible judiciary is evidenced by the establishment of the Judicial Appointments Commission (see p. 428) and the Office for Judicial Complaints, as a consequence of the Constitutional Reform Act of 2005. The Office for Judicial Complaints considers and determines complaints about the personal conduct of all judicial office holders in England and Wales. Both these bodies have their own websites, again indicating a greater openness to public scrutiny.

QUESTION BREAK

- Using evidence from the section above and from other sources, to what extent do you agree with Malleson's comment?
- How much individual discretion do you feel judges should have?

Sentencing activity

The training for those who have been appointed as judges in the Crown Courts and above involves doing 'sentencing exercises' in which they consider what sentence they would give for particular cases.

The scenarios surrounding two cases are set out below. Read them and consider the issues listed after them. Then, as a judge decide how you would sentence.

Susan's case

On a night out Susan's husband gets into a fight in a club. At the end of the incident Susan throws a half pint glass across the room. It hits an innocent bystander who is injured and loses the sight in one of his eyes.

Susan is charged with Grievous Bodily Harm. She pleads not guilty. She has no previous convictions. She has children to look after. Her husband has already received a custodial sentence for his part in the incident.

Should Susan get either (a) a custodial sentence; (b) a suspended sentence; or (c) community service?

What issues do you need to taken into consideration?

Tyrone's case

When drunk, Tyrone followed a woman into a lift in a block of flats. He indecently assaulted her. Her screams led to him being arrested.

Tyrone is charged with indecent assault. He had previous convictions (including for rape). He pleaded guilty and is very remorseful. The assault was not premeditated. He says he has given up drink. He is receptive to treatment.

What sentence should Tyrone receive?

What issues do you need to take into consideration?

(Answer –

These were based on real cases. Susan was given a 12-month custodial sentence and Tyrone an 18-month sentence)

FURTHER READING

Gibson, B. (2008) *The New Ministry of Justice.* This short text provides an overview of the duties and responsibilities of the Ministry of Justice, created in 2007 to rationalize the workings of the criminal justice system in England and Wales (and taking over the role of the Lord Chancellor's Department and the Department of Constitutional Affairs).

Griffiths, J. A. G. (1997) *The Politics of the Judiciary* (5th edn). First published in 1981 and now in a fifth edition this has established itself as the definitive text on the role of the judiciary. Specific cases are used to question the impartiality of the judiciary.

Malleson, K, (1999) *The New Judiciary: The Effects of Expansion and Activism.* A detailed examination of the developments in the appointment, training and scrutiny of judges as a result of the massive expansion in the size and power of our judiciary over the last 30 or so years. In particular it highlights the tension between the requirements that judges are independent with the need for them to be accountable.

Watkins, M. and Gordon, W. (2000) *The Sentence of the Court: A Handbook for Magistrates.* This is a very clear introduction to and outline of the law and practice of sentencing in magistrates' courts, where the vast majority of criminal trails are conducted.

WEBSITES

The following websites provide plenty of current information on the judiciary.

www.judiciary.gov.uk
www.jsboard.co.uk
www.magistrates-association.org.uk

The judiciary website provides a range of key facts and data on the background (including gender and ethnicity) of judges and magistrates (and the Judicial Appointments Commission and the Office for Judicial Complaints have their own websites providing further information). The Judicial Studies Board is the body which provides training and instruction for all judges; while the Magistrates' Association applies particularly to magistrates.

The Criminal Justice System: Prisons and Imprisonment

INTRODUCTION

When we examined the history of punishment (Chapter 9) a good deal of the focus was on the history of imprisonment. Essentially, this was because when considering history punishment is often used almost synonymously with imprisonment. For example, an examination of the history of the different approaches to punishment, such as retribution and deterrence, is typically based around changes in the forms and styles of incarceration. We will not, therefore, need to delve into the origins and history of imprisonment in great detail or catalogue the various pieces of legislation in this chapter. However a brief overview of the key periods in the development of the prison in the last 200 or so years will help provide the context for looking at the contemporary prison system and the major current issues that face it.

THE HISTORY OF PRISONS

Prison histories of the last 200-plus years generally highlight three major periods which were characterized by differing rationales for prison and imprisonment. In the late eighteenth and early nineteenth centuries the emphasis was on reform – of both prisons and prisoners – and this period saw what Foucault described as the 'birth of the modern prison'. In the mid-nineteenth century a much more repressive approach was adopted. Partly as reaction to this, by the end of the nineteenth century and into the twentieth century new notions of reform and rehabilitation emerged. Of course the history of imprisoning people goes back much further than the eighteenth century. Holding people before some form of trial, not necessarily in purpose built prisons but perhaps in castles, goes back centuries. Private gaols existed from at least 1166 (when Henry II tried to set up a gaol in every English county) through to the eighteenth century; these were often privately run, commercial undertakings with prisoners charged for food and other services (including the hammering on and off of leg irons) and conditions – for those with no money at least – dreadful.

Although our starting period here is the reforms of the late 1700s, there were examples of more humane, reformative approaches prior to this. While there are different interpretations for the emergence of the houses of correction and bridewells in the sixteenth century, such a development certainly suggests an early reformative interest and agenda (see p. 293). Bridewell was the name of the first house of correction established in 1553 in London. It lasted until 1700 and its name became a generic term for these early forms of prison.

Early reforms – the late eighteenth century

Throughout the eighteenth century conditions in prisons continued to be appalling, with no segregation of men, women or children, no classifying of offenders (even between tried and untried), the sale of alcohol, extortion by prison staff, among other things, commonplace. These sorts of conditions were described most graphically by John Howard (examples of whose writings on the state of prisons can be found in most texts covering the history of prisons). Howard made a detailed survey of the state of prisons in the 1770s and argued that prisons should operate as secure but healthy and efficient institutions. His inspections and writings did have an impact; the 1779 Penitentiary Act, for instance, promoted the view that prison should have both a punitive and reformative purpose (the very name penitentiary implies prisoners being sorry or repentant for their behaviour, and thinking about it while doing some penance). More specifically, prisoners were to be put to hard work with any profits earned from this work being used to improve prisons (with the notion of paying staff introduced). It was believed that the stress on hard physical work would be morally and physically helpful for offenders. Also, there was a move to start classifying prisoners into different categories. In highlighting the importance of the 1779 Act, Wilson (2002) commented that:

> [It] synthesised everything that was believed at that time about what should be done with prisoners, in that they were to be subjected to solitary confinement, have regular religious instruction, be required to work – but not for profit, would have to wear a uniform, and be subjected to a coarse diet.

Following on from Howard's account of prison regimes and the 1779 Act, there was a spate of prison building in the late 1700s and early 1800s. Another key factor behind the expansion of prisons at this time was the ending of transportation to America after the American Declaration of Independence in 1776. Transportation to Botany Bay, Australia did not begin until 1787 and as an estimated 30,000 people had been transported to America between 1718 and 1775, the authorities were left with a problem as to what they should do with law breakers who would not be executed (Wilson 2002). The use of prison as a punishment for criminals rather than just a holding place for vagrants was linked by Coyle (2005) to the decline in transportation in the early nineteenth century. The culmination of these developments was the opening in 1842 of Pentonville prison in London. This was seen as the 'model prison' and demonstrated the transformation from the small, privately run prisons of the past. It had 500 identical cells in which prisoners lived separately and in silence; they followed a detailed, meticulous routine, in line with that described by Foucault at the start of his famous account of the 'birth of the prison' in *Discipline and Punish*. Foucault examined prisons alongside the development of other institutions, such as the new factories of the industrial revolution period, workhouses for the poor and asylums for the insane, and saw them as making up what he termed the 'great confinement' (see pp. 274–282 for a fuller discussion of Foucault's account). The better regulated sort of prisons advocated by Howard can be compared to the sort of managerial changes going on in the mills and factories of the period, and often run by philanthropists with similar ideas to Howard, such as Arkwright (mills) and Wedgwood (pottery). The move away from public and localized punishments, including privately run local jails, to the 'reformed', state financed and managed penitentiaries of the nineteenth century was completed by the Prison Act of 1877 which placed the entire penal system under state control.

There are two main theoretical positions that have put forward explanations for this move to reform prisons in the late eighteenth century – a *humanitarian* model that saw idealism and philanthropy as the key factors and a *radical* model that emphasized the regulation of dangerous groups. The basic question posed by the 'debate' between these two positions was whether the new prisons indicate a humanitarian idealism or a more insidious regulation of the 'deviant', lower classes.

The humanitarian explanation makes the point that the eighteenth-century penal reformers (best illustrated by John Howard) were invariably motivated by a strong religious faith and believed that they were pursuing an idealistic mission. In addition to this a more general humanitarian mood was evidenced by the fact that there was also a good deal of public concern and even revulsion about the extent of capital and corporal punishments. This view of history is associated with the political position of the Whigs (a viewpoint which became almost synonymous with the Liberal Party after the early 1800s). Such an interpretation of history sees the ideas and visions of key individuals as being the major factor affecting social change and moving history along. Change and reform, then, are seen as motivated by benevolence and philanthropy and histories advocating this approach tend to highlight and glorify the role played by a few great individuals. As regards the history of punishment and prisons, the starting point tends to be Beccaria's condemnation of unjust penalties (and particularly the death penalty) in his treatise *Crime and Punishment* (1764), the seminal text in the application of classicist and utilitarian philosophy to punishment and justice. Beccaria's legacy was taken on and practically applied to the criminal justice process by Jeremy Bentham; while other key figures in this humanitarian history included John Howard and Elizabeth Fry (see pp. 298–299 for fuller discussion of the importance of these early penal reformers).

The radical explanation and model for the emergence of prisons has been seen as part of a more critical 'revisionist' history (Mathews 1999) that has seen the humanitarianism of this period as being more rhetoric than reality. The emphasis here is on social control born out of class conflict and the attendant fears and the protecting of the vested interests of powerful groups in society. There are different variations of this broad approach, in particular an orthodox Marxist position, exemplified by Rusche and Kirchheimer's classic work (see pp. 274–280), whereby punishment is seen as helping to maintain a cheap and reliable workforce, and a position adopted by theorists such as Foucault and Ignatieff which focuses more on the ideological, and political elements involved in establishing and maintaining order (Muncie 1996). Both Foucault (1977) and Ignatieff (1978) described the move from punishments of the body to those of the mind. Ignatieff emphasized the ideological and symbolic functions of the new forms of punishment centred around imprisonment (such as the treadmill and crank) and considered their role in maintaining order. Foucault's attention was more on the power of ideas, knowledge and discourses and he interpreted the various reforms and penal developments as part of an emerging 'carceral society' (see p. 280).

The nineteenth century – (a return to) repressive measures

Following on from the pioneering work of John Howard and other early penal reformers, there were improvements to certain aspects of penal policy in the nineteenth century. However, although physical punishments, such as public whippings and corporal punishment in general, declined there was also a clear decline in the support for the reformation of prisons. This reaction to the early reforms described above occurred in tandem with a strong push toward a greater centralization of prisons, with a more uniform and rational prison regime introduced across the country. These developments were evidenced by the rigid application of strict rules and a strong emphasis on obedience, with the nineteenth-century prisons becoming impersonal and highly regimented institutions, characterized by an array of internal disciplinary procedures and punishments attached to all aspects of daily prison life (for example, prisoners only being allowed to eat after they had completed certain tasks, such as turning the crank a specified number of times). This repressive approach was well established and widely supported by the mid 1800s, helped by the panic over street crimes such as garrotting in the 1860s and given governmental backing by the Carnarvon report (1864) which highlighted an 'insufficiency of penal discipline'. The language of this report, while typical of the time, was indicative of this more repressive approach: 'the large majority of criminals were low and brutish, mainly swayed by self gratification and animal appetite' (quoted in Muncie 1996).

The mid nineteenth century also saw the establishment of the separate cell system. In general terms, then, prisons were extremely harsh and austere establishments up until the 1890s, and completely lacked the religious and moral overtones of the early 1800s. There was still a belief that imprisonment might allow for the reform of prisoners based on the notion of hard industrial work developed through the separate and the silent systems (Coyle 2005). In the separate system prisoners worked in large communal workshops but were not allowed to talk to one another; the silent system had prisoners doing work on their own in their individual cells. In each case then work might have had some use (such as sewing or mending) but often was just there to keep the prisoner busy and to encourage 'good work habits' (such as turning the crank or working the treadmill).

Of course, these comments only provide the overall picture and highlight the general tenor of the time. It is important to remember that even at the same time as an overall move to greater discipline and repression, there were still some reformist moves and developments, such as attempts to classify and categorize different groups of prisoners, reflecting a realization that not all fitted the 'brutish animal' stereotype.

QUESTION BREAK: HARD LABOUR IN VICTORIAN PRISONS

The extract below is taken from Priestley's study of Victorian prison lives and refers to one of the common forms of hard labour expected of prisoners – oakum picking (oakum was the old tarred ropes of ships' rigging, from an inch upwards in thickness).

Three images dramatise Victorian prison work in the popular imagination: men climbing the endless staircase of the treadwheel; convicts breaking rocks; and the picking of Oakum. Oakum was picked by prisoners in cells and workhouses for the greater part of the nineteenth century . . .

Oakum was extremely dirty: after working for an hour or so one's fingers would be covered with tar, and stick to everything you touched.

To the dirt and the difficulty was added, under the threat of punishment, the daily 'task', that of picking 'three pounds per diem' . . . [and] every day several [were] reported just by way of keeping the discipline up to the recognised standard of severity . . .

Oakum picking was a difficult and dirty and distressing occupation . . . But it went on being picked, because of its simplicity and its tediousness and because no one could think of any better way of keeping so many unskilled hands from idleness . . . Its great convenience, though, was as cell task for men in separate confinement, where it continued to keep afloat the leaky vessel of penal labour policy until into the twentieth century.

(From P. Priestley 1985: 121–3)

- How might hard prison labour be seen to provide the potential to reform prisoners?
- What sort of theoretical explanations could be offered for forcing prisoners to engage in hard labour for no other purpose than to keep them busy?

New approaches to reform and rehabilitation – the late nineteenth and early twentieth centuries

As mentioned above, at the same time as the imposition of harsh and repressive regimes within prisons, there was also the introduction of some reformative measures. In the latter part of the nineteenth century there were attempts to classify prisoners and, in particular, to focus on young offenders and to ensure that they were not subject to the same regimes as older prisoners. A key figure here is Mary Carpenter, who campaigned for young offenders to be placed in educational homes and who helped establish the 'reformatory school' as a separate penal institution, and one that developed into the approved schools at the start of the twentieth century. Apart from juveniles, there was little differentiation of prisoners, even between male and female regimes, up until the 1890s. However, by the end of the nineteenth century the harsh prison regime was being questioned, fuelled in part by the high cost of prisons and the continued high rates of recidivism. These concerns were clearly evident in the Gladstone Report of 1895. This report examined several issues including prison accommodation, prison labour and the treatment of juveniles; it emphasized reformation and rehabilitation and helped pave the way for a more scientific, treatment based model and regime to emerge. It led to the Prison Act of 1898 which limited the use of corporal punishment and introduced remission of sentences for prisoners.

Changes to the prison regime from 1900 included the replacement of unproductive labour for the sake of it with more useful work, with particular prison industries being developed, the phasing out of the separate system and an increase in association between prisoners. The Borstal system (named after the first custodial unit for young males opened in Borstal, Kent) based around indeterminate sentences (see p. 241) and the notion that juveniles should leave custody when they had demonstrated that they had been rehabilitated, was introduced for young offenders. As well as changes within the prison regime, the most significant developments in punishment and criminal justice in the early years of the twentieth century occurred outside of the prison, with the probation service established by the Probation of Offenders Act of 1907. Building on the work of police court missionaries, probation was made available for all offences except murder and treason, and involved the offender being supervised by a probation officer, whose basic duty, according to the act, was 'to advise, assist and befriend' the offender (see pp. 465–468 for more details).

The improvements in and liberalization of the treatment of prisoners continued in the first half of the twentieth century. In the 1920s, the shaving of prisoners' heads was abolished and the arrows on prisoners' uniforms were removed; prisoners were allowed to talk to each while working and were paid (a little) for their work (Coyle 2005).

This brief history of the emergence of the modern prison system should not necessarily be interpreted as an uninterrupted movement from harshness to greater humanitarianism. While being in a nineteenth-century prison might be considered preferable to the 'bloody codes' of the late 1700s when there were so many capital offences, whether the mid-Victorian prison regimes based around solitary confinement and hard unproductive labour was 'better' than the Houses of Correction of the 1600s (see p. 293) is perhaps debatable. Indeed this raises the general issue of whether punishment aimed at the mind is any more rational and humane that that aimed at the body.

BOX 13.1 PRIVATE PRISONS

Private prisons have existed in the UK since the twelfth century – and until the emergence of the 'modern' prison in the late eighteenth and early nineteenth century most prisons were privately managed. So the development of private prisons as part of the overall prison estate in the last 20 years is not a completely new phenomenon. As a way of managing the increased prison population the 1991 Criminal Justice Act allowed prisons to be contracted out to private companies. The first privately contracted prison was the Wolds in Yorkshire, which was run by the Group 4 security company and opened to prisoners in 1992. Currently there are 11 privately run prisons in England and Wales (out of an overall figure of 139 prisons), holding around 11 per cent of the overall prison population; this is higher than any other European country and even higher than the USA (which has just over 7 per cent of its prisoners in privately run prisons). While it is difficult to assess the success or not of these prisons, there have been some criticisms. According to data obtained by the *Independent* newspaper under the Freedom of Information Act, private prisons are 'performing worse than those run by the state', scoring lower on the Ministry of Justice's Performance Assessment ratings than state-run prisons. Furthermore, nearly twice as many complaints from prisoners are upheld in private prisons compared to state-run ones (*Independent*, 29 June 2009). None the less, private prisons are now an integral part of the prison system in the UK.

PRISONS AND IMPRISONMENT: THE CURRENT CONTEXT

Probably the most crucial current issue facing the prison service is the massive increase in the prison population in recent years. And there seems to be a general assumption and an acceptance of the fact that the number of prisoners will continue to rise. However, the continual, year on year, rise in these numbers is not inevitable. As recently as the 1980s the prison population remained relatively stable and it is only since 1993 and the hard-line policy promoted by the then Home Secretary, Michael Howard, that the prison population in England and Wales has risen at what can only be described as a phenomenal rate. This situation mirrors to some extent that of the United States and raises the question as to whether this country will follow the sort of 'mass incarceration' being experienced there. With that in mind it would be useful to say something about the United States' jail situation by way of comparison.

In terms of the major aims of punishment, it would seem that deterrence, reform and even retribution have become less important than just incarceration as a basic justification for imprisonment. The United States contains roughly 5 per cent of the world's population yet is responsible for about 25 per cent of the world's prisoners and has a higher proportion of its citizens in prison than any other country. In 2005 it had an incarceration rate of 714 prisoners per 100,000 of the population; the next highest rates were from Russia and South Africa (at 532 and 413 respectively), with England and Wales having a rate of 142 prisoners per 100,000 population and Canada 116 (figures cited in Newburn 2007). This type of mass imprisonment has been justified on a sort of cost-benefit basis. As crime rates in the United States have fallen in the last few years and with estimates of the cost of the average crime put at $300, with the average criminal committing 15 crimes a year, it can be seen how an 'economic argument' might be made for putting more offenders in prison. In addition, the fact that prisons in the United States are quite efficient (in terms of the cost per prisoner per year) adds another element to this utilitarian calculation and approach. However even within the United States there are significant differences in rates of imprisonment from state to state. The prison population of California, for instance, has increased massively in recent years from under 30,000 in the late 1970s to around 170,000 in 2009. As Abramsky (2009) comments, this is not because the crime rate has risen, indeed for most of the last 15 years it has gone down; rather it is because of 'laws like Three Strikes and You're Out and mandatory minimum sentences for categories of drug offenders'. An illustration of the hard-line approach adopted in California was the sentencing in March 2010 of a Californian man for up to eight years in prison for stealing a $3.99 bag of shredded cheese (other examples of the 'Three Strikes' legislation can be found in Chapter 4, p. 133).

This sort of mass containment strategy is very different from the 'traditional' aims of punishment and imprisonment. Deterrent, retributive and reformist justifications for imprisonment recognize the human nature of offenders and their capacity for choice. Containment and incapacitation require little acknowledgement of the human and moral nature of offenders; rather it is a sort of social hygiene approach that assumes it is not worth bothering to try to intervene or influence them.

Of course, it may be that indefinite containment is the only option for certain offenders from whom the wider public needs to be protected. However, on a widespread scale such an approach and policy is based on a pretty depressing picture of humanity and on the notion that people do not change much (and that even if they may change for the better it is impossible to know for sure that this has happened and so it is safer and easier to assume they cannot).

QUESTION BREAK: INCAPACITATION

There would appear to be a lot of public support for a hard-line, containment style policy both in the United States and Britain.

Why do you think a containment/incapacitation approach might be popular?

What arguments can you think of to suggest that people (a) can change and be reformed; and (b) are essentially unchangeable?

To return to the British context, it is commonly held that the expansion of the prison population constitutes a 'penal crisis'. We will consider this notion of a crisis in relation to four main areas: numbers and cost; conditions; security and containment; and legitimacy. This will provide a structure for examining some of the major current issues that are faced by the prison service. Before looking at the prison population a brief comment on the notion of 'penal crisis' might be appropriate. For many years, commentators have described the British prison system as being in crisis. Over 20 years ago, for instance, Bottoms wrote a study entitled *The Coming Penal Crisis* (1980); and reference to our prison system as being in such a state would seem to be generally and widely accepted. This, though, does beg the question of what constitutes a crisis in the prison context. If a crisis is viewed as something that is relatively rare and takes place over a short period of time (Sparks 1996), it is perhaps debatable how useful it is to describe the current situation. As Cavadino (1992) put it, 'how long can a situation remain at crisis point before it is not a crisis?'. However accurate or appropriate the term crisis might be, it is clear that the British prison service has faced many problems throughout its existence and that as we move into the twenty-first century these problems are arguably greater than ever. And whether we use the dramatic term crisis or not, it is important to examine the current state of the prison system and how the different problems it faces relate to one another.

Numbers and cost

The size of the prison population is commented on regularly in the press and in recent years these figures have been setting new records on an almost weekly basis. Official figures can be found in Home Office publications such as the *Annual Abstract of Statistics and Social Trends*, as well as the HM Prison website and other official websites. Here we can only provide a snapshot picture of the current situation.

Despite different initiatives over the years, there has been little effect on the size of the prison population or on rates of re-offending, both of which have risen inexorably. Although there have been slight dips in the prison population from time to time, for instance in the late 1980s, the overall trend has been a regular and pretty continual rise. In April 2010, Alan Travis, *Guardian* Home Affairs editor, reported that the 'prison population has hit a record 85,000 after Labour's decision to end the 18-day early releases scheme just before the election campaign got under way' (*Guardian* 23 April 2010). On 30 April 2010 the Ministry of Justice Prison Population Briefing gave the total number of prisoners as 85,086, compared with 82,868 on the corresponding day a year before. While projecting the future prison population is a tricky task, recent estimates from the Ministry of Justice suggest it will rise to almost 96,000 by 2015. This sort of rise is likely because of the government's target of ensuring that more offenders are 'brought to book' (and if there are more convictions, there will inevitably be more people sent to prison). In terms of explaining these rises in the prison population, Newburn (2007) points out that there are three basic possibilities: more offenders being caught and sentenced, an increase in the seriousness of crimes prosecuted and an increase in severity of sentences. He suggests that there is no evidence of more offenders being caught but that there has been a general increase in sentence lengths.

These record numbers demonstrate quite a change from the situation just over 50 years ago when there were roughly 15,000 prisoners in 40 prisons. And before then at the end of the First World War (1918) the prison population stood at only just over 9,000. In terms of more recent comparisons, the number of prisoners in England and Wales has increased by over 25,000 in the last ten years; and when the Labour government took office in May 1997 the prison population was 60,131 (over 25,000 fewer than it is at the time of writing – in 2010). This growth in the prison population has necessitated a major prison building programme. Between 1985 and 2006, 25 new prisons have been opened. As well as new prisons, existing ones have been developed and extended so there are now 21 prisons holding more than 1,000 inmates.

However, following the general election of May 2010 and the forming of a coalition government, there are signs that the current Justice Secretary, Kenneth Clarke, is intent on reducing the prison population in England and Wales and has questioned why the prison population has virtually doubled since he was Home Secretary in the early 1990s. Whereas the previous government was planning for 96,000 prison places by 2014, Clarke has said that he aims to have only 82,000 people in jail by then. This shift will involve the shutting of prisons and the loss of jobs within the prison service as the present government implements huge budget reduction at the Ministry of Justice.

Within the overall prison population figures there are different categories of prisoner and one area of particular 'growth' has been in the number of women prisoners. Between 1992 and 2002 the female prison population rose from 1,577 to 4,408, an increase of 179 per cent. Since then the female prison population has remained relatively stable – indeed it fell to just over 4,300 in March 2010 (we will consider women prisoners as a separate group below, see pp. 456–460). Another growing part of the prison population is made up of foreign nationals. In March 2010 there were 11,400 foreign nationals in prison compared to 4,259 in 1996. The largest group of foreign nationals were Jamaican, followed by Nigeria, Republic of Ireland, Vietnam and Poland (Ministry of Justice Statistics bulletin, April 2010). These prisoners provide different concerns for the prison service, with issues of language and communication and cultural differences having to be addressed.

As regards the overall numbers, much of the recent rise can be explained by the increase in the numbers of long-term, including life sentence, prisoners.

Long-term and life sentence prisoners

Although most prison sentences are relatively short, with up to 80 per cent of prisoners being released within one year of being sentenced, the number of long-term prisoners has increased enormously over the last few years. In 1965, the year that the death penalty was abolished, 88 new prisoners were sentenced to 10 or more years; this figure had risen to 556 in 1995, 862 in 2000 and 979 in 2004 . As well as there being more long-term and life sentence prisoners, those who are sentenced to life serve longer in prison than they used to; the average time for a lifer in 1985 was just under 11 years, whereas in 2004 it was around 14 years (figures from Morgan and Liebling 2007). In an attempt to halt this upward drift in the number of years served by life sentence prisoners, in 2002 the Lord Chief Justice published guidelines cutting the minimum sentence for offenders convicted of murders to 12 years rather than 14. However, the effects of this were somewhat mitigated because adult murderers involved in the most serious cases will now serve a longer minimum term of 16 years and those convicted of the most serious murders would be given a minimum term with little or no hope of release – so serial killers, for instance, would serve a minimum of 30 years.

The Lord Chief Justice's guidelines were undermined by the then Home Secretary, David Blunkett, in May 2003 in an attack on 'inconsistent' judges in which he insisted that Parliament must have the right to lay down the principles of sentencing. The Home Secretary said that anyone who abducts and murders a child should die in jail, rather than face the current practice of a 20-year minimum sentence, with similar 'whole life' terms also to be imposed on terrorists or multiple murderers and on murderers who have killed before. Other serious crimes such as the murder of a police or prison officer or a race-motivated murder would lead to a minimum 30-year sentence, an increase of 10 years on current practice. His comments were opposed by leading figures from within the criminal justice system. The Bar Council said David Blunkett was trying to ensure the government tightened its grip around 'the neck of the judiciary', while the Howard League for Penal Reform said such measures would increase the present number of life-sentence prisoners by 50 per cent. The assistant general secretary of the probation officers' union, Harry Fletcher, commented that, 'The proposals suggest that there could never be room for redemption. Each case and release date must remain with the parole authorities to reflect remorse, change in the offender and the risk they may pose.'

As well as the fact that life sentence prisoners are serving longer, the number of life sentences has been extended, as a result of the Crime Sentences Act 1997, to include those convicted of a second serious violent or sexual offence. The introduction of the indeterminate sentence of Imprisonment for Public Protection (IPP) in the Criminal Justice Act of 2003 has also increased the number and proportion of long-term prisoners. Indeed the numbers serving indeterminate sentences (life sentences and IPPs) increased by 8 per cent (around 900) between March 2009 and March 2010 and it is worth saying a little about these new life and long-term sentences. Most prisoners serve a determinate sentence in that they have to be released at the end of that sentence. However, prisoners sentenced to life or to an IPP have no automatic right to be released – they have to serve a minimum period, known as the 'tariff', which is set by the judge at the trial. After the minimum period there is no automatic right to release; their release is dependent on the Parole Board being satisfied that the prisoner is ready for release (of course there are a small number of cases where life sentenced prisoners will never be released – where they serve a whole life order).

Different offences can lead to a sentence of life imprisonment. It is a mandatory sentence for murder committed by someone aged 21 or over and a discretionary maximum sentence for a number of other serious offences, including manslaughter, arson, robbery and rape. Also, as mentioned above, it is now a mandatory sentence under the 'two strikes' provision of the 1997 Act. This 'two strikes' legislation has attracted a good deal of concern and is worth commenting on briefly. It is based on the policy introduced in California in 1994 of giving a life sentence to any offender who committed three indictable offences of any severity. This led to some absurd cases where offenders were getting life sentences for committing minor thefts or burglaries. None the less the British government proposed an automatic life sentence for offenders convicted for the second time of a serious violent or sexual offence (unless there were very exceptional circumstances). As mentioned above, the 2003 Criminal Justice Act led to the replacement of the automatic life sentence by the Imprisonment for Public Protection sentence for offences committed after 4 April 2005.

As we have seen, a life or indeterminate sentence does not mean the prisoner will remain in prison for life; however, this legislation has undoubtedly increased the length of sentence for many offenders and so increased the prison population figures. As well as the resource implications of legislation that increases the prison population, such developments also raise issues of justice and fairness (see the extract from *The Times* in the question break below).

QUESTION BREAK: LONG-TERM PRISONERS

It is long-term prisoners who tend to dominate the routines of prisoner life rather than those who are only in prison for a few months. This creates a dilemma for the Prison Service which has to cater for most prisoners who have a brief, transitory experience of prison, while at the same time having to accommodate more and more prisoners who will be inside for many years.

List the main differences between the needs of long-term and shorter-term prisoners.

* What tensions might there be between the two groups?
* How might these factors affect the administration and management of prisons?

Read the extract below and suggest the advantages and disadvantages of the 'two strikes' policy. What ethical issues does it raise?

Robber gets life for his second serious offence

A robber has been jailed for life for stealing £520 under the 'two strikes and you're out' law.

It was Noel Boylan's second serious offence in four years: in 1994 he was jailed for four years for a robbery he committed with a pistol-shaped cigarette lighter.

Judge Jeremy Griggs told Truro Crown Court that there was no alternative to a mandatory life sentence for Boylan under the 1997 Crime Sentence Act.

He would normally have jailed him for nine years, which, with good behaviour, would have entitled him to release after six years . . .

The 1997 Act . . . was inspired by the similar American 'three strikes and you're out' law which became notorious after a vagrant was jailed for life for stealing a pizza.

The sentence was condemned by civil liberties groups. Paul Cavadino of the National Association for the Care and Resettlement of Offenders said: This was a serious offence but we do not think it is right to require courts to pass a life sentence regardless of the circumstances. It is clear the offender deserved a severe sentence but the judge should have been able to decide its length.

There is a risk the new law will deter offenders from pleading guilty, which could lead to unnecessary trials and the possible acquittal of some dangerous offenders. It will also provide an incentive to plea-bargaining to avoid the automatic sentence.

(From S. De Bruxelles, 'Robber gets life for his second serious offence', *The Times*, 8 October 1998)

Cullen and Newell (1999), in their study *Murderers and Life Imprisonment,* consider the question of how many life sentence prisoners might be innocent. While it is impossible to ascertain the numbers, it is an important issue in that innocent life sentence prisoners are likely to serve longer than other lifers as they are seen as not admitting their guilt and demonstrating remorse. And the likelihood that such prisoners will protest their innocence often leads to them being seen as more awkward than other prisoners. The Criminal Cases Review Commission was set up in 1995 to investigate suspected miscarriages of justice and, according to Cullen and Newell, receives new cases at the rate of five a day. Although, again, it is impossible to establish how many who allege they are innocent are 'genuinely' innocent even the Prison Officers Association estimated in 1992 that there could be around 700 innocent convicted prisoners. Of course any estimates are liable to be on the low side as there are many reasons for prisoners not to maintain their innocence, with parole and transfer to other prisons possibly depending on a willingness to own up to crimes and admit guilt. As Cullen and Newell put it: 'It is quite clear that to get parole any sex offender would have to admit guilt, and participate in programmes to work on his offence and any cognitive distortions' (1999: 65). They also cite a comment from the former *Observer* journalist David Rose that, 'for the life sentenced prisoners, protesting innocence is a sure-fire way to remain in gaol forever'.

The various, high profile and infamous miscarriages of justice in recent years have illustrated the extent of this issue. However, it could be argued that the innocence or otherwise of prisoners is not really an area where the prison service can get involved, as it is the courts that convict and sentence offenders. Cullen and Newell argue that such a view is short-sighted in that prisons are an integral part of the criminal justice system; and prisoners who feel they are innocent are more likely to refuse to accept the realities of prison life and more likely to engage in protest about their conditions.

There is an obvious link between the numbers of prisoners and the costs of running the prison service, and the massive rise in the prison population and consequent prison building programme is obviously costing a great deal. It is not cheap to keep someone in prison and it is difficult to estimate the actual costs. Morgan and Liebling (2007) estimate that it costs around £27,000 per prisoner per year, or about £510 a week, whereas the Prison Reform Trust suggest the figure is around £40,000 a year. On top of this there is the phenomenal cost of building new prisons to cope with the rising prison population; according to Prison Reform Trust figures, the average cost of each additional prison place built since 2000 has been just under £100,00, and the rise in places since then clearly illustrates the massive cost of running the prison estate.

Before turning to prison conditions, it is important to bear in mind when considering the prison numbers that the prison population is not determined by levels of crime; essentially it is politically determined and it could be considerably smaller, as it is in other European countries, or, presumably, larger, as it is in the United States. And if there is no clear political drive to restrain the current expansion then prison numbers will undoubtedly continue to rise. As a final point, in this section we have referred to different categories of prisoners, for instance lifers, but one area where there is potential to greatly reduce the prison population is with regard to the number of fine defaulters sent to prison each year. These offenders were not originally sentenced to prison (presumably because their crime did not merit it); when they default on their fines and end up in prison, the government does not get the money from the fine anyway and there is the additional (and as we saw above, heavy) cost of keeping the offender in prison. The number of people sent to prison for not paying fines is considerable, making up roughly a quarter of all people imprisoned per year.

Conditions

It is probably fair to say that the material conditions in which prisoners live are better nowadays, in terms of food and hygiene for instance, than they have ever been. Although the old Victorian prison buildings are still in use there are also many new, purpose-built prisons and daily life in prisons has changed with there no longer being rows of prisoners working in silence. However it is only in recent years that some very degrading practices have been eliminated. It was not until the Strangeways prison riot of 1990 and the subsequent Woolf Report that a target date was set for ending 'slopping out'; this daily ritual whereby prisoners were allowed out of their cells to empty the buckets which they had used for toilets the previous night was only finally ended in 1994. Slopping out will probably be looked back on as an archaic, even barbaric, relic – like the crank and treadmill of nineteenth century prisons, but one which lasted until the end of the twentieth century.

The recent improvements, though, do not mean that bad conditions and repressive regimes in prisons are a thing of the past. There is still a lack of constructive activities for most inmates and, due in large part to the massive increase in numbers, many prisoners spend longer periods alone in their cells and consequently less time working outside of them. Other pressures come from the longer periods served in prison and from the overcrowding consequent on rising numbers; while the much stricter and pervasive security and surveillance in prisons has led to a reduction in communal activities such as eating in dining halls (prisoners taking their food back to their cells is felt to pose a lesser security risk). So while many prison cells may be better equipped and more comfortable than in the past this is perhaps scant consolation if ever longer periods of time are spent in them. And it is also clear that poor conditions remain a major area of concern and dispute for prisoners and so work against the smooth running of prisons.

In terms of day-to-day prison life, fear is a prominent and pervasive feature. For instance, there are more and more drugs of all kinds in prisons and the consequent violence and intimidation that stems from them exacerbates this fear. The quality of prison life is also affected by pressure on prison staff and the extra demands on staff caused by ever increasing numbers can lead to cancellation of work and can limit the opportunities for inmates to engage in useful activities, such as educational programmes, and in leisure activities. Although it is easier to manage with fewer staff if prisoners are locked in their cells, again this will affect the quality of life for prisoners and thereby increase degrees of dissatisfaction. A report by the Chief Inspector of Prisons, Anne Owers, into Norwich prison published in January 2003 showed that more than 200 out of 250 inmates on one wing had no access to meaningful work or education, while on the prison's 'training wing' only eight out of 45 inmates were in education and none was undertaking what might be termed meaningful work (Travis 2003). More recently, in October 2007 another report on Norwich prison from environmental health inspectors was so damning that it led to the closure of one of the prison wings there. The report referred to a lack of heating due to vents being blocked by paint, to dampness and a risk of rodent infestation – indeed the particular wing of the prison (Gurney wing) had been declared 'unfit for animals' by a previous report in January 2007 but was reopened after three days because of overcrowding at the prison (Travis 2007).

It is difficult to assess the extent of prison overcrowding accurately because the data will fluctuate as offenders enter and leave prisons and as prisoners themselves are moved around the system. According to figures from the Penal Reform Trust in 2009 over two thirds of prisons in England and Wales were overcrowded; their report published a 'league table' of the most overcrowded prisons. Shrewsbury, with 316 inmates in its 177 spaces, came out as 'top', followed by Swansea (395 in 230 spaces) and Dorchester (229 in 137 spaces).

QUESTION BREAK: PRISON OVERCROWDING

The current level of overcrowding is undesirable but very limited. Only 20% of prisoners are currently having to double up in a cell designed for one. Regimes are still being delivered, and prisoners are still receiving education, purposeful activity, offending behaviour programmes, and getting exercise and time out of their cells . . . No prison is being required to take more than its operational capacity and we are committed to ensuring that overcrowding does not impact on safety in any way, and we recognise the pressures it creates for prisoners and staff.

(Hilary Benn, Prisons Minister, quoted in *The Times*, 29 August 2002)

Our prisons are becoming no more than warehouses once again . . . The consequences of overcrowding are jeopardising both the safe running of the prison system and the rehabilitation of individual offenders . . . Although 20% of inmates are 'doubling up' in cells designed for one the prison service does not collect data on overcrowding in other types of cells, such as when three inmates have to share facilities designed for two.

(Frances Crook, Director of The Howard League, quoted in *The Times*, 29 August 2002)

Compare the comments of the Prisons Minister and the Howard League with the report of the Chief Inspector of Prisons on Norwich prison (above) on the extent and impact of overcrowding, then answer the following questions:

- Which interpretation of the same data do you find most convincing? Why?
- What additional problems is overcrowding likely to lead to for (a) the management of prisons; (b) the rehabilitation of prisoners?

As well as affecting the day-to-day quality of life in prisons, poor conditions, exacerbated by overcrowding, have been linked with prison disturbances and with increased suicides within prisons. While perhaps not as spectacular as the prison riots of the early 1990s at Strangeways prison in Manchester and elsewhere, there have been a number of disturbances in British prisons in recent years. The prison service admitted to there being 'disturbances and acts of indiscipline' at four prisons in August 2002. Four days of disturbances at Holme House prison, Teesside led to 34 cells being damaged beyond use after about 60 inmates refused to return to their cells, and there were similar disturbances and damage at Swaleside prison in Kent, Pentonville, London and Ashfield in Bristol. The prison service acknowledged that overcrowding and staff shortages were at least partly to blame. The Deputy Head of the Prison Service, Phil Wheatley, referred to the record prison population as having 'increased instability and contributed to a small but significant number of incidents of mass disorder'; he went on to highlight the 'real risk that such incidents could escalate to involve large numbers of prisoners leading to a riot' (quoted in Travis, 'Crowding Fuels Prison Violence', *The Times*, 29 August 2002). Prior to these disturbances, in June 2002, the Lord Chief Justice, Lord Woolf, had warned that 'the intolerable conditions in Britain's overcrowded jails risk further prison riots like those that occurred in the early 1990s' (*Guardian*, 21 June 2002). These kinds of fears were realized in the full-scale riot that occurred at Lincoln prison in October 2002. Prisoners forced the 25 prison officers on duty (in a prison holding 571 inmates) to withdraw to the prison gates and effectively controlled the prison for three hours on October 24th. After a prison officer had been assaulted and his keys taken, hundreds of prisoners were unlocked and went on the rampage, smashing cells and furnishings and lighting fires in two of the prison's wings. The riot ended after 250 prison officers from 17 jails and equipped with riot gear took back control of the prison wing by wing. The General Secretary of the Prison Officers' Association, Brian Caton, said:

> We have been warning the Prison Service that unless they resourced us correctly for the very large increase in the prison population, that these kind of events would become more frequent. We believe that there are many overcrowded prisons now that are reaching crisis point.
>
> (*The Times*, 25 October 2002)

In a more recent comment, in October 2009 the president of the Prison Governors' Association, Paul Tidball, commented that the prison population was now so large that there was potential for a 'widespread disorder' by inmates and that there was a potential for prisons 'to blow' (*Guardian*, 5 October 2009). And in 2010 there was a major riot at Ford open prison.

Poor conditions and increased overcrowding have also been linked to the increased suicide rate within prisons. While the number of suicides in prison, and hence the suicide rate, varies from year to year it is much higher than the suicide rate amongst the wider population. The suicide rate in the prison population has varied from 72 to 133 for every 100,000 inmates between 2000 and 2009 (and from 60 to 95 actual suicides), with the highest rates in 2002, 2003 and 2004, while, as a snapshot comparison, in 2008 the general suicide rate across the whole country was 17.7 per 100,000 for males and 5.4 per 100,000 for females. So men in prison are five times more likely to commit suicide than those in the general population; and this is especially the case for young male prisoners aged between 15 and 17. The Chief Inspector of Prisons, Anne Owers, has regularly referred to prison suicides; in her first annual report she commented: 'Recently there were eight suicides in one week, five of them within 24 hours. These shocking statistics are, of course, directly connected to prison overcrowding and the consequential "churn" as prisoners continually move into and out of prisons throughout the estate' (quoted in *The Times*, 11 December 2002).

In a similar vein, five years later in the annual report of 2007, Ann Owers said:

> During the reporting year, the prison population went from one all time high to another . . . At the same time, there has been a dramatic rise in self-inflicted deaths in custody . . . Many were amongst some of the most vulnerable – foreign nationals, indeterminate-sentenced and unsentenced prisoners and women, at the most vulnerable times, in the early days in an establishment.
>
> (from www.prisonreformtrust.org.uk)

In commenting on this report, the director of the Prison Reform Trust, Juliet Lyons said: 'This massive increase in prison suicides of almost 40% on 2006 results is a result of the pressure of chronic overcrowding across the prison estate' (from www.prisonreformtrust.org.uk).

In a more general consideration of how prisoners adapt to imprisonment, Mathews (1999) points to the tendency to explain suicides in prison 'as a function of the mental instability of some prisoners with histories of psychiatric disorder'. However, those who commit suicide in prison are less likely to have a history of psychiatric disorder than suicides among the general population, 'whereas some 90 per cent of the recorded suicides in the community have a history of psychiatric disorder, only a third of those who commit suicide in prison have similar histories' (Mathews 1999: 70). Mathews suggests that explaining suicides in prison in individualistic terms ignores the effects of the prison regimes and the control strategies in prisons, with little attention paid to the depersonalizing nature of prison life and the range of activities and social stimuli that are available to prisoners. He argues that 'those most likely to attempt suicide are those who are physically and socially isolated in prisons with few activities and with little contact with home and family' (ibid.).

Security and containment

Another aspect of prison life that is affected by increased numbers and poor conditions is prison security, with overcrowding leading to many inmates being held in unsuitable parts of prisons and in the wrong security conditions. Prison security and containment became a prominent issue in the 1960s with a number of spectacular escapes by high profile prisoners, including the Great Train Robbers, Ronnie Biggs and Charlie Wilson, in 1965 and the spy, George Blake, in 1966. Until then security considerations had been relatively low on the prison agenda, but these escapes led to the Mountbatten Report (*Inquiry into Prison Escapes and Security*, Home Office, 1966) which highlighted weaknesses in prison security and established a new categorization of all prisoners in terms of their security risk. This categorization, which determines where prisoners are allocated to serve their sentences, is still in place today in much the same form as suggested by Mountbatten.

As suggested, the escape of George Blake, in particular, was a key factor in these developments and is worth referring to briefly here. Blake was employed by MI6 after the Second World War and while serving in Berlin offered his services to the KGB; after twelve years of spying for the Soviet Union he was sentenced to 42 years' imprisonment in 1961, the longest ever determinate sentence passed in Britain. Essentially George Blake seems to have managed to escape from Wormwood Scrubs five years later without meeting any real obstacles – an accomplice threw a rope ladder over the prison wall and then drove Blake to a house a few minutes away from the prison. He was smuggled out of the country and to East Berlin in December 1966 and is still alive and living in Moscow with a Russian wife, son and grandson.

At the time of Blake's escape prisoners were classified as either 'stars' (first time prisoners) or 'ordinaries' (those who had served at least one previous sentence). The categorization system introduced by the Mountbatten Report included four categories of prisoner according to the level of security felt necessary to hold them in custody. These categories were defined as follows:

- *Category A* – Prisoners who must in no circumstances be allowed to get out either because of security considerations affecting spies, or because their violent behaviour is such that members of the public or the police would be in danger of their lives if they were to get out.
- *Category B* – Prisoners for whom the very high expenditure on the most modern escape barriers may not be justified, but who ought to be kept in secure conditions.
- *Category C* – Prisoners who lack the resources and will to make escape attempts, (but) have not the stability to be kept in conditions where there is no barrier to escape.
- *Category D* – Prisoners who can reasonably be entrusted to serve their sentences in open conditions.

(Home Office, 1966)

As mentioned, this security categorization is still in place today and is perhaps the most important of the prison's internal procedures. In the HM Prison Service's published list of Performance Standards the key aspect of security is the categorization and allocation of prisoners. On reception, all prisoners are risk assessed to determine their security category on reception and then accommodated in accordance with the results of this assessment – they are allocated to a prison in line with their security category. As Price puts it:

[I]t structures the use of the prison estate, acting as a first line of defence against escapes, determining living conditions and allocation possibilities for convicted prisoners. Almost every other internal procedure within the prison system is conditional on the results of this one decision.

(Price 2000: 3)

However, it is a decision and a procedure that offers the prisoner little opportunity to question or appeal against.

One of the main issues addressed by the Mountbatten Inquiry was that of what to do with the category A prisoners. It recommended one, specially built maximum security prison, which was going to be known as 'Vectis'. However, this did not become policy. The Home Office was not in favour of one fortress-type prison for a number of reasons; in the wake of the Blake escape there was a concern about the consequences of a mass break-out and there were misgivings around issues of staffing and control in such a prison. Instead a further inquiry by the Advisory Council on the Penal System (1968) proposed that the most dangerous prisoners be spread around a number of high security prisoners most of whose inmates would be categories B or C. It is understandable that the prison service is particularly concerned about containing and controlling a small number of very dangerous prisoners and the advantages and disadvantages of either the concentration or dispersal of such prisoners has been an ongoing area of debate. Indeed, discussion of how a prisoner comes to be classified as a maximum security risk in the first place has been overshadowed by the debate about what to do with such prisoners (Price 2000).

Problems of security and control in prison are not necessarily one and the same, for instance there will be prisoners who may well have the connections and capacity to organize an escape but who will pose few problems in terms of day-to-day control within prison and might be very compliant prisoners. This raises the question of how to distinguish between a prisoner who is a security risk and one who is a control risk and highlights a particular problem with the fourfold categorization of prisoners. The categories A and B relate to the risk and danger if a prisoner escapes while C and D refer to the likelihood of an escape. As Price (2000) points out, this leaves 'a large hole in the centre of the four categories', in that category B is defined as being almost but not quite A and category C as not quite the same as D but the distinction between categories B and C is much less clear. And how the categories are applied in practice often becomes rather subjective, even depending on which part of the country prisoners serve their sentence. In 1981, for instance, a Prison Department Working Party found that the Midland region placed over 22 per cent of its prison population in category D, open, conditions and just 11 per cent in category B, while the South-West had close to 30 per cent in category B conditions and 10 per cent in category D, open prisons. These differences were simply due to the different levels of prison accommodation available in the different regions.

Since the mid 1960s there have been few escapes by prisoners who pose a genuine danger, although many prisoners who are deemed lower risk do walk out of open prison conditions or abscond when working outside of prison. However, there were two exceptional and dramatic escapes from high security prisons in the 1990s. Six prisoners escaped from the secure unit of Whitemoor prison in Cambridgeshire in 1994, injuring a prison officer with one of two guns used in the escape. In 1995 three prisoners from Parkhurst prison, who were identified by the prison service as some of the most dangerous in the prison system, managed to make a master key and a ladder that could be dismantled into smaller parts in the prison workshops, to obtain wire cutters, pliers and a gun, to evade the CCTV cameras and dog patrols at the prison perimeter and to break through two fences without setting off any alarms. They were at large on the Isle of Wight for four days before being spotted by an off-duty prison officer and recaptured.

These escapes led to separate inquiries, the Woodcock report into the Whitemoor escape and the Learmont report into that at Parkhurst. Both recommended and have led to increases in prison security and surveillance and to more restrictions on long-term prisoners, with the Learmont report stressing that custody should be the primary purpose of the prison service. While it is clear that some prisoners are dangerous and need to be held securely at all time, the vast majority of prisoners are not; and there is a danger that in reacting to specific situations with harsher restrictions, opportunities that may help prisoners to settle into outside life after their release, such as pre-release home leaves, might well be missed.

There have been more recent escapes, more usually from prison escorts. In January 2009 Wayne Connor escaped from a prison van taking him to court after two armed accomplices held it up. He was recaptured within a few days. More spectacularly, in March 2009 Julien Chautard, a French-born arsonist who had been sentenced to seven years' imprisonment, escaped from Pentonville prison by clinging to the underside of the prison van that had brought him there from court. He handed himself in to the police after being on the run for a few days. However, such escapes are few and far between. One of the Key Performance Indicators used by the prison service is that the rate of escapes from prison and prison escorts should be no more than 0.05 per cent of the prison population (www.justice.gov.uk). The prison service easily meets this target. In 2006, for example, there were four such escapes from a prison population of getting on for 80,000 (roughly 0.005 per cent); while the 'prison escape' figures for 2007, 2008 and 2009 were three, one and three respectively (www.parliament.uk).

Legitimacy

The Woolf report (1991) highlighted the sense of injustice held by inmates as a key factor behind the Strangeways disturbances of 1990. This sense of injustice was related to internal prison practices and procedures. As Woolf put it, 'a recurring theme in the evidence from prisoners who . . . were involved in the riots was that their actions were a response to the manner in which they were treated by the prison system. Although they did not always use these terms, they felt a lack of justice.' The report argued that the prison service should seek to achieve and maintain a balance between justice, security and control. This justice should not be seen as some sort of privilege or award for good behaviour; rather it should be a basic requirement that prisoners would receive humane treatment, be subject to fair procedures and be provided with reasoned explanations for decisions made that affected their situation.

Although not explicitly referring to the term 'legitimacy', the Woolf report advocated what could be seen as a 'theory of legitimacy' (Cavadino and Dignan 2007):

> The evidence is that prisoners will not join in disturbances in any numbers if they feel conditions are reasonable and relationships are satisfactory. These are matters which the prison service must address more closely. They are fundamental to maintaining a stable prison system which is able to withstand and reject the depradations of disruptive and violent prisoners. These are matters which must be resolved if we are to have peace in our prisons.

As regards the balance between justice and security and control, the emphasis since the Woolf report has been on implementing the security recommendations, such as installing metal detectors and X-ray machines. This emphasis has been sharpened by the Woodcock and Learmont Inquiries into the prison escapes of the mid 1990s (see above) and has led to some incredibly detailed monitoring of inmates' possessions. The *Prisons Handbook* (Leech and Cheney 1999) illustrates the detailed control over prisoners' property: 'The basic rule is that the standard limit, for all prisoners, for all property held in possession is that which fits into two volumetric control boxes. The volumetric control box measures 0.7m × 0.55m × 0.25m and has a volume of 0.9625 cubic metres' (p. 242). In contrast, there has been much slower progress made on other recommendations of the Woolf report, such as on action to end over-crowding and to improve prison officer and inmates' relationships. It would seem that security has become the top priority and that another detailed and thoughtful inquiry, with some useful recommendations, has become another missed opportunity.

Woolf found that the standard response when dealing with prison disorders was to identify the 'trouble makers' and to subject them to some form of punishment, such as solitary confinement, or to ship them out to another prison. There was little attempt to investigate the grievances that the inmates had. This sort of approach illustrates a general concern of prisoners that the grievance procedures within prisons are inadequate. In addition, the internal prison disciplinary system is felt to operate in a manner that works against the interests of prisoners. As regards internal disciplinary offences, prison governors carry out the initial investigation and deal with the vast majority of cases themselves – a procedure which is perhaps unlikely to be viewed very positively by prisoners. More serious offences can be referred to the police if they also constitute a crime (cases of assault or possession of drugs for example). Until 1992 the prison Board of Visitors used to be involved with more serious disciplinary cases. This was felt by the Woolf report to compromise the impartiality of the Board of Visitors and their main role now is to find out about and draw attention to any abuse of prisoners. Boards of Visitors were established by the prison Act of 1895; they changed their name to Independent Monitoring Boards in April 2003 with each Board being responsible for a particular prison. They are meant to act as independent watchdogs, safeguarding the well-being and rights of prisoners. However, although they are meant to be independent of the prison service, members are appointed by the Home Office and tend to be local dignitaries (including magistrates) who do not inspire a great deal of confidence in prisoners themselves.

Justice within prison does not just refer to how grievances or disciplinary offences are dealt with. The emphasis on prisoners' having to 'earn' privileges and, in particular, to earn remission from their sentences raises further concerns about justice in prison. The Crime Sentences Act 1997 proposed that prisoners would have to 'earn' their early release, rather than it being a right. However, it is difficult to apply such a policy with justice (and in a way that is felt legitimate by prisoners) as such decisions will almost inevitably involve the day-to-day appraisal of prison officers; and these decisions about early release or not are bound to cause all sorts of ill feelings. They might result in many extra months of a sentence being served by some prisoners but not by others.

QUESTION BREAK: RELEASE FROM PRISON

While the idea of prisoners having to earn remission from a sentence is not new – it is similar to the indeterminate sentence idea that has been used in the past (see p. 240), it can increase tension among inmates and raises awkward questions.

What do you think should determine a prisoner's release from prison?

List the arguments for and against linking the release date for prisoners to their behaviour while in prison.

IMPRISONMENT: EXPERIENCES AND ISSUES

Now that we have considered the current situation in British prisons in relation to numbers, conditions, security and legitimacy, the focus of this next section is on the 'experiences of prison life'. This is obviously a vast area and here we will focus on two particular areas: the experiences of female prisoners and the question of whether prison can 'work' in terms of rehabilitating those convicted for serious offences.

Women and prison

According to data from the Ministry of Justice (from their website and statistics bulletins 2010), out of a prison population of just over 85,000 on 30 April 2010, just under 4,400 (slightly over 5 per cent) were female. So with around 95 per cent of prisoners being male it is perhaps not surprising that the prison system has been dominated by the needs of male rather than female prisoners. Although a figure of 5 per cent may seem very low given that just over half the total population of England and Wales is female, the female prison population grew at a much faster rate than the male prison population around the turn of the twenty-first century. Between 1995 and 2005 there was a 150 per cent increase in the number of female prisoners compared to a 40 per cent increase for men (Morgan and Liebling 2007). More recently the female prison population has stabilized – indeed between March 2009 and March 2010 it fell slightly (albeit by just 6), following a small decrease the year before also.

However, the massive rise in the late 1990s has affected the experiences of women prisoners. In a report from the Prison Reform Trust (2003) into Newton Hall prison, Durham, overcrowding was highlighted as a real cause for concern, with the report finding almost half of the female prisons in England and Wales suffering from overcrowding. It made the point that few women offenders are a 'real risk' to the public, with director of the Prison Reform Trust, Juliet Lyon, commenting that, 'for all but the most serious and violent offenders, support and supervision centres in local communities offer the best chance for women offenders to get out of trouble'. However, as we have seen in looking at prison numbers generally, attempts to reduce the prison population do not seem to have much success. The Youth Justice Board, for instance, has recommended that all girls aged 16 and younger should be removed from prisons but has said that these plans have been frustrated by an increase in the number of teenagers being jailed.

As regards the make-up of the female prison population there are some differences from male prisoners. A higher proportion of female prisoners are on remand awaiting trial (in March 2010, 18 per cent compared to 15 per cent for males); while sentenced female prisoners are usually older and serving shorter sentences and are substantially less likely to be reconvicted (Morgan and Liebling 2007). Another development that has affected the female prison population has been the increase in foreign nationals held in British prisons, many for drug-related offences, including drug smuggling, which tend to carry relatively long sentences (Mathews 1999). Ministry of Justice figures from March 2009 showed that 27 per cent of female prisoners were held for drug offences and 18 per cent were classed as foreign nationals (compared to 13 per cent of male prisoners).

The increase in the number of women in prison and the fact that the prison service tries to place women in female only institutions affects the experience of female prisoners. As Morgan and Liebling (2007) point out, with only 19 out of the 142 prison establishments accommodating women it is difficult to place female prisoners near to their homes. And as almost two thirds of female prisoners have at least one child below the age of 18, being in a prison close to their home is the highest priority for most of these prisoners. These sorts of practical issues are likely to intensify the tensions that occur in women's prisons.

Although the female prison population has risen dramatically in recent years, the proportion of female prisoners has not always been as low as it is now. During the Victorian era women made up around one in five of those sent to local prisons and between 1860 and 1890 the average daily population of women in local prisons increased from 4,567 to 4,840 – higher numbers than today and in relation to a male prison population of less than 20,000 at the end of the nineteenth century (Zedner 1991). The female prison population was declining at the end of the nineteenth century and continued to do so into the twentieth, partly due to a decline in the number of women prosecuted for public order offences such as prostitution and because of a growing emphasis on explaining female offending in terms of 'feeblemindedness' alongside a policy of sending those prosecuted for drunkenness to reformatories rather than prisons. Between 1898 and 1914 a number of inebriate reformatories for female drunkards were founded (Zedner 1991). The female prison population continued to fall in the first half of the twentieth century and was less than 2000 by the 1960s. As mentioned above, the figures have increased from that low in recent years.

However, it was during the Victorian era that approaches to female imprisonment (as well as female offending) that are still in vogue today were introduced: for instance, the notion that women should be held separately from men and that women prisoners would benefit from the sort of personal attention that was best provided by prison officers of their own sex (Mathews 1999). There was also a different approach to prison labour for female prisoners; while it was agreed that all prisoners should engage in some form of work to aid their reform the following contemporary comment indicates the different regime advocated for women prisoners:

> The work done by the women prisoners is, of course, of different character to that performed (at) the hulks . . . the hard labour of prisoners working in the arsenal and dockyard is here replaced by the more feminine occupation of the laundry.
> (Mayhew and Binny, 1860, in Mathews 1999)

While there will clearly be common aspects and some overlap between the experiences of and responses to imprisonment for both male and female prisoners, there are some issues which relate more strongly to female prisoners. And, as Heidensohn (2002) points out, while there may be some debate as to how 'gendered' women's experience of imprisonment is, there is a general consensus that women offenders should be treated differently. She refers to the Prison Reform Trust inquiry led by Dorothy Wedderburn which pointed to the prison system not providing for the particular needs of women and highlighted four distinctive characteristics of women prisoners. These were: different patterns of offending from men and lower risk to the public; their role as mothers and primary carers; their history of psychiatric illness; and the effects of the proportionately low numbers of women prisoners ('Justice for Women: The Need for Reform', Prison Reform Trust, 2000, in Heidensohn 2002).

The point about the small proportion of the prison population was referred to earlier as leading to female prisoners typically being held some distance from their homes, with consequent difficulties for arranging visits and so maintaining family contact. A further implication of this is that women's prisons have to cope with a wider range of offenders than men's prisons; and that the range of work, training and educational opportunities are likely to be more limited (Mathews 1999). These sorts of 'structural' factors attendant on numbers and space will also affect the 'culture' within women's prisons. The fact that the majority of female prisoners are mothers affects the nature of and culture within women's prisons. As mentioned above, roughly two thirds of female prisoners are mothers and according to estimates from the Prison Reform Trust each year up to 20,000 children are affected by the imprisonment of their mother. Only around 5 per cent of women prisoners' children remain in their own home once their mother is sent to prison, with most being looked after by their grandmothers, other family members or friends. The question break below considers how women respond to their imprisonment.

QUESTION BREAK: WOMEN BEHIND BARS

The first extract below is taken from the section of Mary Eaton's study *Women After Prison*, which considers how women responded to their imprisonment. The second and third refer to more recent reports and comments on the experiences of women prisoners.

The women described ways of coping with the regimes in which they were held . . .

1 Withdrawal

To preserve something of the sense of self with which one entered prison it is necessary to withhold that self from engagement with the world of the prison. In withdrawing from the situation, women may feel that they are keeping the institution at a distance; however, they are actively conforming to the regime which defines docility as an appropriate characteristic for women . . .

2 Retaliation

I used to get into every kind of skulduggery that was going – like making drink – alcohol . . . That was the way I did my prison sentence – messing around and getting them back all the time . . .

For some women, confrontation with the prison authorities was one way of preserving a sense of self-dignity . . .

3 Incorporation

. . . Women may play an active part in maintaining the hierarchy that characterizes prison life, and so endorse the relative positions within that hierarchy. Experiencing exclusion themselves they practise exclusion on others. Being subject to power, they wield a limited power. 'What I hated more than anything was that there was so much bad feeling and aggression between the women' . . . Prison life does not encourage the creation of community . . . In such a situation many women felt that they changed in response to perceived aggression from others. If there was to be a hierarchy to be reinforced then they determined not to be at the bottom, not to be victims . . . 'I abhor physical violence, but in prison I was totally different . . . It was more like being in care where if you didn't physically stand up to someone who you thought could possibly bully you then you were going to be in trouble.'

(From M. Eaton, 1993, *Women After Prison*,
Open University Press, pp. 41–47)

Women Prisoners Need Life Support

There are more than 4,400 women prisoners in England. Four out of five women prisoners have mental health problems, most commonly depression and anxiety. Almost half have been subject to abuse during their lives. One in three has a child under five. For many women, even a short spell in prison can achieve nothing positive but create havoc with their family life and further damage their mental health.

With only 17 women's prisons in England and none in Wales, many women are imprisoned long distance from their families. For some, a spell in prison is just long enough for them to lose their children and their home.

The Corston report, published in March 2007 following a major inquiry led by Baroness Corston, made far-reaching recommendations about the future of women's prisons. It called for a more 'distinctive approach' to women in the criminal justice system, replacing women's prisons with a network of smaller, urban units for women in custody and for far greater use of community alternatives to prison . . . The report also made specific recommendations for the health of women in the criminal justice system, including improved arrangements for psychiatric assessments and for diverting women in courts and police stations towards mental health services.

The government published its response in December 2007, accepting many of the report's recommendations . . . (it) stopped short, however, of committing to develop the small, local centres Corston proposed to replace existing women's prisons . . .

Very few women prisoners actually need to be in custody. Most need a package of support that spans several public service: from health and social care to housing and employment support.

(From A. Greatly, 'Women Prisoners Need
Life Support', *Guardian*, 29 January 2008)

Female Ex-inmates Talk About Prison Abuse

Sexual abuse is 'part and parcel' of prison life, with staff harassing female inmates in exchange for drugs, cigarettes and even early release, according to former prisoners. Here, they tell their tales . . .

Jade Thompson, 32, is a former drug addict who served several prison sentences for drug-related crimes. Last released in 2003, she has turned her life around, training and working as a drugs abuse support worker. She served time in four prisons – Holloway, Highpoint, Cookham Wood and Foston Hall – and says she witnessed and experienced sexual approaches from staff, male and female, in every jail. 'It was part and parcel of prison life, and very intimidating. If you are not going to buy into the approaches made by staff, you will not progress, you will not get the good jobs, or get on to the courses that will help you get early release' . . .

Susan May, 64, served 12 years of a life sentence for the murder of her aunt in 1992 . . . She has always maintained her innocence . . . She has been imprisoned in six different jails. May agrees with Jade Thompson that Holloway contained a number of predatory female staff. In every jail she was in, she says, there were illicit relationships between staff and inmates. 'Some inmates complied, in return for cigarettes and other treats . . .' May says many women prisoners felt lonely and were more susceptible to the illicit approaches.

(From E. Allison, 'Female Ex-inmates Talk
About Prison Abuse', *Guardian*, 18 July 2009)

- What do you think are the major differences and similarities between the responses of the women interviewed by Eaton and those of male prisoners?
- In what other ways might prisoners, and particularly female prisoners, respond to imprisonment?
- Why do you think women 'react more adversely to custody than men'? Assess the arguments, put forward by the Corston Report, that very few women prisoners should be in custody.

Can prison work?

This sub-section will consider some examples of treatment programmes designed to rehabilitate long-term, dangerous prisoners. David Rose (2002) studied the effects of a year-long Cognitive Self-Change Programme (CSCP) run at Channings Wood prison, Devon. Seven of the eight prisoners on the programme that he examined were serving life sentences and all were judged by psychologists as at risk of offending again. The programme aims to reduce those risks and is one example of rehabilitative programmes that are in place across the majority of prisons in the United Kingdom. The existence of these programmes is seen by Rose as part of 'radical transformation in philosophy and practice now sweeping the British prison system'. In 2001, over 6,000 prisoners completed offending behaviour programmes, more than 11 times as many as in 1994, with the figure set to rise substantially in the next few years. This new rehabilitative emphasis was strongly supported by the then director-general of the Prison Service, Martin Narey: 'Like many who work in the service, I've never seen my job as being about just locking people up . . . If we can get people off drugs, on to offending behaviour programmes and into education, then we're going to reduce crime' (quoted in Rose 2002). Not all the prisoners were so enthusiastic about the CSCP programme and expressed a degree of scepticism, as illustrated by the comment from one of the participants: 'The psychology department have to put you through a stringent risk assessment. It's a year on a microscope slide. If you get your rubberstamp at the end of it, you're OK for D cat (open prison). If not . . .' However, most of the prisoners were positive. As one of the lifers said:

> I didn't want to do this course, but it has given me a lot of insights: why I killed the person I killed and why I've committed violent offences through my life. It's given me a lot of tools that I'm already using, to assess my own and other people's actions.

As well as programmes for serious offenders there are also less intensive courses for prisoners serving shorter sentences. The Enhanced Thinking Skills (ETS) course, for instance, is used in 79 jails. Rose refers to research by prison psychologist Caroline Friendship which demonstrated the relative success of such courses. Offenders who had followed a rehabilitation programme were found to be significantly less likely to be reconvicted within two years compared to offenders matched in terms of offence and social background but who hadn't followed any programme.

However, these positive developments are threatened by the ever increasing prison population and the consequent overcrowding, with many prisoners disappearing from courses just as they get going on them. As well as affecting the living standards within prisons, large rises in the prison population make it more difficult for prison staff to supervise and work with prisoners in tackling re-offending. Indeed this situation has been made worse with the continued rise in the prison population over the last few years, which has had a particular impact on the efforts to rehabilitate short-term prisoners. According to a report published by the National Audit Office in March 2010 the failure to do anything about the criminality of 60,000 prisoners who serve sentences of less than twelve months is costing the country between

£7 billion and £10 billion annually in reoffending (Travis 2010). The report found that more than half of such offenders spend all day in their cells because they have no work or educational courses. Overcrowding is compounded by the long waiting lists for courses that tackle offending behaviour. As the report states: 'Only a small proportion of prison budgets is spent on activity intended to reduce reoffending by prisoners on short sentences, despite the fact that 60 per cent of such prisoners are reconvicted within a year of release.'

Commenting on the Audit Office report, Edward Leigh, chairman of the House of Commons public accounts committee, said: 'The uncomfortable truth is they are not working, studying or doing almost anything constructive with their time. Indeed, half of them spend all day, every day sitting in their cells.'

Grendon is Britain's only therapeutic prison. It opened in 1962 and is a category B prison taking only the most difficult and dangerous offenders who it is felt might benefit from the psychological treatment offered. The therapeutic process at Grendon is based around group therapy sessions in which prisoners confront their crimes and learn to take responsibility for their actions and the effects those actions have on others. According to Weale (2001) it is proof that prison can be 'humane, constructive and life-changing' and can work. Mark Leech, now an author (he is editor of the *Prisons Handbook* for instance) and campaigner for penal reform, served 20 years in prison and is an ex-Grendon prisoner. He agrees with Weale, saying, 'It certainly worked for me . . . Grendon made me realise there were other options I could choose.'

Certainly reconviction rates from Grendon inmates are encouraging. The 24 per cent re-offending rate for life prisoners in general contrasts with an 8 per cent rate at Grendon, while for non-lifers the re-offending rate is 10 per cent lower at Grendon than elsewhere. Grendon is run as a democratic community that sets its own rules based around three policies that everyone is expected to follow – no drugs, no sex and no violence. Such a regime does not suit all prisoners and the comparative freedom within the prison comes as a culture shock to many; prison cells are open all day from 8 in the morning until lock up at 9 p.m., allowing prisoners to eat and talk together freely. While this relative freedom might seem like a soft option to some prisoners, staff and inmates regularly refer to it being the toughest way to 'do your bird', with the therapy being intensive and gruelling. However, not all prisoners respond positively to Grendon's regime. Convicted sex offender Gary Watkins volunteered for Grendon but within a month of his release kidnapped and sexually assaulted a 17-year-old girl, saying at his trial that he had maintained fantasies of assaulting and killing a young girl throughout his treatment. As Grendon's director of research and development, John Shine, commented, 'Some people here make enormous changes. Other people we have to be extremely cautious about . . . We don't know what goes on in their head.' In concluding her examination of the Grendon regime, Weale (2001) makes the point that while Grendon could certainly be seen as a success it should not distract from the bigger issue of why we keep expanding our prison system when we know it creates more problems than it solves.

To some extent, examples such as Grendon and other offending behaviour programmes could be seen as merely papering over the cracks of our prison system.

In responding to David Rose's positive review of rehabilitation programmes, director of the Prison Reform Trust, Juliet Lyon (2002) argues that while prison regimes have improved over recent years, it is misleading to claim that 'prison works' on the basis of a review of therapeutic programmes for long-term prisoners when the 'immense pressure of prison overcrowding' means that 'purposeful activity has increased for each prisoner by just ten minutes a day in ten years' and 'prisons are being turned back into human warehouses'. In concluding her article, Lyon comments that: 'the debate on whether prison works or not is futile. What matters is that prison is allowed to take its proper place in the criminal justice system, one of excellent last resort, properly equipped and able to cope with those who really need to be there.'

QUESTION BREAK: PRISON INSPECTIONS

The following extracts are taken from reviews of reports into prison between 1996 and 2006.

An unannounced short inspection at Aldington prison revealed that it was 'not operating successfully as a resettlement prison and is providing a "poor" standard of throughcare' . . . Too few prisoners received any meaningful training and the prison did not fulfil any of the criteria necessary for resettling prisoners into the community at the end of their sentences. It was remote from any external employment, education and training facilities and there was little purposeful activity for inmates within the prison. The accommodation was 'flimsy', grubby and failed security standards. There had been little improvement since the 1992 inspection.

(*The Howard Journal of Criminal Justice*, 1996, 35: 3, 274)

The inspection at HMP Chelmsford disclosed 'a collective failure over a period of time of a number of senior members of the Prison Service to recognise and eliminate too many unacceptable practices and deficiencies in the running of the prison'. Among elements making Chelmsford 'dreadful' were 'the appalling and 19th century attitude to the treatment of young offenders' which the chief inspector felt may breach the UN convention on children's rights, and finance/staffing problems. Adult and young offenders were freely mixing in the same accommodation and 'it was not difficult to find young men of 17 clearly lost and often afraid within the prison'.

(*The Howard Journal of Criminal Justice*, 1998, 37: 1, 105)

The jail overcrowding crisis, poor industrial relations, and a lack of a clear purpose have led to an 'unacceptable regime' at Liverpool prison, the largest in Britain, according to the chief inspector of prisons.

The report by Anne Owers published today said conditions for new inmates were among the worst her inspectors had seen – with cockroaches, broken windows and dirty cells and toilets . . . Prisoners were able to shower and change their underwear once a week and in some cases not even that frequently, according to the report . . .

There were fewer opportunities for work and education despite criticism in the 1999 inspector's report. 'Only 18% of prisoners had access to education, though the prison's own statistics showed that 95% needed help with basic literacy and numeracy. No national vocational qualifications were being offered', Ms Owers said.

The inspectors also found that, like many local prisons, Liverpool suffered severely from overcrowding.

'Many single cells held two prisoners with an unscreened toilet, and there was considerable difficulty in safely managing the large number of prisoners coming through reception every day.'

(From A. Travis, 'Regime at Biggest Jail Found Wanting', *Guardian*, 28 May 2003)

One of the UK's biggest Victorian jails is a dirty, vermin-infested institution where 40% of inmates have been assaulted or insulted by staff, according to an official inspection report published today.

Pentonville prison, where 14 staff were last month suspended on corruption allegations, is so poorly run that new prisoners were told on arrival not to expect to be given a pillow or a toothbrush, says the chief inspector of prisons, Anne Owers. One evening during the inspection there was not enough food to go round at the only cooked meal of the day. She says the basic operations at the prison are at best patchy, at worst non-existent. Her follow-up inspection carried out in July found that while external areas of the north London prison were better cared for, many internal areas remained dirty and vermin-infested, and overcrowding was so acute that it held 1,125 prisoners when it was only built for 897.

(From A. Travis, 'Inspector Lists Basic Failures at Prison in Corruption Inquiry', *Guardian*, 28 September 2006)

- In spite of numerous critical reports, why do you think prison conditions are still found to be of such poor standards?
- Suggest the possible long-term effects on prisoners and prison officers of experiences and institutions such as those illustrated above.
- How might those who favour (a) retribution and (b) rehabilitation respond to these extracts?

COMMUNITY PENALTIES

In the final part of this chapter we will look briefly at non-custodial, community penalties, often referred to as 'alternatives to prison'. Imprisonment is the most severe penalty available within our criminal justice system and has tended therefore to attract much greater interest than 'less severe' penalties. There is a vast amount of literature on prisons yet relatively little on non-custodial punishments. As Worrall (1997) puts it in the introduction to her study on community punishment, 'there is no market for the autobiographies of offenders' experiences of community service'. She suggests that academic and political debate 'tends to assume that penalty is synonymous with prison'. However, it is important to remember that the vast majority of offenders will never be given a custodial sentence.

Although non-custodial, including community, penalties might be thought of as a relatively recent addition to our criminal justice system, they are by no means new and in this section we will briefly trace their history. Before the twentieth century fines and release on recognisances were the only sentences apart from imprisonment that were regularly used by the courts, although non-payment of fines led to many people being imprisoned anyway. A recognisance was a bond by which the offender agreed to do, or refrain from doing, something; often it involved the offender being required simply to 'keep the peace'. By the mid nineteenth century release on recognisance normally involved some form of surety guaranteeing the future behaviour of the offender; these guarantees were often given by Police Court Missionaries, who were founded in 1876 and seen as the forerunners of the modern probation service (Worrall 1997). The Probation of First Offenders Act in 1887 recognized the role of these missionaries in helping the courts identify suitable offenders for probation (Brownlee 1998).

So probation has its origins in the nineteenth century when minor offenders could be bound over if a suitable person could be found to supervise their future conduct. This sort of supervision in place of another punishment was seen as providing the offender with an opportunity to 'prove' themselves, hence the term 'probation'.

A system of supervision based around missionary work was developed in the USA in the mid nineteenth century and was followed by penal reformers in Britain, and can be seen in the 1907 Probation of Offenders Act, which spelt out the role of the probation officer as being 'to advise, assist and befriend [the person under supervision] and, when necessary, to endeavour to find him suitable employment' (from Brownlee 1998). However, it took many more years before a system of paid, full-time probation officers was in place.

The first half of the twentieth century saw a move away from the missionary aspect of probation to a 'treatment model', based around therapeutic work related to the offender's needs and motivations. This reflected developments in criminology and the notion that crime was something which might be 'cured' through treating the social and psychological conditions and needs of offenders. The probation service itself became a more bureaucratic and professional organization based around therapeutic treatment of offenders. Although religious and philanthropic elements of the nineteenth century continued to influence both the recruitment to and organization of the probation service in the first decades of the twentieth century, the move to professionalism led to a gradual abandonment of the old view of the probation officer being someone who saw the job as a religious calling. This trend continued through the twentieth century. The development of the welfare state after the Second World War ensured that the principles of diagnosing and treating individuals were firmly established as basic probation practice in the 1950s and 1960s. During this post-war period the probation service expanded enormously. The number of probation officers increased from 1,006 in 1950 to 5,033 in 1976, while the number of offenders supervised rose from just over 55,000 in 1951 to more than 120,000 by 1971 (Brownlee 1998).

By the end of the 1970s the treatment model was being criticized on both empirical and ethical grounds (Raynor 2007). Studies into the effectiveness of punishments in general provided disappointing results and the 'nothing works' philosophy came to the fore. The 'treatment' model was also criticized on ethical grounds as dehumanizing individuals. This encouraged a move back to a more retributivist approach. Although the term 'nothing works' is associated with an American writer Martinson and his 1974 article 'What works? Questions and answers about prison reform', the notion was more widely applied and accepted in Britain. By the 1980s there was, according to Raynor, greater emphasis on avoiding unnecessary harm to offenders through imprisonment, with probation seen essentially as a means of reducing imprisonment, reflecting a move away from the earlier emphasis on 'doing good' through treatment.

Greater optimism about rehabilitation began to occur in the late 1980s and into the 1990s, with moves to avoid what had become almost a competition between community sentences and prisons – illustrated by the phrase 'alternatives to prison'. As Raynor puts it, cooperation across criminal justice agencies 'would not be helped if one service continued to define its mission as saving people from the other'. These changes were reflected in the 1991 Criminal Justice Act which advocated a key role for the Probation Service.

The new developments are characterized by a shift in focus to 'what works' rather than the 'nothing works' philosophy. These rehabilitative-based approaches have been centred largely around the work of psychological criminologists. In his overview, Raynor (2007) highlights Andrews and Bonta's theory of offending which relates social disadvantage to personality traits in developing a model of how offending occurs and develops. Social disadvantages such as poverty are seen as making it difficult for families to provide a supportive environment for children; while personality characteristics such as impulsiveness can be reinforced by peer pressure, which may provide access to illegitimate opportunities and delinquent activities and may work against succeeding in formal education. This sort of approach, bringing in both social and psychological factors, has encouraged intervention strategies based on trying to reduce the 'risk' factors faced by potential offenders.

As the 'what works' approach of the 1990s developed, examples of community penalty programmes which seemed to have a positive effect in reducing re-offending came to the fore. As Raynor puts it, 'rather than being the focus of interest for only a few researchers and practitioners [by the end of the 1990s there was] an officially recognized and endorsed strategy . . . prompting a considerable reorganization of the process of supervising offenders' (2002: 1192).

Brownlee summarizes the changing role of the probation service as proceeding,

from its earliest days as a branch of the Church's missionary work among the alcoholic and destitute, through its quasi-medical diagnostic and normalising phase, to its current position as an integral part of a systematised criminal justice apparatus, having special responsibility for the supervision of punishment in the community

(1998: 98)

The probation service does not just supervise offenders who are 'on probation', but also oversees a number of other community penalties. The current range of community penalties are detailed in Chapter 12 (pp. 414–415). The 1991 Criminal Justice Act attempted to clarify the concept of community penalty through defining six 'community orders' – probation order, community service order, combination order, curfew order, supervision order and an attendance centre order. While this framework provides the basis for the current situation, there have been various changes both to the types and the management of community penalties. As regards changes to the actual form or type of community penalty, as a result of the Criminal Justice Act of 2000, the well-established term 'probation order' was replaced by 'community rehabilitation order' and the community service order became a 'community punishment order'. These orders were, in turn, replaced by a single, general community order under the 2003 Criminal Justice Act. Judges and magistrates now consider the crime committed and the likelihood of re-offending and decide on the specific sort of community sentence an offender should get. The order can last up to three years and has a number of requirements attached to it. The requirements might involve unpaid work, completing training programmes or curfews (see p. 415 for the full list of 12 possible requirements). That act also introduced a Suspended Sentence Order which is essentially meant to provide an alternative to a custodial sentence.

In terms of how the probation service and community penalties are 'managed', the National Probation Service became part of the newly created NOMS (National Offender Management Service) in 2004. NOMS brought the prison service and probation service together under a single organizational structure in an attempt to provide what was termed 'end-to-end offender management', with a named offender manager having responsibility for an offender throughout his or her sentence, whether in custody, the community or both. NOMS itself became part of the Ministry of Justice in 2007 – it now consists of nine regional offices in England and one in Wales that aim to deliver and co-ordinate both the prison and probation services. It is difficult to assess the effect on the probation service of these changes – as Whitehead (2009) suggests, they may well have been introduced with the laudable aim of reducing costs, as well as to encourage multi-agency partnerships within the criminal justice system. However, he makes the point that the management changes are liable to weaken the autonomy of the probation service; and so work against a strong probation service 'which has a distinctive and separate voice within NOMS and which is allowed to promote its ideals, can help to ensure prisons are used as a last resort for more serious offenders'.

The continued growth of community penalties is shown in figures provided by Raynor (2007). At the end of 2004, the probation service was responsible for supervising over 220,000 offenders on various community penalty orders, including 7,000 on drug treatment and training orders. In addition it supervises all people released from prison and other custodial institutions and on a statutory supervision order (over

81,000 at end of 2004) – for instance all young offenders who received custodial sentences are supervised after their release and although such supervision is not a community penalty it involves the probation service.

Community penalties are an established and important part of our sentencing system and clearly have a future; however there will always be need to deal with the 'high-risk' offenders and this may lead to an increase in 'bifurcation', providing very different types of services according to (a risk analysis of) the dangerousness of the offender. Of course any changes and developments are dependent on the political climate of the day and there is always a danger that notions of community penalty are not perceived as grabbing the popular imagination (or vote!) as much as hard-line rhetoric and approaches.

This 'danger' highlights the difficulties for establishing and developing community penalties. Worrall (1997) suggests that there are four 'obstacles to community punishment. First, as suggested above, is the public and media perception that community penalties are 'soft' and that prison is the only appropriate punishment. Second, there is the problem of unfair or inconsistent sentencing. Community sentences tend to be given to those who are socially advantaged (and deemed by probation officers to be able to 'benefit' from supervision), whereas less advantaged groups seem to be over-represented in prison. Third, there is a danger that an increase in 'alternatives to custody' will lead to more and more people being drawn into the 'net' of the criminal justice system, so that rather than keeping people out of prison, community penalties will increase the numbers of people with criminal records. Finally, Worrall highlights problems with enforcing community penalties. Probation and community orders are fine if followed by the offenders but if not then such penalties have to be 'backed up' with prison, which can lead to the use of such penalties actually increasing the prison population (although Worrall does point out that probation officers do not lightly institute proceedings against offenders who don't comply with community penalties and are reluctant to return offenders to court if they can possibly avoid it).

In his overview of community penalties, Raynor (2007) suggests that a way forward is to including reparative elements in a wider range of community sentences, so as to emphasize (to the general population and the government) that rehabilitation is basically restorative and that it benefits the community as well as the offender – in other words to try to change public perceptions of rehabilitation as being 'soft' and only 'offender focused'. As he puts it:

> [P]robation services should try to present rehabilitation as work that offenders undertake as a consequence of a crime: work which is directed toward changing their own behaviour and attitudes in a more pro-social direction, to the advantage of the communities in which they live.
>
> (Raynor 2007: 1088)

FURTHER READING

Coyle, A. (2005) *Understanding Prisons: Key Issues in Policy and Practice.* Andrew Coyle was a prison governor before becoming a professor at the University of

London and this introductory text benefits from his first-hand as well as his academic knowledge of the prison service. The book considers how prisons function, what they achieve and their historical and political context.

Leech, M. and Cheney, D. (2009) *The Prisons Handbook 2009*. This is an annual guide to the prison service in England and Wales. Supported by the Prison Service (and published by www.prisons.org.uk) it offers practical information and advice for prisoners and those who work with them. It provides a brief description of every penal establishment and is a mine of useful information.

Liebling, A. and Price, D. (2010) *The Prison Officer* (2nd edn) The focus of the discussion in this chapter has been on prison and prisoners and, as its title implies, this text looks at the role of the prison officer – although a vitally important role for the running of our prison system, an area which is often ignored in studies of prison and imprisonment. This text provides an accessible guide to the work of prison officers.

Mathews, R. (1999) *Doing Time: An Introduction to the Sociology of Imprisonment.* This text provides a clear introduction to the main sociological debates surrounding imprisonment. After examining the history of and current practices within prisons, it examines the impact of imprisonment on different social groups, including young people, women and ethnic minorities.

Rawlings, P. (1999) *Crime and Power: A History of Criminal Justice 1688-1998.* Chapters 4 and 6 of this general historical text provide detail on the early prisons of the eighteenth and nineteenth centuries.

Raynor, P. (2007) *Community Penalties: Probation, 'What Works' and Offender Management,* in Maguire, M., Morgan, R. and Reiner, R. (eds) *The Oxford Handbook of Criminology* (4th edn). An up-to-date review of the history and contemporary practice of community punishment. It details recent changes in the structure and management of community penalties and highlights the obstacles faced in trying to provide rehabilitative punishments.

WEBSITES

Useful websites that focus specifically on prisons include:

www.hmprisonservice.gov.uk the official site of the HM Prison Service – this provides operational details of the prison service in general and of specific prisons.

www.guardian.co.uk/prisons which provides a range of journalistic and critical articles on prisons and life in them.

www.prisonreformtrust.org.uk provides a more critical perspective, focusing on issues of justice within prisons.

www.cjsonline.gov.uk under the section on offenders, this site includes a very useful and informative 'prison walkthrough' which looks at the prison experience from the prisoner's point of views; it includes issues such as arrival in prison, accommodation and the routines of daily life.

REFERENCES

AACAP (1997) 'AACAP official action. Practice parameters for the assessment and treatment of children and adolescents with conduct disorder', *Journal of the American Academy of Child and Adolescent Psychiatry*, 36 (supplement), 122–39.

Abramsky, S. (2009a) 'Emptying California's crowded prisons', *Guardian* 6 August.

Abramsky, S. (2009b) 'Finding cash behind bars', *Guardian* 16 February.

Adler, F. (1975) *Sisters in Crime*. New York: McGraw-Hill.

Advisory Council on the Penal System (1968) *The Regime for Long-Term Prisoners in Conditions of Maximum Security* (the Radzinowicz Report). London: HMSO.

Ainley, P. (2005) 'Open your arms', *Guardian* 14 June.

Ainsworth, M., Blehar, M., Waters, E. and Wall, S. (1978) *Patterns of Attachment: A Psychological Study of the Strange Situation*. Hillsdale, NJ: Erlbaum.

Alford, F. (2000) 'What would it matter if everything Foucault said about prison were wrong? Discipline and punish after twenty years', *Theory and Society*, 29 (1): 125–46.

Allen, G. (1976) 'Scope and methodology of twin studies', *Acta Genetica Medicae Gemellolgiae*, 25: 79–85.

Allen, R. (2001) 'Informing the public', *Criminal Justice Matters*, 43: 40–1.

Allison, R. (2003) 'Secret film catches PC apeing Ku Klux Klan', *Guardian* 23 October.

Althusser, L. (1969) *For Marx*. London: Allen Lane.

American Psychiatric Association (1997) 'Biological reductionism said to be linked to economic reductionism', *Psychiatric News*. http://www.psych.org/pnews/97-12-05/scully.html. Last accessed 12 November 2004.

Amir, M. (1971) *Patterns in Forcible Rape*. Chicago: University of Chicago Press.

Anderson, D. M. and Killingray, D. (1991) *Policing the Empire: Government Authority and Control, 1830–1940*. Manchester: Manchester University Press.

Andersen, S. L. (2003) 'Trajectories of brain development: point of vulnerability or window of opportunity?' *Neuroscience and Biobehaviouiral Reviews*, 27: 3–18.

Anderson, S., Grove-Smith, C., Kinsey, R. and Wood, J. (1990) *The Edinburgh Crime Survey*, Edinburgh: Scottish Office.

Anderson, S., Bechara, A., Damasio, H., Tranel, D. and Damasio, A. (1999) 'Impairment of social and moral behaviour related to early damage in human prefrontal cortex', *Nature Neuroscience*, 2: 1032–7.

Appel, R. (1995) 'Mother Simpson', *The Simpsons*. Production code 3F06.

Aron, R. (1970) *Main Current in Sociological Thought 2*. Harmondsworth: Pelican.

Babiak, P., Neumann, C. and Hare, R. (2010) 'Corporate psychopathy: talking the walk', *Behavioural Sciences & the Law*, 28: 174–93.

Back, L. (2002) 'Aryans reading Adorno: cyber-culture and twenty-first century Racism', *Ethnic and Racial Studies,* 25 (4): 628–51.

Ballinger, A. (2000) *Dead Woman Walking: Executed Women in England and Wales, 1900–1955.* Dartmouth: Ashgate.

Bandura, A. (1963) *Social Learning and Personality Development.* New York: Holt, Rinehart and Winston.

Bandura, A. (1990) 'Selective activation and disengagement of moral control', *Journal of Social Issues,* 46: 27–46.

Banks, M. (2005) 'Spaces of (in)security: Media and fear of crime in a local context', *Crime, Media and Culture,* 1 (2): 169–87.

Barbalet, J. M. (1993) 'Citizenship, class inequality and resentment', in B. S. Turner (ed.) *Citizenship and Social Theory.* London: Sage.

Barclay, G. and Mhlanga, B. (2000) 'Ethnic differences in decisions on young defendants dealt with by the Crown Prosecution Service', Home Office Section 95 Findings no.1, London: HMSO.

Barkham, P. (2005) 'How a top can turn a teen into a hoodlum', *Guardian* 14 May.

Barrett, L., Dunbar, R. and Lycett, J. (2006) *Human Evolutionary Psychology.* London: Palgrave Macmillan.

Barton, A. R. (2001) 'Fragile moralities and dangerous sexualities: A case study of women and semi-penal institutions on Merseyside, 1823–1994', PhD thesis, Liverpool John Moores University.

Batchelor, S. (2001) 'The myth of girl gangs'. *Criminal Justice Matters,* 43.

Baumrind, D. (1978) 'Parental disciplinary patterns and social competence in children', *Youth and Society,* 9: 238–76.

Beaver, K. M., Wright, J. P. and DeLisi, M. (2008) 'Delinquent peer group formation: evidence of a gene x environment correlation', *Journal of Genetic Psychology,* 169 (3): 227–44.

Beaver, K. M., Boutwell, B. B., Barnes, J. C., Cooper, J. A. (2009) 'The biosocial underpinnings to adolescence victimization: results from a longitudinal sample of twins', *Youth Violence and Juvenile Justice,* 7 (3): 223–38.

Beccaria, C. (1963 [1764]) *On Crimes and Punishment.* Indianapolis: Bobbs-Merrill Educational.

Beck, U. (1992) *Risk Society: Towards a New Modernity.* London: Sage.

Becker, H. S. (1963) *Outsiders: Studies in the Sociology of Deviance.* New York: Free Press.

Becker, H. S. (1973) 'Labelling theory reconsidered', in *Outsiders: Studies in the Sociology of Deviance,* second edition. New York: Free Press.

Begley, S. (2002) 'Genes don't give humans edge over their primate relations', *Wall Street Journal,* April 2.

Benedict, H. (1992) *Virgin or Vamp: How the Press Covers Sex Crimes.* Oxford: Oxford University Press.

Berman, M., McCloskey, M., Fanning, J., Schumacher, J. and Coccaro, E. (2008) 'Serotonin augmentation reduces response to attack in aggressive individuals', *Psychological Science,* 20: 714–20.

Berry-Dee, C. *Talking with Serial Killers.* London: John Blake.

Bindel, J. (2007) 'The rise of the cyber-stalker', *Guardian* 10 January.

Binder, E. R. Bradley, R. G., Liu, W. *et al.* (2008) 'Association of FKBP5 polymorphisms and childhood abuse with risk of posttraumatic stress disorder symptoms in adults', *Journal of the American Medical Association,* 299 (11): 1291–305.

Binks, G. (2005) 'Pretty girls get the best', CBC News, 10 June.

Blackburn, R. (1999) *The Psychology of Criminal Conduct: Theory, Research and Practice.* Chichester: Wiley.

Blass, T. (ed.) (2000) *Obedience to Authority: Current Perspectives on the Milgram Paradigm.* Mahwah, NJ: Lawrence Erlbaum Associates.

Bohman, M. (1996) 'Predisposition to criminality: Swedish adoption studies in retrospect', *Ciba Foundation Symposium,* 194: 99–109.

Bohman, M., Cloninger, R., Sigvardsson, S. and von Knoring, A. (1982) 'Predisposition to petty criminality in Swedish adoptees. I Genetic and environmental heterogeneity', *Archives of General Psychiatry,* 39: 1233–41.

Boland, F. J., Burrill, R., Duwyn, M. and Karp, J. (1998) *Fetal Alcohol Syndrome: Implications for Correctional Service.* Research Report R-71. Ottawa, ON: Correctional Service of Canada.

Bond, M. (2004) 'The making of a suicide bomber', *New Scientist* 182, 2447, 15 May.

Bottoms, A. E. (1980) *The Coming Penal Crisis.* Edinburgh: Scottish Academic Press.

Bowlby, J. (1946) *Forty-Four Juvenile Thieves: Their Character and Home Life.* London: Hogarth.

Bowlby, J. (1951) *Maternal Care and Mental Health.* Geneva: WHO monograph series.

Bowling, B. and Phillips, C. (2002) *Race, Crime and Justice.* Harlow: Longman.

Box, S. (1981) *Deviance, Reality and Society,* second edition. Eastbourne: Holt, Rinehart and Winston.

Box, S. (1983) *Power, Crime and Mystification.* London: Tavistock.

Boyle, K. (2005) *Media and Violence.* London: Sage.

Braithwaite, J. (1984) *Corporate Crime in the Pharmaceutical Industry.* London: Routledge.

Braithwaite, J. (1989) *Crime, Shame and Reintegration.* Cambridge: Cambridge University Press.

Bratingham, P. J. and Bratingham, P. L. (1984) *Patterns in Crime.* New York: Macmillan.

Breggin, P. (1995) 'Campaigns against racist federal programs by the center for the study of psychiatry and psychology', *Journal of African American Men,* 1: 3–22. http://www.breggin.com/racist fedpol.html.

Bridges, G. S. and Stone, J. A. (1986) 'Effects of criminal punishment on perceived threat of punishment: toward an understanding of specific deterrence', *Journal of Research in Crime and Delinquency,* 23: 207–39.

Britton, P. (1997) *The Jigsaw Man.* London: Corgi.

Brooks, L. (2009) 'A weekend behind bars showed me why this prison is precious' *Guardian* 29 October.

Brown, J. (2006) 'Your task: selling the real Liverpool', *The Independent,* 27 November.

Brown, J. (1997) 'Equal opportunities and the police in England and Wales: past, present and future possibilities', in P. Francis, P. Davies and V. Jupp (eds) *Policing Futures: The Police, Law Enforcement and the Twenty-first Century.* London: Macmillan.

Brown, S. (2005) *Understanding Youth and Crime,* second edition. Milton Keynes: Open University Press.

Brownlee, I. (1998) *Community Punishment: A Critical Introduction.* Harlow: Longman.

Brownmiller, S. (1975) *Against Our Wills: Men, Women, and Rape.* New York: Bantam.

Brunas-Wagstaff, J., Tilley, A., Verity, M., Ford, S. and Thompson, D. (1997) 'Functional and dysfunctional impulsivity in children and their relationship to Eysenck's impulsiveness and venturesomeness dimensions', *Personality and Individual Differences,* 22 (1): 25–9.

Brune, M. (2008) *Textbook of Evolutionary Psychiatry: The Origins of Psychopathology.* Oxford: Oxford University Press.

Brunner, H., Nelen, M., van Zandvoort, P. *et al.* (1991) 'X-linked borderline mental retardation with prominent behavioral disturbance: phenotype, genetic localisation and evidence for disturbed monoamine metabolism', *American Journal of Human Genetics,* 52: 1032–9.

Bufkin, J. and Luttrell, V. (2005) 'Neuroimaging studies of aggressive and violent behaviour: current findings and implications for criminology and criminal justice', *Trauma, Violence and Abuse,* 6: 176–91.

Budge, I., Crewe, I., MacKay, D. and Newton, K. (1998) *The New British Politics*, Harlow: Longman.

Bull, R. (2010) 'The investigative interviewing of children and other vulnerable witnesses: psychological research and working/professional practice', *Legal and Criminological Psychology*, 15: 5–23.

Burgess, A. (1962) *A Clockwork Orange*. London: Heinemann.

Burke, R. Hopkins (2005) *An Introduction to Criminological Theory*, second edition. Cullompton: Willan Publishing.

Burn, G. (2001) 'Watching Jill', *Guardian* 3 July.

Burns, J. and Swerdlow, R. (2003) 'Right orbitofrontal tumor with pedophilia symptom and constructional apraxia sign', *Archives of Neurology*, 60: 437–40.

Calavita, K. and Pontell, H. N. (1994) 'The state and white-collar crime', *Law and Society Review*, 28: 2.

Cameron, D. and Fraser, E. (1987) *The Lust to Kill: A Feminist Investigation of Sexual Murder*. Oxford: Polity Press.

Campbell, A. (1993) *Out of Control: Men, Women and Aggression*. London: Pandora.

Canter, D. (1994) *Criminal Shadows*. London: HarperCollins.

Cantor, J. M., Kabani, N., Christensen, B. K. *et al.* (2008) 'Cerebral white matter deficiencies in paedophilic men', *Journal of Psychiatric Research,* 4: 167–83.

Carlen, P. (1985) *Criminal Women*. Oxford: Polity Press.

Carlen, P. (1988) *Women, Crime and Poverty*. Milton Keynes: Open University Press.

Cashmore, E. (2001) 'The experience of ethnic minority police officers in Britain: under-recruitment and racial profiling in a performance culture', *Ethnic and Racial Studies*, 24 (4).

Caspi, A., McClay, J., Moffitt, T. E., *et al.* (2002), 'Role of genotype in the cycle of violence in maltreated children', *Science,* 297 (5582): 851–4.

Castells, M. (1996a) *The Information Age*, vol. I: *The Rise of the Network Society*. OxfordBlackwell.

Castells, M. (1996b) *The Information Age*, vol. II: *The Power of Identity*. Oxford: Blackwell.

Cavadino, M. (1992) 'Explaining the Penal Crisis', *Prison Service Journal*, 87.

Cavadino, M. and Dignan, J. (2002) (fourth edition 2007) *The Penal System: An Introduction*, third edition, London: Sage.

Cavanagh, A. (2007) 'Taxonomies of anxiety: risk, panics, paedophila and the Internet', *Electronic Journal of Sociology.*

Cavior, N. and Howard, L. (1973) 'Facial attractiveness and juvenile delinquency among black and white offenders', *Journal of Abnormal Child Psychology*, 1.

Cecil, D. K. (2007) 'Looking beyond caged heat: media images of women in Prison', *Feminist Criminology*, 2 (4): 304–26.

Cernkovich, S. A. and Giordano, P. C. (1987) 'Family relationships and delinquency', *Criminology*, 25: 295–321.

Chambliss, W. J. (1978) *On the Take: From Petty Crooks to Presidents*. Bloomington: Indiana University Press.

Chan, J. (1996) 'Changing police culture', *British Journal of Criminology*, 36: 1.

Chan, J. (1997) *Changing Police Culture: Policing in a Multicultural Society*. Cambridge: University Press.

Chaney, D. (1972) *Processes of Mass Communication*. London: Macmillan.

Chesney-Lind, M. (1989) 'Girls' crime and women's place: toward a feminist world of female delinquency', *Crime and Delinquency*, 35.

Chesney-Lind, M. (1997) *The Female Offender*. Thousand Oaks, CA: Sage.

Chomsky, N. (1989) *Necessary Illusions: Thought Control in Democratic Societies*. Boston: South End Press.

Christiansen, K. (1977) 'A preliminary study of criminality among twins' in S. Mednick and K. Christiansen (eds) *Biosocial Bases of Criminal Behavior*, 89–108. New York: Gardner Press.

Cicchetti, D. and Barnett, D. (1991) 'Attachment organization in maltreated preschoolers', *Development and Psychopathology*, 3: 397–412.

Cicourel, A.V. (1968) (second edition 1976) *The Social Organisation of Juvenile Justice*. New York: Wiley.

Claes, L., Vertommen, H. and Braspenning, N. (2000) 'Psychometric properties of the Dickman Impulsivity Inventory', *Personality and Individual Differences*, 29: 27–35.

Clark, A. (2005) 'Jail bait: rethinking images of incarcerated women', *Bitch* 27: 37–41.

Clark, L. M. G. and Lewis, D. J. (1977) *Rape: The Price of Coercive Sexuality*, Toronto: Women's Press.

Clarke, R. V. (1980) '"Situational" crime prevention: theory and practice', *British Journal of Criminology* 20.

Clegg, N. (2007) 'Justice and liberty: a third way' in J. Margo (ed.) *Beyond Liberty: Is the Future of Liberalism Progressive?* London: IPPR.

Cloninger, C. and Gottesman, I. (1987) 'Genetic and environmental factors in anti-social behaviour disorders' in S. Mednick, T. Moffitt and S. Stack (eds) *The Causes of Crime: New Biological Approaches*. Cambridge: Cambridge University Press.

Cloninger, C., Sigvardsson, S., Bohman, M. and von Knorring, A. (1982) 'Predispositions to petty criminality in Swedish adoptees: II. Cross-fostering analysis of gene-environment interactions', *Archives of General Psychiatry*, 39: 1242–7.

Clough, B. and Mungo, P. (1992) *Approaching Zero: Data Crime and the Computer Underworld*. London: Faber and Faber.

Cloward, R. and Ohlin, L. (1960) *Delinquency and Opportunity*. London: Collier Macmillan.

Coccaro, E., Kavoussi, R., Coper, T. and Hauger, R. (1997) 'Central serotonin activity and aggression: inverse relationship with prolactin response to d-fenfluramine, but not CSF 5-HIAA concebtration in human subjects', *American Journal of Psychiatry*, 154: 1430–5.

Coffey, J. (2000) *Persecution and Toleration in Protestant England, 1558–1689*. Harlow: Longman.

Cohen, A. K. (1955) *Delinquent Boys: The Culture of the Gang*. New York: Free Press.

Cohen, L. E. and Felson, M. (1979) 'Social change and crime rate trends: a routine activity approach', *American Sociological Review*, 44: 588–608.

Cohen, P. C. (1998) *The Murder of Helen Jewett: The Life and Death of a Prostitute in Nineteenth-Century New York*. New York: Alfred A Knopf.

Cohen, S. (1972) (second edition 1980) *Folk Devils and Moral Panics,* London: MacGibbon and Kee.

Cohen, S. (1985) *Visions of Social Control*. Cambridge: Polity Press.

Cohen, S. (1996) 'Human rights and crimes of the state', in Muncie, J., McLaughlin, E. and Langan, M. (eds) *Criminological Perspective: A Reader*. London: Sage.

Cohen, S. and Scull, A. (eds) (1985) *Social Control and the State: Historical and Comparative Essays*. Oxford: Oxford University Press.

Cohen, S. and Young, J. (eds) (1981) *The Manufacture of News*. London: Constable.

Coleman, L. (2004) *The Copycat Effect: How the Media and Popular Culture Trigger the Mayhem in Tomorrow's Headlines*. New York: Simon and Schuster.

Coll, S. and Glasser, S. B. (2005) 'Terrorists turn to the Web as base of operations', *Washington Post*, 7 August.

Collins, D. R. and Bird, R. (2006) 'The penitentiary visit – a new role of geriatricians?' *Age and Ageing*, 36(1): 11–13.

Colman, C. and Moyniham, J. (1996) *Understanding Crime Data: Haunted by the Dark Figure*, Milton Keynes: Open University Press.

Commission for Racial Equality (2003) *Racial Equality in Prisons*. London: CRE.

Cook, D. (1989) *Rich Law, Poor Law: Different Responses to Tax and Supplementary Benefit Fraud*. Milton Keynes: Open University Press.

Cook, P. J. (1980) 'Research in criminal deterrence: laying the groundwork for the second decade' in M. Tonry and N. Morris (eds) *Crime and Justice: An Annual Review of Research*. Chicago: University of Chicago Press.

Conway, M. (2006) 'Terrorism and the Internet: new media – new threat?', *Parliamentary Affairs*, 59 (2): 283–298.

Cornish, D. and Clarke, R. V. (1987) 'Understanding crime application of rational choice theory', *Criminology*, 25: 933–47.

Cornish, D. B. and Clarke, R. V. (2008) 'The rational choice perspective', in Wortley, R. and Mazerolle, L. (eds) *Environmental Criminology and Crime Analysis*. Cullompton: Willan Publishing.

Cosmides, L. and Tooby, J. (eds), (1992) *The Adapted Mind: Evolutionary Psychology and the Generation of Culture*. New York: Oxford University Press, 19–136.

Court, G. (1995) *Women in the Labour Market: Two Decades of Change and Continuity*, IES Report 294. Institute for Employment Studies, London.

Cox, B., Shirley, J. and Short, M. (1977) *The Fall of Scotland Yard*. Harmondsworth: Penguin.

Cox, D., Hallam, R., O'Connor, K. and Rachman, S. (1983) 'An experimental study of fearlessness and courage', *British Journal of Psychology*, 74: 107–17.

Coyle, A. (2005) *Understanding Prisons*. Milton Keynes: Open University Press.

Craig, M. C., Catani, M., Deeley, Q. *et al.* (2009) 'Altered connections on the road to psychopathy', *Molecular Psychiatry*, 14: 946–53.

Crain, C. (2002) 'In Search of Lost Crime', *Legal Affairs*, August (www.legalaffairs.org).

Creaton, H. (2003) 'Recent scholarship on Jack the Ripper and the Victorian media', *Institute of Historical Research, University of London* (www.history.ac.uk).

Critcher, C. (2003) *Moral Panics and the Media*. Milton Keynes: Open University Press.

Croall, H. (1992) *Understanding White Collar Crime*. Milton Keynes: Open University Press.

Croall, H. and Wall, S. (2002) 'Hate crimes', *Criminal Justice Matters*, 48.(1) [PAGE NRS NEEDED]

Crutchfield, R. D. and Kubrin, C. E. (2007) 'Urban crime: are crime rates higher in urban areas, explaining urban crime' (www.law.jrank.org).

Cullen, E. and Newell, T. (1999) *Murderers and Life Imprisonment: Containment, Treatment, Safety and Risk*. Winchester: Waterside Press.

Curran, J. (1977) 'Capitalism and control of the press 1800–1975' in J. Curran, M. Gurevitch and J. Woolacott J (eds) *Mass Communication and Society*. London: Edward Arnold.

Curtis, L. P. (2001) *Jack the Ripper and the London Press*. New Haven, CT: Yale University Press.

Dalgaard, O. and Kringlen, E. (1976) 'A Norwegian twin study of criminality', *British Journal of Criminal Psychology*, 16: 213–32.

Dalton, K. (1961) 'Menstruation and crime', *British Medical Journal*, 2: 1752.

Daly, K. (1989) 'Gender and varieties of white collar crime', *Criminology*, 27 (November).

Daly, M. and Wilson, M. (1988) 'Evolutionary social psychology and family homicide', *Science*, 242: 519–24.

Daly, M. and Wilson, M. (1998) *The Truth about Cinderella*. London: Weidenfeld & Nicolson.

Daly, M. and Wilson, M. (1999) 'Human evolutionary psychology and animal behaviour', *Animal Behaviour*, 57: 509–19.

Daly, M. and Wilson, M. (2002) 'The Cinderella Effect: parental discrimination against stepchildren', *Samfundsøkonomen*, 4: 39–46.

Damasio, A. (2003) *Looking for Spinoza: Joy, Sorrow and the Feeling Brain*. New York: Harvest.

Darwin, C. (1964[1850]) *On the Origin of the Species by Means of Natural Selection: The Preservation of Favoured Races in the Struggle for Life*. Chicago: University of Chicago Press.

Darwin, C. (1871) *The Descent of Man*. London: Murray.

Davidson, R. (2001) 'Towards a biology of personality and emotion', *Annals of the New York Academy of Sciences*, 935: 191–207.

Davies, H., Croall, H. and Tyrer, J. (1998) *Criminal Justice*, second edition. Harlow: Longman.

Davies, R. (2008) 'Low levels of assaults and drug use at Grendon', *Community Care*, 2 September.

Davies, M., Croall, H. and Tyrer, J. (2005) *Criminal Justice: An Introduction to the Criminal Justice System in England and Wales*, third edition. London: Pearson.

Dawkins, R. (1976) *The Selfish Gene*. Oxford: Oxford University Press.

Deno, D. (1996) 'Legal implications of genetics and crime research' in G. Bock and J. Goode (eds) *Genetics of Criminal and Antisocial Behavior*. Chichester: John Wiley & Sons, 248–56.

Dickens, C. (2004 [1897]) *Oliver Twist*. Harmondsworth: Penguin Books.

Dickman, S. J. (1990) 'Functional and dysfunctional impulsivity: personality and cognitive correlates', *Journal of Personality and Social Psychology*, 58: 95–102.

Dignan, J. (2007) 'The victim in restorative justice' in S. Walklate (ed.) *Handbook of Victims and Victimology*. Cullompton: Willan Publishing.

Dobash, R. P. and Dobash, R. E. (1998) *Rethinking Violence Against Women*. London: Sage.

Dobash, R. P., Dobash, R. E. and Gutteridge, S. (1986) *The Imprisonment of Women*. Oxford: Blackwell.

Dobzhansky, T. (1973) 'Nothing in biology makes sense except in the light of evolution', *American Biology Teacher*, 35: 125–9.

Dolan, M., Deakin, W., Roberts, N. and Anderson, L. (2002) 'Serotonergic and cognitive impairments in impulsive aggressive personality disordered offenders: are there implications for treatment?', *Psychological Medicine*, 32: 105–17.

Donovan, P. (2007) 'British justice's shaky history', *New Statesman*, 15 November.

Dorfman, L. (2001) 'Off balance: youth, race and crime in the news', *Building Blocks for Youth* (www.buildingblocksforyouth.org).

Dostoyevsky, F. (1997[1886]) *Crime and Punishment*. Harmondsworth: Penguin Books.

Douglas, K. (2006) 'Are we still evolving?', *New Scientist* 2452, 11 March.

Dowie, M. (1977) 'Pinto madness', reprinted in Hills, S. J. (ed.) *Corporate Violence: Injury and Death for Profit*. Totowa, NJ: Rowman and Littlefield.

Doyle, N. (2005) *Terror Tracker; An Odyssey into Pure Fear*. Edinburgh: Mainstream Publishing.

Draper, R. and Burgess, P. (1989) 'The explanations of violence: The role of biological, behavioural and cultural selection', in Ohlin, L. and Tonry, M. (eds) *Family Violence* Chicago: University of Chicago Press.

Dunbar, R. and Barrett, L. (2010) *Oxford Handbook of Evolutionary Psychology*. Oxford: Oxford University Press.

Durkheim, E. (1960 [1893]) *The Division of Labour in Society*. New York: Free Press.

Durkheim, E. (1964 [1895]) *The Rules of Sociological Method*. New York: Free Press.

Durkheim, E. (1984 [1901]) 'The two laws of penal evolution', in Lukes, S. and Scull, A. (eds) *Durkheim and the Law*, Oxford: Blackwell.

Eaton, M. (1993) *Women after Prison*, Milton Keynes: Open University Press.

Ebstein, R., Novick, O., Umansky, R. *et al.* (1996) 'Dopamine D4 receptor (D4DR) exon iii polymorphism associated with the human personality trait of novelty seeking', *Nature Genetics*, 12: 78–80.

Ebstein, R., Novick, O., Umansky, R. *et al.* (1999) 'Sex differences in the etiology of aggressive and nonaggressive antisocial behavior: results from two twin studies', *Child Development*, 70: 155–68.

Edwards, S. (1989) *Policing domestic violence: Women, the law and the state*, London: Sage.

Einstadter, W. and Henry, S. (1995) *Criminological Theory: An Analysis of its Underlying Assumptions.* Fort Worth, TX: Harcourt Brace College.

Eisenberg, L. (2005) 'Violence and the mentally ill: victims not perpetrators', *Archives of General Psychiatry*, 62: 825–6.

Eley, T., Lichtenstien, P. and Stevenson, J. (1999) 'Sex differences in the etiology of aggressive and non aggressive anti-social behaviour: results from two twin studies'. *Child Development*, 70: 155–68.

Elliott, D. S. and Voss, H. L. (1974) *Delinquency and Dropout.* Lexington, MA: Lexington Books.

Ellis, D. and Austin, P. (1971) 'Menstruation and aggressive behavior in a correctional center for women', *Journal of Criminal Law, Criminology and Police Science*, 62: 388–95.

Ellis, L. (2005) 'A theory explaining biological correlates of criminality', *European Journal of Criminology*, 2: 287–315.

Ellis, T. and Winstone, J. (2001/2002) 'Halliday, sentencers and the National Probation Service', *Criminal Justice Matters*, 46: 20–1.

Emsley, C. (1996) *The English Police: A Political and Social History*, second edition. Harlow: Longman.

Emsley, C. (2003) 'The Birth and Development of the Police' in T. Newburn (ed.) *Handbook of Policing*, Cullompton: Willan Publishing.

Emsley, C. (2005) *Crime and Society in England*, third edition. Harlow: Longman.

Ericson, R., Baranek, P. and Chan, J. (1991) *Representing Order.* Milton Keynes: Open University Press.

Eron, L. D. (1987) 'The development of aggressive behaviour from the perspective of a developing behaviourism', *American Psychologist*, 42: 435–43.

Evansburg, A. (2001) '"But your honour, it's in his genes." The case for genetic impairments as grounds for a downward departure under the federal sentencing guidelines', *American Criminal Law Review*, 38: 1565–87.

Eysenck, H. J. (1974) *Crime and Personality*, third edition. London: Paladin Press.

Eysenck, H. J. (1987) 'Personality theory and the problems of criminality' in B. J. McGurk, D.M. Thornton and M. Williams (eds), *Applying Psychology to Imprisonment: Theory and Practice*. London: HMSO, 29–58.

Eysenck, H. J. and Nias, D. K. B. (1978) *Sex, Violence and the Media.* London: Paladin.

Eysenck, S. B. G. and Eysenck, H. J. (1971) 'Crime and personality: item analysis of questionnaire responses', *British Journal of Criminology*, 11: 49–62.

Faraone, S., Doyle, A., Mick, E. and Diederman, J. (2001) 'Meta-analysis of the association between the dopamine D4 gene seven-repeat allele and attention deficit hyperactivity disorder', *American Journal of Psychiatry*, 158: 1052–7.

Farrington, D. P. (1972) 'Delinquency begins at home', *New Society*, 21: 495–7.

Farrington, D. P. (1992) 'Explaining the beginning, progress, and ending of anti-social behaviour from birth to adulthood' in J. McCord (ed.) *Facts, Frameworks, and Forecasts: Advances in Criminological Theory*, Vol. 3. New Brunswick, NJ: Transactional Publishers.

Farrington, D. P. (1995) 'The development of offending and antisocial behaviour from childhood: key findings in the Cambridge Study in Delinquent Development', *Journal of Child Psychology and Psychiatry*, 36: 929–64.

Farrington, D. P. and Morris, A. (1983) 'Sex, sentencing and reconviction', *British Journal of Criminology*, 23: 229–48.

Farrington, D. P., Barnes, G. C. and Lambert, S. (1996) 'The concentration of offending in families', *Legal and Criminological Psychology*, 1: 47–63.

Fattah, E. A. (1986) 'Prologue on some visible and hidden dangers of the victims movement', in Fattah, E. A. (ed.) *From Crime Policy to Victim Policy*. London: Macmillan.

Faulkner, D. (2001) *Crime, State and Citizen: A Field Full of Folk*, Winchester: Waterside Press.

Ferrell, J. (1999) 'Cultural criminology', *Annual Review of Criminology*, 25: 1.

Ferrell, J. (2001) 'Cultural criminology' in E. McLaughlin and J. Muncie (eds) *Sage Dictionary of Criminology*. London: Sage.

Finlay, L. (1996) 'The pharmaceutical industry and women's reproductive health', in Szockyj, E. and Fox, J. G. (eds) *Invisible Crimes: Their Nature and Control*. London: Macmillan.

Fletcher, J. and Wolfe, B. (2009) 'Long-term consequences of childhood ADHD on criminal activities', *Journal of Mental Health Policy and Economics*, 12: 119–38.

Foglia, W. (2000) *Sigmund Freud: Encyclopaedia of Criminology and Deviant Behaviour*. Blacksburg, VA: Taylor & Francis.

Ford, R. (2007) 'Police "let down" by prison chaos as judges urged to lock up fewer criminals', *The Times*, 25 January.

Ford, R. (2009) 'Police mapping out mission to count every spy camera', *The Times*, 7 March.

Foster, J. (2003) 'Police cultures' in T. Newburn (ed.) *Handbook of Policing*. Cullompton: Willan Publishing.

Foster, J., Newburn, T. and Souhami, A. (2005) *Assessing the Impact of the Stephen Lawrence Inquiry*. London: Home Office.

Foucault, M. (1977) *Discipline and Punish: The Birth of the Prison*. London: Allen Lane.

Foucault, M. (1978) *The History of Sexuality*. London: Penguin.

Fowles, J. (1999) *The Case for Television Violence*. Thousand Oaks, CA: Sage.

Freedman, B. J., Rosenthal, L., Donahoe, C. P. *et al.* (1978) 'A social behavioural analysis of skills deficits in delinquent and non delinquent adolescent boys', *Journal of Consulting and Clinical Psychology*, 46: 1448–62.

Freeman, R. B. (1983) 'Crime and unemployment' in J. Q. Wilson (ed.) *Crime and Public Policy*. San Francisco: ICS Press.

Freud, S. (1953) 'Criminals form a sense of guilt' in S. Freud, *The Standard Edition of the Collected Works of Sigmund Freud*, vol. 14. London: The Hogarth Press, 332–3.

Freund, K. (1994) 'In search of an etiological model of pedophilia', *Sexological Review*, 2: 171–84.

Frigon, S. (1995) 'A genealogy of women's madness', in R. E. Dobash, R. P. Dobash and L. Noaks (eds) *Gender and Crime*. Cardiff: University of Wales Press.

Galen, E. (2000) 'US chemical pollution threatens child health and development', *World Socialist Website*. http://www.wsws.org/articles/2000/oct2000/poll-o06.shtml. Accessed 28 October 2005.

Gao, Y., Raine, A., Venables, P. H., Dawson, M. E. and Mednick, S. A. (2009) 'Association childhood fear conditioning and adult crime', *American Journal of Psychiatry*, November.

Garland, D. (1985) *Punishment and Welfare: A History of Penal Strategies*. Aldershot: Gower.

Garland, D. (1990) *Punishment and Modern Society: A Study in Social Theory*. Oxford: Clarendon.

Garland, D. (1997) 'Of crimes and criminals: the development of criminology in Britain' in M. Maguire, R. Morgan and R. Reiner (eds) *The Oxford Handbook of Criminology*, second edition. Oxford: Oxford University Press.

Garland, D. (1999) Editorial: 'Punishment and society today', *Punishment and Society*, 1: 1.

Garland, D. (2001) *The Culture of Control: Crime and Social Order in Contemporary Society*. Oxford: Clarendon.

Gatrell, V. A. C. (1994) *The Hanging Tree: Execution and the English People, 1770–1868*, Oxford: Clarendon Press.

Gauntlett, D. (2007) 'Ten things wrong with the media "effects" model', www.theory.org.uk

Geis, G. (1967) 'The Heavy Electrical Equipment Antitrust Cases of 1961', in Ermann, M. D. and Lundman, R. (eds) (1992) *Corporate and Governmental Deviance*. Oxford: Oxford University Press.

Gelles, R. (1997) *Intimate Violence in Families*. Thousand Oaks, CA: Sage.

Genders, E. and Player, E. (1989) *Race Relations in Prison*. Oxford: Clarendon Press.

George, C. and West, M. (1999) 'Developmental vs social personality models of adult attachment and mental ill health', *British Journal of Medical Psychology*, 72: 285–303.

Gerber, J. and Weeks, S. L. (1992) 'Women as victims of corporate crime: a case for research on a neglected topic', *Deviant Behaviour*, 13:4.

Gesch, C. B., Hammond, S. M., Hampson, S. E., Eves, A. and, Crowder, M. J. (2002) 'Influence of supplementary vitamins, minerals and essential fatty acids on the antisocial behaviour of young adult prisoners. Randomised, placebo-controlled trial', *British Journal of Psychiatry*, 181: 22–8.

Gibb, F. (2009) 'Judges put on trial to test their courtroom skills', *The Times* 1 September.

Giddens, A. (1984) *The Constitution of Society.* Cambridge: Polity Press.

Giddens, A. (1993) *Sociology*, second edition. Cambridge: Polity Press.

Gilchrist, E. and Blisset, J. (2002) 'Magistrates' attitudes to domestic violence and sentencing', *Howard Journal of Criminal Justice*, 41: 4.

Gill, M. (1999) 'Crimes, victims and workplace', *Criminal Justice Matters*, 35.

Gill, M. and Spriggs, A. (2005) 'Assessing the impact of CCTV', Home Office Research, Development and Statistics Directorate 43. London: Home Office.

Gilligan, C. (1993) *In a Different Voice: Psychological Theory and Women's Development*, second edition. Cambridge, MA: Harvard University Press.

Gilroy, P. (1987) *'There Ain't No Black in the Union Jack': The Cultural Politics of Race and Nation*. London: Hutchinson.

Glasgow University Media Group (1980) *More Bad News*. London: Routledge & Kegan Paul.

Glover, V. and O'Connor, T. (2002) 'Effects of antenatal stress and anxiety: implications for development and psychiatry', *The British Journal of Psychiatry*, 180: 389–91.

Glueck, S. and Glueck, E. (1950) *Unraveling Juvenile Delinquency*. Cambridge, MA: Harvard University Press.

Goddard, H. H. (1914) *Feeble-Mindedness: Its Causes and Consequences*. New York: Macmillan.

Goffman, E. (1968) *Asylums: Essays on the Social Situation of Mental Patients and Other Inmates*. Harmondsworth: Penguin.

Goffman, E. (1969) *The Presentation of Self in Everyday Life*. Harmondsworth: Penguin.

Goode, E. and Ben-Yehuda, N. (1994) *Moral Panics: The Social Construction of Deviance*. Oxford: Blackwell.

Gordon, B. (2008) *The New Ministry of Justice: An Introduction*. London: Waterside Press.

Goring, C. (1913) *The English Convict: A Statistical Study*. London: HMSO.

Gottfredson, M .R. and Hirschi, T. (1990) *A General Theory of Crime*. Stanford, CA: Stanford University Press.

Grace, S. (1995) 'Policing domestic violence in the 1990s'. London: HMSO.

Gramsci, A. (1971) *Selections from the Prison Notebooks*. London: Lawrence and Wishart.

Green, D. A. (2006) 'Public opinion versus public judgment about crime', *British Journal of Criminology,* 46: 131–54.

Greenbaum, R. L., Stevens, S. A., Nash, K., Koren, G. and Rovet, J. (2009) 'Social cognitive and emotion processing abilities of children with fetal alcohol spectrum disorders: A comparison with attention deficit hyperactivity disorder', *Alcoholism: Clinical and Experimental Research,* July 15.

Gregori, J. (ed.) (1998) *What Will Become of US: Counting Down to Y2K*. Academic Freedom Foundation.

Griffiths, J. A. G. (1997) *The Politics of the Judiciary*, fifth edition. London: Fontana.

Grove, T. (2002) 'A light on the lay magistracy', *Criminal Justice Matters*, 49: 24–5.

Grover, C. (2008) *Crime and Inequality*. Cullompton: Willan Publishing.

Groza, V., Ryan, S. D. and Cash, S. J. (2003) 'Institutionalisation, behavior and international adoption: predictors of behavior problems', *Journal of Immigrant Health*, 5 (1): 5–17.

Hagan, J. (1990) 'The structuration of gender and deviance: a power-control theory of vulnerability to crime and the search for deviant role exits', *The Canadian Review of Sociology and Anthropology*, 27 (2): 137–56.

Hagell, A. and Newburn, T. (1994) *Young Offenders and the Media: Viewing Habits and Preferences.* London: Policy Studies Institute.

Hall, C. (2005) 'New look at dangers of drinking in pregnancy', *Daily Telegraph*, 24 October.

Hall, S., Critcher, C., Jefferson T., Clarke, J. and Roberts, B. (1978) *Policing the Crisis: Mugging, the State and Law and Order*. London: Macmillan.

Haralambos, M. and Holborn, M. (2004) *Sociology: Themes and Perspectives*. London: Collins.

Hare, R. D. (1980) 'A research scale for the assessment of psychopathy in criminal populations', *Personality and Individual Differences*, 1: 111–19.

Hare, R. (1996) 'Psychopathy and anti-social personality disorder: a case of diagnostic confusion', *Psychiatric Times*, 13: 39–40. Available at http://www.psychiatrictimes.com/p960239.html. Accessed 28 October 2005.

Harlow, H. (1962) 'The heterosexual affectional system in monkeys', *American Psychologist*, 17: 17–19.

Hart, L. (1994) *Fatal Women: Lesbian Sexuality and the Mark of Aggression*. London: Routledge.

Hart, N. (1993) 'Famine, maternal nutrition and infant mortality: a re-examination of the Dutch Hunger Winter', *Population Studies*, 47: 1.

Hawkings, D. T. (1992) *Criminal Ancestors: A Guide to Historical Criminal Records in England and Wales.* Lewes: Sutton.

Hay, D., Linebaugh, P., Rule, J. G., Thompson, E. P. and Winslow, C. (1975) *Albion's Fatal Tree: Crime and Society in Eighteenth-century England*. London: Allen Lane.

Health and Safety Commission (1997) *Annual Report of Accounts 1996/97*. London: The Stationery Office.

Heidensohn, F. (1996) *Women and Crime*, second edition. Basingstoke: Macmillan.

Heidensohn, F. (1997) 'Gender and crime' in M. Maguire, R. Morgan and R. Reiner (eds) *The Oxford Handbook of Criminology*, second edition. Oxford: Oxford University Press.

Heidensohn, F. (1998) 'Women in policing', *Criminal Justice Matters*, 32.

Heidensohn, F. (2002) 'Gender and crime', in Maguire, M., Morgan, R. and Reiner, R. (eds) *The Oxford Handbook of Criminology*, third edition. Oxford: Oxford University Press.

Henriques, U. R. Q. (1979) *Before the Welfare State: Social Administration in Early Industrial Britain,* Harlow: Longman.

Henslin (2009) *Sociology: A Down-to-Earth Approach*, tenth edition. London: Pearson.

Hentig, H. von (1948) *The Criminal and His Victim*. New Haven, CT: Yale University Press.

Herbert, W. (1997) 'Politics of biology: how the nature vs nurture debate shapes public policy – and our view of ourselves', *US News and World Report*, 27 April. Accessed 28 October 2005.

Herrnstein, R. J. (1995) 'Criminological traits' in J. Q. Wilson and J. Petersilia (eds) *Crime*. San Francisco: ICS Press.

Herrnstein, R. J. and Murray, C. (1994) *The Bell Curve: Intelligence and Class Structure in American Life*. New York: Free Press.

Hills, S. L. (1987) *Corporate Violence: Injury and Death for Profit*. Totowa, NJ: Rowman and Littlefield.

Hillyard, P. and Tombs, S. (2004) 'Beyond Criminology?', in P. Hillyard, C. Pantazis, S. Tombs and D. Gordon (eds) *Beyond Criminology: Taking Crime Seriously*. London: Pluto Press.

Hindelang, M. J., Gottfredson, M. R. and Garofalo, J. (1978) *Victims of Personal Crime: An Empirical Foundation for a Theory of Personal Victimization*. Cambridge, MA: Ballinger.

Hirschi, T. (1969) *Causes of Delinquency*. Berkeley: University of California Press.

Hirschi, T. (1995) 'The family' in J. Q. Wilson and J. Petersilia, *Crime*. San Francisco: San Francisco Institute for Contemporary Studies.

Hirschi, T. and Gottfredson, M. (1994) *The Generality of Deviance*. New Brunswick, NJ: Transaction.

Hirschi, T. and Hindelang, M. J. (1977) 'Intelligence and delinquency: a revisionist review', *American Sociological Review*, 42: 571–87.

Hobsbawm, E. (1964) *Labouring Men*. London: Weidenfeld and Nicolson.

Hoffman, M. L. (1977) 'Moral internalisation: current theory and research' in L. Berkowitz (ed.) *Advances in Experimental Social Psychology*, Vol. 10. New York: Academic Press.

Holdaway, S. (1996) *The Racialisation of British Policing*. London: Macmillan.

Holdaway, S. (1997) 'Some recent approaches to the study of race in criminological research: race as social process', *British Journal of Criminology*, 37: 3.

Hollin, C. (1989) *Psychology and Crime: An Introduction to Criminological Psychology*. London: Routledge.

Hollin, C. R. (1992) *Criminal Behaviour: A Psychological Approach to Explanation and Prevention*. London: The Falmer Press.

Holmes, B. (2005) 'Here's looking at you, chimp', *New Scientist*, 2531.

Holmes, R. M. and Holmes, S. T. (1996) *Profiling Violent Crimes: An Investigative Tool*, second edition. Thousand Oaks, CA: Sage.

Holmlund, C, (2002) *Impossible Bodies: Femininity and Masculinity at the Movies*. London: Routledge.

Home Office (1966) *Inquiry into Prison Escapes and Security* (Mountbatten Report). London: HMSO.

Home Office (1990) *Crime, Justice and Protecting the Public*. London: HMSO.

Home Office (1997) 'A reconviction study of HMP Grendon Therapeutic Community', *Research Findings* 53, Home Office Research and Statistics Directorate.

Home Office (2001) *Making Punishments Work: Report of a Review of the Sentencing Framework* (Halliday Report). London: HMSO.

Home Office (2002) *Protecting the Public: Strengthening Protection Against Sex Offenders and Reforming the Law on Sexual Offences*. London: HMSO.

Hood, R. (1992) *Race and Sentencing*. Oxford: Clarendon Press.

Hooten, E. (1939) *The American Criminal*. Cambridge, MA: Harvard University Press.

Hough, J. M. and Mayhew, P. (1983) *The British Crime Survey*. London: Home Office Research and Statistics Department.

Hough, M. and Roberts, J. V. (1998) *Attitudes to Punishment: Findings from the British Crime Survey*, Home Office Research Study 179. London: Home Office.

Hough, M. and Roberts, J. V. (1999) 'Sentencing trends in Britain', *Punishment and Society*, 1 (1): 11–26.

Howarth, G. and Rock, P. (2000) 'Aftermath and the construction of victimisation: the other victims of crime', *Howard Journal of Criminal Justice*, 39: 1.

Hoyle, C. (1999) *Negotiating Domestic Violence*. Oxford: Clarendon.

Hoyle, C., Young, R. and Hill, R. (2002) *Proceed with caution: an evaluation of the Thames Valley Police Initiative in restorative cautioning*. York: Joseph Rowntree Foundation.

Hucklesby, A. (1993) 'Women, crime and deviance' in S. Jackson and S. Scott, *Women's Studies: A Reader*. London: Harvester Wheatsheaf.

Hudson, B. (2003) *Understanding Justice: An Introduction to Ideas, Perspectives and Controversies in Modern Penal Theory*, second edition. Milton Keynes: Open University Press.

Hughes, R. (2003) *The Fatal Shore: A History of the Transportation of Convicts to Australia 1787–1868*. London: Vintage.

Hughes, P. (1965) *Witchcraft*. Harmondsworth: Penguin.

Hutton, N. (2005) 'Beyond populist punitiveness', *Punishment and Society*, 7: 243–8.

Hyder, K. (1995) 'Black marks', *Police Review*, 14 July.

Hyland, J. (2000) 'British media incites lynch-mob atmosphere over child sex abuse', World Socialist Website (www.wsws.org), 12 August.

Ignatieff, M. (1978) *A Just Measure of Pain: The Penitentiary in the Industrial Revolution, 1750–1850*. London: Macmillan.

Inman, M. (2005) 'Human brains enjoy ongoing evolution', NewScientist.com news service, http://www.newscientist.com/article.ns?id=dn7974. Accessed 4 March 2006.

Innes, M. (2001) '"Crimewatching": homicide investigations in the age of Innocence', *Criminal Justice Matters*, 43: 42–3.

Innes, M. (2003) 'Signal crimes: detective work, mass media and constructing collective memory' in P. Mason (ed.) *Criminal Visions: Media Representations of Crime and Justice*. Cullompton: Willan Publishing.

Institute of Race Relations (2002) *The Criminal Justice System*. www.irr.org.uk.

James, E. (2005) 'Doing time with porridge', *Guardian* 5 October.

James, E. (2007) 'Lost lifers', *Guardian* 17 October.

Jefferson, T. (1990) *The Case against Paramilitary Policing*. Milton Keynes: Open University Press.

Jefferson, T. and Shapland, J. (1990) 'Criminal justice and the production and order of control: trends since 1980 in the UK', paper presented to GERN Seminar on the Production of Order and Control, Paris: CESDIP.

Jeffery, C. R. (1977) *Crime Prevention Through Environmental Design*. Beverly Hills, CA: Sage Publications.

Jenkins, P. (1986) 'From gallows to prison? The execution rate in Early Modern England', *Criminal Justice History*, 7.

Jenkins, P. (2001) *Beyond Tolerance: Child Pornography on the Internet*. New York: New York University Press.

Jensen, P., Mrazek, D., Knapp, P. *et al.* (1997) 'Evolution and revolution in child psychiatry: ADHD as a disorder of adaptation', *Journal of American Child & Adolescent Psychiatry*, vol. 36.

Jewkes, Y. (2004) *Media and Crime*. London: Sage.

Jewkes, Y. (2005) 'High-tech solutions to low-tech crimes? Crime and terror in the surveillance assemblage', *Criminal Justice Matters*, 58.

Jewkes, Y. (2006) 'Creating a stir? Prisons, popular media and the power to reform' in P. Mason (ed.) *Captured by the Media: Prison Discourse in Popular Culture*. Cullompton: Willan Publishing.

Jewkes, Y. (ed.) (2007) *Crime Online*. Cullompton: Willan Publishing.

John, G. (2003) *Race for Justice*. London: Crown Prosecution Service.

Johnson, A. G. (1989) *Human Arrangements: An Introduction to Sociology*. New York: Harcourt Brace Jovanovich.

Jones, H. R. (1894) 'The perils and protection of infant life', *Journal of the Royal Statistical Society*, March.

Jones, S. (2005) 'Darwinism and genes' in J. Stangroom, *What Scientists Think*. London: Routledge.

Jones, S. (2006) *Criminology*. Oxford: Oxford University Press.

Jones, T., McClean, B. and Young, J. (1986) *The Islington Crime Survey*. Aldershot: Gower.

Johnson, J. G. and Smailes, E. (2004) 'Anti-social parental behaviour, problematic parenting and aggressive offspring behaviour during adulthood: a 25-year longitudinal investigation', *British Journal of Criminology*, 44: 915–30.

Johnston, H. (2006) '"Buried alive": representations of the separate system in Victorian England' in P. Mason (ed.) *Captured by the Media: Prison Discourse in Popular Culture*. Cullompton: Willan Publishing.

Jordison, S. and Kieran, D. (eds) (2003) *The Idler Book of Crap Towns*. Boxtree. London

Joseph, J. (2003) *The Gene Illusion: Genetic Research in Psychiatry and Psychology under the Microscope*. Manchester: UK: PCCS Books.

Julien, R. (2007) *A Primer of Drug Action,* eleventh edition. New York: Worth.

Kanazawa, S. (2003a) 'A general evolutionary psychological theory of criminality and related male-typical behaviour' in A. Walsh and L. Ellis (eds) *Biosocial Criminology: Challenging Environmentalism's Supremacy*. Hauppauge, NY: Nova Science.

Kanazawa, S. (2003b) 'Why productivity fades with age: the crime-genius connection', *Journal of Research in Personality*, 37: 257–72, at http://www.lse.ac.uk/collections/methodology Institute/pdf/SKanazawa/JRP2003.pdf.

Karman, A. (1990) *Crime Victims: An Introduction to Victimology*. Pacific Grove, CA: Brookes Cole.

Katz, E. and Lazersfeld, P. (1955) *Personal Influence*. New York: The Free Press.

Katz, L. (2000) *Evolutionary Origins of Morality*. Thorneston: Imprint Academic.

Kempe, C. H. and Kempe, R. E. (1981) *The Battered Child*, second edition. Chicago: University of Chicago Press.

Kerr, D. C. and Lopez, N. L. (2004) 'Parental discipline and externalizing behaviour problems in early childhood: the roles of moral regulation and child gender', *Journal of Abnormal Child Psychology*, 32: 4.

Kershaw, C., Budd, T., Kinshott, G. *et al.* (2000) *The British Crime Survey.* London: HMSO.

Kesey, K. (1962) *One Flew Over the Cuckoo's Nest*. New York: The Viking Press.

Kiehl, K., Smith, A., Hare, R. *et al.* (2001) 'Limbic abnormalities in affective precessing by criminal psychopaths as revealed by functional magnetic resonance imaging', *Biological Psychiatry*, 50: 677–84.

Kinsey, R. (1984) *Merseyside Crime Survey: First Report*. Merseyside Metropolitan Council.

Kirby, A., Woodward, A., Jackson, S. and Crawford, M. A. (2010) 'Children's learning and behaviour and the association with check cell polyunsaturated fatty acid levels', *Research in Development Disabilities,* February.

Kohlberg, L. (1978) 'Revisions in the theory and practice of moral development', *Directions for Child Development*, 2: 83–8.

Krueger, R. F., Schmutte, P. S., Caspi, A. and Moffitt, T. E. (1994) 'Personality traits are linked to crime among men and women', *Journal of Abnormal Psychology*, 103: 328–38.

Kurtzberg, R., Mandell, W., Levin, M. *et al.* (1978) 'Plastic surgery on offenders' in N. Johnston and L. Savitz, *Justice and Corrections*. New York: McGraw-Hill.

Ladd-Taylor, M. and Umansky, L. (1998) *'Bad' Mothers: The Politics of Blame in Twentieth Century America*. New York: New York University Press.

Lahey, B. B., Hart, E. L., Pliszka, S., Applegate, B. and McBurnett, K. (1993) 'Neurophysical correlates of conduct disorder: a rationale and a review', *Journal of Clinical Child Psychology*, 22: 141–53.

Lambert, J. R. (1970) *Crime, Police and Race Relations*. London: Oxford University Press.

Langbein, J. (1983) 'Albion's fatal flaws', *Past and Present*, 98.

Laub, J. H. (1990) 'Patterns of criminal victimization in the United States', in Lurigio, A. J., Skogan, W. G. and Davis, R. C. (eds) *Victims of Crime*. Beverly Hills, CA: Sage.

Lavater, J. (1775) *Physiognomical Fragments*. Leipzig: Weidmann.

Laville, S. (2010) 'Serious and organised crime agency turns spotlight on police corruption', *Guardian* 14 February.

Lawson, W. (2003) 'Fighting crime one bite at a time: diet supplements cut violence in prisons', *Psychology Today*, 22 (1).

Lawton, G. (2004) 'Urban legends', *New Scientist*, 183 (2465), 18 September, 32–5.

Lea, J. and Young, J. (1984) *What Is to Be Done about Law and Order?* Harmondsworth: Penguin.

Learmont Report (1995) *Review of Prison Service Security in England and Wales and the Escape from Parkhurst Prison on Tuesday 3 January 1995*, Cmnd 3020. London: HMSO.

Leech, M. and Cheney, D. (1999) *The Prisons Handbook 2000*. Winchester: Waterside Press.

Leishman, F., Loveday, B. and Savage, S. (eds) (2002) *Core Issues in Policing*, 2nd edn. Harlow: Longman.

Leishman, F. and Mason, P. (2003) *Policing and the Media: Facts, Fictions and Factions*. Cullompton: Willan Publishing.

Lemert, E. M. (1951) *Social Pathology*. New York: McGraw-Hill.

Lemert, E. M. (1967) *Human Deviance, Social Problems and Social Control*. Englewood Cliffs, NJ: Prentice-Hall.

Leonard, M. (1995) 'Masculinity, femininity and crime', *Sociology Review*, 7.

Levenson, J. (2001) 'Inside information: prisons and the media', *Criminal Justice Matters*, 43: 14–15.

Levi, M. (1987) *Regulating Fraud: White Collar Crime and the Process*, London: Tavistock.

Levi, M. (1992) 'White collar crime victimisation', in Schlegel, K. and Weisburd, D. (eds) *White Collar Crime Reconsidered*. Boston: North Eastern University Press.

Lewis, P. (2009) 'Big Brother is watching: surveillance box to track drivers is backed', *Guardian* 31 March.

Lewontin, R., Rose, S. and Kamin, L. (1984) *Not in Our Genes*. London: Penguin.

Liebert, R. M. and Baron, R. A. (1972) 'Some immediate effects of televised violence on children's behaviour', *Developmental Psychology*, 6: 469–75.

Liebling, A. and Price, D. (2001) *The Prison Officer*. London: HM Prison Service.

Lloyd, A. (1995) *Doubly Deviant, Doubly Damned: Society's Treatment of Violent Women*. Harmondsworth: Penguin.

Loeber, R. and Farrington, D. P. (1994) 'Problems and solutions in longitudinal and experimental treatment studies of child psychopathology and delinquency', *Journal of Consulting and Clinical Psychology*, 62: 887–900.

Lombroso, C. (1876) *L'Uomo Delinquente*. Milan: Hoepli.

Lombroso, C. and Ferrero, W. (1920 [1885]) *The Female Offender*. London: Unwin.

Lovatt, P. (2010) Dad dancing. *Dr Peter Lovatt Home Page*. http://dancedrdance.com/DadDancing.aspx. Accessed 18 June 2010.

Lukes, E. (1973) *Emile Durkheim: His Life and Work*. Harmondsworth: Penguin.

Lyon, J. (2002) 'The last resort', *Observer*, 19 May.

Lytton, C. (1988 [1914]) *Prisoners: The Stirring Testimony of a Suffragette*. London: Heinemann.

MacLeod, M. (n.d.) Charles Whitman: the Texas Tower sniper. *Court TV's Crime Library*. http://www.crimelibrary.com/notorious_murders/mass/whitman/index_1.html. Accessed 28 October 2005.

Mackinnon, C. A. (1989) *Towards a Feminist Theory of the State*. Cambridge, MA: Harvard University Press.

Macmillan, M. (1999/2005) The Phineas Gage Information Page. http://www.deakin.edu.au/hbs/GAGEPAGE/index.html. Accessed 10 April 2005.

Macmillan, M. (2000) *An Odd Kind of Fame: Stories of Phineas Gage*. Cambridge, MA: MIT Press.

Macpherson, W. (1999) *The Stephen Lawrence Inquiry. Report of an Inquiry by Sir William Macpherson of Cluny*. London: HMSO.

Maguire, M., Morgan, R. and Reiner, R. (eds) (2002) *The Oxford Handbook of Criminology*, third edition. Oxford: Oxford University Press.

Malleson, K. (1999) *The New Judiciary: The Effects of Expansion and Activism*. Dartmouth: Ashgate.

Margolin, G. and Gordis, E. B. (2000) 'The effect of family and community violence on children', *Annual Review of Psychology*, 51: 445–79.

Martin, C. (1996) 'The impact of equal opportunities policies on the day-to-day experience of women police constables', *British Journal of Criminology*, 36 (1): 510–27.

Martinson, R. (1974) 'What works? Questions and answers about prison reform', *The Public Interest*, 35: 22–54.

Marsh, I., Melville, G., Morgan, K., Norris, G. and Walkington, Z. (2006) *Theories of Crime*. London: Routledge.

Martens, W. (2002) 'Criminality and moral dysfunctions: neurological, biochemical, and genetic dimensions', *International Journal of Offender Therapy and Comparative Criminology*, 46: 170–82.

Mason, P. (2001) 'Courts, cameras and genocide', *Criminal Justice Matters*, 43: 36–8.

Mason, P. (ed.) (2003) *Criminal Visions: Media Representations of Crime and Justice*. Cullompton: Willan Publishing.

Mason, P. (ed.) (2006) *Captured by the Media: Prison Discourse in Popular Culture*. Cullompton: Willan Publishing.

Mathews, R. (1999) *Doing Time: An Introduction to the Sociology of Imprisonment*, London: Palgrave.

Matza, D. (1964) *Delinquency and Drift*. New York: Wiley.

Mawby, R. (2001) 'Promoting the police? The rise of police image work', *Criminal Justice Matters*, 43: 44–5.

Mawby, R. (2003) 'Completing the 'half-formed picture'? Media images of policing' in P. Mason (ed.) *Criminal Visions: Media Representations of Crime and Justice*. Cullompton: Willan Publishing.

Mawby, R. and Walklate, S. (1994) *Critical Victimology: International Perspectives*. London: Sage.

Mayhew, P., Elliott, D. and Dowds, L. (1989) *The 1988 British Crime Survey*. London: HMSO.

Mayr, E. (1982) *The Growth of Biological Thought: Diversity, Evolution, and Inheritance*. Cambridge, MA: Belknap Press.

McCahill, M. and Norris, C. (2003) 'Estimating the extent, sophistication and legality of CCTV in London' in M. Gill (ed.) *CCTV*. Leicester: Perpetuity.

McCord, J. (1979) 'Some child-rearing antecedents of criminal behaviour in adult men', *Journal of Personality and Social Psychology*, 37: 1477–86.

McCord, J. (1982) 'A longitudinal view of the relationship between parental absence and crime' in J. Gunn and D. P. Farrington (eds) *Abnormal Offenders, Delinquency and the Criminal Justice System*, Vol. 1. Chichester: Wiley.

McDermott, K. (1990) 'We have no problems: the experience of racism in prison', *New Community*, 16: 2.

McDermott, R., Tingley, D., Cowden, J., Frazzetto, G. and Johnson, D. P. (2009) 'Monoamine oxidase A gene (MAOA) predicts behavioural aggression following provocation', *Proceedings of the National Academy of Sciences*, January 23.

McEwen, B. (1999) 'Development of the cerebral cortex XIII: Stress and brain development – II', *Journal of the Academy of Child and Adolescent Psychiatry*, 38: 101–3.

McGinn, L. K. (2000) 'Cognitive behavioral therapy of depression: theory, treatment, and empirical status', *American Journal of Psychotherapy*, 54: 254–60.

McGowan, R. (1998) 'The well-ordered prison: England, 1780–1865', in Morris, N. and Rothman, D. J. (eds) *The Oxford History of the Prison: The Practice of Punishment in Western Society*. Oxford: Oxford University Press.

McGurk, B. J. and McDougall, C. (1981) 'A new approach to Eysenck's theory of criminal personality', *Personality and Individual Differences*, 2: 338–40.

McKinlay, A., Grace, R., Horwood, J., Fergusson, D. and McFarlane, M. (2009) 'Adolescent psychiatric symptoms following preschool childhood mild traumatic brain injury: evidence from a birth cohort', *Journal of Head Trauma Rehabilitation*, 24 (3): 221–7.

McLaughlin, E. (1996) 'Political violence, terrorism and crimes of the state', in Muncie, J. and McLaughlin, E. (eds) *Social Problems and the Family*. Milton Keynes: Open University Press.

McLaughlin, E., Fergusson, R., Hughes, G. and Westmarland, L. (eds) (2003) *Restorative Justice: Critical Issues*. London: Sage.

McLaughlin, E. and Muncie, J. (eds) (1996). *Controlling Crime*. London: Sage.

McLean, G. (2005) 'In the hood', *Guardian* 13 May.

McMillan, T. and Rachman, S. (1987) 'Fearlessness and courage: a laboratory study of paratrooper veterans of the Falklands war', *British Journal of Psychology*, 78: 375–83.

McNally, R. (1995) 'Homicidal youth in England and Wales 1982–1992: profile and policy', *Psychology, Crime and Law*, 1: 333–42.

Meadow, R. (ed.) (2000) *The ABC of Child Abuse*. London: BMA.

Mealey, L. (1995) 'The sociobiology of sociopathy: an integrated evolutionary model', *Behavioral and Brain Science*, 18: 523–99.

Mealey, L. (1999) 'The multiplicity of rape: from life history strategies to prevention strategies', *Jurimetrics Journal*, 39: 217–26.

MedlinePlus (2005) Pregnancy and substance abuse. http://www.nlm.nih.gov/medlineplus/pregnancy andsubstanceabuse.html. Last accessed 29 October 2005.

Mednick, S., Gabrielli, W. and Hutchings, B. (1984) 'Genetic factors in the etiology of criminal behaviour' in S. Mednick, T. Moffitt and S. Stack (eds) *The Causes of Crime: New Biological Approaches*. Cambridge: Cambridge University Press, 74–91.

Melossi, D. and Pavarini, M. (1981) *The Prison and the Factory: Origins of the Penitentiary System*. Basingstoke: Macmillan.

Mendelsohn, B. (1963) 'The origin and doctrine of victimology' in P. Rock (ed.) *Victimology*. Aldershot: Dartmouth.

Mendez, M., Chow, T., Ringman, J., Twitchell, G. and Hinkin, C. (2000) 'Pedophilia and temporal lobe disturbances', *Journal of Neuropsychiatry and Clinical Neuroscience*, 12: 71–6.

Merton, R. K. (1938) 'Social structure and anomie', *American Sociological Review*, 3: 672–82.

Meyers, M. (1997) *News Coverage of Violence Against Women: Engendering Blame.* Thousand Oaks, CA: Sage.

Miers, D. (1978) *Responses to Victimisation.* Abingdon: Professional Books.

Miers, D. (1989) 'Positivist victimology', *International Review of Victimology*, 2: 29–59.

Miers, D. (1990) 'Victimology: a critique', *International Review of Victimology*, 3.

Miethe, T. D., Stafford, M. C. and Long, J. S. (1987) 'Social differentiation in criminal victimisation: a test of routine activities/lifestyle theories', *American Sociological Review*, 52: 184–94.

Milband, R. (1973) *The State in Capitalist Society.* Harmondsworth: Penguin.

Milgram, S. (1983) *Obedience to Authority: An Experimental View.* New York: HarperCollins.

Miller, B., Darby, A., Benson, D., Cummings, J. and Miller, M. (1997) 'Aggressive, socially disruptive and antisocial behaviour associated with frontotemporal dementia', *British Journal of Psychiatry*, 170: 150–5.

Miller, G. (2001) *The Mating Mind.* London: Vintage.

Miller, W. (1958) 'Lower class culture as a generalising milieu of gang delinquency', *Journal of Social Issues*, 14: 3.

Mills, C. W. (1970) *The Sociological Imagination.* Harmondsworth: Penguin.

Ministry of Justice (2009) *Statistics on Race and the Criminal Justice System 2007/8.* London: HMSO.

Ministry of Justice (2010) *Statistics on Women and the Criminal Justice System.* Home Office: Ministry of Justice.

Mirels, H. L. (1970) 'Dimensions of internal and external control', *Journal of Consulting and Clinical Psychology*, 34: 226–8.

Mirlees-Black, C., Mayhew, P. and Percy, A. (1996) *The 1996 British Crime Survey.* London: HMSO.

Moffitt, T. E. (1990) 'Juvenile delinquency and attention deficit disorder: boys' development trajectories from age 13 to age 15', *Child Development*, 61: 893–910.

Moffitt, T. E. (1993) 'Adolescence-limited and life-course-persistent antisocial behaviour: a developmental taxonomy', *Psychological Review*, 100: 674–701.

Moffitt, T., Bramner, G., Caspi, A. *et al.* (1998) 'Whole blood serotonin relates to violence in an epidemiological study', *Biological Psychiatry*, 43: 446–57.

Moiré, A. and Jessel, D. (1997) *Brainsex: Real Difference Between Men and Women.* London: Mandarin.

Moore, L. (2000) *Conmen and Cutpurses: Scenes from the Hogarthian Underworld.* London: Penguin.

Moore, S. C., Carter, L. M. and van Goozen, S. H. M. (2009) 'Confectionery consumption in childhood and adult violence', *British Journal of Psychiatry*, 195 (4): 366–7.

Morgan, K. and Norris, G. (2010) 'An exploration into the relevance of Dickman's functional and dysfunctional impulsivity dichotomy for understanding ADHD-type behaviors', *Individual Differences Research* 8 (1): 34–44.

Morgan, R. (2002) 'Imprisonment: A brief history, the contemporary scene and likely prospects', in M. Maguire, R. Morgan and R. Reiner (eds) *The Oxford Handbook of Criminology*, third edition. Oxford: Oxford University Press.

Morgan, R. and Liebling, A. (2007) 'Imprisonment and expanding scene' in M. Maguire, R. Morgan and R. Reiner R (eds) *The Oxford Handbook of Criminology*, fourth edition. Oxford: Oxford University Press.

Morgan, R. and Newburn, T. (1997) *The Future of Policing*, Oxford: Oxford University Press.

Morley, R. and Mullender, A. (1994) 'Preventing domestic violence to women', Crime Prevention Unit, Paper 48. London: Home Office Police Department.

Morris, N. and Rothman, D. J. (eds) (1998) *The Oxford History of the Prison: The Practice of Punishment in Western Society*. Oxford: Oxford University Press.

Motluk, A. (2004) 'Life sentence', *New Scientist*, 2471.

Mulley, K. (2001) 'Victimized by the media', *Criminal Justice Matters,* 43: 30–1.

Muncie, J. (1996) 'Prison histories: reform, repression and rehabilitation', in E. McLaughlin and J. Muncie (eds) *Controlling Crime*, London: Sage.

Murray, C. (1990) *The Emerging Underclass*. London: Institute of Economic Affairs.

Naffine, N. (1981) 'Theorizing about female crime' in S. Mukherjee and J. A. Scutt (eds) *Women and Crime*. North Sydney: Allen & Unwin.

Naffine, N. (1987) *Female Crime: The Construction of Women in Criminology*. Boston: Allen & Unwin.

Naffine, N. (1997) *Feminism and Criminology*. Cambridge: Polity Press.

Naylor, B. (2001) 'Reporting violence in the British Print Media: Gendered Stories', *Howard Journal of Criminal Justice,* 40 (2): 180–94.

Nelken, D. (2007) 'White collar and corporate crime' in M. Maguire, R. Morgan and R. Reiner (eds) *The Oxford Handbook of Criminology*. Oxford: Oxford University Press.

Newburn, T. (2007) *Criminology*. Cullompton: Willan Publishing.

Newburn, T. (ed.) (2003) *A Handbook of Policing*. Cullompton. Devon: Willan Publishing.

Newburn, T. and Hayman, S. (2001) 'Keeping Watch', *Police Review*, 5 October.

Newburn, T. and Reiner, T. (2007) 'Policing and the Police', in M. Maguire, R. Morgan and T. Reiner, (eds) *The Oxford Handbook of Criminology*, fourth edition. Oxford: Oxford University Press.

Newson, J., Newson, E. and Adams, M. (1993) 'The social origins of delinquency', *Criminal Behaviour and Mental Health*, 3: 19–29.

Nicholas, S., Kershaw, C. and Walker, A. (2007) *The British Crime Survey 2006–2007*. London: HMSO.

Nisbet, R. (1970) *The Sociological Tradition*. London: Heinemann.

Nozick, R. (1981) *Philosophical Explanations*. Oxford: Clarendon Press.

Oakley, A. (1972) *Sex, Gender and Society*. London: Temple Smith.

Orwell, G. (1989[1949]) *1984*. Harmondsworth: Penguin.

Parens, E. (2004) *Genetic Differences and Human Identities*. A supplement to the Hastings Centre Report, January–February.

Parker, D. (1996) *Fighting Computer Crime*. New York: Wiley Computer Publishing.

Parker, H., Sumner, M. and Jarvis, G. (1989) *Unmasking the Magistrates*. Milton Keynes: Open University Press.

Parsons, T. (1951) *The Social System*. London: Routledge & Kegan Paul.

Pashukanis, P. (1978) *Law and Marxism: A General Theory*. London: Ink Links.

Passer, M. W. and Smith, R. E. (2001) *Psychology: Frontiers and Applications*. Boston, MA: McGraw-Hill.

Patterson, G. R. and Dishion, T. J. (1985) 'Contributions of families and peers to delinquency', *Criminology*, 23: 63–79.

Pavlac, B. A. (2006) 'Ten general historical theories about the origins and causes of the witch hunts', *Prof Pavlac's Women's Historical Resource Site* (www.departments.kings.educ/womens_history).

Pavlov, I.V. (1960) *Conditional Reflexes*. New York: Dover.

Peak, S. (ed.) (2003) *The Media Guide*. London: Guardian Books.

Pearce, F. (1990) *Second Islington Crime Survey: Commercial and Conventional Crime in Islington*. London: Middlesex Polytechnic, Centre for Criminology.

Pearce, F. and Tombs, S. (1998) *Toxic Capitalism: Corporate Crime and the Chemical Industry*. Aldershot: Ashgate.

Pearce, F. (1976) *Crimes of the Powerful*. London: Pluto Press.

Pearson, G. (1983) *Hooligan: A History of Respectable Fears*. London: Macmillan.

Pearson, J. (1972) *The Profession of Violence: The Rise and Fall of the Kray Twins*. London: Weidenfeld & Nicolson.

Pellegrini, A. and Bartini, M. (2001) 'Dominance in early adolescent boys: affiliative and aggressive dimensions and possible functions', *Merrill-Palmer Quarterly*, 47: 142–63.

Pennington, B. and Bennetto, L. (1993) 'Main effects or transactions in the neuropsychology of conduct disorder? Commentary on "The neuropsychology of conduct disorder"', *Development and Psychopathology*, 5: 153–64.

Perron, B. E. and Howard, M. O. (2008) 'Prevalence and correlates of traumatic brain injury among delinquent youths', *Criminal Behaviour and Mental Health*, 18 (4): 243–55.

Perry, S. and Dawson, J. (1985) *Nightmare: Women and the Dalkon Shield*, New York: Macmillan.

Peters, E. M. (1998) 'Prison before the prison: the ancient and medieval worlds', in N. Morris and D. J. Rothman (eds) *The Oxford History of the Prison: The Practice of Punishment in Western Society*. Oxford: Oxford University Press.

Phillips, C. and Bowling, B. (2007) 'Ethnicities, racism, crime and criminal justice' in M. Maguire, R. Morgan and R. Reiner (eds) *The Oxford Handbook of Criminology*, fourth edition. Oxford: Oxford University Press.

Phillips, D. (1983) 'A just measure of crime, authority, hunters and blue locusts: the "revisionist" social history of crime and law in Britain, 1780–1850', in S. Cohen and A. Scull (eds) *Social Control and the State: Historical and Comparative Essays*. Oxford: Oxford University Press.

Phoenix, J. (1999) *Making Sense of Prostitution*. London: Methuen.

Pinker, S. (2005) 'Evolutionary psychology and the blank slate' in J. Stangroom (ed.), *What Scientists Think*. London: Routledge.

Pizzey, E. (1974) *Scream Quietly or the Neighbours Will Hear*. Harmondsworth: Penguin.

Pollak, O. (1950) *The Criminality of Women*. New York: A. S. Barnes.

Pollard, C. (1998) 'Keeping the Queen's Peace', *Criminal Justice Matters*, 31: 14–16.

Poole, M. (1994) 'A critique of aspects of the philosophy and theology of Richard Dawkins', *Science and Christian Belief*, 6: 41–59.

Povery, D., Coleman, C., Kaiza, P., Hoare, J. and Jansson, K. (2008) 'Homicide, firearm offences and intimate violence', Home Office Statistical Bulletin, London: HMSO.

Power, M. J., Alderson, M. R., Phillipson, C. M. and Morris, J. N. (1967) 'Delinquent schools?' *New Society*, 10: 542–3.

Price, D. (2000) 'The origins and durability of security categorisation: a study in penological pragmatism or Spies, Dickie and Prison Security', in *British Criminology Conference: Selected Proceedings*, vol. 3 (edited by G. Mair and R. Tarling), Liverpool.

Priestley, P. (1985) *Victorian Prison Lives: English Prison Biography, 1830–1914*. London: Methuen.

Punch, M. (1996) *Dirty Business: Exploring Corporate Misconduct*. London: Sage.

Punch, M. (2009) *Police Corruption*. Cullompton: Willan Publishing.

Quay, H. C. (1987) 'Intelligence' in H. C. Quay (ed.) *Handbook of Juvenile Delinquency*. New York: Wiley.

Quinney, R. (1971) 'Who is the victim?', *Criminology*, November.

Quinney, R. (1977) *Class, State and Crime*. Harlow: Longman.

Quist, J., Barr, C., Schachar, R. *et al.* (2000) 'Evidence for the serotonin HTR2A receptor gene as a susceptiblilty factor in attention deficit hyperactivity disorder (ADHD)', *Molecular Psychiatry*, 5: 537–41.

Radzinowicz, L. (1968) *A History of the English Criminal Law*, vol. 4. London: Stevens.

Rafter, N. (2006) *Shots in the Mirror: Crime Films and Society.* New York: Oxford University Press.

Rafter, N. and Heidensohn, F. (eds) (1995) *International Feminist Perspectives in Criminology: Engendering a Discipline*. Buckingham and Philadelphia: Open University Press.

Rafter, N. H. (1983) 'Chastising the unchaste: social control functions of a women's reformatory, 1894–1931', in S. Cohen and A. Scull (eds) *Social Control and the State: Historical and Comparative Essays*, Oxford: Oxford University Press.

Raine, A. (1993) *The Psychopathology of Crime*. New York: Academic Press.

Raine, A. (2002a) 'Annotation: the role of prefrontal deficits, low autonomic arousal, and early health factors in the development of antisocial and aggressive behaviour in children', *Journal of Child Psychology and Psychiatry*, 43: 417–34.

Raine, A. (2002b) 'Biosocial studies of antisocial and violent behaviour in children and adults: a review', *Journal of Abnormal Child Psychology*, 30: 311–26.

Raine, A., Lencz, T., Taylor, K. *et al.* (2003b) 'Corpus callosum abnormalities in psychopathic antisocial individuals', *Archives of General Psychiatry*, 60: 1134–42.

Raine, A., Mellingen, K., Liu, J., Venables, P. and Mednick, S. (2003a) 'Effects of environmental enrichment at age 3–5 years on schizotypal personality and antisocial behavior at ages 17 and 23 years', *American Journal of Psychiatry*, 160: 1–9.

Rankin, J. H. and Kern, R. (1994) 'Parental attachments and delinquency', *Criminology*, 32: 495–515.

Rawlings, P. (1999) *Crime and Power: A History of Criminal Justice, 1688–1998*. Harlow: Longman.

Rawlings, P. (2002) *Policing: A Short History*, Cullompton. Devon: Willan Publishing.

Rawlings, P. (2003) 'Policing before the police' in T. Newburn (ed.) *Handbook of Policing*. Cullompton: Willan Publishing.

Raynor, P. (2007) 'Community penalties; probation, "what works" and offender management' in M. Maguire, R. Morgan and R. Reiner (eds) *The Oxford Handbook of Criminology*, fourth edition. Oxford: Oxford University Press.

Reid, I. and Wormald, E. (1982) *Sex Differences in Britain*. London: Grant MacIntyre.

Reiner, R. (1993) 'Race, crime and justice: models of interpretation' in L. Gelsthorpe and W. McWilliams (eds) *Minority Ethnic Groups and the Criminal Justice System*. Cambridge: University of Cambridge Institute of Criminology.

Reiner, R. (1994) 'The dialectics of Dixon' in M. Stephens and S. Becker (eds) *Police Force, Police Service*. London: Macmillan.

Reiner, R. (1997) 'Policing and the Police', in Maguire, M., Morgan, R. and Reiner, R. (eds) *The Oxford Handbook of Criminology*, second edition, Oxford: Oxford University Press.

Reiner, R. (2000) *The Politics of the Police*, third edition. Oxford: Oxford University Press.

Reiner, R., Livingstone, S. and Allen, J. (2003) 'From law and order to lynch mobs: crime news since the Second World War' in P. Mason (ed.) *Criminal Visions: Media Representations of Crime and Justice*. Cullompton: Willan Publishing.

Reith, C. (1938) *The Police Idea*. Oxford: Oxford University Press.

Reith, C. (1943) *British Police and the Democratic Idea*. Oxford: Oxford University Press.

Renzetti, C. M. (2011) *Feminist Criminology*. London: Routledge.

Ressler, R. K., Burgess, A.W. and Douglas, J. E. (1988) *Sexual Homicide: Patterns and Motives*. New York: Lexington Books.

Revere, C. (1999) 'Ticking bomb baby', *Tucson Citizen*, 29 April. Available at http://www.comeover.to/FAS/Citizen/part3_5.html.

Rex, J. and Moore, R. (1967) *Race, Community and Conflict*. Oxford: Oxford University Press.

Rhee, S. and Waldman, I. (2002) 'Genetic and environmental influences on antisocial behaviour: a meta-analysis of twin and adoption studies', *Psychological Bulletin*, 128: 490–529.

Ridley, M. (1996) *The Origins of Virtue*. London: Viking.

Robson Rhodes, R. M. S. (2004) *Home Office Economic Crime Survey*. London: Home Office.

Roberts, J. V. and Hough, M. (2005) *Understanding Public Attitudes to Criminal Justice*. Milton Keynes: Open University Press.

Rock, P. (1990) *Helping the Victims of Crime*. Oxford: Clarendon Press.

Rock, P. (1999) 'Acknowledging victims' Needs and Rights', *Criminal Justice Matters*, 35.

Rock, P. (2007) 'Sociological theories of crime', in M. Maguire, R. Morgan and R. Reiner (eds) *The Oxford Handbook of Criminology*, fourth edition. Oxford: Oxford University Press.

Rose, D. (2002) 'It's official: prison does work after all', *Observer*, 5 May.

Rose, D. (2003) 'Our jails are full to bursting', *The Observer*, 9 February.

Rose, L. (1986) *Massacre of the Innocents: Infanticide in Great Britain 1800–1939*. London: Routledge & Kegan Paul.

Rose, S. (1997) *The Mismeasure of Man*, second edition. Harmondsworth: Penguin Science.

Rose, S. (2003a) *Lifelines: Life Beyond the Gene*. Oxford: Oxford University Press.

Rose, S. (2003b) 'Belief.' Transcript of Radio 3 programme broadcast 23/12/03. http://www.bbc.co.uk/religion/programmes/belief/scripts/steven_rose.shtml. Last accessed 12 November 2004.

Rosenham, D. L. (1973) 'On being sane in insane places', *Science*, 179: 250–8.

Ross, R. and Fabiano, E. (1985) *The Time to Think: A Cognitive Model of Delinquency Prevention and Offender Rehabilitation*. Johnson City: Institute of Social Sciences and Arts.

Rossi, P. H., Berk, R. A. and Lenihan, K. J. (1980) *Money, Work and Crime: Experimental Evidence*. New York: Academic Press.

Rotter, J. B. (1975) 'Some problems and misconceptions related to the construct of internal versus external control of reinforcement', *Journal of Consulting and Clinical Psychology*, 43: 56–67.

Rowe, D. (2002) *Biology and Crime*. Los Angeles: Roxbury.

Rowe, D., Stever, D., Chase, S., Sherman, A., Abramowitz, A. and Waldman, I. (2001) 'Two dopamine genes related to reports of childhood retrospective inattention and conduct disorder', *Molecular Psychiatry*, 6: 429–33.

Rowe, M. (ed.) (2007) *Policing Beyond MacPherson: Issues in Policing, Race and Society*. Cullompton: Willan Publishing

Runnymede Trust (2008) *A Tale of Two Englands : 'Race' and Violent Crime in the Press*. Runnymede Trust, 29 April.

Runnymede Trust (2009) *The Stephen Lawrence Inquiry 10 Years On*. London: Runnymede Trust.

Rusche, G. and Kirchheimer, O. (1939) *Punishment and Social Structure*. New York: Columbia University Press.

Rutter, M. (1971) 'Parent–child separation: psychological effects on the children', *Journal of Child Psychology and Psychiatry*, 12: 233–60.

Rutter, M. and Giller, H. (1983) *Juvenile Delinquency: Trends and Perspectives*. Harmondsworth: Penguin.

Rybrant, L. and Kramer, R. (1995) 'Hybrid nonwomen and corporate violence: the silicone implant case', *Violence against Women*, 1: 3.

Rymer, S. (1993) *Genie: A Scientific Tragedy*. New York: Harper Perennial.

Saladin, M., Saper, Z. and Breen, L. (1988) 'Perceived attractiveness and attributions of criminality: what is beautiful is not criminal', *Canadian Journal of Criminology*, 30: 251–9.

Salmon, C. A. and Shackleford, T. K. (2007) *Family Relationships: An Evolutionary Perspective*. Oxford: Oxford University Press.

Sampson, R. (2007) 'Old inside', Prison Reform Trust (www.prisonreformtrust.org).

Sanders, A. and Young, R. (2000) *Criminal Justice*, second edition. London: Butterworth.

Scarman Report (1982) *The Brixton Disorders, 10–12 April 1981: Report of an Enquiry by the Rt Hon. Lord Scarman.* London: HMSO.

Schelsinger, P. and Tumbler, H. (1992) 'Crime and criminal justice in the media' in D. Downes (ed.) *Unravelling Criminal Justice.* London: Macmillan.

Schiffer, B., Peschel, T., Paul, T. *et al.* (2007) 'Structural brain abnormalities in the frontostriatal system and cerebellum in paedophilia', *Journal of Psychiatric Research,* 41 (9): 753–62.

Schmid, D. (2005) *Natural Born Celebrities.* Chicago: University of Chicago Press.

Schore, A. N. (1997) 'Interdisciplinary developmental research as a source of clinical models' in M. Moskowitz, C. Monk, C. Kaye and S. Ellman (eds) *The Neurobiological and Developmental Basis for Psychotherapeutic Intervention.* Northvale, NJ: Jason Aronson.

Schwartz, T. (1999) *Millennium Bomb.* New Brunswick, NJ: Global Communications.

Scraton, P., Sim, J. and Skidmore, P. (1991) *Prisons under Protest.* Milton Keynes: Open University Press.

Seager, J. (2003) *The Atlas of Women.* London: The Women's Press.

Seago, P., Walker, C. and Wall, D. (2000) 'The professionalisation of local courts' justice', *Criminal Justice Matters,* 38.

Seaton, J. (1981) 'Broadcasting history' in J. Curran and J. Seaton, *Power Without Responsibility: The Press and Broadcasting in Britain.* London: Fontana.

Segerstråle, U. (2000) *Defenders of the Truth: The Battle for Science in the Sociobiology Debate and Beyond.* Oxford: Oxford University Press.

Sennett, R. (1977) *The Fall of Public Man.* London: Faber.

Sharpe, J. A. (1995) *Early Modern England: A Social History 1550–1750*, second edition. London: Oxford University Press

Sharpe, J. A. (1999) *Crime in Early Modern England 1550–1750*, second edition. Harlow: Longman

Shaw, C. S. and McKay, H. D. (1942) *Juvenile Delinquency and Urban Areas.* Chicago: University of Chicago Press.

Sheldon, W. H. (1949) *Varieties of Delinquent Youth.* New York: Harper.

Shute, S., Hood, R. and Seemungal, F. (2005) *A Fair Hearing? Ethnic Minorities in the Criminal Courts.* Cullompton: Willan Publishing.

Siegel, L. (1992) *Criminology*, fourth edition. St Paul, MN: West Publishing.

Simon, R. (1975) *Women and Crime.* Toronto: Lexington Books.

Skinner, B. F. (1974) *About Behaviourism.* New York: Knopf.

Slutske, W., Heath, A. C., Dinwiddie, S. H. and Madden, P. (1997) 'Modelling genetic and environmental influences in the etiology of conduct disorder: a study of 2,682 adult twin pairs', *Journal of Abnormal Psychology*, 106: 266–79.

Smart, C. (1976) *Women, Crime and Criminology: A Feminist Critique.* London: Routledge & Kegan Paul.

Smith, B. L. (1985) 'Trends in the victims' rights movement and implications for future research', *Victimology*, 10.

Smith, D. and Gray, J. (1983) *Police and People in London.* London: Policy Studies Institute (PSI).

Snell, J. E., Rosenwald, R. J. and Robey, A. (1964) 'The wife beater's wife: a study of family interaction', *Archives of General Psychiatry*, 11.

Solomon, E. (2005) 'Is the press the real power behind punitivism?' *Criminal Justice Matters,* 59: 34–5.

Sparks, R. (2001) 'The media, populism, public opinion and crime', *Criminal Justice Matters,* 43: 6–7.

Sparks, R. F. (1996) 'Prisons, punishment and penality', in E. McLaughlin and J. Muncie (eds) *Controlling Crime*. London: Sage.

Sparks, R. F., Genn, D. and Dodd, D. J. (1977) *Surveying Victims*, Chichester: John Wiley.

Stanford, P. (2009) 'Is this Britain's most successful prison?', *The Independent*, 7 March.

Stanko, E. (1990) *Everyday Violence*. Pandora: London.

Stanley, E. (1990) *Feminist Praxis: Research, Theory and Epistemology in Feminist Research*. London: Routledge.

Stangroom, J. (2005) 'Introduction' in J. Stangroom, *What Scientists Think*. London: Routledge.

Stedman Jones, G. (1984) *Outcast London. A Study in the Relationship between Classes in Victorian Society*. Harmondsworth: Penguin.

Steffensmeier, D. J. (1978) 'Crime and the contemporary woman: an analysis of changing levels of female property crime 1960–1975', *Social Forces*, December, 566–84.

Steffensmeier, D. J. and Allan, E. (1996) 'Gender and crime: toward a gendered theory of female offending', *Annual Review of Sociology*, 22: 459–87.

Steffensmeier, D. J. and Steffensmeier, R. H. (1980) 'Trends in female delinquency', *Criminology*, 18: 62–85.

Steinberg, L. (2010) 'A behavioural scientist looks at the science of adolescent brain development', *Brain and Cognition*, 72: 160–64.

Steinberg, L. and Morris, A. S. (2001) 'Adolescent development', *Annual Review of Psychology*, 52: 83–110.

Stepniak, D. (2003) 'British justice: not suitable for public viewing' in P. Mason (ed.) *Criminal Visions: Media Representations of Crime and Justice*. Cullompton: Willan Publishing.

Stevens, P. and Willis, C. (1979) *Race, Crime and Arrests*. London: HMSO.

Storch, R. D. (1975) 'The plague of blue locusts: police reform and popular resistance in northern England, 1840–57', *International Review of Social History*, 20.

Strauss, M. A. (1980) 'Sexual inequality and wife beating', in M. A. Strauss and G. T. Hotaling (eds) *The Social Causes of Husband–Wife Violence*. Minneapolis: University of Minnesota Press.

Strinati, D. (1992) 'Postmodernism and popular culture', *Sociology Review*, April.

Strong, B. and DeVault, C. (1995) *The Marriage and Family Experience*, sixth edition. St Paul: West.

Sutherland, E. H. (1960) *White Collar Crime*. New York: Holt, Rinehart and Winston.

Sutton, M. (2002) 'Race hatred and the far right on the internet', *Criminal Justice Matters*, 48.

Taylor, I., Walton, P. and Young, J. (eds) (1975) *Critical Criminology*. London: Routledge.

Taylor, J., Iacono, G. and McGue, M. (2000) 'Evidence for a genetic aetiology of early-onset delinquency', *Journal of Abnormal Psychology*, 109: 634–43.

Taylor, N. (1999) 'Fixing the price for spoiled lives', *Criminal Justice Matters*, 35.

Taylor, P. (1999) *Hackers: Crime and the Digital Sublime*. London: Routledge.

The Social Exclusion Unit (2002) *Reducing Reoffending by Ex Prisoners*. London: HM Prison Service.

Thomas, K. (1978) *Religion and the Decline of Magic*. Perthshire: Peregrine.

Thomas, W. I. (1907) *Sex and Society*. Chicago: University of Chicago Press.

Thomas, W. I. (1923) *The Unadjusted Girl*. Boston: Little, Brown.

Thompson, E. P. (1985) *Whigs and Hunters: The Origins of the Black Act*. Harmondsworth: Penguin.

Thornhill, R. and Palmer, C. (2000) *A Natural History of Rape: Biological bases of Sexual Coercion*. Cambridge, MA: MIT Press.

Tierney, J. (2010) *Criminology: Theory and Context*, third edition. Harlow: Longman.

Tobias, J. J. (1967) *Crime and Industrial Society in the 19th Century*. London: Batsford.

Tocqueville, A. de (2000[1835]) *Democracy in America.* Chicago: University of Chicago Press.

Tolstoy, L. (2005[1869]) *War and Peace.* (Translated by A. Briggs.) Harmondsworth: Penguin Classics.

Tombs, S. (1990) 'Industrial injuries in British manufacturing industry', *Sociological Review*, 38: 2.

Tombs, S. and Whyte, D. (2001) 'Media reporting of crime: defining corporate crime out of existence?', *Criminal Justice Matters,* 43: 22–3.

Tonnies, F. (1957) *Community and Society.* New York: Harper & Row.

Tooby, J. and Cosmides, L. (1992) 'The psychological foundations of culture' in J. Barkow, H. Tost, C. Vollmert *et al.* (2004) 'Pedophilia: neuropsychological evidence encouraging a brain network perspective', *Medical Hypotheses*, 63: 528–31.

Tost, H., Vollmert, C., Brassen, S., Schmitt, A., Dressing, H., Braus, D. (2004) 'Paedophilia: neuropsychological evidence encouraging a brain network perspective' *Medical Hypotheses*, 63, 528–531.

Travis, A. (2003) 'Record jail numbers insupportable says Lord Irvine', *Guardian*, 7 January.

Travis, A. (2007) 'Prison wing "unfit for animals" closed down', *Guardian* 5 October.

Travis, A. (2010) 'Failure to tackle reoffending rates of short sentence prisoners costs £10bn', *Guardian*, 10 March.

Trevor-Roper, H. (1967) *The European Witch Craze of the 16th and 17th Centuries.* Harmondsworth: Penguin.

Trimble, J. and Fay, M. (1986) 'PMS in today's society', *Hamline Law Review*, 9: 1.

Tuchman, G. (1978) 'The symbolic annihilation of women by the mass media' in G. Tuchman, A. K. Daniel and J. Bennet (eds) *Hearth and Home.* Oxford: Oxford University Press.

UNIFEM (2002) UNIFEM Annual Report 2001, United Nations Development Fund for Women (www.unifem.org).

Valier, C. (2002) *Theories of Crime and Punishment,* Harlow: Longman.

Vandermassen, G. (2005) *Who's Afraid of Charles Darwin?: Debating Feminism and Evolutionary Theory.* Lanham, MD: Rowman & Littlefield.

Vargha-Khadem, F., Cowan, J. and Mishkin, M. (2000) 'Sociopathic behaviour after early damage to prefrontal cortex', Presentation to the Society for Neuroscience, New Orleans, November.

Vines, G. (1998) 'Life sentence', *New Scientist*, 2162.

Waddington, D., Jones, K. and Critcher, C. (1989) *Flashpoints: Studies in Public Disorder.* London: Routledge.

Waddington, P. (1991) *The Strong Arm of the Law: Armed Police and Public Order Policing.* Oxford: Oxford University Press.

Waddington, P. (1993) *Calling the Police: The Interpretation of, and Responses to, Calls for Assistance from the Public.* Aldershot: Avebury.

Waddington, P. (2000) 'Public order policing: Citizenship and Moral Ambiguity', in Leishman, F., Loveday, B. and Savage, S. (eds) *Core Issues in Policing*, second edition. Harlow: Pearson.

Wade, T. D. and Kendler, K. S. (2001) 'Parent, child and social correlates of parental discipline style: a retrospective, multi-informant investigation with female twins', *Social Psychiatry and Psychiatric Epidemiology*, 36 (4): 177–85.

Wadsworth, M. (1979) *Roots of Delinquency.* London: Martin Robertson.

Walker, N. (1991) *Why Punish?* Oxford: Oxford University Press.

Walker, N. (1999) *Aggravation, Mitigation and Mercy in English Criminal Justice.* London: Blackstone.

Walklate, S. (1989) *Victimology: The Victim and the Criminal Justice Process.* London: Unwin Hyman.

Walklate, S. (1990) 'Researching victims of crime: critical victimology', *Social Justice,* 17: 2.

Walklate, S. (2000) 'Equal opportunities and the future of policing', in F. Leishman, B. Loveday and S. P. Savage (eds) *Core Issues in Policing*, second edition. Harlow: Pearson.

Walklate, S. (2000) 'Reflections on "New Labour" or "Back to the Future"?', *Criminal Justice Matters*, 38: 7–8.

Walklate, S. (2004) *Gender, Crime and Criminal Justice*, second edition. Cullompton: Willan Publishing.

Walkowitz, J. R. (1982) *Prostitution and Victorian Society: Women, Class and the State*. Cambridge: Cambridge University Press

Wall, D. S. (1998) 'Policing and the regulation of cyberspace', *Criminal Law Review*, December, 79–91.

Wall, D. S. (1999) 'Cybercrimes: new wine, no bottle?' in P. Davies, P. Francis and V. Jupp (eds) *Invisible Crimes: Their Victims and their Regulation*. London: Macmillan.

Wall, D. S. (ed.) (2001) *Crime and the Internet*. London: Routledge.

Wall, D. S. (2004) 'Policing cyberspace: law and order on the cyberbeat', *Criminal Justice Review 2003–2004*, Centre for Criminal Justice Studies, University of Leeds.

Wall, D. S. (2005) 'The internet as a conduit for criminal activity' in A. Pattavina (ed.) *Information Technology and the Criminal Justice System*. London: Sage.

Walsh, A. (2002) *Biosocial Criminology: Introduction and Integration*. Cincinnati, OH: Anderson Publishing.

Walsh, M. and Schram, D. (1980) 'The victims of white-collar crime: accuser or accused?', in Geis, G. and Stotland, E. (eds) *White-Collar Crime*. Beverly Hills, CA: Sage.

Walvin, J. (2001) *Black Ivory: A History of British Slavery*, second edition. London: Blackwell.

Ward, T. and Maruna, S. (2007) *Rehabilitation: Beyond the Risk Paradigm*. London: Routledge.

Wardle, C. (2007) 'Monsters and angels: visual press coverage of child murders in the USA and UK, 1930–2000', *Journalism*, 8: 263–84.

Watkins, M. and Gordon, W. (2000) *The Sentence of the Court: A Handbook for Magistrates*, Winchester: Waterside Press.

Watson, J. B. (1925) *Behaviourism*. New York: Norton.

Weale, S. (2001) 'Prison – the therapeutic way', *Guardian*, 2 February.

Weber, M. (1978 (1920)) *Economy and Society*, ed. Roth, G. and Wittich, C., Berkeley: University of California Press.

Webster, D. (1989) ' "Whodunnit? America did": *Rambo* and post-Hungerford rhetoric', *Cultural Studies*, 3 (2): 173–93.

Weimann, G. (2006) *Terror on the Internet*, Washington, DC: US Institute of Peace Press.

Weiner, J. (1995) *The Beak of the Finch: A Story of Evolution in Our Time*. New York: Vintage.

Wells, C. (1989) 'What about the Victim?', *The Investigator*, 5: 26–7.

Wells, L. E. and Rankin, J. H. (1991) 'Families and delinquency: a meta-analysis of the impact of broken homes', *Social Problems*, 38: 71–93.

Werner, E. E. (1989) 'High-risk children in young adulthood: a longitudinal study from birth to 32 years', *American Journal of Orthopsychiatry*, 59: 72–81.

Wertham, F. (1949) *The Show of Violence*. New York: Doubleday.

West, D. J. and Farrington, D. P. (1973) *Who Becomes Delinquent?* London: Heinemann.

West, D. J. and Farrington, D. P. (1977) *The Delinquent Way of Life*. London: Heinemann.

Westmarland, L. (2010) 'Transnational policing and security' in D. Drake, J. Muncie and L. Westmarland, *Criminal Justice: Local and Global*. Cullompton: Willan Publishing.

Whine, M. (2006) 'Common motifs on Jihadi and far right websites', NATO Advanced Research Workshop on Hypermedia Seduction for Terrorist Recruiting.

Whitehead, P. (2009) 'Restructuring NOMS and reducing cultural divides between prisons and probation: a cautionary note', *Criminal Justice Matters*, 77.

WHO (1997) *Poverty and Health: An Overview of the Basic Linkages and Public Policy Measures*. Geneva: WHO.

WHO (2002) *World Report on Violence and Health*. Geneva: WHO.

Williams, A, and Thompson,W. (2004) 'Vigilance or vigilantes: The Paulsgrove riots and policing paedophiles in the community', *Police Journal*, 1 June.

Williams, K. S. (2004) *Criminology*, fifth edition. Oxford: Oxford University Press.

Williams, M. (2005) 'Cybercrime' in Mitchell Miller, J. (ed.) *Encyclopaedia of Criminology*. London: Routledge.

Williams, M. (2006) *Virtually Criminal: Crime, Deviance and Regulation Online*. London: Routledge.

Wilson, D. (2002) 'Millbank, the panopticon and their Victorian audiences', *Howard Journal of Criminal Justice*, 41 (4): pp. 364–81.

Wilson, D. and O'Sullivan, S. (2004) *Representations of Prison in Film and Television Drama*. Winchester: Waterside Press.

Wilson, E. O. (1975) *Sociobiology: A New Synthesis*. Cambridge, MA: Harvard University Press.

Wilson, J. and Herrnstein, R. (1985) *Crime and Human Nature*. New York: Simon & Schuster.

Wisdom, C. S. (1989) 'The cycle of violence', *Science*, 244: 160–6.

Wolak, J., Finkelhor, D. and Mitchell, K. (2005) *Child Pornography Possessors Arrested in Internet-Related Crime: A National Study*. Alexandria, VA: National Centre for Missing and Exploited Children.

Wolfgang, M. E. *Patterns in Criminal Homicide*. Philadelphia: University of Pennsylvania Press.

Wolfgang, M. E. (1998) 'We do not deserve to kill', *Crime and Delinquency*, 44 (1): 19–31.

Woodcock Report (1994) *Report of the Enquiry into the Escape of Six Prisoners from the Special Secure Unit at Whitemoor Prison on Friday 9 September 1994*, Cmnd 2741. London: HMSO.

Woolf Report (1991) *Prison Disturbances April 1990: Report of an Inquiry by the Rt Hon. Lord Justice Woolf*. London: HMSO.

Worrall, A. (1997) *Punishment in the Community: The Future of Criminal Justice*. Harlow: Longman.

Wortley, R. and Mazerolle, L. (eds) (2008) *Environmental Criminology and Crime Analysis*. Cullompton: Willan Publishing.

Wright, R. A. and Miller, J. M. (1998) 'Taboo until today? The coverage of biological arguments in criminology textbooks, 1961 to 1970 and 1987 to 1996', *Journal of Criminal Justice*, 26: 1–19.

Wykes, M. and Gunter, B. (2004) *Media and Body Image: If Looks Could Kill*. London: Sage.

Yates, N. (2003) *Beyond Evil*. London: Blake Publishing.

Yochelson, S. and Samenow, S. (1976) *The Criminal Personality. Volume One: A Profile for Change*. New York: Jason Aronson.

Young, J. (1971a) 'The role of the police as amplifiers of deviancy' in S. Cohen (ed.) *Images of Deviance*. Harmondsworth: Penguin.

Young, J. (1971b) *The Drugtakers: The Social Meaning of Drug Use*. London: McGibbon and Kee.

Young, J. (1986) 'The failure of criminology: the need for a radical realism', in R. Mathews and J. Young (eds) *Confronting Crime*, London: Sage.

Young, J. (1992) 'Ten points of realism', in J. Young and R. Mathews (eds) *Rethinking Criminology: The Realist Debate*, London: Sage.

Young, J. (1996) 'The failure of criminology: the need for a radical realism', reprinted in McLaughlin, J., Muncie, E. and Langan, M. (eds) (1996) *Criminological Perspectives: A Reader*. London: Sage.

Young, J. (1997) 'Left realist criminology: radical in its analysis, realist in its policy', in Maguire, M., Morgan, R. and Reiner, R. (eds) *The Oxford Handbook of Criminology*, second edition. Oxford: Oxford University Press.

Zedner, L. (1991) *Women, Crime and Custody in Victorian England*, Oxford: Clarendon Press.

Zedner, L. (1992) 'Sexual offences', in S. Casale and E. Stockdale (eds) *Criminal Justice under Stress*, London: Blackstone.

Zedner, L. (1998) 'Wayward sisters: the prison for women', in N. Morris and D. J. Rothman (eds) *The Oxford History of the Prison: The Practice of Punishment in Western Society*. Oxford: Oxford University Press.

Zeleny, L. (1933) 'Feeblemindedness and criminal conduct', *American Journal of Sociology*, 38: 564–76.

INDEX